*To Ma and Pa*

Being deeply loved by someone gives you strength, while loving someone deeply gives you courage.

— ATTRIBUTED TO LAO TZU

# CONTENTS

# PART THREE

# INTRODUCTION

Beatrice Ayer Patton never wished to be known; all she ever wanted was for people to know her husband, General George S. Patton Jr. Her efforts to remain in the background indeed were successful. The multitude of books on General Patton end with his death and leave her a mere footnote, while she gets nothing more than a passing mention in the three-hour-long movie *Patton*. Yet, it was no exaggeration when biographer Martin Blumenson wrote that General Patton was "as man and legend, to a large degree, the creation of his wife."[1]

*Lady of the Army* tells the story of Beatrice Banning Ayer Patton. However, it is impossible to do so without bringing George Patton along for the ride because the two of them together were the most interesting and unusual couple. They were so connected in everything they did that throughout the Army, it was said that "to know one of the Pattons is to know the other."[2]

Even though the Pattons were apart for long periods throughout their marriage, their hearts spoke. They wrote to each other almost daily, during peacetime and war, on topics ranging from George's career to trivial details about their many shared passions. Beatrice ensured all her husband's letters and papers were preserved, except for a series of love letters she burned after his death. The George S. Patton Papers are now housed in the Manuscript Division of the Library of Congress and contain over twenty-six thousand items. While most researchers focus on the military aspect of this and other Patton collections, focusing on the personal side of their correspondence opens a revealing window into the private George Patton.

Beatrice Ayer Patton lived by a set of rules, a list of maxims she gathered throughout her life. She carefully noted them in her diary—her thought book —and passed them on to family, friends, and strangers. Each of the following chapters opens with one aphorism Beatrice lived by, a little nugget of wisdom that sustained her throughout the highs and lows of her fascinating life.[3]

General Patton depended on his wife's sage advice. There has been speculation that he had dyslexia, a valid explanation for the spelling and punctuation mistakes in many of his personal letters. George agonized over the problem when young, thinking himself stupid and lazy until he discovered Napoleon was bad at spelling too. He decided it took more imagination to spell a word several ways than continuously spelling it the same way, leaving it up to Beatrice to correct important letters and papers.[4] To maintain the individual character of his letters, they are quoted here as written. However, for the sake of brevity, mistakes are not marked with [sic].

# BEDFORD ARMY AIRFIELD, MASSACHUSETTS

## JUNE 7, 1945

*LIVE EACH DAY TO THE BEST OF YOUR ABILITY AND THE FUTURE WILL TAKE CARE OF ITSELF.*

Nine hundred and fifty-eight days. Beatrice Ayer Patton knew exactly how long it had been since she last saw her husband when she awoke on June 7, 1945. After enduring the wait for so long, slightly trembling inside whenever the phone rang or a reporter showed up on her doorstep, she finally allowed herself to count the minutes until George would arrive at Bedford Army Airfield.

All she hoped as she stepped out of bed, the house coming to life with the sound of her three children, together for the first time in years, was for better weather.[1] Massachusetts' North Shore had been unseasonably cold and wet for weeks, worrying Beatrice. She opened the curtains and looked across the foggy lawn of Green Meadows, an eighteenth-century Colonial surrounded by three hundred acres of top-notch fox hunting country and most of her family. Unfortunately, the oxidized cannon on the back porch was shrouded in mist.

Beatrice loved the excitement on her four grandchildren's faces when she made them believe the cannon pointed west toward the Ipswich River to protect the house from pirates. The adults sat no less spellbound when she recounted George's World War II exploits, reading from his letters so often she knew them almost by heart.

A few months after General Patton successfully led the I Armored Corps in the invasion of Morocco in November 1942, Beatrice received a phone call from the South Hamilton train station asking her to pick up a large crate. When told to bring along a handful of strong men, she knew it had to be the cannon George shipped her on an empty military transport from North Africa. No one could explain how a Portuguese bronze cannon barrel dating from the time of Henry IV ended up on a Moroccan shore in the aftermath of Operation Torch.[2] However, when General Truscott heard of the salvage, he knew an inveterate collector and military historian like General Patton would appreciate a gift of this caliber.

Green Meadows slowly evolved from a home into something resembling a museum as George sent over more and more trophies from the battlefield. Beatrice could retrace her husband's steps as commander of the Western Task Force, the Seventh Army, and the Third Army as she walked around the house. In the living room hung a pair of tusks from a wild boar George shot in the Atlas Mountains with the Sultan of Marrakesh, and the closet was filled with blood-stained German uniforms and matching bullet-riddled helmets. Hidden in the garden was a bust of Hitler, which George sent with an accompanying note to place it somewhere the dogs could pee on it, and on the piano lay an 1893 satin spread from Palermo, embroidered with doves and posies. "He has the name and fame of being the toughest, most hard-boiled general in the U.S. Army," she told a reporter when asked about the curious gift. "And he sends me his love, with a bedspread!"[3]

Deep down, Beatrice never expected George to return, yet she never moved the half-finished model boat that stood on his desk, a replica of Napoleon's at St. Helena. Although it had been two years and seven months, she could still hear him say he expected to die fighting as he boarded the battleship *Augusta* on his way to North Africa, but she was comforted by the knowledge that he was finally fulfilling what he considered his destiny.

For as long as she had known George Patton, she had known he fervently believed that he would one day lead a great army in battle. Most people would have found that belief preposterous, especially coming from a seventeen-year-old boy, but Beatrice found his burning ambition endearing. He spoke so passionately that she not only believed him but also decided that she would be the one to accompany him on his quest for glory. It was a decision she never regretted despite the hardships.

Being married to George Patton was a constant challenge, but Beatrice loved a challenge as much as she loved defying social conventions. Her small stature belied a woman of incredible strength, with a personality that radiated "like a brilliant gem."[4] Her daughter Ruth Ellen once said she was "a pocket Venus" with a heart of gold, but Beatrice was also fierce, independent, and incredibly strong-willed. Those who met her in her travels as an emissary of the War Department were surprised that the wife of General Patton was a dainty and charming woman, yet she was as tough and volatile as he was.

After years of waiting and anxiety, Beatrice got down on her knees to pray when the bells had pealed across South Hamilton a month earlier to signify the end of the war in Europe.[5] It truly was a miracle that George survived, never shirking danger as he led from the front, yet she knew him well enough to realize he would now try everything in his power to join the continuing war in the Pacific. But first, he would be given the hero's welcome he'd always dreamed of.

June 7 was an unusually cold day even for Boston, with temperatures not expected to rise above sixty-six degrees. Beatrice hesitated to wear the new floral dress she bought for the occasion but decided to add a black coat to ward off the chill, and completed her outfit with a green sailor's hat with white felt seagulls.[6] When she looked in the mirror, she was happy to note that she had kept her svelte figure, practicing what she preached to army wives across the country: "Keep faith in God, keep fit, and keep well."

George Patton was the only man Beatrice ever loved, and her heart fluttered at the thought of seeing him again. Over the last two-and-a-half years, she'd often gone to the theater to watch the latest *United News* presentations, hoping to catch a glimpse of him in the short news clippings. He appeared larger than life to the strangers surrounding her, but she recognized his face as the one he had practiced in the mirror for decades. She was the one who gave him the strength to put on his war face, to become General Patton, a persona he cultivated his whole life based on how he thought a true general should look and act.

Beatrice could hardly wait to see the real George Patton again, the kind and generous man she fell in love with forty-three years earlier.

GENERAL PATTON GLIMPSED the Massachusetts countryside below as the C-54 Skymaster circled Bedford Army Airfield looking for a passage through the clouds. The lush fields were in stark contrast to the destroyed land he had left behind in Germany three days earlier. If only people could see it through his eyes, they'd realize "what your soldiers have kept from you."[7] Except for his family, no one seemed to understand "that one cannot fight for two-and-a-half years and be the same. Yet you are expected to get back into the identical groove from which you departed and from which your non-warlike compatriots have never moved."[8]

George always expected, and even hoped, to die fighting in Europe, an end befitting a true warrior who dies "with the last bullet of the last battle of the war." But instead, his Third Army had stopped fighting on May 8, 1945, after Nazi Germany signed an unconditional surrender at the Allied headquarters in Reims. While the world's reaction was one of endless joy and relief, the end of the war in Europe left General Patton feeling "nervous."[9] It was a big letdown for someone who loved the challenge of war, who "loved the mechanics and the interplay of intelligence and historical memory."[10] He couldn't adequately explain it, but he considered war "as much or more of an art than sculpture, it is really a very beautiful intelectual contest."[11]

George was looking forward to all the accolades afforded a war hero, but he was itching to join the war in the Pacific. The tremendous responsibility of commanding hundreds of thousands of soldiers occasionally felt "like a ton of bricks," but in his opinion, war was the only thing he was good at.[12] The record certainly agreed: he led the first Americans into battle during Operation Torch in North Africa, he invaded Sicily with the Seventh Army, and after a few tense months in the doghouse because of his customary forthrightness, he drove the Third Army "farther and faster than any army in history."[13]

Many of the forty-five Third Army officers and enlisted men on board the C-54 Skymaster had been by General Patton's side for years, including Master Sergeant George Meeks, his African American orderly for the last seven years, and Colonel Charles Codman, his aide-de-camp and an aristocratic Bostonian who loved conversing with his boss in French.[14] These men stood by his side, sticking to him like limpets, as dedicated and loyal as the woman who continuously stood by his side in spirit. He hadn't made things easy on his "Beat" the last few years, but she unfailingly shared in his burdens. There was no denying he owed much of his success to her, without question the only woman in the world who could have stayed married to him for thirty-five years.

At six foot two, George stood more than a head taller than Beatrice, yet she was the rock he'd leaned on since he was seventeen. "I wish you were a coach," he wrote her in 1907, "for some how you seem to be able to make me try harder, sort of give me extra willpower."[15] Beatrice was his inspiration, the one who allayed his doubts and fears, stroked his ego, tempered his anger, and delivered the flowers while he delivered the blows.[16] She never curbed his fighting spirit, accepting without complaint that he might one day make the ultimate sacrifice in order to become a great battlefield commander.[17]

George couldn't wait to look into Beatrice's "brave loyal eyes" again.[18] Even after all these years, he still felt a sense of wonder that she chose to spend her life with him. Since the Ayers were entrepreneurs with no military tradition, he worried at first that being an army wife might not come easy to her. However, Beatrice turned out to be "a good soldier" who fought the war on the home front three times, earning her the title of "number one Army woman."[19] George always remained conscious of Beatrice's sacrifices, so his efforts to fulfill his destiny were as much for her as for himself. He had said it most eloquently in 1928 in a toast to the ladies of the Army, hoping that "we [the officers] live to make them happy, or, and the Great Day come, so die as to make them proud."[20]

It had always been George's "plan to be killed in this war, and I damned near accomplished it," but his luck had held and he was on his way back to the United States, victorious and alive.[21] He believed that one was born with a certain amount of luck, but by the end of the war, each shell seemed to land closer and closer, and recently an oxcart had barreled down a street in Germany and narrowly missed his car. Deep down, George Patton felt the reunion with his family would also be his farewell.

AT 3:44 P.M., the fleet of three C-54s and their six Flying Fortress escorts landed at Bedford Army Airfield, twenty minutes early. The fifty-nine-year-old general had a spring in his step as he emerged from the plane despite being ill with strep throat, and the sun started to shine when he put his feet on American soil for the first time in nearly three years. As soon as he saluted Major General Sherman Miles, commanding officer of the First Service Command in Boston, and shook hands with Massachusetts Governor Maurice J. Tobin, he searched the crowd for his wife.

Beatrice's heart skipped a beat as the plane's door opened and her displeasure at being relegated to the sidelines disappeared as soon as she caught sight of George. Her eyes were immediately drawn to the patchwork of battle ribbons on his chest. She waited patiently in the reviewing stand with her children, but she had been counting the minutes since the moment she found out he was returning home, and joy overtook her. She pushed the reporters and photographers aside and ran up to George, who took off his helmet to welcome her embrace.

*Figure 1. A twenty-second reunion at Bedford Army Airfield on June 7, 1945. (Library of Congress)*

"Hello," Beatrice said as she threw her arms around her husband's neck and kissed him on the cheek. "I am so glad to have you back." She was so overcome with emotions that she couldn't say more, so she briefly placed her hand on his face to make sure it wasn't all a dream.[22] The moment lasted a mere twenty seconds, then George IV, granted a two-day leave from West Point, embraced his father with a heartfelt, "Hi'ya, Pop!" Next came kisses and hugs from his daughters, Little Bee and Ruth Ellen, and a handshake from his son-in-law, Lieutenant Colonel James Totten.

These few minutes were all the family had before duty called again. When George walked away to receive a seventeen-gun salute and review the honor guard, he winked at Beatrice. "He looks well," she whispered to her daughters, wiping tears from her eyes. He appeared trim and slender in his gray riding breeches, with the four stars of a full general on his shiny helmet. Some journalists described General Patton as an old man coming home from the war. Still, he had never felt better than during the last three years, despite the heavy workload and the continuous proximity to death and destruction.

General Patton's arrival had been carefully planned. A mere fifteen minutes after landing, it was time to join the motorcade destined for the Charles River Esplanade in the Back Bay area of Boston. Beatrice took a seat in the second car with her son and daughters, while George rode in the lead car with Governor Tobin and General Miles. Close to one million people lined the twenty-five-mile route, part of which covered, in reverse, the same path of Paul Revere's midnight ride some 170 years earlier.[23]

As the motorcade drove at ten miles per hour through the villages of Lexington, Arlington, and Cambridge, George sat on the back of his seat and waved to the crowd with his riding crop. "The only excuses for the horrors of war are glories," he would exclaim later that month, and the crowd certainly did not disappoint.[24] Beatrice felt like her heart would burst with pride as she watched the people of Massachusetts throw flowers at his car while fire trucks lined the route and turned on their sirens as he passed.[25] When she saw his beaming face look back at her, she knew this was the culmination of everything they had worked so hard for.

Beatrice's mind filled with memories as the motorcade crossed the Cottage Farm Bridge across the Charles River into Boston. Turning left onto Commonwealth Avenue, they drove past number 395, better known as the Ayer Mansion because it had been commissioned by her parents—Frederick and Ellie Ayer—from Louis Comfort Tiffany in 1902. Her family sold the home a long time ago, but the memories remained: the living room with the grand piano she played with remarkable skill; the foyer, covered in Tiffany mosaics, which acted like a stage; the library where George had finally admitted his love; and the third-floor bedroom in which she had locked herself when her father was reluctant to give his permission to marry.

Frederick Ayer had been a hardworking and humble entrepreneur who had been the wealthiest man in New England. He was ahead of his time in many of his beliefs and raised his seven children in a nurturing environment that allowed all of them to thrive. Beatrice enjoyed a loving childhood in the lap of luxury, yet she gave it all up to follow George Patton wherever the Army sent him. While it was hard at first to adjust to the simple life of dusty camp-grounds and forlorn towns, she never regretted becoming Mrs. Patton. The joy she felt today in sharing this moment of glory with George was worth all their sacrifices.

At 6:30 P.M., an hour late because of the crowds, the motorcade arrived at the Hatch Shell, an outdoor amphitheater on the Charles River Esplanade. More than twenty-thousand people awaited General Patton's nine-minute speech, but he had eyes only for the roughly three hundred officers and soldiers sitting in the front rows.

"Those heroes are first in my heart," he said in his surprisingly high-pitched voice, which was completely incongruous with the image he portrayed. "I speak of the men who regardless of ice, regardless of snow, went on and on." As he would repeatedly proclaim over the next few days, he was just "a hook" on which the honors of the Third Army were hung, "This great ovation by Boston is not for Patton the General, but Patton as a symbol for the Third Army."[26]

He reminded his audience of the unspeakable horrors of war most people only read about, and his voice began to quiver when he mentioned "the soldier with his naked bosom . . . [who] crossed rivers that couldn't be crossed and plowed through where nobody could plow through." Those soldiers now looked at him from the front rows, many still recovering from wounds they had sustained during the Third Army's fighting in France and Germany. "I can't say anymore," George abruptly concluded his speech when his gentle character broke through his much-practiced war face.[27]

Some might have found General Patton's demeanor rather incredible considering that he slapped two battle-fatigued soldiers in Sicily, but he cared deeply for his men. Few people realized there were actually two George Pattons, and Beatrice was intimately acquainted with both: the warrior who spoke "a song of hate" to motivate his soldiers and the tender-hearted man who once compared her "to the dawning day, What day was e'er so beautiful as you?"[28] Those who knew George personally were aware he possessed a wonderful side that the public never knew, a side which surfaced again a few hours later at the state dinner given in his honor.[29]

*Figure 2. Arriving at the Copley Plaza Hotel: Cadet Patton, General Patton, Beatrice Ayer Patton, Ruth Ellen Patton Totten, and Beatrice Patton Waters. (Patton Museum)*

After a frantic search for Beatrice's bag containing her evening gown, the motorcade proceeded to the Copley Plaza Hotel, where the Patton family spent an hour and a half together in the privacy of a suite. When they finally entered the hotel's ballroom at 8:30 p.m., the band struck up the "2nd Armored Division March," composed by Beatrice in 1941 when George was commander of the 2nd Armored Division at Fort Benning.

Over five hundred guests were seated in the ballroom, many of them people who had supported Beatrice during George's absence, from Ayer family members such as her sister Katharine "Kay" Merrill and nephew Count Mario Guardabassi, to close family friends such as Mr. and Mrs. Gordon Prince, and Dr. and Mrs. Franc Ingraham. Thousands more waited outside to catch a glimpse of the famous general, yet for all but a handful of those in attendance, tonight would be the last time they ever saw him.[30]

Beatrice sat between Governor Dale of New Hampshire and Governor Tobin, who began his speech by paying tribute to her, "the model of a soldier's wife." George vigorously applauded that statement as he took the stage next, hoping "that everyone noticed the enthusiasm with which I cheered the most appropriate words of the Governor in respect to my wife and not the most inappropriate words in regard to me." Any medal or accolade he ever received, he proudly shared with Beatrice because "without my Generals, and my wife, the war with the Germans might have lasted a great deal longer."[31] Beatrice smiled politely, as usual giving little outward indication of her feelings, a stark contrast with her husband, who was soon overcome with emotions again.

George would be castigated for his next remark, infuriating Beatrice, who was sick and tired of his words being misconstrued by the press. "When we foolishly mourn for those men who have died, we are wrong," he spoke off the cuff. "We should thank God that such men were born." Once again, he could "say no more," and he sat back down between Governor and Mrs. Tobin, wiping his tears with a handkerchief without any hint of embarrassment.[32] While this open show of emotion surprised most people in the audience, his family knew George was an impassioned man whose dashing manner camouflaged a sensitive soul. He was a study in contradictions: brutal yet sensitive, gregarious yet lonesome, volatile yet loyal. He was an enigma of his own creation, which few people knew how to crack.

Separated from her husband by Mr. Tobin, Beatrice watched as George was constantly interrupted by autograph seekers while he tried to finish his lobster cocktail. She understood him without words, though, and she knew he was happy to indulge every single one of them. George enjoyed adulation and recognition since he was a little boy, and she provided both in abundance throughout their marriage. George Patton was the center of his own universe, and he was the center of Beatrice's. Such a man would have crushed those less confident and determined than she was, but she thrived on it. If George was indeed living his life ordained by destiny, then Beatrice was part of the plan all along.

*Figure 3. The Pattons return to Green Meadows in the early morning of June 8, 1945, exhausted after a long day of public appearances. (Library of Congress)*

The evening finally ended at 1:15 a.m. with a press conference, albeit brief, because the Pattons had a train to catch so George could finally sleep in his own bed again. It was a very short night; by 8:00 a.m., Beatrice and George were already on their way to the airport to continue his war bond selling tour on the West Coast. They would not return to Green Meadows until June 16th for a well-earned rest.

Besides horseback riding, sailing, and social calls, Beatrice and George just sat quietly holding hands while looking out over the rolling hills of Myopia Hunt country. "When there is so much to go into," Beatrice reminisced years later, "where does one begin?"[33]

## Part I[1]

Your summits crowned with gold and jade-
Your shores with sapphire touched.
Your seas alive with white sails set,
Your deeps with wonders filled.

Your hills and vales where wild things live
'Mid beauty's sweet content.
The beauty of the green wild woods,
The sunset glow on mountain tops-

The homes where love and peace abide,
The dainty flowers that spring and bloom,
In sweetness in the clear pure air
That we were meant to breathe.

All made by God's own gracious will-
In His great love for us,
That we be free in His own world,
His blessings to enjoy.

O mountain tops!
O restless seas!
Do you e'er miss those cherished ones
Who wandered o'er your slopes?

Or sailed around your lovely shores,
In care-free days of youth?
Then from your midst send up your plea
To Him who gave you form,

To guide and guard with his own hand
Those brave and dear young souls
Now struggling in those far off lands,
That God's plan be redeemed.

— *"AN INVOCATION TO AVALON-OUR ISLE OF THE BLEST!" BY*
*BEATRICE AYER PATTON*

# 1

# THE FARM

## NEWTON, MASSACHUSETTS

### 1757–1902

*When in doubt about what to do, the kind thing is usually the right thing.*

Six-year-old Beatrice Banning Ayer awoke to the neighing of horses on a beautiful summer's day in 1892. She traveled three thousand miles by private railroad car from Lowell, Massachusetts, with her parents, Frederick and Ellie, and her younger siblings, Fred and Kay, to visit the extended California branch of the Banning family in Wilmington. The Barn was the home of Captain William Banning, an eternal bachelor. He forswore marriage when his brother Joseph married their cousin Katharine Banning, the love of his life and Beatrice's maternal aunt.

When Beatrice looked outside, she could see the stagecoaches her great-uncle Phineas Banning used to drive. She never met the general, but the stories of his life were legendary. Phineas, an imposing man known as "the father of the port of Los Angeles," was a successful businessman who, among many other ventures, operated several steam-powered tenders along the shallow Wilmington coast.

When the *Ada Hancock* took off for the *S.S. Senator* five miles out at sea on April 27, 1863, with about fifty passengers—including two Mormon missionaries on their way to Hawaii and a messenger from Wells Fargo & Company carrying $11,000 worth of gold dust—it got caught in a violent squall which caused cold seawater to be dumped on the boiler. Passengers on the *S.S. Senator* watched in horror as the *Ada Hancock* was torn to pieces just before five, the detonation of the boiler like the explosion of a bomb. The tragedy left a lasting mark on Phineas, his family, and the family of his business partner, Benjamin Wilson.

Phineas awoke dazed and confused with a concussion on Deadman's Island, a rocky sandbar near the Wilmington shore. His pregnant wife and mother-in-law suffered internal injuries and multiple fractures, while his two young sons escaped largely unscathed. His brother-in-law did not survive the blast, nor did his colleague Henry Miles, whose fiancée, Medora Hereford, suffered a head injury and severe burns. She died three months later after "enduring indescribable sufferings with the fortitude of a martyr." By her bedside were her sister Margaret Hereford Wilson and her step-niece, Maria de Jésús Wilson, who had survived the blast with a mere contusion.[1]

**Figure 4.** *Beatrice (Bea), Frederick (Fred), and Katharine (Kay) with their mother in early 1891.*

The tragedy of the *Ada Hancock* was still talked about twenty-nine years later when the Ayers were getting ready to visit Hancock Banning, a third brother, and Anne Ophelia Smith, his new wife. Beatrice was expected to join her family, but carriage rides made her sick, and she refused to go along, preferring to keep reading the book she had her head buried in for the last few days. Known to be exceptionally skilled at getting her way, she eventually waved goodbye as her family took off for Lake Vineyard in San Marino, the home of Anne Ophelia's half brother, George Smith Patton; his wife Ruth Wilson; their two children, George and Nita Patton; and their grandmother, Margaret Hereford Wilson.

Always keen on making an entrance, the flamboyant Ellie walked into the Pattons' dining room after all the guests had been seated. The heated political discussion between the Republican Ayers and the Democratic Pattons halted when she paused in the doorway before taking a seat next to Mr. Patton. Five-year-old Nita could not help staring at Ellie, who had a lace shawl wrapped around her shoulders, a characteristic pink rose in her hair, and eight gold bangles on her arm, one for each year of marriage. A hush again descended over the dining room when Ellie suddenly got up in the middle of dinner and walked over to Anne Ophelia. She placed her finger under her cousin-in-law's chin and dramatically asked, "Annie, dear, what do you think of life?"[2]

The reaction of seven-year-old George Patton is unknown, but his future mother-in-law's performance left a lasting impression. While the Pattons spent the rest of the evening trying to figure out Ellie, the Ayers could not stop talking about little Georgie. Just a few months older than Beatrice, he was such a good boy who would never have defied his parents and stayed home to read a book.[3] Tired of hearing the story repeated over and over, Beatrice defiantly told her parents she hoped never to meet that "Georgie." And if she did ever have the misfortune of meeting him, she certainly wouldn't be playing with him.

Beatrice and George were fated to meet, though. The Ayers and the Pattons were linked through family and business connections, despite one being an enterprising New England family and the other being patriotic Virginians who settled in California.

---

ALTHOUGH HE HAD ONLY JUST TURNED three, Frederick Ayer never forgot the last time he saw his father and namesake. The man who just a few weeks earlier carried his son on his shoulders as they walked home from the mills, regaling him with stories of the local Pequot Indians and his own experiences in the War of 1812, was "lying on the bed with his arm stretched out over the side," too weak to move. "[T]he splashing of the blood on the yellow bowl" was the last image the boy had of his father, who died on December 21, 1825, at the age of thirty-two, just three days before the birth of his daughter Lovisa.[4]

Frederick always attributed his father's death to hard work, an Ayer family trait that would form the cornerstone of his own life. His grandfather, Elisha Ayer, co-owned the *Falcon,* a privateer commissioned by the Second Continental Congress to capture British vessels along the New England coast.[5] In May 1775, the *Falcon* was forced to surrender to a British Man O' War ship several times her size, and Elisha was impressed into the British Navy. So the surprise was great when he suddenly appeared on his parents' doorstep in Stonington, Connecticut, a few months after his capture.[6]

His escape from the British Man O' War while it lay at anchor in Quebec made him the town's hero, and by 1782 he married Hope Fanning, the twenty-five-year-old daughter of a local farmer, Captain Thomas Fanning. Hope was a great catch; she was a member of a distinguished family whose members served in the Legislature, commissioned their portraits from John Singleton Copley, and developed a friendship with the Marquis de Lafayette.[7] The newlyweds moved into the Fanning Farm in Ledyard, Connecticut, where they raised their eight children, including the first Frederick Ayer, born in 1792.

While there was "no bad blood in the Ayer family," Beatrice's father couldn't deny there hadn't been "a wag or two."[8] This label certainly applied to his uncle, Elisha Jr., who was bound to take over the family business—a group of mills along the Poquetanuck Brook—but disappeared when his fiancée suddenly broke off their engagement. Then, several years later, he reappeared with a flock of Merino sheep, a stallion, and some mares. After crossing the Atlantic Ocean on a privateer, Elisha Jr. had spent most of his time in Spain, where he was introduced to the fine qualities of Merino wool.[9]

The Ayers' second son, Frederick, proved more reliable than his wayward brother and took charge of the family business in his absence. Never one to shy away from hard work or danger, not only did he grow the farm to include a blacksmith shop and wagon factory, but he also fought in the War of 1812 with his brother-in-law, James Cook Jr. The relationship between the Cooks and the Ayers was two-fold: James Jr. married Frederick's sister, Lovisa Ayer, while Frederick married James's sister, Persis Cook Jr.

The Cook family lived on a mill farm a mere two miles from the Ayers and specialized in woolen manufacturing. Several of their sons continued in the textile business, most notably James Jr. and his brother Calvin. The two moved to Northampton, Massachusetts, where they opened a woolen mill in 1820. When the mill burned down, they used their know-how to set up the Middlesex Woolen Mills in Lowell, Massachusetts. James Jr. moved to Lowell permanently, becoming a pillar of the community and eventually the town's mayor. Despite the distance between Lowell and Ledyard, James and Lovisa Cook would play a significant role in the lives of their nephews.

LEFT a widow at age twenty-nine with four young children—James Cook Ayer, Fanny Ayer, Frederick Ayer, and Lovisa Ayer—Persis had a hard time dealing with the sudden loss of her husband. Uncomfortable living with her in-laws at the Fanning Farm, she returned to Preston. Even though James and Frederick were equally responsible for the terror they caused in the neighborhood—including throwing rocks into a neighbor's pond until the wheel of his grist mill clogged up—it was Frederick who was eventually sent back to the Fanning Farm to live with his paternal grandparents.

The Fanning Farm was already crowded when Frederick moved back in 1826, and he found himself living with his uncle and two spinster aunts. His grandmother Hope "spread happiness wherever she went" and could always be found knitting in front of the fire while taking snuff, rarely leaving the house since she became deaf.[10] His grandfather Elisha Sr. was as hardworking as ever and abhorred idleness. He expected everyone around him to be as industrious as he was, including his four-year-old grandson.

At first, Frederick's tiny hands were only capable of picking up sticks and stones, but as he grew older, he sought wood to start the fire, drove the cows to pasture, and took lunch to the men working on the fields. A mile and a half from the farm, "through a lonely wood," stood a barn with Uncle Elisha's Merino sheep. They were not used to the cold Connecticut winters and needed to be brought inside whenever the weather turned bad. Frederick learned to care for the fickle Spanish animals who subsisted on a diet of turnips and carrots. He would trudge through the snow after school to feed them, making sure no Pequots were spending the night in the barn on their way to and from Preston.

Long before the first European settlers arrived on the Eastern shores, the area of Ledyard and Groton was home to the Pequot tribe. Its approximately eight thousand members lived on 250 square miles of land until the tribe was almost completely decimated in 1636 during the Pequot War. Frederick grew up hearing stories of Sassacus, a Pequot sachem born in Groton, around 1560. He valiantly led his men during the Pequot War but fled to New York after his defeat in 1636, only to be killed by the Iroquois Mohawks who wanted to stand in the colonists' good graces. The Pequots who survived the war were either taken into slavery or put under the control of other tribes.[11]

By the time Frederick was born, a few hundred Pequots had returned to the area, living in reservations near Groton, Ledyard, and Mashantucket. Not only was Uncle George superintendent of one of these reservations, but the Fanning Farm lay on an Indian trail connecting Groton to Preston, where the Pequots went to buy rum and tobacco. Frederick was in charge of offering them cider whenever they passed through and occasionally found himself rooming with a local Pequot who spun the family's thread and suffered from "crazy spells."[12]

THERE WAS neither time nor money to have fun at the Fanning Farm. While the family never wanted for anything, not a single penny was made available to enjoy life's little pleasures. Frederick longingly watched his friends skate on the neighborhood's frozen lake, until one day he decided to make his own money so he could buy himself some skates. Even though his efforts of selling animal bones to the local button factory were mostly in vain, the young boy learned to exercise his entrepreneurial mind and never stopped looking for new opportunities to make money.

Despite the hardships, Frederick was an obedient grandson who remembered growing up on the Fanning Farm as some of the "pleasantest hours of my life."[13] For most of his childhood, his mother and three siblings lived about two miles away at the Cook Farm. As the years progressed, Persis grew increasingly worried about her sons. Both James and Frederick possessed an entrepreneurial spirit and were thirsty for knowledge, so nine years after the death of her first husband, she decided to remarry to reunite her family.

Frederick wore his first real suit on August 3, 1834, at his mother's wedding to Hezekiah Ripley Parke, a momentous occasion for the twelve-year-old boy who up until that point had only worn his grandfather's hand-me-downs with the legs and sleeves cut short. Persis married the tailor from Jewett City, Connecticut, to give her children a better future, but Hezekiah provided anything but a stable home. Frederick had only just moved in when the family relocated to Norwich. Perpetually looking for better opportunities, Hezekiah uprooted his family again three years later.

The Parkes loaded their few possessions into a chartered sloop and sailed first to New York, then up the Hudson River to Albany. Their destination was Baldwinsville, a small village along the Erie Canal fifteen miles from Syracuse. Sixteen-year-old Frederick attended some school during the winter and worked as a driver on the canal during the summer. Being a "hoggee" was rough work; while one driver guided the barge through the canal by walking his two horses along the towpath, his colleague rested in the bow. The job only paid five cents a day, but Frederick loved working with horses and even dreamed of being a jockey one day.

After two years on the canal, Frederick took a job at the country store of John Tomlinson in Syracuse. Mr. Tomlinson was well known in the community and "carried on more business than ten ordinary men could well accomplish." Hence, he took a quick liking to Frederick, who considered himself "a restless sort of person" who always had to work.[14] Taking note of his young protégé's keen curiosity and exceptional work ethic, Mr. Tomlinson made Frederick the manager of his new store in Canton after just one year of employment. By the time he opened another store in nearby Lysander, the two men were business partners. The $600 Frederick borrowed from his grandfather Elisha Sr., uncle James Cook, and brother James Ayer was quickly repaid.

As Frederick ventured out on his own as a "Yankee trader," his mother was all but widowed for the second time and left with nothing but two more young children—Persis and William Ayer Parke. Since Hezekiah seemed perpetually unable to support his family, Persis sold their house in Baldwinsville in 1843 and used the money to secure a spot in John Anderson Collins's Skaneateles Community. Unfortunately, it took less than three years for Collins's utopian ideal to fall apart, so the Parkes moved further south, fueled by Hezekiah's newfound obsession with spiritualism and religion. His behavior became so erratic, though, that Persis saw no other recourse but to have her husband committed.

Frederick immediately came to his mother's aid and admitted his stepfather to the Utica Insane Asylum near Syracuse. Hezekiah remained there for a year and was never heard from again after that. From now on, Frederick would take care of his family; he rented his mother a tenement in Baldwinsville and paid for Persis and William's schooling. When he moved to Lowell, Massachusetts, in 1855, to go into business with his brother James, his mother and siblings moved with him.

JAMES COOK AYER spent his childhood with his mother at the Cook Farm, learning the ropes of farming and milling while fervently yearning for a liberal education. When uncle James Cook visited the family in 1836, he took an immediate liking to his namesake and took him to Lowell where he paid for his education at the Westford Academy. When he graduated in 1838, James hoped to continue his education at a prestigious college, but his dreams were quickly shattered. Instead of pursuing "an intellectual, cultured life" as he had hoped, he had no choice but to start working.[15]

It didn't take James long to realize that he could pursue knowledge "solitary and alone." He took a job as a clerk at Mr. Jacob Robbins's apothecary shop in Lowell, learning all about chemistry and compounds. He also befriended the leading physicians in town and often joined them on house calls. These connections proved invaluable when he bought the apothecary shop in April 1841 with money borrowed from Uncle James. He renamed the store after himself and introduced his first original product: Cherry Pectoral, a cough and cold remedy. The syrup contained one-sixteenth of a grain of heroin and was a favorite of new mothers who used it to pacify their babies. Over seventy years later, Beatrice would give her children a few drops of Cherry Pectoral to ensure peace and quiet on long trips.[16]

When the business became too much for one man, James sold one-third of the company to his brother. Frederick's first job was to grow the J. C. Ayer & Co. nationally, so during the winter of 1855 and 1856, he traveled on horseback through Texas, Louisiana, Alabama, and Georgia. Norfolk and Portsmouth had just experienced the worst yellow fever epidemic in U.S. history, and interest was high in the company's products. Frederick didn't peddle his merchandise from door to door; instead, he traveled with a limited number of samples for chemists and local agents to try before ordering.

With Frederick now in charge of selling, James could focus on developing new products. Besides Cherry Pectoral, the J. C. Ayer & Co. would be known for: Cathartic Pills (1853), sugar-coated pills mainly used as a laxative; Sarsaparilla (1858), a syrup made from the root of the sarsaparilla plant which promised a cure against a range of diseases, including syphilis and scrofula; Ague Cure (1858), a remedy against fever and malaria; and Hair Vigor (1867), the company's most lucrative product, which promised to regrow hair and which would be vigorously applied by George Patton.

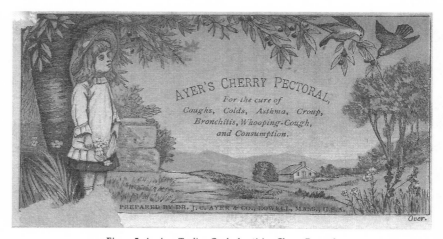

*Figure 5. An Ayer Trading Card advertising Cherry Pectoral.*

James "was always intensely interested in his business and very jealous of any unfavorable allusion to it."[17] Patent medicine was often the only hope for sick people in the nineteenth century. The vast expanse of the United States made it impossible for doctors to see more than a few patients a day, and traveling on horseback prohibited them from carrying an adequate supply of medicine. James had earned the public's trust, but the medical community would always look down upon patent medicine because of its over-the-counter availability; its secret formulas (which James tried to counter by freely making them available); its claim to cure many diseases; and its reliance on advertising.[18]

Dr. Ayer, as he began calling himself, was a master advertiser who took advantage of new print technologies—like color lithography—to cheaply mass-produce advertisements. The J. C. Ayer & Co. employed two unique marketing strategies: the Ayer Trading Cards, featuring the company's name, product information, and original artwork; and the Ayer American Almanac, a yellow booklet containing ads, short historical tidbits, and important dates for the coming year. The cards soon became sought-after collectibles, and the almanac claimed to be "second only to the Bible in circulation," with sixteen million copies distributed each year in twenty-one languages.[19]

AFTER YEARS of "hard work and hard thinking," Frederick had "to show for it my situation in life and standing in society." However, he was always too busy to even think about love, so by the age of thirty-five, he was still single. Back in Syracuse, the town's society ladies he befriended took it upon themselves to find him a wife, but after countless dinners, the love of Frederick's life ended up walking into his store with her mother sometime in the early eighteen-fifties.

Born in Pompey, New York, in 1835, Cornelia Wheaton was the eldest daughter of Charles and Ellen Birdseye Wheaton, abolitionists whose Syracuse home was a way station for enslaved people escaping to Canada on the Underground Railroad. Mrs. Wheaton had twelve children, but she was a staunch suffragist and better educated than most women of her time. Mr. Wheaton was a successful hardware merchant until a failed 1854 investment in the Blue Ridge Railroad Co. left him struggling. Just a few months after Frederick moved to Lowell, Cornelia moved to Shocco Springs, North Carolina, to teach the children of planter John C. Davis and so "relieve her Father somewhat, in this time of trial."[20]

When Cornelia returned to Syracuse in June 1857, her mother invited Frederick for a visit. By the end of his stay, his life's ambition was to have Cornelia's "regard" and "confidence," which she ultimately gave him at noon on December 15, 1858.[21] The Syracuse wedding was "very beautiful and impressive" and a great relief to Mrs. Wheaton, who had stressed about the preparations like so many mothers-of-the-bride. Mr. and Mrs. Ayer spent their wedding night at the Delavan House in Albany, but they never made it home to Lowell.

On the morning of the seventeenth, the newlyweds received a telegram informing them that Mrs. Wheaton, who went to bed in a "lovely frame of mind," died during the night of heart failure at the age of forty-two. Frederick and Cornelia immediately returned to Syracuse, where they found a bereaved Mr. Wheaton and a house in disarray. No one who looked into Frederick's eyes ever failed to see kindness and compassion, and he immediately offered to care for Cornelia's youngest sibling, three-year-old little Mabel.

It was no exaggeration when Ellen Louisa Wheaton, another of Frederick's sisters-in-law, wrote in her diary that there weren't "many young men that would take a little stranger right into his affections, as he has Mabel, and I think it shows pretty plainly that he carries a large heart with him."[22] The same large heart made Frederick open his home to his mother Persis (who lived with him until she died in July 1880) and countless other family members who needed a helping hand.

Little Mabel lived with her sister and brother-in-law until the fall of 1859, when Mr. Wheaton moved his family to Northfield, Minnesota. Meanwhile, Frederick and Cornelia started a family of their own in Lowell. In October 1859, they moved into a house on the corner of Pawtucket and School Streets, just in time for the arrival of their first child, a daughter named Ellen Wheaton Ayer. They would have three more children: James (Jamie) Cook in 1862, Charles (Chilly) Fanning in 1865, and Louise Raynor in 1876.

ONE OF FREDERICK'S favorite stories to tell was his visit with President Lincoln at the White House in 1862 upon his return from a six-month business trip to the West Coast. He and four acquaintances found the commander in chief in his office with his vest unbuttoned and his shirt wet with perspiration.

"Mr. President," Frederick said. "We have called to pay our respects to our President, but none of us has a favor to ask—not even a country post office."

The relief was evident on President Lincoln's face as he rushed over and grabbed both of Frederick's hands. "Gentlemen, I am glad to see you. You are the first men I have seen since I have been here that didn't want something."[23]

Frederick never entertained political ambitions, but as a successful businessman, he understood all too well the responsibilities the president faced. Whether it was a lumber business, an interoceanic canal, railroads, or the textile mills of Lowell, Frederick and James were always looking for new opportunities. The brothers were prudent capitalists who saw it as their duty to become involved with the day-to-day running of the companies they invested in. They never resorted to wild speculation and possessed a visionary character that made them open to investment in companies others often shunned.

Among his countless achievements throughout his life, Frederick took most "pride in suppressing the 1871 smallpox epidemic in Lowell," which began in January at the home of the Kennedys who had just returned from Liverpool, England.[24] Highly contagious and with a mortality rate of 30 percent, cases rose quickly. The authorities, however, were reluctant to enforce the law in the hopes of preventing the mills from closing.

The North Middlesex District Medical Society agreed "that by proper measures this epidemic could be suppressed in a short time," and advised creating a commission to aid in the matter. Their recommendation languished with the City Council for six weeks, during which "the epidemic was raging to an alarming extent, and many lives were being sacrificed." When more than one hundred cases were recorded in the first half of September alone, the citizens of Lowell finally had enough of "the political smallpox."

Frederick Ayer, a city alderman for many years, was "a leader because others were proud to follow" and "powerful because he was kind and just."[25] On September 15, he arrived at a special meeting convened by the City Council carrying a petition signed by hundreds of Lowell residents. It protested the inefficiency of the Board of Health and urged prompt action against the smallpox epidemic. A hefty debate with a "political tone" ensued, which resulted in Frederick—ill with an attack of boils—and four other aldermen being declared the new Board of Health "against our will and most earnest protest."[26]

The faith that the community placed in Frederick was well-founded. The Board exterminated the disease in about six weeks, demonstrating "what skill and science can do, sustained by wise management and efficient action."[27] *The Complete Report of the Board of Health and Board of Consulting Physicians* concluded this sudden turnaround was due "to the prompt report of cases; to the removal and isolation of all cases as soon as reported; to the immediate destruction or thorough fumigation of all infected material; to every precautionary measure, to prevent spread of the disease, that could be devised; and to vaccination."[28]

FLOWING for 117 miles through New Hampshire and Massachusetts, the powerful Merrimack River was the perfect fuel for the booming textile industry of the 1820s. By the time the Ayers moved to 357 Pawtucket Street, the Lowell Power Canal System measured almost six miles and counted seven canals. Frederick and his family lived right next to the Northern Canal, across from the oldest bridge over the Merrimack, on a piece of property purchased in 1859 from farmer Phineas Whiting.[29] Seventeen years later, they replaced Whiting's old house with the most ornate home in Lowell.[30]

Frederick was a humble man of simple tastes, but he spared neither money nor effort to enhance the happiness of his wife and children. The Frederick Ayer Mansion was a two-and-a-half story, red brick house built in the Second Empire style and designed by noted Boston architect Shepard S. Woodstock. As visitors walked up the front steps to the entry portico, they were surrounded by ten carved Corinthian columns with pink granite details. The house was dotted with beautiful stained glass windows, and most of the bedrooms overlooked the Merrimack. The woods surrounding the mansion were a haven for Frederick and his children, who enjoyed riding on horseback along the many trails he established.

*Figure 6. The Saint Paul Globe called the Ayer Mansion "one of the finest homes of New England." (Huntington Library)*

Unfortunately, Frederick and Cornelia would have less than two years to enjoy their new home together. Just a few months after moving into the Frederick Ayer Mansion and barely a year after giving birth to their fourth child, Cornelia was diagnosed with cancer, presumably of the liver. Her spinster sister, Florence Wheaton, moved in and cared for her with the help of eighteen-year-old Ellen, a strong and free-spirited woman like her mother who had studied at Les Ruches, a young ladies' school in Fontainebleau, France.

The family's tender ministrations and access to the best medical care were no match for a cancer which even today only has a survival rate of 33 percent. Cornelia passed away on January 9, 1878, just a few months after her forty-second birthday. Frederick suddenly found himself thrust into the exact same situation as his father-in-law twenty years earlier. After burying his wife in the Ayers' family plot at the Lowell Cemetery, he came home to four devastated children between the ages of two and eighteen. Aunt Florence stayed on to take care of little Louise, some say, in the hope of marrying Frederick next.

A mere six months after the death of his wife, Frederick's brother also succumbed to a long illness. James's problems began in February 1875, when he returned from a trip to Europe where he was fêted at the courts of Germany and Russia. Despite calling himself a "private capitalist" without any political ambition, James gave in to public pressure and ran for Congress. The humiliating defeat he suffered, together with years of hard work and mental strain, led to a bizarre episode in February 1876. He inexplicably wrote several improper letters to acquaintances and was sent to a farm in New Jersey to rest. His behavior continued to be erratic and he eventually ended up in New Jersey's Pleasantville Asylum.

Because of the severity of his overstrain, doctors believed nothing more could be done for James except protect him against himself. A judge ruled him to remain committed and appointed three legal guardians in March 1877, leaving Frederick in sole charge of the business. Since he knew all too well how difficult and expensive it was to care for a sick spouse, Frederick allowed money from the company account to be given to his sister-in-law, Josephine Mellen Southwick, a cold-mannered woman whose only ambition in life was to become the next Mrs. Astor. Worried James might recover at some point and accuse his brother of taking funds without proper authority, Frederick's lawyer advised him to stop until a legal document could be drafted. From that point forward, Josephine considered her brother-in-law the enemy.

James succumbed to "a general paralysis of the insane" on July 3, 1878, at a private insane asylum in Winchester, Massachusetts. He left behind his wife, three children, and a "colossal private fortune" estimated at $20 million (approximately $600 million in 2022).[31] Grieving for both his wife and brother, Frederick withdrew as executor of James's estate when the animosity with Josephine grew. Not only did she take her brother-in-law to court to break James's will, but she also forced the family to choose sides. Josephine ended up losing both battles and left Lowell, dividing her time between houses in Newport, Bar Harbor, and New York, in search of the high-society life.

IN THE SPAN of two years, Frederick lost his wife, brother, and mother. By 1883, his sons were off to Harvard, Ellen found love but was in no rush to marry, and little Louise was still cared for by Florence. Frederick threw himself headlong into his work and probably wouldn't have remarried but for the interference of his sisters-in-law, Emma and Clara Wheaton. Whenever Frederick visited them in St. Paul, Minnesota, they made sure to seat a single lady next to their still sprightly brother-in-law at dinner. One of those friends they hoped to introduce was Miss Ellen "Ellie" Barrows Banning, a vivacious actress whose family history was as colorful as her personality.

Born in Philadelphia on May 7, 1853, she was the daughter of William Lowber Banning and Mary Alicia Sweeney. The Banning name originated in Denmark and spread to England and Holland in the seventeenth century. The Dutch Frans Banning-Cocq was a dedicated public servant who served as captain of the militia and mayor of Amsterdam in 1650. He is the man wearing the red sash in Rembrandt's *The Night Watch*, originally titled *The Company of Captain Frans Banning-Cocq and Lieutenant Willem van Ruytenburch*.[32] This call to public service was also present in the English branch of the Banning family once they crossed the Atlantic. John Banning, Ellie's great-grandfather, was instrumental in the founding of Delaware and cast his vote for George Washington at the first Electoral College in 1788.[33]

William Lowber Banning was born in 1814 on the family farm near Wilmington, Delaware. He studied law in Philadelphia, opened a successful practice, and married Mary Alicia Sweeney. Just two years after Ellie's birth, the Bannings moved to St. Paul at the instigation of Robert Ormsby Sweeney. Rachel's brother was a pharmacist and artist who went to the Minnesota Territory in 1852, looking for opportunities. He found plenty and consequently convinced his sisters, Mrs. William L. Banning and Mrs. Jacob H. Stewart, to move their families in 1854.[34]

The story of how Frederick and Ellie ultimately met in 1883 is full of inconsistencies, embellished throughout the years by Ellie's flair for the dramatic. The *Saint Paul Globe* called her "one of the best known and most highly esteemed young ladies of St. Paul." She was the eldest daughter of the Honorable William Lowber Banning, and a talented Shakespearean actress who made a name for herself in St. Paul's drama societies. Her dedication to her profession was so great that when she had to choose between meeting a wealthy widower and watching Edwin Booth perform *Hamlet,* she could not resist the temptation to choose the latter. She sent Mrs. Wheaton a note of apology and declined her dinner invitation.

When Ellie stepped out of the theater that evening, "the handsomest man," like "a knight in shining armor," walked up to her and asked if she was Miss Ellen Banning. She immediately felt a little flutter in her stomach, but after a stiff yes so as not to encourage the five-foot-nine stranger with the impeccable white beard, she turned around and walked away. But, she recalled, "Once I looked into those piercing blue eyes, if he had said 'Ellen Banning, will you follow me to the world's end?' I would have gone right with him just as I was."

Frederick was similarly intrigued. "Miss Banning," he approached her again, "when I understood that there was one young lady in the town of such good sense and judgment that she preferred going to see a performance by America's greatest living actor to going to an evening party, I decided that she should have both treats, and I have come for you in my carriage with a chaperone to take you to the party."[35]

Frederick and Ellie were married in a private ceremony at the majestic Banning residence in St. Paul on July 15, 1884. The bride's embroidered cream satin wedding dress with diamond details was set to become a family heirloom worn by at least two future generations. In her hair, she wore orange blossoms that uncle Phineas Banning brought from California. Except for his impressive white beard, the sixty-two-year-old Frederick looked as trim and youthful as his thirty-one-year-old bride.

**Figure 7.** *Ellie saying goodbye to her "Sir Frederick" as he leaves on his daily ride.*

No one objected to the couple's significant age difference. In the case of the Ayers, age was just a number. According to all who knew them, theirs was a true love story based on mutual respect and devotion. When his "little daughter" Beatrice asked Frederick years later how he could have loved both Cornelia and Ellie, he explained that both were extraordinary women in their own way, "but perhaps the Frederick Ayer that fell in love with Cornelia Wheaton would never have looked at Ellen Banning."[36]

Ellie was the polar opposite of Cornelia. She was half an inch short of five-foot-seven and always a little chubby, with dimples in her hands and cheeks. She was a force of nature whose bluish-gray eyes could home in on any prey, leaving no one she met indifferent to her attentions. Calling her a little eccentric was an understatement, but beneath the drama was a generous and warm heart. Her four stepchildren immediately accepted her into their lives; to all of them, she would always be "Mama."

Frederick and Ellie's life was one most happily lived, especially with the addition of three children. Beatrice Banning Ayer was born in one of the upstairs bedrooms at the Frederick Ayer Mansion in Lowell on January 12, 1886. She had blue eyes, blond hair, and a little dimple in her chin, just like her mother. Ellie named her daughter Beatrice not because of a family connection but because of its meaning: the bringer of joy and blessings. Frederick Ayer, named for his father but known henceforth as Fred or Freddie, was born on May 7, 1888, and Mary Katharine, named for her aunt but known henceforth as Kay, was born on September 3, 1890.

Beatrice always remembered how her parents "made our family life so happy." Her first recollection of her father was of him coming home from the J. C. Ayer & Co. for lunch, making time to lead her "around the driveway on his horse," to "straighten out some carpentry problem" for Fred, or to take Kay "on his knee and [explain] to her the mystery of the finding and cutting of his garnet shirt-studs."[37] Ellie often gave readings like she used to do in St. Paul, and Beatrice loved mimicking her mother when she dramatized her favorite, *Lorraine Lorraine Lorre,* by Charles Kingsley.[38] On weekends, the family went to The Farm, a stately mansion in the town of Newton, about ten miles outside of Boston, which Frederick purchased as a wedding present for Ellie.

*Figure 8. Baby Beatrice, undated. (Huntington Library)*

The husband Ellie forever called Sir Frederick was happy to leave the spotlight to his wife. While he continued to work as hard as ever, she created a comfortable world for her family in which she was the leading lady. Ellie had a gift for entertaining, and on Sunday night, the dining room table was opened, and guests from all walks of life joined the family for dinner. The Ayers were a tight-knit family, and on those Sundays when no guests were expected, they piled into the surrey—while one person was lucky enough to ride with Frederick in the buggy—for the ten-mile drive to the town of Andover to visit Ellen and her new husband, William Wood. When the snow was piled high in wintertime, they made the trip by sleigh. Beatrice, bundled up in furs, looked up at the night sky and imagined the stars guiding them home.[39]

THE TOWN of Lowell had grown into the largest industrial complex in the United States by the time Frederick moved there in 1855. Its backbone was the textile industry, which held a particular affinity for the Ayers. Not only did both brothers grow up on farms where textiles were produced in small quantities, but James also lived for many years with Uncle James Cook, manager of Lowell's Middlesex Mills. So it was only natural that James would invest his first hard-earned money in the mills of Lowell and Lawrence, an endeavor in which his brother soon followed him.

Frederick had been a major stockholder in Lawrence's Washington Mills for twenty-six years when he received word that the company suddenly filed for bankruptcy in 1885. He suspected Harding, Colby, and Company—the mills' selling house, a powerful component of the manufacturing process—engineered the mills' collapse to purchase it for themselves at auction. His suspicions were confirmed when he showed up at the hastily arranged auction and only found two bidders present: himself and Harding, Colby, and Company.

Frederick bought the Washington Mills for $328,000, sold its equipment for the same amount a few days later, and replaced the nine-story mill with one of the most modern of its time.[40] The new company was formed with $1 million capital, most of the stock purchased by Frederick as many investors thought his business practices were too forward thinking. Frederick hired Thomas Sampson, a textile manufacturer from Rhode Island, as mill manager. However, it was Mr. Sampson's young associate who had the business smarts to get the Washington Mills out of the red.[41]

Born in 1858 on Martha's Vineyard to Portuguese immigrants, William Madison Wood left school at age twelve when his father died of consumption. His good fortune began when he took a job as an office boy in the counting room of the Wamsutta Cotton Mills in New Bedford, Massachusetts. He continued to learn the ins and outs of the textile business by working in different departments, and he was in the process of raising funds to open his own mill when he agreed to run the Washington Mills' cotton manufacturing department in 1886. His meteoric rise began when Frederick agreed to implement one of his novel and risky suggestions: establishing an in-house sales department to eliminate the selling houses. The move proved successful, mainly because Frederick was eventually willing and able to endorse his own notes, instead of relying on selling houses to borrow money like other mills had to do.[42]

William was a self-made man who grew up under similar circumstances to his boss, which might be why Frederick took an immediate liking to him. The "dashing, swarthy, mustachioed, emotional, generous" William became a frequent guest at the Ayers' Sunday dinners, where he quickly fell in love with Ellen Wheaton Ayer, a vivacious, beautiful but petite woman with "the heart of a lion and the constitution of an eggshell." While a Dr. Greenleaf had been waiting for years for her hand in marriage, giving her the time to grieve the loss of her mother, Ellen accepted William's "hand and heart" after a whirlwind courtship.[43] They married in the drawing room of the Ayer Mansion in 1888. A year later, Ellen gave birth to Frederick's first grandchild, a girl named Rosalind, followed by William Madison, Cornelius Ayer, and Irene.


DESPITE MORE THAN sixty years of hard work, Frederick was not ready to retire when his doctors suggested he do so at the age of seventy-three. Ellie knew her husband wasn't meant to sit at home, so she proposed a break from business for Sir Frederick and a break from running a large household for herself. With his companies in the capable hands of his son Chilly, a Harvard Law School graduate, and son-in-law William, now the treasurer of the Washington Mills, Frederick felt comfortable making the grandest of grand tours. In February 1896, he and Ellie sailed for Europe with Louise (20), Beatrice (10), Fred (8), Kay (6), and Mary Ryan (28), the family's nanny and nurse. Their first stop was Paris, where the family made their home for the next two years while they traveled across Europe and the Orient.

The Ayers were avid travelers who took their children along from a young age. "We studied history in the land where the events took place," Beatrice remembered later, and the same went for languages.[44] Frederick always regretted not being able to speak French, so he made sure all his children became proficient. By the end of their stay, Beatrice would be fluent in both classical and conversational French, expertly taught by a governess called Mademoiselle Gogo. As a reward for not speaking English for three months, Beatrice received a doll with blue glass eyes and real auburn hair. For the next six years, Marguerite would travel everywhere with her, but how fooled people would be by the young girl and her doll.[45]

*Figure 9.* Fred, Frederick, Beatrice, and Ellie in Paris, circa 1896.

Like any respectable American family living in Europe at the time, the Ayers had their likeness painted by the most eminent artists of Paris, leaving Beatrice with a lifelong love of portraits. Renowned portraitist François Léopold Flaming painted Ellie, while Jean-Joseph Benjamin-Constant immortalized Frederick. Known for his Orientalism, Constant painted his subject seated in front of "a background of stamped Venetian leather of the fifteenth century," wearing "a fur pelisse of imperial sable." The artist had hoped to show *Portrait of Mr. Frederick Ayer of Boston* at the Paris Exposition since he considered it "one of my best portraits . . . but Mrs. Ayer and her children wished no more to be separated from the portrait than from the original."[46]

Paris was a joy for a horticulturalist like Ellie, who passed along her love of gardening to Beatrice. A member of the Massachusetts Horticultural Society who took home many first prizes—for her flower arrangements, and the breeding of roses, tomatoes, and even asparagus—Ellie must have particularly enjoyed strolling the Jardin des Tuileries. Meanwhile, Beatrice gave her first public piano recital when she turned eleven in January 1897. She was a gifted pianist and would seriously consider pursuing a professional career in the coming years, but it was Frederick who found the most joy in listening to his daughter play after dinner.

When the weather was nice, Mary Ryan took the children for walks along the Champs-Élysées. They were always on the lookout for Aunt Josephine in her landau, the color of her poodles matching that of her hair and outfit. Estranged from the Ayer family since James's death and the bitter contest over his will, Josephine had been living in Paris since 1889. While New York society never accepted her, in Paris, "her great wealth, her lavish expenditures, her brilliant entertainments, and her gowns and jewels were talked about everywhere." She leased one of Paris's finest residences—the Duc de Mouchy's near the Hôtel des Invalides—and became "one of the most generous entertainers in Paris." Parisians clamored for an invitation to her entertainments, her most extravagant being the dinner she gave in honor of Mrs. William Astor in 1897. Soprano Nellie Melba entertained the crowd with "Les Anges Pleurent," but people only had eyes for Josephine, who even outshone the bedazzling Mrs. Astor. [47]

THE COLD PARISIAN winters were no more beneficial to Frederick's health than Lowell's, so the family spent several months in Egypt to take advantage of the warm and dry climate. Almost a century after Napoleon invaded Egypt and a certain 'Egyptomania' gripped the world, tourism in the land of the pharaohs was rampant because of Thomas Cook. The British travel agent's guidebooks democratized travel, as did his economic twenty-one-day trips down the Nile on steamboats. The Ayers, however, traveled down the river on a private *dahabiyeh,* a traditional house barge pulled by mules and horses, similar to how Frederick used to tow barges on the Erie Canal. Once the sole means of transportation on the Nile, the *dahabiyeh* was now "reserved only for the most wealthy, leisured travelers."[48]

The Ayers embarked in Cairo and took approximately three months to sail 760 miles to Wadi Halfa, just across the border of current-day Sudan. With enough money and the right connections—possibly family friend Theodore Davis, an amateur archaeologist and lawyer who made his fortune helping Frederick—they were able to gain access to historical sites such as the Great Pyramid of Giza.

Beatrice and Fred hung over the railing of the *dahabiyeh* searching the muddy waters for the Tropic of Cancer, which their private tutor, Mr. Smith, described as a dotted line.[49] They went on daily excursions under the watchful eye of Mary Ryan and the captain's young son, who acted as their interpreter and guide. Many of the tombs dotting the desert hadn't been emptied yet, so Beatrice's strong sense of curiosity compelled her to jump inside one. Luckily the guide grabbed her before she could do so because staring up from the pit were the "soulless eyes" of a group of cobras. It was the beginning of Beatrice's lifelong tendency to take leaps of faith, both literally and figuratively.[50]

When Chilly joined the party for an extended visit and gave his sister $10 as a twelfth birthday present, she intended to spend the money getting a ship tattooed on her chest like the captain. She and the captain's son made it as far as the quay before Mary Ryan caught up with them and brought them back to the *dahabiyeh.* It was apparent that Beatrice was predisposed toward a certain eccentricity, and all it would take was the right person to fully develop that side of her character.

Beatrice's journey down the Nile only intensified an inborn curiosity that would never be satisfied. When she came upon a partially unwrapped mummy outside its sarcophagus during another tomb visit, she couldn't resist the temptation to touch its brittle foot. A piece broke off, and for the rest of her life, she carried a jelly jar containing the toe of a four-thousand-year-old mummy. Occasionally she would lift the lid, releasing the "odor of eternity," which her daughter Ruth Ellen later described as a faint smell of tar and sweetness.

Unlike the tourists on Thomas Cook's steamboats, the Ayers were not shielded from the local population who lived in squalor along the Nile. Their hardships were never more evident than during the few weeks Jamie spent with his parents and siblings on the *dahabiyeh.* Frederick's eldest son had taken a job at the Washington Mills when he graduated from Harvard in 1886, but he quickly grew disillusioned. So he convinced his father—whom he and Chilly called The Governor—to allow him to pursue his dream of becoming a doctor, and he had recently graduated from Columbia's College of Physicians and Surgeons in New York City.

It was very rare for a doctor to pass through the area, so when Jamie extracted a thorn from a laborer's foot, news spread fast along the banks of the Nile. It was heartbreaking to see hundreds of people with desperation in their eyes waiting each night by the river's edge, many of them wailing and praying for a miracle Jamie often could not perform. Beatrice, Fred, and Kay peeked through a window as Jamie tried to help as many people as possible, but without specialized equipment and skilled help, there was only so much their brother could do.[51] It was a useful lesson that not everyone was as fortunate as they were.

The Ayers traveled around the Middle East and North Africa for a year before returning to France via Algiers. They sailed on the *Maréchal Bugeaud*—named after the conqueror of Algeria—but were caught in a violent storm that soaked everything in their cabins. Only when they made it to Marseilles did they see the extent of the damage: the deck was destroyed and covered in the artichokes the ship had been carrying. Arriving at their hotel, Frederick and Ellie took off the children's wet clothes, wrapped them in blankets, and sat them in front of the fire "like a lot of papooses."

"Sir Fred, don't you think that Beatrice is a little under the influence?" Ellie asked when her daughter finished the hot toddy her father made her and asked for a second one.

"What if she is?" Frederick replied. "It will do her good."

The last thing Beatrice remembered of that night was lying on her bed and "watching the bay window go round and round like a whirligig, and wishing we had one like that at home in Lowell." Even though she couldn't remember, Beatrice assumed she was sick that night because since then, "I have never cared for either whiskey nor green artichokes."[52]

It was back to business for Frederick upon the family's return from Europe in June 1898. William Wood, a master of efficiency, finally eliminated the company's $3 million debt that year and even made a modest profit. In February 1899, he and Frederick solidified their position as major forces in the textile industry with the creation of the American Woolen Company, a conglomerate of eight mills that manufactured clothing, cashmere, worsted yarns, etc. Opposition was steep as concerns over monopolization were raised, but nothing could stop Frederick and William, the company's largest investor and brain-child, respectively.

The American Woolen Company was bound to become one of the largest textile manufacturers in the world. As president of the company, Frederick commuted daily by train to his office at Boston's Ames building. He could have easily employed a chauffeur to drive him the thirty miles from Lowell to Boston, but "[a]s illustrative of his modesty," he preferred to take public transportation and "permitted only a Ford truck to take him to and from the train."[53] Ellie, however, thought the commute too arduous for her seventy-seven-year-old husband during the cold winter months and insisted they move into the city immediately. At the turn of the century, the Ayers left Lowell for a series of rentals in Boston while they awaited the completion of their dream home at 395 Commonwealth Avenue.[54]

Frederick, an inveterate land speculator and real estate investor from New York to Chicago, purchased two lots sandwiched between Boston's Commonwealth Avenue and Marlborough Street in April 1899. Construction on the new Ayer Mansion began by the end of the year.[55] The five-story masterpiece designed by architect A. J. Manning and Louis Comfort Tiffany was a slap in the face of the Boston Brahmins, the traditional upper class who ruled Commonwealth Avenue. The word—derived from the Hindu caste system in India—referred to old-money New England families who were instrumental in founding the United States. They were restrained, disdained new money, and looked down upon a self-made man like Frederick Ayer, who only had a sixth-grade education.

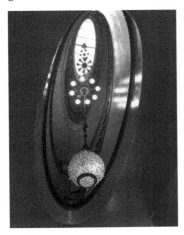

*Figure 10. Looking up the staircase of the Ayer-Tiffany Mansion.*

Neither Frederick nor Ellie "made any pretense of being 'Proper Bostonians.'"[56] If they were not accepted by Boston society, they would just have to transcend them, and in doing so, they distinguished themselves as "forward-looking and worldly patrons."[57] The Ayer Mansion lay west of Massachusetts Avenue, away from all other fashionable houses along the mall, and its white-marbled exterior with colorful mosaics and stained glass windows still stands out among the red brick townhouses prevalent along Commonwealth Avenue. The home was "unusually progressive for turn-of-the-century Boston," not surprising since Frederick's "thoughts were always of the future." Commissioning Manning and Tiffany to build an Art Nouveau-influenced home inspired by the family's recent travels came as easy to him as investing in Alexander Bell's telephone and the New York subway.[58]

The Ayers probably first encountered Tiffany's work at the 1893 Chicago World's Fair. The impressive Tiffany Chapel made the Tiffany Glass and Decorating Company world-famous and was so moving that men took off their hats when they first laid eyes on it.[59] No doubt Ellie marveled at the company's Magnolia Vase, representing the diverse flora of the United States. Tiffany's opulence and use of flowers were right up her alley, as were his Oriental and Moorish influences.

When the family moved into the Ayer Mansion in 1902, it was the tallest house on Commonwealth Avenue, with the most modern conveniences. The inventory list for the insurance company was 352 pages long and included Favrile green-glass vases and a tiger rug with claws. Tiffany specified almost every detail of the house, from walls to light fixtures, and designed custom furniture.[60] His favorite motif throughout the house was the lotus, a detail that blended well with the Ayers' exotic decorations they brought back from their grand tour.[61]

Ellie might have left the stage, but the stage never left her. She was an "outgoing, attractive, fun-loving, person who enjoyed company" and loved being the center of attention. According to her beloved son-in-law George Patton, Ellie had an air of grandiosity about her that "would drive a saint crazy," but family was all that mattered to her.[62] Her style and personality were reflected in the Ayer Mansion, nowhere more so than in the staircase, which doubled as a stage. The wall was a mosaic trompe l'oeil of an ancient Greek temple, the columns "composed of semi-transparent glass backed by gold foil, so when they reflect light, the temple appears to glow from a rising sun."[63] Ellie loved to hold readings there, and the children often performed plays while friends and family sat in the foyer.

Frederick never cared much for the Ayer Mansion. Despite all he accomplished in his long life, he was a man of simple tastes, modest and inconspicuous. He only owned two pairs of boots (albeit of the finest leather and made specifically for him because he had small feet) and cared little for his own comfort as long as his wife and children were cared for.[64] He lived life with an easiness about him, common to those who have nothing to prove, and he couldn't care less about what others thought of him as long as his family was left in peace.

Frederick was one of the wealthiest men on Commonwealth Avenue and also one of the least known. He hated talking about himself so much that Beatrice, the family historian, practically had to beg him to tell her the story of his life on a train ride home from California in 1908. For seven years, she persistently asked him for more details, writing down the information on whatever piece of paper was at hand. Every time she asked her father to reminisce, though, he would merely smile at the perseverant Beatrice.

"Quit, quit, my daughter; you are making a joke of me," he would say, claiming no one would find his life interesting.[65]

IF THE BOSTON BRAHMINS weren't already affronted enough by the brashness of the Ayer Mansion, they were even more shocked by the family's behavior. Frederick Ayer never held to the conventions of the day and always based his decisions on his own innate common sense. He was seen riding along the Commonwealth Avenue Mall daily, accompanied by his wife and daughters. Sidesaddle would remain the norm for female riders until 1930, but Frederick considered it bad for the back and insisted Beatrice and Kay ride astride wearing divided skirts. Then there was Ellie, who was considered avant-garde for allowing her children to volunteer at the settlement house where they might catch a disease. The only thing Ellie expected her children to catch there was a sense of how lucky they were.

Beatrice was homeschooled by a governess, except for finishing school at Miss Carroll in Newton, Massachusetts. In summer, she joined her brother on *The Tempest*, their father's schooner moored twenty miles away at the Eastern Yacht Club in Marblehead. She would return many times in the future, becoming an excellent racing sailor who often took home first prize. The Myopia Hunt Club in nearby South Hamilton—one of the oldest clubs in the United States and one which Beatrice would be associated with until the day she died—was the scene of action in fall with fox hunting, polo, skeet shooting, tennis, and horse shows. Even though she was nearsighted and required glasses from a young age (which she refused to wear for most of her life), Beatrice was a fearless participant in any activity.

Beatrice, Fred, and Kay enjoyed an idyllic childhood and wanted for nothing, but they learned to do as they were told.[66] They grew up with enormous respect and love for their parents and would remain as devoted to them as they did to each other. All seven brothers and sisters were inseparable; if you spotted one Ayer sibling, you were bound to see the remaining six as well. They were so devoted to each other that Ellie "used to accuse [them] of behaving at parties like birds on a telegraph wire."[67] It didn't matter where they lived, how old they were, or whether they had their own families, the Ayers would always come to each other's aid.

Because of the significant age difference, Frederick's children with Cornelia had already moved out of the house long before Beatrice was grown up. Most of them, however, at one point or another, all lived within walking distance of the Ayer Mansion. Ellen, William, and their four children lived at 21 Fairfield Street; Chilly and his wife Sara Theodora Ilsley, whom he married in 1904, lived at 127 Commonwealth Avenue; and Louise married Fred's tutor, a Boston lawyer named Donald Gordon, in 1900, and settled a mere twenty miles away at Drumlin Farm. Only Jamie moved away and settled in New York with his wife, May Hancock Boyd, whom he married in 1907.

Despite her privileged upbringing, Beatrice was never sheltered. She was allowed to develop into a confident and independent woman capable of thinking for herself and speaking her mind. She had just turned sixteen when she moved into her third-floor bedroom in the Ayer Mansion and was the next one up to leave the nest. Just like her parents, Beatrice did not adhere to the standards of her class and continually defied expectations and social conventions. There was "a rebel inside the pampered society girl, and that rebel fell in love with another rebel."[68]

As a beautiful and talented heiress, Beatrice had already been proposed to three times—including once by an American musician and once by a Russian count—but she only showed interest in the young man she met in the summer of 1902. Beatrice was always proud of her family, but this boy worshipped his ancestors and the military tradition they stood for. He was ambitious yet insecure, gregarious yet lonesome, and he had only one goal in life. He had an all-encompassing desire to become a great commander on the field of battle, so finding love was the last thing on his mind.

# 2

## LAKE VINEYARD
### SAN GABRIEL, CALIFORNIA

#### 1770–1903

*DRESS LIKE A SERVANT AND YOU'LL END UP ACTING LIKE ONE.*

Those who met George Smith Patton Jr. for the first time either hated him with a vengeance or loved him with intense devotion. For Beatrice, it was a case of the latter. When she stepped off her family's private railroad car upon its arrival at the Los Angeles train station on or about June 28, 1902, she immediately forgot the promise she had made her parents ten years earlier during her first visit to California. It was love at first sight when she came eye-to-eye with the blond-haired, blue-eyed boy she vowed never to play with, now seventeen years old and almost six foot two.

George, however, felt only dismay when he saw the sixteen-year-old Miss Ayer step off the train with her doll Marguerite. Beatrice was unlike any girl he had ever seen and nothing like he expected after being told this was one of Boston's most coveted young ladies. Beatrice had beautiful blue eyes, a dimple in her chin like her mother, and thick auburn hair that reached her waist, but she looked like a child. She was only five foot two and wore the same outfit as Marguerite, whom she had grabbed from her trunk "for fear she would smother."[1]

Beatrice and her family planned to spend the next two months on Catalina Island, located twenty-three miles off the Southern California coast. The island was owned by Ellie's three Banning cousins: Hancock, who was married to George's half-aunt Anne Ophelia Smith; Joseph, who was married to Beatrice's aunt Katharine Banning; and Captain William, the eternal bachelor. Frederick was looking forward to Captain William teaching him tandem driving, whereby two horses pull a carriage, one in front of the other. It was one of the most complex driving configurations to learn, but that did not deter the eighty-year-old Frederick. Like Beatrice, he loved a challenge and he was equally determined to reach his goals.

George was embarrassed as *The Falcon* sailed toward Catalina Island, his playground for the last seven years since his father bought a stake in the Santa Catalina Island Company from his Banning in-laws. He would always yearn for its "looks and smells . . . [climbing] on rocks that look down into the blue-black water with the yellow fishes and the brown kelp" and "[walking] over those hills on the short grass and [smelling] the clean warm salt wind and [killing] goats or quail."[2]

Tasked with keeping Beatrice company during her stay, George tried hard to shake her, but she relentlessly followed him. Already very image conscious, he worried about what his friends would think when they saw him walking around the island with this "little girl."[3] After all, he was a rough-and-tumble kind of guy who had his mind set on a military career.

*Figure 11. The summer of 1902 on Catalina Island: Katharine S. Banning (later Mrs. Francis Graves), Katharine (Kay) Ayer, Anne (Nita) Wilson Patton, J. B. Banning Sr., Beatrice Ayer, and Frederick Ayer. (Huntington Library)*

THE FIRST PATTON TO set foot on American soil was Robert, a fugitive who was forced to flee Scotland in the mid-1760s.[4] Within five years of his arrival, the flamboyant and egocentric Robert was running a thriving merchant business in Fredericksburg, Virginia. He became a fugitive once again after killing a British soldier in a bar brawl, his whereabouts unknown until he resurfaced in Fredericksburg at the end of the American Revolution.

Luck always seemed to be on Robert's side. He became the superintendent of the Fredericksburg Bank and, in 1792, married Anne Gordon Mercer, the eldest daughter of Brigadier General Hugh Mercer. He was George Washington's close confidant, who died during the Battle of Princeton in 1777, as famously depicted in John Trumbull's aptly named painting.[5]

John Mercer Patton was born in Fredericksburg in 1797, the second of Robert and Anne's six children. His success as a lawyer led him to Virginia politics, first as a member of the U.S. House of Representatives and later as lieutenant governor. His domineering wife, Margaret "Peggy" French Williams, raised their eight sons, and one daughter, in the spirit of Southern gentility. It would be impossible to find a Virginian prouder of her heritage than Peggy, who grew up surrounded by enslaved people on the Spring Farm in Culpeper. She was a hardheaded "southern grande dame" who considered her way of living superior to everyone else's, so when the Civil War broke out in 1861, she expected her sons to fight "and, if necessary, die for the Confederacy."[6]

John and Peggy's fourth child was the first George Smith Patton of the family, born on June 26, 1833. When he graduated from the Virginia Military Institute in 1852, he fell in love with Susan Thornton Glassell, a well-to-do young woman from Alabama whose frail appearance belied "an inner toughness" acquired through years of suffering. Madly in love as he was, George Smith was also terribly insecure, and he felt unable to ask Susan for her hand in marriage until he made something of himself.

Susan patiently waited while George taught at the Virginia Military Institute and studied law, continuously bolstering his fragile ego in reply to his anxiety-filled letters. She had enough by 1855, though, and threatened to go to Europe—tantamount to breaking up—unless he finally proposed. The couple married within months and settled in Charleston, Virginia, where Susan gave birth to George William Patton on September 30, 1856. The family moved into a stately Greek Revival house called Elmgrove, but the Civil War brought an end to the Pattons' idyllic life.

WHEN THE EIGHT PATTON BROTHERS—ROBERT, John, Isaac, George, Waller, Hugh, James, and William—reunited in March 1861 at the ancestral home in Culpeper, it was to fulfill their father's deathbed wish. While John wanted his sons to help Virginia secede from the North merely to defend its genteel way of living, Peggy wanted them to fight for the institution of slavery. Instead of freeing their slaves upon the outbreak of war as her husband had asked, she gave each of her sons not only the finest mounts and uniforms but befitting true "officers and gentlemen," also a slave. One by one, the Patton brothers left Spring Farm, the desire to join the cause so great that George Smith would have moved farther south if necessary to join the Confederacy. His grandson would itch to get on the battlefield just as much, but he would initially do so without political or ideological convictions.

Waller Tazewell Patton was the first brother to die in the Civil War, but he would always be remembered as "the most courageous ... [because] he'd been the most afraid." He graduated from VMI in 1855 and ran the family plantation in Culpeper while maintaining a successful law practice. He became company commander of the Culpeper Minutemen and got his first taste of battle during the John Brown Raid in 1859. After recuperating from a wound sustained during the Second Battle of Bull Run in August 1862, he was killed a year later at Gettysburg during Pickett's Charge. The twenty-eight-year-old colonel, who had a premonition he would die that day, was shot in the mouth as he jumped a stone wall running up Cemetery Hill. When Peggy heard of her son's death, she broke down crying; she now only had "seven sons left to fight the Yankees."[7]

George Smith Patton received his first taste of battle commanding the 22nd Virginia Regiment at Scary Creek on July 17, 1861. While rallying his men, a minié ball shattered his right arm and threw him off his horse. Colonel Patton was captured by the Union Army and faced amputation, but he vehemently resisted and placed his faith in the hands of an ingenious medical student. He was paroled a few weeks later and spent the next eight months recuperating with his family in Richmond, Virginia. In typical Patton fashion, neither pain nor injury diminished his zeal. Despite an offer to teach at VMI, George Smith chose to break the law and returned to his regiment.

The ten-dollar gold coin Susan gave her husband upon his departure ended up saving his life at the Battle of Giles Courthouse on May 10, 1862, but not in the way she imagined. When General Wharton surveyed the battlefield, he noticed a wounded Colonel Patton sitting underneath a tree, writing a farewell letter to his wife. The division commander examined the wound in the colonel's stomach, but instead of a bullet, he extracted a ten-dollar gold piece. The coin, which was meant to get him good treatment in case of capture, caused the bullet to ricochet, but the dirty fingers of General Wharton subsequently caused blood poisoning. Once again, George Smith returned home to recuperate, his wife attributing his survival to his "old luck."[8]

While his father was fighting, George William was taking in the sights of war from his bedroom window. He was a "quiet and passive" boy of six who watched wounded soldiers arriving at the hospital and "cart loads of arms and legs being taken away," leaving him with a "hysterical dread of doctors" for the rest of his life.[9] He had watched in wonder from the shoulders of Uncle Waller when Virginia voted to secede from the Union in May 1861, but the responsibility of being the man of the house weighed heavily upon the sensitive boy's shoulders. So when his father left for the third and final time, George William decided he would be the one to take care of his mother and three siblings—Eleanor (Nellie), Andrew, and Susan.

After surviving the Battle of New Market unscathed in May 1864, George Smith's luck finally ran out on September 19 when a piece of shell struck him in the right hip during the Third Battle of Winchester. Brought to the home of a cousin, he once again vehemently opposed amputation and rallied until gangrene unexpectedly set in. George Smith Patton died on September 25, 1864, at the age of thirty-one. Endowed with a sixth sense when it came to her husband, Susan was not surprised when she opened the front door of her home in Lewisburg, Virginia, to find her husband's servant standing there with his master's saddle, sword, bloodied shirt, shell fragment, and gold coin.

GEORGE WILLIAM PATTON was seething inside; not only had the Yankees killed his father and favorite uncle, but they had also destroyed his mother's happiness and the family's idyllic way of living. The South's economy was devastated when the Civil War ended in April 1865, and the Pattons were destitute. Susan settled into a rundown colonial in Madison County with her four children, her father Andrew Glassell, her brother William Glassell, her mother-in-law Peggy Patton, her brother-in-law Hugh Patton, and her servant Mary. With Andrew blind, and impoverished since investing his fortune in now worthless Confederate war bonds, Hugh recovering from wounds sustained during the Second Battle of Bull Run, and William severely weakened by tuberculosis he contracted in a Union prison, it was up to nine-year-old George William to tend to the vegetable garden. Watching his family go hungry and cold created an intense loathing of poverty, and he vowed never to let the same fate befall his own family.

In the fall of 1866, Susan received $600 from her brother Andrew Glassell to join him in California. He himself had started over on the West Coast thirteen years earlier when he was rejected thirteen times by Eliza Patton, Susan's sister-in-law and the love of his life. Inspired by the success her brother had made of himself, Susan made the arduous trip to the West Coast in November, accompanied by her children, her father, and her brother. Night after night, however, she regaled her children with stories of the Old Dominion and their heroic father, instilling in them a sense that the Pattons were better than any Californian they would ever meet. George William, a born sentimentalist who came to believe strongly in the "power of fate," was especially susceptible to these words. His mother's continued sense of superiority left him with a constant yearning for the romanticism of the Lost Cause and a certain snobbery that he would eventually pass down to his own son.

Susan might have had a reputation for being spoiled before the war, but she refused to be a burden on her brother and immediately looked for a job. She cleaned local schools and churches with the help of her eldest son until she saved enough money to open a small all-girls school. Susan had no formal education, but she was soon known in the area as a "superb, no-nonsense teacher who could handle even the most ill-behaved pupil."[10] Her success allowed her to buy a small adobe house, yet she continued to pine for all she had lost. She occasionally took to drink until one day in 1869, a member of her Virginian past showed up on her doorstep. When George Hugh Smith had lost Susan to George Smith Patton in 1852, he never imagined he'd get a second chance at winning her heart.

Colonel George Hugh Smith was the son of Peggy Patton's sister, Ophelia Anne Williams, and consequently the first cousin of George Smith Patton.[11] The close friends had followed a similar trajectory in life, from attending VMI and practicing law to falling in love with the same woman and fighting for the Confederacy. Wounded, captured, and paroled several times over the course of the Civil War, Colonel Smith refused to sign the Oath of Allegiance in 1865 and moved to Mexico to grow cotton. The endeavor proved harder than expected, and he returned to the United States in 1868. He took a job at Andrew Glassel's law firm—eventually making partner and becoming a well-respected judge and California State senator—and gave Susan a new lease on life. After a year-long courtship, George Hugh Smith married his cousin's widow and legally adopted her four children—the family then expanded with the addition of Anne Ophelia Smith (future wife of Hancock Banning) and Ettinge Smith.

GEORGE WILLIAM never forgot the last time he saw his father, "leaning against a gun and [waving] us goodbye."[12] Four years after watching him pursue the train bound for the Shenandoah Valley from the garden of his Uncle John's home, George William Patton officially changed his name to George Smith Patton in honor of his heroic father. George Sr. (or George I as he confusingly would henceforth be known) hoped to be worthy of the name, but it turned out not all Pattons were "natural-born warriors," as Colonel Smith raised his stepson to believe.[13]

An excellent student and debater, George Sr. entered VMI in 1873 on a full scholarship afforded to sons of killed Confederate soldiers. He was class valedictorian when he graduated with honors in 1877, his speech filled with continued anger against the North, stoked by his grandmother Peggy whom he had watched whip a former Confederate officer across the face because the man said Amen when the priest prayed for the president of the United States. George Sr., however, was by nature quiet and gentle, and his words often came across as forced.[14] He would always portray himself as someone he was not, forever pushing aside his desires and dreams in the interest of his family.

Instead of following his heart to New York City or pursuing his dream of becoming a career officer, George Sr. returned to California in 1878 when he heard his mother was sick and his family's law firm was in trouble. Susan Glassell Patton Smith died five years later after a long battle with breast cancer, four months shy of her forty-ninth birthday. By then, her son had passed the bar and was working at the newly renamed law offices of Glassell, Smith, and Patton.

A mirror image of his father and lauded as an exceptional orator, George Sr. was named Los Angeles's most eligible bachelor in 1884. However, his heart was already taken by twenty-three-year-old Ruth Wilson, daughter of one of California's "most distinguished pioneers."[15]

BENJAMIN "DON BENITO" Davis Wilson was born in 1811 in Nashville, Tennessee. At fifteen, he already possessed an entrepreneurial spirit, and he opened a trading post in Yazoo City, Mississippi. His business dealings with the Choctaw and Chickasaw Indians were the beginning of a long collaboration that would ultimately mean the difference between life and death.[16] In 1833, he moved farther west to become a mountain man, living off the land and trading furs for provisions. After two years, however, Benjamin realized that trappers risked their lives while traders made all the money—John Jacob Astor made his first fortune as a fur trader—so he organized his own company.

When famed American trapper James Johnson killed the chief of the Apache Indians for bounty at the behest of Mexico in 1837, the tribe took revenge by killing twenty-two innocent mountain men. Returning from their murderous spree, the Apache came upon Benjamin and four of his colleagues. Two managed to escape, but Benjamin and the others were taken back to camp, made to undress, and forced to watch as the wood pile was stoked to burn them alive. Luck was on Benjamin's side, though, and he managed to escape with the help of one of the Apache's former chiefs, who recognized him as an old friend. After fleeing on foot through hostile terrain for more than 120 miles, Benjamin arrived penniless in Santa Fe, New Mexico. He started afresh but ultimately decided to test his luck in the yet unnamed and unexplored Far West.

Benjamin joined the Workman-Rowland Party and arrived at the San Gabriel Mission in Southern California on November 5, 1841. He and about sixty-five other trappers, doctors, and traders of varying ethnicities traveled along the 1200-mile Old Spanish Trail through Colorado, Utah, and the Mojave Desert for two months. Benjamin finally settled in Southern California once he was thrice unable to secure passage to China, and purchased Rancho Jurupa—currently the city of Riverdale—for one thousand dollars two years after his arrival.[17]

Don Benito found a wife—Ramona Yorba, the sixteen-year-old daughter of his neighbor, the great Mexican landowner Don Bernardo Yorba—and "true happiness and ... friendship" among the Native Californians and Mexicans.[18] He was reluctant to get involved with the Mexican-American War of 1846 but was pressured into a commission as captain in the United States Army. Ramona, unfortunately, died in 1849, not long after the war ended, leaving him with two children: Maria de Jésús (Sue) and John Bernardo.

Don Benito married Margaret Short Hereford four years later, one of the first female pioneers who made the trip West from the American frontier where she grew up. Her first husband had died not too long after their arrival, and Margaret must have met Don Benito while working either as a house-keeper or a governess to his two children.[19] She already had a child, Edward Sublette, and subsequently had three more with Don Benito: Margaret, who died at the age of three; Annie, born in 1858; and Ruth, born in 1861.


GEORGE PATTON SR. likely met Ruth Wilson as he stood in for his father at the funeral of Don Benito Wilson on March 13, 1878. Don Benito had recently been lobbying Colonel Smith, the newly elected state senator, for government support to build a breakwater in Wilmington. By the time of his death, Don Benito was one of Los Angeles's most prominent citizens and one of the wealthiest men in Southern California, reinventing "himself again and again as the local economy shifted and as technology evolved."[20] He was twice elected to the California State Senate, was the second mayor of Los Angeles, and was a successful merchant and real estate investor in downtown L.A.[21]

Don Benito's closest business partner for many years was Phineas Banning, the uncle of Ellie Banning Ayer. When he was just thirteen years old, Phineas left the family farm in Wilmington and walked thirty miles to Philadelphia to start working as a law clerk at his brother William's firm. After two years, he took a job as a dockworker at the busy Philadelphia seaport, not hesitating at all when offered the chance to work a passage to California in 1851. The twenty-one-year-old Phineas settled in L.A. and quickly made a fortune in staging and freighting, organizing transports between the small pueblo of Los Angeles and the harbor of San Pedro. In this capacity, Phineas first met the formidable Don Benito Wilson.

In 1854, the two men purchased a piece of land they named after Phineas's city of birth, Wilmington. They immediately began construction on what would become one of the busiest ports in the world, followed by a railroad connecting L.A. and Wilmington. Until the project's completion in 1868, horse and carriage was the only means of transportation. "Admiral of the Port" Phineas Banning made sure to meet every boat upon arrival, sending a vaquero (a Spanish-Mexican cowboy) to Don Benito's house if any important passengers were on board.

The Wilsons lived at Lake Vineyard—in what is now San Marino—a sprawling thirteen-hundred-acre estate that was the largest vineyard in Los Angeles. In addition to grape vines, the estate grew various grains and fruits, including oranges, lemons, limes, olives, and walnuts. The house was built in the Spanish style popular in the area, made from adobe brick and featuring a large porch visitors reached by climbing a steep staircase. Wine was part of the Lake Vineyard culture, and a bucket with a silver-handled dipper could always be found in the estate's entryway, waiting to quench the thirst of any gentleman who came back from hunting, riding, or managing the estate.

Lake Vineyard was the home where Annie and Ruth Wilson grew up, where they sat next to their father's bedside when he suddenly died of a heart attack at the age of sixty-seven, and where they continued to live with their mother Margaret as she grew ever more distant and unbalanced. Reading was the only escape for the sheltered Wilson girls, but they enjoyed life at Lake Vineyard so much that they never wanted to leave. Annie hoped to remain single and grow old on the estate with her sister, but then George Patton Sr. entered the scene.

Both sisters fell head-over-heels in love with the dashing young lawyer who had melancholic brown eyes and wavy brown hair. For several years he drifted in and out of their lives, Annie convinced she would be the chosen one. After all, she was prettier and smarter than her younger sister, whom many considered a bit simple. Annie believed there was no way that George Sr.'s interest in her sister was anything more than a distraction upon the death of his mother, but then he asked Ruth for her hand in marriage.

George Smith Patton Sr. married Ruth Wilson on December 10, 1884, at the Church of Our Savior in San Gabriel. Don Benito, who refused to change his religion to Catholicism when he arrived in California, had been instrumental in building the Episcopal church in 1867. The newlyweds left for the train station after the wedding en route to New Orleans. They were shocked to see Annie there as well, suitcase in hand and fully intending to join them. It took Margaret to drag her daughter back to Lake Vineyard, but Annie never accepted that George Sr. had chosen her sister, and she remained single for the rest of her life.

GEORGE SMITH PATTON JR. was born at 6:30 a.m. on November 11, 1885, in the same bedroom as his mother, overlooking the lake for which the estate was named. Georgie, as only his family and closest friends ever dared call him, was a sweet baby who possessed boundless energy and a restlessness which would never be satiated. His adoring family catered to his every whim, but his father was his best friend. Nothing else mattered to Mr. Patton once his namesake was born. Plagued by feelings of inadequacy that he disgraced his ancestors by not becoming an officer, and longing for the genteel way of living he had known in Virginia, Mr. Patton placed all his hopes and ambitions on his son's shoulders.

The Boy—Mr. Patton's name for his son, regardless of his age—followed his father all over Lake Vineyard. He grew up in the blood-stained saddle of Colonel Patton, inspecting the vineyard and orchards of which Mr. Patton was now the manager. George didn't have a care in the world, remembering years later how he went "to the stable at night when I was supposed to be studying and laying by Polvo [his dog] looking at Marmion [his horse] and thinking that I must be the happiest boy in the world."[22]

Nothing was ever good enough for Mr. Patton's family, which grew with the addition of Anne "Nita" Wilson Patton in 1887. He bought his children the best of everything, even if it meant he had to do with less. The family owned a lot of land but was cash-poor, and Mr. Patton often could not work because of ill health. His eternal dread of poverty was exacerbated by James DeBarth Shorb, the husband of his sister-in-law Sue Wilson.

James DeBarth Shorb was a lawyer by training who had turned the San Gabriel Wine Company into one of the largest wineries in the world and then squandered most of the Wilson fortune through spendthrift and bad investments. In its heyday around 1880, Lake Vineyard's 2,500 fruit trees and 129,000 vines could produce one million oranges per year and 1.5 million gallons of exquisitely tasting wine (especially sweet white wine, port, and brandy).[23] But then disease destroyed the vineyard, and inclement weather ruined most of the citrus, forcing James to mortgage Lake Vineyard in order to maintain his lavish lifestyle.

The extent of his debt was not revealed until he died in 1896, leaving his family and in-laws to clean up the mess. Mr. Patton first managed the Shorb estate for the bank. Then, when it was sold to his friend Henry Huntington in 1903, he became the estate manager of the Huntington Land and Improvement Company (now the Huntington Library and Museum). George always remembered James as "either a fool or a crook," and he was furious his uncle robbed him of his father's undivided attention.[24] So even though he grew up surrounded by the Wilson legacy—Mount Wilson in the distance loomed large over the estate—he spent most of his life avoiding any reference to his maternal grandfather.

*Figure 12. George S. Patton Jr. riding Galahad at Lake Vineyard.*
(Huntington Library)

By selling some of the family's land to the city of Los Angeles, Mr. Patton managed to keep a significant share of the original Lake Vineyard. He never forgot the promise he made himself to take care of his family, so he gave part of his salary to his sister-in-law, Sue, and opened the doors of Lake Vineyard to his extended family. Living with the Pattons, besides nanny Mary Scally, were Mr. Patton's mother-in-law, Margaret Hereford Wilson; his unmarried sister, Susan Patton; his widowed sister, Nellie Patton Brown, and her six children; and his sister-in-law Aunt Nannie.[25]

IN ALL MATTERS CONCERNING her son's upbringing, Ruth Patton was overshadowed by her husband and overbearing sister. Mr. Patton easily forgave the Boy his mishaps, and a cunning Aunt Nannie made it a habit to faint at the onset of any disciplinary action. From the moment her nephew was born, she pretty much claimed him as her own. George never questioned the rather bizarre arrangement he grew up in, basking in his parents' love and his aunt's adoration as he grew accustomed to being the center of attention.

When Ruth saw the mangled bodies of the turkeys inadvertently killed by George careening down the hill in a wagon, she for once began the elaborate process of punishing him by calling the doctor and turning down Aunt Nannie's bed. George's stunt, however, was more than simple childhood mischief. He had hurtled toward the turkey patch to imitate John the Blind, King of Bohemia, riding valiantly into combat during the Battle of Crécy in 1346.[26]

George claimed to know what happened because he was there, but the history of the Hundred Years' War between France and England was just one of the many heroic tales his father and aunt regaled him with. Homeschooled for the first eleven years of his life, George sat in front of the roaring fire listening to his father read from *The Iliad* and *The Odyssey* and his aunt from *Pilgrim's Progress* and the Bible. He soaked up information like a sponge, enthralled by stories of Alexander the Great, Napoleon, and his own heroic Patton ancestors.

George Patton knew from the age of three that he was born to be a soldier. According to his sister, "unlike countless other small boys [who] think the same at that age, [he] never deviated from his objective." With Nita often assuming the role of enemy, George "trained in everything he thought would help him excel in his chosen profession." He built a Roman catapult with his closest friend, Ignacio Callahan, the grandson of Lake Vineyard's first gardener, and used it to fire mud at arriving guests. His first horse, a Shetland pony, did quadruple duty as "a knight's charger, a frontier scout's canny mount, a polo pony or a steeplechaser."[27] His father taught him the skills of an outdoorsman, while his step-grandfather taught him that heroism was real and tangible.

**Figure 13.** *George at Lake Vineyard, ready to start his first day of school in October 1897. (Huntington Library)*

George's idyllic childhood ended two months before his twelfth birthday when his father dropped him off at the Classical School for Boys in Pasadena with the words, "Hence forth our paths diverge forever." Being among peers was a rude awakening for the boy who was led to believe that he was perfect. When he realized that he was neither smarter nor better than everyone else, he hid his insecurities behind a mask of self-deprecating humor and bravado. From then on, he would only be able to be himself in the sanctity of his own home.

The Classical School for Boys, with its focus on history, was a perfect fit for George. His performance was mostly average, but he excelled in history. His photographic memory allowed him to memorize entire textbooks and recite them verbatim, the same reason he remembered the details of Caesar's campaigns and Genghis Khan's conquests from Aunt Nannie's and Mr. Patton's readings. Encouraged and inspired by his headmaster, George soaked up his teachers' lessons on self-sacrifice. Everything he learned confirmed what he already knew: there was no more honorable and noble death than dying for a cause on the battlefield, like George Smith and Waller Tazewell Patton.[28]

As THE *FALCON* sailed toward the town of Avalon on Catalina Island, Beatrice Banning Ayer looked like a child next to George Patton Jr. She was so only in appearance, though, because the worldly Beatrice was mature beyond her years and exuded an air of confidence that dwarfed her unsophisticated escort. While Beatrice learned history where it took place, George only read about the military battles of Napoleon, Xenophon, and Caesar. He spent most of his summers at his family's home on Catalina Island.

The Ayers checked into the Hotel Metropole for the duration of their extended stay. The hotel, with its distinct green color located right next to the pier, offered stunning views of mainland California. It was also a few miles from the Pattons' cottage, but that did not deter Beatrice from following George across the seventy-four-square-mile island.

Santa Catalina was the perfect playground for an adventurous boy like George, already an expert marksman who loved hunting. When he was nowhere to be found, it usually meant he was sailing his boat, the *Elaine,* hoping to catch one of the giant tunas so prevalent in the area. If George thought he could shake off Beatrice by participating in some of the island's more adventurous activities, he was mistaken; the more determined he was to get rid of her, the more relentless she became in her pursuit.

How wrong he was in his assessment of the little girl, quickly noticing that she had no problem keeping up with him, even if it meant getting her hands dirty. Beatrice felt no apprehension at sharing any of the risks George enjoyed taking, setting her further apart from the California girls he had known growing up. Underneath her frilly dress was a true tomboy—she also loved skiing, tobogganing, and skating—with grit and determination that would only grow stronger over time.

Even though years later, George would apologize for acting "disgraceful" during the first few weeks of their acquaintanceship, Beatrice never interpreted his behavior that way.[29] Her quiet composure hid a perceptiveness that easily saw through George's boastfulness, and she quickly figured out he acted the way he did to hide his insecurities. The boy who went around boasting of the number of goats he had killed was actually quite innocent and vulnerable, qualities which she found strangely appealing.

*Figure 14. Nita (2nd row, 2nd from left) her birthday party on August 24, 1902, brought together the Ayers, Bannings, and Pattons. George stands in the middle, with Beatrice to his left. (Huntington Library)*

The summer of 1902 was an endless array of entertainments, including women's golf tournaments, picnics on the Isthmus, and an epic barbecue on Hamilton Beach organized by William Banning.[30] On September 5, the theatrical Ayers staged Dugan's *Undine* at the home of Joseph and Katharine Banning. The magical children's play tells the story of Undine, a water sprite who marries a knight to obtain a soul. Joseph Banning Jr. and George and Nita Patton joined Beatrice, Fred, and Kay on stage.[31] George refused to play the romantic lead against Beatrice and forced the role on his sister, preferring to play Kühleborn while he figured out Beatrice and his growing feelings for her.

When George said goodbye to Beatrice two weeks later, he was in "a hell of a fix," wondering why the "little girl who I thought I did not like" had such an effect on him. His whole life had been perfectly planned down to the last detail, but he hadn't counted on meeting a five-foot-two, sophisticated Yankee from Boston who was determined to get what she wanted.

By the time Beatrice left Catalina Island, her long hair was tied up in a bun, and her doll Marguerite was nowhere to be seen. Ruth Ellen was correct in stating that her parents were in love for the rest of their lives from the moment they met, but her father took much longer than her mother to realize it. Beatrice heard all the stories of unrequited love in the Patton and Ayer families, from Aunt Nannie, who wiled her life away waiting for Mr. Patton, to Aunt Florence, who desperately wanted to marry Frederick after Cornelia died. She was determined not to let the same fate befall her.

A wily Beatrice took matters into her own hands and made the first move on October 1. Writing from the Hotel Colorado in Glenwood Springs, where she had just visited the Fairy Caves, Beatrice contacted Aunt Nannie. She casually asked about Nita, then wondered "if Georgie shot any very large goats at the island." She informed Aunt Nannie that she would be returning to school within the week, and she was "beginning to dream of declensions, theorems, and new girls, harmlessly swearing to myself the while (Hm! That doesn't sound very nice, does it?)."[32]

The groundwork laid, Beatrice reached out to Ruth Patton a month later, "I know that Georgie's birthday comes sometime this month, but not the exact date. When it comes, please, spank him seventeen times for me and give him my very best birthday compliments."[33] She finally contacted "Kühleborn" himself at Christmas, receiving her first reply on January 10, 1903. George awkwardly thanked her for the tie pin of a fox's head, "the very thing I most wanted," and concluded his letter with a taste of what life with him would be like. "As to Kuhlborns self there is little to say except that owing to his immortal nature he lived through the football season and did not even brake a bon[e] (worse luck) and that he is now devoting more time than he should to making a polo team; (for above all things he is desirus of an early and glorious death)." He signed his letter, "Your faithful friend."[34]

---

MR. PATTON KNEW he had done the right thing by going home and taking care of his mother in 1878, but he never stopped thinking about the path not taken. The idea that he was an embarrassment to his ancestors consumed him so much that he had signed up for a commission under British Colonel Hicks in 1883. Once again, however, his sense of responsibility toward his family had been greater than his desire for glory and he pulled out at the last minute.[35]

The burden of his ancestors was too heavy for Mr. Patton, but his Boy possessed the one thing he lacked: drive.

Joining the Army had been a necessity brought on by circumstances for most of the Pattons, but for George, it was a choice made of his own free will. Consumed with the desire to become a career officer, he decided to break with family tradition and set his sights on West Point. Graduating from the United States Military Academy meant immediate entry into the Regular Army as a second lieutenant, but it was notoriously hard to get in.[36]

Mr. Patton learned that California's Senator Thomas R. Bard would be nominating a new cadet in 1904. Far from the best choice—not only would George be left with a gap year upon graduating from high school, but Senator Bard was a Republican—he was pretty much the only choice. Putting politics aside, Mr. Patton began a charm offensive in February 1903. He was willing to do anything short of bribery, so his first tactic was to flood the senator's office with letters of recommendation. He sent his own and then "the cordial endorsement of the leading men of Los Angeles in business and politics."[37]

"I recognize that he possesses a strain of blood which ought to result in a successful Army career," Senator Bard replied to all of them, but he refused to appoint George outright. He wanted to compare him "physically and mentally" to other applicants and did not waver from his decision to base his choice on the result of a competitive exam he intended to hold at the beginning of 1904.[38]

Worried his son might not be able to pass certain subjects on Senator Bard's test—especially spelling and algebra—Mr. Patton devised a new plan. Instead of attending a military prep school during his gap year, George would begin his military training at VMI. The Patton name guaranteed him a spot, and the school provided the perfect safety net: either he would not receive the appointment and just finish his education at VMI, or he would be nominated and allowed to transfer to West Point without having to take its admission exam.

Meanwhile, after eighteen years of confiding in his father, George increasingly turned to Beatrice in time of need. After just one year of knowing her, he no longer felt any qualms about sharing his deepest feelings with her, and she wholeheartedly offered him the encouragement he desperately needed and the admiration he craved.

Beatrice had known right away that George Smith Patton Jr. was the one for her, and she quietly bided her time until he realized she was the one for him.

# 3
## THE AYER MANSION
### BOSTON, MASSACHUSETTS

#### 1903–1910

*IF YOU CAN'T CONVINCE HIM, LICK HIM. IF YOU CAN'T LICK HIM, KEEP STILL.*

The clock struck midnight on a freezing February night in 1910 when Beatrice quietly opened her bedroom door and peeked her head outside. The moon illuminated the hallway through the sky parlor, the Ayer Mansion's stained glass, elliptical skylight on the fifth floor. All was quiet on the landing when Beatrice leaned over the third-floor balustrade and lowered a small basket to where her sister was waiting. The "staid, thoughtful, and organized" Kay was a willing accomplice in her sister's efforts to get their father's permission to marry George Smith Patton Jr., and she kept her often impulsive sister supplied with food throughout a weeklong hunger strike.[1]

After being the perfect daughter for twenty-four years, Beatrice now defied her father and locked herself in her bedroom. Her performance did not disappoint; despite her clandestine midnight meals, she grew "paler and more fragile each day" as she leaned sadly on her windowsill.[2] Beatrice inherited a flair for the dramatic from her mother, as well as her steadfastness, self-awareness, and resoluteness. The Honorable William Banning never wanted his daughter to become an actress, yet Ellie made such a success of herself that her departure from St. Paul was deemed a great loss.

The Ayers always treated George with an abundance of hospitality. Still, now that Beatrice finally broached the subject of marriage, Frederick balked at the idea of his daughter being taken away to a "godforsaken Army post in the middle of nowhere."[3] He was convinced he could get the second lieutenant to resign his commission and come work for the American Woolen Company, but he underestimated his adversary. After all, George made it clear to Beatrice that he "would rather risk this life in its entirety than by not risking not getting anything."[4]

Why did fate have to deal him such a cruel blow by making him fall in love with Beatrice Banning Ayer? George couldn't help but feel that it was "horribly wicked to have caused such a wonderful girl as you to love such a fool."[5] He called himself her "devoted slave" who "would give any thing to be able to express the absolute magnitude and wonderful depth of my love," but then he was gripped by fear that she "could not stand army life" even if she said she was willing to.[6] He made it clear that the Army was "a hard unpleasant life with lots of unfairness and lots of unpleasant places where every one is against every one else, where people of small narrow spirits are taken and placed over you," but Beatrice was adamant about marrying him. She was as steadfast on becoming Mrs. Patton as he had been on becoming Second Lieutenant Patton.

---

A QUIET GLOOM hung over the Pattons' sleeping car as the train approached Lexington, Virginia, in September 1903. George and his entourage had been beset with doubts as they watched the landscape gradually change from the desolate desert of Joshua Tree National Park to the luscious woods of the Blue Ridge Mountains. Despite all his swashbuckling behavior at Lake Vineyard in the presence of his adoring family, George was deeply insecure and incessantly wondered whether he would be worthy of the Patton name. In the weeks before his departure for VMI, he had spoken with Colonel Smith and other family members about his fear that he might be a coward.[7]

George was the only one who doubted his courage; everyone else worried he might be unable to adjust to being away from home. Even his great-uncle Colonel John Mercer Patton agreed that "it would be well for Georgie to be 'broken in.'"[8] Mr. Patton's idea of breaking in his son was to leave his wife at a hotel in Lexington to be ready at George's beck and call, an arrangement that set a precedent for his time at West Point. Ruth Ellen wondered years later how her father "grew up to be the man he was with two strong-minded women babysitting him until he married Ma."[9] Ruth and Aunt Nannie alternately spent time on the East Coast, visiting so often that George once jokingly asked his father if he was bankrupted yet by all their "transcontinental vageries."[10]

Cadet Patton made up for his lack of academic skills with studiousness, character, and a will to succeed. He was also one of three candidates recommended by the examination committee when he took Senator Bard's informal competitive exam in February 1904. The eighteen months of hard work by Mr.

Patton on his son's behalf had not been in vain; on March 3, 1904, he received a telegram from Senator Bard, which stated that he chose George Smith Patton Jr. as his newest West Point appointment.

After a "long and tiresome quest," George finally reported to West Point on June 16, 1904.[11] "At times I can scarcely believe my good luck," he wrote Beatrice a month later, halfway through plebe camp, a seven-week intense physical course to transform new arrivals into cadets.[12] He would have been named first corporal had he stayed at VMI, but at West Point, he was once again a plebe, subjected to the merciless hazing of the upperclassmen.

With his future secure and Beatrice now a mere two hundred miles away in Boston, George began replying more prodigiously to the letters she never stopped writing. The more he thought about it, the more he realized he was in love with Beatrice. However, it would take him years to figure out the feeling was mutual, even though she was anything but subtle about the way she felt.

WHILE GEORGE ENDURED the Spartan life of a West Point cadet, the *Boston Globe* announced the presentation of Miss Beatrice Ayer at "one of the loveliest of the debutante parties of the season."[13] The reception took place on December 15, 1904, from four to seven o'clock at the Ayer residence on 395 Commonwealth Avenue. The drawing room, with its floral-patterned ceiling and Byzantinesque stained glass windows, was filled with lilies, violets, and orchids. Among the guests were Beatrice's brother, Dr. James C. Ayer, now practicing medicine in New York; her California cousin Katharine Banning, daughter of Joseph and Katharine Banning; her grandmother, Mary Alicia, in town from St. Paul; and her future sister-in-law, Nita, studying at the Miss Spence finishing school in Manhattan. Ellie, resplendent in a pink velvet dress with a bouquet of her beloved roses in her hands, stage-managed the afternoon as if it were one of her plays.

Beatrice, "one of the prettiest girls of the season," wore a white dress of point d'esprit over silk, accentuated by satin ribbons tied in true lover's knots.[14] In her hands, she carried lilies of the valley sent by George, who was over the moon that she liked his flowers.[15] He, unfortunately, had to decline her invitation due to West Point's draconian rules and the upcoming December reviews. Feeling increasingly comfortable opening up to Beatrice, he confessed he feigned illness "simply because I got frightened at an examination that we are having and thought that I had better go to the hospital and not take it." His plan turned out to be a "perfect 'Gordion knot'" and completely backfired; forced to take the test anyway and put on a liquid diet for a week, he felt like a flower who lived on air.[16]

In an unusual role reversal, George had to reassure his "Dear Beatrice" when she felt "the world is so big" that she would get lost. "I ride horseback with Papa nearly every day and sail and fish and drive the rest of the time," she wrote Aunt Nannie. "Last week I spent in making jelly and pickles, of which I am very proud, for they turned out well . . . Pretty soon I am to be taken to call on some of Mama's friends down here, which is very exciting as I have never been calling with her before. I don't expect it will be interesting at all, but then, it is grown up, which is something."[17]

In the months leading up to her debut, in a letter to George, Beatrice contemplated the futility of society life. He reassured her she would eventually learn to like the shopping and social obligations, like all "proper 'buds' do," but Beatrice wanted more.[18] She was a talented pianist and considered continuing her studies, a move which prompted George to predict that "your mad career will be a great success and am quite certain that none of those dreadful things that you fear will happen." He couldn't imagine, though, why she "should be so glad to take lessons again" when he considered it "beastly hard" to learn.[19]

George passed his December exams, but Christmas was another lonely affair. It had been two years since he spent the holidays with his family at Lake Vineyard, and he had "partly forgotten how to laugh and play." What he found so hard about "hell-on-the-Hudson" was the regimented life that was often the cause of his having to decline Beatrice's invitations. The institute's regulations allowed "no pleasures in its self and at the same time [kept] us from the possibility of enjoyment out side."[20] Two months later, however, an opportunity presented itself which would be a turning point in George and Beatrice's relationship as both converged on the capital for the inauguration of President-elect Theodore Roosevelt.

MARCHING in the inaugural parade along Pennsylvania Avenue with the West Point Corps of Cadets, George couldn't help but notice that "the whole avenue looked like one vast wave or human rover of which we with our grey clothes and shining brasses formed the foaming crest." Washington was still covered in patches of snow when the twenty-sixth president of the United States was sworn in on March 4, 1905, and the Cadets faced a "threatening storm and fierce wind through every back street in the city."[21] George exulted in the militarism of the occasion, but once he completed his official duties and washed the dust off his face, he rushed to The Shoreham Hotel where the Ayers were staying.

He "nearly had a fit of joy" the day before when he returned to his muddy barracks after a night at the theater and found a letter from Beatrice inviting him to spend all his free time with her and her parents.[22] He immediately telephoned his acceptance, excited to get away from the humdrum of cadet life and see Beatrice again. She recently sent him a Valentine's Day card with a dried rose leaf, underneath which she wrote, "Under the rose." It baffled George so much that he asked his father in confidence if he knew what she meant.[23]

The Shoreham, located a mere three blocks from the White House, was one of the most fashionable addresses in Washington. George was about to send up his calling card when "B. grabbed me. She seemed realy very glad to see me, [and] I was of course similarly effected." Mrs. Ayer told him to get something to eat at the Continental Grill while they finished getting ready, so George ordered every dessert on the menu. Cursed with an extreme sweet tooth, his indulgences often cost him dearly, but not tonight; he was about to have "the finest time in the world" at the inaugural ball with Beatrice.[24]

Fireworks illuminated the night sky as the Ayers made their way to the Pension Building (now the National Building Museum). Crowds waited to enter the red brick structure built in 1887 as a memorial to Civil War veterans. The inaugural ball committee was indignant when they found out the company in charge of selling $5 inaugural tickets "had not exercised the discrimination which was promised, and it was feared many 'unrefined' guests would be in attendance."[25] George, however, couldn't care less about who was there because he was "suffering from a bad attack of puppy love even if it has lasted a long time."[26]

After mandatory dancing lessons at West Point, it was a nice treat to test his newfound skills on "the prettiest girl [he] ever saw." Even though "it was pretty hard work and the floor was of stone," in his "state of mind [he] would have danced with equal eagerness on a hot stove." As they two-stepped to Edwards's "My Own United States," George realized "comeing out certainly had a wonderfully good effect on Beatrice," as she was now even "nicer and a lot prettier."

On the other hand, Beatrice couldn't help but notice George's military bearing and impeccable uniform, so she stuck a pin in him and "pretended that she was surprised that I did not burst [and] I came down to a more normal chest expansion."

At the end of the evening, George accompanied the Ayers back to The Shoreham for dinner, but "then twelve o'clock came and with it ended my permit so like a Sinderela (?) I had to go." "[I]f she was having half as good a time as I was," he wrote his father a week later, "I can't blame her had she lost both her slippers."[27] It was finally beginning to dawn on George that Beatrice liked him, but he asked his father not to tell "any of those gushing Bannings or they will certainly tell her and I would have to end my unhappy life in a violent manner."[28]

CADET PATTON COULDN'T THINK of anything more pleasing than Beatrice's suggestion of her staying on at West Point after the graduation ceremonies for the Class of 1905, but despair set in when he began taking his examinations. His plebe year had been a constant struggle in English and math, and he realized he was "neither quicker nor brighter in any respect than other men." He called himself "a characterless, lazy, stupid yet ambitious dreamer," admitting to his father that he "always thought that I was a military genius or at least that I was or would be a great general."[29] He was disappointed that his classmates didn't look upon him as a leader but instead thought him standoffish and remote. Endowed with his father's snobbishness, George considered himself "as far removed from these lazy, patriotic, or peace soldiers as heaven is from hell."[30]

The letters Mr. Patton received from his Boy were heart-wrenching to read. "Pa I am stupid there is no use talking I am stupid," George wrote to Lake Vineyard on June 3. "It is truly unfortunate that such earnestness and tenacity and so much ambition should have been put into a body incapable of doing anything but wish."[31] The reply his father wrote him a week later was one of the most important letters George ever received: "It is a good thing to be ambitious and to strive mightily to win in every contest in which you engage, but you must school yourself to meet defeat and failure without bitterness—and to take your comfort in having striven worthily and done your best ... and that is all you can do. When you have done that—for me you have won."[32]

Two days later, George was turned back for failing math. Worried "because B. will think I am stupid" and she might not wait another year, he felt reassured by the letter she wrote him about trying his hardest.[33] "I think I did," he replied, "but results do not seem to confirm my opinion so to have you say so is very nice."[34] He was allowed to skip plebe camp and "had a peach of a time" on Catalina Island, but he hoped Beatrice could "get the automobile to break down and all your friends to become just slightly ill about the twenty fifth [of August] so that I may see you for a little while."[35]

The Ayers welcomed George with open arms and gave him "a perfect time" in Boston. Out sailing under extremely windy conditions in Frederick's boat, *The Tempest*, George was impressed that Beatrice "never got the least frightened" even though she "knew the danger better than I did." As he wrote his father upon his return to West Point, he "swallowed her [Beatrice] hook to the swivle," and invited her to "every dance to be given at West Point from now until I graduate."[36] When Beatrice attended one Saturday hop in November to celebrate George's twentieth birthday, she gifted him a pocketbook with his initials and wore a new dress in his favorite color—a sign she really liked him, he wrote his mother.[37]

George's entourage at West Point included not only Aunt Nannie and Ruth —Mr. Patton rarely came east, despite his son's urgings to sell his property, stop working, and live a life of leisure—but also Nita, Kay, and Beatrice. Nestled between the majestic Hudson River and the United States Military Academy was the quaint little town of Highland Falls. "The gateway to West Point" counted less than twenty-four hundred residents in 1905.[38] Main Street was barely half-a-mile long and had but few shops, and there were only two hotels to house the thousands of visitors each year. The West Point Hotel and The Villa were not "fit for barns," according to George, yet his efforts to book a room for Beatrice at either one usually resulted in a "cold fess," West Point slang for a dismal failure.[39]

Every weekend, there was an influx of women who came to attend the West Point football games or dance with the dashing officers at Cullum Hall. Beatrice was not opposed to George participating in some "spooning" or fooling around with the ladies because, in the upper classes, it was acceptable to call on other men and women if one was not engaged. She also knew George's reputation for being "easy" came about because he was always available to be anyone's date, just in case it could give him some career advantage.

Beatrice, meanwhile, wondered why only George and "a powerful football player" wrote their name on her dance card, "for I was not unpopular other places." It wasn't until years later that she discovered "Georgie had broadcast the fact that he would lick anyone who invited me," and the football player, "fortunately, could lick him."[40]


WHEN GEORGE finally passed his plebe year in June 1906 and spent the summer in charge of supervising the newly arrived plebes, Beatrice and Kay went down to West Point. The two sisters enjoyed some wonderful picnics with George and his fellow cadets, seated by the banks of the Hudson River. George "never thought West Point could be so nice before" as he took Beatrice strolling along Flirtation Walk, a wooded path along the shore that offered the privacy sorely lacking on the rest of campus.[41] They would have stopped at the Kissing Rock, compelled to kiss per tradition, lest the rock hanging over the precipice break free and drag the Military Academy into the river.

West Point, established in 1802 as a school for engineers and located on a strategic bend in the Hudson River about sixty miles north of New York City, had breathtaking vistas. Immense forests surrounded the campus, and overlooking the Academy was Crow's Nest, a 1,407 ft. (429 m) mountain with panoramic views of the river. Beatrice climbed to the top one day, a feat which impelled a proud George to tell another cadet, who scarcely believed him, that "he knew a girl who had gone up the side of Crows Nest to the top and back again in an after noon."[42] Beatrice was less laudatory about George—she repeatedly pointed out he was always "fishing" for compliments—and he was surprised that she wasn't even awed when he escorted President Roosevelt at an Army-Navy game.[43]

A talented athlete who excelled mainly in individual sports, George was nevertheless obsessed with proving himself as a football player on the Army Cadet team. He tried out year after year but practiced with such exuberance that he always got injured before the game got underway. Having sworn never to ask Beatrice to another game unless he was on the team, she and Kay nonetheless continued to attend as "an act of charity."[44] During one West Point-Yale game, Beatrice observed him prancing "down the field at inspection, chest bulging and chevrons shining, serenely unconscious of the two pairs of cousinly eyes anxiously fixed upon him. He seemed by far the most military person on the post that day; our only anxiety was that he might break in two at the waistline."[45]

At the start of his yearling (sophomore) year, George was demoted from Second to Sixth Corporal for being "too damed military," despite Beatrice's repeated warnings not to become overzealous in his effort "to be a good soldier."[46] No one had ever stood up to George Patton before, but Beatrice somehow knew the perfect combination of compliments, criticisms, and suggestions to make him not feel offended. She was adept at reading between the lines and always knew what to say in reply to his letters, whether they were upbeat or depressing. As a result, George's morale went up as she made him feel good about himself, at one time thanking her "for what you said about me it was the finest thing I ever heard about my self."[47]

Beatrice knew she could not cure George of his self-centeredness and vanity, but she made it clear that he was always taking up too much space in his letters with "that old favorite subject (I)."[48] She was the first person who dared to tell him the truth, and he surprisingly took it in stride. He realized Beatrice was endowed with "a good deal of sense" and began adding her advice to his little black book, writing a B in the margin.[49] She found him "one of the few people in the world who can be courteous without being idiotic," and she advised him about arguing: "If you can't convince him lick him. If you can't lick him keep still."[50] He especially liked her advice that "things not worth failing for were not worth trying."[51]


A HOT AND dusty George stepped off the train at the Pride's Crossing station on August 19, 1907, embarrassed to be late when he saw Mrs. Ayer waiting for him on the platform. He had been reluctant to accept the Ayers' invitation, but Beatrice reassured him, "When Mama asked you to spend a month with us she meant it; and Papa says: 'Tell George that he must spend two weeks with us at the very least. We want him to have time to unpack his trunk and feel at home before he has to leave again.'"[52]

The Ayers had always been so nice to George that it was "positively oppressive." For the next ten days, he would enjoy himself at the family's majestic country home in Beverly, thirty miles from Boston in the Pride's Crossing section of town.

George, who enjoyed the finer things in life ever since his father bought him his first thoroughbred, was surrounded by luxury whenever he spent time with the Ayers, a marked contrast with his regimented life at West Point, where he slept on an iron bed and a hair mattress. He had spent Christmas 1906 at the Ayer Mansion, but the beauty of 395 Commonwealth Avenue paled when compared to the home he now approached, a magical place along the rocky Massachusetts North Shore he described as "almost more beautiful than it is possible to imagine."[53]

*Figure 15. Avalon as seen from the beach. (Huntington Library)*

Avalon was considered one of the most breathtaking homes along the coastline. The ten thousand square foot Renaissance Revival mansion, designed by Parker, Thomas & Rice, featured a three-story main building flanked by two-story wings. The elliptical hallway was three stories high with a striking spiral staircase, its black-and-white marbled tiles leading to the living room, which faced the ocean and measured 65 ft. in length and 30 ft. in width. A mezzanine gallery, where musicians regularly played afternoon concerts, flanked the walls of the living room, which contained a fireplace big enough to roast an ox. There was a library with "handsomely finished bookcases . . . their shelves filled with numerous rare volumes," and a room for flower arranging that included a trash chute for dead flowers.[54] The firm of Frederick Law Olmsted designed the grounds, including a rose garden, two greenhouses, three vegetable gardens, a garage, and stables.

*Figure 16. A garden party at Avalon; Ellie stands in the foreground.*
*(Huntington Library)*

In 1905, Ellie had been adamant about finding a new summer home for her aging husband. She traveled along the North Shore by train to look at properties, requiring only that they be close enough to Boston for the eighty-four-year-old Frederick to continue going into the office three times a week. Eventually, Ellie settled on Pride's Crossing, one of the shore communities inhabited each summer by industrial and political tycoons like Henry Frick, President William Howard Taft, and Alice Roosevelt Longworth. The Ayers bought the twenty-two-acre Robbins estate and tore down the old mansion to build "Avalon-By-The-Sea." Completed in 1906 in a mere eight months, Avalon was named after the little town on Catalina Island and the mythological place where King Arthur's legendary sword was forged.

The summer homes along the North Shore were not sporting estates—for that, there were private clubs like the Myopia Hunt Club in neighboring Essex County—but places of relaxation.[55] The area's permanent residents, wealthy descendants from old whaling and seafaring families who were "cold roast Boston's best," once again snubbed the Ayers.[56] Katharine Peabody Loring and Louisa Putnam Loring were longtime members of Beverly society who were active in social reform and philanthropy. The sisters lived in a shingle-style cottage called Burnside and were scandalized when they observed the ostentatious taste of their new neighbors. They asked their brother, the prominent

Judge William Loring, to put up a fence between the properties extending from the house, across the rocks, and into the ocean. When Judge Loring discovered what a "capital fellow" Frederick was when seated next to him on the train to Boston, he tore down the fence with his bare hands.[57]

Avalon's most striking feature was the terrace which ran from one side of the building to the other, flanked on either side by covered verandas. Guests enjoyed unobstructed views of the Atlantic Ocean, which could be reached by walking down the terrace's set of stairs and the grassy hill. Several years later, possibly in the summer of 1909, Beatrice and her family stood on the terrace breathing in the salty air when they noticed a horse approaching in the distance. It was a beautiful white charger, the kind of horse the cavalry would ride into battle, mounted by Second Lieutenant George S. Patton Jr. He effortlessly rode up the stairs, stopped in front of his sweetheart, and doffed his cap as he made his horse bow in front of her.

*Figure 17. Beatrice (third from left) chatting on the veranda at Avalon. (Huntington Library)*

The ten days at Avalon in August 1907 with "the only girl [he] ever loved" were pure bliss for George. Being with Beatrice felt so natural he didn't even feel the need to put on an act. Not that she would have tolerated that kind of behavior anyway because there was nothing Beatrice hated more than posers, and she was not afraid to tell him so. While George had shared his dreams and insecurities only with his father in the past, he now felt comfortable opening up to Beatrice. She didn't mock him when he said he had once fought with the Vikings and Napoleon, and she didn't think him crazy when he told her of his fervent belief in his destiny. As Robert Patton later wrote about his grandfather in *The Pattons*, "[h]e needed someone above him, someone to steer him, anchor him, hold his reins." More and more, Beatrice took over that role from Mr. Patton.

As George returned to West Point for his Cow (third) year, he worried Beatrice might find him worthless unless he made something of himself. His self-doubt resurfaced while he waited for news of the cadet promotions, so when he finally became Adjutant of the Cadet Battalion, she was the first person he wrote. He reminded her of the time they were riding together, and he feared he would never be adjutant but "you said I would. Since then I decided to get it and thanks to you have so they are realy your chevrons."[58]

THE AYERS RECEIVED QUITE the fright on January 28, 1908, when Beatrice underwent an emergency appendectomy. Setting a pattern that would be repeated whenever something happened to her, George went to pieces. He worried incessantly for weeks, relieved that he had to repeat his plebe year; otherwise, he would have been stationed outside the country, and "that would be worse than an extra year." Beatrice spent the next two weeks on her back in bed, a horrible predicament for George, who thought "it would be hard for me at least to do nothing but think for a week." He entertained her with numerous letters, "very anxious to hear how you are getting along yet dont wish to bother you to write in bed." Instead, he requested her to return his letter after checking the appropriate box: "splendidly, only fairly or still ill."[59]

While Ellie dramatically fussed over her daughter, Fred and Kay amused their sister with a little song they wrote:

Georgie Porgie, so they say
goes a-courting every day
Sword and pistol by his side
Beatrice Ayer for his bride
Doctor, Doctor, can you tell
What will make poor Beatrice well?
She is sick and she might die
That would make poor Georgie cry.
Down in the valley where the green grass grows
There sits Beatrice, sweet as a rose
And she sings and she sings, and she sings all day
And she sings for Georgie to pass that way.[60]

George was "in love with B. to the point of madness," yet, after six years, he still couldn't tell whether she was "only fooling or befooling me."[61] Confident on the parade ground, when it came to matters of the heart, Ruth Ellen later reasoned her father was "too humble at that point in his life" to realize "that Ma was in love with him."[62] Only once did he consider someone else, briefly factoring in his lust for glory as he "put Kate's [Kate Grosvenor Merle-Smith, whose son would be his aide during WWII] $40,000,000 against the B. I fear that I would take the B. ass that I am when with the money I could be a general in no time." He seemed to have forgotten that Beatrice's father was reportedly worth $19 million.

Days before heading to Boston to spend Christmas 1908 with the Ayers, George sat down with his father in the West Point library and admitted that he "was in love with Beatrice but was afraid to propose." His biggest fear was that she would not wait for him, but Mr. Patton assured his Boy that if Beatrice, "a fine little woman," were worth having, she would wait. As to George's lack of courage, his father advised him that the "times in one's life when one feels impelled to speak and to follow that impulse, which comes after long thought, is natural and generally wise."[63]

With just six months to go before graduating, George contemplated his future one final time on the train ride north. His whole life revolved around his firm conviction of one day attaining "what I consider - - wrongly perhaps - - my destiny," and he wondered where Beatrice fit in that picture. He knew his ambition was "selfish and cold," a destiny that was probably best attained alone in case he needed to make the ultimate sacrifice.[64] Yet Beatrice was the only person he could truly be himself with, the only one he could mention his "foolishness" to because she took an interest in everything he did. Despite his tendency to suck "the life out of anyone venturing too near," she stuck around for six years, offering encouragement and support.[65]

Heartened by his father's words, George decided to take the plunge but took along a fake telegram recalling him to West Point. The last thing he wanted to do was embarrass Beatrice in her own home, so at least he could make a graceful exit if she did not feel the same way about him.

The tension at the Ayer Mansion was high while the whole household awaited the big moment they knew was coming. Still, George couldn't bring himself to tell Beatrice, comparing the moment to "pointing a gun at yourself and pulling the trigger in order to prove it is not loaded." He was having "a peach of a time" and wanted to kiss Beatrice every time he saw her, yet it took until the end of his stay, when "God or brains of the family ordained we were left in the library all afternoon." According to Beatrice, the housekeeper had just stepped into the adjacent cold storage room and decided to remain there, afraid "she would ruin the moment they had all hoped and waited for."[66]

December 30, 1908, was "the most perfect afternoon" George ever spent. He told Beatrice how he felt but "asked nothing of her."[67] After "keeping her heart down for so long that it was like a cold storage turkey," relief washed over her, and she returned the sentiment.[68] "The strange part is I think she has known it a long long time six years," George wrote his mother about the fateful moment. "She said I should have known it too what an ass I have been." A week after the pseudo-proposal, Beatrice wrote Ruth as well. It won't come as "a great surprise to you—but we love each other very much indeed and since we have found our tongues to tell one another, you are next in our hearts."[69]

At the end of the day, though, George stopped short of proposing, and the couple was not officially engaged. It was a mutual decision based on Beatrice's belief that George needed a fair chance of discovering the world after six years in military school, and George's belief that he did not want Beatrice bound "by foolish notions of honor" if he was sent to the Philippines for two years.

However, when George finally expressed his love, there was no stopping him. He began addressing her as darling or dearest and ended his letters with kisses (an O with a + inside). A month after the revelation, they met for lunch at The Plaza in New York, George revealing "a little more than I should" about the day in a letter to his parents. They left their chaperone at The Palm Court and found some privacy in an empty corridor. They were soon discovered, though, "as it takes a long time to get long hair unfouled from small buttons."[70]

FREDERICK AYER genuinely liked George S. Patton Jr. but he didn't like soon-to-be Second Lieutenant Patton. As George saw it, the Ayers didn't "understand the army business at all. It is inconceavable to them that a man can have no desire to gain wealth and can wish to kill a fellow being by any such coarse method as shooting."[71] Unlike the Pattons, who identified by the battles they fought, Frederick thought soldiering was a profession for scoundrels.

George's forebears took immense pride in being soldiers—both the men and their wives—but Frederick was a man of peace and didn't think it right for his beloved daughter to marry an officer.[72] He was convinced that he, a man of standing, experience, and considerable age (eighty-seven to be precise), would have no problem changing the mind of a twenty-four-year-old boy. After all, Chilly and (later) Fred returned to work with him in the family business after suffering in their youth from what he called wild oats, wanting to go into forestry and medicine, respectively.

George was "at that stage of youth where one makes axioms and rules for ones self," one of those self-imposed rules being that he destroyed most of Beatrice's letters of that time.[73] However, his correspondence with Frederick was preserved. Their back-and-forth began on January 3, 1909, with the lovelorn "loon" respectfully explaining his intentions concerning Beatrice and his profession.

I know sir that my profession is one of slow and in cases uncertain rise that the lives of those connected with it are not easy. For some reasons therefore I could have wished that I had chosen another course. But after examining all the possible ones for which I might have any ability I believe that I am only capable of being a soldier. Bearing these things in mind I told Beatrice that I loved her, but I asked nothing in return. That I may do some thing which shall make her think me not too unworthy is all I hope for.[74]

George's hands trembled when he received a reply three days later, but he was relieved to find a "generous letter" from Frederick.

It is no wonder to me that you, and I may say Beatrice, have felt a growing admiration for each other, and I admire the delicate way in which you have treated the matter. Beatrice has a pretty well developed mature mind of her own and can speak for herself.

Referring to your profession, I believe that it is narrowing in its tendency. A man in the army must develop mainly in one direction, always feel unsettled, and that his location and home life are, in a measure, subject to the dictation and possible freak of another who he may despise or even hate.

A man like you should be independent of such control. His own man - Free to act and develop in the open world. I would compare the military man to a tree grown in the forest - as against one in the field with plenty of room to spread! Should you, at any time, adopt civil life, I have no doubt that your skill and patriotism will be in requisition with equal chance of preferment, as if you had remained in the service.

You must pardon my assumption in commenting upon an occupation known to be most respectable, and earnestly sought & won with great labor, and this without suggesting a better one, but I do it from the point of a free man—always at liberty to go and come—governed only by surrounding conditions, and my own judgement.

The above views I give from my experience and observation. Every independent man should choose his own course in life but must think carefully as to the road, and where it may lead him.[75]

One final time, George turned to the man who had supported him in word and deed for twenty-four years, baring his soul as he tried to reconcile his love for Beatrice with the heavy burden of his destiny.

All my life I have done every thing I could to be a soldier for I feel inside that it is my job and that war will come. When however I proposed to Beatrice I did something from instinct and against reason at least it seems unlogical because she does not like war because she is not as rich as another girl "Kate"

~~who would I think have married me and because a soldier should not marry.~~
~~This because money seems an excellent tool, not for my own use, but to buy~~
~~success and if I were unmarried I could get more things by paying attention to~~
~~daughters of prominent people if necessary marrying one of them. Now these~~
~~things are not nice but they are logical and I had carefully planned to climb the~~
~~ladder and I had a pretty clear field.~~ But when I see B. all logic goes to hell. It
was so clear at Xmas that she loved me that I played the fool and would do it
again.

Realy I have no strength of character. I know what is right but I think of Beat
and straight way stop all sane mental manoevers and fall down and worship her
and enjoy doing it better than any thing else in the world. Am I an ass or just
human would an embrionic great man have acted as I did or do I show my self a
mess. God knows I am worried to death I have got to, do you understand got to
be great it is no foolish child dream it is me as I ever will be. I am different from
other men my age all they want to do is live happily and die old I would be
willing to live in torture die tomorrow if for one day I could be realy great . . .

. . . there is inside me a burning something that makes me want to do I wake
up at night in a cold sweat imagining that I have lived and done nothing perhaps
all people have it but I dont believe they do. Perhaps I am crazy. There is no use
concealing things from you for you might help and ought to know . . . Would I in
justice to my self do right to stay in the army during long years of peace and by
so doing become pot bound and without ambition. Could I do better by
resigning in a year or so and trying to do something as a cit while waiting for a
chance to do somewhat as a soldier.[76]

BEATRICE READ the correspondence between her father and her sweetheart,
realizing most of it concerned George's profession. She had encouraged him
throughout his five years at West Point, yet she had never shied away from
challenging him on the subject. Would he still like the military if "heredity, and
love of excitement, and desire of reputation" were taken away?[77] How much
glory did he expect to find in a world at peace? Wouldn't life be easier if he
didn't have to bear the weight of the Patton legacy?

When she learned George considered resigning from the Army after a two-
year stint—long enough to learn the practical groundwork for him to be ready
when war did come—Beatrice decided she could only push him so far before
she risked losing him. "A woman who hampers a man at the beginning of his
career is a hateful abomination," she wrote him on January 17, 1909, "and he
always thinks so sooner or later. So you had best not consider me at all in
making your decision. The family might not thank me for telling you this but I
think it. A girl might just ruin a man's life by upsetting it at the beginning. You

can decide better if you consider your self as one instead of as two. You must decide alone and then I will go with you <u>any</u> where."[78]

George contemplated civilian life for Beatrice's sake, but it felt like pulling teeth. He didn't "know or care about other things," having spent every waking moment since he was a little boy imagining himself a great commander. Earning money was unimportant to him—even though he enjoyed spending it generously—as "that is all success in business amounts to." He had the will to pursue a business career, "but it would be self murder," especially since "the chances seem to point to my being some thing in the army out of it nothing." He hoped Beatrice would come to realize "that the army is a profession just like any thing else."[79]

Then again, he worried his ambition was nothing more than "the folly of a boy dreamer who has so long lived in a world of imaginary battles that they only seem real and every thing else un real."[80] When Frederick asked him why he wanted to be a soldier, George admitted there was no logical reason, "I only feel it inside. It is as natural for me to be a soldier as it is to breath and would be as hard to give up all thought of it as it would be to stop breathing."[81] However, his hopes and views were "so insane that I don't think he [Frederick] understands them no one does, not even you [Beatrice], and lord knows I bother you seven days in the week with them - poor B."[82]

After much soul-searching, George resolved to make the army his perma-nent career, concluding that "it is not right to go around and continually apolo-gize for ones profession when one is proud of it and knows it."[83] He had carefully considered Frederick's advice and tried to combat that "unexplained force called instinct . . . but find that it still impels me to the army as my primary to the civil only as my secondary occupation."[84] Aware of the sacri-fices he was asking Beatrice to make if she followed her heart, he decided to be completely honest with her. He wrote her a five-page letter—without punctua-tion in his excitement—preferring to make "her mad now instead of disap-pointing her later."

> Beaty do you understand can you know how much I love you oh it makes me sick at my inability to express it it is so intense that it makes my eyes hurt does it affect you ever that way . . . But one thing I must clear up in your mind though it hurt you. I am <u>not</u> a <u>patriot</u> the only thing I care for are you and my self my self in that I may be worthy of you. I would just as gladly fight for any country against any country, except this one. I say this because I am what you should know me. War is to me simply a matter of business and business is simply a step up for even I must try to go up I won't run along as others run if I can avoid it. Therefore I will probably live a sad life and make others sad yet it is the truth and I could not, nor would I, change it. I may never rise but by even trying I will be sad hence having set the star so high I must of necessity be old before I get there

hence if you should some day like me more I can never offer any peace as others of less insane desire may offer I may never have a home nor real friends of course I may loose ambition and become a cleark and sit by a fire and be what the world calls happy but God forbid. I may be crazy but if with sanity comes contentment with the middle of life may I never be sane. I don't fear failure I only fear a slowing up of the engine which is pounding on the in side saying up - up - some one must be on top why not you. Darling you cant know what that which I have just said cost me.

Dear you may laugh at me hate me think me a fool but if you think I do not love you then you will be wrong. Please love me inspite of my folly but don't love me by reason of ignorance of it. You see the chance of my doing what I wish is so small that I will be very likely to be disappointed and being so disappointed it might revert to others who I love so I must tell them.[85]

June 11, 1909, was "the end of a long and not unhappy period."[86] Beatrice sat on the West Point plain with the Patton family as Secretary of War Dickinson gave the commencement address and handed out diplomas to the 103 graduates of the Class of 1909. Newly commissioned Second Lieutenant George Smith Patton, Cavalry, U.S. Army, was number forty-six based on merit, an accomplishment he ascribed not only to himself but especially to Beatrice. "How fortunate almost unthinkably fortunate I was to meet you," he wrote a week before graduating.[87] "During the five years I was there you were my last thought on going to sleep and my first thought on waking. I never did a thing without calculating its effect on you. I even skinned less than I wanted to because I thought that if I got too unpopular you would not have so nice a time."[88]

Beatrice had made him the cadet he was; now, George could only hope he would be worthy of her as an officer. As he left for California on a three-month furlough, he handed her a picture of himself in uniform (she was always coy in giving him a photo of herself). Before she placed the picture in a silver frame, which she would keep for the rest of her life, Beatrice wrote on the back, "An unwritten page. I wonder what will be written on it. June 1909."[89] As madly in love as she was, though, Beatrice was no longer convinced she was the right person to help George write that story.

"How I appreciate your having spared him to us; we have been so happy," Beatrice wrote Aunt Nannie from Avalon in September 1909.[90] Her outward joy, however, was in marked contrast with her inner turmoil now that George didn't have to leave for the Philippines—he somehow managed to get assigned to the 15th Cavalry at Fort Sheridan, Illinois. Every day she was away from him seemed "such a simple waste of time," but now that he was an officer in the U.S. Army, living in two filthy rooms on the third floor of some bachelor quarters in the middle of nowhere, Beatrice had to confront two problems truthfully before she felt able to move on to the next step.[91]

First, she worried whether she could get accustomed to army life. She knew an officer's wife could make or break her husband's career, but she was clueless about the rigid customs that regulated life on an army post. Since "the vast majority of people die with out one tenth the comforts [she] commanded at birth," Beatrice didn't even know how to keep house or cook.[92] George would have a striker to help with his officer's duties and uniforms, but there would be no Mamie Ryan, her mother's lifelong housekeeper, to sit down with every morning.

Even though George admitted that "both of us have had all we want and more than was good for us," it still bothered him that army life "might be awful for you and even all the love I will give you might not make up."[93] He now asked Beatrice, "If you could not go to the opera and dances and dinners and things and perhaps only liked me to talk to would you be very miserable, would you have nothing to do but cuss your self for being what you were?"[94]

Second, and more importantly, Beatrice was torn between her love for George and duty to her family. She was bored with the traditional life of a debutante, but the idea of leaving behind her eighty-seven-year-old father made the devoted Beatrice waver. George, who once declined an invitation from Mrs. Ayer because "it would be quite square to Papa and Mama," understood her conundrum.[95] "She wants to marry me right away but can't on account of thinking it wrong to leave her father who is pretty old," George wrote Mr. Patton. "That is the reason she does not want to be thought engaged for fear that it would have to last too long a time, until he dies to be brutil and exact."[96]

George respected her request for time, very much aware that he was "asking a lot of a girl raised as B has been."[97] However, "not having the longevity of her family," he feared he would be unable to break the record of "Abraham being engaged 107 years."[98] By the end of the year, the couple was still stuck in the status quo, despite the holidays being "more perfect than hours on this earth are."[99] Some serious issues must have been discussed, though, because George requested new quarters when he returned to Fort Sheridan.

Once again, he wrote his father:

As I told you that B. for reasons of any best known to her self will not say definitely that she will marry me but as she has no objection or appears to have none to my telling her family I fancy she will not object to their decision and I am pretty darned sure I know what that will be. She certainly is an awful ass but then I suppose it is hard to blame a person for clinging to the present happiness and being slightly scared at changing it for any other even though it may be better for it might be worse. I think that the only thing that scares her is the thought of leaving her family not of leaving her wealth for she does not give a dam for that. Any way she has got to or never leave them for I would look like an ass hanging around much longer.[100]

BY FEBRUARY 1910, George no longer cared if the Ayers were going to be "morally sure she is a martyr and I am a monster," and he wrote to Beatrice officially asking for her hand in marriage.[101] After a weeklong hunger strike, she was able to write her betrothed, "Pa and Ma willing for June if you are, rejoice."[102]

Frederick, who never doubted George's love for his daughter, wrote his soon-to-be son-in-law on March 7, 1910. Henceforth, they each would focus on what they did best: Frederick would earn the money and George would earn the glory.[103]

Am sorry that you have hesitated to write me or that you should have any misgivings about doing so. Also sorry that Beatrice should have had any hesitancy about speaking to me freely on any subject pertaining to herself or her interests. I have always endeavored to cultivate the most confidential relations with my children and to make them feel free to confide in me and consult me in all matters. I invite you to the same confidential relations and freedom of intercourse.

You know how Beatrice lights our lives and how dearly we all love her. Our beloved younger children, so full of promise, will always remember Beatrice, who brought happiness as a shining example, who strained every nerve to do her best to be the light of our house, to be the moving spirit for the good of all, to improve every gift, and never to withhold from father, mother, sister or brother the constant expression of her love and devotion.

She has no discounts, no minus traits—all is to the good. She has made us all happy always, and we hope she will always be a joy to you, as she has always been to us. Of course we feel that half the house will be gone when our Beatrice goes, and we confide her to you with our love and fullest confidence. Her frequent return to us we shall look for with longing. Will you keep this ever in mind?

I know that your accommodations are not what you would have them in private life but think Beatrice enjoys roughing it to some extent, as all good soldiers and sailors must, and you know she is a pretty good sailor.

I did not know you had such a fine nest egg in your property. I would not sell the land. It has been my custom when my children have married and left our home to give them a monthly income, and shall do the same to Beatrice and the younger ones. This is without regard to their circumstances and for reasons which I will explain later.

I am hoping to take Beatrice to Chicago, and if so, will, of course, see you but it is not certain. I admire your firmness of purpose in sticking to the army until more strongly tempted by another occupation, and with every good wish for your early and steady advancement, I am sincerely your friend F. Ayer[104]

ANY SUITORS BEATRICE and George still entertained became aware on March 12, 1910, that all was ended, when Mr. and Mrs. Ayer announced the engagement of their daughter Beatrice Banning Ayer to Lieutenant George S. Patton of the Fifteenth U.S. Cavalry.[105] While both their parents were very much in favor of the match, Beatrice would hear whispers for years to come at family gatherings how "her 'Yankee' family thought she had fallen from grace, while George's 'southern' family thought he had spoiled the lineage by marrying a Yankee."[106] Neither could some of her friends understand why she would willingly give up her gilded life to go live on a "frontier post."

The peacetime army was not what Second Lieutenant Patton had expected, and after just one month, he was already pining for action. His quarters were awful, life was monotonous, and he was left eating dinner "in lonely grandure" while kissing Beatrice's picture goodnight.[107] He created a polo team and often traveled to Chicago to visit Aunt Nannie or attend the opera with young ladies from the post (at least until he was officially engaged). "Did you ever think how strange it would be to be like most people not in love and expecting to see in every new girl the possible only one," George wrote Beatrice. "I never felt that way for since I have been old enough to think sensibly on the subject I have only had one girl in mind the others only appealed to me as amusing boys who by some chance wore long hair."[108]

Since his arrival on September 13, 1909, George had grown close with Fort Sheridan's commandant, Captain Frank Marshall, and his wife, "one of the greatest ladies of the Old Army."[109] When they learned of Beatrice's lingering doubts, they invited her to Fort Sheridan to experience army life. Even though Beatrice spent the last five years visiting George at West Point and learning all she could about the Army, nothing could have prepared her for the grittiness of Fort Sheridan when she arrived with her parents six weeks before the wedding.[110] The scoundrels Mr. Ayer worried about were indeed present, many of them foul-mouthed soldiers without ambition or education who made George "positively . . . ill when I think of the effect they would have on a girl I know."[111]

A small cavalry post thirty miles north of the Windy City on the western shore of Lake Michigan, Fort Sheridan was known for freezing cold winters and blazing hot summers, which turned the unpaved roads into either muddy marshes or dusty sandpits. Established in 1887 at the request of wealthy Chicagoans who feared a working-class revolution after years of labor unrest, it was named by and for famed General of the Army, Philip Sheridan.[112]

The ladies of the post primed Beatrice on army etiquette, but on the third night, she broke down crying and offered to give "her true love" his freedom. "You're ambitious," she remembered telling him. "Why don't you marry some nice Army girl who knows all the ropes? I'll never make a success of it."[113] George quickly "kissed her out of that fancy," even though he wrote his father a year earlier that it seemed "ridiculous that I should have fallen in love with a girl so completely useless as a wife for an army officer."[114]

George had crossed out that sentence before mailing his letter, and he now had ample proof that he greatly underestimated his betrothed. Returning to quarters after attending a reception held in Beatrice's honor by one of the post ladies, George once again wrote his father, "Really I think that she will be ever so much more efficient than I had dared to hope. She made such a hit with the Q.M. [quartermaster] that I think our chance of getting a house went up a number of points."[115]

With the "formation of matrimony at a thousand miles from the leading lady" a difficult thing to stage, the weeks before the wedding were especially hard on Beatrice.[116] She cried continually at the thought of leaving her family, with George admonishing her to stop or "you will hurt your looks."[117] Her brother-in-law, William Wood, took her shopping for her wedding gift at the best jeweler in Boston, where she was free to pick whatever she wanted. As Beatrice debated between a diamond brooch and a diamond bracelet with pearls, William, who loved Beatrice dearly and enjoyed nothing more than spoiling his family, bought her both.

Jewelry was a tradition in the Ayer family and one of Beatrice's favorite gifts. For her engagement ring, she chose a miniature of George's West Point class ring—a Citrine Topaz, his birthstone—and for her wedding ring she chose a gold band with two hands wrapped around a heart. It was the same as George's, whose hands were equally bejeweled. On his right middle finger, he sported a gold ring of a snake wrapped around itself—given to him by Aunt Nannie when he was sixteen—and on his left hand, he wore a gold and diamond ring given to him by Beatrice, his West Point class ring, and his wedding band.

Beatrice spent her last days as a single woman in New York shopping for her trousseau, and she received one last letter from "her lover" four days before the wedding, only hereafter I shall still be your lover but also your husband. Darling since I wrote my first letter to you almost eight years ago I have grown older and wiser and have thus been enabled to better understand and more clearly see your infinite perfection. So that in a way I may be said to love you more now than then for I have ever loved you to the fullest of my power. God grant that if I develop in no other way my capacity for loving you may increase for it is only by a divine love that I can express to you my gratitude for all you are, have been, and will be to me. Beaty you are so wonderful in all things that an infinity of love were still too little for you . . .

As I have so often told you, never a day hardly an hour has passed that you have not been the subject of my thoughts, the object of my life. The little that I have done has been for you and the greatest sting of failure in the much that I have not done has been the fear of your displeasure . . .

My letters to you have been, though they were poor, the expression—not always expressed I fear—of the best that is in me. I have turned to you, through them, when I was sad or out of luck or disheartened and they have helped me to do more and better. They were the holiest part of many, many Sundays. And their answeres the brightest spot in many many weeks. The inspirations for a weak and cowardly nature. Yes even if these letters have never given you pleasure they are at least justified by the good they have done me. Yet I hope they have made you a little happy.

Part of this might sound as though I have had a hard life, but that is not the case. Only small hills seen against the sky line of an unknown horizon assume the size of mountains through uncertainty and lack of comparison. And I have always so wanted to win that I have ever feared lest I might loose . . .

I have prayed that you should love and marry me yet not at the expense of your happiness so now that my prayer is to be granted it seems certain that you will be happy. God grant it! May our love never be less than now And our ambition as fortunate and as great as our love. Amen.[118]

---

FELLED by a bad case of influenza, Ruth Patton was too sick to attend her son's wedding on May 26, 1910. It was the only shadow on an otherwise perfect day, although Aunt Nannie didn't think so because it finally gave her the opportunity to live out her fantasy. While her sister spent the day in bed at the Hotel Touraine, she unashamedly assumed the role of mother-of-the-groom.

At 2:15 p.m., Aunt Nannie and Mr. Patton left Boston's North Station on a private railroad car with the other out-of-town guests for the twenty-five-mile ride to Beverly Farms. Mr. Patton carried a wooden box filled with orange spring blossoms from Lake Vineyard for his "Dear Little Girl." He missed out on the wedding preparations because he was "looking a little into politics," but it was "without fear or misgivings" that he surrendered "his only 'little boy' to your [Beatrice's] loving keeping 'for always.'" After eight long years, it was finally "the joyful day—when I shall find another daughter."[119]

Horse-drawn carriages were waiting at the Pride's Crossing station to take the guests to St. John's Episcopal Church. The small Gothic church, designed by Henry Vaughn in 1902 and decorated with white and green spring blossoms for the occasion, fell quiet at 3:30 p.m. when the first notes of *Lohengrin's* wedding march filled the nave. The choir marched down the aisle, singing the words intended by Wagner to accompany the music but which were usually left out.

George, dressed in his full dress blue uniform, was hardly able to keep standing when he saw Beatrice approach on the arm of her eighty-eight-year-old father. She was wearing the same embroidered satin wedding gown Ellie had worn at her wedding to Frederick twenty-six years earlier, and her tulle veil was fastened with the orange blossoms she had just received from her soon-to-be father-in-law.[120] After a short ceremony—with Kay being maid of honor, Fred being best man, and Nita being a bridesmaid—the new Mr. and Mrs. Patton left the church under an arch of sabers drawn by George's ushers.

The wedding—according to some the first military one in the area since the Civil War—was written up in newspapers from Boston to Los Angeles, and was considered the social event of the season on the North Shore. Ellie, who wore a dress of pale blue satin with a white feathered hat, prepared the wedding party with her usual eye for detail. The sun had started to shine when the nuptials were exchanged, so the twenty-five-musician orchestra was able to play out on the terrace when the guests arrived at Avalon. Immediately after the Pattons cut the wedding cake with the groom's gift to his bride—a cavalry saber with their names and wedding date engraved on the side— the ushers gave their Army cheers, and the band played their interpretation of "The Star-Spangled Banner."

The guests returned to Boston on the 6:53 train, followed by Beatrice and George, who could hardly wait to spend their first night together at the Hotel Touraine. Despite his reputation as a spoonoid at West Point, George was also known to be "safe . . . sort of like the horse with no bad habits."[121] So after eight years of courtship, the wedding night ended up being so passionate that, even years later, the groom apologized to the bride for hurting her.

The next morning, Ellie surprised "her children" by walking into the bridal suite with a white rose, followed by her other children carrying the breakfast tray.[122] Beatrice considered the gesture awfully thoughtful, but George was merely embarrassed, even though "I do and have for a long time loved your family as though they were the nearest people on earth to me." He knew when he married Beatrice that he basically married the whole Ayer family, but he just didn't expect them to be "so close together and so happy" so soon.[123]

**Figures 18 & 19.** *Beatrice with the two most important men in her life.*
*(Huntington Library)*

George had been able to get a thirty-six-day furlough with Captain Marshall's help, just enough time for a quick honeymoon to England. "The privacy of a cabin [is] as good a place as any other in which to make love," Beatrice reasoned when she and her husband boarded the *S.S. Deutschland* in New York on May 28, except that she was terribly seasick and George spent most of the time "massaging her tummy."[124] When they arrived in Plymouth on June 3, she immediately had a taste of what life would be like as Mrs. Patton.

First, she married the man but also the soldier. Intensely interested in history, George dragged her to every fortification and castle from Cornwall to London. Beatrice's curiosity perfectly matched his thirst for knowledge, and she happily took up his interests and made them her own. Second, her husband attracted bad luck—they had three tire blowouts in just as many weeks. He was so injury-prone that she wondered if she should feed him "powdered china ... [to] make his bones less brittle," but she had "such fun curing him."[125]

Their return to the United States five weeks later marked the beginning of the "chores of married life." After a quick visit to Avalon, where Frederick was "tickled to death" to see his children, the Pattons continued to Fort Sheridan.[126] Kay, an "exquisite and meticulous housekeeper," much more than her sister, accompanied the newlyweds.[127] "B is all that I thought her and a little more," George wrote Aunt Nannie on the thousand-mile train ride, and he fervently hoped "that when we love each other as we do that we can be happy any where."[128]

# 4

## CUSTER HILL
### FORT RILEY, KANSAS

### 1910–1916

*BE FRIENDS WITH EVERYONE BUT CONFIDE IN NO ONE.*

M rs. Mary Biddle Lane Garrard exemplified the Old Army. Born in 1857 at Fort Clark, Texas, in a "rat-infested log cabin," she was the first child of Colonel William Bartlett and Lydia Spencer Lane. Mary grew up on the frontier, traveling for days by caravan every time her father was sent to a new garrison. Her mother—author of the seminal *I Married a Soldier; Or, Old Days in the Old Army*—crossed the Great Plains five times and was temporarily left in charge of Fort Fillmore, New Mexico, when the Civil War broke out in 1861.[1]

Neither the hardships nor the dangers deterred Mary from marrying West Point graduate Joseph Garrard, joining him, among many other places, at Fort Robinson, Nebraska, during the last days of the Sioux Wars. Once accused of rude conduct against a lieutenant, Mrs. Garrard considered it her duty to share her knowledge with young army brides.[2]

When Beatrice saw the senior lady of Fort Sheridan approach her front door one frosty February morning in 1911, she quickly threw on a shawl to hide her dress, which no longer fit around her belly. As she let Mrs. Garrard into her modest living room, Beatrice couldn't help but wonder what the wife of the post commandant would want with the wife of a mere second lieutenant.

Mrs. Garrard spoke first, breaking the tension with a trite weather statement before turning the subject to Beatrice and her frequent absences from post functions. Wasn't she enjoying army life? Or was she having problems getting along with Mister—the title of a second lieutenant—Patton?

The eight months since Beatrice married had been one long adjustment, to army life and matrimony. She was still learning about what she later called the Army's "undercurrent—the thing that colors all our lives. We are reminded of it throughout our waking hours by the uniforms, the drills, and, most of all by the bugle calls; reveille, when the junior officers' wives get up to cook the junior officers' breakfasts; mess call, at noon, when our husbands come home to lunch; retreat, when the flag is hauled down and folded for the night, while the children at play on the parade ground stand at attention in imitation of their father, and, last of all, at eleven o'clock, Taps, the soldiers' goodnight."[3]

"I'm the oldest wife on the post," Mrs. Garrard said when she observed Beatrice's reluctance, "and the others have delegated me to ask you a rather delicate question."

"I'll be glad to answer if I can," Beatrice replied.

"My dear little Mrs. Patton, you must think we are a bunch of old busybodies, sticking our noses into other people's affairs, but we have all been thinking about you, and since you have confided in no one, not even the post doctor, we wondered if you know you are going to have a baby."[4]

Beatrice's first reaction was to be insulted. On Commonwealth Avenue, strangers didn't show up on one's doorstep without first leaving a calling card, and they certainly didn't stop by to talk about their personal lives. Of course she knew that she was eight months pregnant; she just chose not to see the post doctor, preferring to take the streetcar into Chicago to see an obstetrician recommended by the Ayers' family physician. She hated sitting in a room full of sick soldiers, waiting for a doctor she found repulsive and unqualified.[5]

Neither did she feel the need to confide in anyone, mainly keeping to herself as she remembered the advice her mother shared on her wedding day, "Never get intimate with your next-door neighbor; never borrow anything; never confide in anyone except your husband, doctor, pastor, and mother."[6]

Beatrice came from "a family in very comfortable circumstances," into what she thought was the "pretty hard" and "terribly serious" life of an army wife. She wondered how the ladies of the Old Army could be so debonair while one of them had lived "through a cholera epidemic in the Philippine Islands," and another had sat "on the stern of a tugboat on the Yalu River, watching the corpses float past, wondering if she could identify her husband's."

Over time, Beatrice would come to understand that the women "of the Old Army were inoculating me little by little with the store of courage which is the legacy of every Army woman and which we hand on from one generation to the next."[7] Mrs. Garrard wasn't meddling; it was the job of a wife born and reared in the Army to teach her stuff to a wife recruited from civilian life.

---

THE PATTONS ARRIVED at Fort Sheridan on June 29, 1910, shocked to find the walls of Quarters 92A painted a peacock blue, the color of the local train station and the only one available to the quartermaster.[8] Not that there were many walls to paint because number 92A consisted of a dining room hardly big enough to fit a table and four chairs, a bathroom with space for just one person, and a bedroom without the closet space Beatrice liked so much.

Finding adequate housing had been a significant headache for Second Lieutenant Patton in the weeks leading up to his wedding, as he tried to please all the women in his life. He had worried incessantly about Ellie's reaction upon her first visit to an army post. Yet, he was pleasantly surprised to hear that both Mr. and Mrs. Ayer thought Fort Sheridan exceptionally nice. He did ask Beatrice to help her mother understand that they had no choice in the matter of housing as quarters were assigned based on rank, and neither money nor "the love I have for you [Beatrice] and the love she [Ellie] has for me . . . increase my rank one bit."[9]

So much for the joy of not losing Beatrice every minute because George was ordered to Camp Robinson, Wisconsin, on maneuvers with Troop K just one month later. Beatrice had her mind set on joining her husband and looked into the possibility of staying at a hotel in nearby Sparta, but Captain Marshall discouraged her. Even if she made the arduous trip, which no other spouse was making, she would only get the see George for a few hours on Sundays. Defeated and "feeling like a dog" while she packed George's suitcase, she decided to return to Avalon with Kay instead.

Friday, July 30, was the first of many goodbyes the Pattons said over the years. Tears marked the moment of departure; a habit Beatrice would take years to break. The last she saw of George for five weeks was him loading mules on a boxcar, her train pulling out of the station in the opposite direction. A letter chased her to Avalon—apologizing for not being grateful and promising to "be a better sweetheart"—as did the annoying stomach issues which persisted throughout her monthlong stay.[10]

Beatrice even delayed her return to Fort Sheridan, a logical decision, according to George, but hardly romantic since she "had then been away from me nearly half of our married life . . . At first I thought you were unwell and so agreed with what ever your decision was to be but all the reason you mention was a few tears which God knows I had a better cause to shed at the disappointment of not seeing you than your mother had at the thought of loosing you when you had been there a month already."[11]

Torn between her mother and George, Beatrice finally made up her mind and returned home on September 18. She was over the moon to announce that her stomach issues turned out to be morning sickness, and she was three months pregnant.[12] After all, she believed a woman's ultimate goal in life was to "find love, to have it returned, and to be able to bear a child to sanctify that love." However, all George could think of was how he managed to get his wife pregnant on their honeymoon. He knew it was selfish, but after eight long years of courting Beatrice, he had been looking forward to months, if not years, of alone time with her.

Beatrice was thrilled "that <u>both</u> my families are glad of God's little present to us," and she hoped "that it may be a joy to them as well as to us."[13] While Ellie and Frederick were just firm believers in the more, the merrier, Mr. Patton was elated that the continuation of the heroic Patton bloodline was assured with the imminent arrival of a boy. Beatrice was well aware of her father-in-law's obsession, but being realistic, she asked George one day if he would "terribly mind if the baby was a girl?" She couldn't have been more relieved when he replied, "What do you think, Beaty? I married one, didn't I?"[14]

BEATRICE HAD BEEN "A VERY outgoing young person" growing up, but she largely kept to herself at Fort Sheridan. "You are going among strangers," Ellie had warned her daughter. "Be friends with everyone but confide in no one."[15] Worried she took her mother's advice a little too much to heart, Beatrice decided to make an effort and reach out to her neighbors. First Lieutenant and Mrs. Osborne lived in the other half of the two-family, two-and-a-half story home and shared a porch with the Pattons.[16] The door flew open as Beatrice was about to knock, and Mister Osborne ran out with shaving cream on his face and his suspenders down to his knees. Mrs. Osborne was in hot pursuit, still wearing her nightgown and swinging a rolling pin.

Beatrice quietly retreated to 92A, wondering if she, who (according to George) was "not by nature intended for such a life being too grand and bright and well educated," would ever have anything in common with the other wives of Fort Sheridan. Maybe George was right when he wrote her that "a woman to like the army ought to be narrow minded not over bright and half educated."[17]

Both Beatrice and George thirsted for knowledge, and it was not uncommon for them to spend twelve hours reading on Sundays. She continually asked Aunt Nannie for advice on books, particularly ones "that would be a help with regard to coming events." Each letter of recommendation arrived with fresh oranges and pomegranates from Lake Vineyard to keep her and the baby healthy, and each new book felt like "a drink of water."[18]

Beatrice remembered her first few months at Fort Sheridan as "new and exciting."[19] The Pattons were the only ones who ventured out onto Lake Michigan in a canoe, and on weekends they drove into the city to catch an opera or to have dinner with Aunt Nannie. After developing a passion for driving and mechanics on his honeymoon, George bought himself his first car at a price higher than his yearly salary. He also purchased a pedigreed blood-hound called Flipper and the first of many thoroughbred horses because riding in steeplechases, on the polo field, or out hunting was "a fine advertisement" for an officer.[20]

Beatrice began "living the life of a turnip" as her pregnancy progressed.[21] She taught her "butter fingers" to sew so she could make curtains and "some of the dear little clothes myself" and tried her hand at cooking. Despite her "bum housekeeping," George soon developed "a double chin," although the culprit might have been the maid sent over by the Ayers.[22] Beatrice made many adjustments, but her parents always ensured someone was around to help. If space was lacking to house either a cook, a nanny, or a maid, George just created extra space. After all, Beatrice happily reported to Aunt Nannie that her husband had "added to his other accomplishments that of champion furniture polisher, varnish-and-painter, cook, plumber, carpenter, gardener and heavy chaperone."[23]

As winter approached, George kept "busy heaving coal on the furnace" while Beatrice worked on his papers to get his name in circulation.[24] "I may be famous yet thanks to her," George wrote to Aunt Nannie when one of his military essays appeared in the *Cavalry Journal*.[25] A prolific writer adept at putting organized thoughts on paper, George needed his wife to edit his work, correct his spelling, and translate French source material.

Looking outside the window as she worked, Beatrice saw Fort Sheridan's famous landmark, a 227-foot water tower, which loomed large over the parade ground. The creamy-yellow structure, which housed a 90,000-gallon water tank, was the tallest in Illinois upon its completion in 1891 and was made from clay bricks mined from the bluffs overlooking Lake Michigan. Beatrice was reminded of her trip to Venice as a child whenever she looked at the tower's terra cotta roof, meant to resemble St. Mark's campanile on the Piazza San Marco.

---

WHEN THE BUGLE called retreat and the last notes of "The Star-Spangled Banner" faded away like the sun, cries were heard coming from the upstairs bedroom at number 92A. The door almost hit Ellie and Frederick in the face when their son-in-law rushed past them, down the stairs, and into the kitchen, where he summarily threw up in the sink. Beatrice insisted George be present on March 19, 1911, when she gave birth to a healthy baby girl named Beatrice Smith Patton. Known as Smith for the first two years of her life, her name then changed to Beatrice Ayer Patton and, consequently, Baby Bee and Little Bee.[26]

Growing up at Lake Vineyard, George saw plenty of foals and puppies being born, but nothing prepared him for what he conceived as "the horror" of watching his first child come into the world. While he possessed a very high pain tolerance, he could not stomach seeing his wife suffer. Beatrice had a long and difficult labor, and George looked on helplessly as the "wonder of a lady" he had married ten months earlier was "torn to pieces (in his eyes) by a monstrous stranger . . ."[27] Luckily, mother and child were fine, and within two weeks Beatrice recuperated sufficiently to come down for meals while the baby enjoyed fresh air out on the porch.

Used to being the center of attention, George grew sulky and depressed as Smith took up Beatrice's (and everyone else's) attention. "The ~~accursed~~ infant has black hair is very ugly and is said by some dastardly people to slightly resemble me which it does not, since it is ugly," George wrote to Aunt Nannie two days after his daughter was born.[28] There is no record of how Beatrice felt about her husband's petulant behavior. However, he apologized years later, admitting that he "was very jealous at the time. You were not so mad as circumstances justified you in being."[29]

If Beatrice was not as upset as she should have been, it was because she knew George's behavior was not due to a lack of love for her and Little Bee but due to an abundance of love for himself. Over time, she was happy to note that "Georgie is perfectly crazy over her and she over him." He taught his daughter to ride on Peach Blossom—the Shetland pony he had received as a child—and took her to Ringling Bros. Circus, where he laughed "at the clowns like all the other kids."[30]

In June 1911, Beatrice and Smith escaped the oppressive heat at Fort Sheridan by heading to Avalon, only to get caught in the worst heatwave in New England history, an eleven-day disaster that killed two thousand people by heatstroke, suicide, and drowning. Horses dropped dead in the streets, and cows stopped producing milk when the temperature in Boston reached 104 degrees on July 4.[31] Meanwhile, George was getting "pretty lonesome" at Fort Sheridan, but Beatrice didn't dare to "take Smithy in this heat, although I have not told him that. I am just hoping for it to let up without that, for I don't want to make him jealous - dear soul."[32]

"I thought the little devil would never come back," George wrote when his family finally returned on July 23.[33] Beatrice was the cure for his insecurities, but she was also the cause of them whenever she left town. Marrying Beatrice had been both frightening and surprising: frightening "at the thought of the wonder of it and of the vastness of my responsibility," and surprising "that I should ever have dared to ask such a blessing, and that having asked it, it should have been granted."[34] He didn't seem to realize yet that Beatrice would always come back to him, usually with minimal effort on his part, but at a terrible price to her health, as she worried continuously about all the people she loved.

Beatrice finally settled into a routine when she returned from Avalon. Every morning she and Little Bee waved goodbye to their "handsome" officer from the front porch and went for a walk along the canyons of Fort Sheridan with Flipper. She lunched with the "lovely ladies" from the post, invited high-ranking officers and their wives to dinner, and even gave her first concert, a reading accompanied by music. One afternoon, though, Mrs. Garrard showed up on her doorstep again. The conversation proceeded pleasantly until she segued into the happiness of the Patton marriage since the baby's arrival.

Beatrice's face first registered embarrassment, then offense as her guest bluntly asked whether everything was going well in the bedroom. Sensing Beatrice's unease, Mrs. Garrard explained that her husband had seen Mister Patton sitting on his rifle butt between two targets while teaching some green recruits to shoot. He "wondered if some circumstance had occurred of such a nature that Mister Patton was trying to take his own life without causing any comment, perhaps because of some misunderstanding at home."[35]

Beatrice often indulged her husband's idiosyncrasies—he did warn her that he wasn't normal—but she was nobody's fool. When Second Lieutenant Patton returned home that evening, she was waiting in the tiny entryway with Little Bee, the nanny, and a pile of suitcases. Insulted that the Garrards saw her as the cause of George's apparent malaise, she furiously awaited an explanation and threatened to leave for Avalon.

George assured her that he was not trying to take his own life but had merely been testing out a theory he had read about in a book on George Washington. He was intrigued by a letter the future president wrote to his brother about the opening battle of the French and Indian War, and he wanted to see if there indeed was "something charming in the sound" of bullets whistling by one's ear.[36]

BARON DE COUBERTIN created the modern pentathlon in 1912 to test "the fitness of a perfect man at arms" through five competitions: shooting, swimming, riding, fencing, and cross-country running.[37] Since Second Lieutenant Patton graduated from West Point as an expert rifleman, received his coveted Army "A" for breaking a school record in track and field, and competed skillfully with the broadsword, it was hardly surprising that the Army selected him to represent the United States at the 1912 Olympics in Stockholm, Sweden.

With just one month to go before his departure, George was at a marked disadvantage despite being in excellent physical condition. To catch up with the months of preparation most of his competitors enjoyed, he immediately began training like a maniac, to the detriment of his body and family. George subsisted primarily on a diet of raw steak and salad while working out from morning till evening, and Beatrice remembered him being "unfit for human companionship."[38] His training intensified on June 14 when he sailed for Stockholm on the *S.S. Finland,* joined by his wife, parents, and sister. (Fifteen-month-old Little Bee stayed behind with her grandparents at Avalon.)

Every day for the next two weeks, George joined the cross-country team at 6 a.m. for a two-mile run across the deck, followed by shooting practice "with the revolver team from ten to twelve [and] fencing with the fencing team from three to five." He ended the day at swimming practice, in a canvas water tank with a rope tied around his waist.[39] He didn't even let up during a short layover in Belgium, preferring to go for a run around the countryside while Beatrice and her in-laws explored Antwerp and Brussels.

Since the Pattons were paying for their own transportation and accommodation, they moved into the Grand Hotel when they finally arrived in Stockholm on June 29.[40] Nearly 2500 athletes from twenty-eight countries converged on the capital, precisely what Baron de Coubertin hoped would happen when he conceived the modern Olympics in 1896 to promote international goodwill. The thirty-three athletes who competed in the modern pentathlon "felt more like good friends and comrades than rivals in a severe competition." They would remain friends for life, Gustaf Wersäll writing Beatrice thirty-three years later that he had been "rather intimidated by your eyes looking so critically at me" when they first met.[41]

The six-day event got underway on July 7 with the shooting competition.[42] To everyone's surprise, George missed three of the twenty shots he fired from his .38 Colt at a target twenty-five feet away, leaving him a dismal twenty-first. Theories abound to this day about how an outstanding marksman like George Patton could have missed three times, especially since he achieved an almost perfect record-setting score during a practice run. George always believed the missing bullets passed seamlessly through the hole created by his first bullseye, but Beatrice took the blame upon herself. Her husband could only have missed the target if he was too tired, and she was the one who had kept him out late partying.

George fared better the next four days: he ended up seventh in the 300-meter freestyle swimming, although the effort left him so exhausted he had to be dragged from the pool by a boat hook; fourth in fencing with the dueling sword (épée); and sixth in the five-kilometer cross-country steeplechase.[43]

*Figure 20. George Patton (second from right) in the cross-country run. (Library of Congress)*

The last day of the competition, July 12, was unusually sweltering for Stockholm, and only twenty-two competitors remained for the four-kilometer cross-country run. Instead of pacing himself as Beatrice had advised him, George took off "like a 100 yards sprinter."[44] He was spent by the time he reentered the stadium, and it was a "fearful experience" for Beatrice to watch her husband throw himself forward across the finish line and faint dead away in the grass in front of the royal box.[45] He regained consciousness either a few minutes (according to the newspapers) or a few hours (according to George) later with his family hovering over him, and learned that he had finished third in the race and fifth in the overall competition.

While George was disappointed and embarrassed that he lost out on a medal because of pistol shooting, he was not a sore loser. He always played to win, but doing one's best was what counted. So when Beatrice once found her husband on his knees before a polo game, she asked him whether he was praying to win. He replied with one of the lessons he had learned from his father upon failing his plebe year at West Point, "No, just that I would do my best."[46] Second Lieutenant Patton had done more than his best at the Olympic Games, and his performance brought him front-page coverage at home.

Instead of returning home on the *S.S. Finland*, the Pattons left Stockholm on July 17 for a tour of Europe. They visited Berlin, Dresden, and Nuremberg, where Beatrice and her father-in-law satiated their curiosity by eating donkey meat sandwiches washed down with German beer.[47] Leaving the rest of the family to continue their continental tour on their own, Beatrice and George then drove to the École de Cavalerie in Saumur, France.

Always looking to perfect his game, George arranged for daily fencing lessons with Sergeant Major Cléry, fencing instructor at The Cavalry School and, according to his Swedish comrades, "the best master in Europe."[48] The Pattons stayed for two weeks before finally sailing for New York on August 12. However, they were not returning to Fort Sheridan but to Fort Myer, where George had been with Troop A of the 15th Cavalry since December 1911.

ACROSS THE POTOMAC from Washington DC sits Fort Myer, on land abandoned by Robert E. Lee's wife when Virginia seceded from the Union. Fort Whipple, as it was known at its inception in June 1863, was one of over seventy forts tasked with defending the capital during the Civil War. Half a century later, the troops at Fort Myer provided mostly ceremonial support, from inaugurations of presidents and escorting visiting dignitaries to burials at Arlington National Cemetery.

By the time the Pattons arrived in December 1911, Fort Myer was the pinnacle of the U.S. Cavalry and the Army's most prestigious post. It was the place, according to George, "where all people with aspirations should attempt to dwell," so he lobbied for months to be posted there when his two years at Fort Sheridan were up.[49] An excellent practice on "how to use influence," he had Frederick "employ the Mass people"; his father "would try to fix it in California and in Texas"; and Kay was seeing a Major Horton, who had quite the clout in Washington.[50]

Life at Fort Myer had been wonderful in the months preceding the Pattons' departure for Sweden and continued to be so upon their return. Their new home had a white-tiled bathroom with unlimited hot water, a big room with lots of windows for the baby, plenty of space for visiting Ayers and Pattons, and even a plethora of fleas.[51] Since everyone apparently had a driver, they soon employed a chauffeur who regularly took Beatrice to the National Mall to visit the recently opened U.S. National Museum (now known as the National Museum of Natural History) or attend sessions of Congress.[52]

Beatrice was in her element, and her confidence grew. She knew the wife of a career officer had certain obligations, and she began using all the skills her mother taught her to entertain the powerhouses of Washington and the most important people on the post. George, who considered himself and his family "well fitted for society," was busy keeping his name in circulation among the Washington elite and the Army establishment.[53] Secretary of War Henry L. Stimson was impressed by the charm and appearance of the young officer he met along Fort Myer's bridle path, and the two forged a lifelong friendship. George also joined the Fort Myer polo team and participated in a series of races along the East Coast, including the exclusive Piping Rock and Belmont Park Races on Long Island.

Chastised by Frederick for being away from his family so often, George explained that "what I am doing looks like play to you but in my business it is the best sort of advertising. It makes people talk and that is a sign they are noticing. And you know that the notice of others has been the start of many successful men." He ended by pointing out that if Frederick "had not done more work than other people when you were my age you would not be now what you are."[54]

BEATRICE SPENT the first few years of her marriage trying to find the perfect balance between her husband, her children, and her parents, but the scale almost always tipped in favor of George. If she wanted to spend time with him, she needed to make sacrifices, and this meant leaving her daughter in the loving hands of her parents for weeks at a time.

Since his return from Sweden, George had been lobbying the Army Chief of Staff and the Secretary of War for permission to continue his sword training with Adjutant Cléry at Saumur. They finally consented on the condition that he foot the bill, so the Pattons sailed for France on July 14, 1913, for a six-week stay at Saumur. The trip felt like a second honeymoon, especially to George, who imagined his first years of marriage to be exactly like this, just the two of them without children or family around.

The Pattons were a team interested in everything, so there was hardly a time they occupied their room at the Hôtel Budan. Located in the center of town on the banks of the Loire River on the Quai Carnot, the hotel was within walking distance of Saumur's historical attractions. Towering over the picturesque village, where Gabrielle Bonheur "Coco" Chanel was born in 1883, was the Château de Saumur, constructed in the $10^{th}$ century to protect against Norman attacks (and rebuilt in the $12^{th}$ century by Henry II). The Écoles Militaires de Saumur was founded in 1763 by the Duc de Choiseul as part of Louis XV's effort to reorganize the French Cavalry.

While his fellow Olympians told George that he would find the best fencing master in Europe at the Écoles Militaires—Adjutant Cléry, "beau sabreur" of the French Army, and the European champion with the foil, dueling sword, and saber—the school was best known as the capital of the French military equestrian tradition. The Pattons spent many evenings with future General Houdemon, who became a lifelong friend and always remembered George's "proud and elegant figure accompanied by Mrs. Patton, brightening the threshold of my house ..."[55]

Beatrice was elated to be back in France. She felt a close affinity with the people ever since her sojourn in Paris during her childhood, and she loved the language so much that she even dreamed in French. Every morning she walked the half mile to the Écoles Militaires with George, often joining his lectures so she could help him with his French. On the way back, she paused to watch the Cadre Noir—the corps of instructors named for their black uniforms with gold trimmings—showcase the talent which made the school one of the most prestigious riding academies in the world (on par with the Spanish Riding School in Vienna).

If Beatrice wasn't translating lectures after having lunch at one of the many sidewalk cafés, she could be found in the library researching the Fulks, a prominent family who ruled the Saumur area for hundreds of years. The first Duc D'Anjou, its most eccentric member, occupied Saumur in 1025 after a long battle with the Duc de Blois.[56] Known as "Fulk the Black," D'Anjou's cruelty was legendary, and because George always "told it like it was," he made sure to include every gruesome detail of the Duc's career when he turned Beatrice's research into a history book for his children.

George was "such a dear," but as always, he couldn't help being class-conscious.[57] The snobbism he inherited from his father first showed itself at West Point—his classmates were "nice fellows but very few indeed are born gentlemen"—and occasionally resurfaced throughout his life in "an almost violent streak of disdain and prejudice against what he clearly regarded as inferior peoples."[58] On August 15, George and Beatrice walked to a nearby church where the local children were being blessed during the Feast of the Assumption.

"George and I went over this afternoon, but he certainly does hate the masses!" Beatrice wrote in a letter to Aunt Nannie, who could not join them in Saumur because of illness.

> I couldn't get him to stay, so he left me in high dudgeon—'no decent French woman would want to stay here alone to watch all these flea-bitten, ignorant people.' I [Beatrice] couldn't tear myself away for over an hour—hundreds of round, red-faced peasants in curious caps there were, with round red babies of every age, going up to be blessed; and being rewarded with doughnuts and wine afterward! . . . I returned home to find Georgie patting himself on the back for having been so broad-minded in letting me stay.[59]

An Englishman had told Beatrice on her honeymoon that one traveled to North America for the scenery and to Europe for the history. Hence, every weekend she and George went exploring the French countryside, either by horse or car (which they brought from the U.S.). They drove across the Loire Valley, visiting "all the chateaux in that part of the country," from Blois to Amboise.[60] With their Michelin map and camera in hand, they "personally reconnoitered the Normandy Bocage country, using only the watershed roads used in William the Conqueror's time [circa 1047], passable in any weather."[61] They always returned to the hotel exhausted and covered in dust, but with each excursion, George grew his knowledge of the area for the next time. A prodigious student of history since he was a child, he fervently believed that history continuously repeated itself. He believed that he had traveled these roads before, and he confidently told Beatrice that he would one day be back.

It took Beatrice days to pack the multitude of souvenirs she and George purchased—including a $75 antique chest, which would forever hold her sheet music—but she finally finished by the time Adjutant Cléry's "meilleur élève" returned to the Hôtel Budan from his last class.[62] As George looked around the empty hotel room, he casually asked his wife whether she had packed all the military memorabilia hiding under the bed. Confronted with a pile of swords and scabbards, Beatrice grabbed one with both hands and chased him around the room. She never complained about the work involved with being the wife of George S. Patton Jr., but she refused to be taken for granted. She dropped the heavy sword with such force that the blade got stuck in the corner of a table, and George dutifully got down on his knees and helped her pack the rest of their possessions.

"If I have said any thing of a detonating nature," George once wrote his wife, "please don't explode."[63] More than a head shorter than the husband she was devoted to, she possessed an explosive temper George had known about since he met her. Years earlier, when he hoped she would finally do him the "kindness" of sending him a picture, he asked "with much inward fear . . . as I never have gotten quite over the way you squelched me once before."[64]

*Figure 21. Portrait of the Patton family in 1914 at Fort Riley. (University of Kansas)*

BEATRICE COMPARED the peripatetic nature of military life to a turtle who carries its shell, bringing "whatever background we have . . . wherever we go."[65] So when the Pattons returned to Fort Myer on September 17, it was time to begin packing again. Moving to a new post was routine by now: while Beatrice packed up the old place and visited her parents for an extended stay, George went ahead to spruce up the new place.

Unfortunately, the first house he was assigned at Fort Riley, Kansas, turned out to be a nightmare; built in 1881 and "never since been cleaned," there was barely enough space even with the additional shelving he installed.[66] Worried about Beatrice's reaction and very much aware that she had "to give up a lot on my account," George told her not "to come until every thing is all right here."[67] It took a lot of pull, but he eventually managed to secure the "hottest," meaning warmest, house on the post with a laundry room and space for servants.

Beatrice seemed to have adapted well to life in the army after three and a half years of marriage, but the honeymoon phase ended when she arrived at the old frontier post, so remote that letters took weeks to arrive. As she stepped off the train at Junction City on October 25, 1913, she realized this was "the mud of the road" George warned her about before their engagement.[68] The closest town was nothing more than a train junction without any theaters or museums to stimulate her, and George even doubted the water and milk were safe for human consumption.

Fort Riley was a rude awakening for Beatrice after Fort Sheridan, where she was occupied with the arrival of her first child, and Fort Myer, where she could engage with sophisticated friends. The only thing that took "some of the pain out of being so far from home" was that "Riley was so near California."[69]

Established in 1853 to protect travelers from marauding Indian tribes along the Oregon and Santa Fe trails, Fort Riley became the home of the Mounted Service School in 1892. George had been clamoring to attend the two-year course since he graduated from West Point, and he took on "more work than I have ever done in the Army."[70] He attended the Cavalry School from eight to twelve and taught fencing with "much energy and enthusiasm" in the afternoon.[71]

The newly minted Master of the Sword proved to be a very competent teacher, and he improved his skills even further with the help of his wife, who sat in the back of his class to take notes and make suggestions. At five o'clock, when the bugle sounded, Beatrice walked to the flagpole with Little Bee to observe the retreat ceremony. With his official duties for the day completed, George walked up from the stables and strolled home with his family.

**Figure 22.** *George and Little Bee at Fort Riley in 1914. According to her father, she was "a natural born hunter" and a talented equestrian from a young age. (University of Kansas)*

The heat at Fort Riley was oppressive—temperatures often reached into the nineties during the summer, and the area was prone to flooding and tornadoes —but the lack of activities was even more stifling to Beatrice. George had warned her that "to survive this place at all you will have to ride horse back as there is not another thing to do there is not even a place to go to in an automobile."[72] There were hunts along the prairie, polo games, a biweekly dance, and a weekly movie on Sunday night, but this was not enough for a cultivated woman who felt inspired by music, art, and poetry.

With nowhere to go, Beatrice also had no one to see, as everyone "seemed very wild and crude and savage." She did her best to fit in, but "her heart was not in it." Not only was she unable to relate to her neighbors' favorite topics of conversation—the good old days, (lack of) money, and cooking—but she also had trouble understanding their heavy southern accents, the language of the "downstairs' staff" as she called it. Moreover, with Hannah and Kane taking care of the household, Beatrice had even more time on her hands to brood, and she began "to feel she was a terrible failure as an Army wife."[73]

Maybe she was not cut out for this life after all, no matter how much she loved George. Lonely and bored, she returned to Boston as often as she could, egged on by her mother, who played on Beatrice's feelings of guilt. With her father getting on in age (he was now ninety-one years old), Ellie loved reminding her daughter how much Frederick missed his precious daughter.

George wholeheartedly encouraged his wife to visit her family while at Fort Riley, knowing he was to blame for her unhappiness.

A week after returning from a monthlong visit to Avalon in the summer of 1914, Beatrice finally "woke up." It all began one evening when she joined George on the porch, and the silence was interrupted by the near-deaf mother of a neighbor who yelled, "What say?"

Unaware that Beatrice had returned that afternoon, the daughter-in-law replied with a loud shout, "I said that with that pretty little Mrs. Patton gone so much to see her folks, Mrs. Merchant seems to be getting her hooks into young Mr. Patton."

Beatrice didn't doubt George's fidelity, but the sudden understanding that she was the butt of gossip made her realize that she needed to make some changes.

The pivotal moment in her life came to pass a few days later when she took Little Bee for her daily stroll out on the prairie. Beatrice had walked to the top of Custer Hill many times before, but this time it felt as if she were seeing the rimrock—the sheer rock wall at the upper edge of a canyon—for the first time. When she bent down to take a closer look, she noticed the rock was made from tiny shells and sand. It suddenly dawned on her that she was standing on the shore of what once was a giant body of water. Beatrice grabbed her daughter, ran home as fast as she could, and immediately wrote her favorite bookstore in Boston to order all the books they carried on American marine fossils.

That day out on the prairie, Beatrice discovered Kansas was the bottom of the Permian Sea approximately 250 to 290 million years ago.[74] Far more important, though, "her inner eye had been opened, [and] she had discovered the whole world."[75] Her life changed when she realized that beauty and knowledge could be found even in a place as desolate as Fort Riley, as long as she made an effort to look. Never again would she doubt the army life, embracing it with the same passion she brought to every endeavor she undertook.


It was akin to a miracle that Beatrice got on the train without shedding a tear, saying goodbye to George and Little Bee as she headed fifteen hundred miles to Lake Vineyard to give birth to the long-hoped-for Patton son.[76] Ever since her daughter was born, an indomitable Beatrice had the same reply every time George asked her what she wanted for her birthday, anniversary, or Christmas: "I want a baby."[77]

Beatrice wanted to give her husband a son, but George "never got over" the events of March 19, 1911, and remained unmoved by her exhortations. He could live without a son but not without his Beat, yet here he was four years later, feeling both relieved and frightened as the train pulled out of a snowy Junction City carrying his wife, sister, and mother. Work prevented him from having to witness another massacre, but George made it clear where his priorities lay. "She is a brave woman and I hope she will have no trouble," he wrote his father on February 11, 1915. "You must tell the doctor that if there is the least question between her life and that of the child The child must go. This is probably an unnecessary caution but I insist on it. If he will not subscribe to it get another doctor who will."[78] To Beatrice, he wrote to "[p]lease try and rest all you can . . . you are more tired than you know. Above all don't sew too much it tires your back and is of realy no importance."[79]

The grief enveloping Lake Vineyard after the recent death of Colonel Smith changed to excitement when Beatrice arrived. She planned to give birth to G.W.—George Washington, the temporary name she gave the baby so as not to tempt fate—in the same ugly bed, but not the same house, where his father and grandmother had been born. After his boy got married, Mr. Patton had finally felt able to walk "hand-in-hand into the sunset" with his wife and built her a new home at Lake Vineyard.[80]

Uncle George and Aunt Ruth, as Beatrice called her in-laws, fixed things up nicely for her and even planted flowers outside her window so she, and the baby boy, would have something nice to look at in the coming weeks. She was waited on like a queen as she enjoyed the mild winter climate on the porch, eating fresh oranges and grapes while watching George's freshly washed baby clothes drying in the wind. The only damper on the occasion was the ill health of the Ayers, who were spending the winter in nearby Pasadena.

Dr. Wernick first met Frederick in 1908 after he was "thrown from the upper berth of his Pullman compartment," but he turned out to be "in the very best of health." When he was called on December 23, 1914, the doctor once again "found Mr. Ayer in fine health and spirits," but Mrs. Ayer "was in bad health."[81] Ellie, who was plagued by a lingering illness, took months to recover. And delaying their departure from California even further, Frederick suffered "an attack of acute bronchitis" shortly after his twelfth grandchild was born.

With fear and trepidation, Kane awoke Lieutenant Patton at two in the morning to deliver a telegram, convinced something terrible had happened to Beatrice. The whole household had been walking on eggshells, and George "was getting more and more worried every day." So it was an immense relief to read "that it has happened and that you had no complications." "In the words of our immortal ex president," he was "D E L I G H T E D" with his new baby daughter, born on February 28, 1915.

According to George, Hannah notified the whole post, "more delighted than if it had been her own," and he "steared clear of her all day for fear she would embarrass me." Since no one expected another girl, he suggested Beatrice "have it named out there where you can get more advice. All I know is that I don't like the sound of either Ruth or Ellen. You might call it Beatrice

Second like a race horse. I certainly like the sound of that name the best of any." He ended his letter with one kiss for "it" and twelve for Beatrice, hoping she had not suffered "or are not suffering more than necessary."[82]

Since Beatrice was still able to write George a letter "on the twenty-seventh in which you speak of no symptoms," he assumed "it must have come all of a rush so to speak," but the birth of M.W. (Martha Washington since "it" turned out to be a girl) had been another long ordeal. George was "very proud" to be the husband of a woman who showed so much "uncomplaining courage," especially since the ineptitude of the attending physician left Beatrice in considerable discomfort.[83]

Despite the safe arrival of a healthy baby girl, a sense of disappointment was palpable at Lake Vineyard. Everyone had hoped for a boy, mostly Mr. Patton, who still fixated on having a grandson to carry on the Patton name. Beatrice bravely wished for "better luck next time," upon which Aunt Ruth exclaimed, "Beatrice, dear, please don't mention 'next time' to your Uncle George. He has had a very hard day!"

The rumor that Beatrice had returned to Fort Riley because a baby carriage was spotted on the Pattons' front porch finally proved true at the beginning of May when she arrived at Junction City with Ruth Ellen, named after her two grandmothers. According to family consensus, "R E" was the ugliest baby anyone had ever seen. When George held her for the first time, he could only marvel at how such a tiny baby could produce so many decibels. After days of constant wailing, the members of the Patton household were ready to kill each other, so a desperate Beatrice took Ruth Ellen to a doctor in Junction City, who diagnosed her as "starving to death."

Put on a strict diet by a "Dr. C." in California to get back her "lines of Venus" for George, Beatrice was neither producing the right amount nor the right quality of milk.[84] The doctor suggested feeding Ruth Ellen cream laced with a touch of brandy, and within days she became "a most awfully <u>good</u> baby," adored by her sister, who was "just a little bit jealous."[85]

AFTER COMPLETING his second year at the Mounted Service School in June 1915, George was bound to return to the 15th Cavalry, which he had left at Fort Myer two years earlier. This would have been joyous news had it not been that the 15th Cavalry was going to the Philippines in October to relieve the 8th Cavalry. The news reverberated throughout the family, but Beatrice was convinced that "it will all turn out right in the end" as George left her and the children at Avalon to go use his influence in Washington. "I am so happy when we are together," Beatrice told Aunt Nannie, "and now he will very soon be gone. But I would not keep him here for the world."[86]

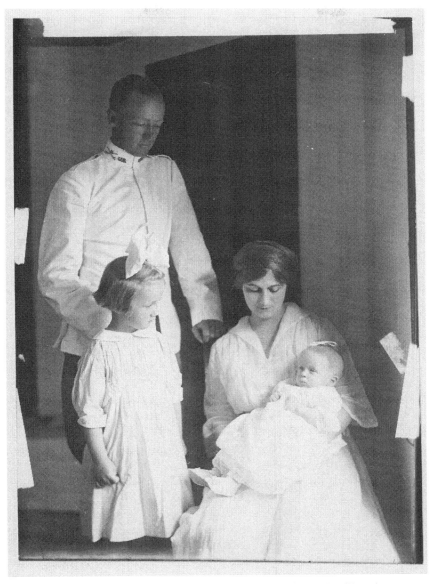

*Figure 23. Portrait of the Patton family at Fort Riley in 1915. (University of Kansas)*

"Some day I will make them all know me," George wrote from the capital, but he knew enough people to affect a transfer to Fort Bliss, Texas, with the returning 8th Cavalry.[87] As usual, George planned to go ahead to spruce up their living quarters, but on the day of his departure, Beatrice decided to join him. There was no sense arguing with her; "she was very nearvous," and George "thought it as well to let her come as she wanted to so much."[88] Beatrice was not about to miss another second with her husband, not with a war on the horizon and not after he came within minutes of asphyxiating a year earlier during their annual summer vacation along the North Shore.

Mr. Robert Reese was driving along Topsfield Road at 3:30 p.m. on August 10, 1914, when he came across an overturned touring car. He saw a body pinned beneath the wreckage, so he used all his strength to lift the vehicle and pull the unconscious driver to safety. Mr. Reese dragged the stranger into his car and drove two-and-a-half miles to Turner Hill in Ipswich, the 200-room home of his friends, mining magnate Charles G. Rice and his wife, Anne Proctor Rice. While they waited for the doctors to arrive, Mrs. Rice, a tiny woman with the heart of a lion, cleared the stranger's throat and checked his clothes for some form of identification, covered as he was in motor oil with pieces of gravel embedded in his face.[89]

Mrs. Rice was surprised to see the name Frederick Ayer Jr. sewn in the collar of the man's polo shirt because she knew him to be out of town. Fred was her son-in-law; her daughter Hilda married him a week earlier, and the couple was on their honeymoon. Theirs was a "romance of the hunting field" which began after Fred graduated from Harvard and returned from a sabbath year circling the globe in 1912.[90] The newlyweds even rode off into the sunset on horseback, wearing their riding habits. In their possession was a check for $1 million (approximately $25 million), which Fred received from his father with the words, "Son, this should start your married life right. Make it grow and may it bring you happiness."[91]

Only after Mrs. Rice carefully cleaned the stranger's face did she realize the man was George Patton Jr., who had borrowed his brother-in-law's polo shirt on his way to a game. Four doctors from neighboring towns were summoned, including Dr. Peer Johnson, a close family friend who was present at many of the most important life events of the Ayers and the Pattons. They diagnosed the critically injured patient with a bad concussion, partial paralysis of his right arm, and severe chest injuries from being crushed by the steering wheel. It would take months for George to recover fully but despite the distress, the near-fatal accident was a blessing in disguise for Beatrice. In the weeks preceding his "annual mishap," George had been determined to obtain a leave of absence to join the war in Europe.

*Figure 24. Three generations of Frederick Ayers, circa 1916.*

On July 28, 1914—one month after the assassination of Archduke Franz Ferdinand and his wife—Austria-Hungary declared war on Serbia. As neutrality laws were broken and mutual defense pacts kicked in, half of Europe soon joined the fight, but President Wilson called on all Americans "to act and speak in the true spirit of neutrality."[92] To George, "all other forms of human endeavor shrink to insignificance [when] compared to war," a view he shared with men like Theodore Roosevelt and Winston Churchill, who considered war to be man's ultimate test. So, George was beside himself that he might miss out on finally proving his mettle because of a cowardly president.[93]

Since "my family does not rely on me for support [and] I would only be risking my self," George asked General Wood for "a years leave on some pretext" so he could "go to France and take part in this war." He even offered to pay all expenses and promised "never [to] apply to the United States for help if I get in trouble or captured." The chief of staff replied that the Army did not "want to waste youngsters of your sort in the service of foreign nations," but Beatrice knew full well her husband would have kept looking for a way had fate not intervened.[94]

George always attributed his survival to Mrs. Rice, writing her affectionately a few years later, "Ever since you so foolishly prevented my untimely departure to another world I have taken occasion to remind you of your error."[95] George was "disgusted with human frailty," admiring those, like himself, who always tried to do a little "more than the ordinary." Known for her "perfect candor" and "indomitable courage," Mrs. Rice was a talented equestrian like himself. She was bold and spirited, jumping over the highest fences when she could have taken an easier route, and no amount of broken bones—both arms, both legs, her neck, her back, her pelvis, her collarbone, and countless ribs—ever stopped her from pursuing her passion.[96]

LEAVING Little Bee and the four-month-old baby with her parents at Avalon, Beatrice and George returned to Fort Riley on July 8, 1915, to pack up their belongings. Since George hadn't secured quarters yet at Fort Bliss, they shipped their household goods and eleven horses to Lake Vineyard. The Pattons followed in their car, driving fifteen hundred miles over unpaved roads along the Santa Fe Trail that Don Benito Wilson had traveled seventy-three years earlier. They managed to drive 114 miles in five hours on a good day, but on a bad one, when they got stuck in three different mud holes, they only managed 138 miles in nine-and-a-half hours.[97]

When they arrived in San Bernardino, California, they were "so dirty that we had lunch at the station restaurant instead of at the hotel," but a few days of rest at Lake Vineyard brought some respite.[98] Mr. Patton hoped to dissuade Beatrice from going to Fort Bliss, a border station that was looking increasingly dangerous because of ongoing political unrest in Mexico, but she was adamant about dropping off George before heading back to Avalon.

Beatrice's worries shifted from her parents and children to her husband as she read about the worsening tensions at the Mexican border in the *Boston Globe*. Though filled with romantic longing, George's letters were no more reassuring as he hunted for danger. In November, he spent eleven hours in the saddle, riding over sixty miles in the hopes of leading a saber attack against a band of Carrancistas—one of the factions in the Mexican Revolution—who had been spotted along the border. While George liked "this sort of work a lot," Beatrice began to worry she would never see him alive again.[99] When she learned he would not be able to come to Avalon for Christmas, she packed her bags after an exciting Thanksgiving and returned to Fort Bliss. Because of the dangerous territory and the lack of amenities, she once again left Little Bee and Ruth Ellen with their grandparents.

Beatrice's relief was evident when she was reunited with George at the El Paso train station on December 22. Since he had been ordered to Sierra Blanca for border patrol duty a month after his arrival, he still hadn't secured quarters at Fort Bliss. So instead, he took Beatrice to the Hotel Paso del Norte for the night, the safest and most ornate building in town, even though it was just a mile from the Mexican border.[100] The next day George drove them the ninety miles to Sierra Blanca—a trip which took them four hours—the roughest and most dangerous place Beatrice had ever been.

*Figure 25. Beatrice along the Mexican border. (Library of Congress)*

A vital railroad junction sixteen miles from the Mexican border and founded in 1881, Sierra Blanca had a post office, a hotel, a local newspaper, two general stores, and two cattle breeders.[101] George rented the only house available, a three-room adobe he occasionally shared with Major Langhorne, another well-off officer who drove through town in a Cadillac. Thirty-year-old Lieutenant Patton was already the most popular man in Sierra Blanca, and the cowboys considered him a kindred spirit for his profanity and marksmanship. Beatrice added to his popularity; it didn't happen very often that an elegant young lady came to town, especially one who was unpretentious, knowledgeable about horses, and not afraid to partake in the local culture.

Coming home from the border one day, George accosted his wife with "genial oaths, matter-of-fact invective and picturesque complaints."[102] Unperturbed, Beatrice continued serving her guests, ladies of the post who didn't know how to react when a husband addressed his wife in such a manner or when a wife exhibited such unladylike behavior. George already made his reputation as an expert marksman when he "hit a jack rabbit running at about fifteen yards while riding at a trot," but Beatrice was equally up for hunting along the Rio Grande.[103] One Saturday morning, they left on a twenty-six-mile ride, hunted all afternoon, "slept in the open then hunted till two [the] next day." They shot "thirteen fine duck most of them Mallard and B killed two of them besides a quail and a plover so she had a fine time."[104]

Beatrice became as fascinated with the town as the town's 350 residents were with her. Sheriff Richard "Dick" Love was Beatrice's greatest admirer. One of seven siblings, he lived on a ranch thirty miles outside of town surrounded by natural hot springs. He invited the Pattons, Major Stuart Cramer, and some local businessmen for dinner just three months after his ranch was raided by General Pascual Orozco, the right-hand man of deposed Mexican President Huerta. While Orozco and his men pressed the cook to prepare a meal and forced the ranch hand to shoe their horses, Sheriff Love caught them red-handed. He pursued them into the hills, and by nightfall Orozco and his four companions were killed in a posse fight with the help of the 13th Cavalry and a group of prominent Sierra Blanca citizens.[105]

The situation along the border had only gotten worse since then, but no one batted an eye when a shot suddenly rang out in the middle of dinner. While Ruth Ellen tells the story one way in *The Button Box,* Major Cramer's recounting in 1943 is likely more accurate.[106] In an effort to emulate the local cowboys and shoot faster, George had filed down the sear of his pistol and wore it in his waistband. Unfortunately, all the gun now needed to go off was a bump across the hammer, so as he moved about at the table, a bullet accidentally discharged, creasing his thigh and embedding itself in the floor. Since no one was seriously injured, dinner continued without anyone bringing up the mishap.[107]

Driving home that night under the bright light of a full moon, George managed to run the car into a cattle gate without even attempting to brake. "God dammit," he sobbed, "I suppose you don't give a damn whether I kill my fool self or not!"

Beatrice looked at her husband to see tears streaming down his face, then calmly replied, "Why, Georgie, you always told me not to notice things like that. Besides, I knew you weren't hurt much, because you weren't bleeding. Are you really hurt?"

Only his ego was hurt, because of Beatrice's cavalier reaction, but he was the one who taught her that "worrying does not help any thing and hurts every thing."[108] She reassured her husband that she still loved him dearly, but it wasn't unusual for George to become insecure after a long separation.

Their grandson Robert Patton later explained that his grandfather "often felt, sometimes with reason, that he was on the verge of losing Beatrice and had to win her affection anew."[109] When a man got married, George wrote in his West Point notebook in 1909, "he must be just as careful to keep his wifes love as he was to get it. That is he should always be spoony and make love to her so she will continue to like him for it would make her most sad if he said as it were 'Now I have got you I will take a rest.' Don't do that ever."[110]

SAYING goodbye to Sierra Blanca in January 1916 with a barbecue and square dance organized by the local townspeople, Beatrice returned to Avalon to pick up the children while George prepared the new homestead at Fort Bliss. Fortunately, he was allocated a large two-story house with tall windows and a sleeping porch because Ellie sent along a retinue of servants: Julie Gould, the cook; a Chinese houseboy; and Catherine "Taty" Breen, the children's beloved Irish governess. There was also a steady stream of visiting family members, beginning in February with "sensible, loyal and loving" Nita Patton. Twenty-eight, unmarried, and still living with her parents at Lake Vineyard, her life was beginning to frighteningly remind her of Aunt Nannie's.

None of the suitors Nita brought home over the years lived up to her standards, nor were they good enough for her father and brother. But then she caught the eye of fifty-five-year-old Brigadier General John J. Pershing. Black Jack Pershing—so named for having served two years with the all-black 10th Cavalry Regiment—tragically lost his wife and three daughters in a fire at the Presidio in San Francisco on August 27, 1915. He lived with his sister and five-year-old son Warren at Fort Bliss while post commander. The strict disciplinarian possessed a temper as hot as his personality was cold and inspired fear in all those who stood before him. Nita must have been the only person in the U.S. Army to describe the dashing officer with his commanding presence as "entertaining."[111]

Tensions with Mexico came to a head on March 9, 1916, when Mexican revolutionary Pancho Villa and his troops raided Columbus, New Mexico. President Wilson ordered General Pershing to hunt down those responsible for the death of eighteen innocent Americans, and there was no one more eager to join the Mexican Punitive Expedition than George. Unfortunately, the 8th Cavalry was instructed to remain at Fort Bliss as a garrison. Not about to miss a war just miles from his front door, George relentlessly pursued Pershing, willing to accept any job. Whether it was his need for a temporary aide, his friendly relations with Nita, or his recognizing himself in young Lieutenant Patton, Pershing called the following morning and made George's dearest wish a reality.

"White and little looking" as she packed George's bag, Beatrice managed to hold it together at the moment of parting. But when soon-to-be First Lieutenant George Patton rode off on March 16, 1916, with a framed picture of his wife in his pocket, he was pleasantly surprised to see that "B acted fine and did not cry or anything." Beatrice wouldn't see her husband for five months, but she would prove her mettle, despite Nita's fear that her sister-in-law was "not fitted for the strenuous life," getting "too excited over mishaps."[112]

The next three years of Beatrice's life were marked by constant worry—for George, her children, and her parents—but they were also the years that she would "learn to take it." As she stood by George's side in circumstances beyond her control in order for him to pursue his dream, she realized that "instead of making ourselves sick with worry and fear and selfish thoughts, we ought to remember that our men are going to be talking all the rest of their lives of the places they've been, the men they've known, the battles they've won."[113]

The Mexican Punitive Expedition and World War I would be the most challenging years of Beatrice's life, but as she told the next generation of army wives years later, "Struggles make us strong. Life knocks us to our knees but this leaves us in a better position to pray."[114]

# 5

## AVALON

## PRIDE'S CROSSING, MASSACHUSETTS

### 1916–1919

*YOU OWN NOTHING UNTIL YOU HAVE GIVEN IT AWAY FREELY.*

The dust cloud, which appeared on the southern horizon on June 4, 1916, was not caused by a band of Villistas but by Mother Nature. Just fifteen minutes after the crowd at Rio Grande Park spotted it, El Paso became engulfed in darkness.[1] Beatrice described the storm as "quite a fierce one" in a letter to her mother, who wrote her almost daily. Wind speeds reached fifty miles per hour, "enough to blow one inside out, like an umbrella," and the whole house "was creaking like a ship." When she went to sleep, "all the curtains in the room were standing out straight ... [and] the bed was rocking in the wind."[2]

Dust storms were frequent in the Chihuahuan Desert, and they plagued both George in Colonia Dublán and Beatrice in El Paso on an equal basis. When she experienced her first one just days before Christmas 1915, she broke down crying and wished her husband would resign from the Army. It was one of the few times Beatrice's resolve faltered, but she possessed "the heart of a pioneer woman," according to Ruth Ellen, and soldiered on.[3]

Despite its harsh environment, Beatrice still considered Fort Bliss "a fine place to keep house in," and she refused to go to Avalon despite George's suggestion that she would be better off at home if he got killed, "... which I shant be."[4] She wanted to be nearby in case something happened, a decision which must have disappointed Ellie, a "kindly and lovable woman" with "a penchant for imperious histrionics."[5]

One would be hard-pressed to find three siblings more devoted to their parents—not to mention each other—than Beatrice, Fred, and Kay. Fred began working in his father's company despite his strong desire to become either a doctor or a writer; Kay returned from The Masters School at Dobbs Ferry, New York, to take care of her parents, who had become somewhat dependent on her; and Beatrice could not resist the pull of her family despite missing George "every single minute" she was away.[6]

Beatrice's absence was hard on her family, but as long as their health allowed it, Frederick and Ellie traveled across the country to visit the Pattons. By 1917, however, both Ayers were plagued by health issues, and Ellie liked to remind "ma fleur qui pense [her thinking flower]" how much the aging Sir Frederick missed his little daughter.[7]

**Figure 26**. *Portrait of Ellen "Ellie" Banning Ayer, date unknown.*

Extremely close to his own parents, George was very understanding of his wife's dilemma, even though he felt as if he were leading "a double sort of existence," with Beatrice and away from Beatrice, each with its own "time scale."[8] He was reluctant to keep her away from her father, despite a tendency for his life to unravel when she was not around, and he never asked her to come home, merely sending her a few subtle hints if she stayed away too long. George knew how sad the Ayers were whenever Beatrice left them, but he hoped Ellie would at least "take a little comfort out of the thought at my happiness at seeing them."[9]

Married for seven years, the Pattons already spent a third of that time apart. In hindsight, Beatrice would regret how complaisant she became upon her first visit to Avalon after her wedding, returning again and again and again. Forced to choose over and over between duty to her parents and duty to her husband, she was wracked with guilt and self-reproach no matter what decision she made. Thinking back later to the days when she was separated from George, not by necessity but by choice, she couldn't help but lament what a stupid fool she had been all those years.

RETURNING from a trip to El Paso on or about May 15, 1916, an unopened newspaper on the seat beside her, Beatrice was greeted by Mrs. Duncan sticking her head outside her kitchen door. She remembered everything going black and driving straight into the garage door when she heard her neighbor call out, "Your husband's a Medal of Honor man now, Mrs. Patton!"[10] The news out of Mexico had been slow, but when an unscathed Beatrice checked the paper, she realized that it was Lieutenant George Patton Jr. who had at last succeeded in getting into a fight. His exploits were not worthy of a Medal of Honor—to his lasting regret, he would never receive one—but they were front-page news for days. "Thank Heaven he is a dead shot," Beatrice exclaimed when she read her husband's interview with the *New York Times*.

*Figure 27. Lieutenant Patton in Mexico. (Library of Congress)*

Even though the Mexican Punitive Expedition was a cavalry mission, George instigated the U.S. Army's first motorized attack on May 14. Until that day, the Punitive Expedition was not what he had expected. Pancho Villa was nowhere to be found—unbeknownst to the Americans, he had gone into hiding after being shot in the leg a few days before the start of the expedition—and there was not much to do around camp except hunting and going on inspection trips. So, when George heard that the commander of the Dorados, Villa's bodyguards, was rumored to be hiding near Rubio, he pestered Pershing until he received "permission to go out with the 13th Cavalry to hunt for Mr. Julio Cardenes."[11]

Lieutenant Patton and approximately ten men of the 13th Cavalry left their encampment near Rubio, about 250 miles from the border, and drove into town to buy a fresh supply of maize. Their guide, Holmdahl, was an ex-Villista and recognized some of his old compadres in a group of men gathered in the town square, so George decided to "combine business with pleasure" and took his men to reconnoiter Cárdenas's nearby ranches. The story of what happened next has been told many times—per George in many different ways—but it always ends with three dead Villistas strapped to the hood of three Dodge touring cars.

George had waited his whole life for a moment like this, yet he was neither scared nor excited when he and his men "sprang directly from their cars into the fight."[12] Prohibited from firing at the locals until it was established they were hostile, he was so schooled not to shoot that when "three armed men dashed out on horseback . . . I merely drew my pistol and waited to see what would happen." It wasn't until the threesome galloped toward him, shooting, that he fired back.

George ran for cover to reload when suddenly, "a man on a horse came right in front of me, I started to shoot at him but remembered that Dave Allison [a ranger he befriended at Sierra Blanca] had always said to shoot at the horse of an escaping man and I did so and broke the horses hip, he fell on his rider and as it was only about ten yards, we all hit him. He crumpled up." Two more Mexicans were killed in the scrimmage as they tried to flee, one of whom was Julio Cárdenas.[13]

While three men kept skinning a cow outside without interruption, George discovered Cárdenas's wife, mother, and baby inside the hacienda. They "expressed neither horror, hate, nor grief," unlike the two women who were trembling in a corner behind a locked door and called "on God the Father and Christ the Son and the saints to have mercy on her and hers" before wishing the wrath of God on "los Americanos."[14] Chased by a band of Villistas for part of the way, George and his men returned to camp with three rapidly decomposing bodies tied to their cars. Pershing dubbed George the "Bandit" and allowed him to take home Cárdenas's silver-mounted saddle and saber as his first spoils of war.[15]

When Beatrice read George's account and saw his picture in the newspapers, she was "so proud of him I am nearly dead."[16] Frederick wrote his "dear Son & Daughter" that he was "trying to think of words to express my feelings and admiration of your courage and bravery, and our joy that you came away alive." But, surprisingly, Nita was "sick at the thought" that her brother had potentially killed someone.[17] While it isn't certain that any of George's bullets killed any of the three men, it didn't seem to bother him if one is to believe what he wrote Beatrice: "You are probably wondering if my conscience hurts me for killing a man. It does not. I feel about it just as I did when I got my sword fish, surprised at my luck."[18] Yet, as Ruth Ellen later told an interviewer, "You can't kill without something inside you also being killed," and it was in Mexico that her father started in earnest the practice of writing poetry to deal with the death and destruction of war.[19]

JUST FIVE MILES north of El Paso and within walking distance of Mexico, Fort Bliss's primary duties were not that different from those at its inception in 1848: secure the Southern border, train for war, and protect the local civilians. Tensions were still high in El Paso after race riots broke out in January 1916 over the killing of eighteen Americans by Villista Pablo López, and the town's population exploded with the arrival of thousands of soldiers and National Guardsmen. Temporarily billeted in tents in less-than-ideal conditions, many of them could be found in El Paso on payday, spending the little they earned on liquor. Whenever Nita drove into town to visit the El Paso City Market or take the children to Elite Confectionery for ice cream, she made sure to have her gun on hand.

Beatrice would always remember her time at Fort Bliss for the invaluable lessons it taught her, most importantly, the value of keeping busy. Her relationships with the families on the post were outstanding, and she was a fixture in the society pages of the *El Paso Times* as she hosted lunches and handled the receiving line at the bi-weekly hops. The children adapted well, and Nita was a valuable addition to the family, so much so that Beatrice didn't "know how I could possibly get along without her!"[20]

Still, Nita was under the impression that her sister-in-law thought her to be "awfully slow … and [without] music in my soul." When Kay came to El Paso in July to visit with two of her suitors—Keith Merrill and Stuart Cramer—Nita felt like the fifth wheel, "except when people want things done." She frequently unburdened herself during her months-long stay at Fort Bliss in lengthy letters to her mother, writing with a certain gleeful satisfaction that Beatrice seemed entirely out of her element.[21]

In August, General Pershing returned for a weeklong vacation in Columbus, New Mexico, joined by Lieutenant Patton so as not to arouse suspicion. Whether the tension Nita described to her mother was real or only imagined, she felt vindicated when Pershing asked her to sit in the lead car. "Bea is quite peevish because she had to ride behind with mere colonels, and the dust gave her hay fever," she wrote Ruth, her belief confirmed that her sister-in-law was too good and too delicate for army life.[22]

Why the sudden veiled animosity? Maybe Nita was aware of Beatrice's ambivalent feelings toward her relationship with General Pershing. George had jokingly said, "Nita may rank us yet," but Beatrice did not relish her sister-in-law becoming Mrs. General.[23]

Or maybe Nita was just a little bit annoyed at the excellent relationship Beatrice enjoyed with Mr. Patton. Bamps, as his grandchildren called him, considered Beatrice "the dearest little daughter a man has ever had - and the finest and truest son's wife."[24] Reading those words brought tears to Beatrice's eyes, "tears of joy they were, to think that you should love your Son's wife so much. I always think of myself as your daughter, and it makes me very happy to know that you look on me in the same way."[25]

Like Beatrice, Mr. Patton worried a lot and he tended to be "nervous & anxious about all sorts of imaginary possibilities." Yet, he subjected himself to the "suspicions and meanness" of politics for years while all he wanted to do was enjoy "the path of old age" with his wife.[26] His Boy spurred him on like a horse at the races, convinced that "if there is a war your presence in Washington would be more useful to me than at any other time."[27]

When the "Harry Hotspur of the South" once again sought the Democratic Party's nomination for U.S. Senator in the fall of 1916, he was haunted by his words on women's suffrage. "A Virginian, with all the fire and chivalry of the south," he once said women were "incapable of balloting discreetly and wisely."[28] Beatrice's thoughts on the subject are unknown, but she did believe that "a family should have a head, and a normal man wants to be head of the family."[29]

THE LAST THING Beatrice expected was to be waiting at the Columbus train station for the third time in two months. She had been campaigning for her father-in-law in California when she received word that her husband was reluctantly returning to Fort Bliss on sick leave, but luckily he wrote her a "long tale to keep you from being worried."

On October 2, 1916, George returned from an evening at the movies and decided to work on a paper before going to bed. Unfortunately, burning gasoline spewed from his lamp as he tried to make it work properly. Once he extinguished his face, hair, and tent, he calmly notified Pershing that he was going to the hospital, where he spent the next five days "hurting like hell" and eating through a straw. Diagnosed with "severe first degree burns of his entire face and the dorsal or upper surface of the right hand," he only cared that his eyes were okay as he "would have hated worst to have been blinded because I could not have seen you [Beatrice]."[30]

In family lore, there was such a thing as the "famous Patton luck," first experienced by George's great-uncle John Mercer Patton during the Civil War. John survived more attacks than all his brothers combined, including Tazewell and George, who were each shot three times. George Patton Jr. possessed that same amount of luck. Despite suffering at least one misadventure a month, he always managed to escape permanent injury or death, whether it was at West Point where he almost brought his "fiery life to a sudden and tragic conclusion" when he tripped jumping a hurdle, or at Fort Sheridan where he "looked like a stuck pig" when his horse threw its head back and hit him in the face.[31]

Warned by his father at just two years of age to be more careful or he would break his neck, the boy replied almost presciently that he "wouldn't break it for any 'mount of money."[32] George believed that he was born to be hung. If he wasn't accidentally getting hurt, he put himself in harm's way on purpose to test his luck. Every mishap he survived gave him confidence that "the Lord . . . must be holding me for some other job."[33]

When George arrived from Colonia Dublán on October 13, his face looked like "an old after-birth of a Mexican cow on which had been smeared several very much decomposed eggs."[34] Beatrice offered to change his dressings on the two-day train ride to Lake Vineyard, but to her embarrassment, she got sick to her stomach when she had to pull "yards of skin off his face."[35] Fortunately for a vain man like George Patton, his face healed without scarring—he merely felt the cold on his ears for the rest of his life—and two weeks later, he was able to join the campaign trail. He basked in the glory of his father's adoration, who exalted "the bandit killer" at every campaign stop and introduced him at his private club as his "hero son."

Beatrice, George, and the girls returned to Fort Bliss two days after the election, unsure of the outcome since Mr. Patton refused to concede until all votes were counted. It wasn't until November 12 that newspapers called his loss to Hiram Johnson, the Republican governor of California. At Beatrice's instigation, which meant George's, he traveled to Washington to procure a job in President Wilson's second administration, but he was "too high souled to be a good advocate for him self and [he] lost out."[36] Mr. Patton never told his Boy, but he was relieved he had lost. He would never run for political office again, content with remaining the mayor of San Marino until 1924.

While George possessed the drive his father lacked, he still occasionally found himself in these "worthless streaks when I don't seem to do or care to do any thing."[37] With war raging in Europe and the Punitive Expedition a dead end, he became as despondent and insecure as he had once been at West Point. Beatrice once again became his solace. "If we were doing any good here I would not mind," George wrote her from Mexico a few days before Christmas, "but to just sit and see things go to hell is not very pleasant."[38]

Then, almost one year since Beatrice broke down at Sierra Blanca, a similar dust storm brought George to the edge.

It has been awful here for the last two days. I have never seen such dust. And it made me wish I was out of it. If I could only be sure of the future I would get out. That is if I was sure that I would never be above the average army officer I would for I don't like the dirt and all except as a means to fame. If I knew that I would never be famous I would settle down and raise horses and have a good time. It is a great gamble to spoil your and my own happiness for the hope of greatness. I wish I was less ambitious, then too some times I think that I am not ambitious at all only a dreamer. That I don't realy do my damdest even when I think I do.[39]

Time dragged during the last two months of the expedition, and being away from Beatrice for so long was a high price to pay.[40] George apologized on January 12, "both for your having a birthday and also for my absence," and had a colleague deliver her roses.[41] He absolutely "[hated] to get old and also for you to get old," and he urged her not to "worry about me and get gray hair" and "ride a little or you will loose your figure."[42] Having grown up with a father who was sixty-four when she was born, Beatrice knew old age could be beautiful, but George dreaded the idea. "Realy all joking aside I don't expect ever to be sixty not that it is old but simply that I would prefer to wear out from hard work before then," he wrote Beatrice in 1909.[43]

It was a great relief when President Wilson officially recalled the Mexican Punitive Expedition in January 1917 after months of political maneuvering. At five past ten, on the morning of February 5, General Pershing crossed the border into the United States after a nine-day journey. Behind him, as he entered Columbus, New Mexico, were the members of his general staff and a caravan of ten thousand men stretching over fifteen miles long. To watch "the arrival of Gen. Pershing, George, & the army was an occasion of a lifetime," which Beatrice described in "a most picturesque & entertaining" letter to her father.[44]

Despite an eleven-month manhunt, Pancho Villa eluded capture in the mountains he knew so well, but at least George learned "a lot about my profession and a lot how much I love you [Beatrice]. The first was necessary the second was not."[45]

---

BARELY SICK A DAY in his life, Frederick attributed his longevity to a quiet life of moderation. "Mr. Ayer has probably eaten less every year and taken more exercise upon the ounces of food he consumed than any other man," it was reported of the nonagenarian. "For years he has supplemented his walking and riding with the heaviest massage so that there is not a superfluous ounce on his bones, his nerves are in perfect tune, and his skin as flexible as a baby's."[46]

Frederick made two concessions to old age—taking breakfast in bed and dictating his letters as tremors affected his hands—but he remained a striking presence on his horse, even at ninety-four. He still went on a daily ride, no matter the weather, because it was all about leading a "rational life of recreation blended with routine, rather than long periods of grinding intensiveness followed by long periods of recuperation."[47]

The United States had just declared war on Germany on April 6, 1917— President Wilson could no longer ignore the Germans' aggression toward neutral and unarmed vessels on the Atlantic—when Beatrice received word at

Fort Bliss that her father was desperately ill with double pneumonia. Advised to come home as fast as possible, George requested emergency leave on April 11 and took Beatrice and the children to Avalon. When they arrived at the "combined Hospital and matrimonial establishment," Frederick had just regained consciousness, but Ellie had also taken ill. In addition, Beatrice had been so worried on the ride over that she soon added "to the general jollity by being also in bed sick."[48]

*Figure 28. Portrait of Katharine "Kay" Ayer. (Huntington Library)*

The matrimony George alluded to in his letter to Pershing was the impending wedding of Kay to Keith Merrill, a lawyer and Minnesota National Guardsman who had been stationed on the Mexican border. He first met the Ayer family in 1903, when Frederick took his fifteen-year-old son on a tour of The Hill School in Pottstown, Pennsylvania, leaving him there to "room with a love of a boy named Keith Merrill." When the entire Ayer family returned a few months later to visit Fred, Keith was introduced to eighteen-year-old Beatrice, whom he found "very attractive and charming," and Kay, "a chubby child of fourteen."[49]

Seven years later, during Yale's Class of 1911 senior prom, Keith recognized a classmate's "slim, dark-haired, dark-blue-eyed" date as Kay.[50] He was so smitten after just one waltz that he decided to continue his studies at Harvard Law School because it was within walking distance of the Ayer Mansion. Kay, however, turned out to be very elusive; when she wasn't taking care of her parents or entertaining a long line of suitors, she was traveling extensively.

Despite three years of persistence—an exasperated Ellie remarked that the family couldn't "even go to church without my finding Keith Merrill in our pew again!"—Kay preferred to remain single when asked for her hand in marriage. Dejected and lost without her guiding "idealism," it wasn't until Keith joined the National Guard in 1915 that he found the confidence to start corresponding with Kay again.[51]

Initially planned for the summer of 1917, the wedding was moved up to May 7 because of the Ayers' declining health and the outbreak of war with Germany. Frederick recuperated sufficiently from his bout with pneumonia that he was able to haltingly walk his youngest daughter down the makeshift aisle in the living room of Avalon.[52] The newlyweds left on their honeymoon the next day, a trip to Washington for Keith's interview with the Consular

Service of the State Department. Honorably discharged from the National Guard and turned down from serving in the Army, he was intent on serving his country one way or another. George, however, saw this as "an evident desire not to be killed" and called his new brother-in-law "un embusqué."[53]

George had already been in Washington to look for a new assignment, "nearer Boston so Mrs. Patton can be near her parents" because they "are too sick to be left alone."[54] What he really wanted, though, was to go to France as soon as possible. The opportunity finally presented itself on May 18. Upon returning from an afternoon ride with Mrs. Rice at Turner Hill, a wire awaited George, requesting him to report to General Pershing in Washington immediately. His father, who was already in the capital with Ruth and Nita, advised him to bring Beatrice but couldn't provide any more details. Before speeding off to Boston to catch the 12:30 a.m. train to New York, George kissed his daughters goodbye and said a hasty and unwittingly final farewell to his in-laws.[55]

At Penn Station, the Pattons purchased the *New York Times*, its headline leaving little to the imagination: "President Calls The Nation To Arms; Draft Bill Signed; Registration on June 5; Regulars Under Pershing To Go To France."[56] Tasked with creating an American Expeditionary Force to join the Allies in their fight against Germany—a tall order because the American Army was woefully small and pathetically undersupplied—Pershing selected roughly 180 men to join his general staff and set up headquarters in France. The recently promoted Captain Patton hated to leave Beatrice while she was having so much trouble with her "insides," but this was the moment he had been waiting for his whole life.

On May 28, just two days after his seventh wedding anniversary, George noted the near despair on the faces of his family, but he and Beatrice were convinced they would see each other in Paris soon. He appreciated Beatrice's attempt to keep her emotions in check, but she didn't accompany him to Lower Manhattan, where the ferry to Governor's Island awaited. A reluctant Mr. Patton accompanied him instead, very much aware that this was the moment he had always dreamed of but never dared to pursue.

WITH GERMAN U-BOATS patrolling the Atlantic and torpedoing Allied ships, Beatrice was relieved to learn the *H.M.S. Baltic* made it to Liverpool on June 8 and to Paris five days later. The French capital was seemingly unaffected by the war of attrition being fought a mere sixty miles away. Still, Paris was "a stupid place" without Beatrice, "just as heaven would be under the same conditions."[57]

As soon as George ascertained that his wife would be as safe in Paris as she was at Avalon, he wrote her to follow him across the Atlantic the moment she was feeling better. He suggested she bring along Little Bee to keep her company, an immersion suit in case they got torpedoed, and a letter of credit for $10,000 (about $230,000) because life in the city was expensive.[58] By the time Beatrice finalized her travel plans a month later—first sailing to Cuba, then to Spain, and continuing to Paris by train—General Pershing directed the War Department to issue an order banning all military spouses from entering the war zone.

When Kay left for Washington on July 6 after an elaborate goodbye dinner, it was another "link out of the chain" for the Ayers. Just two days prior, Kay had pulled her sister into a bathroom at Avalon to confer in private. Keith had just called from Washington with the news that he was sailing for London in four days as the newly appointed vice-consul. He had booked a cabin with two berths in case Kay thought it right to join him, but her duty to her parents prevented her from making an immediate decision. Beatrice's advice was to the point, "You must go. There's no question about it. I can't go with my husband, but you can go with yours."[59]

For Beatrice, it was now almost impossible to procure a passport except with the proper influence. If she couldn't make any headway with the secretary of state, George suggested she become a secretary to either Mr. Patton, if he managed to get a diplomatic appointment, or to Mr. Henry Cabot Lodge, a friend of her brother Chilly who was about to embark to France with his Boston unit. Beatrice was willing to go to any length to get to Paris and even considered becoming a correspondent with the *Boston Transcript* or a Red Cross nurse, an idea George opposed at first because Red Cross nurses worked so hard under terrible circumstances. On top of that, he and Beatrice "would be so far apart we could never meet," and she would be unable to bring the children.[60]

"If you come here and leave the children you will start getting sick in about a month," George reasoned. "If you don't see me you will probably do the same."[61] Leaving both children "will just about finish me," but it was a sacrifice Beatrice was willing to make. The Pattons suggested they would care for their grandchildren at Lake Vineyard, but since Little Bee and Ruth Ellen would be her parents' "only joy" if she went to France, Beatrice thought it best to leave them at Avalon. After all, "they (Pa & Ma) are well enough to get loads of pleasure with them & don't mind the responsibility; and without them they'd be all sole alone in this great house."[62]

By August, Beatrice accepted what she referred to as "the Munroe job." She got as far as securing passage and a letter of credit, but the War Department ultimately denied her request for a passport. She was so distressed by the situation that Stuart Cramer and his father "kidnapped" her and took her to Maymont, North Carolina, to recover. "This disappointment was so unexpected & cruel," Beatrice wrote Aunt Nannie on August 16, especially since her "poor Georgie" had already found them a little apartment in Paris.[63]

She didn't care about herself, but George kept reminding her that he missed her "in all I do or think; we are so united I don't function well alone."[64] The thought of Beatrice coming over even consumed his dreams: "I dreamed that I had a letter from you saying you had sailed and I put it in my mouth to keep someone from seeing it and it got stuck in my teeth and choked me. I tried so hard to get it out that I woke up."[65] He even constructed a table detailing the exact number of days they had been separated since getting married: "27 1/2 months or 2 years, 3 1/2 months."[66]

Beatrice realized doing something for somebody else was "the best way to minimize our own troubles & disappointments," but she "was simply knocked up."[67] She was "stirred up & cranky," and felt "very nervous & mean as a dog" all summer long, her letters to George filled with sadness.[68] Then, when she returned to Avalon, she found a letter from Mr. Patton "about putting our minds on getting ready for the years of happiness after the war. Do you know I never thought of that. Life has been all storm for me the past few months, and I had lost sight of anything but the present."

Her father-in-law suggested she come to Lake Vineyard for "a real rest cure," but since she couldn't be with Georgie, her place was at Avalon, where she could make "the greatest difference, not only in the family's pleasure, but in their actual comfort & health . . . And I am sure that, as soon as I get my poise back, I can do it without the least hurt to my own health, & shall make it my business to take care of myself - looking ahead to the happiness to come."[69]

IT UNNERVED Beatrice to talk to her family about Georgie "any more than I have to," and when she read his letters, she left out "the parts about how much he wants me near him."[70] George hated to excite and worry her by writing in such a way. Yet, when he heard through the grapevine that a Major Conger's wife received a passport at the behest of President Wilson even though the War Department first denied her request, he thought this a viable option for his wife. In an enclosure he sent to both Beatrice and his father to help them in their quest, George listed all the reasons why Beatrice should be allowed to come to France:

1) We were separated for 11 months while I was in Mexico.

2) She speaks and writes French like a native having been educated in France, hence she would be a great help to me. Also Mrs. Robert Munroe of the Red Cross has promised her a position in the Red Cross here. This position is still open.

3) B and her family have given over $40,000 to the Red Cross, hence should be entitled to some consideration.

4) Unlike most Army women, B is very rich so there is no possibility of her ever being a tax on the government here.

Beatrice was willing to sacrifice her life to be with her husband, but she wasn't willing to sacrifice his career.[71] When she heard the War Department threatened to recall an officer whose wife planned to go to France, Beatrice abandoned her efforts and changed tack. If she couldn't be with George in France, she could at least wait for him in England like she had waited for him at the border in El Paso. She secured a business position with the E. T. Slattery Company—a high-end department store across from the Boston Common—to be their buyer in London. Since Slattery's local agent would do the actual buying, Beatrice would refund the $2,500 salary, but at least it would give her a three-month passport to go on a business trip to England. George was intrigued by Beatrice's scheme, but Mr. Patton thought her plan "wrong and very dangerous."[72]

"Dear Uncle George," she replied on September 9,

Your telegram & letter each cost me a meal – the first I've lost since the day Georgie was hurt by the Ford. However. Of course I had already thought over the whole thing just as you put it and understand your feelings perfectly. Freddie & I think, though, that if the Secy had intended to do anything against officers' wifes [sic] going to England, he would have said so - it would have been so easy. It is pretty hard to get about 2 cables a week from G. suggesting all sorts of plans, and letters all the time saying definitely that he would rather have me geographically near him even though he mightn't be able to see me, than here – and have a way to go and not take it; but I will, as long as you seem to think it so dangerous for me to go. Please don't think I am just silly, wanting or willing to jeopardize G's career; if that were the case I would have sailed for France on this same job, Sept. 8th – yesterday. I will keep your letter until I find out about the censorship. You see, I don't want to get G. into trouble, but he wants me to go & I am certainly going if there is any way I can do it that will be safe for him.

You are lovely to always want me to go to you this winter; but, if I don't go to Europe, the only thing I can possibly do is to stick by the family. If they go South they will need the kids & me more, even, than if they were here with all their children around them, and I could not leave them except to be near Georgie. They are perfectly willing I should go to Europe, but I would break their hearts if I were anywhere else. And I don't wear myself out! Don't worry. If I have to get used to the idea of staying this side of the water, I will get along all right. Few army wives have two Pas & Mas wanting them – or any other kind of wives either.

When I got home from North Carolina I was so down & out I wasn't even glad to see the children; then I got this offer of a job & cheered up; and, if it does nothing else, it has tided me over some nasty weather in my own soul!

The family couldn't go to Cal. It's too far; but are thinking of going to Aiken & taking a house. I am very much against their trying to move at this time but I guess we'll have to be governed by what the Drs. say. The kids are fine. B. goes to "outing class" twice a week, a class of about 20 kids her age where they play all sorts of games. She has 2 music lessons a week & is doing beautifully – writes everything she plays; and has a tutoress for regular lessons 3 times a week. I hate to give her up so much (I only help her with practising now) but I haven't much time to be with the babies, & the regular work is good for her; and of course I take them a good deal, just to play, when I do have time, some part of every day. We went for a long walk (about 2 miles) yesterday. Just before we got home we met 3 little boys of about 10, who stopped dead in their tracks – Ruth Ellen had given them a most illuminating & flirtatious smile. As we passed on she remarked, "I was dest shining at de boys." What do you think of that?

I am so glad Aunt Ruth finally got to Catalina & hope she's still there & enjoying life again. I send you this to Lake Vineyard as I know you don't stay away from there any more than you can help. I love you all, always; and you have a right to say anything you want to - Aunt Ruth too; though I notice she didn't. I would just as soon she would. Your loving B[73]

After postponing once to ensure she wouldn't get her husband in trouble, Beatrice booked herself on the next available crossing, leaving October 22 on the *S.S. Saxonia*. Resigned to the idea that she might not even get to see George if he couldn't secure leave, at least she would be able to spend time with her sister in London. Excited at the prospect, Kay shared the news with George and a friend, who immediately notified General Pershing.[74] Made aware of his duplicity over the last five months, he asked Captain Patton straight out if Beatrice was planning to cross the Atlantic despite his orders. Desperate to have his wife by his side and convinced he would not be sent home as he had "a rather unfair advantage over J [code for Pershing]," George defiantly said there were no orders against wives going to England.[75]

Convinced by her father-in-law that her arrival would look like "favoritism and influence, and all sorts of innuendoes would be started that might hurt Georgie's career," Beatrice finally abandoned her plans "with an aching heart."[76] The general staff was already rife with rumors. After a somewhat unusual courtship that began at El Paso and lasted about a year, Pershing had asked for Nita's hand in marriage in March 1917, just before he was recalled to Washington to form the American Expeditionary Force. Nita accepted his diamond engagement ring, but since everyone's lives were awash in uncertainty, no official announcement was made.

The saga of the Pershing-Patton relationship was a three-year affair that spanned two continents, a world war, and the involvement of many meddling family members. Pershing often talked about Nita to her brother when they met up socially during WWI, and in November, he asked George to write Beatrice for a favor. He could tell from Nita's letters that "she is very much alive to the responsibilities she will one day assume," but she felt "tied too much to her mother's apron strings." Because Beatrice had such a tremendous influence on her sister-in-law, Pershing hoped she might invite Nita for a stay.

THE CONSTITUTION'S splendor was something the residents of Thomasville, Georgia, hadn't seen in a long time when it pulled into the Thomasville Depot on October 27, 1917. The crème de la crème of Pullman's private railroad cars, the Constitution came with a fully equipped galley and a staff of two, offered accommodations for up to fourteen guests, and had a mahogany-paneled dining room with a rear observation deck.[77] On board were Frederick, Ellie, Beatrice, Little Bee, Ruth Ellen, two of Frederick's cousins, Nanny Taty, and a retinue of nurses and servants. In addition, an express train arrived earlier that day carrying the Ayers' horses, cars, and everything necessary to reside for six months in what was once known as the "Winter Resort of the South."[78]

*Figure 29. Beatrice (in the white skirt) and Nita (behind her) at Sunny Hill Plantation in 1918, attending the Georgia-Florida Field Trials. (Thomasville History Center)*

Longleaf pine forests running wild with bobwhite quail surrounded Thomasville. It offered a mild winter climate, and the sweet scent of pine that permeated the air was said to provide relief to those suffering from pulmonary conditions. Wealthy northerners had been hibernating in the town since 1875, first in grand hotels on Broad Street, then in private mansions they built. While the resort era had ended by the time the Ayers arrived, the town of approximately eight thousand retained its Southern charm. The family moved into the Crozier House on oak-lined Dawson Street and were joined a few weeks later by Nita.[79]

Beatrice was beside herself when she discovered a Boston funeral parlor stashed two of their most expensive bronze caskets on the same train she and her family traveled on. The incident left her with an intense hatred of undertakers and a desire to be cremated. While one source claimed that Frederick wanted the caskets taken along in case he died en route, based on Beatrice's reaction, it is more likely that the funeral parlor acted of their own accord. After all, Boston had been awash with rumors for months that both Mr. and Mrs. Ayer's health was declining.[80] For the most part, Frederick recuperated from his bout with pneumonia and would celebrate his ninety-fifth birthday in near-perfect physical condition, but Ellie's health was most concerning. The sixty-four-year-old had been frail since just before Kay's wedding and suffered from an unspecified heart condition.

Thomasville's warm, soothing air quickly proved beneficial to Beatrice's parents. Ellie soon felt "refreshed and invigorated by her daily drives and open air diversion," while Frederick enjoyed riding through the Georgia woods on Newport, his favorite horse, purchased in 1903.[81] The friends he made in town were all "delighted with his optimism, his love of life and energy, his cordiality and rugged honesty of manner and bearing."[82] Beatrice, meanwhile, continued to have issues with her insides and underwent a minor operation at the beginning of December.[83]

"We each owe it to the other to take care of our selves so we can make up when we meet for the long time we have been separated," George wrote.[84]

... I am sorry you feel so blue over having been operated on instead of coming to Kay. There is no reason for it if you had come you might have been a wreck for life and we could not have had a good time together. It is ever so much better that you are all fixed up with new plumbing and will stay fixed. But remember if you start rushing around and try to come before you are absolutely fit you will not only undo all the good of the operation but will also probably die so for heavens sake don't risk it. It seems as a direct act of god to me that you did not get my wire until you were in the hospital for had it gone a few days sooner you might have been foolish enough to have tried to have come and might now be dead. Realy the correct point of view is that of happiness not sadness and it is another evidence of the direct interposition of fate or destiny in our behalf that you did not come while in so bad a condition. I feel confident that this forced delay will allow you to not only come to England but to F. also but don't think of doing it till you are well and have been for a long time. Sea voyages now are most long and uncomfortable and if you had to get in the water or a small boat before you were quite strong it would kill you and I don't want you dead. Cheer up Beat. You are a sport now keep it up. I am sorry that you have been so sick all by yourself with no one to either comfort or pick on you.[85]

George implored Beatrice not to worry, but she worried all the time: about her husband, who volunteered to walk across a bridge known to be wired; about her children, who might grow up without a father; and about her parents, who were struggling a little more each day. Because "letters certainly are the devil for leaving out things everyone is sure you know," Chilly took it upon himself to inform his brother-in-law that Beatrice was suffering greatly under the strain of not knowing whether he was at the front.[86] George reassured his "Beat" that he was "a lot safer here than I usually am at home because I don't play polo or race or jump or do any other interesting thing."[87]

Indeed, in George's case, it was almost "safer to go to war than to take a bath in a slippery tub" because a month later, he suffered "his usual yearly accident." Returning from a visit to the front where he watched "the flash of the guns and the trench rockets going up," he drove his car into a closed railroad gate. His head went through the windshield, cutting his face badly but missing the carotid artery, jugular "and facial nerve about an 1/8 of an inch."[88] It was more detail than most officers would feel comfortable sharing with their wives, but George knew Beatrice worried no matter what, so he figured he might as well tell her everything.[89]


WHEN THE AMERICAN EXPEDITIONARY FORCE moved its headquarters from Paris to Chaumont at the beginning of September, George and his friend Colonel Fox Conner completed the 150-mile journey in George's Packard, which he had shipped from the U.S. at considerable cost and to the resentment of many. The Conners had been close friends with the Pattons since October 1913, when they met on a train from Kansas City to Fort Riley. Fox and his wife Virginia (a.k.a. Bug) could not stop staring at the young officer who sat down at the other end of the car, carrying the biggest sword Bug had ever seen. His immaculate appearance was striking, as was his ramrod straight posture, which never faltered no matter how much the train shook. Intrigued by the young man's fierce face, Captain Conner decided to introduce himself, and so began a friendship that lasted a lifetime.[90]

Driving through the French countryside reminded George of his trips with Beatrice in 1912 and 1913, and finding her galoshes in the trunk inspired a poem "full of concealed pathos."[91]

While searching in my motor car
To get a can of grease
I came upon some rubber shoes
The shoes of Beatrice.

You who have never met her
Of course can hardly know
The train of deep emotions
Those rubbers set aglow.

For gazing on them brought to mind
The picture of her feet
And dainty legs in stockings trim
Duckwalking up the street.

The memory of her cunningness
And of her crooked tooth
The tragic thought that far from her
I'd passed the half our youth.

So picking up the grease can
I sadly turned aside
And jammed a hub cap full of goo
My woeful thoughts to hide.[92]

George's experience on the general staff made it clear "that I would have been no good in business for the daily grind in an office is not what I like."[93] He saw no future in his job as head of the motor pool, which consisted of being "a sort of 'Pooh-Bah'" in charge of the enlisted men, but suddenly fate tapped him on the shoulder. A firm believer in progress and innovation, George's interest was piqued at the end of September by talks of a rumored tank force. For years the British and French had been developing an armored vehicle that would ease the infantry's job by crushing barbed wire, traversing trenches, and crossing no-man's-land. A tank force was the opportunity George had been waiting for, not only to set him apart but also to get away from Pershing so no one could ever say he "rode up on the train."[94]

Individualistic and egocentric, George nonetheless admitted that he was "apt to make mistakes of judgment" without his Beatrice.[95] After the whole passport incident, she pointed out that he probably overestimated his "drag with J." It was the kind of solid advice and astute observation George had come to rely on from his wife.[96] Unfortunately, instead of being able to discuss his future with Beatrice in England as he had hoped, he found himself debating his future in a Chaumont hospital room with Fox Conner. Admitted with catarrhal jaundice, George shared a room with his old friend who was recuperating from surgery on an obstructed bowel.

Beatrice worried about his safety if he were to join the Tank Corps, but George reassured his wife that he loved her "too much to try to get killed but also too much to be willing to sit on my tail and do nothing."[97] The more he thought about it, the more he realized tanks were the perfect vehicle for becoming "one of the two or three at the top," especially for someone like himself with "imagination and daring and exceptional mechanical knowledge." As to getting off the general staff, he explained to Beatrice "that for a man of my age and experience it is a cemetary of ambition . . . Besides I am conscientiously opposed to it. I have always talked blood and murder and am looked on as an advocate of close up fighting. I could never look my self in the face if I was a staff officer and comparatively safe. The men who get on the staffs now will stay on them and see other men from the line pass and beat them."[98]

When asked twenty-six years later about her proudest moment, Beatrice passionately replied, "Did you know my husband was the first man in the United States Army in the Tank Corps, back in the World War?"[99]

On November 10, 1917, Captain Patton was tasked with establishing the School for Light Tanks from the ground up. The "really spectacular" spelling in some of his recent writings made it clear to Mr. Patton that his son missed his "Editor," but the fifty-eight-page memo coined "the Basis of the U.S. Tank Corps" turned out to be the best technical paper George ever wrote.[100] Still, despite the compliments he received from his superiors and the progress he made, George got the blues. For the first time ever, he felt as if he lacked backbone.[101]

Named director of the new Army Tank School at Bourg and promoted to major in January 1918, he still felt "unusually small in self esteem. I have been so long a small but important cog in a machine . . . it is hard to go off and be the last word all by myself."[102] His letters to Beatrice covered the full spectrum of human emotion, from elation and confidence to sadness and self-doubt, and he eagerly awaited her every reply. He lamented not having her around "to sympathize and correct spelling for me" and constantly craved her reassurances. With Beatrice by his side, George felt confident, knowing that her common sense evened out his impetuous nature. "I would give a lot to have you consol me," he wrote her, "and tell me that I amounted to a lot even when I know I don't."[103]

**Figure 30.** *Little Bee, Ellie, and Frederick, circa 1918. (Library of Congress)*

FREDERICK AYER, whose single purpose in life had been to use his wealth to give "pleasure and happiness where he could," died a few minutes after 4 p.m. on March 14, 1918, three months into his ninety-sixth year. He had been battling bronchitis since the end of January when he got caught in the rain riding Newport, and while the man who avoided "the use of any habit-forming drugs" seemed to rally once again, his heart ultimately succumbed.[104]

Beatrice was on her way to Washington to meet with Lieutenant Braine—George's new assistant and his liaison with the U.S. government in setting up the Tank Corps—when her father passed away. "Frederick Ayer died as he had lived, surrounded by those he loved, and planning for the future," she wrote in *The Reminiscences of Frederick Ayer,* a small family-published book bringing together all the anecdotes her devoted father reluctantly told her.[105]

According to the *Boston Globe*'s obituary, there was "no clearer brain in New England" than that of Frederick Ayer, who was "striking in appearance, his remarkable vigor showing in every move" until the end of his life.[106] "Vitally interested in modern day affairs," among other things, he was a major stockholder in the American Telephone and Telegraph Company, one of the largest real estate owners in Boston, an investor with industrialist John Munro Longyear in the development of coal on the island of Spitsbergen, and a director of numerous companies. Unostentatious, modest, and unassuming, Frederick "never paraded his achievements nor permitted others to do so."[107] His "honesty was as well known as his wealth"—he proudly told Beatrice he never earned a dollar he was ashamed of—and his mind remained "as elastic as his step" until the day he died.[108]

Twenty-five years after his passing, Beatrice still vividly remembered the last conversation she had with her father. Sitting by his bedside the evening before she left for Washington, Frederick asked "his little daughter" to give George "what he needs. [He] is bringing in much glory to our family and we must always see that he is as comfortable as we can make him."[109]

Despite his initial reluctance, Frederick made peace with his son-in-law's chosen profession and took great pride in all his hard work. "Pa," Beatrice reminded her husband decades later, "always loved you and trusted you." Meanwhile, Ellie kept the first picture of her son-in-law in his lieutenant's uniform on her nightstand for the rest of her life, written across the back: "The bravest are the tenderest; the loving are the daring."[110]

Frederick had been a dreamer, "but where many merely dreamed, he both dreamed and achieved."[111] In this regard, he was not that different from his son-in-law, with whom he had regularly corresponded. Blessed with an "extraordinary youthfulness of mind" which allowed him to understand and discuss "all manner of subjects, however foreign to the interests which had always crowded his life," Frederick advised George to be open to "new means to win the Great War, particularly the adoption and development of the tank."[112] When Ellie cleaned out Sir Frederick's wallet upon his death, she found George's reply tucked inside: "In November I got a letter from you saying that war was so wasteful of life and that some means ought to be devised of reducing the killing . . . Your letter decided me and next morning I asked for the tanks."[113]

While waiting like "an expectant mother" for the arrival of his first tanks, George learned of his father-in-law's passing.[114] After wiring his condolences, he sat down to write Beatrice one of his most compassionate letters, unaware that his wife's travails were only just beginning as their letters crisscrossed the ocean.

"My darling little Beatrice," he began,

Yesterday evening I recieved a telegram from your mother saying "Our Commander has gone his love for you shown in every word and deed." Darling one I know what the death of your father must mean to you but you ought to take great very great comfort in the fact that most of his pleasure in the last years of his life were due to you and your beautiful and unselfish love for him.

Personally I thank God that you were able to be with him so constantly and it is without question a direct interposition of the Almighty God that this war made it necessary and possible for you to be with him for had it not occurred you would have been in the Philippines and absent at the time so priceless to him.

It is a great source of pleasure and pride to me that Mr. Ayer who is the most perfect mortal I know of took an interest and pride in my present work, and his last letter to me will ever be an inspiration to me in this or any other work.

Beatrice Jr and Ruth Ellen should be wonderful children with such a grandfather.

It is futile to attempt to comfort you words, especially written words, are totally inadequate to consol for such a loss but reason shows clearly that you ought not grieve too much. He went at the end of a magnificent career his last months blessed with a divotion few men ever know because few or none have ever deserved so much.

I know Darling that you are suffering all that the human soul can suffer but hope that the spirit of your father will help and support you in the hours now passing. Your whole duty is now to stay with your mother and I hope and have prayed that she is not utterly prostrated. She is so brave that I feel sure she will behave wonderfully.

Beaty my whole heart is at your feet and if feelings can traverse space I am helping you the little that even he, who loves you more than any thing on earth, can help.

My poor Darling Please take comfort if you can. May God help and strengthen you.[115]

Ellie "bore up wonderfully well as far as could be observed and never gave in to her grief," but her health was so precarious she was unable to return to Boston for the funeral.[116] So instead, she said goodbye to Sir Frederick at an intimate family service held at the Ayers' Thomasville residence on Sunday, March 17, placing one last letter between the hands of the love of her life. The train with Frederick's body, escorted by his sons Jamie and Fred, who came from New York and Washington, left for Boston the next day.

A devastated Beatrice remained at Thomasville to care for her mother. Still, her letters to her husband were both "brave and sensible."[117] George believed Mr. Ayer's death would be "easier to bear than the constant dread of its arrival under which dread you have been suffering for so long," but he seemed to forget that he was the source of a similar kind of anxiety.[118]

Sitting by her mother's bedside on March 26, Beatrice went to pieces when Ellie read William Wood's telegram: "GEORGE KILLED IN ACTION DEEPEST SYMPATHY TO BEATRICE."[119] A policy debate was currently raging in Congress on the distribution of casualty lists, and Beatrice experienced firsthand the heartbreak of newspapers printing said lists before the War Department had time to notify the next-of-kin. Despite her serious condition, Ellie remained level-headed and tried to reassure her daughter.

"What makes you think that you are married to the only George Patton in the Army?" she asked before suggesting Beatrice call the *Boston Transcript*.

Beatrice remembered finally getting through to Atlanta and hearing the operator "call Louisville, then—fainter—Richmond. Then Washington. Then silence." She had learned long ago that part of falling in love with an officer was waiting, and it took until well into the night for a call to come in from Atlanta relaying a message from the *Boston Transcript*.

The deceased George Patton Jr. was in the Medical Corps and one of seven currently in Europe. "For one consumingly selfish moment I thought God had been good to the Pattons," Beatrice admitted. "Then I thought of the family that was really bereaved and my heart went out to that wife." Even though it didn't feel so at the time, Beatrice realized there were many things worse than suspense. "Give me suspense, every time," she said during WWII. "A woman never knows her luck."[120]

**Figure 31.** *Frederick and Ellie were reunited in the family plot at the Lowell Cemetery. Just a few paces away stood the Ayer lion, which marks the burial plot of Dr. James C. Ayer and his wife.*

IF CATASTROPHES COME IN THREES, the third one to befall Beatrice in just three weeks was the most heartbreaking of all. While Ellie's condition "improved to the extent that it was thought possible that she would regain her strength and vitality," she suddenly took a turn for the worse. Fred sped back to Thomasville with his wife Hilda and the family physician, but the grief over Frederick's loss was too much for Ellie's frail body.[121] On April 3, Ellen Banning Ayer died of heart failure in her son's arms while Beatrice whispered in her ear, one month shy of her sixty-fifth birthday.[122] Brother and sister agreed the grief over their father's loss hastened their mother's death, a view supported by Dr. Washburn, whose only explanation for Ellie's sudden demise was a broken heart.

On April 7, friends and family gathered in the opulent hall of the Tiffany Mansion for the second time in less than a month. Ellie was remembered as "a beloved mother, a noble woman, and a worthy, capable friend ... [whose] cheery disposition and generous qualities were notable characteristics."[123] She had lived for her husband, her laughter keeping him young during the thirty-four years of their marriage.

"Poor Beat has the worst of it," George wrote Kay when he heard the news. "You have Keith. Fred has Hilda but B is alone poor child I feel so sorry for her."[124]

He wrote his wife another heartfelt letter, regretting that he wasn't there to help when her parents died.

What has happened has quite reconciled me to your not having come to France. You would have felt so terribly to have been away. It seems a heartless thing to say but I think that Ellie is happier than she would have been to have continued on without your father. They were as nearly one as is possible to be - as nearly as one as we are. I do not think I would care much about keeping on if you were gone. Because if you were not around to admire what I did what the rest thought would make little difference.

From the stand point of your health things are better as they are also. Because the human heart can only suffer so much and yours I know was fully crushed by your father so that this will only add a little more to your grief. Also your dear little heart will not be laden with the worry of something to come . . .

You can always know that no child has ever been more devoted or unselfish in care and love for parents than you have been you can also feel sure that they both know it. I wish I could cuddle you in my arms and comfort you in spirit I do. Don't worry about me I am safe and well. I love you with all my heart and will try to replace by my love and tenderness a little of their love also.[125]

According to George, Ellie was better off death than had she lived "a help-less and unhappy invalid," and he urged his wife not to make "the mistake of useless memories and reproaches which lead to nothing but renewed grief."[126] Despite the care and devotion Beatrice had always shown her parents, she was consumed with guilt upon their death and blamed herself for not spending enough time with them in the last years of their lives. Everyone knew there was nothing Beatrice could have done to be a better daughter, but as grandson Robert Patton later wrote, "in trying to mother Georgie, her parents, her kids, she imagined she was failing at all three."

"For once in your life you have no obligation to fulfill so for heavens sake do what pleases you," George wrote as Beatrice contemplated the future.[127] Mr. Patton knew the death of her parents was a "very severe ordeal," and he hoped she would "be able to force herself to be as quiet as possible for the next few months" so as not to break down her health by too much.[128] He invited her to spend some time at Lake Vineyard before renting a house of her own, an offer George hoped she would accept if she thought she needed rest more than stimulation.[129] Ultimately, Beatrice thought it prudent to remain on the East Coast and moved in with Fred, Hilda, and their two children. They were living at Highwood, a country home in Washington's Chevy Chase neighborhood, since Fred was a volunteer with the U.S. Navy and served on Herbert Hoover's food relief program.

From the moment her parents died, George sent his wife a monthly present.[130] Even twenty-four years later, Beatrice could still name all ten of them. The two most memorable ones were a bunch of dried daisies he gath-ered crawling around no-man's-land while reconnoitering for the St. Mihiel offensive, getting so close to the German side that he could hear them whistle; and a piece of shrapnel from a shell which exploded a mere hundred yards from where he was standing. He took the piece to his tank repair unit and had them put Beatrice's name on one side and May 30, 1918, on the other side. While back in Paris, he took it to Cartier to have it turned into a bracelet, hoping Beatrice would like it "for it might have made you a widow."[131]

"Unless the shock has been too great" of losing both her parents, George hoped Beatrice at least would enjoy better health now. The worst was over, so he thought she had "nothing to look forward to with anxiety," seemingly unaware that he was as much a constant source of worry as his in-laws had been.[132] He continued to write in his "usual style," not because "of lack of feeling, but rather an evidence of consideration" since his letters, which took on average two weeks to arrive, "will simply serve to reopen the wounds which by that time will have grown less sensative."[133] One can only imagine Beatrice's feelings when her husband proudly shared that he removed his helmet and lit a cigarette in sight of the Bosch.[134]

BEATRICE LATER ADMITTED that she took World War I (and the Mexican Punitive Expedition) hard, and she suffered from insomnia and tachycardia, an abnormally fast heart rate that comes on without exertion.[135] She eventually "learned to take it," but at thirty-three, she didn't know yet "that worry is a senseless and an evil thing." Her emotions in turmoil over her parents' death and her nerves frayed at the realization that she might never see her Georgie again, Beatrice frightened herself when she slapped Ruth Ellen because the three-year-old broke her doll.

"I was often scared," she remembered of those days, "and it took all the courage I could summon" to get through the days. Only with experience would she learn that "war is not half so deadly as most people think. Women exaggerate the horrors of war. Some imagine that their men are under fire all the time. As a matter of fact, being shot at is a very small part of the war."[136]

**Figure 32.** *The two sisters wore the same outfits until one day Little Bee had enough and she cut her dress to pieces.*

Indeed, George was still "distressingly," "shamefully," and "disgustingly" safe after being in France for over a year, and all the waiting had him "dreading lest the war should finish before I can really do any fighting."[137] General Pershing had made it clear from the very start that the American Expeditionary Force would fight independently from the British and French under the sole command of an American general; he refused to fight until his army was fully equipped, trained, and over 1.3 million strong.

In addition to his duties in the Tank Corps, George took a course at the Staff College so he wouldn't have too much time to think about Beatrice, whom he wanted "both spiritually and physically."[138] How much the body was "meddling in the affairs of the heart" was evident from a hilarious letter he wrote Beatrice from Paris.[139] When he returned to his hotel room,

I heard much rustling of paper and laughing in the next room so I went to the door to listen. It was an english officer and his wife. She had just arrived. I know I should not have listened but I felt lonesome so I did. It was most amusing. They talked in a most impersonal way and every few minutes would stop and kiss. At last curiosity got the better of me and I looked through the key hole. They were both very properly clad in gray dressing gowns like mine and were sitting quite a ways apart eating crackers. At last they decided to go to bed. They had been seperated only five months but she said it was years. I could not help thinking of us.

Well they went to bed she in a nitie as thick as sail cloth he in canton flannel and in twin beds. At this point the thought occured to me, "No wonder the Bosch beat the British if they are that cold blooded." Soon however he asked her if she was tired. Foolish question! she said no but that he must be and that he should go to sleep at once.

I feared for a moment that the cracker dirt had clogged his soul but was reasured on hearing him say that he was not at all tired at the same time there was much squeaking of beds and I felt assured he had gotten into hers (her bed). Then all grew quiet again and I feared that they had gone to sleep.

But soon my ears told me that I was in error. I should say that just after they got in bed they turned out the light.

xxxxxxx (Indicating part that Aunt Nannie would skip if reading aloud) The lights came on and he of the flannels above mentioned rose perfectly unclothed. Here I went to bed. It is sort of funny yet verges on the tragic for as other wise I would not have observed.

I hope you are not too shocked at my conduct. I bet under the circumstances you would have acted just the same . . . I love you with all my heart and will never use twin beds or canton flannel pajamas when I see you.[140]

No longer duty-bound to her parents, Beatrice once again considered traveling to England to visit Kay, who was expecting her first child. However, in June 1918, George definitively told her to stop because "after all the work I have done I should hate to be sent home that way."[141] No detail was too small for Lieutenant Colonel Patton as he built the Tank School from the ground up, including the design of a shoulder patch still in use today. Once the final design was picked, he took a $100 bill from his wallet and handed it to a startled soldier to have the patches made in town.

George often used his wealth to advance his Army causes and would continue to do so for the rest of his career. When First Lieutenant Braine traveled to the U.S. in April 1918 to procure more tanks, his travel allowance was insufficient to cover all his expenses. He went to Highwood at George's behest to receive $1000 from Fred (to be deducted as war bonds) and to give Beatrice an eyewitness account of her husband.[142]

Beatrice offered more than monetary support. George's career was a joint affair—when she became "Mrs. Colonel" in April, George remarked, "we never thought to reach it so soon did we"—and she often acted as his emissary and sounding board.[143] "Next time you go to Washington make it a point to see Brigadier Gen. Hugh S. Johnson who lived with me in Mexico. He is now very close to the Chief of Staff and is also a good friend of mine," George wrote home as he anxiously awaited an opportunity to get in the fight. "You could talk to him quite freely about me and might pump him about John [Pershing] but he is pretty smart so you will have to be careful on the pumping. Still I think that he is susceptible to good looks and you have them. That is one of the many reasons why I love you."[144]

When Beatrice received George's June 22nd letter, it was accompanied by one he had written a month earlier. Captain Viner would have sent it to her in case George didn't return from a two-week stint with a French Tank Group, but since he already wired that he was home safe, he thought it might amuse her. He offered Beatrice his sword and pistol, and permitted her to marry should she ever fall in love again. "Few men can be so fortunate as to have such a wife," he wrote, and his only regret was not marrying her sooner and being "mean to you at first." He ended his letter with the hope that if he got killed, "it will be in a manner such as to be worthy of you and of my ideals. Kiss Beatrice Jr and Ruth Ellen for me and tell them that I love them very much and that I know they will be good."[145]

THE FIRST MAJOR American offensive took place on September 12 near St. Mihiel. The First Brigade Tank Corps performed exemplarily, with fifty officers and nine hundred enlisted men under the command of Colonel Patton. Instructed by Brigadier General Rockenbach to remain in his command post, a frustrated George quickly disobeyed orders and rode into battle on a tank, personally leading his men to victory. Most of the tanks either broke down, got bogged down in the mud, or outran the infantry, but General Pershing was happy with the new Tank Corps' performance. George finally proved to himself that he had the nerve, and with Beatrice's picture in his pocket, he felt "quite safe" when the Meuse-Argonne offensive commenced two weeks later on September 26.[146]

The beginning of battle left George feeling nervous, like the start of a polo match, but his unease disappeared as soon as he watched his tanks disappear into the fog.[147] Despite the severe reprimand he had received from Brigadier General Rockenbach, he couldn't resist the call of battle. He followed the sound of gunfire until he reached the town of Cheppy, where a hundred lost infantrymen were desperately trying to find cover from German machine gun fire. Losing patience when none of the soldiers were doing "a damned thing to kill Bosch" or bring up his bogged down tanks, George took matters into his own hands.[148] He exhorted the terrified men to dig out the one tank holding up the whole column, spearheading the effort as bullets whistled around his ears and he cursed the Germans.

Pinned down by machine gun fire as he made it back up the hill, fear overtook George for the first time. Just as his grandmother Susan had described how a calm came over her when she thought the end was near during her perilous trip from Virginia to California, a calm descended over George as he looked at the sky. He saw his ancestors who died in battle "leaning out of a cloud bank": General Hugh Mercer, Colonel George Patton, and Colonel Waller Tazewell Patton.[149] "[I]f I had not thought of you and mama & B and my ancestors I would never have charged," George reminisced to his father a month later. "That is I would not have started for it is hell to go into rifle fire so heavy that one fancies the air is thick like molases with it."[150]

Lieutenant Colonel Patton favored a glorious death over a long and comfortable life, so he stood up to face the Germans. He tried to make the infantry charge, but only six men followed him across the open field, all of whom were shot down until only George and his orderly, Private Joseph "Joe" Angelo, remained standing. George understood "all men are afraid in battle," but only the coward "lets his fear overcome his sense of duty," so he kept going until a bullet entered his groin at 11:15 a.m. and exited through his buttocks, leaving a hole the size of a teacup.

When George took his children years later to visit the man who risked his life to save him, they couldn't help but wonder how a little man like Private Angelo could have dragged their father forty meters into a shell hole. Numb with shock but also blessed with a certain insensitivity toward pain which made him "suffer less than most people," he remained in the shell hole for almost two hours, guarded by a tank "like a watch dog."[151]

Always the consummate officer, George kept directing his tanks against the machine gun nests and, once extracted, insisted on making a detour to his command post to give a brief report on the morning's events. Before going into surgery, he paid an orderly to send a wire to his wife. The man took the money but never sent the message, and it wouldn't be until September 29 that Beatrice received a wire with the cryptic words: "Slightly wounded no danger love."

BEATRICE FELT a familiar lump in her throat and a funny feeling in her stomach when she read the *Boston Globe*'s headline of Friday, September 27, 1918: "Americans Crush Hun Line, Capture 5000 Prisoners."

"As you seem to think that I am in every fight you read of, that ought not to bother you," George had reassured her, "especially as I personally will be in some deep hole miles in the rear of the fight on the telephone in a most useful and inglorious position."[152] While she never knew the specifics, Beatrice did know pretty much everything George was up to since he talked to her as much about his tanks "as you used to talk about children."[153]

Letters from the home front were a lifeline for soldiers off to war. George anxiously awaited Beatrice's replies, feeling down in the dumps whenever he didn't get any, but the unreliability of the mail service meant one week no letters might arrive, while the next a stack of twenty came at once. Some never arrived at all because the boats that carried them were torpedoed, leading to miscommunication. Back in Thomasville a few months earlier, Beatrice had collapsed by the side of her bed when she read George was heading to the front, but Nita pointed out the letter was six weeks old. "If he'd been killed, you'd have heard," she comforted her sister-in-law. "You're crying for nothing."[154]

When Fred left Washington in August 1918 to run the family business with his brother Chilly, Beatrice and her daughters moved to Avalon. She kept busy sorting through her parents' possessions and schooled herself in not always expecting the worst. She didn't know it at the time, but "only two out of every hundred who fought were killed . . . more soldiers died of disease than were killed . . . [and] 85% of the wounded returned to duty."[155] Ignorance wasn't always bliss, and it paid to educate oneself. It was advice she would take to heart in the next war and share so others would not have to go through what she did.

It took every ounce of reserve not to get alarmed when the phone rang at 11:30 p.m. in the days following the Battle of the Argonne; on the line was a young reporter who wanted to know some biographical data about Colonel Patton. Beatrice interrupted the man, asking him whether something had happened to her husband. When she made him transfer her to his boss, the editor informed Beatrice that the story broke off just as he received news that "Colonel Patton was leading a charge."

Beatrice sat by the telephone for three hours without losing hope, surrounded by four Catholic maids who kept praying the rosary, until the editor called back to say Colonel Patton was seriously wounded but alive. It would take twelve days before Beatrice was convinced she was not going to be a widow, but "when the good news came, I drove all over town, ringing door bells and telling people. I couldn't trust myself to telephone."[156]

When she finally heard from George, he explained that the doctor thought it a miracle "the bullet went where it did without crippling me for life. He says he could not have run a probe without getting either the hip joint, the siatic nerve or the big artery yet none of these were touched. 'Fate' again." Was it also fate which impelled him to keep walking? He told Beatrice he would never have gone forward had he "not thought of you and my ancestors. I felt that I could not be false to my 'cast' and your opinion."[157]

That opinion came in her reply: "Georgie, you are the fulfillment of all the ideals of manliness and high courage & bravery I have always held for you, ever since I have known you. And I have expected more of you than any one else in the world ever has or will."[158]

Everything George did was "for the effect" it would have on Beatrice, and he took many of the risks he did in order "to prove that she had been right in marrying him."[159] It was a terrible blow when he learned he wouldn't be receiving the Distinguished Service Cross because it was "all I can ever get out of two years away from you."[160] Promoted to (temporary) Colonel in October, he preferred the decoration to the promotion, especially since the higher one's rank, "the harder it is to get into a fight."[161]

Luckily the bureaucratic mishap would be fixed, and George ultimately received the DSC (and a year later also the Distinguished Service Medal) because he would not get another chance to earn one. The Great War ended at 11 a.m. on November 11, 1918—on George's thirty-third birthday of all days. Tenor Enrico Caruso opened his second-floor window at the Knickerbocker Hotel on Times Square and sang "The Star-Spangled Banner," Cecil B. DeMille called "cut" on the set of *Don't Change Your Husband,* and Beatrice Ayer Patton stopped packing her bags when she heard the bells of St. John's peal across Pride's Crossing.[162] She dropped to the floor and hugged Little Bee and Ruth Ellen tight, crying, "The war is over! The war is over! Your father will be coming home."[163]

George, however, would not be returning stateside anytime soon. He returned to the Tank School once the wound in his leg began to heal, but it was "a hellish stupid world now and life has lost its zest."[164] He kept busy organizing reviews and maneuvers, giving lectures, and writing a tank manual and a book on the war, but he longed to take Beatrice "in my arms and squeeze you." He closed out 1918 with the following entry in his diary: "End of a fine year full of interest. I hope it will be the only one in which I am away from B. for such a long time. Sat up until 12 reading French history from 1814 to 1914. Got letter from Frenchman again accusing me of all sorts of vice and saying he would write Gen. P. I hope he does."[165]

His men, who were apt to be killed, deserved "as much pleasure as they can get," but he was not one of those "pleasure seekers."[166] George planned to "drink a gallon of black coffee so I will stay awake and can make love to you [Beatrice]."[167] Upon his return from a second visit to the U.S. in October, Lt. Braine reported that Beatrice didn't have gray hair, "or at least that you had fixed them." As obsessed with Beatrice's appearance as with his own, this gave George great pleasure as he always thought of her "as Undine so I don't want you to look 33, even if I do."[168] (To his great consternation, he must have looked even older because a doctor in the hospital put his age at forty-five.) He advised Beatrice to stop her "fool idea" of war work and "attend only to your self. Your hair, your chin and your tummie. I have done plenty of war work for the family."[169]

Beatrice was again having a "hell of a time" with her health at the start of the new year, so it was a devastating blow that George would be part of the occupying forces in Germany.[170] He submitted a request to be allowed to return home at the same time as the First Tank Corps, citing his long absence from home, the death of his in-laws, the "very poor health" of his wife, and the pride he would feel at taking his men home.[171] Despite his compelling arguments, his request was denied until General Pershing personally intervened.

THE FRENCH OCEAN liner *S.S. Patria* sailed into Brooklyn under cover of fog at noon on March 17, 1919, after a seventeen-day voyage from Marseille. On board were 2110 soldiers, including Colonel George S. Patton Jr., commander of the 304th Tank Brigade. Beatrice, supposedly "as good as ever" after her most recent health scare, was anxiously awaiting George's debarkation. Unfortunately, the process stalled when a group of unruly soldiers showed their contempt for pro-German newspaper mogul William Randolph Hearst, who was supposedly on board the police boat that escorted the *S.S. Patria* into the harbor at 31st Street.

After one year, nine months, and seventeen days, Beatrice saw with her own eyes that George looked "well and happy," but he had aged.[172] He walked with a slight limp and had lost a lot of weight, but he hadn't lost his elan; as soon as he caught sight of his comrade-in-arms, he dramatically threw his cane in the East River and hugged his wife close. The couple was quickly swept up in the roaring reception, and George basked in the attention of the waiting press who welcomed "Pershing's aide" as a hero. The first American to lead a tank battalion, Colonel Patton enthusiastically told reporters how tanks "are the natural answer to the machine gun, and in warfare they have come to stay, just as much as the airplanes have."[173]

While the Great War was supposed to be the war to end all wars, a student of military history like George Patton knew that idea to be folly. There would always be another war, and he fervently hoped to be around for the next one. He had survived the Meuse-Argonne Offensive without any lasting effect, while 26,000 other U.S. soldiers died, indicating that God had something bigger planned for him. It would be a long and infuriating wait, however. The advent of isolationism spelled doom for a career officer like George Patton, both professionally and personally.

Whether it was weeks or years, the Pattons always went through some "initial awkwardness" after a separation, but one of the first lessons Beatrice learned as an Army wife was the need to be "elastic."[174] She knew George was no longer the same person who had sailed for Europe in 1917. As she would explain to a group of green army wives during WWII, "Some of them [returning soldiers] won't be fit to be heads of families. Then their wives, who may have been the cherished and protected type before the war, must become the captains. Some men will have been going at full gear for so long that they won't be able to go into reverse for a while. Wives must be ready for anything and able to do whatever is indicated. They must take charge, if necessary, or step down."[175]

The first nine years of Beatrice's marriage revolved around George Patton and her efforts to juggle her duty to her husband and her family. In a cruel kind of way, her parents' passing was a release.[176] While she would continue to be the dutiful wife whose life centered around her husband, Beatrice would come to realize there was a different side to her which could exist independently. The tiny seed of eccentricity that Beatrice possessed since birth would finally mature under the tutelage of her husband.

The years between the two world wars would be marked by self-destructiveness and pathos for George Patton, but Beatrice would blossom. She admitted making "rather a mess of things" during WWI, but she muddled through and came out stronger. Beatrice suffered terrible losses and likely damaged her health permanently, but she had grown as a woman and an army wife. It was all preparation for what she knew would one day come so that she could take it by then.[177]

## Part II[1]

Oh! loveliest of women,
What ere I gain or do,
Is naught if in achieving,
I bring not joy to you.

I know I often grieve you,
All earthly folk are frail;
But if this grief I knowing wrought,
My life's desire would fail.

The mandates of stern duty,
Oft take us far apart,
But space is impotent to check,
The heart which calls to heart.

Perhaps by future hidden,
Some greatness waits in store;
If, so the hope your praise to gain,
Shall make my efforts more.

For victory apart from you,
Would be an empty gain;
A laurel crown you could not share,
Would be reward in vain.

You are my inspiration,
Light of my brain and soul,
Your guiding love by night and day,
Will keep my valor whole.

— *"TO BEATRICE" BY GEORGE S. PATTON JR.*

# 6

## SUNSET ROCK
### BEVERLY, MASSACHUSETTS

### 1919–1925

*Open all the doors for the children and even if they don't go through the doors at the time, if they have been opened, some day they will come back and go through them.*

While a Pierce Arrow looked peculiarly out of place on an army base—especially when parked in front of the home of a young colonel—it blended in perfectly when driven through Washington's Dupont Circle neighborhood. The area's major thoroughfare is known today as Embassy Row, but in the first quarter of the twentieth century, the mansions lining Massachusetts Avenue were the private residences of the capital's most prominent families. The triangular Wadsworth house, on the intersection of Dupont Circle and Massachusetts Avenue, was the winter home of oilcloth manufacturer Herbert Wadsworth and his wife Martha—like Beatrice, an accomplished horsewoman and pianist.[1]

The Beaux-Arts residence, completed in 1902, was made for entertaining; its two-story mirrored ballroom was the perfect setting for a white-tie dinner party. Perhaps the Wadsworths knew Beatrice from the time they spent in Boston, or maybe they met George at one of the many East Coast horse shows, but the reason for the Pattons' invitation remains as much a mystery as the date of the invitation (possibly between April and September 1919 when George was on temporary duty in Washington). Nevertheless, whether the details of what happened that day are family lore or not, the incident cemented Beatrice's reputation as a fiercely protective and devoted wife.

Driving through the residence's porte-cochère and along the circular drive-way, George dropped off Beatrice at the front door before parking the car. She joined a corpulent reserve officer in the foyer who stood waiting for his wife. Her opinion of such officers was rather low, informed as she was by George that "any man, especially a professional soldier, who did not maintain himself in fine physical trim through routine exercise was not being true to himself and his profession."[2] George certainly took his own advice to heart—eat less, exercise more—and Beatrice beamed with pride as she watched him approach in the distance, an officer to the hilt wearing his full dress uniform with his medals and wound chevron.

It was an accepted practice for officers to wear their dress uniform in place of white-tie, yet the older colonel casually remarked to no one in particular, "Just look at the little boys they are promoting to Colonel these days; look at that young chicken still wet behind the ears, wearing a Colonel's eagle."

The longer George was married to his Beat, the more he loved her. "She is the most interesting lady that it has ever been my pleasure to meet," an old friend wrote upon meeting her. It was a sentiment George wholeheartedly agreed with as she was "forever doing the most gracious and thoughtful things."[3] Beatrice possessed enough diplomacy for two, yet she was a high-spirited woman who could be as unpredictable as she was sensible. Her temper was legendary, and she had a fighting spirit that frightened even the soldiers at Fort Bliss. Yet, the last thing George expected to see as he entered the Wadsworth house was his wife, "petite but powerful," resplendent in her evening gown, sitting on the floor astride a stunned reserve colonel.[4]

Beatrice's natural inhibitions went out the window when it concerned George and woe betide anyone who stood in his way or insulted his honor. It was evident this colonel spent most of his days behind a desk and never a day in battle, and she had hit him with such force that both landed on the floor. It took a stunned George and another bystander to pull her off the bewildered man.[5]

Thirty years later, General Marshall still recounted Mrs. Patton tearing up an unsuspecting officer's face as evidence that "she adored him [George] to the point of making him worse."[6] Everyone in the Army knew Beatrice was so protective of her husband that she took it to heart when someone criticized him. She had an unwavering belief in his greatness and was uncompromising in her defense of him. Ultimately her anger would be directed at those who came out against him, "ingrates and simpletons who did not realize this was the great George Patton, the best among them."[7]

ADHERING to a new philosophy that anything she did "spells advancement for Georgie," Beatrice insisted on trading in the plush Washington home she rented in November 1918 for a ramshackle barrack at Camp Meade, Maryland.[8] George would have been happy to commute the twenty-five miles from the capital, "an hour and a quarter . . . by auto or trolley," but Beatrice was tired of being separated from him.[9] It was one of the advantages of the army in peacetime that George pointed out a long time ago, "It is true that families get separated but when they are together they see lots more of each other."[10]

Beatrice felt a sense of déjà vu when she arrived at Camp Meade in April 1919; the walls of the abandoned barrack George requisitioned were once again painted yellow and blue. She immediately got to work turning the shack into a home, because "even if you think you'll be moving within a few years, treat each new house as a permanent home. Really move in. Pretend it's your home forever. Make it as nice as you can and be sure to have the things you really care about always with you. It gives one a feeling of permanence."[11]

Because their new home was made of wood planks covered in tar paper, a kitchen was considered a fire hazard, and Beatrice was obliged to take her daughters to the mess hall once a day. On Sundays, they got to try the rolling kitchens out in the field, a familiar sight to all the soldiers who fought in WWI. The colossal iron contraption with its distinctive chimney was pulled by horses like a piece of artillery and could feed up to two hundred men at a time.

*Figure 33. The Patton family, either in 1917 or 1919. (Patton Museum)*

Little Bee and Ruth Ellen loved the excitement, but after one week of eating canned food, Beatrice put down her foot and insisted George fix the problem. Riding around camp looking for a solution, he came across an abandoned signal house, which he dragged home behind his tank. According to Ruth Ellen, her mother's "reactions to some of our predicaments were extraordinarily sensible," and Beatrice didn't mind her "outhouse" kitchen that George connected to the house with a covered walkway. After all, that was how they did things at George Washington's Mount Vernon.[12]

While Little Bee had a decent memory of her father, Ruth Ellen had only her mother's stories to go on. Beatrice had portrayed George as a knight in shining armor, so it was a massive letdown to Ruth Ellen when her father did not live up to her high expectations. Instead, he was a skinny, "disagreeable man" who walked with a limp and perpetually looked as if he carried the weight of the world upon his shoulders. She could not understand what her mother found so fantastic about this "ogre."[13] After being absent for most of the last three years, George had an easier time commanding a tank brigade than dealing with four-year-old Ruth Ellen, whose temperament was beginning to match his own.

Only with age would Ruth Ellen understand why her father behaved the way he did. Peace was an immense letdown for a man who forever feared laziness, "which has ever pursued me [and] is closing in on me at last." George had long known that "being a soldier and being a member of the army in time of peace, are two different things." He "would only accept the latter" as a means to the former because "peace service is narrowing, tedious, perhaps unpleasant, and above all distructive of initiative which is the one quality necessary to a successful soldier."[14]

While impatiently awaiting his next assignment in Casablanca in 1943, George wondered whether he was "being made perfect through suffering, for I do suffer when I cannot move."[15] That was how each day felt to him once he returned from WWI: constantly looking for ways to burn off the inordinate amount of energy he had since childhood and relive the rush he experienced briefly in battle. His solution was to escape into a life of extreme physical exertion, and he began to collect cups and ribbons at horse shows, polo matches, steeplechases, and fox hunts.

FOUR MONTHS after his return from France, George requested a leave of absence for forty-five days to travel to Lake Vineyard to invest his share of the sale of Catalina Island.

Unfortunately, a fire had broken out at the Grand View Hotel on the island at 2:30 a.m. on November 29, 1915. It had quickly spread like a chain of dominos to hundreds of surrounding cottages, the Hotel Metropole, and the

Tuna and Pilgrim Clubs. Luckily it was the off-season, and no one was injured, but the Catalina Island Company—basically the Banning brothers who owned the island and all of Avalon—estimated their losses between $1 million and $1.5 million.[16]

"Bigger and better city to rise out of [the] ashes," the residents cried within days of the inferno. Even though William and Hancock Banning had completed the Hotel St. Catherine in the Descanso Canyon two and a half years later, mounting debt and declining tourism during the war had left them no choice but to sell in February 1919. In one of California's biggest real estate deals up to that point, the Catalina Island Company and all its assets were sold for $4 million to chewing gum magnate William Wrigley Jr.[17]

The Pattons' trip to the West Coast would be their first vacation since 1915, but the second honeymoon George hoped for upon his return from Europe never came to pass. However, lack of money, as he had feared, was not the issue. Through hard work, solid vision, and keen judgment, Frederick Ayer left a fortune of $20 million upon his death (approximately $400 million). Because of his diverse financial holdings, settling his estate was "an involved process" that would take years.[18]

Beatrice inherited her father's modesty. George, however, enjoyed money's benefits in the most ostentatious ways, even though he couldn't understand how some people defined ambition as merely amassing a fortune.[19] Never "satisfied with any thing but the best," able to "afford it," and believing "in enjoying my self between wars," George bought a second car when most people could not afford even one, and his personal stable at Camp Meade grew to include ten horses.[20]

The $3 million (about $50 million today) Beatrice inherited—and an additional $3 million in an investment trust run by Fred and Chilly—meant the Pattons never wanted for anything.[21] Beatrice made her children "thank Granfer Ayer in our hearts" whenever they received something nice. Through his example, she taught them that wealth was a responsibility and not a privilege, reminding them that their grandfather worked hard all his life so his children and grandchildren could live a comfortable life.[22]

The Pattons' lifestyle was in marked contrast to their neighbors at Camp Meade, who would never be able to afford the housekeeper, governess, cook, and six servants Beatrice now employed. Infantry officer Dwight David "Ike" Eisenhower moved into his own rundown barrack in September 1919 with his wife Mamie and two-year-old son Doud (known to all as Icky).

Mamie Geneva Doud, the daughter of a successful meatpacking executive, spent a privileged childhood in Iowa, Colorado, and Texas. Mr. Doud consented to his daughter marrying the young officer she met at Fort Sam Houston in October 1915, but he refused to give her an allowance. Forced to turn "an orange crate into a dressing table," Mamie quickly learned to be frugal with the paychecks Ike handed her to manage, $320 per month by the time they arrived at Camp Meade.[23]

"I sure like them," Mamie said of the Pattons, but Beatrice and Mamie's personalities were too different for them to become more than casual friends.[24] Beatrice enjoyed exploring history, attending the theater, and reading poetry; Mamie was happiest listening to show tunes, reading grocery store romances, and playing mah-jongg. Beatrice was a skilled conversationalist who organized sophisticated dinner parties and traveled extensively; Mamie preferred organizing potlucks and sitting on her lawn enjoying the home life. Beatrice lived life at breakneck speed like her husband, sailing and horseback riding competitively; Mamie abhorred sports and only watched football because Ike was the talented coach of the Camp Meade team. Both women had a tendency toward frailty, but while Mamie often gave in to illness, Beatrice did not. Like George, she believed that "the body is never tired if the mind is not tired."[25]

"Mamie had been raised like a Southern belle," her granddaughter Susan Eisenhower wrote in *Mrs. Ike*, "to do nothing but run a great house, manage the servants, and please a man." Ten years younger than her worldly neighbor, Mamie considered Beatrice matronly, while Little Bee and Ruth Ellen thought Mamie was "the most glamorous creature" they had ever seen. Insisting they call her Mamie, as Mrs. Eisenhower made her sound old—a more reserved and proper Beatrice disapproved of her children calling adults by their first name— the Patton girls could not stop staring through the fence whenever Mamie sat down in her yard wearing a flimsy negligee and swirling a glass of iced tea.

Icky was the darling of Camp Meade and often trailed along with eight-year-old Little Bee and four-year-old Ruth Ellen as they played in the bullet-riddled tank stationed in front of Camp Meade's headquarters, or fished in the ditch behind the house. After proudly showing his catch around the post one day, Icky asked Beatrice, who was always worried when the little boy showed up on her doorstep alone, to prepare his fish. His catch looked a little worse for wear, so Beatrice tactfully sent him outside to play while she prepared his dinner. She threw his fish in the garbage and opened a can of sardines instead, arranging them on a piece of buttered toast with a lemon wedge and a sprig of parsley.[26]

DESPITE ALL THEIR DIFFERENCES, Mrs. Patton and Mrs. Eisenhower were very much alike when it came to their husbands. "Ike was my career," Mamie once said, words Beatrice could easily have spoken about her own spouse.[27]

Five years younger than George and graduated from West Point in 1915 with the "Class the Stars Fell On," Ike was an affable and easygoing man. He grew up in relative poverty in Abilene, Kansas, where his mother's books awakened in him an interest in military history. Unlike George, whose brazen ambition was clear from his earliest years, Ike only took the Naval Academy and West Point admission exams because a friend told him he could attend tuition-free. While his performance at West Point was considered average, during WWI he became noted for his organizational skills at Camp Colt, the country's largest tank training center in Pennsylvania.

George and Ike immediately got along when they met in September 1919, bonding over a belief in the bright future of the tank and the sudden realization that they were but a handful of people who shared that belief. When they weren't spending the weekend driving George's Pierce Arrow along the highway looking for a group of thieves involved in a string of holdups, they were taking apart a tank down to its smallest part. Twice they came within inches of making their wives widows as they tested military equipment.[28]

Isolationism and demobilization made George feel as if "we are like people in a boat floating down the beautiful river of fictitious prosperity and thinking that the moaning of the none too distant waterfall—which is going to ingulf us —is but the song of the wind in the trees."[29] With the Army's budget severely cut, it quickly dawned on George and Ike that the Tank Corps was sent to Camp Meade to die. Whatever remained would be incorporated into the infantry, a move they vehemently opposed. However, the men making the decisions at the War Department, the ones who "never heard a shot fired in anger," as George derisively liked to say, had their heads stuck in the sand.

In the summer of 1920, Beatrice watched full of pride as Major Patton gave one of his lively presentations to seven visiting generals from the War Department. (After reverting to his prewar grade of captain in June 1920, he was immediately promoted to major, but he would not reattain the rank of colonel until 1938.) She immediately recognized the disgust on her husband's face when all seven generals refused, "with cold superiority," to go on a ride with him. After all, "tanks were known to blow up, topple over and even turn turtle on a steep hill." Yet, despite being dressed "fit for a garden party," Beatrice didn't hesitate when George suggested she join him for a ride instead.

She nimbly climbed into the turret of a small whippet tank—known not only for its speed and mobility but also for its unpredictability—and smiled brightly despite losing her hat as George handled "the tank as he would a polo pony." The generals took one look at the disheveled Beatrice—her hair tangled, her dress covered in oil stains, and her body in bruises—and once again refused George's offer, leaving nothing but snide remarks about Beatrice's "unladylike behavior" in their wake.

Ultimately, Mamie came to Beatrice's defense, explaining that "generals were afraid of soiling their uniforms" while her neighbor had shown true sportsmanship.[30] Beatrice had ample warning before her marriage that her husband was consumed with war, and she quickly realized if she wanted to be part of his life, she would have to learn it all. If her demonstration did nothing to convince the War Department, it at least highlighted her commitment to, and her belief in, George's career.

When the Tank Corps was incorporated into the Infantry at the end of the summer, George made the difficult decision of returning to the Cavalry, where he could at least expend his boundless energy doing the things he loved best. In an unofficial capacity, however, he would spend the next twenty years studying tanks, convinced that he "would yet be in the biggest war in history."[31] Before leaving Camp Meade in October 1920, he organized a meeting that brought Eisenhower under the tutelage of his true mentor, Brigadier General (later Major General) Fox Conner.[32]

Inspecting Camp Meade's Infantry Tank School in September, Fox wondered if George could recommend a competent executive officer to join him at Camp Gaillard in Panama, where he was to be the new commanding officer. George suggested Major Eisenhower without hesitation and invited Fox and his wife Bug to one of Beatrice's famous Sunday brunches so they could meet. These get-togethers were a Camp Meade highlight during an otherwise dull time of demobilization, with Beatrice the gracious hostess and George the amiable raconteur.[33]

After three years in each other's company, George ended his last review of the 304th Tank Brigade with an emotional speech reminiscent of those he would give on his war bond selling tour in 1945, praising his men for winning him the DSC and DSM. While he realized some might have considered him a tough leader, he "never asked any of you to brace more, work more, fight more, than I have been willing to do myself."[34] Beatrice followed her husband with an equally teary farewell speech, touched by the silver cup she received and the many offers to help them move to Fort Myer.[35]

---

EXCEPT FOR THE addition of three wireless communication towers known as the Three Sisters, Fort Myer had changed very little since the Pattons left in 1913. However, a lot had changed for the family when they returned in the fall of 1920: George had fought in two wars, Beatrice had lost both her parents, and the family had grown with the addition of Ruth Ellen and Tank, a deaf bull terrier George bought at his wife's behest to help build a rapport with his children. All these experiences gave the Pattons a sense of confidence that would sit them well as they returned to the pleasant prewar lifestyle they so enjoyed before. From now on, though, Beatrice would focus on just two things: raising her children and helping George further his career.

The Pattons moved back into their old home on Officer's Row, a pleasant brick house that was "rather small, but anyway very pretty and a good location."[36] It stood a mere stone's throw from Arlington Cemetery, which soon became the favorite playground of nine-year-old Little Bee and five-year-old Ruth Ellen. Beatrice made it clear that Arlington Cemetery was not a macabre and sad place, but one steeped in glory and history. While she taught Ruth Ellen to read by tracing the letters on the gravestones, George taught his daughters there was nothing strange about dying and blamed the education system for "picturing death as such a terrible thing."[37]

*Figure 34.* A quiet moment in a hectic life. *(Huntington Library)*

Snow began to blanket the manicured lawn of Quarters Five on the after-noon of January 27, 1922, while George lay recuperating from a freak allergic reaction to shellfish. As the worst snowstorm in the capital's history got underway—with a record-setting thirty-two inches—he was busy organizing his rapidly growing military library. "We were indeed lucky that an Army offi-cer's professional library is transported free," Beatrice recalled. "No matter where we moved, there was never enough room for the books."

These books weren't for show, as she made clear. Her husband "made notes on all the important ones he read" and kept a list of helpful quotes that he could conjure up on a dime when the situation called for it. If there were no faithful translations of German or French books he was interested in, he asked Beatrice to make him "a workable translation." Besides military volumes, the Pattons' library also held "many works on horsemanship, fox hunting, polo and sailing, all sports with a spice of danger to keep a soldier on his toes in time of peace."[38]

Meanwhile, the snowfall outside was about to cause "the greatest disaster" in the capital's history.[39] Over two feet of snow accumulated in just twenty-four hours, severely hobbling transportation across the region. Yet, hundreds of adults and children braved the elements to attend Comedy Night at the Knickerbocker Theater on January 28. Just as the opening credits of *Get-Rich-Quick Wallingford* appeared on the screen at nine o'clock, a hissing sound emitted from the theater's ceiling as its flat roof struggled under the weight of the snow. An eyewitness who was just about to enter the building then experi-enced "the most heart-rending thing I ever want to witness," as the roof split in half and caved in on itself, taking down the balcony and part of the exterior wall.[40]

Summoned by General Pershing—now the Army's chief of staff—Major Patton was one of the first to arrive on the scene with one hundred men of the 3rd Cavalry. It was still snowing, so it took four teams of mules to pull the trucks through Washington's deserted and snowbank-covered streets.[41] To George and his men, it felt as if they entered a battlefield when they neared the Knickerbocker Theater, the screams of survivors and the smell of blood filling the air. Freeing the one hundred and thirty-three injured and recovering the ninety-eight bodies was a task that "tried the souls of men." Still, the 3rd Cavalry soldiered on through the night under the "highly efficient" leadership of Major Patton.[42]

When an exhausted George came home the following morning just as the last snowflakes were falling from the sky, grime covered his pale face. The scene at the Knickerbocker Theater had been horrible, but in his typical bravado—which to anyone not part of the family might come across as insensi-tivity—he described the night in gruesome detail to his daughters. Beatrice admonished her husband for recounting how he pulled a woman's body clean of her head when he tried to free her from the rubble, but he disagreed that his daughters were too young for such stories. "Bee, goddammit," he yelled, "they've got to know things like that do happen. They can't go through life with blinders on."[43]

During the Pattons' forthcoming tour in Hawaii, Ruth Ellen recited one of her father's more gruesome poems at school, hoping to dispel the sissy image her classmates had of her. "The Mercenary's Song" included such colorful stanzas as, "The women I have ravished, / The infants I have slain. / The priests and nuns I've roasted, / They haunt me not again."[44] What shocked the headmaster even more than the words was Ruth Ellen's admission that she hadn't recited it in ignorance of its true meaning.

George found the whole situation hilarious, but Beatrice used the opportunity to sit down with Ruth Ellen and explain that most parents were not as frank with their children as she and George were. If Ruth Ellen ever planned to share anything else with her classmates—poetry, knowledge, or books—she was to check with Beatrice whether it was okay to do so.

ACCORDING TO GEORGE, BEATRICE "BEHAVED FINE" and never looked "prettier" when she sailed out of New York Harbor on April 15, 1922.[45] Two days earlier, the State Department issued her an emergency passport to visit Kay in England, who had fallen ill with perpetual fever after the birth of her third child. Beatrice didn't hesitate a second to travel thousands of miles to help. Her brothers and sisters were her best friends and, except for George and their children, "the closest kin there is."[46]

Ellen, Jamie, Chilly, Louise, Bea, Fred, and Kay all had families of their own now, but they were as devoted to each other as they had always been. Beatrice was the first to arrive at Miss Lancaster's Nursing Home in the heart of London—where Kay was recuperating from "four operations in as many weeks"—followed by Fred and Hilda, and Jamie and May.

The Merrills' first two children were born in London—Keith Merrill Jr. in 1918 and Rosemary Katharine Merrill in 1920—where Keith remained vice-consul until the spring of 1921. Then, after a brief respite at Avalon, he was sent to Madrid in August 1921 to take on the duties of the American consul. Spain was beset by political unrest and general strikes, and its hospitals "were little better than pest-houses."[47] Wanting nothing but the best for himself and his family, Keith rented a palatial residence markedly nicer than the American embassy, to the envy of the ambassador.

Two days after welcoming Eugenia "Gene" Ayer Merrill into the world on March 11, 1922, Kay developed a high fever and began to suffer from severe abdominal pain. Doctors quickly diagnosed perpetual or childbed fever, a potentially lethal infection caused by unsterilized instruments that had been the leading cause of maternal death for centuries. Told there was nothing to be done for his wife, Keith bought an operating table which he fashioned into a stretcher, hired a nurse, and took Kay by sleeper train to Paris and across the Channel to Miss Lancaster's Nursing Home, where she spent the next three months.

Ever since the spring of 1919, when Mr. Patton lost out on the opportunity to become the U.S. Ambassador to Italy—a prospect Beatrice liked so much that she was even willing to pay half of the $30,000 annual cost [about $475,000]—he had wanted to take his family to Europe.[48] So when word reached Lake Vineyard of Kay's illness and Beatrice's impending departure, the Pattons immediately left for Fort Myer to take care of their grandchildren.

Since George would be spending most of the upcoming summer at New York's Mitchel Field, participating in the Junior Championship Polo Tournament, Mr. Patton thought this was the perfect opportunity to take his family across the pond. Beatrice could not wait to travel together—the trip from the west coast through the Panama Canal took sixteen days—so Mr. Patton booked passage on the next crossing for himself, his wife, their daughter, and their two granddaughters. They sailed on the *Rotterdam* on May 13th, arriving in Plymouth on the 21st.

*Figure 35. Portrait of Mr. Patton, during his tenure as mayor of San Marino. (Huntington Library)*

Mr. Patton rented Sir Harry Stonor's Elizabethan manor called Turville Park, forty-five miles west of London in the quaint village of Turville, replete with servants, gardeners, a dairy farm, and greenhouses. A smart dresser who "displayed classic chivalry toward ladies, making him a dashing, romantic figure," Mr. Patton immediately fit in.[49] Every morning he could be seen walking the fields carrying his walking stick, his dreamy brown-gray eyes gazing above a perfectly manicured mustache, and his five-eleven frame as erect as an officer's. While Beatrice spent most of her time in London looking after her sister and the new baby, Bamps read his granddaughters all the English classics as he took them around the countryside.

A real romance was infinitely more interesting, though, and Little Bee and Ruth Ellen loved spying on Aunt Nita as Harry Brain pursued her. She had met him in 1919 when she lived with the Merrills in "the choicest residential area of London" while working for the Red Cross. At that time, Nita had asked General Pershing point-blank about the state of their relationship, and he callously asked her to keep their engagement a secret until "his feelings returned."[50] Black Jack could get anyone in the world now that he was a conquering hero, and he figured Nita "could more or less be propped in a corner until he had time to regroup and reconsider."[51]

On July 19, 1919, Nita had convinced herself she caught Pershing's eye as he rode a magnificent bay horse at the head of the American contingent during London's Victory Parade. However, she received neither an acknowledgment nor an invitation to one of the many victory balls, and two months later she returned her engagement ring. Nita never spoke about her relationship with Pershing again, but when Harry Brain asked for her hand in marriage while rowing on the Thames, she reluctantly rejected his proposal, realizing "that unless I could mate with a master, I'd better stay clear of the shoals."[52]

When Kay was finally released from the hospital in June 1922, she spent another month recuperating before leaving for St. Jean-de-Luz, a small fishing village in France's Basque country near the border with Spain. The Pattons crossed the Channel with the Merrills, but they went on to tour the sites of World War I where George had fought. He hoped they "had a nice time at the battle fields," but unfortunately, he could not show them in person the hill where he was shot. His vague descriptions were useless, and the Pattons spent days looking in vain.[53]

THE SUMMER of 1923 "couldn't have been more perfect," according to Beatrice.[54] The Pattons had been married for thirteen years, "13 years of variegated tapestry with the warp of love," as she wrote her father-in-law.[55] George completed the five-month Advanced Officers' Course at Fort Riley in June and was offered a coveted spot at the Command and General Staff School at Fort Leavenworth, Kansas, a yearlong course offered only to the best. Meanwhile, Beatrice was pregnant for the third and, in her own words, "really . . . the last time!"[56] She put off having another child for George's sake but realizing that she could have lost him in 1918 added a sense of urgency to the mission.

When she first brought up the subject in a letter to George after he was shot in 1918—and after Kay had just given birth to her first child, a son—he replied, "Your childish proclivities of which you boast do not interest me at all. I love you too much and am jealous, or something of the children. Besides I may run into some gas. Your only chance to have another child is accident or Immaculate Conception. You ought to be complimented but being pig-headed, I suppose you are not. I love you too much."[57] In the end, George "was not altered by the gas as I was not gased," but it took Beatrice another five years to prevail upon her husband.[58]

*Figure 36. Miss Beatrice Patton ready to compete in March 1922.*
*(Library of Congress)*

Without a house of their own, the Pattons spent an idyllic three-month vacation at Avalon, the family's "general gathering spot" now owned by the Merrills. (Kay "wished to keep the place in the family and she wished to keep it a family place," so she and Keith bought out her six siblings in the summer of 1921.)[59] Beatrice had never been happier in her life than during those leisurely days she spent watching Ruth Ellen play on the beach and Little Bee riding along one of the wooded trails with her father. She was filled with joy that George "seems like his old self again—he has been so changed since the war I feared it was permanent! But this summer he is just like a kid—every stern line has gone out of his face and he fished on the pier with the kids till 7 last evening. They are having a grand time with him."[60]

It was such a relief to Beatrice to have her old Georgie back, the man she had said goodbye to in May 1917. While George appeared to have been the same effervescent guy he was before, Beatrice knew he had been "so changed since the war, so serious and restless." He had been difficult to live with at times as his moods swung between "manic self-assurance and incapacitating despondency," but now, with his morale and confidence boosted by his acceptance to the Command and General Staff School, it seemed like he was back to his old self.[61]

The highlight of the Pattons' vacation took place on August 21, 1923, when they saved three boys from drowning in Salem Harbor during a sudden storm. Beatrice was a phenomenal sailor who knew the North Shore like the inside of her pocket, and she was often out on the water in a "sweet little 17-footer."

Even though their little Manchester Skiff boat held only two people, George and Beatrice got all three boys on board—two brothers, aged sixteen and ten, and their sixteen-year-old friend—and made it back to land safely. The affidavit Beatrice submitted to the Treasury Department describing the harrowing ordeal speaks for itself:

On August 21st 1923 Major Patton and I were sailing off our place at Pride's Crossing, marked Plum Cove on the chart of Salem Harbor. Our boat was an unseaworthy 14 foot skiff. Halfway across the harbor we realized that the wind was rising and getting very squally. Our boat began to leak badly and became almost unmanageable. To turn around and go home meant coming about and sailing before the wind and we felt our boat would not stand it, so we decided to try for the opposite (Salem) shore.

Just then we heard a shout behind us. The water was covered with white foam and black squally patches, making it difficult to distinguish any object. At last we saw three boys, apparently standing up to their armpits in the sea about 300 feet from the Great Haste, a barren slippery lone rock. We were too full of water to go about, so Major Patton maneuvered the skiff so as to drift toward the boys. This threw us into the trough of the waves so that we slipped more water, but the tide was running in the right direction and we finally managed it. As we approached the boys, they sank to their chins. One of them called to us that his two companions could not swim. They were all astride a capsized sailing dory larger [18 1/2 foot] than our boat and had unstepped their mast. Their sails and rigging floating about in the water made our approach very awkward.

Major Patton stretched an oar to them and took them off one by one, lifting them over the stern to prevent our capsizing. They were gray and chattering with cold. With five in the boat we almost had no freeboard and I suggested rowing home, as, if we tried to carry sail, we should probably all be drowned. Major Patton however [?] that the boys' condition necessitated the quickest method of travel in spite of the extra risk. We stowed the boys in the bottom for warmth and sat in the stern to keep out the following seas, which broke over our backs many times before we reached the lee of the land. Later, the boys told us that two other boats had passed them without attempting their rescue.[62]

While Beatrice was just as instrumental in the rescue effort, all while five months pregnant, she allowed George to take the spotlight. He received a medal from the State of Massachusetts, and Beatrice decided to surprise him with the Silver Lifesaving Medal from the U.S. Treasury Department. She submitted a mountain of paperwork, but it wasn't until February 1926 that her request was approved. When George finally had the Silver Lifesaving Medal pinned on his chest, his greatest champion remarked, "I have never been prouder of him in my life."[63]

With Kay's near-death experience still fresh in everyone's minds, the Pattons decided not to take any risks, and George moved to Fort Leavenworth on his own in September 1923. General Sherman had established the School for Application for Cavalry and Infantry in 1881, and it had rapidly grown into the top military education program in the country. It was as close to war as an officer could get without actual combat and the course load was so heavy that many students became suicidally depressed, quit, or divorced.

George attended classes from 8:30 a.m. until 5 p.m. when he took his daily exercise. He then sat up well into the night studying or solving tactical problems, often with a blue light emanating from his bedroom window as he sat "baking my head with no apparent results."[64] When a fellow student became suspicious, George embarrassingly admitted to his superiors that the lamp was not some form of cheating but merely another failed attempt at regrowing his thinning hair.

His family remained at Avalon, where Beatrice had access to the best medical care and the support of the Merrills, who returned from abroad in November 1923. Keith "respected the obligations to the service," but unless his next assignment was in the United States, he considered resigning and accepting Fred's offer of managing the J. C. Ayer & Co. It had been running a deficit for years, and many thought it "practically impossible to resurrect the business." Still, Keith was willing to take on the challenge "if it was the only way to do my best for the family, which has always done so much for me and has never yet asked me to do anything for them." After long consideration, he decided to remain in the Foreign Service, but not before satisfying "his sense of obligation to the Ayer family" by suggesting his brother-in-law as an alternative for the job.[65]

"Anxious" to give birth to "George and Martha" so she could be "slim and lively" before George arrived for his Christmas break on the twenty-third, even Little Bee's suggestion of taking a bumpy ride on a pony was to no avail.[66] Beatrice was "getting very tired waiting" and hoped "It"—avoidance of gender was carefully practiced—would at least be born on the twenty-second as her doctor predicted, but the only place Beatrice checked into that day was the Hotel Puritan in Boston, "exactly opposite the old Ayer house [it was sold in 1921]."[67] With the loss of her parents, the arrival of Nita and Ruth earlier that month was a great "comfort" to Beatrice.

"For the first time," Ruth wrote her husband at Lake Vineyard, "I have come East and felt it was worthwhile."[68] Little Bee and Ruth Ellen were happy to see their grandmother and "crazy to go to California" once the baby was born.[69] According to Nita, "the whole family have been very nice to us this time" as Beatrice took her in-laws to visit all her siblings.[70] They had dinner with Mrs. Wood; visited Fred and Hilda at Ledyard Farm; went with Theodora Ayer to her social club; and drove to Lincoln to see Louise Gordon, recently widowed but acting very "brave."

On Sunday morning, December 23, Beatrice, Nita, and Ruth picked George up at the train station in Boston and drove to Pride's Crossing to spend the night at Avalon. Ruth continued the story in another letter to her husband,

> Sure enough at half past eleven, Georgie came flying down my hall calling to me to get up so B, Kay, Keith, Georgie and I started for Boston in the pouring rain. Keith driving fifty miles an hour, but he drove well and we arrived at the "Phillips House" safe, and sound, and waited all night for the baby to be born. We all had breakfast at the hospital, and soon afterwards we were rewarded by the arrival of the fine baby boy.[71]

Three weeks before her thirty-eighth birthday, at 9:15 a.m. on December 24, 1923, Beatrice's most fervent wish came true with the birth of George Patton IV. According to his proud grandmother, the baby was "a husky little fellow," weighing ten pounds and a half, and endowed with "fine lungs."[72] He had "a determined little face … a very broad, fine forehead … [and] a round chin with no cleft in it," as all the Ayers had.[73] Little Bee thought her long-awaited brother "might amount to something when he gets big," while Ruth Ellen, who had been praying for a baby brother for months, described him as "very sweet, he has a turned up nose and a red face."[74] Beatrice dubbed him "the hospital beauty … a real blonde like Georgie" with blue eyes and a round face.[75]

There was no doubt that the new addition to the family would be named after his grandfather, but there was some discussion about the suffix. "What's in a name?" George wrote regarding the use of numerals, but he favored the "3rd . . . as it shows that the race at least knows its own grandfather." In the end, accuracy prevailed over logic; even though his father was called George Smith Patton Jr., young George was the fourth generation to carry that name.

Beatrice came through the delivery exhausted but in fine shape and had "plenty of milk" for the baby. But, despite her glowing health, the doctor decided to keep her in the hospital for a month. "When one has money," Nita wrote her father, "the doctors surely do worry over one's health, and make Bee an easy prey to their pretended anxieties."[76]

While Beatrice and the baby "got along nicely" in the hospital, George returned to Fort Leavenworth, and Nita and Ruth returned to Lake Vineyard with Little Bee, Ruth Ellen, and Tank. They were joined by Miss Dennett, the children's newest governess from England since Nanny Taty had been fired for taking the children to a rally outside the White House. "'Denty is a real educator," Beatrice wrote Mr. Patton, "giving the children an appetite for more, which I hope will never have to be blunted by poor teaching."[77]

*Figure 37. Mr. Patton holding his namesake. He is joined by Beatrice, Little Bee, Ruth, and Ruth Ellen. (Huntington Library)*

Since his arrival at Fort Leavenworth in September, George had been "studying to beat hell." He managed to prepare a small room with abundant light for his son, but the house was too small for three children. Saying goodbye to her daughters left "an ache down somewhere around my heart," but Beatrice loved "to think of them at Lake V.—as long as I can't have them. To feel not only that they are happy but that they are so <u>wanted</u> and so <u>welcome</u> makes me happy."[78]

Neither George's warning about how busy he was nor the statistics of the school's impact on its students' marriages stopped Beatrice from moving to Fort Leavenworth in January 1924 with baby George and his English nanny, Alice Holmes. Beatrice had "such a lovely time at home" that "it was never so hard to leave before," so it took her a while "to settle down to brass tacks again."[79] She could have easily gone to California or stayed at Avalon until George finished his course in June, but husband and wife had been apart so often in the last two years that she was willing to make any sacrifice.

George came home for lunch on Wednesdays and Saturdays,

> & does not have to go back again; but so far, he studies every minute that he is at home. However—he can do far better work here than if he had to stay in the quarters assigned to him, in a shack, with shouting men & pounding typewriters noon & night. Here, he has a big quiet study to work in. He has no time at all, even to write a letter, but I plan to do all the odd jobs & will typewrite his notes for him daily. He is required to ride two hours daily, so should keep in good shape.[80]

There was nothing to do at Fort Leavenworth—located just one hundred and forty miles west of Fort Riley and known for being the birthplace of the Buffalo Soldiers—but Beatrice unfolded into a social butterfly from the moment she arrived. "Major and Mrs. George S. Patton entertained with one of the very handsome dinners of the season at the golf club last evening for one hundred and thirty guests," the *Leavenworth Times* reported.

Beatrice added such cachet to George's performance that Fort Leavenworth's commandant wanted to keep him on as instructor after the course finished. Of course, George graduating 25th out of 248 students—making him an honor graduate and a member of the General Staff Corps—might also have had something to do with it. Still, there was no denying how valuable an asset Beatrice was to her husband's career.

AFTER THIRTEEN YEARS, an ecstatic Beatrice found herself back in familiar surroundings when George was ordered to Boston to assume the duties of G-1 (Personnel Officer) at First Corps Area headquarters. Instead of moving in with the Merrills at Avalon in July 1924, the Pattons rented Sunset Rock a scant distance away. Like Avalon in scope and amenities, the mansion was built in 1897 for the Spaulding brothers, who struck it rich in the sugar refining business. There were plenty of excellent trails to exercise the horses, terraced gardens leading down to the beach, and a big stable.

It took a squad to run a household like Sunset Rock, and Beatrice did not relish being its sergeant. She wholeheartedly agreed with George that "homes are more of a bother than a blessing," unlike Kay, who employed "so many servants they are falling over each other."[81] Living in England for four years, Kay had taken on the habits of the British upper class, and Avalon was kept in meticulous order with the help of liveried butlers. Even though a certain amount of formality was important to the Pattons—especially at the dining room table where they always dressed in evening wear—the formality at Avalon was too much. In addition, George thought his brother-in-law "too G.D. 'Nice'" and often wrote disparaging remarks about him to Beatrice during WWI. (He had much preferred Kay's other suitor, Stuart Cramer.)[82]

Rumor had it that George was once temporarily banished from Avalon for publicly insulting Keith. Everyone who knew George Patton could tell at least one story showcasing his powerful and often infuriatingly maddening personality. For the Merrills, this happened at 2535 Belmont Road, at the new mansion they built near Rock Creek Park in Washington, where Keith continued his career at the State Department.

*Figure 38. The Pattons loved to play dress-up. (Huntington Library)*

At a dinner party for foreign dignitaries, George finished his main course, unobtrusively wrapped his steak bone in a napkin, and quietly left the room. He returned five minutes later, waving the cleaned bone in the air and exclaiming he never had enough to eat at the Merrills. He then invited anyone who felt the same way to join him in front of the fire to gnaw on their bone. Instead of the laughter he had anticipated, a hush fell over the room, and one can only imagine Beatrice's embarrassment as George pulled another one of his antics.

What about George Patton made people put up with his tendency to "create tension for the sake of diversion"? As his grandson Robert Patton wrote in *The Pattons*, "His colleagues forgave him because his strength as a commander outweighed the annoyances of him. His children forgave him because while he acted outrageous, he always made up for it." His most "gauche behavior," however, his family could only forgive for Beatrice's sake, and Beatrice forgave him because she enjoyed the life of "exhilarating drama of passionate highs and lows."[83]

She also understood her Georgie better than anyone else. His behavior must have exasperated Beatrice at times—like when he scandalized Washington's society ladies by asking them to help take off his pants so he could show them his scar—but she always handled every situation with grace and diplomacy and never showed her displeasure in public. She knew the man who dominated a room telling stories, "which kept everybody killing themselves with laughter," was not the "perpetual fountain of boyish exuberance" everyone else saw but "a deeply troubled man" who hid behind a carefully crafted façade.[84]

Beatrice reveled in the cultural life of Boston while living at Sunset Rock. She enjoyed attending the Boston Symphony Orchestra and took Little Bee and Ruth Ellen to see Anna Pavlova's "Dying Swan." With the theatrical flair she inherited from her mother, albeit in a slightly more subdued way, Beatrice not only encouraged her daughters to enjoy the performing arts but to actively participate in them as well. She also insisted her children learn several languages because "it is only polite to speak the language of the place you are at." She taught Little Bee to play the piano, while Ruth Ellen learned a bunch of raunchy songs to perform with her sister at cocktail parties. "I think we had a better time than anybody I've ever met," Ruth Ellen remembered of her youth. "We had very interesting parents . . . who were interested in everything."

Tutored by governesses and spending every day in each other's company, Little Bee and Ruth Ellen were best friends, despite their differing personalities and four-year age difference. Little Bee was as sensible and responsible as her mother and "good as gold." Serious and practical, the outstanding equestrian was also caring, quiet, and eager to please. Upon learning that Santa Claus was not real, and parents were just the "earthly agents" who delivered gifts in his name, Little Bee filled Beatrice's stocking with gifts because she no longer had any parents.[85]

On the other hand, Ruth Ellen was "a cute rascally boy" who resembled her father both in looks and temperament. Beatrice described her as "a rogue" who wandered out of the yard at Fort Bliss at two years old. She waited until Little Bee turned her head before following three cows and a dog down the street, intent on bringing them home as a gift for her mother.[86]

The Patton children were not your typical army brats, and this bothered thirteen-year-old Little Bee, who hated standing out. She preferred life on Boston's North Shore, where she blended in with the crowd and could spend time with the multitude of cousins who lived within driving (and riding) distance.

The family spent July 4 at Avalon shooting off fireworks and holding a clambake, while they spent Thanksgiving hunting at Ledyard Farm. Fred and Hilda's home, named after the Connecticut town where Frederick Ayer was born, was located five miles from Avalon in the small equestrian town of Wenham. The Ayers already had sixteen horses and three children—Frederick Ayer, Jr.; Anne Proctor Ayer; and Ethan Ayer—but the family was soon to grow with the addition of twins, "the squeaks," and a string of George's horses.

---

LIFE in the army was always unsettled. As Frederick once warned his future son-in-law, a soldier's "location and home life are, in a measure, subject to the dictation and possible freak of another." A mere eight months after the Pattons moved to Sunset Rock, George was reassigned to the Hawaiian Division at Schofield Barracks to become its G-1 and G-2 (personnel and intelligence officer). He was convinced the move "was not the intention of the W.D. [War Department] but . . . some inside politics of the island."[87]

"While, as you surmised, we are very reluctant to leave Boston," George wrote General Harbord, Pershing's chief of staff during the war and George IV's godfather, "I imagine that professionally the move is for my own betterment, for if I remained here having a good time for several years I might become soft and fat, and forget how to say 'Charge.'"[88]

Beatrice was devastated to leave behind her idyllic life at Sunset Rock so soon. She usually didn't mind her "movies" lifestyle, but this transfer was particularly disappointing.[89] She was leaving behind a life she thoroughly enjoyed to go to a somewhat mystical location halfway across the world while still dealing with lingering health issues from young George's breech birth. Beatrice's doctor insisted on making some "minor repairs" before she left, so George had no choice but to leave her at a Boston hospital in February 1925.

Beatrice was no longer the newlywed who cried at every departure, and the lessons she taught herself at Fort Riley stood her in good stead. She ordered every book on Hawaii from Lauriat—including Mark Twain's *Letters from Hawaii*—and devoured them as she lay recuperating at Sunset Rock for another month. She learned Hawaii's first inhabitants arrived about 400 AD on canoes from the Marquesas Islands in French Polynesia, a distance of about 2,336 miles. More than a thousand years later, on January 20, 1778, the Native Hawaiians spotted the *Resolution* and the *Discovery*, bringing Captain James Cook and the first Europeans to Hawaii's shores.

While this knowledge intrigued Beatrice, what truly caught her attention was the arrival of two Massachusetts whale ships on September 29, 1819, at Kealakekua Bay. Some of the first missionaries to arrive in Hawaii were on board, many of whom hailed from Boston. Could there have been an Ayer ancestor on board? Beatrice's interest was also piqued by the Mormonism that prevailed on the islands. She was familiar with the Book of Mormon, the sacred text of the Latter-Day Saints, after George escorted a group of Mormons back to safety during the Mexican Punitive Expedition.

The Pattons were inveterate believers in the power of history. By the time Beatrice left for Hawaii, she was already steeped in its lore and culture. She left with an open heart and mind, and any preconceived notions she had about Hawaii's past and present melted away the moment she saw Oahu for the first time, not through the eyes of a missionary but as a pioneer.

# 7

# THE PARKER RANCH

## WAIMEA, HAWAII

### 1925–1928

*INTERESTED PEOPLE ARE INTERESTING.*

A short headline on the front page of the *Pasadena Evening Post* immediately caught Beatrice's eye on July 7, 1927: "Fountains of Fire, Liquid Rock Shoot from Hilo Volcano." Despite the death and destruction associated with an erupting volcano, the Native Hawaiians welcomed the reappearance of Pele, the goddess of fire, as it signaled the return of prosperity.

The sudden eruption of Kīlauea was first noticed around 1 a.m. on July 7 by the night watchman of Volcano House, a hotel on the slopes of Kīlauea whose fireplace had been burning continuously since 1877. The first hotel guests parked their cars next to the edge of the crater within twenty minutes, and by morning, all anyone could talk about was the reawakening of the "House of Everlasting Fire." Volcano fever gripped the islands as residents and tourists booked passage on one of the inter-island steamers, many even willing to sleep on mattresses laid out on deck.[1]

The eruption surprised the Native Hawaiians and the scientists who found the lack of seismic activity beforehand unusual. Dr. Jaggar, the noted volcanologist who made Kīlauea his life's work, was not even on the islands . . . and neither was Beatrice.[2] She had no choice but to follow the events in the newspapers until she returned from Lake Vineyard on July 20. Kīlauea was still creating lava and great clouds of steam after a fortnight, so she booked herself on the first available passage on the *Haleakala* and sailed for Hilo on the Big Island, a sixteen-hour trip. Beatrice, who brought along her car but was not the best driver, informed George that she "managed that long twisty drive" up to the Halema'uma'u crater without any problems.[3]

For almost a century, the Halema'uma'u crater at the top of Kīlauea contained an active lava lake, until it suddenly drained into the ocean in February 1924. Three months later, groundwater came into contact with magma and smoldering rocks, causing an explosion that left the crater measuring approximately eight miles wide.[4] "There are no mounds of ashes, nor cinder cones to warn that one has reached the edge of the firepit ..." Beatrice wrote of an earlier visit in April, "and it is very startling to be suddenly on the brink of the yawning 700-foot-deep hole: dry, sandy, constantly rumbling with avalanches that are heard but are too far away to see."

Halema'uma'u was filled with boiling lava when Beatrice reached the top in July 1927. Occasional gusts of heavy wind blew sulfur fumes, dust, and volcanic glass fibers, known as Pele's hair, into the direction of the spectators. Many of those crowding around the edge were Kānaka Maolis, the Native Hawaiians whose ancestors first arrived from Polynesia around 400 or 500 CE. They had been making offerings, or ho'okupu, to Pele for generations, often tossing a handful of freshly picked 'ōhelo berries into the fiery pit. The 'ōhelo —a tart, scarlet berry related to the blueberry—grew on the volcanic rocks of the Kīlauea and was Pele's favorite ho'okupu.[5]

When Beatrice threw her cluster of berries into the Halema'uma'u crater, a gust of wind threw one of the branches back at her feet. Her friend Emma Ahuena Taylor, an expert on Hawaiian anthropology and a Native Hawaiian high chiefess, explained that was a good sign. "It is clear that Pele wanted to share with you," but so did everyone else.[6] While the Native Hawaiians were usually reluctant to open up to foreigners, they recognized Beatrice as a kindred spirit filled with genuine enthusiasm. From the moment Beatrice arrived in Hawaii, she felt right at home.

---

BEATRICE's Hawaiian adventure began on April 30, 1925. That day she boarded the *S.S. President Adams* with her three children, their three dogs, and nanny Alice Holmes for the first leg of their trip, from New York to Los Angeles. The *S.S. President Adams*—one of seven in a series of presidential liners run by the Dollar Steamship Line—was a markedly more comfortable vessel than the military transport George had taken a month-and-a-half earlier. The amenities on board were on par with those of a luxury hotel and included a writing room, a social club, world-class dining, and staterooms with private baths and real beds instead of berths.[7]

There were plenty of things to do on the ship during the three-week crossing, from deck games for the children to five o'clock tea before dinner. Beatrice quickly befriended her fellow passengers, including singer, comedian, and actor Al Jolson. Always looking for a way to keep busy, Beatrice charmed the entertainer and roped him into organizing a concert with her even though he told reporters he was going "to take a complete rest."[8]

Beatrice hadn't been to Panama since her youth—when the canal was still under construction—and she couldn't help but marvel at the modern feat of engineering completed in 1914. She told her daughters of their grandfathers' very different experiences as they made the same transcontinental journey: Mr. Ayer in 1862 when he returned East via the San Juan River through Nicaragua after selling patent medicine, and Mr. Patton in 1866 when he traversed the Isthmus of Panama on a mule, his mother looking to begin anew in California.

Ruth Ellen was the same age as her paternal grandfather when she made the trip, but she enjoyed the spectacular vistas from the comfort of the tearoom. It took twelve hours to sail the forty-mile waterway, half a day wherein time stood still for the passengers on board the *S.S. President Adams*. As mulas (small locomotives) pulled the ship through the last set of locks, the silence was broken by Beatrice's conversation with Mrs. Simonds—sister of Mrs. Marshall, who took Beatrice under her wing at Fort Sheridan in 1910— who walked alongside the boat.

*Figure 39. Aunt Nita with her nephew. (Huntington Library)*

After sixteen years in the Army, the Pattons had built a network of friends across the country. Mrs. Marshall arranged for her sister to personally welcome the Pattons when the *S.S. President Adams* made a brief stop in Balboa, a district of Panama City on the Pacific side of the canal.[9] Mrs. Simonds, who was married to the commanding officer of the Canal Zone, stood waiting on the quay to take her guests on a whirlwind tour of the city in a carreta, a colorful horse-drawn carriage on two big wheels.

When the travelers finally arrived in Los Angeles on May 18, they spent just a few days at Lake Vineyard before boarding the *S.S. City of Los Angeles*. It would take six days to sail the 2,558 miles to Honolulu, and it was a voyage Beatrice would make at least five times in the next three years. As the boat left port on May 23, she hoped her first crossing would be smoother sailing than George's, who not only had been besieged by screaming wives and crying children but also had to contend with a fire on board. He had taken along the Packard, the horses, and the furniture, but just two days into the crossing, the hold caught fire, and anything that didn't burn was ruined by seawater.

"As distance removes sorrow to a degree," George immediately informed Beatrice that "practically every thing is ruined" except for the bed and the Packard, which traveled on deck.[10] Beatrice's Chickering piano was "floating happily" in the hold, but George decided to salvage it, knowing how much her parents' wedding gift meant to his wife.[11]

While it had taken George a few days for the "beauty of the place" to grow on him, it was love at first sight for Beatrice.[12] One "could smell the islands as much as six miles off shore," and the first thing she noticed as the ship pulled into Honolulu Harbor was the partially constructed Aloha Tower, the soon-to-be tallest manmade structure in all of Hawaii, which was still dwarfed by the shadow of Diamond Head.[13]

While the S.S. City of Los Angeles moored at Kulolia and Ke Awa O Kou on May 29, the sound of ukuleles welcomed its passengers to paradise. It didn't take Beatrice and the children long to spot George on the quay, already tanned from the continuous sun and carrying an armload of leis. He quickly went on board to welcome his family, then walked off the gangplank carrying his seventeen-month-old son, who summarily kicked his shoe into the blue waters of the Pacific with a joyful squeal.


SITUATED at the foot of the Waianae Mountain, Schofield Barracks felt like a country club where, according to George, "not one person in a hundred seems to ever do any thing."[14] A posting there could easily feel like one long vacation, but the base played a critical role. Oahu was known as the key to the Pacific and crucial to the defense of the United States, hence why construction began on Pearl Harbor after the annexation of the Hawaiian Islands in 1898. In turn, Schofield Barracks was established in 1908 to help defend Pearl Harbor. There were schools, hospitals, and recreational facilities, and anything unavailable on base could easily be procured in Honolulu, just twenty miles away.

On one side of Schofield Barracks lay the village of Wahiawa; on the other side lay the pineapple plantations. Oahu—the most populous island in a chain of eight despite only being the third largest—was known as "the gathering place." Honolulu was the center of commerce and a melting pot of nationalities, the streets lined with curiosity shops and international cuisines, from Japanese teahouses to Chinese restaurants.[15]

Approximately 75 percent of Honolulu's ninety thousand residents were of Japanese descent, and many worked as servants in the officers' quarters of Schofield Barracks. For the more senior officers who could afford it, the best option was to hire a live-in Japanese couple for $100 per month, precisely what the Pattons did. Goto cooked and gardened while his wife, Kani, cleaned and served the food.

The Pattons moved into a traditional U-shaped Hawaiian home with an open court and a lanai (a roofed and screened-in porch). The house was spacious and included a living room with fireplace, dining room, kitchen, four bedrooms, two bathrooms, two servants' rooms, and lots of closets.[16] The climate on Oahu was cool but humid, making one "wet like a melon in an ice box," as per George's description, but it reminded him of growing up in California.[17]

Hawaii was an ideal location for those who enjoyed active and outdoor living. Beatrice was soon gardening, inspired by the beautiful flowers and luscious trees she saw everywhere. Nearby were plenty of places to picnic and a "valley full of burial caves where chiefs in their armor were buried."[18] While no one else seemed to go to these remote locations, the Pattons were always out and about. In a note to her father-in-law, Beatrice described a visit to Māui as "heavenly,"

> Georgie has been in bed by 9 (!!!) every night & takes a long nap every after-noon!!! . . . we have a lot of horses which the kids catch & ride around & I lead the small fry on a pony with the cutest little stock saddle you ever saw. This is <u>much</u> nicer than we expected in every way. We don't dress up at all & the Dillingham crowd is just near enough for society - about 3 miles. This place is a sort of paradise for children—everything to play with & nothing to hurt them. Monday, B., R.E., & I are going on a 5 day camping trip into the crater & out the ditch trail.[19]

One of the most famous beaches in the world was just a stone's throw away from Schofield Barracks. Waikiki Beach was once the playground of Hawaiian royalty who enjoyed the fantastic surf on an early version of a longboard. However, by 1925, there were only monied visitors from the mainland who enjoyed partaking in Hawaiian luaus—a beach feast with traditional food, like poi and poke, and entertainment, like the ukulele and the hula.

Despite a name that translates as 'spouting fresh water,' Waikiki Beach was originally a wetland and a breeding ground for disease. The man responsible for draining almost a thousand acres of swamp was Walter Dillingham, the most prominent member of Hawaiian society and husband of Louise Gaylord, an old school friend of Kay. The Pattons and the Dillinghams, whom the children called Uncle Walter and Aunt Louise, became immediate and lifelong friends. "Of all the men I have met in a long life," George wrote Walter in 1942, as he embarked on his greatest adventure, "I have liked you best."

Walter Dillingham was born in Honolulu in 1885 to Emma Louise Smith, a missionary's daughter, and Benjamin Franklin Dillingham, a successful busi-nessman who was the founder of the Oahu Railway and Land Company.[20] Benjamin had ended up in Hawaii by happenstance in 1865—he was the first officer on a clipper when he broke his leg riding a horse—but he played a significant role in the development of the islands. His son followed in his footsteps. After attending school in Massachusetts, Walter returned to Oahu and founded the Hawaiian Dredging Company. Around the time of the Pattons' arrival, Walter had just about completed the Ala Wai Canal near Waikiki Beach, but he was also responsible for the dredging of Pearl Harbor and the building of its dry docks.

When Walter was not at La Pietra—his villa on the slopes of Diamond Head where he lived with his wife and four children—he could be found on the polo fields of the Dillingham Ranch, on the North Shore of Oahu. He was the organizer of the first polo team on the island, the co-founder of the Hawaii Polo and Racing Club, and a frequent victor at the Inter-Island Tournament. Until now, the Army's performance had been below par, but when George assumed command of the Army Polo team, Walter Dillingham finally met his match.

POLO IS ARGUABLY one of the oldest team sports in the world, originating with Central Asian nomads who played it in preparation for war.[21] Centuries later, the U.S. Army recognized the game as good preparation for leadership and they footed the bill for the first Army Polo team to be established in 1896. George himself believed that polo was "a vital professional asset . . . [and] the nearest approach to mounted combat which can be secured in peace."[22] So, he built and organized the first polo field and team at Fort Sheridan in 1910. And since there wasn't much chance of winning a game riding a horse provided by the Army, he often loaned his personal horses to his teammates.

There was a good reason polo was known as the 'sport of kings,' because one needed a fortune to be able to play. A polo game comprises between six and eight chukkers—also known as chukkas or periods—of seven-and-a-half minutes each, wherein two teams of four vie to hit a wooden ball between two posts on either end of a grassy field.[23] Since the game is so taxing, a player in a high-caliber game needs to change his horse after almost every chukker, meaning each team can require up to twenty-four polo ponies, so named not because of their size but because of their agility.

George brought part of his stable to Hawaii—including Barbara Breeze, Javelin, Star Shell, and Bull Run (chosen as the best polo pony in the Hawaiian Department in 1926)—and soon employed three grooms to help care for them in addition to his family.[24] A stickler for rules and regulations whose high standards applied as much to his soldiers as to his family, George was highly particular about how his ten horses were exercised daily. Little Bee and Ruth Ellen were already accomplished equestrians, but exercising polo ponies was a different matter.

Every morning the whole family rode along the pineapple plantations surrounding Schofield Barracks. When the Inter-Island Tournament took place at the end of August—the social event of the season since 1902, with teams from Oahu, Māui, and Kauai competing against each other in a weeklong contest—the Pattons rented a bungalow at the Halekulani Hotel and rode the horses across the park into the warm waters of Waikiki Beach for an invigorating swim.

"The polo here is not much," was George's astute assessment of Army polo when he first arrived on the islands. However, by the time of his first Inter-Island Tournament in August 1925, the newspapers hailed the new team as "Schofield's Crack Polo Quartet."[25] A year later, with the Crown Prince of Sweden and his wife in attendance, the Army team won the tournament for the first time since 1912, beating Dillingham's Oahu team and the Māui team of the Baldwins.[26]

*Figure 40. Walter Dillingham (left) and George Patton competing in 1926. (Library of Congress)*

Polo is a spectator sport, and the eight chukkers of each tournament game made for an exciting afternoon. Nowhere else in the world could one enjoy a polo game with a backdrop of luscious mountains and the sound of crashing waves in the distance. Shiny black cars lined the playing field as guests prepared to tailgate, while the grandstand filled with the Army and high society of Hawaii.

Whether the experience was as much fun for the worrying Beatrice is in doubt, but she gamely took part in the heart-pounding experience of watching her husband ride his ponies at thirty miles an hour across a 300-by-160-yard field. George's ardor bordered on recklessness but nowhere more so than on the polo field, where neither pain nor Beatrice could stop him from playing as if his life depended on it.

Being accident-prone did not make George any more careful, and his medical file grew thicker by the month. One time when his head was split open by a mallet, he merely wedged an iodine-soaked cotton wad underneath his hat and continued the game, while another time, he held his head over a bucket to protect his clothes from blood while a veterinarian, the only doctor in the vicinity, stitched his umpteenth head wound.

George praised himself lucky to have a wife who had "so much sense about Polo," but her cavalier attitude hid a trembling heart.[27] After a nasty fall during a steeplechase in 1913 where he had sustained serious injuries to his scalp, Beatrice had written Aunt Nannie that there wasn't "a bit of use in worrying about him. I sort of hate to have him race, but the best way to keep him to his senses seems to be not to oppose him in any way."[28]

Beatrice learned to take his mishaps in stride and adopted a laissez-faire attitude, allowing her to remain calm in the most trying circumstances. One day during the thirties, her tea party was interrupted by a gunshot from the upstairs bedroom where George was cleaning his guns. The bullet traveled through the ceiling and landed near Beatrice's feet, but to the consternation of everyone present, she merely shrugged, "I wish he'd be more careful."[29]

"A TOUR of duty in Hawaii cannot fail to enrich one's knowledge and experience and to fill the mind with memories that will be cherished through life," wrote Major General Summerall, commander of the Hawaiian Department from 1921 until 1924 and a close friend of the Pattons.[30] This sentiment was especially true for Beatrice, "who love[d] to study character."[31]

"Every mountain, every valley, every point of land and every bay of the eight islands carries its own story," an exalted Beatrice noted. "When I realized that the scholars, the singers and the cowboys that I met were the grandchildren, and might even be the children of the men whose stone adzes I picked up under the kiawi trees, I began my study of Hawaii Nei . . . visiting remote places, listening to legends, collecting a patchwork scrapbook which has been my keenest pleasure."[32]

The first missionaries had arrived on the Sandwich Islands—a name given by James Cook in 1778—on March 30, 1820, just ten years after King Kamehameha I unified the islands. While the monarchy would survive until the United States annexed Hawaii in 1898, the Kapu system—Hawaii's ancient laws, including a ban on men and women eating together—was already abolished in 1819 when King Kamehameha II shared a symbolic meal with the women of his court. So, it was perfect timing when the *Thaddeus* dropped off fourteen New England missionaries, whose Western practices and beliefs quickly filled the void left by the loss of the Kapu system.

While Beatrice enjoyed socializing with the likes of the Dillinghams, it was the indigenous culture that truly spoke to her. Just three miles from Schofield Barracks lay the Kūkaniloko birthstones, where royal women came to give birth in the presence of up to thirty-six ali'i (chiefs); they uttered no sound, hence its name, "to anchor the cry from within." Her discovery of Oahu's Piko (navel) as she rode through the sugarcane fields changed her thinking. Although she would always admire the missionaries' courage in leaving Boston for the unknown, Beatrice quickly changed her focus to the Kānaka Maoli when she read about the hardships they suffered, from their lack of immunity against the diseases brought from the mainland to the suppression of their local culture.

The true beauty of Hawaii lay in the history and the culture of the Native Hawaiians who arrived from Polynesia almost fourteen hundred years before the missionaries. When Walter Dillingham realized Beatrice's interest went beyond the average tourist's curiosity, he introduced her to Captain Douglas Crane. Friendly with many locals, Captain Crane then introduced Beatrice to Hamana Kalili, a local fisherman who is said to be the originator of the Shaka sign—a fist with a raised thumb and little finger.

Born in 1882 in Laie on Oahu, Hamana lost the three middle fingers of his right hand in an accident at the Kahuku Sugar Mill. No longer able to work as a sugar cane presser, he became a security officer for the Kahuku Station, tasked with preventing local rascals from jumping on the trains. Seeing Kalili gesture with his right hand was a strange sight, but the children quickly adopted the motion to signal that the coast was clear. A traditional Hawaiian greeting was born, and the Shaka eventually became a sign of respect and friendliness to surfers worldwide.[33]

Beatrice first met Kalili, whom she described as a "magnificent example of the pure Hawaiian," when she joined Captain Crane to buy some fresh lobsters. Kalili was a renowned fisherman, and Beatrice looked on in amazement as he dove off the lava rocks and resurfaced a few minutes later, holding a lobster he caught with his bare hands. He took an immediate liking to Beatrice, a "concerned listener" who always showed an interest in what others told her, and he took her to the village of Laie to meet his family and friends.[34]

Normally wary of outsiders, the people of Laie didn't take long to fall under Beatrice's spell. Her respectful behavior and appropriate actions made them open up, and before long, they were sharing ancient songs and stories they had hardly ever shared before. They also taught Beatrice how to prepare poi, a creamy paste made from cooked taro root, which tasted sweet when eaten immediately or sour when left to ferment. Once Beatrice discovered this staple was the secret to the Hawaiians' beautiful teeth, she served poi for breakfast every day. However, George made it abundantly clear from the first bite that he hated the purple dish.

SINCE THERE WAS no room at Schofield Barracks for Miss Dennett and she was let go before the family left Pride's Crossing, Beatrice had no choice but to send her daughters to an actual school in the fall of 1925. To the surprise of everyone, after just one year, Little Bee asked to go to boarding school on the East Coast instead. Unlike Ruth Ellen, who loved learning to dance the hula and play the ukulele, Little Bee yearned for ballet classes and piano lessons.

Beatrice knew "it [would] be a bit hard to leave Punch," but George made her see that their daughter was growing up and it was important to let her go. She consulted her sister-in-law, Theodora, whose daughters—Theodora and Anne—had recently graduated from the Foxcroft School in Middleburg, Virginia.[35] Beatrice bit her tongue for the sake of her brother and daughter when the outspoken and haughty Theodora pointed out the slim chance of Little Bee getting into Foxcroft since the Patton name was unknown in society. They were only in the Army, but Theodora promised to put in a good word with Miss Noland, Foxcroft's founder and headmistress.

Whether Theodora had anything to do with Little Bee ultimately being accepted is unknown, but Big Bee and Little Bee left for Virginia in September 1926 while George began the most domesticated three months of his life. Beatrice left him with a detailed list of instructions on how to care for the house and the children, all with the help of a retinue of servants and neighbors. "My popularity as a elegable bachelor continues to such a degree that I am loved and replete with bad food," he wrote Beatrice on November 22.[36]

Except for the removal of his tonsils, two-and-a-half-year-old George IV was not much trouble since he spent most of his time taken care of by Miss Holmes.[37] However, George had his hands full with eleven-year-old Ruth Ellen, both his greatest nemesis and admirer. As per Beatrice's instructions because she disapproved of the cafeteria food at the Leiehua School, George picked up his daughter for lunch every day. Fresh and healthy food was as important to Beatrice as a clean plate, and she was appalled that George was never made to eat what he didn't like as a child.

Even though George tried to change his behavior for his wife's sake, he remained a difficult eater. So when Goto prepared a Hawaiian delicacy called breadfruit for lunch one day, neither George nor Ruth Ellen had any intention of trying the sweet custardy flesh full of vitamins and antioxidants.[38] Eager to please Beatrice by enforcing discipline, George ordered his daughter to eat the breadfruit or "take a licking," but to his surprise and embarrassment, she chose the latter. While hesitant, George was nonetheless not about to be outmaneuvered by a wily teenager who was as stubborn as he was, and he told her to go pick out a whip.

Watching the proceedings from the children's table in the corner, young George and Miss Holmes's eyes grew wide when Ruth Ellen returned with the meanest looking whip, which was also the least painful. "That didn't hurt," she defiantly told her stoic father after he struck her leg with his hunting whip. Lunch then proceeded with neither one touching their breadfruit, but a guilt-ridden George wrote Beatrice a letter that evening offering her a divorce since he had mistreated their daughter.

Beatrice—who usually sided with her husband anyway—couldn't hold a sin against him that she had regretfully committed herself. "I think I'm a good mother," she once said, "but I can remember all too well punishing my children in the heat of disappointment or shock and wishing later I hadn't. In fact I would have given my right hand—not to have given some of those spankings."[39]

Ruth Ellen's relationship with her father was loving but tempestuous. From the moment she could write, she made notes of the stories he told because she felt there was something special about him, but she refused to accept his authority at face value and always spoke back at him, often more bluntly than even Beatrice. This both intrigued and frustrated George, and his behavior toward Ruth Ellen oscillated between "putting her down, teasing her and loving her."[40] Mr. Patton, however, advised his son that Ruth Ellen "must be ridden with a light rein, and an easy snaffle bit. You will neither do yourself or her any good, by using curb and spur."[41]

AFTER REACHING the pinnacle of success and familial happiness, the Woods were struck by a series of tragedies, which culminated in William's suicide on February 2, 1926. Spending the winter at the Hotel Ormond in Daytona, Florida, for health reasons (both his and his wife's), William drove off with his valet early that Tuesday morning. When the limousine came to a quiet stretch of highway, William asked his driver to pull over. He walked away between the trees, placed a .38-caliber revolver in his mouth, and pulled the trigger. William Wood was dead at the age of sixty-eight.

His problems began with the Lawrence Textile Strike of 1912, caused by a Massachusetts law limiting the workweek for women and children to fifty-four hours. The resulting reduction in the hours of the male employees—because the mills were unable to run without a complete workforce—led to peaceful protests. These quickly turned violent when members of the Industrial Workers of the World (IWW), a labor union formed in Chicago in 1905, took charge of the strike. When dynamite was found across Lawrence to bring discredit to the IWW, William Wood was framed as the mastermind and charged with conspiracy. However, he was eventually acquitted, and the ordeal led him to reconsider his stance on social issues.[42]

*Figure 41. William Wood named the Ayer Mill after his father-in-law, who rang the first bell at 9 p.m. on October 3, 1910. The Ayer Mill Clock Tower — with a clock-face just six inches smaller than Big Ben — forever changed the skyline of Lawrence. (Lawrence Public Library)*

The 'Bread and Roses' strike was nothing compared to the loss of his youngest daughter Irene to the Spanish Flu, and the loss of his son William when his $18,000 car crashed into a telephone pole during an impromptu race on the roads of Reading, Massachusetts. As if losing two of his four children and watching his wife suffer ill health for years wasn't bad enough, William was also forced out of the company he transformed into the greatest textile corporation in the world, with 40,000 employees working across sixty mills. Worried his personal issues were clouding his vision, shareholders of the American Woolen Company were relieved when Wood, who had recently suffered a series of strokes, signed his resignation papers on December 31, 1924.

The fate which befell his brother-in-law "Billy" was exactly like the "nasty morbid thought" George described to Beatrice in 1909. There were moments when "an awful fear" came to him "that some thing horrible is going to happen to me or those I love to sort of eaven up for the wonderful joys I have had lately and those that I may have in the future."[43] Over the years, however, that thought must have faded because it directly juxtaposed with how he now spurred Beatrice to hunt more frequently.

Ever since the birth of George IV, Beatrice felt free to be as daring as her husband, and she took a greater interest in hunting and jumping. During their stay at Sunset Rock, she had started traversing hunting jumps under the watchful eye of her husband and brother. Then, for her thirty-ninth birthday, in

January 1925, George gave her a black mare called Dinah, whom he trained to be the perfect jumping companion. Just like his father-in-law once surprised his wife, by having her favorite tree planted outside her window in the middle of the night, George surprised his own wife, by bringing Dinah into the living room while his daughters kept Beatrice occupied upstairs.

After dropping off Bee at Foxcroft on the beautiful hunting grounds of Middleburg in September 1926, Beatrice went to the North Shore to be entertained for the next few weeks by friends and family.[44] She had some business to attend to regarding her father's estate but spent most of her time on horseback, hunting several times a week. George egged her on in every letter he wrote, even though he hated "to have you hurt more than to be hurt my self."[45]

Not to be outdone by the husband who taught her that the thrill of hunting outweighed the threat of injury, Beatrice became ever bolder while on horseback. Unfortunately, she took a terrible spill one frosty November morning out hunting with the Myopia Hunt Club. She was either thrown from her horse during a jump or crushed when her horse stumbled and fell on top of her, and by the time Fred reached his sister, she was unconscious and remained so for several hours. It is unclear to what extent Beatrice was injured—her departure to Hawaii was delayed by several weeks—but the poem she wrote on November 13 was pretty revealing.

Why must you drag me back?
Death would have been so sweet!
I gallop through the orchard pied with sunlight
My blood fast racing.
The hoofs of all the field pounding accompaniment,
And then, swift as a lightning flash, the fall—
And waken in God's arms.
What's this? No, I do not remember—
Oh, my death!
Please, doctor, let me die—don't bring me back.
Yes, I am winning though—broken, you say?
What matters it, so long as I can live to feel your arms about me;
Never to hear his little feet come pounding down the hall,
Never to feel your lips on mine again—
Dear God, be merciful and grant my prayer;
Grant me a few more years of life![46]

BEATRICE RECOVERED SUFFICIENTLY by December 1926 to travel to Lake Vineyard for the holidays, where she found her father-in-law in one of his wistful moods. Mr. Patton had felt ill since the spring of 1926 when he visited Schofield Barracks with his family (minus Aunt Nannie, who was afraid to catch leprosy), and he revealed at Christmastime that he was recently diagnosed with tuberculosis in his left kidney.[47] He probably contracted the disease from his uncle William Glassell, but his condition was exacerbated by a lifetime of drinking—a habit he shared with Aunt Nannie—and his constant worry over financial ruin.

The Pattons returned to Schofield Barracks on January 22, 1927, only to be notified within days that Mr. Patton's condition suddenly deteriorated to such an extent that an operation to remove his kidney became unavoidable. At Beatrice's urging, George requested a three-week leave and sailed back to Los Angeles. The image of his father waving goodbye as he was wheeled to the operating room stayed with George for the rest of his life, his "calmness and assurance" in the face of death requiring such courage it would "have won the Medal of Honor on any field of battle."[48]

Although very weak, Mr. Patton survived the operation, and he spent the next two weeks recuperating with his Boy by his bedside. He talked an awful lot about mysticism and prophesies—an interest he acquired in 1924 while traveling with Ruth and Nita through Egypt—but it was apparent that he had lost the will to live. "I hear that you have got your self on your mind and dont eat etc.," George wrote upon his return to Hawaii. "Of course if you want to die that is the best way to secure the end desired. You will now say that I dont understand you and that you cant help it. You can if you will. With all the people who love you and want you to live it is selfish and poor sportsmanship to act as you are doing."[49]

George kept up his relentless cheerleading, which bordered on ruthlessness. However, Mr. Patton's slow recovery and the death of his friend, colleague, and neighbor, Henry Huntington, on May 23, hastened his demise.[50] On or about June 8, George received a cablegram at Schofield Barracks that his father was failing rapidly, and he had only been out at sea two days when a radio message awakened him. Mr. Patton passed away at 7:40 a.m. on June 10, 1927, at the Good Samaritan Hospital, three months shy of his seventy-first birthday.

Beatrice immediately booked passage on the *S.S. Cleveland* for herself and Ruth Ellen and chased George across the Pacific Ocean. She felt the loss of Mr. Patton as keenly as the loss of her own father and knew the effect his passing would have on her husband. "He loves you so much," Beatrice wrote Mr. Patton years earlier, "that you can keep him in order better than anyone else in the world."[51] That task would now rest squarely on her shoulders.

While Mr. Patton's death was not the national news that Mr. Ayer's had been, he was nonetheless remembered as a "noted figure in Southern California's history ... whose death severs a close link between the old and the new California."[52] He had been a vestryman at the Church of Our Savior for so long that the reverend was barely able to contain his emotions during the funeral service on June 13.[53]

The small church, built by Benjamin Wilson sixty years earlier, was filled to the brim with friends and family, but George would not arrive until two days later. He sent word from aboard ship not to delay the funeral, a blessing in disguise according to Bee, who happened to be traveling west to begin her summer leave from Foxcroft when her grandfather had died.

Bee confided to her mother that the things she had witnessed in the days before the funeral were so horrendous that she was relieved her father hadn't been there. Lake Vineyard had been filled with an unbearable sound of wailing that cut right through the bone, from the Mexican employees who worked for the family for so long they even remembered Benjamin Wilson, to an Irish contingent led by George's nanny, Mary Scally.

However, this was nothing compared to the screams coming from Aunt Nannie's locked bedroom. No one who set foot in Lake Vineyard between June 10 and June 13 could understand how Ruth and Nita sat in stony silence next to the coffin of their husband and father while Aunt Nannie screamed for Mr. Patton to take her, lamenting that she should have been his wife and Georgie should have been her son.

As soon as he arrived at Lake Vineyard, George went to the San Gabriel Cemetery to say goodbye to his best friend. He stood next to Mr. Patton's grave weeping for an hour, suddenly realizing "that the grave no more held Papa than does one of his discarded suits hanging in a closet."

George first saw his father walking among the gravestones, then again two days later as he was cleaning out his office (a veritable shrine to his Boy). On the wall hung the saddle of Cárdenas whom George had (possibly) killed during the Mexican Punitive Expedition, and the shell of a sea turtle he had harpooned off Catalina Island. In the safe, he found the pieces of family history that spurred him to greatness: the gold piece that saved his grandfather's life during the Civil War and a blood-stained shirttail containing the shell fragment that killed him just a few months later.

Just like Beatrice, George wondered incessantly whether he had been a good son, but these visitations made him realize that his father was all right and their separation was only temporary. He closed this chapter of his life by writing a brief biography titled *My Father as I Knew Him*, ending his epithet on July 9, 1927:

Oh! darling Papa. I never called you that in life as both of us were too self contained but you were and are my darling. I have often thought that life for me was too easy but the loss of you has gone far [to] even my count with those whom before I have pitied. God grant that you see and appreciate my very piteous attempt to show here your lovely life. I never did much for you and you did all for me. Accept this as a slight offering of what I would have done. Your devoted son G S Patton Jr[54]

---

WHEN CAPTAIN VANCOUVER arrived on the Sandwich Islands in 1791—the second to do so after Captain Cook in 1778—he couldn't help but notice how years of chieftain wars had impoverished the inhabitants. Since there were no large animals on the islands, he brought along six cows and one bull for King Kamehameha I when he returned in 1793. To propagate the breed, the king released the animals into the wild and implemented a Kapu, prohibiting anyone from killing them. Unfortunately, things quickly got out of hand; when a young man from Massachusetts named John Parker jumped ship in 1809, the Big Island was overrun with cattle.

Industrious and enterprising, John quickly became the errand boy of King Kamehameha I. He left to fight in the War of 1812, but when he returned three years later carrying a shiny American musket, the king gave his old friend permission to hunt the now thousands of cows that roamed the island. In addition to considerable wealth, John's friendship with Kamehameha also brought him a wife—the king's granddaughter, Chiefess Kipikane—and two acres of land on the slopes of Mauna Kea. When King Kamehameha III opened the door to private land ownership in 1848, with a piece of legislation called The Great Māhele, John purchased over fifteen hundred acres of additional land.

The descendants of John Parker turned out to be somewhat eccentric, and in 1899 a lawyer named Alfred Wellington Carter was brought in as manager of the Parker Ranch to ward off financial ruin. One of the changes he instituted was the shift from mainly breeding cattle to mainly breeding horses, which included providing mounts to the Cavalry Remount Service. So it came to be that Major Patton—an expert horseman whose knowledge of equines was second-to-none—received orders in April 1927 to visit the Parker Ranch and buy one hundred horses for the Field Artillery.

George had the greatest difficulty persuading Beatrice not to flee east when Bee was admitted to the hospital with appendicitis, but the suggestion of turning his first visit to the Parker Ranch into a family vacation did the trick. After all, Beatrice always wanted to visit Volcano House to see the Halema'u-ma'u crater and Punalu'u Beach to walk in the black sand.

*Figure 42.* Anne Ayer Steward—daughter of Chilly and Theodora—
spending her honeymoon on the Parker Ranch with Aunt B and Uncle
Georgie in late 1927. (Courtesy of Scott C. Steward)

The first inter-island flight did not take place until 1929, and steamships remained the go-to mode of transportation between the Hawaiian Islands until the fifties. The *S.S. Hualālai* left Honolulu at 4 p.m. every Tuesday and Friday and arrived at Hilo Harbor on the Island of Hawaii at 8 a.m. after a 211-mile trip. Curiosity getting the best of her as usual, Beatrice immediately befriended the skipper, who was so charmed by her sailing experience that he chattered away all evening, telling her stories of old Hawaii, which she would ultimately weave into a book.

The Pattons debarked on the Big Island, and drove sixty miles along the coastal road to the Parker Ranch. As they traveled north along what is now Route 19, the landscape on their right was dominated by the rugged Hāmākua coastline and countless sugarcane plantations. On their left, they had to crane their necks to search for the top of Mauna Kea, the White Mountain so named for its snowy peak. At one point, they saw the destruction of an old lava stream, then suddenly a rainforest and the Akaka and Kahūnā Falls.

When they finally arrived at the Parker Ranch, situated between the slopes of Mauna Kea and Mauna Loa, near the town of Waimea, their guest house was ready and dinner was served. The paniolos—local cowboys so named because they spoke Español—had already driven down the horses from the mountain by the time the visitors awoke the next morning. After checking the horses their teeth, jaws, nostrils, eyes, legs, and tails, George marked them as either impossible, possible, or probable.

It took him most of the day to select sixty-six horses under the watchful eye of his wife and daughter, and when they returned exhausted to their room after a long day in the sun, they discovered all their belongings had been moved to a bigger house on the ranch. Mr. Carter had been so impressed with George's knowledge of horses, not to mention Beatrice's charm, that he decided to accommodate the Pattons in the nicest guest house near his own so he could get to know them better.

The following day, Mr. Carter took the Pattons to see his world-famous thoroughbreds. They roamed "the slope of a quiescent volcano, rugged enough to develop wonderful feet and bone, and steep enough to give fine endurance." Interested in a "hunter/jumper Thoroughbred," George immediately fell in love with the first horse Mr. Carter showed, a chestnut gelding called Konohiki (Hawaiian for trustee). The second horse Mr. Carter brought out was just as impressive, and the Pattons made another purchase, thus beginning a lifelong professional and personal relationship.

Writing Mr. Carter from Morocco after the invasion of North Africa in 1942, George often thought "of the happy times I had in Hawaii with you and your family and look forward to the day, which I think is distant, when I shall be able to return."[55]

BEATRICE AYER PATTON lived her life according to one adage, "Interested people are interesting." This philosophy made her an exceptional army wife, beloved wherever she went. Those who knew her by reputation only—wasn't she a snobby heiress?—were pleasantly surprised by how down-to-earth she was when first meeting her. Others were instantly charmed by her innate shyness and unaffected nature.

Those who knew only her husband imagined her to be a "big woman, with a tanned skin and a loud voice"; instead, "they saw this little figure with tiny hands and feet, and a tiny face with astounding blue eyes." Her eyes were the first thing people noticed about her—a trait she inherited from her father, who was known to have the kindest eyes—and they sparkled with a genuine interest in, and concern for, others.

Usually a quiet and reserved man, Mr. Carter felt so comfortable with Beatrice that he spewed out stories of Hawaii and his ancestors. First, he proudly showed her and Ruth Ellen around the Parker Ranch, beginning with the Mana Hale, John Parker's ancestral home, which stood next to the family cemetery. Mother and daughter sensed "passing laughter and people moving about" as they toured the house; it was what the Hawaiians called mana, the spiritual energy of power and strength in all persons and objects.[56] Next, they toured the ranch on horseback, from the Humu'ula Sheep Station with its Merino sheep and the slopes of Mauna Kea teeming with wild turkeys and pheasants, to the Paliho'oūkapapa (the old dairy) and Puako Bay.

The paniolos were the lifeblood of the Parker Ranch, with their wide pantaloons and red belly sashes, knife cases on their belts, and catch-ropes within easy reach. Most of the fresh meat consumed on the Hawaiian Islands came from the Parker Ranch, and it was quite the spectacle to watch the paniolos riding their horses into the surf and swimming the cattle to the waiting boats where ropes hoisted them on board. There was so much to see and do at the Parker Ranch, a "quite fudal and most interesting place," that the Pattons left "with six rolls of movie film."[57]

Miles and miles of dried lava tubes ran beneath the Parker Ranch like a labyrinth, but the only signs they existed were the cinder cones that dotted the land—small mounds of dried lava formed around volcanic vents. Beatrice's curiosity was evident in the questions she asked the paniolos, and she wanted to know all about the burial cave not far from the stables. When one paniolo revealed that he had attended the funeral of his great-grandfather inside that cave, surrounded by the mummified bodies of his ancestors who appeared as tall as giants, Beatrice immediately rode out to the cinder cone. She had heard about the giants who once roamed the Hawaiian Islands, and nothing would satisfy her curiosity but seeing one with her own eyes. However, wary of outsiders and afraid of being ridiculed, the Native Hawaiians had closed off the cave decades earlier.

Since the "Hawaiian Islands are honeycombed with caves," Mr. Carter introduced Beatrice to an old friend who knew the location of an accessible one.[58] She and Ruth Ellen drove sixty miles to the southwestern part of the island and the settlement of Pu'uhonua o Hōnaunau (the City of Refuge). When a commoner broke a Kapu, or a warrior suffered defeat in battle, he could escape death (and the wrath of the gods) by fleeing to this place of refuge where his sins were absolved.

The beachfront settlement was dotted with black lava rocks and giant kii— wooden images of the gods protecting the Hale o Keawe Heiau, a sacred temple with the bones of twenty-three ali'i. It was impressive, but the trio was there to hike the 1871 Trail around Alahaka Bay to the Keanae'e Cliff. To get to the entrance of "the grave of the common people," it was necessary to descend the Alahaka Ramp by rope. Beatrice wrote in her notebook about her experience:

> The entrance was not impressive, a roundish hole in the cliff face, but once inside, we saw by our lighted candles rows and rows of coffins, crowded together. Our guide said, "Beyond these are the skeletons of the old people, nine and ten feet tall." But since he did not offer to go further back, I contended

myself with what I could see in the main cave. Some of the coffins were open, the tenants within mummified by the dry air. There were withered leis about their necks, and each with some little treasure to comfort him in the next world. One head rested on a fancy pillow, one had a hairbrush snuggled against his cheek, and my candle caught the glint of more than one pocket mirror.[59]

Adventure always lurked within Beatrice, but unlike the eleven-year-old girl who took a mummified toe while visiting a burial chamber in Egypt, the forty-one-year-old woman didn't take anything from the burial cave. However, she got something much more precious out of her recent exploits across Hawaii: a closer relationship with her youngest daughter.

Until her sister left for boarding school, Ruth Ellen had always felt closer to her father because her mother was much harder to read. Surprisingly, she considered her mother distant and formidable, until the two of them started going on excursions together, and she realized "Ma" was "a lot of fun." They learned to speak Hawaiian, dance the hula, and play the ukulele, and together they waited in high anticipation for a weekly letter from Foxcroft.

ONE OF GEORGE'S most ardent supporters sailed into Honolulu Harbor in January 1928 to become the new commander of the Hawaiian Division. The Pattons were waiting on the quay with their arms filled with leis to welcome their close friends, General and Mrs. Conner. While their friendship began because the Conners were so intrigued by George's remarkable carriage, Beatrice and Bug had much in common.

Not only did their fathers run successful patent medicine businesses, neither Mr. Ayer nor Mr. Brandreth liked the idea of their daughters marrying officers, hence the title of Bug's eventual memoir, *What Father Forbad*. Life as an army wife "was often exhausting [but] it was seldom boring," primarily because of all the interesting people Bug met. Of those, the Pattons "were the most interesting and unusual couple I have ever known."

The last time they all spent quality time together was in the summer of 1921 when the Pattons had invited the Conners to be their guests on a deep-sea fishing trip to Florida. They left Washington's Union Station on June 14, George almost missing his train because "he played polo until the last moment." Bug was intrigued by the Pattons' carry-on bags. Beatrice's contained "a straw hat, a box of pills and a pair of nail scissors," while George's contained "a pair of socks, a bottle of eye drops, four magnificent reels and a small jar of Elizabeth Arden's Orange Skin Food," not for his face, but as "reel lubricant."

*Figure 43. Beatrice and her catch. (Library of Congress)*

Sailing from Boca Grande to Key West on the *Ladyfish*—a 75-foot houseboat more luxurious than some of the army housing the Conners had lived in—the friends spent several days near Captiva Pass fishing tarpon. Beatrice's "first tarpon jumped so near the boat that it struck her and left her entire side bruised, besides plastering a scale on her cheek," while Bug caught a case of beginner's luck and reeled in three tarpons her first day.

The vacation ended with a trip to Havana—where Bug had met her husband in 1900 and where Beatrice had traveled as a child—and a stroll along the Paseo del Prado, where Beatrice suddenly remarked her pants were falling down. "They've gone," she whispered to Bug before she could catch them, so "she stepped out of the filmy garment, tucked it under her arm and our husbands never even saw what happened."[60]

Unfortunately, the Conners arrived at the end of the Pattons' three-year foreign service.[61] Hawaii had been paradise on a personal level, but professionally things had begun to unravel for George as soon as he had arrived. His teetotaling superior, Colonel Lowbar, had asked him to spy on a major he suspected of serving bootlegged liquor. Typically one to follow orders to a T, George had refused, causing the relationship between the two men and their wives to become a little strained.

Mrs. Lowbar condescendingly snubbed Beatrice at social functions, until her husband's reassignment to Boston when she came knocking for some letters of introduction. Mrs. Patton, who hated poseurs, claimed "her family were just simple country folk who lived outside Boston," not the kind of people Mrs. Lowbar would be interested in getting to know.[62]

George's circumstances had brightened considerably when he became the Hawaiian Division's G-3 (Operations Officer) in November 1926, a function he coveted for months as it allowed him to train and prepare troops for combat. Even though there was no war on the horizon, George had been as zealous as ever, and soon his habit of being "too positive in his thinking and too outspoken in his remarks" had cost him his new position.

Coming to the islands had felt like a chore in 1925, but the entire family was having such a marvelous time that three years later they hated "the thought of leaving."[63] Unfortunately, George's request for an extension was denied, and he was reassigned to the Office of the Chief of Cavalry at the War Department in Washington.

At least George's stay ended on a high note, with a glowing performance review written by General Conner: "I have known him for fifteen years, in both peace and war. I know of no one whom I would prefer to have as a subordinate commander."[64]

BEATRICE WORKED on *Légendes Hawaiiennes* for four years, a collection of Hawaiian legends she translated into French to challenge herself. She privately published the book in 1932, to George's great relief, who worried "it will be a great disappointment to her if she does not."[65] *Légendes Hawaiiennes* is quite rare—it was printed in a limited quantity and mainly distributed to Beatrice's friends and family—and valued for its beautiful illustrations by Juliette May Fraser, a local Hawaiian artist. A second book, *Love Without End,* was published posthumously and compared the old and the new Hawaii. In its preface, Beatrice wrote, "Every person I ever met in Hawaii contributed to it. It is with Aloha that I make my offering."

Emma Ahuena Taylor was part ali'i—a Native Hawaiian aristocrat—and part American. She was a fervent suffragist known throughout the islands for her detailed knowledge of Hawaiian history and genealogy.[66] An accomplished writer who wrote in flourishing romantic sentences, which influenced Beatrice's own writing, Emma served as president of the Daughters and Sons of Hawaii for many years.[67]

Upon meeting Beatrice for the first time in 1927, Emma knew she had finally found the perfect person to help "perpetuate the memory and spirit of old Hawaii," precisely what the Daughters and Sons of Hawaii set out to do. Not a day passed that Emma didn't show up on Beatrice's doorstep or call with some important story she suddenly remembered, typical of a kupuna whose job it was to pass on stories to the next generation.[68] Through Emma, Beatrice met the most important Kānaka Maoli, no matter where they lived.

There was nothing Beatrice wouldn't do to satisfy her curiosity. When she visited Ruth Ellen and her cousin Clifford Watson on Māui, where they spent part of their summer vacation at the Ulapalakua Ranch, the three of them went on a four-day camping trip to the Haleakalā Crater. Riding to the top on horseback, they spent their first night in a rundown guesthouse at the edge of the crater, which had a circumference of twenty miles and was 2500 feet deep. When they awoke at five o'clock in the morning, they discovered why the volcano's name translated to 'house of the sun.'

Legend has it that this most spectacular sunrise was created by the demigod Māui, after whom the island was named. His mother, Hina, was an artisan who made kapa, and this Hawaiian bark cloth needed a lot of sun to dry. So when his mother complained about how short the days were, Māui climbed to the top of Haleakalā and waited to capture the rising sun with a lasso, "compelling him to move more slowly through the heavens."[69]

The weather was chilly at 10,023 feet above sea level, and there were clouds as far as the eye could see. As they watched the stars fade away and night turn to day, mother, daughter, and cousin experienced what Mark Twain described as "the sublimest spectacle I ever witnessed."[70] After breakfast, the trio began their descent, camping on the crater floor for their second night. Once they traversed the crater, they spent their third night at the home of a Chinese shop owner and their fourth night at the house of a retired paniolo.

Of the Kānaka Maoli, Beatrice wrote in her notebook, "They were a race of storytellers whose history, stretching back into the twilight of antiquity, was handed down by word of mouth. Battles and love tales, genealogies and voyages of discovery, legends of gods and kings, were sung for hundreds of years by chanters trained for that purpose."[71]

Even though the missionaries brought with them the written language, the Native Hawaiians were afraid to openly talk about their culture, and they continued their ancient traditions mostly in secret. Beatrice, however, "possessed a rare quality of sympathy with native life." Hence, the Kānaka Maoli "told her things not usually told to people of another race because they knew that such inner thoughts and ideas would meet with a sympathetic reception."[72]

Beatrice took the islands home in her heart in April 1928, a home of her own for the first time.

# 8

## WHITE OAKS
### WASHINGTON, DC

### 1928–1935

*A LADY IS A WOMAN WHO BEHAVES LIKE A GENTLEMAN.*

Beginning with the roaring twenties and continuing until the end of the fifties when Mrs. Perle Mesta pushed them off their throne, a trio of hostesses known as the 'Three Mrs. Bs' ruled Washington society. They held such an iron grip on the capital's social life that whoever arrived in Washington should first leave their calling card with them, then at the White House.

The first B was Mrs. Truxtun Beale of Decatur House, an heiress and diplomat's wife who favored discretion, maybe because Mr. Beale once shot a San Francisco editor who refused to issue an apology after slandering the soon-to-be Mrs. Beale. The second B was Mrs. Robert Woods Bliss of Dumbarton Oaks, a famous art collector who married her diplomat stepbrother and was known for cultivating the performing arts. Grandest of all was Mrs. Robert Low Bacon of John Marshall House, a descendant of the last royal governor of Virginia and the most politically connected of the three.[1]

Social climbers across the country considered Washington the perfect location for their daughters' formal presentation to society. Most were so desperate that they blindly accepted the trio's tight control of the schedule, and even their meddling with the selection of caterers, orchestras, and guest lists. The Three Mrs. Bs' practices went unchallenged until the fall of 1930 when they received word that a certain Mrs. George S. Patton Jr. was hell-bent on organizing her eldest daughter's formal presentation all on her own.

Nineteen-year-old Bee was a kind, beautiful young woman with big blue eyes and "a peach complexion with a dusting of freckles like cinnamon on cream."[2] Before the summer holiday was over, the *Washington Post* already wrote about the popular debutante who was much fêted on the North Shore, first at a garden party at Avalon organized by Aunt Kay and Uncle Keith, then at a dance at Juniper Ridge, organized by Aunt Theodora and Uncle Chilly. Beatrice believed "a debut was not about putting your daughter on the auction block," but about having a great time with friends and family.[3]

When the *Washington Post* announced that Miss Patton was to make her bow on December 13 at a tea to be given at White Oaks—the family's residence while George served in the War Department—Beatrice received a call from one of the three Bs. Which B was on the line is unknown, but she warned that Miss Patton's presentation would be a spectacular failure. Unperturbed, Beatrice politely thanked Mrs. B for the advice and apologized for the inconvenience, but she wasn't about to change her plans. Unversed in the art of being rebuffed, especially by an unknown, Mrs. B ended the conversation with a threat: she would schedule another debutante tea that same afternoon.

So it came to be that two buds, Beatrice Patton and Katrina McCormick, were welcomed into society on December 13, 1930.[4] If the capital hostesses thought this would cause no one to attend Bee's coming out, they were badly mistaken, unaware of the powerful connections the Pattons had made throughout the years. Not only was Beatrice assisted in her hostess duties by Mrs. Eisenhower, Mrs. Stimson, and the wives of the Secretary of the Navy and the Assistant Secretary of War, but also in attendance were General Pershing and Secretary of State Stimson.

The afternoon was such a success that Beatrice also charted her own course for Ruth Ellen's debut four years later. No longer living at White Oaks, Beatrice rented the Sulgrave Club (formerly the Wadsworth House, where she had accosted the reserve colonel in 1919). Despite being called one of "capital soci-ety['s] . . . most popular families" by the *Washington Post*, Beatrice once again received a threat veiled as a friendly reminder from a Mrs. B.[5] Her reply was slightly more direct this time: "That will be perfectly all right; I doubt very much that the same people would care to go to both parties as we will be having our own friends."[6]

---

AFTER EIGHTEEN YEARS of marriage and ten moves across the country, the Pattons finally owned a home when they returned from Hawaii in May 1928. While stationed at Schofield Barracks, George became convinced the U.S. would soon be at war with Japan, and he was determined to get into the fray. He wanted Beatrice to be surrounded by friends and family if he were to die on foreign soil, as he had been saying for years. While California and Virginia were viable options, he pushed for "a place in the hunting country [of Massachusetts]," away from Boston because he considered himself "too much of a savage for city life."[7]

In the fall of 1926, while convalescing from her riding accident on the North Shore, Beatrice learned from Fred and Chilly about Green Meadows, the old Burroughs estate at 650 Asbury Street in South Hamilton, Massachusetts. It was a familiar place to the Ayers, right in the middle of Myopia Hunt country. For over a decade, Fred and Chilly attended hunt breakfasts and participated in horse shows at the 363-acre estate, which straddled the town-lines of South Hamilton and Topsfield.

*Figure 44. Green Meadows as it appears today.*

Built in 1786, the remodeled and enlarged colonial farmhouse had been the summer residence of realtor George Burroughs and his wife, Edith.[8] Unfortunately, tragedy struck on July 23, 1925, when a nervous Mr. Burroughs took off on his first pleasure flight in a small Curtis airplane with Lieutenant Hogue, a decorated war veteran. The plane had been in the air for ten minutes when it suddenly nosedived, struck the Boston Revere Beach and Lynn Railroad tracks, and rolled into the water. Nothing remained of the plane except "a twisted, useless mass," and both Lieutenant Hogue and Mr. Burroughs died on impact.[9]

Essex County—a cluster of towns northeast of Boston, some so small it was impossible to tell where one ended and the next began—was one of the premier hunting spots in the country. For generations, gentleman farmers had been buying acres of adjoining land in South Hamilton, Wenham, Topsfield, and Ipswich. Many of the area's residents were lifelong members of the Myopia Hunt Club. They allowed fellow riders 'right of passage' through their property, but outsiders might not be as sympathetic to the plight of the hunters. So when Mrs. Burroughs put Green Meadows up for sale in the fall of 1926, a syndicate of Myopians bought the property to protect their hunting grounds, and subsequently offered it to the Pattons at the instigation of Fred and Chilly.[10]

The location was perfect: Chilly lived three miles away at Juniper Ridge in South Hamilton, Fred three miles away at Ledyard Farm in Wenham, and Kay eight miles away at Avalon in Pride's Crossing. "With respect to the house it seems to me that if you like it you had just as well buy it," George replied to his wife on November 2, 1926, from Schofield Barracks. "As inspite of polo ponies, boats and Squash Courts you don't spend 1/4 of your income I think the house might be fine and certainly no extravagance."[11] So with Fred and Chilly taking care of the details, the Pattons became the proud new owners of Green Meadows on January 29, 1927. Almost a century later, the Patton family remains an integral part of the community.

Green Meadows was aptly named. The nineteen-room, two-and-a-half story house lay on a low hill bordered by a fieldstone wall in the front and nothing but lush fields in the back. French doors in the living room led to a two-story, screened-in porch with views of a pond and the Ipswich River, partly hidden behind the tree line. The sprawling estate included a boathouse, a garage, a stable for ten horses, a barn, a chicken coop, and a private dock on the Ipswich River. When they first returned to South Hamilton in May 1928, Beatrice and the children temporarily moved in with Fred and his family while Green Meadows underwent major renovations.


SINCE GEORGE increasingly worried he'd "live to retire a useless soldier," Beatrice couldn't have picked a better spot for his eventual retirement than the town of South Hamilton.[12] Named after one of America's founding fathers, the town counted a mere 2,044 residents during the 1930 census. Hamilton was a rural farming community until about 1883, when the Myopia Hunt Club was organized. Life in South Hamilton and its neighboring towns revolved around the horse, and wealthy Bostonians interested in the sporting life bought up local farmhouses and remodeled them into summer estates. The sport employed hundreds of people, from laundresses and cooks to blacksmiths and horse traders.

The area's rich equestrian tradition dates to 1638, when the British first settled the land, driven by its resemblance to the countryside they had left behind. During H.R.H Edward Prince of Wales's visit to America in October 1924, the future king spent a day at the Myopia Hunt Club. However, the

Prince of Wales was not the most famous prince in attendance. That distinction belonged to the Prince family, who founded the Myopia Hunt Club, so named because its four founders—the Prince brothers: Gordon Sr., Charles, Frederick, and Morton—were nearsighted.

Frederick Prince was the most illustrious of the four. He amassed a fortune through savvy investments and purchased Princemere, in Beverly Farms, in the 1880s, just two miles from where Avalon now stood. Gordon Chickering Prince, born in 1888 to Myopia cofounder Gordon Prince Sr., became one of George's closest friends in the area. After serving in the Signal Corps' Aviation Branch in France and Italy during WWI, Gordon continued to dabble in aviation, an interest he shared with George, who learned to fly after the Great War.[13]

Gordon was another one of those brave men who possessed the quality George most admired: courage. A fearless steeplechaser, he broke his neck in a horse riding accident in 1927, ending his career with the National Guard but not his daring horsemanship. Nine years later, while inspecting his 40-foot yacht at the Knowles Boat Yard in Beverly, a stray .22-caliber bullet struck him in the neck.

"Guess I've been hit," Gordon remarked calmly as he took himself to the hospital, where he was released that same day. The culprits were found to be three boys—between the ages of nine and thirteen—who were shooting at an abandoned car frame across the river. When George heard the news, he wired, "Sorry you were shot, for God's sake next time marry the girl."[14]

**Figure 45.** *The Patton family at the 1929 Labor Day Horse Show in South Hamilton: Master George, Beatrice, Ruth Ellen, Bee, and George.*
*(Patton Museum)*

Gordon had married Anna Agassiz in 1924—daughter of Rodolphe Agassiz, mining financier, ten-goal polo champion, and Hamilton summer resident —when she became one of the first female graduates of Columbia University's College of Physicians and Surgeons. She was a superb horsewoman, the great-granddaughter of the American scientist Louis Agassiz, and one of Beatrice's best friends.[15]

The Pattons quickly became leaders in the society events and were always greatly missed on the North Shore when not in residence. The highlight of the summer season was the annual Labor Day Horse Show, in which all the Pattons, Ayers, and Princes enjoyed competing. The day-long event, first held in 1896, drew thousands of spectators from across the area to watch riders compete in a long lineup of classes. The family class was always a crowd favorite. It never disappointed to watch the Pattons, with George IV joining on his pony when he was barely five years old, compete against the Ayers, "among the best riders on the North Shore."[16]

Fred "never excelled in any sport," at least not until he married Hilda, one of "the best-known horsewomen on the North Shore," who turned him into an accomplished and fearless rider.[17] Even though he was only five foot eight, Fred was just as courageous as George when on a horse, and a competitive but friendly streak existed between the two best friends. Whether it was hunting, polo, or steeplechase, George, Fred, and the other members of the Myopia Hunt Club went all in, resulting in so many injuries that it was said the club was solely responsible for keeping Beverly Hospital in business. The *Boston Globe* headlines were endless: "Rider Thrown, Also Kicked In The Face," "Runaway Horse Dies After Crashing Auto; Hamilton Rider Safe," "Frederick Ayer Injured In Polo Game At Princemere: Struck in Chest by Ball."

Beverly Hospital, established in 1893, was an institution Fred cared for deeply. When Hilda was nearing her due date in February 1926, Dr. Peer Johnson, a close family friend and the chief of staff at Beverly Hospital, spent three days snowed in at Ledyard Farm awaiting the birth of Neil and Hilda Ayer. While Fred kept his mind occupied by building a sideboard, Dr. Johnson wondered whether he might not be interested in becoming the hospital's president.

"Father believed in honesty and hard work," Neil Ayer wrote later in his memoirs, *Wind Over Willowdale*. "He believed that if you were fortunate enough to be a member of a family that had done well, and to live in a house where you were sure that the next meal was going to be on the table, and to get an education without having to work for it—that you owed it to society to return something to it."[18] So, while Fred was president of Beverly Hospital for the next thirty-four years, Hilda gave back to the community by running the Visiting Nurse Association in Wenham.

LIKE MOST HAMILTONIANS, the Pattons were in residence during the summer only and left a property manager in charge of Green Meadows the rest of the year. Their nomadic life began afresh in the fall of 1928 when they moved into Woodley Mansion, just two miles from Kay's Washington residence and a short drive from George's office at the "tempo" Munitions Building. The Federal-style home, built in 1801 on a hilltop near Washington Cathedral, had an illustrious history—former residents included Presidents Martin Van Buren and Grover Cleveland—and was equipped with stables and a squash court.

Known throughout both military and civilian circles as an excellent hostess, Beatrice soon opened the doors of Woodley Mansion for some serious entertaining. Out of circulation for three years while in Hawaii, it was time to make new connections and renew old friendships. "There is no career, except that of a minister's wife, in which a woman can be more of a help, or a detriment, to her husband than that of an Army wife," Beatrice said. "She lives practically at his place of business, and sees his associates daily, and, if she is a shirk or a gossip, she is known as such throughout the service. Her reputation begins at her first post and sticks to her as closely as her skin until she dies." [19]

Beatrice's reputation was one of total devotion, both to the Army and to her husband. She might have "adored him to the point of making him worse," General Marshall once said, but Beatrice was George's voice of reason. Besides Mr. Patton, she was the only person who was ever able to make George "see his problems clearly," always giving "patient, judicious, and loving counsel," providing "support, advice, and reassurance" without being judgmental. [20] She was "a very high caliber person" who "didn't want to be recognized," but her quiet and steadfast influence on her husband was one of her greatest assets. George depended so much on Beatrice's common sense that he doubted an article he submitted to the *Cavalry Journal* would be accepted because he "failed to have your help either in criticism or punctuation." [21]

George constantly craved Beatrice's approval and attention. He still missed her when they were apart, "thinking how much nicer a trip it would have been had you been there." [22] He was always the first to write upon leaving, usually apologizing for something he said. "I hope I did not leave you with the impression that I thought you were either a poor sailor or mother. I think you are perfect in these rolls as in all others," or, "I did not intend to hurt your feelings this morning when I said you had better not hunt. It was simply because I hate to have you get hurt. I know perfectly well that you ride better than the majority of the people who do hunt." [23]

George was "a man of the moment and when that moment was over, so too was the incident it triggered," unlike Beatrice, whose capacity for forgiving and forgetting did not extend beyond her family. She was an "iron fist in a velvet glove" who could hold "a grudge like no one's business." The Eisenhowers would one day personally experience how near impossible it was to reverse the tide once on Beatrice's wrong side, but when Ike joined the staff of the Assistant Secretary of War in 1929, they were still great friends. Their son John, born a year after the death of Icky from scarlet fever in 1921, "always held the Pattons in considerable awe because of their obvious wealth," but what he remembered most from those early visits was George's love of jokes and penchant for swearing. "I was astonished that he not only swore profusely around ladies but also encouraged all three of his children to do the same."[24]

The mark of any "well educated and cultured man," according to George, was to be able to swear for three minutes without repeating himself.[25] Beatrice, who hated "disloyalty, adultery, divorce, gossip, drink, and coarseness of speech," was very much aware that George's cursing was just a part of his public persona.[26] "He wasn't born that way," Mrs. Paddy Flint surmised. "Underneath the rough-spoken, cold-blooded exterior, he was a gentle and kindly person who had to make himself tough to do the job he had."[27]

From the moment he left Lake Vineyard in 1903, George reinvented himself "in the guise of a rugged, macho male," suppressing a personality which, by nature, was characterized by "Old World gallantry."[28] Despite their volatile relationship, Ruth Ellen considered her father to be the kindest man who ever lived. When anyone got hurt, a frequent occurrence in the Patton family, "he was always there to cut off the riding boot, grab off his shirt and stuff it under the broken collarbone, or apply one of his huge linen handkerchiefs to whatever was bleeding."[29]

Cursed with a "damned mild expression . . . for so fierce a warrior," and "the world's most unfortunate voice," George could "work up a fairly ferocious expression, but I have not got, and never will have, a natural-born fighting face."[30] It took him hours of practice in front of the bathroom mirror, an act so intriguing that Bee and Ruth Ellen never tired of spying on him in the morning. After he covered his hair in a mixture of castor oil, lemon juice, rum, and iodine, he looked himself in the eye and recited the battle speech from Shakespeare's *Henry V*.

EVER SINCE SHE left Bee at Foxcroft in September 1926, Beatrice regretted the decision. She knew her daughter had been looking forward to the experience, but she began questioning whether Foxcroft had been the right choice.[31] When she asked Anne Ayer for her unbiased opinion, her niece said she thoroughly enjoyed her Foxcroft education, except for a troublesome teacher called Miss Alice. Unlike Bee, Anne grew up in the kind of milieu which permeated Foxcroft. Its students were daughters of politicians, captains of industry, and diplomats, but the Pattons were neither famous nor rich enough to make Bee a member of the in-crowd.

Bee had few friends, but she performed well academically. Unfortunately, by her third and last year (1928-1929), an unknown scandal concerning Miss Alice and some students got "gentle, sensitive and humble" Bee in trouble. Clueless as to what was happening, she made herself sick with worry, and her parents found out what was happening only when she was admitted to the infirmary with a hundred-degree fever. While the details are lost to history, the result was that Foxcroft wanted to avoid a public scandal and awarded Bee her diploma early.

Upon her return from France with Aunt Nita in May 1929—a graduation gift from her parents—Bee moved back home for the next four years. Because Beatrice wanted her daughter to do more than just enjoy the good life, Bee volunteered with the Girl Scouts giving riding classes instead of going to college. Meanwhile, a reluctant Ruth Ellen moved out to attend The Masters School in Dobbs Ferry, New York. She was disappointed to miss out on three years of fun, especially now that she had finally figured out her parents' complex personalities. Beatrice never spoke in clichés and abhorred "milk-sop philosophy," but George was a born sentimentalist.[32] He often came across as aloof, but he made a so-called "great sacrifice" in 1932 to ensure his daughters' happiness.

George considered only two jobs worthwhile as he waited for the next war: superintendent of cadets at West Point and military attaché to Great Britain. He had already lost out twice on the former and once on the latter, but in 1932 he was, at last, offered the position of military attaché. Beatrice was elated that the opportunity finally presented itself after thirteen years, even though she knew her husband did not care for the job itself. She hoped this change of pace would do wonders for his ever-diminishing spirit, enjoying the perks of playing world-class polo, hunting in the British countryside, and taking part in international horse shows.

It was a great surprise to Beatrice that George ultimately declined the offer. He did so to save his marriageable daughters from the clutches of the British aristocracy, who always needed "all the money they can lay their hands on to keep up the castle, or the grouse moor, or the stud farm, or whatever it is they have inherited." He overheard their talk during WWI, and he couldn't imagine Bee or Ruth Ellen married to someone who was "totally inconsiderate of their wives and daughters" and gave everything to their sons.

George didn't want his daughters to become, what would later be coined, dollar princesses. The practice became popular after Jennie Jerome, daughter of a self-made American financier, married Lord Randolph Churchill in 1874. While his parents initially opposed the match, once they heard how much Miss Jerome was worth, they even overlooked the rumored tattoo on her wrist. The union was rocky, but it did bring forth a British prime minister and a wave of similar marriages of convenience, which led to the transfer of close to one billion pounds of wealth over the next fifty years.[33]

"Someday, just tell them what I did for them and maybe they won't think I'm such an old bastard after all," George asked Beatrice.[34] Unfortunately, his refusal to take on the assignment of a lifetime meant many more years spent wallowing in the boredom of the peacetime Army. As the years progressed, Beatrice would bear the brunt of his disappointment.

*Figure 46. The Pattons at Fort Myer in 1929. (Patton Museum)*

WITH THE INAUGURATION of Herbert Hoover as the thirty-first president in March 1929, Henry Stimson returned to Washington, this time as secretary of state. With him was his "devoted companion" of thirty-six years and "the greatest happiness" of his life, Mabel, a reluctant hostess who joined her husband in all his varied interests. The Stimsons always had a hard time relaxing in the company of others and didn't socialize much, yet they got along splendidly with the Pattons. Their friendship had been strong for seventeen years, and Lieutenant Colonel Stimson had even boarded with (then) Major Patton at Langres during WWI.

The Stimsons must have fallen in love with Woodley Mansion during the many evenings they spent there having dinner or playing squash because they became its new owners barely a year after the Pattons had moved in. George sent Beatrice to Green Meadows to enjoy the Myopia Hunt—Mrs. Rice, Hilda, Beatrice, and twelve others rode a dangerous hunting course with 140 obstacles—while he and eighteen-year-old Bee went house hunting.

It was the fall of 1929, right around Black Tuesday and Thursday when the New York Stock Exchange crashed. It was the start of one of the bleakest periods in American history, but neither the Pattons nor the Ayers would be impacted much by the Great Depression. George, who was increasingly bothered that he still had nothing to show for the sacrifices Beatrice continued to make, looked for the grandest house money could rent. He settled on White Oaks for $1,000 per month, a Mediterranean-style mansion overlooking Rock Creek Park, which he hoped would remind his wife of her beloved Avalon.

Beatrice never told her husband how much she hated White Oaks, confiding to her daughters that she genuinely enjoyed army life, despite it being "pretty trying too." She might have considered herself "the greenest bride who ever came into the service," but not once did she miss the lavish lifestyle of her childhood.[35] Running a big household was a nuisance, and the family counted twenty members in April 1930: five Pattons, three grooms (including George Kent, who worked for the family for over twenty years), four maids, a nanny (Alice Holmes), two cooks, two housemen, a chauffeur, and two children (belonging to the Clements and the Maidments).[36]

Despite George's insecurities, Beatrice never regretted marrying him, but there was one family member who still regretted her marrying into the army. Being a member of society was important to Theodora Ayer, so once her daughters married—Theodora to Robert Winthrop and Anne to Gilbert Livingston Steward—she decided to take Bee and Ruth Ellen under her wing. Their entrance into society was imminent, and Theodora feared her sister-in-law wasn't putting much thought into the grand occasion.

Bee and Ruth Ellen reluctantly accepted an invitation to Juniper Ridge, where Aunt Theodora subjected them to cross-examination. She explained that everyone was very fond of their father, but it was common knowledge that their mother had "married beneath her." As such, a lot more would be expected of the girls if they ever hoped to be accepted by any potential mother-in-law in Boston's high society. At this point, the sisters stood up and walked home, followed by Aunt Theodora in her chauffeured Rolls-Royce, begging them not to tell their mother what she had said.

Always composed and considerate, Beatrice told her daughters not to worry as Aunt Theodora just got "her priorities a little mixed up. She and your Uncle Chilly are really devoted to your father!"[37] Beatrice was confident enough in her role as Mrs. Patton that Theodora's antics never bothered her, and she certainly never allowed Theodora's feelings to come between her and her brother. It was always a mystery to those who knew Chilly—a quiet, honest, and sensible man who enjoyed the simple life of sitting around the fireplace singing and telling stories—how he managed to put up with his wife.

AUNT NANNIE'S death on November 26, 1931, was as much a surprise to George as his mother's passing had been just three years earlier. Ruth had suffered from debilitating arthritis for many years, causing her to be "very nervous and irritable" at times.[38] Her condition wasn't life-threatening, but her will to live had died with her husband. Nita had suggested her mother accompany her to Washington to visit the grandchildren, but just one day after they departed Lake Vineyard on October 6, 1928, as the train barreled through Albuquerque, New Mexico, Ruth suddenly died of a heart attack. California's "pioneer daughter" had celebrated her sixty-seventh birthday in April and passed away just fifteen months after her husband.

Aunt Nannie lived with her sister and brother-in-law for forty-three years until she moved to a smaller house on the Lake Vineyard estate just one day after Mr. Patton's funeral. Money was never the reason she refused to live her own life; it was always the love for her two Georges. No one could explain why the Pattons tolerated this unusual ménage à trois, but somehow Aunt Nannie's presence became part of life. Beatrice was almost closer to her than to her own mother-in-law, yet it wasn't until the funeral that she learned Aunt Nannie had been dependent on alcohol for a long time.

With the passing of Aunt Nannie, Nita was finally free, and with the help of her brother, she was able to continue living a comfortable life at Lake Vineyard. She never married, but she adored her nephew and two nieces and wanted children of her own. Adopting a child as a single woman in 1935 was difficult enough but trying to do so with George Patton as a brother was almost impossible. Like their father, George considered it a birthright and a privilege to carry the Patton name; it was an honor that was not to be accorded a stranger.

Nita wasn't about to be bullied into forgoing an adoption because of such absurdity. Brother and sister had always been close, but to George's dismay, Nita told him to accept the adoption, or she would walk out of his life. Beatrice tried to be the voice of reason and sent George to talk to a child-rearing expert. Whereas she had been ambivalent about Nita's relationship with General Pershing, she wholeheartedly supported her sister-in-law in her efforts to adopt a child.

As Beatrice matured, she became "wiser about George's foibles." Like others knew all along, she came to see that he wasn't perfect and could be a terrible pain in the neck. She became less forgiving and more impatient with his behavior, especially as the years of peace began to weigh on him and his behavior became increasingly outrageous. In public, however, she would always remain the devoted wife who defended her husband ferociously.

George eventually apologized to his sister, realizing that "it was all a question of invironment and training and not at all a question of blood lines."[39] He became a loving uncle to Peter Wilson Patton and David Wilson Patton—born in England in 1932 and 1933, respectively—and wrote them occasionally during WWII as he did his other nieces and nephews. They turned out to be worthy of the Patton name: Peter became a lieutenant commander in the Navy and David a colonel in the Army after graduating from West Point.

AFTER SERVING on the staff of the Chief of Cavalry and completing with honors a year of study at the U.S. Army War College in June 1932, George became the executive officer of the 3rd Cavalry. Stationed at Fort Myer four times—1911 to 1913, 1920 to 1922, 1932 to 1935, and 1938 to 1940—the Pattons left a lasting mark on the base. They built the Old Post Chapel to provide a formal place of worship for the soldiers, but rest and recreation were equally important.[40] So they paid for the construction of a tennis court and skeet shooting range, and looked for novel ways to raise money for the Soldier's Rest and Recreation Fund.

Horsemanship stood front and center at Fort Myer. The 3rd Cavalry often took part in official functions and military funerals, and its riders were some of the best in the country. They became one with their horses through repeated drills, allowing them to perform ever-bolder tricks as each squadron tried to outdo the other during the annual Fort Myer Horse Show. Having participated many times, George figured plenty of people would be willing to pay to see these daring feats (think Roman Rides on steroids). So, in the early 1920s, he had secured Fort Myer's exhibition hall as the venue for what he dubbed the Society Circus, "a glorified horse show, with circus stunts and all sorts of thrills."[41]

The exhibition rides took place every weekend in January and February. Eventually, they showcased not only the horsemanship of the 3rd Cavalry but also of the soldiers' family members and Washington's debutantes. In addition to organizing lunches and afternoon teas to raise more money, Beatrice and her children were enthusiastic participants. Eleven-year-old "Little Miss Beatrice Patton" had featured prominently in the *Washington Times* in 1922 as a member of the "Woman's Battalion of Death, defying danger and the laws of gravity."[42]

The annual fundraiser had grown into a ten-week affair by the time the Pattons returned to Fort Myer in 1932, and its audience now consisted of entertainers, politicians, and eligible young bachelors. The Society Circus's theme in 1933 was Technocracy, "arguing the case of the horse versus the most modern contraptions of a scientific age." "Knighthood" showcased Crusaders in royal review, while "The Technor Calls for His Mount" was the "outstanding comedy feature of the afternoon." George IV showcased clever maneuvers in "The Germ of Discipline," while Ruth Ellen performed tandem jumping in "Adventure, Or Pioneer Maids in a Beauty Roundup."[43]

**Figure 47.** *After reading and watching Gone with the Wind, Beatrice and George dressed up as Scarlett O'Hara and Rhett Butler for Ruth Ellen's twenty-fifth birthday party in 1940. (Patton Family Archives - Wenham Museum)*

It was no surprise George insisted participants in the Society Circus dress up because the Pattons loved playacting and costume parties. Beatrice moved her wooden box filled with costumes from post to post and always signed her daughters (and herself) up for the drama club. During train travel, they often entertained people by putting on a show. Major Stuart Cramer remembered "they would be a gangster and his accomplice in crime; again a couple eloping from their respective mates, or perhaps a pair of foreign spies."[44]

The Pattons took dressing up very seriously and studied their characters like actors preparing for a play. Their costumes were elaborate and often made at home to make them as historically accurate as possible; comfort always took second place to authenticity. A newspaper article from April 1939 showed Beatrice and Ruth Ellen painting shields while George fitted his son with chainmail made from pot scrubbers.

"Hoofprints of 1939" was their most memorable event at Fort Myer. George and Beatrice could have fooled the Knights of the Round Table as they rode into the exhibition hall dressed as King Arthur and Lady Guinevere. It was the perfect make-believe for a man who had the heart of a romantic warrior and still believed "in the days of chivalry—the golden age of our profession—[when] knights-officers were noted as well for courtesy and gentleness of behavior, as for death-defying courage."[45]


GEORGE HAD JUST TAKEN up his post with the 3rd Cavalry and moved the family into a new rental in Rosslyn, Virginia, when he got dragged into one of the Army's most shameful episodes. It all began in 1924 when Congress approved the World War Adjusted Compensation Act, providing a bonus to the 3.5 million soldiers who had fought in World War I. A soldier's bonus was based on the difference between his army pay and his hypothetical earnings had he not gone to war, and was issued in the form of bonds that wouldn't mature until 1945.

As the country sank deeper into the Great Depression, desperate veterans began demanding their bonuses early and marched on Washington. By the summer of 1932, over forty thousand veterans made it to the nation's capital, and about one-third of them lived in tents on the mudlands of Anacostia, a neighborhood in southeast DC. Makeshift villages like this sprang up across the country and became known as Hoovervilles, named after the president who refused to acquiesce to the Bonus Expeditionary Force's demands.

The man who saved George's life in 1918 was one of the 'residents' of the Anacostia Hooverville. Private Joe Angelo, who weighed a mere 107 pounds, needed his $1,424 now and not in fourteen years. Fueled by desperation, he had left behind his wife and son in New Jersey and walked 160 miles to the capital so he could testify in front of a congressional committee on February 4,

1931. Beatrice took her three children to watch the proceedings and meet the man who saved their father's life. "If you're as good an officer as your Daddy," Angelo told the eight-year-old George IV, "the men will follow you anywhere." Beatrice, however, was quickly irked by what she considered Joe's "enlarging on the truth" and the way he exploited his connection to her family.[46]

Forever grateful for saving her husband's life, Beatrice was all for supporting Joe financially whenever he needed it, but she hated his bringing it up in public. She cringed when he mentioned the watch she sent him and the "stickpin with a bullet mounted in gold, given me by Colonel Patton's mother in memory of the bullet that was taken out of his leg." What he said next really annoyed her, "I could go right over here to this cavalry camp across the river and get all the money I want or need from Colonel Patton. But that ain't right. I don't want him to feel under any obligation to me for saving his life. He owes me nothing. I did my duty."[47]

The situation festered until July 28, 1932, when Army Chief of Staff Douglas MacArthur—whom Beatrice referred to as "Dragon Seed" since paying a social call on his formidable and eccentric mother—pressured President Hoover to mobilize the Army and evict the Bonus Marchers from Washington.[48] The 3rd Cavalry was assigned riot duty. From a military perspective, George considered the whole affair "a most distasteful form of service," but he was not about to miss a chance to get embroiled in a bit of fighting and test his theories on crowd control.[49]

*Figure 48. Major Patton en-route to the Ellipse near the White House. (Library of Congress)*

Major Patton rode across the Memorial Bridge at the head of his two hundred-strong regiment. At 4:30 p.m., a group of six hundred soldiers and several tanks drove the Bonus Marchers from the National Mall. Most veterans left peacefully across the Anacostia Bridge, yet, the Army resorted to tear gas, and the Cavalry drew their sabers in the heat of the moment. Two veterans died, and fifty-five suffered injuries during the melee.

President Hoover's refusal to take the Bonus Marchers' plight into account contributed to Franklin Roosevelt's landslide victory in November 1932. George was apolitical, as he believed any soldier should be, and he never voted. He swore to do his duty regardless of who occupied the White House, but that never stopped him from voicing his opinion in private. The more he learned about President Roosevelt's New Deal, the more he fretted about Beatrice's bank account.

The Pattons never struggled during the Great Depression, but George's beloved Army and his fellow soldiers did. As soon as President Roosevelt took office, the Army's already meager pay was cut once again to balance the budget. The pay was so low that civilians who joined the Civilian Conservation Corps—Roosevelt's environmentally focused public work relief program—made more money than a member of the Regular Army. Yet, life on an army post was quite pleasant, with plenty of food and activities to keep soldiers out of trouble, from hops to horse shows and hunting to polo.

THE PATTONS and the Ayers saw it as a badge of honor to die on the hunting field, doing what they loved best. For Beatrice, overcoming the literal hurdle of the fox hunt was like learning to be an army wife, "I was often scared, and it took all the courage I could summon. My family thinks that I am naturally brave—that courage is congenital, or something. But it isn't. It's acquired."

"But why does your mother do it, if she is so frightened?" a family friend asked Ruth Ellen about the hunt.

"Well," she replied, "Mother is a New Englander, and she doesn't feel that she is getting anywhere unless she has something to overcome."[50] Also, Beatrice was married to George S. Patton Jr. She had realized early on that standing in her husband's way, whether in war or games, would only be detrimental.

"If they are true men, a woman can't hold them back," she told a reporter. "And a true woman wouldn't want to."[51] So one day, Beatrice decided that if she couldn't stop George, she might as well join him. To her great disappointment, she couldn't go to war with him, but she could make all his other activities her own, even if it meant pushing herself to the extreme. If George was going to keep risking life and limb, so was she. At least she would be there if something happened, which beat sitting at home waiting in fear for the phone to ring.

By 1933, Beatrice's transformation into a "fearless" huntress was complete, and she and George became Joint Masters of the Cobbler Hunt in Fauquier County, Virginia. Every Wednesday and Saturday morning from October through May, the Pattons awoke at 4 a.m. and drove to Delaplane, Virginia, fifty miles west of Washington near the Blue Ridge Mountains. Their responsibilities as masters were not only financial but also organizational; they were "expected to pay for everything and please everybody." Their duties ranged from cultivating good relations with local landowners and reimbursing them for property damages to paying the staff and scheduling the meets.[52]

On the day of the hunt, the masters oversaw the field (the hunters who follow) and the pack (the group of hounds). They ensured the field only rode through land they were permitted to use, kept an eye out for property damage, and prevented the field from overtaking the pack as they chased the fox. As Master of Hounds, George owned the fox hounds and oversaw their breeding, while George Kent, the Pattons' whipper-in, or right-hand-man, was responsible for them during the hunt.

No one who saw the Pattons hunt together ever forgot the occasion. George would "pass by the low spots in the fence, in favor of a high place with an unknown landing on the far side . . . steeling himself to danger."[53]

"Come on, Bea! Do you want to live forever?" he would yell as they jumped fences, creeks, and stone walls, some measuring close to five feet with an eight-foot drop on the other side. Beatrice, dressed in a black coat and boots, white stock, and tan breeches, followed George (almost literally) blindly over every obstacle. Nearsighted since she was a child and refusing to wear her glasses out of vanity, she relied on George's red hunting coat—called Pinks—to lead the way.

If George was hard on his daughters, it was because he wanted them to be able to keep up with any man, just as Beatrice could keep up with him. It gave him immense pride and joy to watch her tenaciously stay ahead of the field with him, continuing through rain and snow while others quit early. A typical entry in his hunting diary concluded, "Mrs. Patton had the field and went away in great style with only Dr. Langhorne and Major Blunt well up. We crossed two valleys over fences that every horse hit due to fatigue and finally ran the old customer to ground in the earth by the abandoned saw mill. Time 53 minutes of fast hard going."[54]

No matter if a hunt lasted an hour or six hours, the field was famished by the time they finished. Everyone—even those "who never hunt but always eat"—then met at the home of one of the club members or landowners for a sumptuous hunt breakfast with Virginia hams, warm loaves of bread, farm-fresh eggs, and homemade jams. There was more than one occasion when not all riders returned, but no one batted an eye at injuries because it was an expected and accepted part of the game. After jumping a stone fence and racing downhill, "Memorial pulled b. [Beatrice] off with the reins and stepped on her. So she and Kent went in." George made it sound like no big deal in his diary, and neither did Beatrice because she was present at the next meet three days later. "The moral victory over fear was far behind," she wrote in her thought book. "Hunting, polo, dangerous sports, but they keep us intrepid; for in sport, as in all life, the big jump, if well taken, makes all the rest picayune."[55]

**Figure 49.** *Joint Masters of the Hunt. (Library of Congress)*

The most memorable incident from their three years at the Cobbler Hunt was the fall of Mrs. Gaddis, one of the local landowners who founded the Cobbler Hunt in 1929. Even though her first husband died in a horseback riding accident, she remained an avid huntress who always rode sidesaddle. On December 23, 1933, George and his hunt servants jumped a wall underneath a big tree branch, followed by Beatrice and Mrs. Gaddis, whose "black mare made a huge jump and struck Mrs. Gaddis's head against the limb. When I [George] picked her up she was face down and apparently dead but asked me to turn her over. Dr. Morgan came up and after a thorough examination sent for an ambulance and took her to the Warrenton Hospital. Her skull was fractured, two bones in the neck cracked and one dislocated."[56]

At Mrs. Gaddis's insistence, the hunt continued. It turned into the best meet of the season, George wondering if Mrs. Gaddis had died on the way to the hospital and the hounds had been chasing her ghost instead of a fox, which remained unobserved that day. She didn't die, but it wasn't until a year later that she was well enough to attend her first hunt breakfast.

While Bee joined her parents during their first Cobbler season, Ruth Ellen became their constant companion when she graduated from The Masters School in 1934 and moved back home. Since Beatrice forbade her daughter to join the hunt the day after attending a late-night debutante ball, Ruth Ellen quickly chose to forgo the dancing. There were plenty of eligible bachelors at the Cobbler Hunt, courtesy of Fort Myer. While the Pattons' obsession with fox hunting might seem frivolous during the Great Depression, the Army considered it essential training for cavalry officers. The Chief of Cavalry permitted George to count his hunting hours as time on duty as long as he took along a minimum of two officers so they could gain cross-country riding experience.

An order on Fort Myer's bulletin board read: "Major and Mrs. George S. Patton Jr., Joint Masters of the Cobbler Hunt, invite the officers and ladies of

Fort Myer, Virginia, to hunt as their guest with the Cobbler Hunt." If those interested adhered to the rules and could jump a certain height, George offered them the use of one of twelve horses he stabled at the Cobbler Hunt Club. Each horse possessed a distinctive personality suited to a specific type of rider. Beatrice was a "bruising" rider who rode herself and her horses to the limit, and George trained both Quicksilver and Memorial to be the perfect hunting companions for his wife.

The only horse off-limits to anyone except George was Ho'okupu (a gift to the gods), a huge thoroughbred Beatrice bought him as a present while stationed in Hawaii in 1927. Only George could control the spirited Ho'okupu, who was always so impatient to get the hunt underway that he would rear and walk around on his hind legs. No one was surprised George won the local Hunter Trials on Ho'okupu in 1934 because winning trophies was "a 30-year-old habit of my family," according to Bee.[57]

On October 20, 1934, Beatrice and George organized the Cobbler Hunt opening meet, an unforgettable day with over 2500 guests, including the troops of Fort Myer. While a field of fifty rode to hounds for three hours, the 10th Cavalry's cook took care of lunch. The pièce de résistance was a giant steer roasted on a grate. As the local gazette noted, "the Pattons really stage a show when they get under way," and the day concluded with a jousting event. George personally charged all thirty knights while the military brass looked on, including Colonel Joyce (Fort Myer's commanding officer), General Drum (George's future nemesis), and Billy Mitchell (considered the father of the U.S. Air Force).

According to George's notebook, he and Beatrice spent $160 on food (about $4,000 today), including ten gallons of whiskey for punch. "Beatrice and I both feel," George began the last entry in his hunting diary on March 20, 1935, "that the cost of hunting for the last three years as Masters has been more than offset by the pleasure abtained which no inflation or confiscation can ever take away from us."[58]

ONE COLD AND snowy morning in the winter of 1934, as they awaited the start of the hunt, Beatrice intently watched her husband sit huddled on top of Ho'okupu, lost in thought. "Is it Napoleon again?" she asked, gently touching his arm. George and Beatrice both "believed passionately in reincarnation"— so much so that Ruth Ellen realized only later in life that it was not something everyone believed—and frigid weather always brought back memories of Napoleon's devastating retreat from Moscow in 1812.[59]

No one in the Patton or Ayer family ever laughed at George's idiosyncrasy, knowing he didn't just say these things in jest. He once confided to his nephew, Frederick Ayer Jr., that while he didn't know what others believed, "for myself there has never been any question. I just don't think it. I damn well know there are places I've been before, and not in this life."[60] Some might argue his recollection of past lives was nothing more than his subconscious mind processing years of historical and military studies, but George was always able to "dramatically link the present with the past."[61]

"History seasoned with imagination and applied to the problem in hand was his hobby," Beatrice said of the countless vacations the Pattons took visiting battlefields. "As he had acted out the death of Ajax on the old home ranch, so he and our family acted out Bull Run, Chancellorsville, and Gettysburg." Beatrice "represented everything in those battles from artillery horses at Sudsleigh's Ford to Lt. Cushing, Army of the Potomac, at the Battle of Gettysburg." She never forgot when "the girls jumped over the stone wall into Harper's Wood. Ruth Ellen fell wounded, took a pencil and paper from her pocket and wrote her dying message" just like her great-great-uncle Tazewell Patton had done in the exact same spot. At that moment, Beatrice "heard a sort of groan behind me. As Lt. Cushing, firing my last shot from my last gun, I had been too busy to notice a sightseeing bus had drawn up and was watching the tragedy of Pickett's Charge."

George's behavior on ancient battlefields was the result of his reading. Beatrice explained that after studying a battle, he would play "them out on the ground in a way no one who ever participated in the game can forget."[62] One who certainly never forgot was the German military attaché, General Friedrich von Boetticher. He once joined the Pattons on a trip to Spotsylvania, Virginia, the scene of the Battle of the Wilderness in 1864. Since she always remained a proud Yankee, Beatrice represented the Union, while Ruth Ellen and George IV represented the Confederacy. George took on the role of the Confederate General Early, who stood on a hill overlooking the battlefield, but General von Boetticher noticed a discrepancy in his guidebook and pointed out he, George, stood on the wrong hill. A heated discussion arose until an older man quietly inched away from a nearby tour group and agreed with the "young gentleman." The man had fought in the Battle of the Wilderness and had seen with his own eyes where General Early had stood, as apparently had George, who replied: "Of course General Early was on that rise; I saw him there myself."[63]

Weekends at the Patton homestead followed a set schedule. After piles of waffles for breakfast, George IV remembered that "the whole family would set out to do something active and interesting to us . . . Some people like to spend their spare time at home, but not us. We'd be off and away—seeing, doing and laughing the whole day through. Every weekend or holiday, as I now look back upon them, was an adventure, and no two were alike. Unknown to my mother and my father, they instilled in their children their own passion for 'doing.' It didn't make any difference what we did on those wonderful days, we always had our greatest fun out of doors."[64]

THE HEART of every parent across America was gripped by fear come Memorial Day—until Dr. Jonas Salk released the first polio vaccine in 1955—and the commencement of summer travel was not just an option but a necessity. Movie theaters, churches, and swimming pools closed, and social distancing remained in effect through the polio outbreak's peak in August. Parents tried any remedy to keep their children safe, but for those who had the means, moving away from the big cities during the summer was the best option.

As if war and maneuvers hadn't already separated George and Beatrice enough, polio now added another yearly three months to the tally. Worried about young George, Beatrice left for Green Meadows as soon as newspapers reported the first case. George stayed behind in Washington and visited as often as he could on weekends, taking the earliest train on Saturday morning and returning after dinner on Sunday night. Train travel today is surprisingly slower than a century ago, but it still took about seven hours to cover the approximately 440 miles between Boston and Washington.

**SKIPPER AND CREW AT COHASSET RACES**

The Misses Ruth Ellen and Beatrice Patton are acting as crew for their mother, Mrs. George S. Patton, Jr. of Washington, D. C., and "Green Meadows," South Hamilton, who is racing today in the Women's National Sailing Championship competition at the Cohasset Yacht Club for the cup donated by Mrs. Charles Francis Adams.

*Figure 50. A newspaper clipping from one of Beatrice's scrapbooks.*
*(Library of Congress)*

Since Beatrice thought the ocean was the safest place to be, she went out on the water almost daily. As she had proven when she helped George save those three boys in 1923, the North Shore held no mysteries for her. Beatrice's love of racing was ingrained in her from childhood by her father, who loved boats almost as much as he loved horses. He enjoyed them so much that at ninety-four, he was still taking daily rowing exercises and ended up being the one to drag his son-in-law, William Wood, back on board after their boat capsized.[65]

When Beatrice officially moved to Green Meadows, she joined the Manchester Yacht Club, where she kept her two sloop yachts, the *Dantesk* and the *Ventura*. The tricks she learned growing up—like sailing as close as possible to the islands dotting Manchester Bay, where the warm rocks created an extra draft—stood her in good stead when she raced her fifteen-footer, Herreshoff S Class, to victory. She prepared each race in detail, and "the minute she got at the tiller, she became a different person."[66]

Beatrice always lugged a twenty-pound movie camera with her wherever she went because improving their game was important to the Pattons. At horse shows, for example, they filmed themselves so they could analyze every detail of their performance, from the position of their feet to the timing of their jumps. Beatrice always recreated her races with model sailboats on the pond at Green Meadows, trying to figure out what went wrong, or, more often, what went right. She was known as "a leader in the women's sporting events of the North Shore" and participated in the Women's National Sailing Championship with her daughters in September 1932 and 1933.[67]

Beatrice was a talented racing skipper who understood the tides and the wind, but a captain needs more than that to win. She formed a formidable team with her daughters, but George's feelings about crewing with Beatrice were evident in a letter he wrote her from Washington, "I will even 'bend' so much as to sail with you in the Dantesk if you want me."[68]

George enjoyed being on the water just as much—ever since his father had bought him his first sailboat on Catalina Island when he was thirteen—and he bought a twenty-two-foot powerboat in 1930 to cruise on the Potomac River, christening her the *Moku* (Hawaiian for boat). Grand Colonial houses and plantations from a bygone era dotted the shoreline, many of them in various states of decay because of years of neglect (this was the era before preservation and conservation). As they traveled along the river's many creeks and inlets, Beatrice would occasionally jump ashore to satisfy her curiosity, take pictures, and dig up a bulb or a bush to plant at Green Meadows.[69]

Not surprisingly, the whole point of cruising was lost on George, and he kept his children busy scrubbing the deck or cleaning the brass. Doing nothing was not in the Pattons' vocabulary; they always had to be "doing something." George IV later remembered, "My father was . . . inherently lazy. He said so himself, but he forced himself through his strong self-discipline to do those routine things which he knew would keep his mind alert and his body active and strong."[70]

A lifelong subscriber to *Popular Mechanics*, George used a design from the magazine to build a twenty-foot cabin cruiser in 1932 with George IV and Beatrice's help. After a year of Beatrice sitting on wooden planks so George could nail them together, they realized the boat was too wide to fit through the garage door of their home in Rosslyn, so they had to tear down part of the doorframe. Christened the *Menehune*—mythological Hawaiian dwarfs known to be excellent craftsmen—the name also proved unfortunate when the boat all but capsized when they finally put it to water. The *Menehune* was a labor of love, though, and gave the Pattons many years of pleasure once Fred Ayer helped make her seaworthy.

While George first hired a skipper for longer distances, he soon found the man too cautious and went at it alone. By 1933, he felt confident enough in his abilities that he and Beatrice tried to cruise from Washington to Manchester-by-the-Sea along the inland waterways. Beatrice fell in love with her beautiful surroundings: quaint little towns, endless nature, and locks and drawbridges to move the *Moku* along as they cruised toward Massachusetts. Whenever the opportunity presented itself, they picked up friends along the way to spend a few hours with them.

Experienced at sailing in open sea, they discovered cruising was totally different when they reached Massachusetts Bay. After a journey of four hundred miles, the *Moku*'s engine suddenly died ten miles from their destination, near Marblehead, a rocky area known for its many maritime disasters. With luck still on their side, Beatrice and George did not become another statistic that day and made it to Manchester alive, but George sold the *Moku* the next day and decided to focus on sailboats instead.

JUST LIKE HER MOTHER, the only man Bee ever loved was her first love. John Knight Waters and Beatrice Ayer Patton Jr. were introduced at George's twentieth West Point reunion in June 1929, just weeks after Bee's return from Europe with Aunt Nita. Beatrice was still haunted by what had happened at Foxcroft, so George's reunion sounded like the perfect opportunity for the shy Bee to meet some young men. George asked Mrs. Harriet Rogers, an old friend, and the reunion hostess, for the "best cadet" to escort his daughter for the weekend. There was no doubt in Mrs. Rogers's mind that Cadet Waters was the man George was looking for: a champion fencer, a star football player, and an expert horseman.

Bee fell head over heels in love the moment she laid eyes on Johnnie. She continued dating at her parents' suggestion—they approved of the match, particularly liking the effect Johnnie had on their daughter's self-confidence—

but Bee had made up her mind. Come June 1931, she eagerly awaited a proposal, but Johnnie asked her to wait until he could give her the life he felt she deserved. Unfortunately, the Waterses were hit hard by the depression, and Johnnie moved back home to Baltimore with his two brothers to help their father pay off his debts.

Mr. Waters died in December 1932 (his wife had already passed away in 1915), and the proposal came the following summer at the Pattons' home in Rosslyn, Virginia. Bee first told her father, who immediately gave his blessing. Then, unable to contain her excitement, she ran into her sister's room—where Beatrice was helping Ruth Ellen pack for her last year at The Masters School— and exclaimed, "I'm going to marry Johnnie Waters." Beatrice noted in her diary that evening, "Of course I said yes—and all is well," but that was not really what happened according to Ruth Ellen.

Beatrice started crying, slapped her daughter in the face, and ran from the room, yelling, "You can't! You're much too young!" Hurt feelings were quickly mended, and Beatrice began planning the perfect wedding, but it had been a shocking reaction. Maybe it was the realization that Bee was all grown up. Maybe it was worry because she knew Bee never liked army life, and now she would be tethered to it forever. Or perhaps Beatrice worried about her husband. She had seen a tiny seed of unhappiness germinating in her Georgie for years, even though everyone else only saw the affable and fearless officer.

Beatrice's impulsive side usually surfaced only in connection with George. The more Ruth Ellen pondered her mother's irrational behavior that evening, the more it dawned on her that her father was probably at the root. Bee was "finally taking Georgie's youth away from him," bringing home once again that he still hadn't fulfilled the promise he had made Mr. Ayer in 1910.[71] Twenty-four years had passed since Beatrice put all her faith in him, yet as his daughter embarked on the same adventure, he was still waiting for an opportunity to gain the glory he had promised his wife.

George wrote in a postscript to a cousin, probably only half in jest, "How do you advise birth control for grandchildren—they would cramp my style."[72] Still young at heart with the constitution of a twenty-year-old, he desperately tried to hold back time. Worried complacency would come with age—hence why it was "better to live in the lime light a year than in the wings forever"— he had been obsessed with staying young. He exhorted Beatrice to do the same, but she mostly ignored his admonitions to dye her hair (the first streaks of gray appeared in her thirties) or lose weight (which she didn't need to do, as she was as svelte as ever).

*Figure 51. Beatrice letting her hair loose; Green Meadows stands in the background. (Courtesy of Scott C. Steward)*

Beatrice believed in aging naturally and scorned women who acted like "muttons dressed as lambs."[73] Compared to the other mothers who visited their daughters at The Masters School, Ruth Ellen considered hers less "sophisticated" in appearance—Beatrice was more sophisticated in her conversation topics as she hated irrelevant small talk. While everyone else had manicured fingers and coiffured hair, Beatrice cut her nails short so she could play the piano and always did her long hair up in a braid herself. Her priorities lay with her family, and unlike George, she didn't need to use her appearance as a substitute for self-confidence.

Appearance was everything to George, and he never spared any expense to look, as he put it, like the French aristocrat Beau Brummel. He never forgot the respect his father commanded at Lake Vineyard by his mere comportment, and he believed that "one must look well in order to hold peoples attention."[74] He was proud of his taut riding body and regal bearing, referring to his looks in many of the letters he wrote Beatrice, often wishing she could have seen him in his newest uniform.

Beatrice believed that "if you feel pretty, you'll look pretty." Endowed with a bit of the Bostonians' puritanical streak, she also thought one had to "make it last, wear it out, use it up, do without." Kay, who always dressed in the latest fashions from Paris and with a meticulous eye for detail, visited Green

Meadows once a year with the sole purpose of helping her sister clean out her closet, making sure she donated everything she hadn't worn in over a year.

"Men and women of New England," Beatrice once wrote, "hard to uproot as your native apple trees." After almost a quarter century in different locales, the Pattons were back to where it all began. Beatrice Ayer Patton and John Knight Waters were married on June 27, 1934, at St. John's Episcopal Church in Beverly. The ceremony commenced at 3:30 p.m. with *Lohengrin*'s wedding march and ended with the traditional arch of sabers, followed by a reception on the luscious lawn of Green Meadows. From his viewpoint as a "wedding guest," George marveled at "what a really great organizer I think you [Beatrice] are. No show could have gone better . . ."[75]

A picture of father and daughter taken just before their dance echoes one taken twenty-four years earlier at the Pattons' own wedding. Bee was wearing her grandmother and mother's wedding gown (which still fit Beatrice), and her veil was kept in place with orange blossoms. George was wearing the same ceremonial dress blues he wore back then, and to Beatrice's pride, "he doesn't have to button himself into it with a button hook either." The only difference was that he now sported several decorations and the silver leaf of a Lieutenant Colonel—he was finally promoted to the permanent rank of Lieutenant Colonel in March 1934, fourteen years after his last promotion. As to Beatrice, she wore "an empire model gown of heather gray chiffon and lace," leading George to remark that "no mother of a bride ever looked better or cried less."[76]

**Figure 52.** *Ruth Ellen—the maid of honor—never forgot the look on her father's face as he walked Bee down the aisle, "like a child who is having his favorite toy taken away." (Patton Museum)*

Amid the day's excitement, Beatrice noticed a blank notebook labeled "Mother's Thoughts on Marriage" on Bee's desk. She peeked inside to see what advice her daughter had gathered over the last twenty-three years, but to her surprise, there was only one entry: "To see if he is fresh, look in the fish's eye, but feel under the chicken's arm." So Beatrice took a pen and added a second entry before tucking the notebook away in Bee's suitcase: "Recipe for a successful marriage—the army travels on its stomach."[77]

ON HIS FIRST crossing to Hawaii in 1925, George had mused how "the men who dared this ocean must have been great fellows and fine seamen."[78] Ten years later, in March 1935, when he found out he would be returning to Hawaii to head the G-2 at Fort Shafter—the Army's intelligence section—he decided to dare the same ocean himself. While he tempted fate pretty much every day of his life in small measures, fourteen years after WWI he needed something big to test his luck. In 1934 he bought himself a second-hand, fifty-one-foot schooner called the *Arcturus* (after the brightest star in the Northern Hemisphere) and decided to sail her the 2,238 miles to Hawaii. "Pop was great on exploring new things ..." George IV said of his father, "anything that would round out his professional attainments."[79]

Everyone George talked to considered it a suicide mission, but Beatrice did not object. She knew George meant it when he said, "I would rather be dead than be nobody." As with fox hunting, instead of telling him he couldn't go, she decided to join him; if he was "going to drown, she was going to go drown with him." If the trip didn't kill them, though, Beatrice's cooking might.[80] Since George wanted everyone on board to have a job, and Beatrice wasn't strong enough to work the big sails, she offered to be the cook. She took cooking classes—with Kay at Avalon and with Bee at Fort Riley . . . or more than likely with their cooks—and tried to cultivate perfect balance by standing on a wooden plank set on top of a can.

As was to be expected, George took his job as captain just as seriously. He took a six-week celestial navigation course, and Fred, a more experienced sailor, helped his brother-in-law overhaul the *Arcturus*. The schooner did not have a long-distance radio or a lifeboat, but Fred set everything up so the Pattons could survive the projected fourteen days at sea.

George found five people crazy enough to join him: Beatrice, Anna and Gordon Prince (who had crossed the Atlantic on a schooner in 1920), George's first cousin Francis "Doc" Graves, and Captain Joseph "Joe" Ekeland, a Scandinavian rigger whom George hired in 1934 when he bought the *Arcturus*. George IV was desperate to join his parents, but he was deemed too young for such a dangerous crossing. He stayed behind with Alice Holmes and would travel to Hawaii once the school year finished.

Joe accompanied the *Arcturus* to Los Angeles in April 1935, transported on the afterdeck of the steamer *Kentuckian*. The family's furnishings, two cars, and seven horses were also sent ahead and made the crossing to Hawaii on an army transport. As to the Pattons themselves, they traveled to the West Coast by train and spent a few days with Bee and Johnnie at Fort Riley along the way. Ruth Ellen stayed behind with her sister and would continue the journey to Hawaii two months later on a commercial steamer.

When Beatrice and George arrived in Los Angeles, Joe had completed the final preparations and stocked the *Arcturus* with plenty of canned food, onions, potatoes, and beer. After a few days with Nita, who threw the sailors a big farewell party, the *Arcturus* set sail for Hawaii on May 8, 1935.[81] Beatrice felt none of the apprehension she had felt leaving for Hawaii the first time. Since publishing *Légendes Hawaiiennes* in 1932, she had been working on a historical Hawaiian novel, and being back on Oahu would fill her with the inspiration necessary to complete the project.

While Beatrice would be spared the constant worry of wondering where George was and whether he was safe, this was the riskiest endeavor they had ever undertaken. She was nothing but encouraging and never openly showed any apprehension, but it couldn't have been reassuring when George shrugged his shoulders as the *Arcturus* pulled out of the Wilmington Harbor and whispered to her, "We can learn, can't we?"[82]

# 9

## ARCTURUS

### PEARL HARBOR, HAWAII

#### 1935–1937

*IF WOMEN ONLY REALIZED HOW STRONG THEY WERE, THEY WOULD NOT GO AROUND BEING DISCONTENTED AND TRYING TO BE EQUAL TO MEN.*

Beatrice might have been a haole—one not native to Hawaii—but she truly inhabited the spirit of aloha. More than just a salutation, aloha became a way of living, an inherent part of the Kānaka Maoli's culture. In 1986, the "Aloha Spirit" was encoded into law, defining it as "the coordination of mind and heart within each person," a "mutual regard and affection and . . . warmth in caring with no obligation in return."

It signified Akahai, "kindness, to be expressed with tenderness"; Lōkahi, "unity, to be expressed with harmony"; and 'Olu'olu, "[agreeableness], to be expressed with pleasantness." In addition, it signified Ha'aha'a, "humility, to be expressed with modesty"; and Ahonui, "patience, to be expressed with perseverance."[1]

The spirit of aloha aligned perfectly with Beatrice's personality and her belief that "there is no real happiness in getting unless you get in order to give."[2] Born "down-to-earth humble" and blessed with an open—and rather progressive—mind, putting people at ease was most important to her, regardless of the subject they came to discuss. When an Army Air Corps lieutenant showed up on her doorstep at Fort Shafter with a beautiful woman in tow, she took them into the living room, where the young man awkwardly explained the situation.

He had met Miss Jones a few months earlier, right after she stepped off the boat from San Francisco, where she had worked as a prostitute. Trouble made her flee to a brothel in Honolulu where licensed prostitution existed, but now Miss Jones and the lieutenant were in love and they wanted to get married. Considering the delicate nature of the situation and the fact that his mother lived thousands of miles away, the lieutenant came to ask for the approval of "the greatest lady he ever met."[3]

All and sundry respected Beatrice's opinion on a wide range of subjects, and she never betrayed the trust of those who confided in her. She was discreet because that was how she was raised and because she had "known several able officers to be ruined by malicious gossipy wives."[4] Beatrice was unperturbed by the lieutenant's story and asked him to return in an hour. As she talked with Miss Jones privately, she realized the woman was one of those people "from whom sin departed like water off a duck's back." When the lieutenant returned to pick up his intended, Beatrice whispered to him, "God bless you both; you are a very lucky young man."

"The gift of giving" was what defined Beatrice, whether it was through financial support, hard-earned advice, or friendship. After a quarter-century in the Army, "the greenest bride ever" was now the seasoned veteran. People no longer knocked on her door to offer advice; they now knocked to ask for advice. Beatrice was as much an individualist as George, and she believed the rigid social rules of the Army were meant to be broken. She detested officers' wives who refused to speak to those of lesser rank; her door was open to anyone who needed a listening ear, regardless of rank, race, or social background. She never judged and always kept an open mind to give the most objective and judicious advice possible. And in the case of the lieutenant and Miss Jones, they led a long and happy life together.

---

In many regards, long-distance ocean faring was nothing like small yacht sailing along the East Coast. Despite fair weather and steady wind, once the *Arcturus* hit open waters, Beatrice discovered, to her great surprise, that she suffered from severe seasickness. Unfortunately, there was no medicine against the debilitating malady in 1935, so all she could do was spend most of the day asleep in her berth while Doc Graves took care of the cooking. Occasionally, she came out on deck to enjoy the cool night's air and to regale her crewmates in a Scottish accent with stories of Mr. Glencannon, Guy Gilpatric's tales of a Scottish ship engineer with a walrus mustache. Meanwhile, George recited poetry well into the night, spouting forth half a dozen Kipling poems from memory to every single one Gordon Prince remembered.[5]

*Figure 53. The Arcturus's crew: Gordon and Anna Prince, George, Doc Graves, Beatrice, and Joe Ekeland. (Patton Museum)*

George did rather well as a navigator, working on the small galley table with his maps and compass as he charted the *Arcturus*'s course. Since he had the least sailing experience of anyone on board, he didn't make any navigational decisions until he had consulted the crew, but then "he'd never have any second thoughts or look back."[6] The crossing proceeded surprisingly smoothly, and except for a few dolphins and sampans, the *Arcturus* was all alone until they spotted the *U.S.S Memphis*. After a fifteen-day-and-one-hour trip covering roughly 2,450 miles, the schooner made landfall on May 22, 1935, in the exact spot George intended and within hours of his prognostication.[7]

The *Arcturus* anchored off Coconut Island—a tiny blob of land in Hilo Bay —and her passengers spent a few days exploring the treasures of the Big Island. Beatrice, Doc, and the Princes rode up to Volcano House, the perfect respite from the heat of the tropics. They lunched with noted volcanologist Dr. Jaggar in the hotel's glass-enclosed dining room, which offered views of the Kīlauea volcano on one side and snowcapped mountains on the other side, and embarked on a private tour of Mauna Lao. "The whole forest is so vibrant with life that one can almost hear it growing," Beatrice wrote of one of her excursions up the volcano.

Suddenly, the forest ends and there, incredibly, is a vast dump heap of rock, quivering in its own heat waves, while a chill strikes the watcher—sweating from the climb. And coats are buttoned to step out onto the lava, past spongy volcanic ash called a'a, and over dangerously twisting stretches of the lava called pahoehoe: glassy crumbles, knife-edged. There are steam cracks oozing sulfurous vapor, ancient craters—pits hundreds of feet deep and hundreds of feet across—some filled with dried lava that looks like the scum on cocoa, some filled with giant lehua trees so deep down that only their scarlet-blossomed crowns can be seen. White-tailed tropical birds fly out of nowhere, swoop down and disappear into Halemaumau.[8]

The *Arcturus* continued its voyage on May 27, sailing 110 miles to Māui, the second-largest island in the Hawaiian chain and the lushest of all. Doc reluctantly left the party and returned to Los Angeles on urgent business, but the Pattons and the Princes spent the next few days at the Haleakala Ranch, established by the Baldwin family in 1888 in the shadow of the Haleakala volcano. The Baldwins were one of Hawaii's Big Five—five industrial families whose companies were mainly involved in the sugar business and who wielded enormous political and economic power—and were responsible for introducing polo to the island of Māui (much like Walter Dillingham on Oahu).

Twenty-six days after leaving California, the *Arcturus* finally sailed into Honolulu Harbor at 4:30 p.m. on Monday, June 3, 1935. An official Aloha party greeted the schooner with music and hula dancing and covered the crew with so many leis that only their eyes remained visible. The number of people waiting on Pier 15 was a testament to how well-liked the Pattons were in Hawaii, but the Army brass was in stark contrast to the carefree crew, tanned dark from the sun.

THE PREVALENT TENSIONS between the Native Hawaiians and the military came to a boiling point in 1932 with the Massie Trial, when a young Navy wife accused two Hawaiians, two Japanese, and one Chinese of rape. Just like Beatrice, the twenty-year-old Thalia Massie came from a privileged background, but that was where the similarities ended. Mrs. Massie's marriage was unhappy, her family fell on hard times, she hated mixing with her husband's naval colleagues, and she looked down upon the Native Hawaiian and non-white population.[9]

The case against the five men ended in a mistrial when the jurors deadlocked over the conflicting evidence, so Thalia's mother, Grace Hubbard Bell Fortescue, took justice into her own hands. Mr. Kahahawai, one of the five wrongly accused men, was kidnapped by Grace, her son-in-law, and two of his naval buddies, and shot to death when he refused to confess to a crime he didn't commit. Caught trying to dispose of the body, the criminals were found guilty and sentenced to ten years in prison, but the judge commuted the sentence under pressure from the Department of the Navy. They were released after one hour of community service and returned to the mainland to continue their lives as if nothing had ever happened.

The relationship between the military and civilian communities in Hawaii had always been plagued by "cultural differences, land-use conflicts, and racial discrimination."[10] Major General Wells, commander of the Hawaiian Division from 1930 to 1934, and Charles Judd, who worked at the Ministry of Forestry, founded the Piko Hiking Club, "an association of men who enjoyed hiking and the exploration of the out-of-the-way places on Oahu," in the hopes of improving said relationship.

By the time the Pattons returned to Oahu, the Piko Hiking Club had established several permanent trails and cabins along the island's volcanic terrain. Military membership was dwindling, but Beatrice and George were eager to join, and by June 1936, the two of them, plus Ruth Ellen, completed the membership requirement: cross the Ko'olau or the Wai'anae range three times. Charles Judd was an enthusiastic guide who always wore a yellow handkerchief around his neck and was followed everywhere by his dog, Panache. To ensure everyone was still following him, he would occasionally call out the club's motto and await its echo: "Pehea kou piko? How's your belly button?"[11]

On September 27, 1936, Beatrice, George, and Ruth Ellen took part in the club's most challenging hike ever at twenty-eight miles. The group left at 5:30 in the morning and followed the Pupukea, Kahuku Summit, and Kipapa trails until they reached Uncle Tom's cabin at 6 p.m., where dinner was waiting.[12] They took homing pigeons along in case of an emergency, but all thirty-seven participants—including ten officers and just four women—made it down the mountain by midnight. Unfortunately, this most memorable hike also turned out to be the club's swan song, and the Piko Hiking Club disbanded in March 1937.[13]

LOCATED five miles from downtown Honolulu, Fort Shafter was the oldest military base on Oahu and the home of the Hawaiian high command since its founding in 1907. In June 1935, the Pattons moved into Quarters Six on Palm Circle, a residential loop surrounding a grassy parade field ringed by royal palm trees. Since George was "a man of considerable wealth," and he asked to have the blueprints of his new home sent to him in Washington, rumors quickly circulated "that he intended to completely remodel and make additions to his future home at his own expense."[14]

The three-story home became a veritable hotel during the two years the Pattons lived there, and the first guests already arrived on July 11. Frederick Ayer Jr. and his sister Anne traveled with their cousin George IV and the ever-present Alice Holmes, who now acted more as a housekeeper than a nanny. A week later, Ruth Ellen and Bee, now known in Army circles as Mrs. Waters, also sailed to Hawaii.[15]

*Figure 54. Quarters Six on Palm Court at Fort Shafter. (U.S. Army)*

If Fred and Hilda's eldest children expected to be lounging on Waikiki Beach for the next four weeks, they forgot to take "Auntie Bee" into account. Beatrice was not about to coddle her niece and nephew; she treated them like she always treated her own children: adapt to your environment. She tried to get the youngsters interested in Hawaiian culture by dragging them to countless ruins, but to them, everything looked like "a pile of rocks."

Frederick Jr. remembered traveling with his aunt "about the Hawaiian Islands where she knew and was liked by everyone from the Big Four [Five] families and the governor to Japanese vegetable growers and native fishermen. She knew and could talk on equal terms with the curator of the museum on Oahu and Dr. Jaggar, the famed volcanologist of Mauna Loa."[16]

Beatrice, Frederick Jr., Anne, George IV, Bee, and Ruth Ellen sailed on the *Arcturus* to the Big Island on July 23 for a ten-day visit to the Parker Ranch.[17] One of the reasons George wanted to sail the *Arcturus* to Hawaii was so he would have the freedom to travel between the islands at his leisure. The schooner resided at the Pearl Harbor Yacht Club for the next two years, with Joe remaining on board as captain and Beatrice joining the Pearl Harbor Yacht Club's Star Fleet. She was soon crowned "the First Lady skipper in the Territory" as she raced the *Abba Dabba* and embarrassingly won the Mrs. Patton Trophy, which she put up in January 1936.[18]

The Ayers returned to Massachusetts on August 10, and Bee returned to Fort Riley on September 21. Ruth Ellen, however, had decided to forgo college when she graduated from The Masters School in 1934, and she was eager to spend the next two years with her parents and little brother in Hawaii. She joined the Junior League—an educational, women's volunteer organization aimed at improving communities—and started working at the occupational therapy workshop of Queen's Hospital in Honolulu. She became "a very popular member of the Army set," joined several organizations, and started acting in the community theater.

Eleven-year-old George IV no longer sat at the kiddie table or enjoyed separate activities with Nanny Holmes, so Beatrice urged her daughter to take him along on her outings. Ruth Ellen hadn't felt particularly close to her brother because of their eight-year age difference, but now a bond developed between them that would last a lifetime. Master George, as he was sometimes referred to, was closest to his mother until the Pattons' second tour of duty in Hawaii, when he also developed a more mature relationship with his father.

Unwittingly, the next two years on the islands would be the last time father and son would spend a significant amount of time together. The two Georges often flew to Molokai to hunt spotted deer, sailed to Hawaii to spend a few days at the Parker Ranch—where young George spent the summer of 1936 working as a paniolo—and joined Beatrice and Ruth Ellen as they explored archaeological sites around Oahu.

There are many differing accounts of the Pattons' second tour of duty in Hawaii, but George IV always remembered those two years as some of the best times he spent with his father, mother, and sister.

*Figure 55. Hunting on Molokai. George IV always enjoyed "a fine relationship" with his father, "a magnificent individual who loved life and people and the outdoors and the good things that go with them more than anything else." (Library of Congress)*

"MOST OF US GET SCARED," Beatrice once said, leaving no doubt about where she got the idea. "It's *acting* scared that's cowardly."[19] So she never did, always assuming the role of George's willing sidekick, trying everything in her power to keep him happy and interested.

George often tried his hand at the projects described in *Popular Mechanics,* so not long after he arrived in Hawaii, he made a diving helmet he'd seen in the September 1932 issue. According to the instructions, he used a five-gallon white-lead can, fifty pounds of lead, a heavy plate-glass disk, a fifty-foot garden hose, and a tire pump.

The magazine claimed the helmet was effective up to thirty feet deep, and Beatrice was the first to volunteer as they took the contraption out on the *Arcturus.*[20] The whole family watched in admiration as she dove underneath the heavy helmet and let herself sink slowly to the bottom, about twelve feet below. George patted himself on the back as he saw bubbles rise to the surface until young George stood on the air hose and Beatrice's helmet filled with water. One can only imagine her reaction when George pulled her up, but his wife's performance tickled him. With a proud smile, he said to his children, "Your mother is a fearless woman!"[21]

At fifty, Beatrice was doing things she had never imagined herself doing. While some things she did at first for fear of losing George, she eventually discovered in herself the same eccentricity he possessed. It turned out that Beatrice was more like George than anyone ever suspected, although the clues were there all along. When she was eleven years old, Beatrice had been about to jump feet-first into a freshly opened Egyptian tomb, and it was only the action of the Ayers' quick-thinking guide that prevented her from ending up in a cobra pit.

Nearly four decades later, roaming a deserted beach once inhabited by warring Hawaiian chieftains, Beatrice's tendency to leap before thinking hadn't left her. She knew the islands were honeycombed with undiscovered burial caves, so her heart leaped with joy when George IV excitedly called out in the distance that he had found one. She immediately jumped into the abyss before anyone could stop her and eagerly wandered deeper into the cave, stunned by the number of neatly arranged bones she saw. Everything suddenly made sense when she heard George yell in the distance that she was wandering around a family vault. After dragging her out, he showed her the chained gate with a family name chiseled above; she had gained access through the partially collapsed vault in the back.

Throughout the years, Beatrice found several real burial caves, always with "an old Hawaiian lingering in the vicinity . . . They do not pop out at once unexpectedly, but simply seem to be there as part of the scenery." These "guardians of the sacred places," as she called them, were the perfect deterrent before legislation like the Native American Graves Protection and Repatriation

Act.[22] Except for the mummy's toe in a moment of youthful ignorance, Beatrice was happy to satisfy her curiosity by looking and taking pictures. Historical artifacts were to be respected and experienced in their natural surroundings, which became eerily apparent when she began working at the Bishop Museum in Honolulu. She trembled every time she walked past the glowering statue of Kalai-pahoa, the Poison God, "captive behind lock and key."[23]

Following the publication of *Légendes Hawaiiennes* in 1932, Beatrice began working on a second book on Hawaiian history. She was excited to recommence her research in person and quickly befriended Dr. Peter Buck, the director of the Bishop Museum. A medical doctor from New Zealand, Dr. Buck's interest in ethnology stemmed from the realization that his patients' cultural backgrounds significantly influenced how he could perform his medical duties. It didn't take long for Dr. Buck to be affected by Beatrice's enthusiasm. He not only gave her a job at the museum cataloging fishhooks but also advised her on Hawaiian culture in writing her newest book. While Beatrice's job seemed rather mundane, it allowed her to discover all the artifacts hidden away in the Bishop Museum.[24]

WITH THE OFFICIAL start of the polo season less than two months away, the *Hawaiian Star-Bulletin* heralded the return of Colonel Patton, "one of the leading polo players in the United States Army," as the Army's best chance of winning the Inter-Island Tournament again.[25] However, upon the *Arcturus*'s arrival in Honolulu, George told reporters he merely wished "to continue playing in more or less informal matches" since he wanted to give "the younger men a chance in the actual competitions."[26] However, Beatrice knew her husband well enough to realize that he would not be able to resist the flattery and the call of glory.

Polo was as much a war preparation for George as it was for Beatrice, and she watched "cavalier and unflustered" on August 26, 1935, as the Fort Shafter team took on The Islanders (the Māui team led by the Baldwin brothers). Players became so involved in the game that they lost all semblance of fear, and casual observers felt only excitement as the ground shook with eight horses careening across the polo field at thirty-five miles per hour. However, for those in the crowd who truly understood the risks involved, each seven-and-a-half minute chukker felt like an eternity. Beatrice's heart trembled every time she saw George get on a polo pony, but while some might prefer not to watch, she considered waiting by the phone the worst experience of all.

Known as a "rough player, always on the offensive, noted for headlong dashes and wild swings which might have been intended to terrorize his opponents rather than really to maim them," George played position number three, the team captain and the player with the highest-rated handicap. Aggressiveness and competitiveness defined a good number three, and George "went after polo with the same delighted ferocity that he gives to any enterprise."[27] A "great battle" was seen as Fort Shafter tried to defend its honor after losing the Inter-Island Tournament against California's Midwick team, and by the start of the fourth chukker, they were in the lead.

It was hard to keep track of the players in the heat of battle, but Beatrice had her eyes on George as he rode in pursuit of Richard Baldwin to prevent him from evening the score. She watched in horror when his horse suddenly stopped short, and George made "a somersault over the animal's neck and [landed] in a pile under his forelegs," hitting the ground headfirst. Luckily his horse did not trample him, but Beatrice expected the worst when he let go of the reins—his cardinal rule was never to let go no matter what—and remained motionless on the field.

After being "out cold for several minutes," George unsteadily got on his feet, refused all help, remounted his horse, and finished the match without making a single goal.[28] At the end of the sixth chukker, Fort Shafter lost by one point, and The Islanders received the "handsome cups" paid for and handed out by Beatrice. The big thrill of the day had been George's spectacular fall, and even though he "recovered in a few minutes and resumed play," the incident would have a lasting effect on both Pattons.[29]

The 1935 polo season was "one of great social gayety," but a worried Beatrice suggested they forgo the customary after-game cocktail party.[30] George, however, brushed off the accident and insisted on joining his teammates for a quick drink before leaving on a pleasure cruise on the *Arcturus*. It wasn't until two days later that Beatrice's suspicions were confirmed, and she realized something was indeed quite amiss. While preparing to sail back into Pearl Harbor, George suddenly looked up from the wheel and stared at his wife as if he had just woken up from a deep sleep.

"Where the hell am I?" he asked, confused as he took in his surroundings. The last thing he remembered was "seeing the ground come up and hit my face" when he fell off his horse.

That same day a doctor belatedly diagnosed a concussion and advised Beatrice to keep her husband away from sun and alcohol for a week. George had suffered several concussions in the past without noticeable consequences. This time, however, there was no mistaking to those who knew George Patton best that he somehow no longer was the same man. Over the next few months, he suffered all the classic telltale signs of (what we now call) traumatic brain injury—including irritability, anger, depression, and teariness—exacerbated by his already fragile emotional state at the thought of turning fifty.

"No one that ever sees me now would ever know what a pretty girl I was," turned out to be the only complaint Beatrice's children ever heard their mother make about growing old. George, however, had written Beatrice as far back as

1904 that he "just hate[d] to grow old and be oppressed with the knowledge of how little I have done; it makes me feel absolutely worthless."[31] To have all this talent and ambition and to not be able to utilize it was maddening to George. As he reread Major General Fuller's *Generalship: Its Diseases and their Cure,* he was painfully reminded that all the heroes he admired had found glory by the time they were fifty.

"Uncle George had an overpowering fear of growing old or losing any of his physical powers . . . ," Frederick Jr. said of his uncle and godfather. "Sometimes this feeling on his part resulted in behavior which fell far short of correct."[32] When George awoke on November 11, 1935, he preferred to wallow in self-pity and refused to get up. Beatrice left him alone for some time, then returned to coax him out of bed with female guile: she calmly explained he'd been fifty for the last year and was technically beginning his fifty-first year.

THOUSANDS OF VISITORS attended the Māui County Fair in Kahului every year, attracted by the entertainment and the plethora of stalls selling everything from Hawaiian needlework to local foods. Horse racing stood supreme until Mr. Baldwin introduced exhibition jumping at the eighteenth Māui County Fair in October 1935.[33] George eagerly agreed to give a demonstration, and he sent his best horses ahead so they could get used to their temporary accommodations. George, Beatrice, and Ruth Ellen were all entered to participate in the jumping competition—on Red Fox, Quicksilver, and My Risk, respectively—but the day before the Pattons were to sail for Māui on the *Arcturus,* a severe case of bronchitis brought Beatrice to her knees.

Ruth Ellen offered to stay home, but Beatrice insisted she could manage with the help of Alice Holmes, Emma Ahuena Taylor, and a Hawaiian masseuse, "a descendant of those skillful priests and a devout Catholic." Within a few days, she felt good enough to attend a dinner party organized by Major General and Mrs. Drum in honor of Major General MacArthur, who was on his way to the Philippines to become the chief military adviser to its commonwealth government.

In a chapter of *Love Without End* titled "Doctors, Priests and Tabus," Beatrice described how alternative medicine healed her:

> She [the masseuse] had gone into the hills at dawn to pick the noni leaves [a small fruit-bearing tree in the coffee family that grows on lava flows] for my chest, while the dew was still on them. She arrived with the leaves in one hand and an electric light bulb with an extension cord in the other. She laid the leaves on me and heated them by passing the 100-watt electric light bulb back and forth over them while I lay and coughed and reflected on the blend of old and new that is Hawaii as we know it. When this was done, she kneaded me all over with

mashed kukui nuts [one of the Polynesians' canoe plants that grows nuts particularly useful for easily absorbing oils] squeezed into a cloth, and as she worked,
she talked ...[34]

"The search for truth is common to every age and to every race," Beatrice
discovered when she delved into the magical world of Hawaiian medicine and
healing. "In old Hawaii, all doctors were priests ... [and] roughly divided into
five classes: diagnosticians, bone setters, drug therapists or herbalists, physio-
therapists or masseuses, and psychotherapists." After her experience with the
physiotherapist, Beatrice learned about the herbalists when she told a
Hawaiian friend how "[a] streak of bad luck dogged my family in 1935."

More than three hundred plants were used on the islands to make medicine, but their properties went far beyond medicinal. One friend suggested that
Beatrice not only allowed the evil spirits to run inside but enticed them "by
planting red ti around the house." Then there was the Kahuna-ana-ana, or
psychotherapist, "the lowest class of wizard ... whose power worked through
fear."[35]

Beatrice's bout with bronchitis and subsequent cure awakened a greater
interest in native Hawaiian foods. The best place to satisfy her hunger for
knowledge was at a Hawaiian lū'au, which reminded her of a New England
clambake because many dishes were cooked in an underground oven or imu.
In the morning, a hole was dug in the sand and filled with hot stones; then, the
food was buried and left to simmer while the guests enjoyed themselves on the
beach with live music and hula dancing. The most popular imu dish was the
Kālua pig (shredded pork), served alongside lau lau (steamed meat wrapped
in taro leaves), poi, poke (raw fish), and haupia (coconut pudding). Most of the
lū'aus Beatrice attended were at the invitation of her Kānaka Maoli friends,
and as such, they were authentic.

Beatrice had always been an adventurous eater willing to try anything,
from calf's testicles at the Parker Ranch to the ancient Hawaiian delicacy of
dog liver at a lū'au. The poi dog, or 'īlio, was brought to the islands by the
Polynesians and was a staple of the Hawaiian diet when Captain Cook arrived.
One of his lieutenants described the dogs as dim-witted, with "short, crooked
legs, long backs, and prickly ears." They also had flat heads, possibly because
their diet consisted of poi, which didn't require chewing.[36] The 'īlio tasted like
lamb and was mostly eaten by women, who were forbidden to eat pork until
the tabu was lifted in 1830. However, like so many other facets of the Hawaiian
culture, the arrival of Westerners ended the tradition of eating dogs, and the
'īlio became extinct because of interbreeding with European dogs.

Some Native Hawaiians, however, continued the practice at traditional
lū'aus or private ceremonies, using any stray dog they could find. Beatrice fell
violently ill with dysentery, a gastrointestinal disease that usually cured itself

after about a week of misery. George said it served her right because "anyone who ate dog's liver would eat their own children, like Cronos," but Beatrice took a more philosophical view. To her, it was proof of the ambivalent relationship she had with man's best friend. The Ayers loved their dogs but reasoned they belonged outside, while the Pattons considered their furry friends to be one of the family. Beatrice always lived in harmony with them, but according to Ruth Ellen, "there never was a dog so sick that he couldn't make it to her [Beatrice's] feet before he vomited."[37]

THE WORLD of dating was not one the Pattons were very familiar with—Beatrice promised herself to George when she was just sixteen, and Bee was spoken for at eighteen when she made her debut—hence they were rather strict with Ruth Ellen when it concerned the opposite sex. Beatrice understood the world of hops, horse shows, and the Junior League, but Hawaii was different. As Ruth Ellen started dating men outside of the Army, she was shocked to discover both she and her parents had a reputation around Oahu. Colonel and Mrs. Patton were rumored to belong to Honolulu's fast set—the one who played polo and drank hard, among many other immoral things—and Ruth Ellen was said to be "fast," out with a different man every night.

Ruth Ellen followed her mother's advice of never seeing the same guy twice in one week in case "you run out of conversation, and then what?" However, she considered herself anything but fast and didn't even allow a boy to kiss her on the lips lest she fall into temptation. "What man would want to blow his nose in another man's dirty handkerchief?" her father always told her. Beatrice explained that fast meant an entirely different thing to people of different social classes and that it was perfectly alright to see other men as long as one wasn't engaged.[38]

Mother and daughter shared everything, but there was one incident Ruth Ellen felt unable to share until she married in 1940. Invited to a dinner dance at Schofield Barracks during the mid-thirties, she was set up with a young lieutenant who belonged to a prominent political family but who was known by some to have a bad reputation. Ruth Ellen didn't want to disappoint the evening's hostess and apprehensively agreed. She kept her guard up all evening, and all went well until she asked the young man to drive her home at midnight. Instead of driving toward Honolulu, he pulled into a secluded sugarcane field near the Kūkaniloko birthstones and stopped the car.

Beatrice taught her daughters that a woman had two possessions in life: her reputation and her virginity. The former you inherit from your father and husband, but the latter "is yours and yours alone to give to whom you choose, and if you give it away for nothing you get nothing in return."[39]

Ruth Ellen didn't plan to lose either that night. Years of horseback riding gave her strength beyond what one might expect—like her mother, she stood just a little over five foot three—so she managed to wrestle free from the lieutenant's grasp. She ran from the car and kneed her assailant in the groin when he caught up with her.

Ruth Ellen contemplated driving to the military police, but then she remembered his father was powerful enough to destroy her father's career . . . at least if George didn't ruin his own career first by defending his daughter's honor. With adrenaline coursing through her veins, she managed to drag the lieutenant into the backseat and left him there once she had driven back to Fort Shafter. Beatrice and George—who always remained awake until their daughter gave a gentle knock on their bedroom door upon her safe return—were ready to give her an earful when she arrived way past her 1 a.m. curfew. Ruth Ellen adamantly refused to tell them what happened, but her torn dress, messy hair, and bruised eye spoke volumes.

As Carlo D'Este wrote in *Patton: A Genius for War*, "when it came to his family, there was a puritanical streak in Patton that would lead to the unleashing of his wrath for the slightest real or perceived disrespect to his daughters or his wife."[40] Years earlier, during the Piedmont Hunt in Virginia, George had watched Ruth Ellen set her horse in preparation for clearing a post rail fence, a crucial moment as once committed to the jump, a rider cannot make any changes without risking serious injury. He watched in horror as a careless rider appeared out of nowhere and missed colliding with Ruth Ellen by a hair's breadth. He overtook the sloppily dressed officer with the horrible riding style and cursed him for longer than his customary three minutes.

Only later that afternoon did George learn from his commanding officer that the man he so profusely insulted was Argentina's military attaché, who outranked him. No doubt Beatrice was the author of the apology note the man received; by the time he finished reading, he was convinced the verbal onslaught George unleashed against him was a compliment worded in typical "Anglo-Saxon sporting terms."[41]

"Oh, that Georgie," Beatrice once cried to Ruth Ellen, "he goes around distributing blows to people right and left and I go around distributing roses."[42]

---

DR. THOMAS JAGGAR was a sixty-four-year-old volcanologist from Philadelphia who was as dedicated to the study of volcanoes as George was to the study of war. The Harvard graduate witnessed the devastating 1902 eruption of La Soufrière on St. Vincent, but the 1908 Messina earthquake (and subsequent tsunami), which killed 80,000, made him aware of the importance of long-term observation. So, in 1909, he traveled to Hawaii and decided on the Halema'u-ma'u crater to establish the Hawaiian Volcano Observatory. Dr. Jaggar integrated well with the local population, so well that they believed "he was under the special protection of the goddess [Pele] and doing her great and flattering honor by studying her moods."[43]

When Mauna Loa on the Big Island erupted again on November 21, 1935, five newly formed lava streams began flowing toward Hilo, threatening the town's water supply. Dr. Jaggar had the novel idea to bomb the volcano in the hopes of disrupting the flow and enlisted the help of the U.S. Army Air Corps. Colonel Patton was tasked with organizing "the first-ever aerial bombing of a volcano," which occurred on December 27, 1935.

Whether the bombings had anything to do with the flow ceasing on January 2 was never determined, but "everyone knew that Pele was furious," and she took her revenge on the pilots.[44] According to Beatrice, the wife of one of the pilots committed suicide by drinking "a corrosive poison that burned her throat," and one pilot was killed a few weeks after the bombing in a midair collision that his co-pilot miraculously survived.

George was spared the wrath of Pele, but by the summer of 1936, he was in desperate need of another challenge. He had "too much time on my hands, too much alcohol, and too little perspiration," and his commanding officer, with whom he had cordial social relations, was making his professional life hell. On August 31, George received a severe public reprimand from Major General Drum at the Inter-Island Tournament polo match between the Oahu Blues and the Army.

The score was 8–0 in favor of the Blues at the start of the fourth chukker, when Lowell Dillingham took a nasty spill, and his horse stepped on both his wrists. Walter Dillingham, who had been refereeing, took his son's place, playing his first match since breaking his leg at a tournament in Shanghai two years earlier.[45] The return of the "grand old man of Hawaiian polo" brought excitement both on and off the polo field.

With mallets and horses all bungled up on the edge of the field, George unleashed a steady stream of expletives.[46] Fred once testified in court—in a case where a polo player hit an opponent on the head with a mallet—that swearing "is fairly common in the heat of combat," and he often did it himself. "Some players swear at the world in general, and some swear when they miss the ball, and some swear at their horses, and nobody minds much."[47]

Unfortunately, Major General Drum did mind the meaningless trash talk of an athlete, or he saw his chance to get back at his subordinate. He stood up on the dais, motioned for Colonel Patton to approach, and reprimanded him for "foul language and conduct unbecoming a gentleman." A silence descended over the field as the captain of the "wonder team of 1926" was relieved; George saluted with a firm "Yes, sir" and walked off the field.

As he often did when he disagreed with his superiors, George "suppressed his desire to react" so he wouldn't decrease his chances of commanding a great army one day. However, Major General Drum, the most powerful man in Hawaii in military circles, hadn't counted on Walter Dillingham, the most powerful man in Hawaii in civilian circles. After conferring with Mr. Baldwin, who stood watching on the sidelines, he rode up to Major General Drum and gave him an ultimatum. Unless Colonel Patton was reinstated as captain of the Army team, the game would be finished, and the tournament canceled. Knowing how popular the Inter-Island Tournament was and how important it was to the creation of goodwill between the Army and the Hawaiians, General Drum had no choice but to recall his subordinate and allow the match to continue. Before the game even recommenced, he and his family left the dais and drove home.[48]

The Pattons and the Drums were neighbors on Palm Circle and had known each other for a long time. The men were both members of the Baltic Society—a small club created by General Pershing's staff who sailed from New York on May 28, 1917, on board the H.M.S. Baltic—and yearly commemorated their entrance into WWI with a get-together.[49] As commander of the Hawaiian Department, Major General Drum was the one who requested George as his G-2, but he quickly came to regret the decision when he noticed how popular the Pattons were. It galled him enormously to be overshadowed in social circles by a man six years his junior and two ranks below him.

Possibly Hugh Drum had been jealous of George for years, but Mrs. Drum seemed to be the only one who realized it and continually tried to make amends. Mary Drum was "a wonderful person with a soul of great sensitivity," and she and Beatrice spent a lot of time together organizing events as members of the same organizations.[50] So when Mary heard George had found himself another challenge—sailing the Arcturus to Fanning and Palmyra Island, twelve-hundred miles south of Hawaii in the middle of the South Pacific—she nailed a St. Jude's medal to the schooner's mast. She also promised to keep an eye on Ruth Ellen, who would travel with the Drums to Volcano House in her parents' absence.

The crew could undoubtedly use the protection of the patron saint of hopeless causes and desperate situations because George was still doubting his navigational skills. He thought it would be pretty embarrassing if they got lost at sea, "like a modern example of the flying dutchman," but then again, with how his life was going, "possibly being lost at sea would be a rather convenient way out."[51]

Beatrice signed on without hesitation. She was thrilled to visit three remote islands named after one of her ancestors and relieved to see George enthusiastic about something again. A picture in the local newspaper showed him dressed in a polo shirt and slacks, ticking off the essentials on his clipboard as the *Arcturus* was stocked with cases of canned food and fresh fruit.[52] One of only five private schooners in the Hawaiian Territories capable of making a trip as the one George planned, the *Arcturus* was packed to the gills. In addition to the Pattons, there was Suzuki, the Japanese cook who brought his fishing spears; Lieutenant Levenick, a classmate of son-in-law Johnnie Waters; Jimmie Wilder, a well-known ethnologist; Joe Ekeland; and George IV.

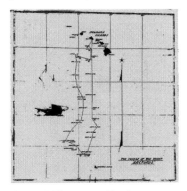

**Figure 56.** *The voyage to Fanning Island. (Library of Congress)*

When the *Arcturus* sailed from Pearl Harbor at 8 a.m. on September 10, 1936, thirteen-year-old George IV was the most excited member on board. He was just a deck boy, but at least he was deemed old enough to come along this time. There was no better person to learn the ropes from than master rigger Joe Ekeland, who laid the foundation for George IV to one day become an experienced sailor in his own right.

The forty-four-year-old Joe was born in Sweden and had been on the water continuously since he was ten years old; he even explained to Beatrice that he had such a strong upper body because he went nowhere on his legs.[53] His back was covered in a tattoo of a dragon he named the Moo Fat, an impressive piece of art from Bali that George loved showing off to the women in the harbor. Joe's personal life was somewhat mysterious and a favorite topic of conversation for Beatrice.[54] He was a fun, modest, and gregarious man "of high principles" and remained a loyal friend of the Pattons for life.

While the crew considered Joe the *Arcturus*'s captain, George remained in charge of navigation. Young George remembered the only time his father "would get a little testy with me was when I tried to talk with him when he was navigating, and he had every right since there were no sophisticated navigation aids in those days."[55] Luckily, conditions were good heading south on the Pacific Ocean, and the *Arcturus* reached Fanning Island after sailing a little over nine hundred miles in ten days. Beatrice couldn't wait to explore the remote island her ancestor, Captain Edmund Fanning, had discovered on June 11, 1798, while sailing to China on the *Betsey*.

Except for the Polynesians who might have passed the chain of three islands on their way to Hawaii, Captain Fanning had been the first to spot what would be called Fanning Island, Washington Island, and Palmyra Island. In typical Fanning fashion, Edmund was "loath to spend his time in needless idleness" and seemed to have had a penchant for the sea. He had left Groton, Connecticut, when he was fourteen to be a cabin boy, and through his industriousness, became captain ten years later. Captured several times by the British during his travels, being the nephew of General Edmund Fanning—a colonial administrator from New York who joined the British Army during the Revolutionary War—always got him and his crew released immediately.

Captain Fanning's great-great-grandfather was Edmund Fanning, who happened to be the great-great-grandfather of Hope Fanning, Beatrice's great-grandmother. Simply put, Captain Fanning was Hope's third cousin and Beatrice's third cousin, third removed. Beatrice eagerly devoured Captain Fanning's two volumes recording his travels through the South Pacific, paying particular attention to his description of numerous ravenous sharks which seized upon "the rudder and the oars, leaving thereon many marks of their sharp teeth and powerful jaws."[56] The shark played an important role in Hawaiian culture, and Beatrice chose it as her 'aumākua or family guardian. Taught a Hawaiian prayer that would protect her, she swam fearlessly in any water, but George thought she was crazy and always stood on deck with a loaded rifle.

Just like Captain Fanning had loaded his boat with fruit, "which seemed to have ripened and thus fallen for many years past," the *Arcturus* was restocked while its crew spent three days exploring Fanning Island, one of the most remote places on earth. Only "the occasional intrepid yachtsman" dared to venture to this speck in the ocean measuring less than five square miles. The atoll's few hundred residents were "polite, gentle and shy," lived in grass huts, and had neither electricity nor running water. They subsisted on the spoils of the ocean and the land, both plentiful. The "abundant and varied plant life," including banana, breadfruit, and coconut trees, also provided relief from the elements; the temperature on Fanning Island could reach up to ninety degrees Fahrenheit in late summer.[57]

The *Arcturus* sailed for Palmyra Island on September 24, three hundred miles northwest of Fanning Island and uninhabited (as was Washington Island, which they passed along the way). Describing his discovery of Palmyra Island in *Voyages Round the World*, Captain Fanning wrote he awoke three times in the night to a premonition he would shipwreck, a warning the *Arcturus* was wise to heed one hundred and thirty-eight years later. Coral reefs surrounded most of the island, and anchorage was possible only about three-quarters of a mile from the atoll. Since the sandy bottom made it hard to anchor the *Arcturus* securely, the crew deemed it prudent to always leave someone on board while the rest explored the tropical island crowded with coconut trees. Joe and George IV stayed on board one afternoon, and it was only with the greatest difficulty that a cursing George and his crew managed to row back to the boat against a strong current.

The *Arcturus* began its return trip on September 27 but got caught in a terrible gale, forcing everyone to hunker down in their bunks except for

George and Joe. When they finally arrived home on October 13, Pearl Harbor was so crowded that friends like Walter Dillingham and Mary Drum had to run from pier to pier with leis in their hands as the *Arcturus* looked for a spot to moor. George looked rejuvenated after his month-long and "relatively uneventful" cruise, but his outward exuberance was nothing more than a charade.[58] It soon dawned on him that Beatrice was the one returning to a bright future, and she would steal the spotlight he craved so much.

THE LAST TIME anyone saw Private William J. Goins alive was on the afternoon of May 18, 1926, when the young man suddenly disappeared beneath the waves at Haleiwa Alii Beach, next to Schofield Barracks. His friends immediately searched for him in the shallow waters, but Private Goins, who couldn't swim, had disappeared without a trace.

Two weeks later, on June 1, Kalili (the fisherman with the missing fingers) went to check on his lines at the Kahuku Plantation, about fourteen miles from Haleiwa Beach.[59] Kalili hoped to find an abundance of ulua—a priceless indigenous Hawaiian fish—but instead, he found a great white shark, measuring twelve-and-a-half feet, with his tail caught on his hooks. The injured shark was still alive, but it exhausted itself trying to break free during the night, and despite the reverence the Hawaiians felt for the shark, Kalili had no choice but to put it out of its misery.

As he cut into the shark's stomach, Kalili noticed it had recently feasted on a lobster, some of his uluas, and a pair of trunks with the inscription "B25." He also "uncovered the bones of both upper arms, both the bones of each forearm, most of the bones of the left hand, except the thumb, the top of the head from about the eyes back to and including the bones by which the head connects to the spinal column, and a wad of black hair about three inches long."[60] Since no sharks were sighted at Haleiwa Beach the day Private Goins (number B25) disappeared, his body must have been dragged out to sea by the current, where he became an easy meal for the passing great white shark.

The news soon spread around Schofield Barracks, where a slightly disbelieving Beatrice immediately jumped in her car to check the phenomenon with her own eyes. By the time she drove the twenty-four miles to the Kahuku Plantation, only the shark's jaw remained, all twenty-four inches hanging from a tree with a stick clenched between its teeth. If a shark had to die, the Hawaiians at least made sure to use every part: the meat became fishcakes; the skin became the head of the pahū pal drum; and the teeth became part of the lei o manō, a traditional Hawaiian club. Since Kalili knew Beatrice well, he invited her to stay for the ceremony that the women of the village were performing that evening. A shark as big as this had to have been someone's ancestor, and the village needed to make amends.

A significant part of the Hawaiians' belief system was based on their powerful bond with nature, and this was nowhere clearer than in the concept of 'aumākua. Deceased family members took on an animal form—lizards, owls, and especially sharks were recognized as family guardians—and appeared in their descendants' dreams to offer spiritual guidance.[61] For this reason, the Native Hawaiians neither killed nor ate shark, and instead of fearing them, they treated the manō with respect and reverence.[62]

That day in 1926, Beatrice was introduced to the power of the shark in Hawaiian culture, and she made it a central theme of her second book, *Blood of the Shark*, published in December 1936. For seven years, she worked to turn the stories the Hawaiian people confided to her into a cohesive novel "of early Hawaiian history and tradition." Described as "a romance of old Hawaii in the days of Kamehameha the Great," *Blood of the Shark* was lauded for its historical accuracy, which "in no way detracts from its dramatic power."[63] Beatrice was able to "cleverly weave an interesting factual background into the narrative" because of Emma Ahuena Taylor, whose family history formed the basis for *Blood of the Shark*.[64]

Emma was the great-granddaughter of Captain George Beckley, an Englishman who arrived in Hawaii in 1801. King Kamehameha I was fighting a war against the many chieftains of the Sandwich Islands, and George fell into the monarch's good graces when he sold him the ships he captured privateering. Eventually, Captain Beckley became a noble, worked as a foreign minister to King Kamehameha I, and married the High Chiefess Elizabeth Ahia. Their marriage was a prime example of the coming together of two unique cultures, the overarching theme of *Blood of the Shark*.

Beatrice conveyed the clash between old and new Hawaii through the story of Adam Gordon, a fictitious shipmate of Captain Vancouver. As a thank you for saving his daughter's life, Chief Kaha offered Adam her hand in marriage. Despite the opposition, Kilohana was intent on marrying her hero, setting in motion a series of events highlighting the struggle the ancient Hawaiians faced when confronted with the culture of white men. While Kilohana's love for Adam is strong enough to overcome any animosity, Adam can never look past his own culture and accept that his wife "is of the blood of the shark."

There was no doubt that Adam Gordon's story was partly Captain Beckley's, but anyone who knew the Pattons could see that Adam Gordon's personality was also partly Colonel Patton's. Not only was Adam a poetry lover who recited long passages by heart, but he was also "a difficult man who swears fulsomely, kills easily in battle, rides a horse with a furious intensity, and yells at his wife, 'You god-damned black wahine [woman].'"[65] One can't help but wonder if Beatrice had her own marriage in mind when she wrote *Blood of the Shark*.

EMMA'S TRUST in Beatrice had not been misguided. Within weeks, the first run of *Blood of the Shark* sold out, and it served "a definite and worthy purpose" of bringing the history of the Pacific Islands to the mainland. Beatrice traveled the islands giving lectures on Hawaiian culture and Pacific cruising, introduced a fashion trend called the Kilohana Kapa—a colorful swing skirt and wrap-around—and became recognized as an authority on Hawaiian culture and history.[66] In addition, she received an authentic Hawaiian name, which she found "a sacred thing to be treasured in love and reverence—a secret not to be shared," and she was fêted in December 1936 at a traditional Hawaiian lū'au in her home at Fort Shafter.

The Native Hawaiian community shared in her success and brought piles of food cooked in imus. Besides giving cultural advice throughout the years, Dr. Buck also wrote the book's introduction and spoke a Polynesian blessing as he sprinkled the corners of the Pattons' living room with salt water. Finally, Emma concluded with a Hawaiian prayer, to have "mercy on thine offspring, Beatrice Patton. Give her ever more knowledge, skill and power … [and] give love and success to Colonel Patton, her husband, and their children."[67]

*Blood of the Shark* was a labor of love for Beatrice. Of all the people celebrating with her that night, George should have been the one who best understood her feeling of accomplishment, yet he couldn't show how proud he was of his wife. Instead, he sulked like a child, irked to be on the sidelines watching his wife's star rise while his only seemed destined to crash and burn.

The boy who grew up the center of attention at Lake Vineyard still couldn't stand sharing the spotlight and even felt jealous of his wife and children. "Photos and press clippings were Georgie's domain," Ruth Ellen remembered. He pouted when he heard Beatrice was complimented for having "the story mind," and when he read that *Blood of the Shark* marked "Mrs. Patton as a writer who can recreate the Hawaiian legends of the past and make them come alive."[68]

Beatrice Ayer Patton so far devoted two-thirds of her life to George S. Patton Jr. *Blood of the Shark* was something she did for herself, without considering her husband or his career. The joy she felt over the success of her book was forever marred by George's childish behavior, so she began keeping what she called a thought book to try and make sense of the demons her husband was fighting. "I don't know how long it takes for a man to spiritually gut himself," she wrote. "Probably depends on how much guts he had to start with."[69]

The Pattons were equal partners, but Beatrice was always happy to take a backseat and allow George to shine. However, now that she had finally accomplished something removed from his sphere, he was unable to reciprocate. She wasn't lying when she said George was always supportive of her writing, but at this moment in his life, he was so self-absorbed and depressed that he could not look past his own perceived failures. Beatrice tried to ignore his behavior while remaining sensitive to his struggles, but whenever she focused on herself, he felt abandoned and acted out.

The concussion George suffered during his polo accident in August 1935 was exacerbated by his days of carefree sailing and led to a sudden inability to hold his liquor. It was disconcerting behavior for a man who was "always standing tall" and in control, a man whom no one could remember ever seeing intoxicated. George enjoyed a good glass of whiskey and the occasional cocktail, but he believed one should never "get drunk because when you get drunk you are no longer your own boss."[70]

Beatrice was not a big fan of alcohol—she enjoyed the occasional glass of wine with dinner, but hard liquor made her fall asleep—and she had absolutely no patience for drunken foolishness, which was why George's recent behavior mortified her so much. It wasn't that he was drinking more than before, but suddenly, just one drink made her once proud husband all sentimental. She philosophically mused, "There is a Mr. Hyde in all of us. Drink is the door through which he slips in easiest. To see Mr. Hyde take possession of a loved one is one of the most terrifying and disgusting things that can ever happen to me."[71]

It broke Beatrice's heart to see the man she loved in such a downward spiral, slowly becoming an embarrassment to himself and those around him. Thinking he might be going through a midlife crisis, she bought him a newly published book by a Dr. Marie Stopes called *Change of Life in Men and Women*. The title didn't leave much to the imagination, and George summarily took the book to the back alley of their home and set it on fire. Even Beatrice would never fully understand her complex husband, but in the past, she had always understood him well enough to know how to handle him.

She was determined to see him through this rough patch, but even she was at her wit's end. "Some of our loved ones we can save from their mistakes by our own experience, but some must make their own," she wrote. "This is hardest to bear—to watch them suffer and do nothing but be ready to help if the time comes." For some, "every experience is their own private possession to be lived thru as if it had never happened before. They do not connect themselves with anything else in books or human experience."[72]

Frederick Jr. remembered the Patton household wasn't "a happy place" when he visited in the summer of 1935, "nor were the lives of his wife and children easy."[73] Although George had always been grateful for Beatrice's advice, now he didn't take it so well when she pointed out his increasingly intolerable behavior. The one person in the entire world who had never criticized him now did, and Beatrice became an easy target as his disagreeableness increased. While he was never physically violent and rarely raised his voice, George now found a cruel enjoyment in picking on his wife. Knowing how much she hated it, he would pour himself a second drink before dinner while tauntingly looking her in the eye.

Beatrice had put up with a lot from her deeply flawed husband, and the self-restraint she showed in the face of his taunts spoke to the strength of her character and her undying love. Grounded and sensible, she never lost sight of who George truly was and recognized this was just a phase that would pass.

If COLONEL and Mrs. Patton were considered members of Hawaii's "fast set," their names were never associated with any of its scandals. Ruth Ellen could say with certainty that in the five years she spent in Hawaii, she never heard the faintest rumor that either of her parents was involved in some "naughty Polynesian fun."[74] Just the opposite, those who knew the Pattons intimately were aware that they were loyal to each other only.

Walter Dillingham considered George "one of my best friends," but he also enjoyed a genuine friendship with Beatrice, secure in the knowledge that she was neither interested in his wealth nor his good looks. Happily married to Louise since 1910, tall and handsome Walter, with brown eyes and olive skin, possessed a certain flair the opposite sex found irresistible. He was wary of women who sought out his company for the wrong reasons, but he knew Beatrice would never cause him any problems. She had eyes for only one man, and everyone knew that man was her Georgie.

Beatrice never worried about leaving her husband alone for weeks on end. The abounding stories of lovelorn women chasing him made her laugh because she knew he never encouraged any of them. Of course, he enjoyed female company as much as any other man, but she knew that "... having seen the world I [George] have yet to see your equal."[75] She felt just as secure during WWII, when the Patton family seemed to grow at a rate equal to George's fame, including (fake) cousins, nephews, and even a daughter by his "first wife."[76]

Maybe it was his uniform and chivalrous attitude mixed with humor or his blue eyes and blond hair (whatever was left of it), but wherever George went, he unwittingly caused a stir. Ruth Ellen never forgot her embarrassment at her graduation when all her classmates and their mothers hung adoringly around her oblivious father, yet it was all innocent until the publication of *Blood of the Shark* when George suddenly started noticing. He basked in the attention Beatrice was now too busy to give him, and he sought out the company of Ruth

Ellen's friends, who enjoyed his drunken antics and boisterous behavior. Angered by the way he was treating her mother, Ruth Ellen was also saddened to see her once proud father act so undignified. "Ma has been so happy here because she has created her book and given herself to it unsparingly,", Ruth Ellen wrote in January 1937. "Daddy has been unhappy because he has lost energy, and where before he gave himself unsparingly, now he has no extra to give and misses it without knowing why."[77]

On October 29, 1936, Jean Gordon—daughter of Louise Ayer Gordon, Beatrice's youngest half sister—arrived for an extended visit together with her aunt and chaperone, Florence Hatheway. They took up residence at the Halekulani Hotel in Honolulu for the next two months, but spent most of their time with the Pattons at Fort Shafter. Jean arrived every morning full of enthusiasm for the day's activities … and Uncle George.

Beatrice was busy preparing her book launch, so she was oblivious to what was happening around her, but a consternated Ruth Ellen, who was just three weeks older than her cousin and one of her best friends, couldn't help but notice Jean's flirtatious behavior. She had seen it before, at Bee's wedding in 1934, but discounted the idea back then. After all, Jean spent a lot of time with the Pattons growing up, and she regarded her uncle as a father figure ever since her own father died of leukemia in 1923.[78]

George had been none the wiser two years earlier, but his fragile emotional state in Hawaii made him highly susceptible to the attentions of a beautiful twenty-one-year-old. He was jealous of Beatrice's success and mad at her because she no longer treated him as the center of the universe. His self-esteem, which depended on her attentiveness and encouragement, hit a new low, and he was depressed. No matter how much he acted out to get her attention, Beatrice refused to be caught up in his little game, intent on focusing on herself for once in her life. Knowing how important *Blood of the Shark* was to her mother, Ruth Ellen tried to mitigate the situation by setting her cousin up with some of her old dates. Jean could have had any man her own age, but she was only interested in Uncle George, who was elated that someone was finally paying him the attention he craved.

George always admired his mother-in-law for her ability "to put away things that hurt and be cheerful in spite of them," but he should have praised himself lucky that his wife possessed that same quality.[79] Whether Beatrice was too focused on her book to notice the warning signs or she was blinded by a rare occurrence of naivete, when she suddenly fell ill, she sent an unchaperoned Jean and George to the Parker Ranch. A tension settled over the Patton household when they returned a few days later; everyone could feel something had happened. Only the parties involved knew whether Jean Gordon was a dalliance, but it was without a doubt a serious flirtation, which forever marred what should have been one of the happiest moments of Beatrice's life.

It wasn't until Jean and Florence left for Massachusetts on December 24 that Beatrice brought up what happened.[80] Watching George wave goodbye like a lovelorn teenager as the *S.S. Empress of Canada* pulled away from its berth, Beatrice turned to her daughter, "You know, it's lucky for us that I don't have a mother because if I did, I'd pack up and go home to her now, but your father needs me. He doesn't know it right now, but he needs me. In fact, right now he needs me more than I need him."

She blinked her tears away before continuing, "Perhaps there is a reason for all of this. I want you to remember this; that even the best and the truest of men can be bedazzled and make fools of themselves. So, if your husband ever does this to you, you can remember that I didn't leave your father. I stuck with him because I am all that he really has and I love him; and he loves me."[81]

It wasn't surprising that an ardent gardener like Beatrice would compare marriage to a tree: "Sometimes it is in bud, sometimes in blossom, sometimes in leaf, sometimes in fruit ... Sometimes the leaves will all fall off and it will look dead, but if you keep on cultivating the roots, always cultivating the roots, it will come alive again."[82]

Beatrice would never stop cultivating the roots; she would not give up on the love of her life after one transgression. "Never brood, be natural, do not regret, fill up life, go forward," she wrote in her thought book.[83] So forward she went, and the gold and silver chalice George had made for her in 1937 always stood as an unspoken "symbol of seeking her forgiveness."[84]

---

ON JUNE 13, 1937, Beatrice wrote the first entry addressed to her "darling children" in the *Arcturus*'s logbook, one day after sailing from Hawaii for the last time. Back in February, George had received news of his transfer to Fort Riley—to become the executive officer of the 9th Cavalry and a faculty member of the Cavalry School. Since then, he'd been preparing to sail the *Arcturus* back to Los Angeles, where he planned to sell her. Captain Ekeland was again in charge of the crew, which included George (navigator), Beatrice (diarist), George IV (deckhand), Doc Graves (unofficial "gourmet" cook), and Suzuki (official cook). Ruth Ellen had been dying to join, but since her arm was in a cast after a bad riding accident, her parents thought it safer for her to sail home on a steamer with Alice Holmes.[85]

When the *Arcturus* pulled away from Pearl Harbor's Pier Six at 9 a.m. on June 12, more than two hundred people were waving goodbye, and the Pattons received "180 leis and a ton of presents enough to sink the ship." Seven airplanes flew overhead to salute them, and even though Beatrice didn't see any real sharks, she saw a "huge shark in the clouds – whether Niuhi or Ukanipo I do not know, but at any rate a good omen."

The first days of the crossing were just how she "pictured a cruise ought to be – lovely weather – everyone happy and comfortably sunburned – and the whole situation most pleasant and congenial."[86]

Beatrice continued her entries, which were a testament to her eye for detail and knack for colorful descriptions:

> June 22: Yesterday we had the best sail, we've ever had on this boat – anywhere from seven to nine knots, cool breeze, blue sparkling water, sunny sky and balloner and staysail set. Then at 9.30 PM when I took the wheel, the wind went down like magic, leaving Arcturus sitting in a heavy swell and here we are still, at 10.30 AM having made four miles.

> June 23: Joe says we are in the latitudes where nothing works and I believe it - we haven't had a radio time tick for days and the barometer is completely hay-wire.

> June 25: Just spotted another small glass ball, and George dove overboard after it, while the gonies [a type of albatross] made passes at him. He had to swim several strokes to get it and his face was quite pale when he finally eluded the gonies and brought it on board. He ran down the companion-ladder, looked up our position on the chart, then came on deck panting; "Mother, do you realize that where you sent me overboard, it was three miles deep?"

> June 27: Good morning, darling Bee and Johnnie; this letter is especially for you on your third wedding anniversary, though we shall probably have to drink to your health in lavender water, as the regular stuff is running low. I picture you at West Point having a little party, and wish that I could see you.

The *Arcturus* covered only 1,340 (of the 2,552) miles in the first two weeks, and then foul weather began to threaten her progress even further. It was blowing so hard on June 30, Beatrice wrote, that "Daddy had to lash me down." A week later, on July 7, the waves were so high "it does not seem possible that the boat can hoist herself over the swells."

> It has been far too bumpy to write. George and I don't even steer after dark, which makes a hardship on the others who have our watch from 8 to 10.30. I think it's safer. Even though we are lashed two ways to the sampson blocks, we cannot stay put on the wheel box, which is like a bucking horse. Our legs are too short. As there is no electric light, he and I crawl into my bunk and gossip, mostly about "Gone with the Wind." I started reading aloud to him the first day of the gale and now he can hardly be torn away from it—I hope it clears up by the time he finishes it! One of his comments is that, "Even the dirtiest soldier wouldn't say some of the words they use in that book."

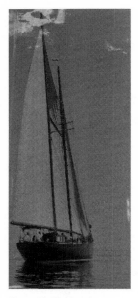

*Figure 59. The Arcturus.*
*(Library of Congress)*

That day Beatrice also caught a few coherent words on the radio and ended her entry with some ominous words: "We don't know how bad the storm has been—bad enough for us, though *Arcturus* has ridden it like a gonie—but we wonder—has there been a disaster at sea?"

On July 9, the crew of the *Arcturus* gathered from the "cluttery-sounding stations on the radio" that "the crash was Amelia Earhart, though we do not know whether she has yet been rescued. It is very strange, to crowd around the radio at night, by the light of the hurricane lantern and hear the voices coming over the air. Not so different from spirit voices; our food is still very plentiful, and though I fear you all may be beginning to worry about us, there is nothing we can do about it."[87]

The *Arcturus* was so far behind schedule that by July 10, the Pattons should have arrived at Green Meadows, but they were still 195 miles from the California coast. The crew was incredibly lucky to have survived the storm, and after ten days, they were finally in calmer waters . . . so calm that they advanced at only three knots (or 3.5 miles per hour).

After one month on the Pacific Ocean wearing mostly the same clothes, the crew was starting to look a bit disheveled, and a favorite topic of conversation between George and Beatrice was how to keep their socks dry. George preferred to hang his, and "I [Beatrice] take mine to bed with me, trying to dry them with my h'animal'eat. Neither system works. George has worn his navy bell-bottoms day and night for three weeks. I expect that I will have to soak him like a postage stamp to get them off when we land."[88]

While they still had plenty of food, the liquor ran out on July 9, except for the "medicinal alcohol, which G. has hidden." The only thing left was

a small bottle of oke [Okolehao, a sweet Hawaiian moonshine made from baked ti root] - the kind with the grass hula skirt around it which holds one drink. He has given Joe a drink out of it nearly every night for four weeks and there is still a lot left in the bottle! The first night, they broached it they each took a sip and George said, "It felt like hitting a brick wall at eighty miles an hour. You should have seen Joe; he just turned all colors of the rainbow, when I think of what it did to him, imagine what it did to me."[89]

Finally, at 12:15 p.m. on July 11, Joe spotted San Miguel Island, 121 miles from the Wilmington Harbor in San Pedro. It would take until midnight for the *Arcturus* to arrive, take care of some business, and then continue to the California Yacht Club. Ruth Ellen, Nita, and a stream of family and friends were waiting there when the *Arcturus* finally landed more than two weeks behind schedule, yet no one seemed to have worried much despite the radio silence.

"Thirty days at sea and not a cross word," Beatrice mused in her last letter before closing the logbook with one final farewell,

Goodbye, Arcturus; May you always answer the helm as handily and ride the seas so buoyantly for your new owners as you have for the Pattons, over 8,000 miles of the Pacific Ocean. And may they love you and care for you as we have done.

## Part III[1]

I will remember happy days, not sad ones;
   I will remember good people, not bad ones;
Forgetting hurts — scar tissue is the strongest
Remembering Love:
       'tis love that lasts the longest.

               — *"ON GROWING OLDER" BY BEATRICE AYER PATTON*

# 10

## SAND HILL

### FORT BENNING, GEORGIA

### 1937–1942

*To wish to reform a man is to set yourself above God.*

On January 14, 1942, the fourteen thousand men of the 2nd Armored Division stood waiting on the parade ground of Fort Benning, Georgia, for one final review with Major General Patton. When the band struck up the "2nd Armored Division March," tears appeared in the commanding officer's eyes. Not only was he emotional to be leaving behind his pride and joy, but for George, there was nothing more beautiful than a well-executed dress parade or military exercise. No one who witnessed one of his mock attacks forgot the experience, from the sound of the 75mms and screaming sirens to smokescreens and advancing infantry with gas masks and bayonets.[1]

Watching from the grandstand was Beatrice, composer of the "2nd Armored Division March." She was born with an "artistic temperament" and an ear not only for languages but also for music.[2] A gifted pianist who could play by ear and compose accompaniments to Kipling's poetry, she also played the mandolin, the steel guitar, the ukulele, and the musical saw.[3] The antique wooden box she had purchased on her honeymoon was now filled with her sheet music and traveled with her everywhere. Whether it was the restored Chickering at Green Meadows or the Steinway at Avalon, Beatrice could always be found behind the piano, calling out to her audience, "What does anyone want to sing next?"[4]

*Figure 60. Mounted review of the 2nd Armored Division on February 14, 1941. (Library of Congress)*

Her musical talents were in stark contrast to her husband's, who once mistook "The Star-Spangled Banner" for a funeral march.[5] George "evolved" a theory of his own, "that people who are not musical are usually not good at languages because their ear is so constructed that the fine differences of sounds do not affect them hence they cannot pronounce." Beatrice tried to teach him to sing during their courtship, but a tone-deaf George was pretty "hopeless" and could barely distinguish between the different bugle calls.[6] "He didn't have a musical ear but he [still] liked music," according to Beatrice, and he always sang with gusto in church and even attempted to learn to play the saxophone. On Sunday evenings, though, when Beatrice sat down at the piano to sing with the children, he stayed behind in his study to read.[7]

With the advent of war in 1941, Beatrice figured a rousing march was just what George needed to boost the morale of the thousands of green recruits arriving at Fort Benning every month. So she had collaborated with the U.S. Army Band and composer Peter DeRose—husband of the "Original Ukulele

Lady," May Singhi Breen—to compose the "2nd Armored Division March." The piece was intended for a full military band and opened with gunshots and a siren—an analogy to George, who rode through town like a charioteer, heralding his arrival with tooting horns and blaring sirens. Beatrice infused the "2nd Armored Division March" with her husband's personality, and even the lyrics echoed his sentiments to the core:

We're Uncle Samuel's men of the great fighting forces
You'll hear from us now and then we're the New Armored Corps
We move to the fight like the stars in their courses
And all we required to know is where is the war!

Armored cars the fighting tanks,
The new armored corps;
Manned inside and out by Red Blood Yanks,
come join us if you want to go to WAR!

Glorious! Glorious! In War we're ever victorious.
We move right in and fight like sin,
In the great Armored Corps.[8]

RETURNING to Green Meadows after a two-year absence, the Pattons were cheerful as they reunited with friends and family, including the Waterses, who came to spend what was left of the summer. But unfortunately, George's ebullience at having tempted fate on the *Arcturus* and surviving once again was short-lived.

According to Bug Conner, George "was mortally afraid of mosquitoes"— she had watched him put on two pairs of pants and three shirts during their Florida fishing trip in 1921—but they often plagued Green Meadows in summer because of the nearby Ipswich River.[9] The pesky little buggers were rampant on Sunday morning, July 25, 1937, when George, Beatrice, and Johnnie left for a ride on the estate. Galloping through the luscious fields, George admittedly broke one of his cardinal rules by riding his horse "in the danger zone," with its head right next to Beatrice's stirrups.

When her horse Memorial suddenly bolted trying to escape a pestering fly, George was riding so close that Memorial's hind leg struck his right shin with such force it broke in three places, "like a dry stick snapping."[10] The pain was so overwhelming that he fell to the ground unconscious, his tibia breaking through the skin.

*Figure 61. Bee riding at Green Meadows. (Courtesy of Scott C. Steward)*

Beatrice rode in the ambulance to Beverly Hospital, where George remained for the next 103 days, "without expense to the government." He was under the care of his good friend Dr. Peer Johnson, a "magnificent big man," who believed it "nonsense" that a real man could work himself to death; instead, "men stop looking forward, stop learning new things and then they rust to death."[11] It was the thing George feared his whole life and which now almost came to pass. X-rays revealed a compound fracture of the right tibia and two complete fractures of the right fibula. It took five hours before George was finally wheeled to his room, his breaks reduced and his leg in a cast that ran from his toes to his groin.[12]

He couldn't wait to tell Beatrice about his out-of-body experience. Instead of lying on the grass at Green Meadows, George saw himself on a Norse battlefield. He watched as two Vikings put him on a shield for the Valkyries to take him to Valhalla—the final resting place of heroic warriors in Norse mythology —but he woke up when they placed the shield back on the ground, indicating that it wasn't his time yet.[13] Cold comfort, because even though Dr. Johnson predicted a swift recovery of eight to ten weeks, George "developed every known complication since being out on my back, including a pestiferous disease known as Phlebitis which consists of unmitigated swelling of the leg."[14] The life-threatening condition, whereby a blood clot forms in the vein that can then potentially dislodge and travel to the lungs or brain, could only be cured by more bed rest and immobilization.

"He was getting on well, when two successive attacks of phlebitis nearly took him from us," Beatrice wrote General Harbord at the end of September, "but now he seems to be mending at last, and has had a normal temperature for a week. Today he completes his seventh week in bed, but he's such a good patient that all the nurses quote him to the other patients, and vie with each other in painting his toenails their favorite ruby, garnet and rose." When a review board came by to investigate the circumstances of George's accident, "the floor nurse had just finished both his fingers and toes in cardinal with platinum tips! He told me he had to keep his hands under cover all the while they were there."[15]

For three months, Beatrice drove the six miles to Beverly Hospital, her husband's room decorated with colored toilet paper and dubbed the "Hula Hula Night Club." George was the center of attention, with daily visits from the multitude of Ayer family members and friends who lived in the area, and doted on by an army of nurses. When he was finally allowed to walk around on crutches, he roamed "the corridor visiting other patients, dispensing ribaldry and cheer."[16] Everyone considered him the life of the ward, friendly and easygoing, but Beatrice knew him well enough to see right through the bravado. Her worst fears became reality when he was finally released from the hospital on November 5.

Beatrice prepared Green Meadows for George's arrival by converting a small reception room next to the entrance hall into a temporary bedroom and bathroom. The room offered easy access for George and to the many visitors who stopped by to raise his spirits. For a man who thrived on activity and possessed boundless energy, being confined to bed was a horrifying experience, and Ruth Ellen soon described her father as "suicidally depressed."

*Figure 62. George IV with his mother outside Green Meadows, January 1938. (Library of Congress)*

She'd seen it before, in 1932, after he had declined the job of military attaché to Great Britain. Recognizing the signs, Ruth Ellen escaped Green Meadows as often as possible and left her mother to carry the heaviest burden of nursing George back to health. Meanwhile, George IV was at boarding school, and Bee was back at Fort Riley, pregnant with the Pattons' first grandchild.

Beatrice's strength of character was tested like never before over the next eighty-seven days. While he was the picture of congeniality in front of visitors, George took his frustrations out on his wife, and the only way for her to stay sane was to leave the house for a daily ride and a semiweekly sailing trip. George, however, felt only resentment as he watched his wife walk out the door to pursue her interests. He'd been injury-prone his whole life, but he always managed to get back on the proverbial horse as soon as he fell off. This time, though, he was still bedridden after more than three months. Despite being a model patient who took his physiotherapy very seriously, there was "nothing much anyone can do except to wait for the damn bones to grow together."[17]

ONLY ONE THOUGHT consumed George as he waited for his bones to "knit": take revenge on Memorial. So the first thing he did on December 15, when a brace finally replaced his cast, was to limp down the driveway to the stables and look his nemesis in the eye. Beatrice followed him, furious to see that he was about to beat up her horse with his crutch. When she chastised him for taking out his frustrations on a dumb animal while he was very much aware he had only himself to blame, George stared down his wife and blamed her for "denying him the one pleasure he still had, the killing of the horse that had ruined his career."[18]

George was Beatrice's "old curmudgeon," and since doing nothing was "tiresome" for him, she looked for ways to keep him busy.[19] As fall turned to winter, she contacted John Alden, one of America's premier naval architects who ran the Alden Design Offices in Boston. When the Pattons had decided to sell the *Arcturus* upon their return from Hawaii, it was with a heavy heart but with the knowledge that they would commission their own schooner one day.[20] After taking the *Arcturus* through hell and high water and experiencing its quality, beauty, and speed firsthand, they knew John Alden was the man they wanted. Hoping a project like this would keep George from brooding too much, Beatrice invited Alden to Green Meadows sooner than expected.

The Pattons' request was simple: a beautiful schooner fast enough for Beatrice to race, sturdy enough to sail the world, and maneuverable enough to be operated by one person.[21] Working with Beatrice and George was an absolute pleasure for Alden, not in the least because they knew what they wanted. They gave him a little notebook titled, "When and If we ever build a boat," a blueprint of their ideal schooner based on their observations while crossing the Pacific Ocean on the *Arcturus*. Alden was so impressed with their ideas that he agreed to incorporate as many of them as possible.

On January 26, 1938, George signed a contract with F. F. Pendleton in Wiscasset, Maine, to build his dream schooner for $12,000 ($225,000 today).[22] Gordon Prince helped him decide on the name during one of the many evenings he spent at Green Meadows, keeping his friend company throughout his rehabilitation. Talking about the future, George said it no longer was a question of "When and If we build a boat," but, "When the war is over, and If I live through it, Bea and I are going to sail her around the world." After WWI, Mr. Patton had assured his Boy that he "would yet be in the biggest war in history," a likely prospect now that Hitler was consolidating power in Europe.[23]

**Figure 63.** *The When and If. (Library of Congress)*

Beatrice had been right; the *When and If* brought George purpose during the darkest hours of his convalescence. She allowed him to take the wheel, happy to see him involved with every detail of the schooner's construction.[24] The *When and If* took about a year to construct and was rigged by Joe Ekeland. When she launched on February 6, 1939, she measured sixty-three-and-a-half feet, weighed thirty tons, and could sail up to 228 miles per day under the right conditions, with a diesel engine for emergencies. The main mast stood eighty feet above the waterline, the double hull was mahogany over cedar, and there was enough space below deck to sleep thirteen people comfortably.[25] She was constructed "like a tank," using only the best materials and with no expenses spared. George even installed a cannon on the starboard side so he could shoot salutes.[26]

The Pattons made their first extensive trip on June 28, 1939, when they sailed to Norfolk, Virginia. It was only a six-day trip, but at least the schooner would now be available for weekend sails along the Chesapeake Bay while George was stationed once again at Fort Myer. When the U.S. entered World War II in December 1941, George put his precious baby in storage as a precaution. All he could think of were the events of May 1940, when any British vessel worthy of crossing the North Sea was asked to help evacuate the over 330,000 stranded British and French troops on the beaches of Dunkirk.

Beatrice "was like a mother to the people who worked for her," and the Pattons' generosity and kindness toward their employees was evident in the loyalty and devotion people such as George Kent, Reggie Maidment, Alice Holmes, and Joe Ekeland showed them.[27] When Beatrice, George, and Ruth Ellen finally arrived at Fort Riley on February 8, 1938, Private George Meeks and his wife Virgie joined the extended family. Bee was the one who serendipitously suggested her mother should retain Virgie's services when she and Johnnie were transferred from Fort Riley to West Point. Virgie was an excellent cook and had lived in the Waterses' maids' quarters with a certain Private George Meeks.

William George Meeks always kept an air of mystery about himself, but he was born on a farm in Georgia to Grant Meeks and Maggie Brooks on July 5, 1896. According to census records, he quit school in second grade, joined the Buffalo Soldiers, and fought in France in WWI. However, because of segregation, he never advanced in rank until he became Colonel Patton's orderly. From that point forward, Meeks received a promotion every time George did, until he reached the rank of master sergeant.

Virgie was worth her weight in gold, but Private Meeks truly blew Beatrice away. Meeks organically assumed the job of George's orderly, requiring no instructions and always keeping one step ahead. The meticulous preparation of George's uniforms had always been the bane of Beatrice's existence, explaining her husband's detailed instructions again and again to each new orderly, but Meeks knew precisely what to do, and he did it better than anyone ever did. George's boots were so shiny he could mirror himself in them, his pants had perfectly straight creases, and his woven belts had a quintessential faded look after soaking in the exact ratio of bleach to water. According to Ruth Ellen, no one knew why George Meeks became devoted to her father, "but what Georgie found in him was Man Friday, the loyal and true."[28]

Fort Riley was "the post nearest our heart," said Beatrice. It was "a place of happy memories," and she had been looking forward to creating more of those with her daughter and son-in-law living nearby, especially now that Bee was finally pregnant. However, because of the Pattons' six-month delay, the Waterses had already moved to Highland Falls, New York, where Johnnie joined the faculty of the U.S. Military Academy at West Point.[29]

The life of an army wife followed a particular pattern, and Beatrice soon saw her own youth reflected in Bee's. She left George and Ruth Ellen to ride the prairie shooting jackrabbits and traveled to New York for the birth of her first grandchild on April 26, 1938, a healthy baby boy named John Knight Waters Jr. While there, Beatrice took the opportunity to spend time with her brother Jamie, Frederick's second child and eldest son. He was the only sibling who had left the Ayers' bubble on the North Shore, a well-respected surgeon, and a "true gentleman and playboy."

In 1907, a forty-five-year-old Jamie had married May Candee Hancock, a widow eleven years his junior who suffered from frequent bouts of ill health. Dr. Ayer and his wife were members of New York's high society and traveled extensively. They divided their time between an apartment on Park Avenue, a villa in the Bahamas, and a mansion in Glen Cove, Long Island, where George often stayed during the polo season. However, their son Frederick II remembered his parents' marriage was not a happy one, and both were "trapped in a vicious circle of misunderstandings, and consequent emotional withdrawals."[30]

Beatrice adored Jamie, so when she found him deeply depressed at a Manhattan hospital in the spring of 1938, she installed an aquarium with exotic fish in his room. Jamie's health had been declining for months, but no one could figure out what was wrong with him. Frederick II reasoned his father never fully recovered from the way Bellevue Hospital passed him over for a promotion that should have been his based on seniority. He sued his employer in 1910 and lost, leaving him "hopeless and humiliated, and without ambition to such an extent that he neglected his family responsibilities." He was never the same after that, even though he continued to run a successful private practice and became quite "distinguished as a painter."[31]

Jamie's mysterious illness was so severe that even General Pershing wrote Beatrice in "the hope that your brother is now well on the road to recovery," but it was not to be.[32] On March 20, 1939, Dr. James C. Ayer was the first Ayer sibling to pass away. Beatrice was devastated by the news, sobbing in George's arms that her "darling Jamie" was so young. "He was only seventy-seven," she replied when George asked his age.[33]

FOR CENTURIES, the grand tour—a months-long vacation through France and Italy emphasizing art and culture—was considered the ultimate coming-of-age ritual for the upper classes of Europe. By the late nineteenth century, Americans also began taking part in this tradition. Even though a grand tour didn't always cure young love, Beatrice and George hoped a trip to Europe would make Ruth Ellen forget all about the Air Corps officer she was in love with.

No doubt George imparted some of the same sage travel advice he recently gave his godson, Frederick Jr. He told him to "see as much as possible because there is going to be one hell of a war (and they're going to blow all kinds of places off the map)," to keep his eyes "open for what the people are doing, and try to do the same," to "always compliment people on what they have which pleases you," and most importantly of all, to "ask all kinds of questions. Be intelligently curious."[34]

Ruth Ellen sailed ahead in May 1938 and spent a month at the Hotel Wagram overlooking the Jardin des Tuileries in Paris, chaperoned by Jean

Gordon's aunt Florence Hatheway. Beatrice and George IV commenced their Atlantic crossing at the beginning of June, once the fourteen-year-old completed his first year at The Hill School in Pottstown, Pennsylvania.

George IV "was suckled and weaned" on a theme of war and history.[35] He sat on the lap of General Pershing, who told him his father was "a great man"; he skipped school to go to a lecture by T. E. Lawrence, more commonly known as Lawrence of Arabia; and he asked Colonel Wild Bill Sterling, a Texas Ranger from George's Mexican days, how many men he'd shot with his pistol.[36] George IV had wanted to attend a military prep school upon his return from Hawaii, but to his great dismay, his father told him he'd seen enough of the military already, and it was now time "to experience the other side."[37]

Beatrice never attended college, yet George IV called her "terribly well educated," and Ruth Ellen described her, using an eighteenth-century quote by Sir Richard Steele from *The Tatler*, "To love her is a liberal education."[38] Besides her myriad interests, Beatrice spoke perfect French and passable German, Hawaiian, Italian, and Spanish. She approached everyone she met in their native language, believing it was politer to make an effort even if her grammar and vocabulary were far from perfect. Since she pretty much approached everyone and everything, it became a running joke in the family that Beatrice would speak to a wax figure at Madame Tussauds . . . and the figure would even reply!

George couldn't take another two months off after being on sick leave for half a year, so before leaving for Europe, Beatrice had spoken with him in detail about his WWI experiences and reread all the letters he had sent her during that period. Florence remained in Paris as Beatrice, George IV, and Ruth Ellen left on their quest to find the spot where Colonel Patton was shot twenty years earlier. Unfortunately, since George could describe the location only as "a little plain between two hills," their mission failed once again, even with the help of an expert guide.

Other spots were easier to find: the bridge across La Beaune near the town of Essey, which he had cockily crossed to find out if it was mined; the ancient Roman ruins of Champlieu, where he remembered camping with Caesar's army; and the haunted Château d'Aulan in Langres, where he had billeted while organizing the tank school in December 1917.

During the two weeks they drove around France, the Pattons managed to see more than anyone thought possible and visited with old friends, from Saumur to Langres. Wherever they went, Beatrice charmed the local population, opening doors that remained closed for other tourists. And because she had so much detailed knowledge of WWI, she ended up playing tour guide to more than just her children on more than one occasion.

Neither Beatrice, nor George IV, nor Ruth Ellen could have imagined that a mere two years later, in the spring of 1940, the roads they traveled would again become a theater of war. Neither could they have imagined their husband and father would be the next one writing history along these roads. One day, they would return to discover exactly where George's tracks had tread.

WAITING for the Pattons at the Ciampino Airport just outside Rome on June 30, 1938, was Count Francesco "Mario" Guardabassi, the fun-loving and long-suffering husband of Beatrice's niece, Rosalind "Didah" Wood. Beatrice had agreed to visit only after multiple assurances that Didah would be out of the country on one of her many familial visits to The Old Fort, the Guardabassis' Pride's Crossing estate.

Didah had a degree from Columbia University and ran a Red Cross convalescent hospital during WWI, but she was a bigot who offered her opinion on every subject and at every opportunity. "She is very peculiar, but he is charming," Beatrice wrote General Harbord. "He and I always have a great time when she is not there - - in spite of being my 1/2 niece she is too full of politics."[39]

The Guardabassis had met in Palm Beach, where Mario worked as the social director of the Hotel Alba, and married in 1928 when he was sixty-one and she was thirty-nine. Mario wore many hats throughout his life: opera singer on the stage of the Metropolitan Opera; decorated grenadier soldier in the Italian army; restaurateur of the Lido-Venice on New York's East 53rd Street; and first-and-foremost, a portrait painter. He studied art in Rome and exhibited his portrait of Pope Leo XIII at the Chicago World's Fair in 1893. His authentic Italian charm made him a favorite of high society, and he painted the likes of Dame Nellie Melba, Mrs. Vincent Astor, Mrs. George Vanderbilt, and Ruth Ellen Patton.

Beatrice loved portraits ever since she watched her parents' likenesses be put to canvas in 1896, and the living room walls at Green Meadows were covered in paintings of the Patton family. She had a fine time having her picture painted in 1919, her face bearing a certain gravitas, which matched the melancholy look on her husband's portrait painted by Donald Gordon Squier in 1932.[40] It was around the same time that Mario painted Ruth Ellen, home for the summer from The Masters School, and laid up at Green Meadows with a broken leg. Opera reverberated throughout the living room as Mario combined his love of painting and singing. Beatrice, whom Mario adoringly called his "zieta [little old auntie]" despite being nineteen years her senior, either bellowed along with him or accompanied him on the piano.

Mario loved telling his "darlings" how he had stood all alone on a bridge-head during WWI and prevented his troops from panicking when they heard of the approaching Austrian Cavalry. He had managed to inspire his men to retreat in an orderly fashion, allowing them to regroup and mount a defense against the Austrians.[41] It won him Italy's highest military recognition and a ticket to America to act as an emissary for the Italian government. His title, though, was a "Facist title," as Beatrice made clear to General Harbord, given to him by Mussolini for his efforts in correcting the "misapprehensions" the Americans felt toward fascism.[42]

Mario loved beauty. In the 1930s, he had purchased a rundown villa in Pila, and had it renovated by Rome's most famous architect, Ugo Tarchi. Villa Torre di Pila and its surroundings were stunning: the stone terraces in the back of the house overlooked an impressive Italian garden with fountains, a swimming pool, and a pond with swans. Climbing to the top of the 14th-century watchtower, one could see the vastness of the surrounding property with its limonaia, farmhouse, and amphitheater. The villa's interior was just as impressive, with frescoed walls, painted ceilings, and a fireplace in every room.[43]

After a whirlwind tour of Rome, Luigi, the Guardabassis' chauffeur and bodyguard, drove the Pattons the 110 miles to Perugia, a picturesque hill town where Mario was born in 1867. The Guardabassis' young sons, Frederico and Junio, were waiting on the front steps of Villa Torre di Pila just seven miles outside of town. Beatrice felt as if she were dropped in the middle of a commedia dell'arte when she saw the waiting staff, all lined up with relief written over their faces that Didah was still away. Present were Porcorossi, Mario's factotum; Philomena, the cook who enjoyed getting into heated arguments with Mario; and Georgio, the waiter who fell instantly in love with Beatrice and Ruth Ellen.

Mario was the perfect host. One day he asked Philomena to prepare a picnic basket with wine and cheese so he and his guests could spend the day searching the countryside for the artifacts Beatrice loved so much, another day, he organized a pool party for Ruth Ellen so she could meet some Italian bachelors. By this time, it was apparent the trip fulfilled its purpose, and Ruth Ellen was intent on breaking things off with her Air Corps pilot, although he was still unaware. To George's embarrassment, he ran into the guy and was surprised by his "fillial" manners and his happiness at having received "several letters from R-E."[44]

After a week, Luigi drove the Pattons back to Ciampino Airport for their flight to London. When they arrived at their hotel, Beatrice was handed a wire from George informing her that he had just been named the new commanding officer of the 5th Cavalry Regiment at Fort Clark, Texas, a job she knew was a dream come true for him. Since their father would be busy for a few weeks getting their new home ready, Ruth Ellen and George IV convinced their mother to extend their vacation. The threesome traveled the British countryside until August 6, 1938, visiting every garden, castle, and cathedral.

AFTER WAITING ALMOST twenty years for an assignment he truly coveted, George expected to be at Fort Clark for a long time. When he arrived there with the Meekses at the beginning of July 1938, he "chose quarter 24 as it has a sleeping porch and is more isolated," but he also built on a butler's pantry and an awning to help fight the oppressive heat which was so terrible that he joked his figure "dwindled perceptiably."[45] He described Fort Clark to Beatrice as "the last frontier post," with nothing to do but ride, read, and swim. The nearby town of Brackettville was nothing more than a speck in the middle of nowhere, and the closest major city was "quaint" San Antonio, 123 miles away.[46]

Since Ruth Ellen was single again, George suggested Beatrice "make arrangements for R-E to visit B or some of the rest of the family quite a lot while we are here" because "all the lieutenants are just out of WP [West Point] and so far are not a very choice lot."[47] Ruth Ellen was having none of it. When her father flew to Green Meadows to see George IV off to school, she returned with her parents to Fort Clark to enjoy the frontier life. However, in hindsight, she would always wonder if her mother was the subconscious reason why she stayed home well into her twenties.

George felt on top of the world for the first time in years, relieved to have his colonel's eagles back after a long-awaited promotion and happy to be actively training troops as commanding officer of the 5th Cavalry. His interest in the tank corps intensified with the situation in Europe worsening; he was writing articles for military journals again; and, despite his horses being "affected by the heat," he was back in the saddle.[48] Because of his excellent physical condition and access to the best doctors, George recovered full function in his leg after his riding accident. Still, phlebitis would remain his (and Ruth Ellen's) Achilles' heel.

George soon struck up "numerous friendships with the ranchers who while crude are real people and have plenty of shooting and fishing to trade for a little politeness."[49] It was a good trade-off: he received permission to ride the ranchers' land while they received invitations to the weekly hops at Fort Clark. Many weekends were spent crisscrossing Texas to participate in horse shows or driving 450 miles to Fort Bliss. The Pattons were always welcomed with open arms by the friends they had made in 1915, each day ending with Beatrice on the piano while George told stories of WWI, quietly hoping he might soon get the chance to make some new memories.

George was looking forward to having his son spend the holidays on one of the last frontier posts, but with just one phone call from the Chief of Cavalry, the Pattons' idyllic time at Fort Clark—so reminiscent of their first years of marriage—ended abruptly after only four months. Effective immediately, Colonel Patton was named the commanding officer of the 3rd Cavalry Regiment at Fort Myer. Since his performance at Fort Clark had been nothing but impeccable, "[t]he order to Myer came as a great surprise" to him.[50] George learned a long time ago, though, that "the only way you get on in this profession is to have the reputation of doing what you are told as thoroughly as possible," and he had built "a reputation from not kicking at peculiar assignments."[51]

As the story goes, General Herr was brutally honest about the reason for this urgent and unexpected transfer: money. Brigadier General Wainwright thoroughly enjoyed being the commanding officer of the 3rd Cavalry, but without an outside source of income, he was no longer able to keep up with the social demands of the job, and he was transferred to Fort Clark. It was more important than ever for the military establishment to cultivate good relations with Washington's political elite, but the budget available to Fort Myer's commanding officer did not suffice to entertain at a level that might influence Congress's military appropriations.

As soon as he hung up, George looked at his wife and spewed out his bitterest reproach ever, "You and your money have ruined my career."[52]

This was the last straw for Beatrice; a huge fight ensued, which ended in a temporary truce only when she went to bed exhausted and exasperated. Both she and George always agreed that "the possession of wealth by an Army officer is a help rather than a hindrance to a military career," mainly to "entertain moderately but in good taste."[53] So to be blamed that the wealth he so ostentatiously flaunted throughout the years caused him to lose out on the opportunity for some real soldiering was more than she was willing to accept. For one of the first times ever, Beatrice was truly angry with George. Jean Gordon disappointed her; this accusation angered her.

At the beginning of their marriage, money had been a frequent topic of conversation between the Pattons. George often pointed out his wife's "perfectly ridiculous" money management skills as she forgot to pay the bills—including the ones he continually sent her—but he was the first to admit he was the only one with "so much money" who "knew so little about it."[54] Luckily their finances were in the capable hands of Arvin "Jerry" Brown, George's cousin (son of Eleanor Thornton Patton) who was mainly involved with Mr. Patton's inheritance, and Fred and Chilly, who managed the Ayer Trust. (In 1923, Beatrice had appointed her brothers "as Trustees of the Trust" she had created for George's benefit.)[55]

George did not understand how some people's only ambition in life was to get rich, even though he enjoyed money's benefits rather spectacularly.[56] His own inheritance would have enabled him to lead a comfortable life inherently better than the average officer, but Beatrice's inheritance ensured George never wanted for anything. He bought the newest cars as soon as they became available, he built an impressive stable of thoroughbreds that were the envy of every horse lover, and he had his uniforms and suits tailor-made so he could walk into a room exuding confidence. "Dangerous modesty is not one of my faults," he once wrote Beatrice, and his extravagant display of wealth was often a source of envy for many of his peers.[57]

Beatrice followed her father's advice to give George "what he needs," and would continue to do so. Just six months after his bitter accusation at Fort Clark, George found it "quite hard to economise" and asked his wife to send "me a check for $5000.00 [about $95,000] as I am getting pretty low."[58] After close to thirty years in the Army, it was a well-known fact that Beatrice was the daughter of industrialist Frederick Ayer. A frequent rumor among the enlisted men was that "every time they took a patented hangover remedy they helped make George Patton rich."[59] George enjoyed the good life too much to change his habits, but he knew there was one thing money could not buy: glory on the battlefield.

RUTH ELLEN REMEMBERED the 1,750-mile drive from Fort Clark to Fort Myer hadn't been pleasant. To add to George's frustrations, Quarters Eight was not yet ready and they had no choice but to move in with the Merrills until after Christmas. Built for the formal entertaining expected of "minor members of the Foreign Service," 2535 Belmont Road was known as "Little Moscow" in the early thirties because of the number of Russian Embassy members Keith invited in the hopes of improving U.S.-Russian relations. Like Beatrice, Kay's "help to her husband in his job was incalculable, both because of her charm and ability as a hostess and her wide acquaintanceship."[60]

Beatrice was in for a lot of entertaining herself, and she was already expected to host members of Congress before she was fully settled. Just a few days after moving into Quarters Eight, the stress of the last few weeks caught up with her. Colonel Albert Kenner—Fort Myer's Post Surgeon and soon-to-be close friend and personal physician of the Pattons—paid a house call and diagnosed renal colic and kidney stones. For one of the few times in her life, Beatrice felt so miserable she was forced to stay in bed. Less than 24 hours later, Colonel Kenner was called back to Quarters Eight to examine George.[61] He turned out to be perfectly fine, so Beatrice explained to her daughter, "All men fall to pieces when their wives get sick because it threatens their comfort and security."[62]

Despite George's criticism, Beatrice was ready to take up her duties like a good soldier. They had come so far together; she was not about to give up when war seemed imminent. Josephine Polk, a green army wife whose husband served with Colonel Patton, remembered a meeting Beatrice held for the officers' wives. Josephine immediately noticed Mrs. Patton's "vibrant" personality and "strong face" as she took the stage to remind everyone that from now on, "your country is FIRST . . . my husband has already fought in two wars, World War I, and the war in Mexico against Pancho Villa—and he may be called again before his career is finished. So you, dear young women, must be prepared to send your husbands off, if the need be."[63]

There wasn't a single day Beatrice managed to complete all she had planned, but she "felt that one should remain flexible and enjoy the process of living."[64] She "made it her business to help her husband," aware that her actions could potentially make or break George's career because "an error [at Fort Myer] is always noted."[65] He was as much a diplomat as an officer, and Beatrice's first obligation was to organize a series of lunches for the capital's foreign diplomats and Congressional leaders. Traditionally held on the first ten Fridays of the new year, Beatrice commenced her customary charm offensive on January 6, 1939, with the help of the Meekses and Ruth Ellen. By the end of the day, Beatrice decided it was time to institute some changes; the guest list would now include not only Fort Myer's high-ranking officers but also newly-weds so they could learn how to engage with Washington's politicians.

The Pattons were a crack at entertaining, but their home was no longer a place of refuge. Beatrice hated the intrusion on her privacy, every detail of her life scrutinized by hundreds of people passing through her home. Mrs. Schuetz, wife of Democratic Congressman Schuetz from Illinois, couldn't help but remark after lunch how Mrs. Patton was "certainly living high off the hog with all her silver and linen marked with her initials and paid for by the poor taxpayers."[66] Keeping cool under trying circumstances was easy for Beatrice, and she calmly explained most items in Quarters Eight were her private possessions, bought with her own money or received as gifts from friends and family. Mrs. Schuetz begged to differ as her husband had informed her that "everything in this house is the property of the United States Government."

Being Fort Myer's commanding officer was the most socially prestigious posting in the U.S. Army, but the endless entertaining was getting on George's nerves. Stuck behind a desk all day instead of training troops, he was stuck behind a dining table at night, and it wasn't getting him anywhere. He acted the perfect Southern gentleman with his big "sissy-baby smile," but no one knew better than Beatrice and Ruth Ellen that the smile that went "so far around the corners of his face that his ears would lie flat" was not a symbol of affection but of dislike.[67]

Moreover, advancement in the U.S. Army had been so slow that every time a general died, "every colonel in Washington [was] like a wolf bitch in heat," yet, in recent months, more and more of George's colleagues were being promoted to general.[68] The cavalry had helped him through the humdrum of peace, but now that Europe was in the throes of a new type of warfare, it looked as if being a member of the cavalry might be a detriment.

Beatrice remembered George saw "the war coming a long time ago and drove everyone crazy worrying over whether or not he was too old to get in."[69] His fears materialized in the summer of 1939 when he learned the new Chief of Staff, General George Marshall, was intent on purging the Army of any officer he deemed too old to command or too opposed to modernization. George had nothing to worry about regarding the latter, but he might fall in the first category at fifty-four. So with Beatrice at Green Meadows for the summer, George "consumated a pretty snappy move": General Marshall would be "batching" with him while his home was being readied.[70]

George impressed upon his roommate both his continuing belief in armored warfare and his vigor (by taking him sailing on the *When and If*), unaware Marshall didn't need impressing. The two had never worked together and barely knew each other, yet George's name appeared in the little black book Marshall carried with him for years, listing those officers he thought fit for high command.

AFTER TWENTY YEARS in the peacetime army and facing an uncertain future, George was in the throes of a "self-indulgent depression." He had been the wonderful companion of old at Fort Clark, but his sour mood returned with a vengeance at Fort Myer. At home from boarding school, George IV remembered his father being so "snappy he could take your head off in a minute."[71] But no matter how big a pain in the neck his father was, he never heard his mother utter a single bad word about him. The older he got, the more George IV realized what an unusual woman his mother was. He worshipped her and stood in awe of her strength, especially when dealing with his temperamental father, whom he'd seen act out most outrageously.

Lieutenant James Polk remembered Colonel Patton as "a wealthy and somewhat eccentric sportsman who had rather novel, but still interesting ideas about modern warfare. He was always beautifully turned out, rode fine blooded horses, and was very active in polo, drag hunting and horse shows as was his whole family. They were very popular and everyone loved Mrs. Patton, a charming woman and very gracious hostess."[72]

Lieutenant Polk was a guest at the equestrian-themed stag dinner George organized while Beatrice was out of town. He covered the floor in sawdust, prepared a punch with floating "doughnuts resembling horse-droppings," and sat his guests on bales of hay. Beatrice returned unexpectedly and discovered her house in disarray and a horse in the pantry. She was enraged—especially since the horse destroyed one of her antique tables on the way out—and all of Fort Myer knew Colonel Patton "spent a week in the dog-house."[73]

George still exuded an air of joie de vivre in front of an audience, but he didn't feel the need to hide his frustrations at home. The same exasperating scene unfolded every day at dinnertime: refusing to come to the table when called, he poured himself a second drink in the living room and remained there until he finished his glass. He then drove Virgie to insanity by sending his food back, complaining it was too hot, too cold, or not cooked properly. Without *Blood of the Shark* to distract her, Beatrice received the full load of George's wrath.

Ruth Ellen—who now ran a nursery school in the post chapel—watched in disgust as her father belittled her mother or yelled at her like a drill sergeant. She knew her Ma didn't take well to hearing her husband criticized, but his insolence reached such levels at Fort Myer that Ruth Ellen could no longer keep quiet. Beatrice admitted she "felt quite powerless" to help George, but she was going to see the crisis through as "men always struck out at the thing they loved best when they were unhappy."

"Young people don't believe older ones can really be in love," Beatrice told a reporter in 1943. "They think love is the possession only of youth. They don't realize that love grows stronger and closer, bigger and finer and more essential, with each year that passes. Especially if it's the only love you ever had."[74] It was this love that made Beatrice more tolerant than others might have been and which allowed her to put George's erratic behavior into perspective. Whenever she did feel the urge to be mean, she closed her eyes and recited Dinah Maria Mulock Craik's "Too Late." The poem talks of a wife's regret as she mourns the loss of her husband, and she promises him to be "so faithful, so loving" if he would just return to her.

Beatrice didn't want to regret something she might have said if George went off to fulfill his destiny—something which looked more likely every day since the atrocities that took place on Kristallnacht in November 1938—so she instituted a "sanity plan" to escape the shouting matches at home. Every morning she went for a ride in the Virginia countryside or the Fort Myer riding hall. Just as George met (now) Secretary of War Henry Stimson on the bridle paths of Rock Creek Park in 1912, Beatrice made an acquaintance with Eleanor Roosevelt, whose horses were stabled at Fort Myer. Beatrice's impression of the First Lady was of a "very shy and very lonely" woman, but one who had "the finest eyes she had ever seen in a woman's face." When a curious George asked his wife what she discussed with the First Lady, Beatrice coyly replied, "Oh, just ordinary things — the children, you and the president, books — she has some very good ideas."[75]

In January 1939, George oversaw the President's Birthday Horse Show, a fundraiser for the March of Dimes, the non-profit founded by President Roosevelt to fund research for a polio vaccine. The event was the start of a weeklong national campaign and a roaring success because of the participation of Errol Flynn. The actor was slated to compete, but his suitcase containing his riding breeches got lost on the train to Washington. Beatrice came to the rescue; she realized Mr. Flynn was about the same size as George and she gave the actor a pair of her husband's brand-new riding breeches.[76]

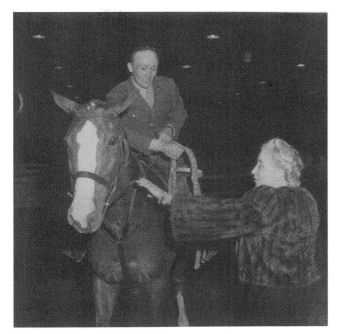

*Figure 64. Beatrice at a horse show, date unknown. (Library of Congress)*

Colonel and Mrs. Patton entertained the president and first lady in the commanding officer's box, watching Ruth Ellen take first prize in the hunters' class on Beatrice's horse, Keonakolu. George took only fourth place in the handy jumpers' class, Errol Flynn did not place at all, and Beatrice was too busy entertaining to participate. After a parade of the president's stable, Jeanne de Arc took a turn around the ring. A relic of what was starting to look like a bygone era, the thirty-two-year-old mare was one of the last surviving horses of WWI and wore her "wound stripe and six combat stars on her service ribbon."[77]


THE U.S. ARMY of the interwar years was small, so small that people either knew each other or of each other. Confined to bed with renal colic in December 1938, Beatrice suggested Ruth Ellen accompany the new commanding officer of the 3rd Cavalry to his first horse show at Fort Myer. Old acquaintances came up to the CO's private box all night long to welcome back the Pattons, including Mrs. Helen Herr Holbrook. She was the daughter of General Herr, the chief of cavalry who had delivered the news of George's reassignment a few weeks earlier; the granddaughter of Mrs. Hoyle, doyenne of the Old Army and one of Beatrice's close friends; mother of Joanne Holbrook, who would one day become George IV's wife; and the one who introduced Ruth Ellen to James "Jim" Willoughby Totten.

Ruth Ellen enjoyed being raised "under the shadow of the flag," and all she ever wanted was to marry an officer.[78] She had met many over the years, but she knew right away the twenty-six-year-old field artillery lieutenant, who came from a long line of illustrious artillerymen and graduated from West Point in 1935, was the one. Within eight months, Jim proposed, and Ruth Ellen accepted, on the condition both her parents consented. Worried about their reaction—Beatrice was bothered by Jim's Catholicism, and George considered him "too fresh"—she first broached the subject with her best friend, George Kent. Ten years her senior and always protective of "Miss Ruth," he gave his approval after a thorough vetting.

Ruth Ellen waited until her mother was visiting the Waterses at West Point to break the news to her father. "What do you think Ma will do when I tell her I am going to marry Jimmie Totten?" she asked over lunch after a relaxing morning riding and skeet shooting. George's reaction was immediate, "God-dammit, you can't marry him! He's too short [just under five foot six], he's a field Artilleryman, and he's a Catholic." This outburst was immediately followed by a request to "make us a pitcher of martinis, and don't put any vermouth in them. I know you're serious, because if you were still just thinking about it, you would have told your mother first."[79]

Beatrice was indeed "quite upset" when father and daughter broke the news; not only had Ruth Ellen known Jim for only eight months, but he was a Catholic. Anti-Catholicism was still rampant in the United States in 1939. Still, it was a surprising reaction for an open-minded woman raised in a family where freedom of religion stood paramount. Ellie never cared for the strict Protestant beliefs forced upon her at home, so she allowed Beatrice, Kay, and Fred to choose their own faith. After attending services at different places of worship throughout Boston, Beatrice became a Congregationalist. However, she agreed with George that God "is quite impartial as to the form in which he is approached," and she had no problem switching to the Episcopal Church when she married.[80]

When Ruth Ellen returned from a visit to Lake Vineyard, Beatrice had changed tactics. She wouldn't stand in the way of her daughter's happiness, but she would have a talk with Jim. George was appalled by her plan and made good on his threat to walk out if she went through with it. In a perfor-mance worthy of an Oscar, Beatrice held forth on the values of the Episcopal Church for half an hour, upon which time she asked Jim, full of confidence, whether he had changed his mind. Instead of replying to her question, he asked her opinion on turncoats. Taken aback, she replied she didn't approve of them. "Neither do I," Jim said as he walked out the door.

Ruth Ellen feared the love of her life was gone forever, but Jim returned a few days later to ask for her hand in marriage. By then, Beatrice's illogical ambivalence had resolved itself, and she was once again caught up in the excitement of wedding planning. The ladies of Fort Myer insisted on organizing a bridal shower in the spring of 1940, but Beatrice knew many were struggling, so she suggested people bring recipes instead of gifts. Ruth Ellen amassed such a cherished collection of recipes passed down from generation to generation that she collected them all in a little book aptly titled, *The Rolling Kitchen.*

The wedding took place at St. John's Episcopal Church—at Jim's insistence —at 4 p.m. on July 6, 1940. Ruth Ellen was the third Patton to get married in the small Beverly church and at least the fourth one to wear Ellie's wedding gown. Bee, pregnant with her second child, was matron-of-honor, while George IV and Johnnie were ushers. The bridesmaids included Rosemary and Eugenia Merrill, Anne and Hilda Ayer, and Jean Gordon. One can only wonder at the reasoning behind this peculiar arrangement, but Beatrice was known for her strong familial ties and always enjoyed a loving relationship with her sister Louise.

It was quiet in the Pattons' 1932 Packard Sedan on the twenty-minute ride from Green Meadows to St. John's, where two hundred guests were waiting. Growing up, Ruth Ellen experienced both sides of George's polarizing effect on people: she loathed him at times yet loved him to death. As they neared the church, George finally found the courage to break the silence, "I guess you know your mother and George and I will miss you. I hope we gave you a happy childhood." The last thing her father told her as they arrived at the church made Ruth Ellen realize all would be well, "If you treat Jim the way your mother has treated me, you will be alright."[81]

MAY 1940 was a pivotal moment in world history as Hitler launched another blitzkrieg and invaded Denmark, Norway, Belgium, the Netherlands, Luxembourg, and France in one sweeping motion. However, the United States remained neutral as President Roosevelt juggled widespread American isolationism, Prime Minister Churchill's urgent request for help, and a run for an unprecedented third term in office.

To test the Army's preparedness and gauge the future of the Cavalry, General Marshall organized a series of war maneuvers in the spring of 1940. The first maneuver occurred in May and pitted Major General Joyce's cavalry against Major General Chaffee's mechanized forces. George was selected umpire, putting him in a tough position. He might have been one of the top horsemen in the U.S. Cavalry, but after years of private study, he was also considered an unofficial expert on mechanization.[82]

Just days after walking his daughter down the aisle, George opened the newspaper and read about his transfer to Fort Benning, Georgia, to organize and train the 2nd Armored Brigade. The depression plaguing him for months, if not years, lifted immediately, but his leave-taking of the 3rd Cavalry was bittersweet. He had finally pushed Beatrice too far.

All of Fort Myer came out to bid Colonel Patton farewell on July 24, 1940, at a moving ceremony that ended in his departing the base in an armored car escorted by a cavalry squadron. He was returning to his "first love," but his true love was not by his side at this critical moment in his life.[83] Only one small act on Beatrice's part gives some insight into what she was thinking at this time. When she left Hawaii, a friend had given her a small idol of a soldier since he, the idol, would be much happier living with a military family. However, "during a period of unrest in my family," Beatrice got angry with him and threw him into the pond at Green Meadows.

She returned from South Hamilton on July 31 to empty Quarters Eight, but she blatantly refused to follow her husband to his new command for the first time ever.[84] While he flicked a switch back to perfect happiness as if nothing had happened, she seemed unwilling or unable to do so this time for reasons lost to posterity. "Most relationships are combined give and take," she said, but George had finally done too much taking.[85] Only George's side of the conversation is known, but it was clear Beatrice had said some choice words, and he was soon packing her "books and things" to ship to Green Meadows.

One of the happiest moments of George's life was at first marred by sadness and despair, and his initial struggle to prepare his men for armored warfare made it clear that he could not have lived without Beatrice. For thirty-eight years, his "lady of the Army" had been so entwined in everything he did on an emotional and professional level.[86] Beatrice had always been attracted to George like iron to a magnet. She had followed him with minimal effort on his part for over thirty years, accommodating herself because she knew a self-centered man like George Patton would change for no one.

Beginning on August 27, when the Meekses were the only ones present at his first Division problem, George wrote Beatrice one melancholic letter after another but she didn't reply to any of them. He reminded her how every time "I have done any thing worth while you have always been in the gallery. It is hard to have no gallery any more and I feel quite sorry for my self but more sorry for you because I have shattered all your ideals . . . I even hate to type that I love you because it sounds like such a lie. But I do."[87] He wrote again four days later after attending General Singleton's final review:

> I felt very sorry for him first because it was his last formation except in Arlington and second because he had no one there. But in his case it was an act of god and not one of insanity as it is with me.

I just heard that Kilner who was with me in Mexico gassed him self on account of a disgrace he got into with another woman. I am inclined to think that he had more guts than I have or perhaps not, it is pretty hard to go on living and wishing one was dead and when I realise that I have made it so hard for you who are inoscent it makes me feel even worse.

. . . I hope some day you may forgive me but I will be damned if I see why you should. I love you anyhow.[88]

He wrote her his third letter in a week on September 3, 1940, "worried all day for fear you got hurt in the Horse Show but if you were some one would probably have told me." General Herr had asked him if he wanted to command a cavalry division, but it made "little difference any how. I am not kicking I have only my self to blame and you are the one I have hurt. I suppose the most charitable thing to this is that I was crazy. But I cant see how you or any other self respecting person could ever forgive me . . . I love you and miss you terribly but can see no future I have hurt you too much. Perhaps when we are both dead you will forgive me. I hope it will be a comfort to us. You are the only person I have ever loved."[89]

When his plane almost crashed upon takeoff a week later, he wrote Beatrice she "almost got [her] wish that I die soon." He had been waiting for over two weeks for a letter from her "about starting our lives anew. But it has not come so I suppose it wont. I dont blame you at all I simply am sorry for both of us."[90]

In Hawaii, Beatrice had discovered a part of herself that could exist without George, but as she pursued her own interests and saw the effect it had on him, she realized he needed her more than she needed him. September 1940 was not the moment to abandon the love of her life, not when the destiny they had sacrificed so much for was finally at hand. So she retrieved the idol—it would ultimately travel to war with George—and joined her husband at Fort Benning at the end of September, recommitted to the mission and each other. She soon entertained the multitude of visiting army brass and proudly sat behind her husband at reviews, her long hair nicely done up and her face shaded by a hat from the hot Georgia sun.

George was a motivated man who excelled at motivating, but he depended on Beatrice to give him the confidence to do so. The moment she stood by his side again, his attempts to train a group of discouraged young men with little or no equipment became successful. In October 1940, his colonel's eagles became general's stars, first one and then a second a mere seven months later, and his swashbuckling style made him the darling of the press. He never forgot the feeling of elation after giving his first speech—a nervous toast to the Ayers during Christmas Eve dinner when he was still a West Point cadet—and he hadn't grown tired of the proverbial pulpit since then. His unique and expressive manner of speech quickly earned him the nickname "Old Blood and Guts," and his picture appeared in magazines and newspapers across the country as the 2nd Armored Division became an exemplary division known as the "Hell on Wheels."

*Figures 65, 66, & 67. "Mrs. Patton's House" at Fort Benning. (Library of Congress)*

Brigadier General Patton was involved with every detail of his command. He designed a tank uniform—a green double-breasted jacket with a diagonal row of brass buttons, a gold football helmet, and green jodhpurs—and he refused to live in the officers' quarters.[91] "We didn't like living an hour's drive away from the men," Beatrice remembered. "The General felt we ought to live out at our own camp." The War Department agreed to build a new house in Fort Benning's regular cantonment area, known as Sand Hill, but Beatrice offered to cover the cost and designed most of the house herself. The log cabin stood hidden among the Georgia pines, "with a great fireplace of native stone and such huge windows that the outdoors and the indoors seemed to mingle." The cabin became known as Mrs. Patton's house when it was 'donated' to Fort Benning upon their departure. "I hated to leave that house more than any of the others," Beatrice said in 1943. "We put down a lot of roots at Benning."[92]

The Pattons were soon the center of social life at Fort Benning and nearby Columbus. Beatrice became such a fixture in the small town that years later, the mere mention of her name still opened doors, "You know Mrs. Patton? Well, what can we do for you?"[93] On Sunday evenings, they drove twelve miles to eat at Spano's on 10th Street, the oldest restaurant in Columbus, established in 1893. The pan-roasted oysters with Spano's secret dipping sauce were a favorite, as was the wine-soaked bread pudding, all served on the restaurant's iconic marble tables. After dinner, the Pattons would stroll to Springer Theater and catch a movie before heading back to Fort Benning, where a busy week of training and entertaining awaited them.[94]

JUST DAYS before Hitler invaded Russia in June 1941, the U.S. Army organized the first of three military maneuvers to test, among other things, its tactics of armored and mechanized warfare. Eleven thousand men, four hundred tanks, and fifteen hundred vehicles of the 2nd Armored Division stealthily made their way from Fort Benning to Chattanooga to participate in Phase II of the Tennessee Maneuvers. Despite ill-suited terrain for mobile warfare, their "aggressive attacks overwhelmed their opponents," and Major General Patton and the 2nd Armored Division were "declared to be equal of Europe's best."[95] A reporter who went along for the ride wondered whether the division commander was even aware that he was a general because "he exposes himself to danger as casually as a strip teaser does to the front row orchestra."[96]

The 1941 maneuvers were as much a test of the Army's doctrine and tactics as they were of its soldiers and commanders. When Phase I of the Louisiana Maneuvers kicked off on September 15, the Red Force of Lieutenant General Lear, which included the 2nd Armored Division, was pitted against the Blue Force of Lieutenant General Krueger and his chief of staff, Colonel Eisenhower. Junior in age and rank, Ike had been trying for a year to effect a transfer to the armored force to command troops under his old comrade. However, he would make such a big impression during the Louisiana Maneuvers that General Marshall found him more valuable behind the planning table and would order him to Washington to work for the War Department instead. From that moment on, Ike's rise was meteoric; by April 1942, he would already outrank George by one star.

Major General Patton cemented his reputation as an audacious officer during Phase II of the Louisiana Maneuvers. In a preview of what was to come in Europe three years hence, he took his division on a 350-mile end-run and outflanked the enemy, ending up at their rear. When he took his men outside the playing field into Texas, he outran his supply lines and resorted to refueling his tanks at local gas stations. Rumors abounded he paid for the fuel out of his own pocket, and for the parts he purchased at Sears when his tanks broke down. Some took umbrage at how he played the game, but George "was unaware of the existence of any rules in war."[97]

While George was making a name for himself, Beatrice retreated to Green Meadows to await the arrival of their third grandchild. It was a full house over the summer: George IV was busy preparing for his final year at The Hill School and his West Point admission exam; Bee was visiting with her two sons, Little Johnnie and George Patton Waters, born just a few months earlier in March 1941; and Ruth Ellen was anxiously awaiting the birth of her first child. The Tottens didn't plan to have children right away, but Jim began to worry he might be leaving sooner than expected, and the last thing he wanted was to go off to war without holding his first child. Like her mother, Ruth

Ellen believed in "the sooner, the better, and the more, the merrier," so she readily agreed.[98]

Michael Walke Totten was born in Boston on October 4, 1941. Complications necessitated a C-section, but a formidable Beatrice, both curious and afraid, convinced the doctor to allow her into the delivery room during the operation. After recuperating at Green Meadows for a few weeks, Ruth Ellen left Michael in the care of his grandmother to join Jim at Fort Knox, Kentucky. Nurse Crowley—a stalwart of the Ayer household, whose first job was nursing Frederick and Ellie in 1918—followed a few weeks later with baby Michael.

When Jim was diagnosed with hepatitis B, caused by a yellow fever vaccination that contained infected human blood serum, Beatrice left for Fort Knox without hesitation.[99] With George going to war becoming more likely every day, Ruth Ellen could only marvel at her mother's strength and determination as she moved in and took over the household.

---

UNAWARE THAT SIX Japanese aircraft carriers were approaching Hawaii, Oahuans were out dancing in nightclubs, having drinks at the Royal Hawaiian, and enjoying lū'aus beneath the stars. Walter Hyde Dillingham (nephew of the Pattons' friend) even woke up in his tuxedo on December 7, 1941, after he crashed with a friend at Hickam Field, the Army's principal airbase adjacent to Pearl Harbor.

The Air Corps reserve officer was just about to pass through the front gate around 8 a.m. when a series of airplanes flew by with Japanese insignia, but it wasn't until bullets whizzed by his car that he realized this wasn't a movie production.[100] When he turned on the radio, he heard Webley Edwards's chilling words, "Attention. This is no exercise. The Japanese are attacking Pearl Harbor. All Army, Navy, and Marine personnel report to duty."

Radio was the fastest way of disseminating news in 1941, so it was no surprise that Beatrice had hers turned on while she was busy caring for two-month-old Michael at Green Meadows. But, unlike most people, she was not surprised the Japanese bombed Pearl Harbor. George had been warning about such an attack since 1935, concerned about Japan's expansionism and the growing number of Japanese on the Hawaiian Islands. He'd written a racially tinted paper when he was the Hawaiian Department's intelligence officer (G-2) and suggested interning the Japanese population to protect U.S. interests in the Pacific, but General Drum and the War Department accused him of warmongering.

Beatrice immediately thought of all her friends in Honolulu and Pearl Harbor; she knew the area so well she could vividly imagine the destruction taking place almost six thousand miles away along the dry docks and airfields.

*Figure 68. Beatrice in front of the Pattons' regular officers' quarters at Fort Benning. (Library of Congress)*

She was devastated by the loss of life—the final tally would bring the number of deaths to 2403 and the number of wounded to a thousand—but at the same time, she felt a wave of relief wash over her. It was the same relief that made Churchill sleep "the sleep of the saved and thankful" that night, the same relief felt by President Roosevelt, who knew "the blow had fallen" and entry into the war was now inevitable.[101]

With most of the Pacific Fleet destroyed, the United States declared war on Japan on December 8; three days later, Germany and Italy declared war on the United States. This was the moment Beatrice both hoped for and dreaded: Georgie would finally get the chance to fulfill his destiny. He had waited twenty-three years for the opportunity, and now her waiting would begin. At least "she'd learned to take it," her new attitude one of hope instead of despair. She hung a print called *The Soldier's Return* in the hallway of Green Meadows, but she refused to make space for its companion, *The Soldier's Farewell*. "That may be over-emphasis on the psychology of something or other," she explained when a journalist asked her about the missing piece. "But we're keyed for hope in this house, and there is no room on our walls, or in our hearts, for despair."[102]

Beatrice returned to Fort Benning as soon as war was declared, to spend time with the husband she had barely seen over the last six months because of the 1941 maneuvers. Her return was not only a boon to George but also very much appreciated by his colleagues. Beatrice was as well-known as George in Army circles and a marvel to many of his fellow officers. She wasn't just his supportive wife; she was his partner, impetus, and pacifier. When General Devers, chief of the armored forces, spent a few days with the Pattons at Fort Benning, a heated discussion arose at the dinner table between the two generals regarding the future of tank design. Beatrice prepared to leave the room, but General Devers stopped her, "No Bea, you better stay in here because George and I are going to have a fight and I'd like to have a referee."[103]

Changes were happening at an ever-increasing speed. George received command of I Armored Corps in January 1942 when General Chaffee died of cancer. A month later, he was ordered to locate, create, equip, and command a Desert Training Center to prepare troops to fight Rommel's Afrika Korps. After he took off for California in his private plane to scout suitable locations, Beatrice was so distraught that her Columbus friends drove her around town to look at gardens. George already had two near misses in the last few months flying his Piper Cub, but the approach of war finally accomplished what she had been unable to do for thirty-two years. As George wrote Walter Dillingham that same month, "I am not playing polo right now, as it would be sort of unfortunate to miss a war for a bad polo game."[104]

As the only person privy to all the details of George's job, Beatrice knew it was only a matter of time before the emerging "star of the Armored Forces" would be called upon to chase his destiny. So, on April 10, 1942, the day before he left Fort Benning for the newly established Desert Training Center near Indio, California, she organized a despedida at their log cabin. She insisted Bee and Ruth Ellen attend their father's goodbye party, but unfortunately, George IV couldn't make it from The Hill School.

Beatrice vehemently objected to George concocting his own punch using the half-empty bottles of Johnnie Walker Red Label, Old Crow, Southern Comfort, and white wine he found in his liquor cabinet, but he reminded her of her favorite saying, "Make it last, wear it out, use it up, do without." The Patton women wisely stuck to beer that evening because the Armored Diesel felled even the most formidable officer.

*Figure 69. Beatrice and George, most likely at his despedida. (Library of Congress)*

As the evening ended, George raised his glass—a goblet he had made from an oil can—and gave a toast "to the wives. My, what pretty widows you're going to make."[105] Bee and Ruth Ellen were now also part of that group. The sisters returned to their husbands the next day, unaware it would be more than three years before they would see their father again. They never got the chance to say goodbye officially, yet no one had any regrets. Not only did they have their own families to worry about, but they had always known this moment would come.

INDIO, located in California's Coachella Valley, about 120 miles from Lake Vineyard, was once known as the last frontier town in America. Its past was as rich as its surroundings were dry, and Beatrice, as she always did when she arrived somewhere new, "immediately put her inquiring mind to work learning the history of the place."[106] Cahuilla Indians first inhabited the area, drawn to that specific spot in the arid Coachella Valley by twelve palm trees that grew there. Access to water was the same reason surveyors of the Southern Pacific Railroad had chosen the location to found the town of Indio in 1876, located midway between Yuma and Los Angeles. Over the years, it evolved into an agricultural town known for its dates, then a mining town, and finally, the supply depot of the Desert Training Center.

Indio was the most extreme environment Beatrice ever found herself in as an officer's wife. Undeterred by temperatures reaching triple digits by June, she rented a 1925 mission-revival ranch-style house with an icehouse roof (a double roof to keep the heat out) and just a few rooms. The home had no air-conditioning, but she learned a few tricks from the locals to fight the dry heat. During the day, wet cloths hung in the windows with fans blowing behind them; during the night, Beatrice slept in a submarine, a bedroom "where water ran slowly down through burlap, reducing the inside temperature by as much as 20 degrees."[107] She was helped by the Meekses, whose transfer George had specifically requested.

"Didn't we have fun this summer?" Beatrice wrote a few months later to George's cousin, Arvin Brown, because she was "pretty busy for an idle woman."[108] When George was out of town, she spent time with Nita at Lake Vineyard or entertained friends and family in Indio. Eugenia "Gene" Merrill had recently married and moved to Los Angeles with her husband, Robert Seamans Jr. She had spent a lot of pleasant time in the company of the Patton family when growing up, and both Uncle George and Aunt Bea were "important role models."

Beatrice was a "positive influence" who always encouraged Gene to be herself, while George "was a fascinating man" with whom she enjoyed "a really fun relationship."[109] One Sunday in the spring of 1942, a Packard stopped in front of Gene's door in Pasadena, a general's flag fluttering on the hood. She immediately accepted Aunt Bea and Uncle George's invitation to spend the week with them in Indio, riding a tank and watching maneuvers.[110]

George spent most of his time at his headquarters at Chiriaco Summit, about twenty-five miles from Indio and bordering what is now Joshua Tree National Park. The fifty-six-year-old Major General wasn't there to "get comfortable" but "to train for war." During the week, he chose to rough it with his men at Camp Young, sleeping in a tar paper structure and limiting his ration of food and water.[111]

He trained his men mercilessly to avoid bloodshed later, but he commanded their respect by never asking them to do anything he wouldn't do himself, whether it was joining them on their daily one-mile run, pulling tanks out of the sand, or directing traffic when chaos ensued. His soldiers came to expect him in the middle of the night as he surprised the night watch, and from the sky in his Stinson plane to observe maneuvers, and at the field hospital to visit those who succumbed to heat, exhaustion, or scorpion bites.

Undoubtedly, Beatrice paved the way for the amicable relationship between the people of Indio and the Army, befriending everyone she met as she rode her bike through town. George occasionally surprised her for supper, but otherwise, just like his men, he only came into town from late Saturday night until early Sunday evening. He was adamant about disrupting the lives of Indio's two thousand residents as little as possible, but many saw the influx of soldiers as a boon to the town's economy.[112]

Since women weren't allowed at the Desert Training Center at first, the female population of Indio soon complained about the many catcalls they received from the thousands of soldiers who descended on the town every weekend. George addressed their concerns during a Memorial Day speech at the Hotel Indio. He would ban whistling if the locals insisted, but he suggested not to worry, "If they didn't whistle at me, then I'd worry." With very little entertainment available when the Desert Training Center was first established, the Pattons ingratiated themselves to tens of thousands of soldiers by purchasing a piano for Camp Coxcomb's officers' club and installing radios in each of the center's ten camps.

*Figure 70. R&R was important to the Pattons. Here they are at Fort Benning in 1941, dedicating the Service Club. (Library of Congress)*

Being so far from political and military powers at this critical juncture in history caused George such anxiety that he wrote countless letters to those in higher office, requesting to "be given a chance to prove in blood what I have learned in sweat." An indomitable Beatrice made it her mission to observe as many maneuvers and reviews as she could, especially when officials arrived at the Chiriaco airstrip, and she could use her charm to represent George's best interests.

Visitors were immediately taken to the "King's Throne," a sand hill overlooking the training area where George narrated and directed the mock battles from a microphone. Protected from the glaring sun by a tarp, Beatrice beamed with pride—or sweat—as she watched divisions of 15,000 men fight with live ammunition, the closest she'd ever get to combat with George in command.[113] She listened intently to his speeches and made notes of things to change, paying close attention to his audience's reaction.

Meanwhile, the British faced a losing battle against Rommel's Afrika Korps in the desert of North Africa. After the fall of Tobruk—the British stronghold in Libya—General Marshall finally agreed to deploy one armored division to the area and put Major General Patton in charge of the operation. But overzealous as he was wont to be, George advocated for two divisions when he arrived in Washington at the end of June 1942. Fed up with his badgering and aware that he needed "a tight rope round his neck," Marshall decided to teach George a lesson and sent him back to Indio. Beatrice was a calming presence while he worried himself to death that he had squandered his chances, until he received a cryptic letter from Eisenhower, stationed in London as commander of all troops in the European Theater of Operations (ETO).

On July 30, 1942, a messenger knocked on the door of Beatrice's Indio home and handed her a quickly scribbled note from George: "Darling B. I have just been ordered to leave for Washington to day preparatory to going over seas on an inspection trip. I will probably be gone 2 or 3 weeks but will return here before going to war. I love you."[114] It was apparent it was "the real thing this time."[115] When Beatrice arrived in Washington two days later and made her "headquarters" at the Merrills' home, George was about to leave for London to meet with Eisenhower.

Two weeks later, he had "an exciting trip back ... as the head winds took so much gas that the pilot left it to me whether to turn back or go ahead & possibly down." He gave the go-ahead to continue, confident his luck would hold now that he was named commander of the Western Task Force—in charge of the invasion of Casablanca—in a joint British-American amphibious operation in North Africa called Operation Torch.[116]

Neither Patton returned to the Desert Training Center. Instead, Beatrice set in motion the long-distance "evacuation of Indio" with the help Arvin Brown "so generously offered." Her car was still at Nita's and could remain there for the time being, but the Meekses closed the Indio home and shipped everything to Green Meadows. Like Beatrice, Virgie wanted to stay with her husband as long as possible and hoped to travel east "at the same time and over the same route" once he received his orders.[117]

Even though "Georgie is terribly busy & I mostly see him only when he is half, or all, asleep," Beatrice was happy "to be together as long as we can."[118] She knew Operation Torch was "bad and mostly political" with "only a 48% chance of success," but at the moment, she felt the same way her husband did before a polo game: waiting for the game to begin was the hardest part.[119] George "went to Mexico on one and a half hour's notice, and on five days' notice to France in 1917," but the eleven weeks to plan Operation Torch felt like an eternity, even though it was but "a short time to organize the greatest expeditionary force ever to sail at once from the U.S."[120] By October they were still together, and at Kay's suggestion Beatrice was "trying to remember all the time how awful my life would be . . . if Georgie <u>didn't</u> get to go." She saw merit in this unusual reasoning, "but it's hard any way you look at it."[121]

On October 6, just a day after she watched George kiss the *When and If* goodbye on the Chesapeake Bay, Beatrice spent the night on Cove Point Beach, Maryland, to observe a trial landing at Solomon's Island. While neither Patton had much trust in the Navy, George started to feel more confident when he realized "that his whole life might have led up to this: Command of tanks in a war, study of the Chauvel and Alenby in the desert in World War I, practice landing operations in our outboard in Oahu, and last, all of our blue water sailing and navigating."[122]

A week later, Beatrice remembered George being "more shaken than I could believe," when he came home for lunch. It took "a strong drink, a glass of beer, [and] two cups of coffee" before he was able to tell her what had happened.

"If you don't succeed, I don't want to see you alive," George had just told Brigadier General Truscott and Major Generals Anderson and Harmon, who had been his friends for years. He planned to see each of them ashore, not to "usurp your deeds, but in order to share with you the dangers of our soldiers." He then asked General Marshall into the room to shake hands with the men who were potentially sacrificing their lives for a mission that seemed bound to fail, but "the General 'had to go to the Senate' and excused himself." Beatrice could tell how much this simple action had "hurt" her husband.[123]

"The last few days have been tough," Beatrice wrote in her diary, "mix-ups, delays, disappointments, and of course grief at parting."[124] As the first leaves turned orange in New York's Hudson Valley, George traveled to West Point to spend an afternoon with his son, who had been accepted "by the skin of his teeth." All George IV ever wanted was to be a soldier, but getting him admitted to the Military Academy proved as hard a battle as it had been for Mr. Patton thirty-six years earlier. Academically challenged like his father, young George was set to attend a year of military preparatory school, but after graduating from high school, "he felt he should enlist if he failed to make West Point this year."[125] His parents consented, but they were "glad" when he passed his admission exam and received an appointment from Massachusetts Congressman Thomas Flaherty in July 1942.

With all his affairs in order and with peace of mind that Beatrice would be well taken care of at Green Meadows, George sat down to write his farewells. He penned letters to his children; his sister; his old nanny, Mary Scally; Mrs. F. C. Marshall, who took Beatrice under her wing at Fort Sheridan; Mrs. Simonds, who welcomed Beatrice as she sailed through the Panama Canal in 1925; the Princes; the Merrills; and Generals Brewster, Singleton, and Harbord.[126]

He wrote Beatrice a paper on how to care for his horses and a heartfelt letter to Fred:

> The job I am going on is about as desperate a venture as has ever been undertaken by any force in the world's history . . . So my proverbial luck will have to be working all out. However I have a convinced belief that I will succeed. If I don't I shall not survive a second Donqurque (if that is how you spell it). Of course there is the off chance that political interests may help and we shall have, at least initially, a pushover. Personally, I would rather have to fight-it would be good practice. However, in any event we will eventually have to fight and fight hard and probably for years. Those of us who come back will have had some interesting experiences. And further, when we get back we will have a hell of a job on our hands. I should like to have a crack at the latter part.
>
> So far as B and the children are concerned, I know that under your supervision they could not be better off. I am inclosing a sealed letter to B. which you are only to give her when and if I am definitely reported dead. I expect you to keep it a long time . . . Letters even to me will probably be censored so avoid political and financial statements you don't want others to read. This all sounds very gloomy, but is not realy so bad. All my life I have wanted to lead a lot of men in a desperate battle, I am going to do it. And at fifty-six one can go with equanimity-there is nothing much one has not done. Thanks to you and B., I have had an exceptionally happy life. "Death is as light as a feather, reputation for valor is as heavy as a mountain."[127]

George's final meeting with General Marshall on October 21 was more "affable and encouraging." Next, he called on General Pershing at Walter Reed Hospital, where he had been a resident for years. At eighty-two, the mentor did not recognize his protégé until George reminded him that his success "as a fighting man began with his taking me to Mexico." After receiving Pershing's blessing, George kissed his hand and saluted him; at that moment, "25 years seemed to drop from him." As George walked away, he realized it was "probably the last time I shall see him, but he may outlive me."[128]

George's last meeting of the day was at 2 p.m. at the White House. President Roosevelt greeted him and Rear Admiral Hewitt (in charge of the Western Task Force's naval operations), "Come in Skipper and Old Cavalryman and give me the good news." George would have preferred to get something more substantial out of the meeting, but the president, who considered George "a joy," focused primarily on bonhomie and asked him "whether he had his old Cavalry saddle to mount on the turret of a tank and if he went into action on the side with his saber drawn."[129] The thirty-minute meeting ended with wishes of Godspeed from the president and a promise from George to "leave the beaches either a conqueror or a corpse."

TWO WARS HAD TAUGHT Beatrice that the trick was "not to say goodbye at all," but to be "very casual about it."[130] The plan had been for the Pattons' leave-taking to take place at Bolling Airfield, just outside Washington, but when they stood on the tarmac on the afternoon of October 22, 1942, Beatrice gratefully accepted General Stratemeyer's offer to come along to Norfolk, Virginia. The C-47 took off at 2 p.m., Beatrice surrounded by some of George's most loyal subordinates who would be with him until the day he died: Deputy Commander General Keyes; Chief of Staff Colonel Gay; Deputy Chief of Staff Colonel Harkins; Captains Jenson and Stiller, George's aides; and finally Meeks, his faithful orderly.[131] She entrusted General Keyes with a letter he was to give George on his fifty-seventh birthday, hopeful that things would go according to plan.[132]

That morning, "G seemed pleased ... that I [Beatrice] had trimmed my black hat with a red bird, but did not remark, for which I was grateful, that my eyes were as red as the bird."[133] It was George, however, who was "considerably upset" when the C-47 landed, and he jumped out of the plane without saying goodbye. Beatrice called him back.[134]

This was the third time she was seeing her husband off to war, but she learned it was "too tough on the man who's going" if you "cry or make a scene."[135] The "only important thing is how he feels," and today, George felt "proud" because his wife "did not cry for once" and her "eyes did not go back on you."[136] As he prepared to leave, Beatrice told him she loved him, kissed him goodbye, and stepped into the waiting car which would drive her the two hundred miles back to Washington whenever she was ready.

Beatrice "was glad, the great strain was over for him at last," but it was only just beginning for her.[137] To have George safe at home would have meant bouts of unhappiness like he had experienced intermittently over the last twenty-four years; to have him participate in the biggest war in history meant years of waiting and anxiety for her.

He told her that "he expected to die fighting," and she believed him. WWII was his last chance to gain the glory he yearned for his whole life, and she knew he would give it his all because "life and happiness [were] small sacrifices."[138] She made herself sick with worry during WWI, but this time around, she was toughened. "Be happy today," she repeated the Old Army's adage. "Who knows what tomorrow may hold?"[139]

It was a cold and wet night, but Beatrice sat in that car for hours, mesmerized by the sight of the flickering lights aboard the one hundred ships in the harbor.[140] The biggest armada to sail from U.S. soil was an impressive sight, but the image which remained with her forever was of the only man she ever loved embarking on his destiny, a figure tall and impressive.

Battle for him was "not a terrifying ordeal to be endured," but "a magnificent experience wherein all the elements that have made man superior to the beast are present: courage, self sacrifice, loyalty, help to others, devotion to duty."[141] She knew his men would be proud to follow him, "galvanized into action by the dynamism of one man," just as she had been for the last thirty years.

George's only regret was that "Bea was not at the Hotel Chamberlin to see us pass" when the *Augusta* left at 8.10 a.m. on October 24. He called her from on board the day before, then penned the first of hundreds of letters he would write her over the next few years, reminding her that he would be "thinking of you and loving you."[142] In his diary, he wrote: "This is my last night in America. It may be for years and it may be forever. God grant that I do my full duty to my men and to myself."[143]

Although "it was alright to be afraid of dying," Major General Patton didn't fear death.[144] Not only did he consider it "foolish" to fear something "we don't know anything about," but he also considered himself "better situated to be killed than most as I have had out of life about all there is to get."[145] All he hoped for was to "have the guts to put my theories of personal leadership into action," and to finally justify the confidence Frederick Ayer and his daughter had put in him.

# 11

## GREEN MEADOWS
## SOUTH HAMILTON, MASSACHUSETTS

### 1942–1945

*LIVE THE BEST YOU KNOW, AND PERHAPS ONE UNHAPPY SEEKER WILL SEE IN YOUR*
*BEHAVIOR THE KEY TO HIS OWN FREEDOM.*

To the woman who determinedly walked the halls of Boston's South Station on a hot summer's night in July 1943, the sight of service members saying goodbye to their loved ones as they left for training camps across the country felt eerily familiar. Most women did not have the experience a veteran like Beatrice Ayer Patton had in seeing their men off to war, so tears flowed liberally to her dismay.

Thirty-three years earlier, Beatrice had learned from one of the Old Army wives to put on her smile every morning, just as she put on her clothes. While she had done "her fair share of crying, [crying] is something that army wives do in private. The smile is for parade." Her smile, however, always "got a little stiff" when dealing with the press, and she was beginning to hate them like undertakers.[1]

South Station was the perfect place for milling journalists looking for a human-interest story, with over 125,000 passengers each day and a hub for soldiers coming from and going to the war. If Beatrice hoped to slip quietly into the South Station Theater to catch the news, then she hadn't counted on the mob of reporters who descended upon her when she rounded the corner. She was now a household name like her husband, and her witty conversation and biting remarks always made for excellent copy.[2]

However, the only thing Beatrice told reporters on July 17 was that she had some time to kill before catching a train to New York, and she "thought it might be fun to see my husband again . . . it helps keep us together to see him in the newsreels."[3]

These twice-weekly newsreels—called *United News* and produced by the newly created Office of War Information—were an essential source of information even for a general's wife. George wrote as often as he could, but his letters were censored and took anywhere from one to six weeks to arrive. Certain officers sent cables, but Beatrice was not in the habit of asking favors and didn't want "to annoy people who are trying to do their stuff under difficulties."

So she wrote letters, just as she traveled under the constant threat of being put off by service personnel. She wrote George full of glee of the time her seat was taken by a technical sergeant who asked her what she cut out of the newspaper.

"Is that Patton of the second armored?" the man asked when Beatrice showed her clipping. Once she told him who she was, "we ate all his sandwiches together."[4]

The audience who sat with her that night in the South Station Theater saw General Patton, whom they vigorously applauded, but Beatrice saw her Georgie, a great man who "has all the flash, and drama, and personality, and everything to back it up with."[5] She got her first look at the three stars on his helmet as he jumped off a landing barge, a cigar clenched between his teeth.

The invasion of Sicily had just been announced, and General Patton waded ashore to command the Seventh Army from the front as the fight for the town of Gela intensified. Reading about his "great personal courage and the magnificent fighting qualities of his troops" was one thing, but witnessing them with her own eyes was even better.[6] Beatrice coyly asked him in a letter to "try and give me a smile" the next time he saw a camera crew approach, although she believed his stern look had been appropriate to the occasion.[7]

George's success brought her such excitement "that I just don't worry or do anything but shine in your reflected light. I feel, as you do, that all your life has pointed to this and that you still have many big things ahead, and that God is with you and guiding your every move. I feel sure that you are marked by destiny and that I am willing to wait on God for that."[8]

The thought that George might get killed at any moment no longer frightened Beatrice the way it had in WWI. After all, "there are lots of things worse than being killed in a good fight."[9]

HOW DIFFERENT THE Second World War was for Beatrice, with news arriving while battles were being fought. When she heard war vessels were concentrating near Gibraltar, she knew it was time to return to the capital. The whole family was wonderful to her, but the Merrills' mansion in Washington was Beatrice's home away from home during the war. "Here I am busy every minute and I meet interesting people and feel in touch with the war all the time and all my life is new to me," she explained when George asked why she didn't spend more time at Green Meadows.[10] In the capital, someone was always knocking on the door with news from her husband or offering to take over a care package she had lovingly prepared.

Operation Torch—three simultaneous landings in Algiers, Oran, and Morocco—was planned to commence sometime in the early morning of November 8 (local time).[11] With zero hour approaching rapidly and the War Department poised to make a major radio announcement at 9 p.m., Beatrice eagerly accepted Secretary and Mrs. Stimson's invitation to dinner at Woodley Mansion. What better place was there to be on the eve of the first major American offensive than at the home of a longtime family friend who also happened to be the secretary of war. The Stimsons were always "wonderful - - a great comfort."[12]

Beatrice couldn't eat a thing as the clock slowly moved toward nine. She believed an army wife could have a "share" in her man's life, "Even though they are away from us, we can read intelligently and keep up with what they are thinking." She prepared herself for this moment by re-reading every book on Hannibal she could find in George's immense military library, just as George spent the last two weeks preparing on board the *Augusta* by reading the Koran. Knowledge was her ally, while "worry and fear and selfish thoughts" were her enemies. She realized George's mission wasn't primed for success—most of it depended on whether Vichy France welcomed the Allies as friends or foes—but "a war like this, for a noble cause, in defense of our ideals of democracy and liberty, is one of the greatest adventures in life a man can have."[13]

While time had taught Beatrice the fortitude necessary to give off a semblance of calm even in times of crisis, the waiting never got easier on the inside. Since there was no immediate announcement at nine o'clock, she demurely asked the Secretary of War for an update. When the news finally came in that "the entire operation had come off as planned," she couldn't describe her feelings. Her heart felt a little lighter when she drove home to the Merrills, knowing the invasion was off to a good start. She sat by the radio for hours that night, but it wasn't until the morning that Katherine Marshall called to inform her that George "had made a successful landing," although no one had heard from him yet.

All hell broke loose at 2535 Belmont Road on November 8 when the War Department released Major General Patton's name as one of the commanding officers of Operation Torch. Beatrice was writing her husband when the *Times Herald* called for an interview. She dutifully gave a few polite answers and then returned upstairs to continue writing when "the doorbell rang and a reporter from the same paper was at the door to get my picture. I sent word that I was out, as I am too busy answering the phone and writing to you to bother with anything like that this afternoon."

Beatrice was well aware that "there are months and perhaps years of waiting and anxiety ahead of me, yet today all I can think of is your triumph, and the thought that rings through my mind like a peal of bells is that the first jump is taken and you will never have to take it again. And I know that it is a success."[14]

Mrs. Patton had "no love for the press," but when Paramount News returned later that evening, she realized she now resided in the spotlight. So she begrudgingly went downstairs and gave a brief statement: "This is America's hour of triumph. Safely our men have crossed the sea to fight our battle. The spirit of victory is in their hearts. They will not fail."[15]

Everything Beatrice did reflected on George, regardless of his being 3,800 miles away. Talking to the *Washington Post* a few days later, she wished she was with him, "shooting at somebody," despite being a "poor shot." No one who knew her doubted her sincerity when she said she wanted "to be there going through that sand and taking a part in the fighting."[16] But, instead, while General Patton was fêted by "about 100,000 people cheering, yelling and clapping," she and Mamie Eisenhower received an invitation to the White House to have tea with the First Lady.[17]

Just hours after the cessation of hostilities on November 11, in a small village near Casablanca called Fedala, General Keyes handed George the birthday letter "that wonderful person . . . his devoted wife" had entrusted to him at Norfolk.[18] Beatrice knew that leading his men to victory was the best birthday gift George could have ever received.

> I wish I were with you; fighting in your army. I would be a better soldier than here at home; but there can be no separation between us except by amputation, as of the fingers of a hand. What hurts you hurts me too and I share in your triumph, even thousands of miles away.[19]

After years of study and sacrifice, George accomplished "exactly what he set out to do." All Beatrice could think of was "how you are doing that which you have longed for and trained for all your life, and how glad I am that you are having your chance to show what you really are."[20]

*Figure 71. Beatrice addressing the women of France. (Library of Congress)*

FROM THE MOMENT George began planning Operation Torch, Beatrice looked to do "something active to win the war," something "brand-new . . . divorced from my life with the general."[21] She would have joined the Women's Army Corps (WAC) but was "a bit too old."[22] So instead, George had suggested in August 1942 that she could write for the War Department. She had visited their offices the next day and offered her services, but they were currently only looking for speakers. Since Beatrice didn't like public speaking, she "thanked them and bowed myself out." However, George disagreed and told her to go back in the morning, "Tell them you are a speaker. If they don't think so, you'll find out soon enough."

As Beatrice's longtime friend, Lieutenant General Charles Herron, said of her, "In her great qualities of heart and head, and even in courage, she was not overshadowed by her distinguished husband." Beatrice returned the next day and began working with a reviewing officer in the Public Relations Office who showed her "ways to put over some points I want to make and still walk the crack."[23] Even though she never thought she could make a speech, she quickly gained a reputation for being a "direct and purposeful speaker," one who was doing "as fine and as well" in her sphere as George was doing in his.[24]

Beatrice didn't "feel at all important to the war effort," but she was "damned sure that I can help it along on the home front."[25] Once in a while, she was discouraged, wondering if she was becoming like the persons she despised the most, the ones taking "people's money and doing no good and who would be more use rolling bandages." But then she reminded herself that the War Department always asked her back, and young army wives sent her letters to thank her for her advice.[26] They appreciated the window she offered into her own life, a life that was as alien to them as it had once been to her:

> Army life is very like the Gulf Stream, which, made of the same watery element as the ocean through which it runs, has no boundaries; yet its temperature and its tempo keep it separate and distinct. It is not only a different color from the rest of the ocean, it supports entirely different fish. Army Officers are highly educated professional men who are content to get along with little of this world's goods, so they must live the life they love; and the women who join them must be of the same sort to be successful and happy, for the lines that prescribe our lives are as definite as the boundaries of the Gulf Stream . . .
>
> It is an interesting thing to notice that in this common life of ours in which we move about from post to post (I have been married thirty-one years and have had nineteen major moves) we still preserve our local differences within our families, carrying our background with us as a turtle packs its shell. In any Army post, if you go into a row of houses exactly alike on the outside, you will find the Boston people using the broad and eating fishballs on Sunday morning, while the family from Mississippi next door eat hot bread twice a day in the atmosphere of the Deep South.[27]

Beatrice spoke at women's clubs and factories, packing her days "full to the brim . . . with every opportunity for usefulness," "jumping around the country so constantly" that Chilly had a hard time keeping track of his sister.[28] In September 1943, she was "booked for the next fortnight every afternoon, and for several evenings a week, to give talks on the need for unity of effort in every war activity."[29]

Around the same time, the Office of War Information recruited her to make a series of broadcasts over shortwave radio to the women of France. She directed her talks at Mademoiselle Gogo, "ma chère bonne institutrice," who taught her the language in Paris in 1896. Beatrice last saw her in 1938 during Ruth Ellen's grand tour, but she hadn't received any letters since 1940 when the octogenarian wrote that she heard "the German soldiers singing in the streets."[30]

Friends and family wrote George constantly of the "grand job" Beatrice was doing "to keep up the civilian morale." He was very proud of her, happy that she was "producing fine publicity for both of us." She sent him transcripts of the speeches she made, and in return, he wrote her useful anecdotes, historical references, and verses she could use in her upcoming talks. He thought most "war broadcasts etc put too much emphasis on sacrifice and not enough on Glory," but Beatrice did him proud.[31] She was excited when the War Department allowed her to "get much more warlike," until she came across as a little "too emphatic" in the drafts she submitted for review.[32]

Talking to the Montpelier Woman's Club in Vermont in April 1944, Beatrice spoke "in a humorous vein, dealing with the personal troubles of an army wife, [but] she concluded her talk on a serious note." She believed it was "nobody's business to criticize the military at this distance," and opposed the constant clamor for information and the demands "that the American public be told everything." She warned that there was "no such thing as a good rumor, they are all poisonous," and took George's advice to advocate for the War Department to release the names of divisions currently in action, "It makes those families proud, and frees from worry the families of those not taking part."[33]

EVERY RING of the telephone made Beatrice pause for a brief second. Warned by George that he worried for Johnnie's safety in the North African desert with the 1st Armored Division, her worst fears were realized in February 1943 when the War Department informed her that Lieutenant Colonel Waters was missing in action. There was a moment of silence when she told her daughter, but then Bee put on a brave face, "I am sure Johnnie's alive. Don't worry, Ma, the Regulars will show. I'll never give up."

Beatrice was an inspiration to her daughters, but she felt almost ashamed when she remembered her reaction when George was reported dead during the last war.[34] Four-year-old Johnnie and one-year-old George were just a little younger than Bee and Ruth Ellen had been in 1918, yet Bee remained calm. According to Beatrice, waiting was "one of the hardest things women have to bear in wartime." As days turned into weeks, the Pattons reminded themselves that "missing men and men accounted dead turn up every day."[35]

When news of the 1st Armored Division's ambush reached George, he was both worried and disgusted. He'd been stuck in Morocco for the last three months acting as proconsul—Beatrice's French lessons finally paid off, as did her entertaining and diplomatic skills—while other less capable commanders were continuing the fight with his troops. He'd been apoplectic when he visited Tunisia, and his son-in-law told him that he was the first general the 1st Armored Division had seen since they started fighting twenty-four days earlier. This glaring lack of leadership finally caught up with the allies on February 14, 1943, at the battle of Sidi Bou Zid.

George personally went to check the battlefield, but neither he nor the Graves Registration found a trace of Johnnie. So instead, he picked up an ammunition clip and sent it to his grandsons as a reminder of the brave fight their father put up.

*Figure 72. In May 1943, Bee and Beatrice look on as John Knight Waters Jr. receives his father's Silver Star. It was one of the thousands of pictures Beatrice pasted in countless scrapbooks. (Library of Congress)*

At the time of the attack, the 1st Battalion was holding a hill in the Kasserine Pass. The small force managed to defend their position for two days and nights against repeated attacks from Rommel's forces, but when they were eventually ordered to retreat, Colonel Waters stayed behind with a small detachment to cover the withdrawal. Knowing Johnnie for almost fifteen years, George was convinced his son-in-law didn't surrender, but he asked Fred "to make little Bea and also Bea senior believe that he did."[36]

General Eisenhower considered Lieutenant Colonel Waters's action that day "one of the finest performed in this war" and called him "the perfect example of a cadet and officer" during a radio broadcast celebrating West Point's 141st anniversary.[37] It was the finest tribute both Bs had ever heard, but it was nothing compared to the news they received on March 17.[38] Colonel

Waters was alive but had been captured by the Germans. Now that her worst fears hadn't been realized, Bee's imagination magnified all other "minor fears and anxieties . . . Is he well-treated? Is he ill, hungry, neglected, unhappy in the dreary surroundings of a prison camp? The sum of these minor worries is sometimes almost harder to bear than the former great anxiety about his life itself."

George expected his daughter "to take the thing in a very matter of fact manner," but he knew her well enough to realize "that she will probably be under a terrific strain," and he asked Fred and the rest of the family to keep an eye on her.[39] Bee spent most of the war in Washington—the best place to learn "something new about prisoners"—working for the American National Red Cross and the Relatives of American Prisoners of War and Civilian Internees.[40] Every morning she opened a stack of newspapers and meticulously searched for any information about German prison camps, then she contacted recently released or escaped Prisoners of War (POW) in the hopes of getting a firsthand account of Johnnie.

On the same day Bee learned Johnnie was a POW, Beatrice received a call from the press informing her that a newly promoted Lieutenant General Patton was assigned temporary command of II Corps. It was the first Beatrice heard of the wonderful news that he was replacing Lieutenant Fredendall, the man partly responsible for the debacle at Kasserine Pass.[41] George's unbending discipline was controversial, but she knew "how lucky they [his soldiers] are to be with General Patton." He believed the least he could do before sending young men onto the battlefield was to prepare them as well as possible—his armies continually had some of the lowest casualty rates of the war—and to never ask of them what he wouldn't do himself.[42]

General Patton's soldiers "swore at him, but by him," and they respected him because he didn't make them fight for him, but with him.[43] Front line soldiers of II Corps, holding the valley heights around El Guettar against heavy counterattack, were surprised to see a group of command cars approaching in the distance. The convoy was shelled, so a "tall, spare figure" got out of the car and continued on foot, climbing a steep hill to the outpost where he observed the battle for an hour. Soldiers peered out of their foxholes to catch sight of "Old Blood and Guts," dressed in a leather aviator jacket and carrying his ivory-handled .45 revolvers, looking taller and more impressive than many imagined. "It sure is good to see him in the front lines," twenty-three-year-old Corporal Davis of Brooklyn told the *Associated Press*. "I hear he wants to get Rommel in one tank and him in another and have it out."[44]

War for George was "the greatest of all games." Still, one of its tragedies, "particularly to a General, is that in order to carry out his mission of defeating the enemy, he has to cause the death of such heroic individuals . . ."[45] On April 1, 1943, he ordered Captain Richard "Dick" Jenson—his aide since he had taken command of the 2nd Armored Division in 1940, and whose family had been friends with his for three generations—to the front with General Omar Bradley. The twenty-seven-year-old's watch stopped at 10:12 a.m., when a German Stuka flew over his forward command post and dropped a bomb within inches of the slit trench he sheltered in.[46] George sank down on his knees when he saw Jenson's unmarked body and "cried like a baby" in plain sight of his staff, acting "like an old fool," kissing the boy's forehead and cutting off a lock of blond hair for his mother. "Had Dick been my own son I could hardly feel worse," he wrote Echo Jenson a few days later. "Words fail me to express to you my sorrow and sympathy."[47]

Beatrice learned of the "dreadful loss" by telegram the next day. She called Echo to offer her condolences, then asked Nita to go over to the bereaved mother's home because "there is probably no one in this world who can sooth a sore heart any better."[48] Dick had been a bachelor, but Beatrice knew "had he lived to have a son," he "would have loved to see him a West Pointer."[49] So, together with Echo and George, she established a scholarship in "reverent, loving memory of Captain Richard Norman Jenson . . . a gallant soldier, honorable gentleman and faithful friend." General Harbord was put in charge of the Richard Jensen Memorial Fund of the Army Relief Society, which consisted of $5,000 to be given to a high school student with a West Point appointment who was the son of an officer who died in WWI.[50]


THE TOWN of South Hamilton was like any other during WWII: food and gasoline were rationed, residents planted victory gardens, and over three hundred men went off to serve in the Armed Forces.[51] Gordon Prince failed his military exam because of debilitating arthritis, but he was appointed Massachusetts Wing Commander of the Civil Air Patrol and flew over 30,000 miles looking for submarines. His wife Anna took the Massachusetts State Board Exam nineteen years after she graduated from medical school and volunteered her services at Beverly Hospital.

Fred managed to keep the hospital running at full capacity with countless volunteers and helped create Massachusetts's civilian defense program. However, he was eager to get in uniform like his son Frederick Jr.[52] George discouraged his brother-in-law because "a great many men of your age and of much less ability" were "delegated to jobs not one tenth as important as what they had been doing in civil life, while the truly important things they had been doing were left to the hands of less competent men."[53]

General George S. Patton Jr. was viewed by "his townspeople, neighbors and friends" as a "true gentleman, affable, warm-hearted, cheery in his greetings, popular with everyone."[54] Beatrice was equally loved in South Hamilton; the chief of police said she was "always law abiding" with a pleasant word for everyone, while the owner of the local diner called her one of the best and often joined her fishing for pickerel in the Ipswich River at the back of Green Meadows.[55] Purchased fifteen years earlier, the old Colonial finally served its true purpose: a home for Beatrice while George was at war, surrounded by friends and family who were as loyal to her as to him.

*Figure 73. The proud grandmother with her namesake on a hot summer's day at Green Meadows. (Library of Congress)*

*Figure 74. Ruth Ellen and Michael Willoughby Totten. (Library of Congress)*

Beatrice split her time between Washington, where Bee worked for the Red Cross; West Point, where George IV struggled through his plebe year like his father had; and Green Meadows, where Ruth Ellen awaited the birth of her second child. Advised to wait at least two years before trying for another baby, Ruth Ellen had decided there was no more time to wait when both her father and brother-in-law were sent to war. Beatrice worried incessantly during her daughter's high-risk pregnancy, so it was a great relief that Ruth Ellen moved to Green Meadows in May 1943. A month later, she gave birth to the Pattons' first granddaughter, Beatrice Willoughby Totten (so named at Jim's insistence). With the help of the War Department and the *Boston Globe*, George received a radio picture of his granddaughter, sound asleep in the family's crib while Beatrice and Ruth Ellen looked on.

Despite strict rationing and loss of manpower, life at Green Meadows was pleasant. Beatrice proudly told a reporter how she and Ruth Ellen grew vegetables, made butter, preserved fruit, bred chickens, and ate "bacon of our own raising."[56] Gardening had always kept Beatrice grounded—she never forgot how her father, at four years old, scavenged for sticks on his grandfather's farm—but it also helped her sleep during the war. The more worried she was, the more vehemently she pruned the chokecherry in her backyard. With George's penchant for leading from the front and attracting scandal, her garden was soon in tip-top shape.

Beatrice was "a violent and vigorous gardener" who got down on her knees to pull weeds wearing her so-called "petit costume du mal": blue overalls and a red bandanna.[57] When a neighbor pointed out the luxury of having help from that "little old man," Beatrice slyly replied: "He's a friend of mine. I have known him all my life and, although he would really like to, he's too old to go into the service."[58] Not that Beatrice didn't try; she filled out a civil service application and was willing to accept a job outside of the country subject to regulations. She didn't expect to get in, "but I certainly should never let anything stand in my way if I were."[59]

Green Meadows was a big property protected by two huge shepherds, Carmichael and Ajax. Every stall in the stable had a horse, each with a set of detailed instructions. Luckily Beatrice was "a wonderful horse nurse" because help was few and far between.[60] When one of the horses fell ill with colic—a gastrointestinal disease that can be fatal if a horse lies down—Beatrice and Ruth Ellen spent most of the night walking it around the stable. Remembering how George always gave his horses whiskey when they suffered from colic, she called Chilly and asked him for a bottle. Feeling sorry for "dear little Bee, all alone with Georgie off at the wars and no one to take care of her," he sent a chauffeur with one of his last pre-WWI bottles. When she called back a few days later to thank him for saving George's horse, Chilly almost had a heart attack when he learned who the whiskey had been for.[61]

*Figure 75. A coveted snapshot. (Library of Congress)*

The air at Green Meadows was heavy with apprehension every morning, and not until the mail and the newspapers had been delivered were mother and daughter able to breathe a little easier. Beatrice was like a detective, using every little piece of information she could get her hands on to figure out where her Georgie might be and how he was doing. Her favorite letters, besides her husband's, were the ones she received from people who had seen him in person. If she was lucky, a snapshot might fall on her lap when she opened the envelope, but she was just as appreciative to read a few simple lines about how he looked. "It may please you to know that I found your General looking, as usual, the splendid soldier which he is . . ." Major General Troy Middleton wrote her in May 1943. "[T]hat is, in the best of health and physical condition."[62]

George equally enjoyed the "glances of the family" he received from the Hamiltonians, while they enjoyed listening to Beatrice read his replies aloud at the Myopia Hunt Club. His letters from Morocco were so detailed that Beatrice almost fancied she was there, especially since they brought back memories from the time she spent in North Africa as a child. His description of the Diffa (a Moroccan feast) given by the pasha of Casablanca reminded her of the time she got lost at a similar dinner in Algiers when she was ten years old. She remembered having

> . . . the very same kind of mutton stew that you had after your wild boar hunt, eating with three fingers from a big common bowl, and [having] our hands washed before and after with exactly the same apparatus you did, with soft soap. I got tired of sitting around with the coffee, and followed one of the sermon boys out, and somehow got into the harem side of the establishment. I had a wonderful time sitting on a sort of bunk in the wall being fed rose petal jelly with a spoon in a tumbler of water, while the women played with my pigtail and from time to time fingered the gold band on my crooked tooth. I can smell the place yet, lots of heavy perfume, hasish smoke and overall the family slopjar, about as tall as I, uncovered and almost full. Mama came bursting in and said Beatrice Ayer, I am going to have you boiled and sterilized, and I believed her, she said it with such conviction.[63]

George was excited to visit all the historical sites he had studied for so many years, places he knew Beatrice also would have enjoyed because she was "one of the few people sufficiently educated to appreciate it."[64] He took hundreds of photos to share his experiences with her and sent her tons of souvenirs, which they eventually planned to put in a museum attached to Green Meadows.[65] Just weeks into the war, Beatrice had already received a swastika flag that flew from a Casablanca hotel, a camel saddle, and the Western Task Force's landing flag. She reciprocated by sending back an equal number of packages. By Christmas, George had already received so many presents that he could "neither count, smoke, nor eat them all," so he shared them with his entourage or strangers in need.[66]

In reply to a Mrs. Sparkes's inquiry about whether the War Department made a mistake regarding her husband's death, George could offer nothing more than his condolences and the suggestion to call "Mrs. Patton as she might be able to lighten your intolerable burden. She is a very understanding soul, and possessed of great human sympathy."[67] According to Ruth Ellen, her mother had a sixth sense for the "unspoken needs" of others, "a real instinct for trouble." Beatrice preferred to keep her good deeds quiet and always made people feel they did her a favor instead of the other way around.

Clare McNair had been friends with the Pattons for a very long time, but it wasn't until both her son and her husband were killed in battle that she discovered what a truly great lady Beatrice was. Besides financial help, "only a Beatrice Patton would have thought" to place a standing order with a local Washington florist to deliver a huge bouquet to Clare's apartment every Friday, turning her living room into "a bower of blossoms each weekend."[68]

"A woman of eminent goodwill," as Lieutenant General Herron later eulogized Beatrice, "she aided literally thousands by her wise counsel and her unobtrusive philanthropy."[69] Beatrice realized how brutal the war was for first-time "war widows," especially with the "constant undertow of hysteria and defeatism that is forever trying to pull us down."[70] It was difficult enough for her to enter the Army as "a very young and very green wife" in peacetime, but in wartime, it was "perhaps even more difficult for the officers are now selected and the wives are not!" Not everyone was primed like Beatrice to see war as "a magnificent adventure, a chance for a man to use and show his most virile qualities—an opportunity to have a share in the winning."[71]

Because of the war, the number of women entering the Army from civil life outnumbered "those brought up in the Army tradition, yet the tradition is still so strong that they are shaping up into Army wives as quickly and proudly as their husbands shape up into uniform." The Women's Interest Section of the War Department asked Beatrice to talk about army etiquette, that which "keeps us homogeneous in times of peace and bolsters our morale in wartime." After thirty-three years, the customs of the service held no more secrets for Beatrice. She explained that a new officer called on his colonel, while the older post residents called upon the new family. It wasn't "toadying to rise when your chief's wife enters the room, you would show that courtesy to any older woman; and it is not belittling yourself to offer to serve at her party. You would do it for your mother. Incidentally, your colonel's wife can do a lot for you . . . if she knows you and likes you."[72]

Beatrice implored the "new crop of Army Reserve brides" to learn the Army's customs and traditions, many of which were rooted in history. She told of Frederick the Great putting buttons on the sleeves of uniforms to prevent his soldiers from wiping their noses on their cuffs. She explained an old Indian expression of the frontier days was at the root of "the apparently meaningless 'How'" in which those of the Regular Army greeted each other at parties when they raised the first glass.[73] Most importantly, she hoped people would come to regard the salute as "an honor instead of a nuisance" when they "realized the gesture is a sign of brotherhood among service people."[74]

Beatrice considered the home front the second front, and it was up to the women to "man" it because "victory lies with us."[75] Even though some of a woman's duties appeared to be of "the simple type, lacking drama," they were essential to winning the war. If you don't save fat, for example, "your own soldier may lack a bullet."[76] She emphasized the importance of rationing, "insuring that the soldiers get plenty of butter at all meals, coffee three times a day, and eggs for breakfast."[77]

At some point, Beatrice even stopped using her gasoline coupons and took a colorful donkey cart George sent her from Sicily to attend Sunday Mass.[78] One time a Rolls Royce pulled up beside her, and her sister-in-law Theodora leaned out the window, "Beatrice, dear, do you think it is quite the thing for an Ayer to be riding to church in that vehicle?"

Never at a loss for words, Beatrice replied, "Well, Fedy [Theodora's nickname], if our Lord could enter Jerusalem on the rear end of an ass, I don't see why I can't go to church in a donkey cart."[79]

The war was both a "challenge" and an "opportunity." Beatrice urged women to "get a job outside the home" and practice "self-improvement." The cornerstone of her own marriage, she suggested that "wives should study their husbands' particular interest or specialty. They should read up on the country where he is stationed—and on other countries too. They should do things to make themselves prettier and more desirable—take good care of their skin, brush their hair, get beautiful figures, and lovely hands! They should learn to cook, if they don't already know how, or study decorating, perhaps. The boys are going to see a lot of pretty women on this grand tour they are getting," so it was necessary to "hang on to every bit of your charm."[80]

A soldier's job "was to win the war," while his wife's job was "to write him cheerful letters, keep a brave face and a brave heart, and pray without ceasing." Beatrice's advice was part of the "ten-point regimen" she lived by in wartime; a "practical philosophy" gleaned from years of experience:

1. Don't worry. Look on the bright side, smile—and if things are piling up and you can't see your way clear, try praying.

2. Keep healthy.

3. Write cheerful letters. You cannot ask advice from a man in Libya or Australia. The problems will be out of date by the time he gets your letters.

4. Never listen to rumors—and never, never repeat one.

5. Don't stop at the headlines when you read the papers. Buy a reliable newspaper and read what the official communiques say and consult a map.

6. Don't turn on the radio every time you come in the house. Set yourself a stated time to listen to it.

7. Get yourself a regular job of war work, outside the home, even if it's only two hours a week.

8. Realize you are not the only one whose husband is away at war. Don't feel sorry for yourself.

9. When the fighting man is home on leave, make a holiday of it—not a family problem study.

10. Keep your family intact—after all, that is what our men are fighting for—their homes.[81]

---

"HE WRITES INTERESTINGLY and tells us nothing," Beatrice said of her husband's voluminous correspondence. Hence, it was a complete surprise when a War Department Public Relations Officer called her on November 21, 1943, "to warn me against the reporters."[82] She skimmed through the letters George had written since his appointment as commanding general of the Seventh Army in July 1943, but the only indications he gave that something had happened was on August 22. In between comments on the successful conclusion of the

Sicilian campaign and his new home near the beach—"many times better than Waikiki"—he casually mentioned, "As usual I seem to have made divine destiny [George's codename for Eisenhower] a little mad but that will pass, I suppose."[83] After that, he continued sending cryptic messages but otherwise saw "no value in spreading my troubles."[84]

Five months earlier, on a hot summer's day at the Oyster Bar in Grand Central Station, Beatrice had just ordered an oyster stew when she unfolded the *New York Times* and saw the headline: "Gen. Patton Waded Ashore To Battle."[85] The thought of oysters suddenly made her feel sick, so the soldier sitting next to her offered a word of advice.

"The thing is," he said, "don't let nothin' worry you, lady. In the Army, a fella gets tough. The first six weeks your feet hurt, and you can't think about anything but your wife. I been in the Army thirteen months now, and them things don't bother me no more. Get tough, lady, get tough!"[86]

It was "all a question of destiny," but George expected his wife to either "be a widow or a radio fan" by the time she received the letter he wrote days before Operation Husky commenced on July 10.[87] The invasion of Sicily was successful but brutal, and thirty-eight days of military and political fighting took their toll on everyone.[88] George claimed not to have a "personal feeling of responsibility for getting them [his soldiers] hurt as I took the same chances." Still, his emotions always betrayed him when he visited the wounded.[89] Walking through the 15th Evacuation Hospital on August 3, commending his men and handing out medals, he came upon a seemingly healthy Private Charles Kuhl sitting on the edge of his bed.[90] When the twenty-seven-year-old confessed he couldn't take the fighting, George slapped him with his glove and kicked him out of the hospital tent.

Seven days later, he was similarly driven over the edge when he visited the 93rd Evacuation Hospital and came across Private Paul Bennett crying on his cot.[91] According to a witness, the General knocked the soldier's helmet off his head, yelled at him that he wouldn't have "these brave men here who have been shot at seeing a yellow bastard sitting here crying," and pulled his gun.[92] George admitted he "acted precipitatly and on insufficient knowledge," but at that moment—possibly suffering from war nerves himself and the first effects of a bad case of sand fly fever—he thought he was restoring the soldiers' manhood by slapping them out of their hysteria.[93]

The Patton Incident had long been settled by the time Drew Pearson revealed its details four days before Thanksgiving on his popular radio show, the *Washington Merry-Go-Round*. Since "Georgie has never mentioned it in his letters except that he had had his ears pinned back really badly," Beatrice puzzled together what had happened over the last three months based on a report from General Eisenhower. She discussed her findings with General Harbord, "about the only person I can talk to freely."[94]

1. Georgie slapped a hysterical patient in a hospital during a battle at St. Stefano.

2. It was officially reported to Eisenhower by a medical officer and "three reputable newspaper men."

3. Eisenhower sent an investigator. He sent a second one. He went himself to investigate & ordered Georgie to apologize to all concerned which he did, and more too.

4. He sent still another man to go about among units of the 7th Army to ascertain whether Georgie had "lost prestige" & found he had not.

5. The correspondents agreed not to publish the tale, as it was damaging to the war effort.

6. Pearson got hold of it & broadcast it.

7. The truth was demanded & Algiers sent an unequivocal denial. They had to take it back!

[8.] Then Eisenhower sent his statement, a request from the W.D., saying that G. had been sufficiently punished & that it was reported to him that, wherever G. went among his men, he was greeted "with thunderous applause."[95]

Beatrice "behaved with wonderful tact and devotion" when the press showed up at the Merrills' home to "interrogate" her.[96] "[A] commanding officer—from a shavetail to a general—is the 'father' of his men and sometimes reacts like one when they disappoint him." She remembered "all too well punishing my children in the heat of disappointment or shock and wishing later I hadn't." The general was a "tough perfectionist" who asked nothing of his men "that he couldn't or wouldn't do himself." He "feels deeply" and "has been known to weep at his men's graves—as well as tear their hides off. The deed is done and the mistake made, and I'm sure Georgie is sorrier and has punished himself more than anyone could possibly realize. I've known George Patton for 41 years and I've never known him to be deliberately unfair. He's made mistakes—and he's paid for them. This was a big mistake, and he's paying a big price for it," but maybe "a few people can understand it if they put themselves in his place."[97]

Just days after Pearson's announcement, *True Confessions* published an article titled "A Hero's Wife." The interview was conducted months earlier, but Beatrice's words were eerily clairvoyant. "The General makes a lot of noise," she began, "but he's quite sweet, really." He maintained that "any man who says he is not afraid in the face of fire is either a liar or an idiot. But that he is a coward only if he lets his fear get the better of him."[98]

George had constructed such a myth around himself that it was inconceivable to the public that he still possessed "an old fear of fear" himself.[99] Yet he wrote Fred that every day "for the first half-hour the palms of my hands sweat and I feel very depressed. Then if one [a shell] hits near you, it seems to break the spell and you don't notice them anymore."[100]

Only in hindsight did George admit that he "acted in a foolish manner . . . and showed lack of judgment as to the locality."[101] He received an unofficial letter of reprimand from General Eisenhower on August 17 and apologized to Privates Kuhl, Bennett, and the whole Seventh Army. Very much aware that a fighting general like Patton was indispensable to the war effort, and given carte blanche by General Marshall, General Eisenhower asked journalists to "use their judgment" and keep the details of the incident quiet.

The story, however, kept floating around the War Department until Drew Pearson got wind of it and went to see Assistant Secretary of War Patterson, who "asked him not to broadcast it—which of course didn't bother him at all."[102] Pearson's reputation had taken a beating since President Roosevelt called him "a chronic liar"—a pro-Russian, he tried to meddle in U.S. war policy—and he was desperate for a good story.[103] He had no qualms publishing information which he knew to be false or detrimental to the war effort, and he had previously gone to battle with General MacArthur and General Pershing.

For the rest of her life, Beatrice considered Drew Pearson "a traitor to America." Most of the statements he made were "pure bunk," according to George, but there was still "sufficient basis of truth" in the broadcast that it left him, as he so eloquently described it, "a passanger floating on the river of destiny."[104] In hindsight, part of the problem was that "the publicity of the incident was not handled in a very fortunate manner."[105] A "phony telegram denying the reprimand" began circulating, but Beatrice knew all too well that George "was never officially reprimanded, and the telegram evidently was trying to cover up the thing—too late."[106]

BEATRICE HOPED that "in the light of history, we will see how unimportant this is," but the weeks following Pearson's announcement were "a tough time for all of us."[107] It was sickening how one day her husband was heralded as the heroic conqueror of North Africa and Sicily, and the next, the country was ready to "kick him to death while he's down."[108] She put her subscription to a news clipping service on hold and curtailed her public appearances, worried she might speak her mind in the heat of the moment. Like George, she believed that cowards "bring discredit on the army and disgrace to their comrades." In the margin of one of his letters, she wrote it was "too bad we have to support cowards." It was deplorable that "their kind" was even allowed to propagate.

George's "chief regret" was to have caused his family "undue worry," especially since "the 'incident' was far harder on you [Beatrice] than on me, as I simply did the ostrich act and would neither see nor hear any evil."[109] He apologized profusely to Beatrice, especially when he heard from Kay that his wife was "all shrunk up (not her words but the idea) over the incident."[110]

This was Beatrice's "first experience of scandal," and it was "a tough one!"[111] When General Harbord heard that General Pershing told Beatrice what he "would have done if he had been in command," he reassured her that "the old gentleman is truly devoted to you and to General Patton and his statements of what he uttered from an atmosphere of age and illness, need not worry you at all."[112] Beatrice replied on December 18:

> I'm sorry General Pershing told you of the cruel things he said to me. I told him that I would never repeat them and that I would try to forget them. No? I shan't let them spoil my Christmas! I am going to spend my second plebe Christmas at West Point wrestling with a home grown turkey and hoping that I can cook it well enough to pass the cadet appetites. Col. Meister, the head medico [?], is going on Xmas leave, and is leaving me his house.
>
> A V-mail from Georgie dated Dec. 1st says that he is beginning to get the repercussions of the "Patton Incident." He says in part, "what hurts most is that no one has ever asked for my side of the story." That is true—
>
> I agree with you that, if it had to be done, the thing should have been made public at the time instead of being allowed to leak out by means of a disreputable columnist; but I cannot imagine, if the cases had been reversed, Georgie lending such an avid ear to anything against one of his own men then in the midst of a battle, and the morale of whose army was well known.
>
> I have not said this to anyone else, but I feel that, under cover of defending his "military value," everything possible has been done, not only to tear down his reputation at home and abroad, but to damage his own morale. It is oftentimes just as easy - or easier - to do this by not doing a thing as by an avert act, and I could trace a whole list of this sort:
>
> i.e. Never featuring the fact that our troops were first into Messina and he with them. In fact, soft pedalling the whole thing. - - And ending with no decorations for Sicily while the President himself decorated Clark & 5 others for Salerno & Georgie looked on.
>
> Georgie is a great man, and nothing like this will sap his courage or break his heart - - is that the way to get the best out of an army? I know he broke the regulations, but as Gen. Summerall wrote me, "he must have been under great provocation." And the fact remains that the patient practically "took up his bed and walked."[113]

A deluge of letters arrived at Green Meadows, 90 percent of which were in support of General Patton. However, the 10 percent who condemned his actions did so in such a despicable manner that it made Beatrice physically ill. Most hate mail came from staunch isolationists who abhorred the war, like the one from an enraged mother who asked Beatrice if she was proud of her husband. The woman thought it rather strange "that a wife does not <u>know</u> her husband. You should write to him and tell him to join the Nazi Army. He fits in very nicely with them. It is too bad a Nazi bullet hasn't gotten to his heart, but there is a God up above, and he sees all." Another writer stated that if she defended "the dirty-mouthed roughneck that [you] have the misfortune to be married to, you are as bad as he is . . . Don't think that because he is a general and you are wealthy that you can get away with such outrageous behavior."[114]

Beatrice kept faith by repeating her mother's advice: "To bear misfortune nobly was itself good fortune." She knew George was "a man furiously fighting for his country," a man who gave a cold soldier the coat off his back, who stopped his jeep by the side of the road to administer morphine to a dying soldier, and who personally ensured that all his men received a hot turkey dinner on Christmas Eve. She hated the name "Old Blood and Guts" as much as George did and always wished people "wouldn't make him so blood-and-gutsy."[115] Growing testy with journalists as the affair dragged on, Beatrice snapped, "The object is to win the war isn't it? . . . He's a good general—I know that and I'll say it—even if I am his wife."

The whole family was "behind him," but George didn't want any "member of the family to make excuses for me or to mention anything. If I cannot stand on my record very few people can."[116] He wondered how "the fate of the only successful general in this war" could depend "on the statement of a discredited writer like Drew Pearson."[117] Since "General Eisenhower decided that the incident was closed after giving George you-know-what and after his numerous apologies," Beatrice thought "that would be that," but those in the U.S. who'd never "heard a shot go off in anger" made a bigger deal of the slapping incident than those personally involved.[118] Congress considered blocking his next promotion and recalling him, a move Beatrice knew "would probably kill him." However, a Gallup Poll revealed that "an overwhelming majority of Americans" believed that the affair "was much overrated and that Gen. George Patton should continue as usual in charge of his troops on the Italian front."

Generals Marshall and Eisenhower thought so, too, although they weren't ready to tell George yet. Day after day, he saw his Seventh Army shrink, "From commanding 240,000 men, I now have less than 5,000."[119] His troops were off to continue the fight in Italy while he was stuck in limbo in a palace in Palermo, "using a toilet previously made malodorous by constipated royalty."[120] He had "absolutely nothing to do and hours of time in which to do it," so he asked Beatrice to send him "some more pink medicine" as "this worry and inactivity has raised hell with my insides."[121]

Despite a physical distance of over four thousand miles, the Pattons felt as connected as ever, and his "pain carried over" to Beatrice.[122] She believed that "having people a long way off doesn't need to separate you from them," and she tried to buoy George's spirits by writing him adoringly, reassuring him he was "a better man in every way than you have ever been and are learning all the time the ways of the dove as well as those of the serpent and the fire dragon."[123]

During a brief stopover in Sicily in December 1943—after meeting Churchill and Stalin in Tehran—an "extremely nice" President Roosevelt informed General Patton that "the matter was a closed incident as far as he was concerned." George walked away crying when the president assured him that he would "have an army command in the great Normandy operation."[124]

However, for several more months, George was kept "in the dark as to his new assignment . . . just another form of punishment," Beatrice thought, "and very small potatoes at that."[125] He was sent around the Mediterranean as a decoy, keeping the Germans guessing where their most-feared general would appear next. George soon expected to "hit bottom and then bounce," though, and when a dud landed mere inches from his feet, he "knew then for certain that I was destined to live to do great things."[126]

ONE DIDN'T NEED to see the dainty woman or recognize the Boston accent to know when General Patton's wife was speaking. Endowed with the same fighting spirit as her husband, albeit with slightly less colorful language, she used "her words as weapons."[127] Of course, Beatrice was not the only officer's wife employed to rally the nation—among others, Mrs. Chester W. Nimitz worked for the American Woman's Voluntary Services, and Mrs. William A. Hastings was president of the National Congress of Parents and Teachers. However, Beatrice was the only one who did it in such a vocal and combative tone, living up to her reputation of being a "two-fisted lady," and a "brutal individualist."[128]

When a captain's wife from Indio described Beatrice as "Dresden China," the captain corrected his wife with a hearty laugh, "Dresden china—oh, sure, filled with TNT!" Beatrice possessed "an eager shyness . . . and friendliness," but she could just as easily turn her "incredibly blue eyes upon you with a 'we are not amused' expression." Formidable and determined did not even begin to describe the woman who was said to be no "bigger than a pint of milk," always wearing the Cartier bracelet George had her made from the first shell that landed near him on May 30, 1918.[129]

The American public quickly learned what those in the Army had known for a long time: Beatrice was her husband's fiercest defender. The story of her attacking the colonel at the Wadsworth house over two decades earlier still did the rounds and would cling to her even after her death. She never took well to George being criticized, and woe behold anyone who did. When people told her she had nothing to worry about since General Patton's "life is too valuable for him to be up in front," she vehemently lambasted those statements: "Well, my General does, and wherever he fights, he will be the first man under fire. His men will follow him over the top as they did in France, and, should he fall, he knows that a thousand of the enemy will die to avenge him."

"My wife . . . is a great soldier, too," George wrote a bereaved father, "and admires brave men."[130] She commanded the stage as her husband did, and her words more often resembled those of a soldier instead of a lady. "Half the time I can't remember what I tell my hearers," she replied to a question about her speaking style. "You know, I don't feel like a speaker—I feel more like a yell leader. I want to start 'em all rooting for a touchdown. It's a great thing for a team to have the gang behind it cheering, working, believing, giving it everything they've got. You can't be the whole American people. But every one of us can be us—and do our working and our sacrificing and our rooting."[131]

Beatrice once remarked rather wistfully, "Women cannot share their [soldier's] glory except by reflected light, but it is for us and our homes and our America that they are fighting." Whenever the War Department launched a new war loan drive, though, she was ready to do her duty. Her audiences loved hearing excerpts from George's letters, and people were even willing to pay for his envelopes. When a "Westerner" agreed to buy a $1,000 war bond in exchange for one of George's envelopes, Beatrice quickly looked through her desk to see how many she had.[132]

Purchasing war bonds was the perfect opportunity "to inflict the most punishment on the enemy with the least casualties to ourselves." On September 26, 1943, Beatrice was the principal speaker at a war bond rally in Salem, which raised $172,000, bringing the town within 10 percent of its $8,000,000 quota.[133] She joined the parade on the back of a fire truck and sat on stage with several wounded veterans from the Sicilian campaign. After the Salem National Band played the "2nd Armored Division March," Beatrice briefly closed her eyes to gather her inner strength before beginning to speak. Everyone in the audience probably had someone in the war,

> . . . but after 33 years in the Regular Army, I have loved ones on every fighting front; not casual acquaintances nor people I know merely by name, but friends and neighbors who have known me in sunshine and shadow, people who call me Bee for short. They are in the Aleutians, they are in Australia, and Africa and

Italy; they are fighting, they are at office desks, they are prisoners of war, and they are dead.

I do not know where my husband is tonight. I should like to be a soldier fighting with them, or a nurse fighting for them, but as it is, I am the wife and mother and grandmother of soldiers and soldiers-to-be, and I must fight the war here on the home front behind the lines. This front, the home front, is the front where the war will be won or lost. We know our armies. They are fighting and defeating the most perfect military machine the world has ever known. They will not let us down, but they cannot land a ship nor a plane nor can they fire a shot unless we here at home back them up.[134]

WHILE MRS. PATTON was continually urged to speak more, General Patton was asked never to speak again. Tact was not his forte, and as far back as 1919, his father had already cautioned him that "the 'gift of gab' you have developed may get you in trouble—unless restrained such a gift is always dangerous."[135] In the tiny British town of Knutsford, however, the furor began with something George supposedly hadn't said. As he wrote his brother-in-law, "It is funny that I have never had any doubts about licking the Germans any place I meet them. The only question in my mind is being able to survive the lapses between campaigns when I always seem to get myself in trouble."[136]

On January 26, 1944, General Patton received his "twenty-seventh start from zero since entering the U.S. Army." Informed by Eisenhower that he would command the Third Army, he was disappointed not to be part of the initial invasion of Normandy, but he had always made a success of each new beginning.[137] It was a relief to Beatrice because recently, several generals had been recalled due to "battle fatigue," and the last thing she wanted was for George to be sent home to teach. "The more he fights, the better he feels," she wrote General Harbord, "and I hope he can keep right on into Berlin."[138] Unfortunately for George, the prospect of a fine fight was still months away, and there was nothing to do but "to possess my soul in patience."[139]

George's appointment was kept a secret, but the first troops arriving from the United States in March 1944 were not surprised to be welcomed by General Patton. Beatrice had unwittingly revealed the secret when she had mailed a letter addressed to "Gen. George S. Patton, Jr., c/o Third Army headquarters," located thirty miles outside Liverpool in the quaint town of Peover.[140] If he wasn't crisscrossing England to greet and train his men, George lunched at The Bells of Peover, played some golf (he longed to play polo but didn't want to risk it), or sauntered over to the house of the Stockdales where he enjoyed a scotch and soda in front of the fire with Willie—his new bull terrier—by his feet.

On April 25, George was again taught a lesson on "the infinite variety of SOBs in the press and politics."[141] That day he reluctantly gave "a perfectly harmless informal talk" at the opening of the nearby Knutsford's Welcome Club, assured that no press would be present.[142] The entertainment these clubs organized for newly arrived American GIs was valuable because "the British and Americans are two people separated by a common language, and since it is the evident destiny of the British and Americans [and, of course, the Russians] to rule the world, the better we know each other, the better job we will do."

Whether George mentioned the Russians would never be known—several audience members gave a sworn statement that he did—but the single journalist stealthily present quoted George's speech the next day without mentioning the third member of the Big Three.

*Figures 76 & 77. Beatrice longed to be in Peover when she received these pictures from Mrs. Stockdale. (Library of Congress)*

Prime Minister Churchill dismissed the ensuing furor as ludicrous, and even General Bradley agreed that "what would have passed as a local boner coming from anybody less than Patton had promptly exploded into a world crisis."[143] George believed the affair "was so trivial in its nature, but so terrible in its effect, that it is not the result of an accident, but the work of God." He sounded so depressed in a letter to Ruth Ellen that she wished "they would invade before something worse happens to him."[144] George felt like the little boy whose father told him "to jump from the mantlepiece and he would catch him, but when the little boy jumped, he let him hit the floor and then said, 'Now, Willie, that should be a lesson to you. Don't trust anybody.'"[145]

After a few days of being "realy badly frightened," George learned he and Beatrice would not get "a chance to put the boat [*When and If*] in commission" sooner than expected.[146] However, his name was again debated in the Senate, and the confirmation of his promotion to the permanent rank of major general was delayed. Just as she had done during the slapping incident, Beatrice wrote letters to those in power and attended as many of the committee hearings as she could, keeping a tally in her thought book of how she thought the voting would proceed—"Senator Downey of California: Apparently favorable, Senator Truman of Missouri: Professes to be a great admirer, Senator Wallgren of Washington: Loudmouthed ignoramus."[147]

Beatrice was never "blue or downhearted," but she knew how much anguish this latest incident caused George. "I love you and need you," he concluded one letter, eventually apologizing for sounding so whiny, "but even I can be pushed just so far."[148] It was unfathomable to Beatrice—as it was to the Germans—that America's fighting general was cast aside like this, and resentment was beginning to grow in her. She was disappointed in his superiors for never openly defending him, driven by the "overriding influence of politics," and she was angry at the press for their unfavorable opinion, always closely following his conduct "in the expectation of playing up some future similar outburst" on his part.[149]

LIKE MILLIONS OF AMERICANS, the Pattons sat huddled around the radio on June 6, 1944. As dawn broke that morning along the French coast, German soldiers witnessed the approach of the largest amphibious invasion force in history. Close to 156,000 American, British, and Canadian troops were about to effect five simultaneous landings along the beaches of Normandy, establishing a long-awaited second front. Beatrice and Ruth Ellen sat up all night at Green Meadows, praying the invasion would succeed with minimal loss of life. Ruth Ellen knew Jim was in Italy with the 69th Armored Field Artillery Battalion, but Beatrice hadn't received mail from George in weeks. His letter urging her not to "get excited when the whistle blows" because he was "not in the opening kick off" would not arrive until weeks later, so she assumed he was "in the thick of things."[150]

Bee sat waiting by the radio in Washington, hoping "dad is on the way to get Johnny out of prison camp," aware that "a lot of other wives of POWs are feeling just that way."[151] Meanwhile, George IV and his classmate William Clark had their ears pressed to the radio at West Point, where later that afternoon the commencement of the Class of '44 would take place (one of the graduates was John Eisenhower, son of Operation Overlord's Supreme Commander). While Cadet Clark knew his father was still commanding the Fifth Army in Italy and had captured Rome two days earlier, Cadet Patton knew only that his father had been seen in England. He fervently hoped his Pop was in on the fight, knowing that for him, it was "hell to be on the side lines and see all the glory eluding" him.[152]

D-Day was "a lovely sunny day for a battle," according to George, yet he found himself sitting in his trailer on the British coast. As he listened to the radio for the latest news of the invasion, he wrote his son a heartfelt letter on the attributes of outstanding leadership. Before leaving for North Africa, he asked several of his friends to keep an eye on his son and "give him such help and advice as you think fit" in case it was "necessary for me to pass out of the picture and not return." George wrote his namesake that he had "no immediate idea of being killed, but one can never tell and none of us can live forever, so if I should go don't worry but set yourself to do better than I have."

A year earlier, George IV's first reaction upon being turned back— because of math, just like his father—had been to quit West Point and enlist, "feeling that the war simply can not end without his participation."[153] "I cannot criticize you for this because the same thing happened to me," George wrote in the midst of planning Operation Husky. He understood "better than anyone the acute pain which you are enduring," but he never pulled strings. The only thing he did was suggest a change to West Point's turn-back system during wartime in a letter to Congressman Wadsworth, thinking it "utterly ridiculous to turn a boy back on one subject during war when at the same time thousands of others are being commissioned through OCS [Officer Candidate School]."[154]

Since George shared all his personal correspondence with Beatrice—who wished she had influence, but didn't—she forwarded a copy of this letter to General Marshall. He replied that the question had been debated for many years, but there simply wasn't enough time for a Cadet "to carry his regular work and devote sufficient time to study to eliminate a condition." Instead, he suggested young George occupy himself a little more with his studies and a little less with his father's battles.[155] Beatrice was piqued, especially since her son had done his best and his self-esteem was currently so "that until he either passes or enlists he is not a person anyone would want to be with."[156]

*Figure 78. Cadet Patton (2nd from right) at West Point. (Library of Congress)*

A year later, in his trailer on the British coast, George commended his son on his "decision to study this summer instead of enjoying your self," proof that "you have character and ambition."[157] He reminded him "SELFCONFIDENCE is the greatest thing a man can have," but that was precisely what he lacked at West Point until Beatrice showed up.[158] How many letters full of desperation had he written her from the Military Academy, afraid he would "degenerate into a third rate second lieutenant and never command any thing more than a platoon."[159] All he ever wanted was to be given a chance to carve his name "on some thing biger than a section room bench," and Beatrice was convinced he finally had his chance on July 12, 1944.[160]

George hated that he couldn't tell his wife all the details, "as after all you are the only one who really counts."[161] An NBC news report that the Third Army was invading greeted Beatrice when she arrived at Juniper Ridge to have dinner with Chilly and Theodora. She came home that night and listened to the radio "at 11, then at 12, and heard the same thing, without giving any location, simply quoted as a German rumor—since then, nothing. Can you imagine? I don't remember much about the dinner."[162] Unfortunately, the report was nothing more than a rumor, and the Third Army would not become operational until August 1.[163]

General Patton did arrive in France on July 6—near the town where he and Beatrice bought a tapestry years earlier—anxious to get started and possessed by "a horrible feeling that the fighting will be over before I get in."[164] He needn't have worried, though, because after the Allies successfully secured the beachheads, they quickly became bogged down in Normandy's bocage country. It wasn't until July 25 that General Omar Bradley—now George's superior —initiated Operation Cobra, a massive aerial bombardment that broke up the Germans' defensive line and opened a path for General Patton's Third Army to exploit.

"ALTHOUGH ARMY WIVES traditionally prefer to let their husbands make the headlines," on August 15, 1944, it was impossible for Mary Elizabeth Bradley, Mildred Hodges, Beatrice Patton, and Georgie Devers to stay in the background. That day General Eisenhower finally revealed that the Third Army, commanded by Lieutenant General George S. Patton Jr., was responsible for cutting off the Breton peninsula and enveloping part of the German Seventh Army.[165]

Beatrice was delighted to know where her husband was, but she already had her suspicions. She read the papers and army communiques daily, noting the Allies' progress on her Michelin map. With most of the Army stuck in Normandy's hedgerow country since clearing the beachheads, Beatrice indicated on July 28 where she thought the Third Army might invade. Her prediction was eerily accurate; George had schooled her in 1912 and 1913, when they drove along the roads used by William the Conqueror in 1064, that "the greatest study of war is the road net."

Just hours after General Eisenhower's announcement, the Senate confirmed Lieutenant General Patton's promotion to the permanent rank of major general (he continued to hold the wartime rank of lieutenant general). His nomination had been held up because of the slapping incident, but suddenly the military committee "was of the opinion that General Patton had been disciplined sufficiently," and unanimously agreed "that he is a great soldier."[166]

Journalists rushed to Green Meadows, despite Beatrice's insistence that "people aren't interested in me."[167] Looking radiant in a sheer black coat and butterfly enamel earrings when she opened the front door—she was just about to leave for Washington, hopeful of finding a seat on the train—she "was terribly pleased" to hear of George's promotion. As to his mad dash across France, she was delighted that he was finally "on the kind of a job he has trained himself for, ever since 1918."

*Figure 79. There had been a few times George thought he'd be able to go stateside, but those visits always fell through at the last minute, and he had to make do with "the imprint of your [Beatrice's] lips on a recent letter," which "looked pretty attractive." (Library of Congress)*

As the Third Army advanced "farther and faster than any army in history," General George S. Patton Jr. won back his reputation. His confidence skyrocketed, and he finally felt that Beatrice's "long loving loyal confidence in me is justified."[168] The Pattons' affectionate epistolary relationship was in full bloom during WWII, and Beatrice wrote him "faithfully . . . and so very entertainingly."[169] Writing letters to George was like talking to him, which is why he coined her letters "outpourings."[170] She added clippings from newspapers, gossip, and the occasional book, including one called *How to Treat Germans.* George's letters were known in the family as "communiques." And after all these years, Beatrice had finally figured out the reason for his "funny" spelling: to confuse the censor. She defied "anyone who hasn't been your Fidus Achates for as long as I have to make head or tail of some of it."[171]

Whether he was sitting in his trailer parked in an apple orchard or in the home of the mayor of a French town with shells falling in the distance, at night George made time to write his wife (as well as other family members, friends, and even strangers). Where did one of the oldest generals in the war, at fifty-nine, find the time and energy to fight, read books, write letters, visit wounded soldiers, and travel to the front? George had prepared mentally and physically for this moment his whole life. Even Bill Mauldin—a staunch critic whom General Patton had berated for the way he depicted soldiers in his Willie and Joe cartoons—admitted that listening to "Old Blood and Guts" was "as if I were hearing Michelangelo on painting."[172] Commanding the Third Army was not a job for George; it was the greatest honor of his life.

When General Marshall returned from a visit to France, he wrote Beatrice that her husband "looked in splendid health and in fine fettle and full of fight." Words like that lifted her heart because no matter how often George wrote that he was doing fine, Beatrice continued to worry about his wellbeing. He was still as accident-prone as ever—from dropping a blackout screen on his toe to falling asleep in front of his sunlamp—yet his luck seemed to hold when it came to attacks from the Germans.

Beatrice hated when people played down her fears by claiming she was used to it, especially because those words were most often uttered by women married to desk officers far removed from the front. She knew they meant well, but there was no point in explaining that it was impossible to get used to the uncertainty. Instead, to keep her calm, she quietly recited Thomas Buchanan Read's Civil War poem, "The Brave at Home."[173]

Her seemingly laissez-faire attitude led to headlines like "Mrs. Patton Takes Heroism of Her Husband in Stride" and "Nothing Surprises Mrs. Patton." Having lived with and among soldiers for almost two-thirds of her life, Beatrice understood what it meant to be one. She understood the adherence to superstition—George carried a St. Christopher's medal, placed in the heel of his custom-made tanker boots—and the importance of luck, often the only reason one soldier survived and the next didn't. Her husband's life had been filled with luck—"never forgotten you [Beatrice] as the greatest"—and when he finally attained command of the Third Army, he chose "Lucky" as its code name.[174]

George's firm belief in his destiny guided his life, and as long as his luck held, he was convinced his number wasn't up. It was a belief Beatrice turned into a short story called "Lucky Shot," based on an anecdote George wrote her from Sicily. "Lucky Shot" begins with four soldiers hiding in a cellar while being shelled by the Germans. When Private Blinley is accused of being "yellow," one of his comrades confesses he "ain't worryin' till my number comes up." Everyone but Private Blinley seemed to agree with that adage until the shelling outside intensified, and a bomb landed in their midst. The men "flattened themselves against the wall, waiting, [a]ching seconds passed before some voice whispered, 'Dud!'" When a lieutenant walked in asking for volunteers and aimed his flashlight at the bomb, "it shone like gold, [a] buried treasure bursting out of the ground." Private Blinley stared at the serial number, "This is my number, sir. I'd like to volunteer. Will the Lieutenant gimme a chance?"[175]

While Beatrice dabbled in writing a book based on the speeches she gave, she also renewed her efforts to get her husband's poetry published. George liked to pick up the pen when he couldn't sleep or "when I am low in my mind," and his "poetic muse" was most active during times of war.[176] Many letters to Beatrice during the Mexican Punitive Expedition and WWI included a sheet of poetry, imploring her not to lose it as "they may be priceless some day." In 1919, Beatrice tested that premise and sent a compilation of his poems to a publisher. She prefaced the work with a disclaimer from the anonymous author:

> These rhymes were written (over a period of years) for his own amusement by a man who having seen something of war is more impressed with the manly virtues it engenders than with the necessary and much exaggerated horrors attendant upon it. They are offered to the public in the hope that they may counteract to a degree the melancholy viewpoint so freely expatiated upon by most writers.[177]

George's vivid imagery describing both the horrors and glories of war was not appreciated in 1919, and Beatrice's proposal was rejected. She shelved the project and planned to publish his work posthumously, but then news outlets began clamoring for any piece of information on General Patton. She couldn't believe her luck when *Woman's Home Companion* paid $50 in October 1943 to print "God of Battles," followed by *Cosmopolitan* in early 1945, which published "Fear." *Collier's*, however, declined to print "The Song of the Bayonet," explaining to Beatrice that "nothing more should be printed that will revive the 'Old Blood and Guts' legend."[178]

PLAGUED by new setbacks and separated for over two years, George wished his "Beat" were with him. He enjoyed Willie's company, but he missed his wife's shoulder to cry on when a war of speed became a war of attrition.[179] Just six weeks after the Third Army was let loose, General Eisenhower diverted gas and ammunition to Field Marshall Montgomery for a major offensive called Operation Market Garden. The Third Army's progress slowed to a crawl, and George adopted the "mournful role of defender." His soldiers were continuously battered by cold and rain as the seasons changed, and trench foot took more casualties than the enemy. Beatrice offered "great assistance" in supplying his men with arctics and socks, so by December, he was at least "particularly relieved at having been able to stop trench foot in his Army."[180]

"Destiny [a.k.a Eisenhower] sent for me in a hurry when things got tight," George wrote home on December 21. "Perhaps God saved me for this effort."[181] A week earlier, two panzer armies had suddenly attacked the densely forested and sparsely defended area of the Belgian Ardennes, a last-ditch effort by the Germans which George compared to the one big flop a tarpon makes before he dies. Then, during an emergency strategy meeting with senior members of the Allied command on December 19, General Eisenhower called General Patton's suggestion of counterattacking in two days with three Third Army divisions "fatuous." Yet George was dead serious; all he needed to do was call his Chief of Staff, General Gay, at Third Army headquarters with a specific codeword to set one of three plans in motion, which he and his staff had prepared over the last few days.[182]

The Battle of the Bulge was George's ultimate date with destiny, a five-week period during which he finally felt like he "earned his pay."[183] Colonel Codman—an old friend of the Ayers who replaced Captain Jenson as aide—said his boss had an "uncanny gift for sweeping men into doing things which they do not believe they are capable of doing, which they do not really want to do."[184] It was a magnificent feat to turn the Third Army ninety degrees, move it seventy-eight miles along icy and snow-covered roads, and then be ready to attack in just two days. Wars were fought with weapons, according to George, "but they are won by men," and it was "the spirit of the men who follow and of the man who leads that gains the victory."

While Beatrice spent another Christmas in Washington with her children and grandchildren, George woke up at 6 a.m. to visit his men. All day long, he drove through the bitter cold in an open jeep—"pneumonia buggies," he called them—making sure every soldier received a hot turkey dinner.[185] Each man carried in his pocket a small card distributed on the 22nd; one side contained a Christmas greeting from General Patton, and the other side contained the prayer for fair weather he asked Chaplain O'Neill to write. Incessant snowfall had made it impossible for the Air Force to aid the Third Army in rescuing the US 101st Airborne Division from Bastogne, but one day after the prayer was issued, the skies miraculously cleared, and Bastogne was liberated three days later.

With approximately 75,000 Americans killed, captured, or missing in action, the Ardennes Offensive was WWII's bloodiest battle in the European theater. When asked how her husband shouldered the immense responsibilities of war, Beatrice replied he did so through his unwavering belief in God, himself, and his men.[186] Both Pattons found "great help and comfort" in religion, despite George's swearing, which was "on equal terms with the most accomplished mule-skinner."[187] He prayed daily "to do my duty, retain my self-confidence, and accomplish my destiny" because "no one can live under the awful responsibility I have without Divine help."[188]

Once the bulge was cleared in January 1945, the Allies were ready for the advance into the Third Reich. Trying to raise America's war spirit for the final stretch, Staff Sergeant Thomas J. Defibaugh toured a war plant in Baltimore on

March 7. The veteran of the Battle of the Bulge kept his audience spellbound as he described the Fourth Infantry Division's crossing of the Sauer on January 18. The first soldiers who crossed the icy river in three-person boats were like "sitting pigeons" for the Germans, so General Patton "figured the men would have a better chance swimming since they would then present only the tops of their heads as targets to the enemy gunners." To inspire his troops, "General Patton jumped into the water and swam across to the opposite bank, then swam back. Thousands of troops followed him."[189]

**Figure 80.** "Not posed and not too fat," George wrote on the back of this picture taken in Sicily. (Library of Congress)

Since George was told not to comment on the episode, the press reached out to Beatrice. She had no idea what the reporter was talking about when he asked about the "story of General Patton swimming the Sauer River under fire" and suggested that he call the War Department to confirm. The reporter didn't bother checking his sources and was adamant about getting Beatrice's reaction, "By the way, Mrs. Patton, can the General swim?"

Beatrice didn't even deign to answer that question and hung up, but the same reporter called again at 1:30 a.m. He was on his way to Green Meadows and told her to meet him "at the door in three quarters of an hour with a picture of the General in a swimsuit." Fed up, she asked the young man if it ever occurred to him if "General Patton did swim the river, he didn't do it in a swimsuit?"[190]

Beatrice knew George "easily could have done it," but she found out the real story a few weeks later in one of his letters: "I crossed over on a partially submerged assault bridge without life lines, and as I had to jump several bodies without being able to see where my feet were going to land, it was quite a feat. To a scared soldier seeing me through a heavy smoke screen, I might have looked as though I was swimming."[191]

Beatrice was "beginning to believe the saying that 'history is a lie that everyone believes. . . . ' I often wonder how in the world historians ever sort the fables from the truth."[192]

BEATRICE HAD BEEN FEELING miserable for weeks with a cold she seemed unable to shake, but her spirits were raised when reporters called to inform her that General Patton was the first to cross the Rhine on March 23. He stopped halfway across the bridge to pee in the river, and then the prolific military student continued his crossing, fell on one knee, and grabbed a handful of dirt, exclaiming, "Thus, William the Conqueror!"[193] It was the "greatest account" Beatrice had ever heard, and it would make "a superb addition to a wonderful scrapbook."[194] Unbeknownst to her, though, a few days later, George took a risky gamble which had the potential of becoming "a new incident."[195]

Jim Totten returned from Italy in October 1944 after a recurrence of his hepatitis B, but by March 1945, Lt. Col. Waters had been a 'Kriegie' for more than two years. Four months after his capture, the Germans took him to Oflag 64, a POW camp for American officers near Szubin, Poland, where he spent the next eighteen months. Two days before the Soviet Army liberated Oflag 64 in January 1945, Johnnie was one of 1,400 POWs forcibly marched to a new location 550 miles away near the town of Hammelburg in Bavaria, Germany. After five horrendous weeks of trudging through heavy snow, only 490 made it to Oflag XIII-B alive.

Having a family member in a POW camp brought many "problems and worries" not fully understood by those not in the same position. "He is out of the conflict and apparently safe, yet he is completely separated from us," Bee wrote in a letter distributed by the War Prisoners Aid of the Y.M.C.A. to relatives of POWs.[196] George always felt "terribly sorry for B," so when he learned of a German POW camp just outside his sector, he pretty much defied orders, hoping to liberate his son-in-law.[197] The task force he sent on March 26, 1945, to free 900 prisoners made it to Hammelburg unopposed, but their problems began when they realized Oflag XIII-B held twice as many POWs as they had expected.

Those taken prisoner just weeks earlier at the Battle of the Bulge were too weak to walk back fifty miles, so Task Force Baum had no choice but to leave most of the POWs behind when a German company tried to recapture the camp. Those sent to liberate Oflag XIII-B who weren't killed or managed to escape were taken prisoner, including George's aide, Major Al Stiller, a rugged man who would walk through fire for his boss. Meanwhile, after surviving two years in a POW camp without a scratch, Lt. Col. Waters was shot by a German soldier who didn't realize he had been sent under a flag of truce to talk to the Americans.

A nervous George felt terrible when he finally learned the fate of Task Force Baum. "I don't know what you and [little] B will think," he wrote to Beatrice. "I tried hard to save him [Johnnie] and may be the cause of his death. Al Stiller was in the column and I fear he is dead."[198]

Just eleven days after the failed raid on Hammelburg, the Seventh Army liberated Oflag XIII-B. Major Al Stiller was being forcibly marched to Nuremberg with the other healthy POWs—he would be rescued a month later, thirty pounds lighter—but Johnnie was found in the care of an old Serbian doctor who managed to save him against all odds.[199] The bullet had entered Johnnie's right thigh, hit his hip bone and the coccyx, and came out his left buttock; just one-sixteenth of an inch higher and he would have been killed or paralyzed.[200]

George immediately called Eisenhower and asked him to inform "Little B" that "Lt. Colonel John K. Waters was safe at the headquarters of the 3rd Army," looking "awfully thin" but with "a good morale."[201] Bee "never lost hope" that her husband would return and always reminded Little Johnnie and Pat "to believe that their daddy . . . would be freed some day." According to Beatrice, when the news finally came, "it filled our house with flowers and our hearts to overflowing." Even the dogs were howling when the press reached 3900 Tunlaw Road NW, again before the War Department did, on April 7.[202] As Beatrice knew all too well, "You never can really gloat until you know your true love is safe."[203]

At the war's end, George could think "of no error I made except that of failing to send a combat command to Hammelburg." Whether he sent Task Force Baum specifically to rescue his son-in-law will never be known with certainty, but the evidence certainly points in that direction despite his vehement denials.[204] The occasion was the one time he let his personal feelings trump his military acumen and one of the only times that the accusation he needlessly wasted lives rang true.

Eisenhower gave him a stern reprimand, and the press was already "trying to make an incident out of my attempt to rescue John."[205] However, the Pattons were spared another scandal when President Roosevelt died just twenty-three days before the end of the war in Europe, on April 12, 1945. What happened at Oflag XIII-B was relegated to the back pages and, except for a brief resurgence in October, would not be fully known until decades later.

*Figure 81. Bee, Johnnie, and Pat visiting Aunt Kay. (Library of Congress)*

George wasn't half joking when he wondered whether his usefulness was at an end now that he had rescued Johnnie. As the war petered out, he became fatalistic and, for one of the first times ever, closed his letters to Beatrice with a reminder for her to remember that he loved her in case the Germans got him.[206]

For General Patton, it was no sacrifice to die for his country.[207] He always shared the dangers with his men at the front—tank warfare was like spaghetti, he said, "you can't push it from behind"—and he hoped to "go as gallantly and as easily" as his close friend Colonel Paddy Flint did during the Normandy invasion.[208] He wrote to Colonel Fletcher that "the best thing that could happen to me would be to get a clean hit in the last minute of the last fight" because he knew "that peace will be much more difficult than war. In fact war for me has not been difficult, but has been a pleasant adventure."[209]

Meanwhile, the Patton women kept "their heads up in good shape." Beatrice had been radiantly happy in her husband's success, but life had become rather dull lately.[210] When George dreamed that he "was in a boat in a muddy creek" and saw Beatrice "running over the mud [calling] 'Georgie' the way you do," he wondered, "were you in any trouble?"[211]

Once Jim began working at the Pentagon, Ruth Ellen and the children moved to Washington, a few blocks from Bee at 2900 45th Street NW. George hated the thought of Beatrice alone at Green Meadows, especially since some reporters had been brazen enough to apply for jobs on the farm. She contemplated moving in with Fred and Hilda for a while, but ultimately she moved back to the Merrills' home in Washington and began working at a museum arranging specimens as she had done in Hawaii.[212]

———

"THIS IS A SOLEMN BUT GLORIOUS HOUR," President Truman addressed the nation at 9 a.m. on May 8, 1945. "General Eisenhower informs me that the forces of Germany have surrendered to the United Nations. The flags of freedom fly all over Europe." To George's great chagrin, he was stopped at the border of Czechoslovakia, but "Patton's Own" had captured over 80,000 square miles of territory and effected close to 1.5 million casualties on the enemy (counting those killed, MIA, and wounded). General Patton won back his reputation in the nine months that the Third Army was operational, but his wife's "modest estimate" meant more to him "than the opinion of the rest of the world."[213]

Beatrice had just enough time to get down on her knees to pray before the phone started ringing off the hook, from reporters to family members of POWs who demanded to talk to Johnnie. "If you hear that I have been sitting astride the roof, dropping slates on the callers' heads, don't be surprised," she wrote

General Harbord. "I am not crazy - only, like Cousin Egbert, in Ruggles of Red Gap, 'I can be pushed just so far.'"[214] Reporters who clamored for her reaction were told it wasn't her place to say anything. The war with Japan was still ongoing, which meant the war was not over for her husband.

For thirty-one months, Beatrice believed her husband had "a date with history" and resigned herself to the idea that she "would never see him again!" Like George, she expected his death to be "spectacular . . . killed in battle, not bombed out of headquarters somewhere to the rear, but blown up, bit by bit in a tank advancing at the head of a victorious attack through the enemy's strongest lines."[215] It certainly wasn't for lack of trying that he didn't die a heroic death in Europe.

George admitted that he was "like a puppy always sticking my nose into trouble." The number of accidents, mishaps, and near-misses throughout the war (and his life) would have been enough to kill a hundred less lucky men. On May 21, he casually mentioned to his wife that he "started flying my self again to day but was pretty rusty."[216] Reporters were constantly amazed by how "little alarmed" Beatrice was when told of yet another of her husband's close calls.[217] She knew his whole military career had been filled with danger because each brush with death was a reconfirmation of his destiny.

When four shells struck the spot George had been standing just thirty seconds earlier to take pictures, he excitedly wrote Beatrice "how much that near miss cheered me up. I know I am needed!"[218] Returning to Morocco from a visit to the front in 1943, his plane "nearly hit several mountains and I was scared till I thought of my destiny. That calmed me. I will not be killed in a crash." Just days before the war was over, he was "nearly killed by a bull cart coming out of a side street," and his Cub plane was shot at by a Polish Spitfire who mistakenly thought he was shooting at Germans.[219]

When the war ended, George was sent to Bad Tölz near Munich to "take up the governing of this part of Germany." He hoped not to stay long because he really wanted "to go home for a while on my way to China."[220] Leaving on a "goddamn bond raising tour" of the United States on June 4, George made it clear at every stop that he was ready and eager to go fight the Japanese, but how much longer could his luck hold?

As Beatrice waited with her family at Bedford Army Airfield for the C-54 to land on the afternoon of June 7, she realized living through three wars "was too much for one lifetime."[221] She remembered waiting with Nita in El Paso on February 5, 1917, as First Lieutenant Patton rode his horse across the border with General Pershing at the head of the defunct Mexican Punitive Expedition. She vividly remembered Colonel Patton, commander of the 304th Tank Brigade, walking down the gangplank in Brooklyn on March 17, 1919, and throwing his cane in the river. She had been relieved that the wound to his leg left him with nothing more than a slight limp, until she had realized that the man who returned from WWI was not the same one who left for WWI.

Now, as the doors of the C-54 opened, she was overwhelmed with pride as General Patton bounded down the steps, wearing a total of twenty stars (eight on his shirt collar, four on each shoulder, and four on his helmet). She was looking forward to having "fun together again hunting and sailing," but George guessed he would "be hard to live with." Peace, to him, was "much more difficult than war . . . a pleasant adventure."[222] As he wrote General Harbord a few months later, "The great tragedy of my life was that I survived the last battle. It had always been my plan to be killed in this war, and I damned near accomplished it, but one cannot resort to suicide."[223]

# 12

## 130TH STATION HOSPITAL
### HEIDELBERG, GERMANY
### JUNE 1945–DECEMBER 1945

*THEY CAN TAKE AWAY YOUR GOODS AND CHATTELS, AND THEY CAN SAY ALL SORTS OF THINGS ABOUT YOU, BUT THEY CAN NEVER TAKE AWAY YOUR MEMORIES, SO BE SURE YOU HAVE LOTS OF LOVELY ONES.*

In her own words, Beatrice Patton tended "to collect unusual Christmases and not necessarily merry ones," and she found "it a mistake to look too far ahead." It made her feel like "the man who fell off the roof, and, as he passed the 7th story window, yelled 'All right so far.'"[1] Still, spending a few days with the Tottens in Washington before heading to Green Meadows to prep for the holidays, the last thing she expected on December 9 was the call she dreaded throughout the war.[2]

General Patton was slated to begin his leave on January 1, but Generals Gay and Keyes assured him it was more than appropriate for him to ask to go home for Christmas. After all, his only real vacation since March 1940 had been the nine days he spent at Green Meadows in July 1945. So, after much contemplation, George finally called General Bedell Smith on December 5 to say that "he would like to go home for Christmas" as long as he wasn't "running out on anything."

His one-month leave granted, George confessed to Eisenhower's Chief of Staff that he didn't expect to return to Europe.[3] He had been at a dead end since September when he was relieved of command of the Third Army, and he had been on the verge of resigning for several weeks "because if I retire, I will still have a gag in my mouth, which as an Army Officer I have worn for forty-one years."[4] Those he confided in, however, suggested he wait to talk to Beatrice and Fred in person before making such a momentous decision.

That night, George unwittingly wrote his last letter to his "Darling B,"

> I just sent you a paragraph on the daily radio that I leave South Hampton on the USS N.Y. 45000 ton battleship [allowing him to travel with his papers] on Dec 14 and should arrive where ever it lands on Dec 19. I have a months leave but dont intend to go back to Europe. If I get a realy good job I will stay in otherwise I will retire.
>
> I will radio you where and when I land and will stay a day or two in Wash to see how the [?] and to hussel jobs for Hap Gay and Harkins.
>
> I hate to think of leaving the army but what is there? We can get a chance at the visiting foxes any how.
>
> Did I tell you that at last I got DSMs for all my old command took three years and it was J [?] H. who put it over.
>
> I was going to shoot pigs today but it was too snowy. I seem to have survived Sweden all right.
>
> I will give George $100.00 before I leave.
>
> Don't bother about throwing an Xmas party. I will try to get Reggie etc some things but it's I fear too late.
>
> I may see you before you see this.
>
> Love
>
> George.
>
> Thanks for the books and candy. George Meeks does not smoke cigars.[5]

The Pattons had been "so long together in spirit" that their "hearts [talked]" when apart.[6] "This has happened to me so many times in my life," Beatrice wrote her husband in November 1943, when she found out he took Casablanca at three in the morning. "I woke up in the night for no reason and looked at the clock. It was just three. I thought, what is G. doing, I wonder ... I did not feel worried, but just lay thinking about you for some time."[7]

Beatrice was writing Christmas cards—"From George and Beatrice Patton with our love always"—while Ruth Ellen was fixing the veneer on a cabinet when the phone suddenly rang that quiet Sunday morning.[8] Beatrice felt a familiar lump in her throat and a funny feeling in her stomach when Ruth Ellen got up to answer the phone. "Something's happened to your father," Beatrice forebodingly remarked when her daughter handed her the receiver.

A reporter from the Associated Press greeted her, asking for a comment on General Patton's condition. Sick and tired of the press's obtrusiveness, Beatrice explained her husband was leaving for the United States the next day, December 10.

"When did this happen?" she interrupted the reporter when informed that the General had been taken to a hospital in Heidelberg following a car accident. Without news from the War Department, she "asked to be kept advised of General Patton's condition and expressed hope that good news would be forthcoming."[9] After all, surviving accidents "fit[s] the pattern of his life."[10]

———————

GEORGE ALWAYS SAID a man should take his wife to the nearest hotel for a few days upon returning from a long absence, but the War Department had other plans. Despite arriving at Green Meadows well past midnight after the celebratory dinner at the Copley Plaza, the Pattons awoke at 6 a.m. on June 8, 1945, to continue their war bond selling tour. George made sure to spend the little time he had available that morning with his son, who was returning to West Point and a summer assignment at Fort Benning.

To George IV, the man sitting across the breakfast table was not just General Patton, an officer he was desperate to join in battle, but also Pops, a father who wrote him at least three times a month to offer advice. And yet, as he remembered the screaming crowd along the streets of Boston, he couldn't help but feel that his father "belonged to history more than he belonged to us."[11] George IV could count on two hands the number of times he'd seen his father in the last five years, yet he would never see him again.

It was merely 8:25 a.m. when the eleven-car motorcade arrived at Bedford Army Airfield, and Beatrice was happy to see the press kept at a safe distance.[12] George's triumphant entry into Boston was "a proud and wonderful day," marred only by the press's behavior and the headlines which greeted her that morning.[13] She was seething with anger that some newspapers accused George of having no respect for those who died in battle, the end he so desired. It had always been easy for his critics to "be ferocious as hell back home on three hot meals a day," but it took guts to do what General Patton and his men had accomplished over the last ten months.[14]

When the C-54 took off for Denver, Colorado, it finally dawned on Beatrice that the last seventeen hours hadn't been a dream. She couldn't stop staring at her Georgie, his battle jacket heavy with ribbons and his helmet gleaming with a fourth star he had received in April, a star he said was "as much yours as mine."[15] She didn't think his appearance had changed much, but she knew the man underneath the uniform had. In the last few weeks of the war, he saw unimaginable horrors, from the concentration camps the Third Army liberated to White Russians in "a pitiable state" who begged to be rescued from the advancing Russians, to displaced people "streaming back utterly forlorn." An Ayer family member already observed that he seemed "more mature and quieter," and Beatrice sensed a certain gravitas in his manners.[16]

Following a parade in Denver, Colorado, where they joined forces with General and Mrs. Doolittle, it was on to Los Angeles, where Nita Patton was the first to greet her brother when he landed on the afternoon of June 9. She proudly told reporters how he knew at age three that "he was going to be a soldier," but he also realized "he was fortunate to be born when he was and under the circumstances he enjoyed, so that he had the training and opportunity to participate in two world wars."[17] She privately called him "a modern knight in shining armor," happy that he had gotten his "revenge on all the slimy jealous toads who tried to do you harm."[18]

Over one million people lined the streets of Los Angeles to welcome home Generals Patton and Doolittle. After a brief stop at city hall and a reception at the Ambassador Hotel, the motorcade reached its final destination: the aptly named LA Memorial Coliseum, where over one hundred thousand people were waiting to enjoy a spectacle only Hollywood could produce.

Humphrey Bogart impersonated General Doolittle in a Tokyo Raid briefing, Edward G. Robinson impersonated General Patton in a tank briefing, Judy Garland sang "God Bless America," and Bette Davis read one of George's poems. As the evening ended, the Coliseum turned dark, and over one hundred thousand matches were lit in memory of those who died. Beatrice was overwhelmed with emotions when the buglers played "Taps," and she could barely bring out the words to the Lord's Prayer and "The Star-Spangled Banner."

**Figure 82.** *Beatrice with Nita and her two sons in San Gabriel, June 1945. (Patton Museum)*

The first thing George did when he arrived at Lake Vineyard was to retreat to the basement with Ignacio Callahan, the estate's third-generation gardener, to share a glass of sixty-five-year-old brandy made from grapes grown on the estate.[19] Next, he drove Beatrice, Nita, and her two sons the two miles to the Church of Our Savior, where he thanked God because He "has been very good to me."[20] When they arrived, the press was waiting in droves, confirming Beatrice's suspicions that George would be "so famous that we will have no private life."[21]

They followed the family as they placed a wreath by the plaque commemorating Dick Jenson, attended a service seated in the family pew, and walked next door to the Sunday school for a brief ceremony. George finally found some privacy at the San Gabriel Cemetery, where he placed red roses on his parents' grave and quietly prayed. No one except Beatrice made as many sacrifices for George as his father, but it hadn't been in vain. "Papa [would be] proud of you these days . . ." Nita wrote her brother during the war, "and yearning over his fair haired boy."[22]

**Figure 83.** *Clockwise from bottom left: Michael Walke Totten, Rosemary Merrill Loring with Caleb Loring II, Beatrice Willoughby Totten, and Ruth Ellen Patton Totten in Washington, April 1945. (Library of Congress)*

"DAMN IT, I'm no politician, I don't smile," General Patton snapped at a photographer on June 13 when he arrived at Washington National Airport.[23] Bee, Ruth Ellen, their children, and Kay—who'd been a great help to Beatrice and her daughters throughout the war—were waiting on the tarmac. John Knight Waters III, George "Pat" Patton Waters, Beatrice Willoughby Totten, and Michael Walke Totten enthusiastically waved when they caught sight of their famous grandfather.

It was the first time George was meeting his granddaughter Beatrice in person—the three-week-old baby in the picture he had received back in Sicily was now two years old—and she greeted him with an exuberant, "Hello, daddy." Explaining to her daughter that this was not her father but her grand-father, Ruth Ellen realized George was as much a stranger to his grandchildren as he had been to his children when he had returned from WWI.[24]

George went straight to the Pentagon for a meeting with General Marshall and Secretary of War Stimson to discuss a possible assignment in the Pacific, then enjoyed a quick lunch with Beatrice before dashing off to see President Truman. When he arrived at the White House gate, an officer warned him photographers were waiting to capture him being disarmed by the Secret Service, so he left his ivory-handled revolvers on the floor of the car.

The smirk on George's face triumphed over the disappointment in the photographers' when he told them he didn't "wear pistols to social engage-ments. Only wear 'em in battle."[25] His family knew the pistols, the grimace, and the immaculate uniform were nothing more than pieces "of an effective military commander's tool kit."[26] George was expected to continue playing the part of General Patton, or people would immediately point out, "look at the old guy." However, the effort was beginning to wear him down.[27]

All George wanted to do when he visited Walter Reed Hospital that after-noon was to give a boost to the Third Army veterans and see Johnnie, but it seemed the War Department was intent on turning his visit into a public spec-tacle.[28] "I'll bet you goddamn buzzards are just following me in here to see if I'll slap another soldier, aren't you? You're all hoping I will!" George barked at the press as he arrived with his family.

Wearing his "olive drab battle jacket, heavy-soled tank-man's shoes, and carrying his 4-starred garrison cap and riding crop," George was the picture of health and vigor as he bounded up and down the stairs, in marked contrast with many of the patients. When he left the amputation ward where Ruth Ellen had been working as an occupational therapist for the last five months, he broke down crying: "Goddammit, if I had been a better general, most of you would not be here."[29]

Beatrice knew her husband felt as if he "might be nearing the end of his life."[30] He was physically and mentally exhausted when he arrived at Bee's and barely had any voice left. He'd been welcomed as a hero wherever he went, but it was becoming increasingly evident to him that "there is no place for a man like me." It seemed "there was nothing more of interest in the world now that the war was over," and "the reaction from intense mental and physical activity to a state of inertia" was difficult.[31] Beatrice hoped George could finally learn to relax now that he had fulfilled his destiny, but she realized peace would be hell on him.

George waited to sit down with his daughters until Beatrice was saying goodbye to their grandchildren. He asked Ruth Ellen and Bee to "take care of your little brother and tell John and Jim to take care of you. I'll be seeing your mother, but I won't be seeing you." They vociferously disagreed, but their father explained that all men were born with a reservoir of luck, "like money in the bank," and some spent it faster than others.

"I've been very lucky," he continued, "but I've used it all up. The last few shells that fell near me, each one was closer; I've had increasingly narrow escapes. It's too damned bad I wasn't killed before the fighting stopped, but I wasn't. So be it."[32] The way her father spoke those words sent shivers down Ruth Ellen's spine, "Sometimes Daddy talked just to hear himself, sometimes to shock people . . . Sometimes he saw things other people couldn't see. I think that was one of those times."[33]

When Beatrice and George finally returned to Green Meadows on June 15, five-year-old David Gordon Richardson was the last one standing between General Patton and his vacation. George's first reaction to the local boy's request for an autograph was a brusque no, but then he called him back, "I'll give you an autograph, but just you—nobody else." The Pattons had hoped to return unobserved, but someone had leaked their arrival time, and ten thousand people lined the streets from Beverly Airport to Green Meadows. The weary travelers indulged the mayor and listened to his welcoming speech at city hall, but at this point, all George wanted was some "rest and quiet" with Beatrice. He was tired after "fighting the war for 31 months" and needed to "get some peace."[34]


As soon as the front door of Green Meadows closed, George changed into his riding habit and took his favorite horse for a ride. However, the photo taken of him that day sitting atop Konohiki shows him looking lost and forlorn. It was certain now that General Patton had fought his last war; instead of going to China to fight, he had just been named military governor of Bavaria.[35] Beatrice greeted the news of George's appointment not with relief but with resentment at those in charge for burdening her husband with the one job he was neither suited for nor interested in. When George's name was not included in the first list for permanent promotion back in March, she began to "believe that, for some reason I do not know, General Marshall dislikes Georgie."[36]

*Figure 84. General Patton with his wife at the South Hamilton High School Field. (Courtesy of the Boston Public Library, Leslie Jones Collection)*

The war was over, and so General Patton's usefulness had ended. However, his status as an outcast in the Army's upper echelons was in stark contrast to the country's appreciation. On June 24, he again became public property when South Hamilton celebrated his triumphant return at the South Hamilton High School Field. The town counted only 2,037 residents in the 1940 census, but five thousand "long-suffering wives, brothers, fathers and sweethearts" applauded the Pattons while the High School Band played the "2nd Armored Division March."[37] After shaking close to three thousand hands—with an accompanying warning that there was to be "no damned squeezing"—the Pattons drove to St. John's Episcopal Church for a service celebrating his safe return.

Seventeen days were not enough time for George and Beatrice to catch up. They were able to make a few short trips around Marblehead on the *When and If*, but they spent most of their time with family and friends. The first night, the Merrills organized a dinner party at Avalon, and the last night, Ellen Wood organized one at Woodstock.[38] Beatrice overheard George talking to Robert Seaman—the husband of Kay's daughter Gene—at the dinner table about the time he married into the Ayer family, and his "father-in-law was very much against war. I told him what I was trying to do in World War I, and he finally said, 'Well, just make sure that, if you're going to be a soldier, you be the best soldier you can be.'" He looked across the table at Beatrice before continuing, "The most wonderful thing about this family is that it energizes people to do the best they can."[39]

WHEN SERGEANT MEEKS first spotted the lights of Le Havre on what was America's 169th Independence Day, he remarked to General Patton that they certainly did their "thirty days in jail" during their stay in the United States. Because Major General Everett Hughes referred to Jean Gordon when he wrote in his diary that George had told him that Beatrice gave him "hell," it is often thought Meeks's remark refers to Beatrice's anger that her niece took a job as a donut girl with the Red Cross in the Third Army. Despite telling others "never to listen to rumors," Beatrice brought up Jean's name a few times during the war, but George wrote in March 1945 not to "worry about Jean I wrote you months ago that she was in this army . . . I have seen her in the company of other Red + several times but I am not a fool so quit worrying."[40]

Beatrice was aware many marriages would "break up after this war," and those that endured were "the ones in which the partnership is so real and close that neither time, distance nor changes can dissolve it."[41] The war brought the Pattons back together in 1941, and their bond only grew stronger during their separation. Beatrice might have said some choice words about Jean Gordon in June 1945, but if George was relieved to be back in Europe, it was because,

> with the exception of my own immediate family, the whole attitude of the people in America is quite inimical to that which exists in Europe. None of them realizes that one cannot fight for two and a half years and be the same ... I was particularly depressed with the attitude of the War Department, where everyone seems to place emphasis on what they call 'planning' and no emphasis at all on fighting.[42]

George felt misunderstood. A pastor had called out his speech at the Coliseum in a sermon titled "Profanity in High Places," and many had taken offense that he told the children at Sunday school they were "the soldiers, sailors, and nurses of the next war."[43] George didn't "want to be regarded as a war monger," but he had seen it a hundred times throughout history: the war to end all wars did not exist. The best way to prevent another armed conflict was to be prepared; after all, "you don't stop fires by eliminating the fire department."[44]

George had always been an outspoken supporter of universal military training, and Beatrice gladly took on the contentious cause in his absence. The guns in Europe had been silent for only two weeks when she had participated in a radio broadcast addressing the twelve million women who volunteered during the war. She hoped they would "keep the faith" and demonstrate "national conscience by the intelligent use of the vote whenever it is our privilege and our duty to exercise it." She also advocated for a year of military training, "to make . . . our boys better men with more pride in themselves, a greater sense of responsibility toward others, and a deeper reverence for the land that bore them and has given them so much."[45]

General Patton's bond with the Third Army was unique, and his men welcomed him to Bad Tölz with an honor guard and a spectacular review that gave him "a very warm feeling in my heart to be back among soldiers." However, he was "still confused as to just what one has to do" when he took office as military governor.[46] As far back as 1925, an efficiency report stated that George Patton was "a man of energy and action, better qualified for active duty than the routine of office work." If ever there were a time George could have benefited from Beatrice's steadying presence, this was it, but spouses were not yet allowed to travel to Europe.

In George's eyes, a disagreement about denazification eventually undid "the friendship of a lifetime."[47] Practically begging Eisenhower to be allowed to take Berlin in the last days of the war, the Supreme Commander merely wondered, "Who would want it?" An incredulous George replied, "I think history will answer that question for you."[48] It annoyed him that "some leaders were just damn fools who had no idea of Russian history." He told Fred that "anybody who wants the Russians to rule any part of this world is a God-damned fool," frustrated that those in high command "have allowed us to kick hell out of one bastard and at the same time forced us to help establish a second one as evil or more evil than the first."[49]

George's priority was to get Bavaria going as fast as possible—to protect against the Russians and prevent people from dying during the winter—even if it meant employing former (low-level) Nazis. This would eventually become an accepted strategy, but in the summer of 1945, this method went squarely against Eisenhower's order to remove all Nazis from every level of society.[50] It didn't matter that Bavaria was the "best-governed area in the ETO [European Theater of Operations]," as Stimson informed Beatrice after a visit to Germany; Chief of Staff Walter Bedell Smith and G-5 Brigadier General Clarence Adcock at SHAEF (Supreme Headquarters Allied Expeditionary Force) thought George was getting a little too friendly with the Germans at the expense of the displaced persons.[51]

General Eisenhower summarily returned from his vacation in Nice and visited George at Bad Tölz on September 16 to discuss his running of the displaced persons camps and the number of Nazis in his administration. The old comrades talked until three in the morning when George announced that he intended to "go home and retire" since none of the jobs he coveted were offered him. Eisenhower asked him to wait until January 1; set to replace General Marshall as Chief of Staff on October 1, he hoped George would remain in his post for at least three months "after he left so as to get things running quietly."[52] Loyal to a fault and always respectful of his superiors, George reluctantly agreed. However, Beatrice and friends like General Harbord wondered "why they are keeping him over there so long."[53]

EVEN WILLIE KNEW it was best to leave General Patton alone when he awoke in the type of mood he was in on September 22. At the end of that morning's press briefing, however, Carl Levin of the *New York Herald Tribune*, Ray Daniels of the *New York Times*, and Ed Morgan of the *Chicago Daily News* were intent on "trying to get Patton to lose his temper."

They got right up in the General's face blowing cigarette smoke, and went after him "with the attitude of a criminal prosecutor interrogating a hardened criminal . . . for permitting a German named Schaeffer to hold public office in Munich." Finally, after much provocation, George remarked that it was "no more possible for a man to be a civil servant in Germany and not have paid lip service to Naziism than it is for a man to be a postmaster in America and not have paid at least lip service to the Democratic Party or Republican Party when it is in power."[54]

General Eisenhower had only political considerations to contend with since the war in the Pacific ended on September 2. He believed even "this tempest" would have blown over, yet he chose to take his ablest fighting commander away from his beloved Third Army, not "for what he has done; I'm firing him for what he'll do next."[55] George was transferred to the Fifteenth Army at Bad Nauheim, a so-called "paper army" in charge of writing the history of the war.

"All good things must come to an end," he said in a quivering voice as he addressed the Third Army one final time on October 8, "and the best thing that has ever come to me thus far is the honor and privilege of having commanded the Third Army."[56] Tears glistened in his eyes as he reviewed his troops and handed the flag to his successor, Lieutenant General Lucian Truscott. He departed for the train station in the pouring rain with his head held high and the band playing "Auld Lang Syne."

George placed the blame squarely on the Communists and the U.S. government's "original inhabitants of Palestine," who "succeeded due to the lack of spine of D.D. [Divine Destiny, a.k.a Eisenhower]."[57] While his self-esteem would have fared better had he resigned immediately, George still felt a particular obligation toward his profession that left him oscillating between retirement and resignation. At least his new assignment was "more in keeping with my natural academic tendencies than is that of governing Bavaria," and the work progressed faster than expected.[58]

**Figure 85.** *A reunion in Sweden on November 29 with the 1912 Modern Pentathlon Olympic Team and Joe Ekeland. George intended "to make a journey with his family to all his different battlefields" and hoped to return with his wife and son the following summer. (Library of Congress)*

George spent most of his time traveling through Europe, becoming an honorary citizen of Metz, Toul, Reims, Luxembourg, Chateau Thierry, Thionville, Épernay, Verdun, etc. Every European city and town welcomed him as a hero, but the American press once again vilified him. He didn't read the news clippings Beatrice sent him because they kept him awake, but he told her to "cheer up . . . the reaction [has] started and I will come out on top sooner than people think."[59]

He had been "terribly hurt for a few days," but his biggest regret was that he had "worried" his wife anew. He apologized for getting her into a situation where she was again "being bothered by reporters," but Beatrice didn't blame him.[60] She had finally reached her breaking point; she felt "so badly about this last incident" that she suggested George ask for a congressional investigation.[61] Her radio message "felt just like a look out of your brave loyal eyes," but now was "not the time to begin the offensive," he wrote back, so "an investigation would be futile."[62] As long as he was in the Army, he wouldn't "raise any stink because, while I think General Eisenhower is most pusillanimous in yielding to the outcry of three very low correspondents, I feel that as an American it would ill become me to discredit him yet—that is, until I shall prove even more conclusively that he lacks moral fortitude."[63]

George Patton had survived the war but wouldn't be able to survive the peace. To Beatrice, the greatest calamity to befall her husband was Eisenhower's decision to make him military governor of Bavaria, "a post which he was unsuited by temperament, training or experience to fill." Even the *New York Times* called it "a mistake to suppose a free-swinging fighter could acquire overnight the capacities of a wise administrator . . . [and] his removal by General Eisenhower was an acknowledgment of that mistake."[64]

Eisenhower's disregard for George's wishes to become head of the Army War College or commanding general of the Army Ground Forces angered Beatrice, but his transfer to the Fifteenth Army infuriated her. In her opinion, George was "crucified and thrown to the wolves" without a single voice "raised in his defense." Eisenhower's "cowardice towards the press" disgusted her.[65]

Beatrice had lost her respect for the press a long time ago, when she realized they would do "anything for sensation." During the war, many American correspondents took issue with General Patton's strict adherence to discipline, and they "were hostile to his enforcement of orders which they considered trivial."[66] Whenever the press brought up the topic, Beatrice defended George's methods by using the example of eight soldiers who had suffered "horrible head injuries" after taking off their helmets to cool down. "It is not enough for us to think of these wounded as heroes," she said, "they are truly victims, but tragically victims because of their lack of obeying orders and living under discipline."[67]

Now that the war was over, the press antagonized George for his refusal to prioritize denazification and his apparent interest in fighting the Russians. Beatrice never stopped believing George was set up, even though Levin, Daniels, and Morgan always denied they were "plotting at the breakfast table how they would get Patton."[68] A correspondent showed up on her doorstep a few months later to apologize. "It is probably too late," the man said as he stood outside, "but I want to tell you, Mrs. Patton, how much I regret having had anything to do with that fatal press conference. After I had spent more time in your husband's presence and observed the problems he faced and how he handled them, I came to admire him greatly."

Beatrice was an excellent hater, and all she remembered of the months following the September conference was the despair in George's letters. "It's still too late," she said before closing the door in the reporter's face.[69]

TRYING to keep up with George Patton was enough to kill a man half his age. He had recently celebrated his sixtieth birthday at the Grand Hotel in Bad Nauheim with his closest friends—Hobart Gay, Paul Harkins, Geoffrey Keyes, and Albert Kenner—but he felt fine "for a man of my advanced age."[70] He informed Fred that it was his "firm determination to spend all the money which you can provide or which I can borrow, beg, or steal on a life of continued amusement," planning to hunt "six days a week in Virginia whenever I am not engaged in shooting or sailing."[71]

Forever burdened with a need to conquer timidity and "compensate for the almost unbearable sense of frustration induced by enforced inaction and passivity," George was again flying, riding, and jumping, just as he had done after WWI.[72] He built a jumping course on the grounds of Bad Tölz but never rode "alone for fear of breaking my neck."[73] Besides a former Nazi and Olympian, his frequent companion was his chief of staff, Hobart "Hap" Gay, who spent most of WWII by his side. The two had met at Fort Myer in 1938 and bonded over a shared passion for history, hunting, and horses.[74]

*Figure 86. George celebrating his 60th birthday on November 11, 1945, with The Old Guard: unidentified, Paul Harkins, unidentified, Geoffrey Keyes, George, Albert Kenner, Hobart "Hap" Gay, unidentified, and George Meeks. (Library of Congress)*

Since George had been feeling lower than the arse of the "species of whale which is said to spend much of its time lying on the bottom of the deepest part of the ocean," Hap thought a hunting trip might cheer up his friend on his last full day in Germany. A fellow officer had told him about a hunting preserve overrun with pheasants eighty miles away near Mannheim. George liked the idea; not only would he be able to get his wife the feathers she so loved putting on her hat, but on the way over, they could stop at Saalburg to explore an old Roman fort dating back to 90 A.D.

Private First Class Horace "Woody" Woodring—a nineteen-year-old demoted several times until he was assigned to the Fifteenth Army as General Patton's driver—sat behind the wheel of the spacious 1938 Cadillac limousine when the hunting party took off at 8:50 a.m. on Sunday, December 9. They drove twenty miles to Bad Homburg, where George regaled his companions for forty minutes with historical anecdotes of Germania and the Roman Empire. Then, his feet wet from the snow, he rode shotgun to dry them under the heater until the Cadillac was stopped at a checkpoint, and he reclaimed his seat next to Hap, making room for the freezing hunting dog, which had been riding in an open truck with Sergeant Spruce.

The mood in the Cadillac was light as Woody drove along the N-38, until they stopped at a closed railroad crossing on the outskirts of Mannheim around 11:45 a.m. and George became pensive. Mannheim was one of those towns he had described as "utterly destroyed," the road strewn with derelict vehicles. "How awful war is; think of the waste," he said, leaning forward in his seat as he stared out the window.

Taking off at a mere ten miles per hour—three times slower than the average polo pony—only Hap and Woody saw the 2 1/2-ton army truck that came from the opposite direction and suddenly cut in front of the Cadillac. Woody turned the wheel and hit the brakes while Hap yelled, "Sit tight," but George was taken by surprise and unable to brace himself. Without the benefit of a seatbelt, which would not be common until the sixties, he was thrown forward six feet and hit his head on the ceiling clock before smashing his face into the glass divider between the front and back seats.

George must have realized something was terribly wrong the moment he fell against Hap with blood streaming down his face, but befitting a true commander, his first concern was for his companions. They were both okay, yet Hap instinctively decided not to move when he felt the dead weight of his friend leaning against him.

"I think I am paralyzed," George said after a momentary silence. "I am having trouble in breathing. Work my fingers for me."

When he calmly repeated his request, despite his chief of staff's earlier compliance, Hap remained "holding General Patton in a more or less steady position until two medical enlisted men arrived on the scene."[75] Then, surveying the scene of the accident as they awaited the ambulance, Hap found Technician Fifth Grade Robert L. Thompson of the 1st Armored Division explaining that he hadn't seen the Cadillac when he had turned across the road to enter a depot.[76]

About fifteen minutes after the accident, Captain Snyder of the 290th Combat Engineers arrived. The young doctor found an alert General Patton leaning against the backseat, quiet except for an occasional curse word and partially scalped with a gash—deep enough to show the white of his skull—running from the bridge of his nose, across his forehead, and along the top of his head. Captain Snyder spoke frankly when contemplating which of the two nearest hospitals to go to, "He broke his neck. He needs the very best we've got."[77]

Unable to move his arms or legs, George was at the mercy of the four men who carefully lifted him out of the Cadillac, and he implored them to "hold up my neck [or] I will die" as they carried him into the waiting ambulance. "I don't feel very much," George replied when asked how he was feeling, but he didn't say another word during the twenty-five-mile ambulance ride, lost in thought as the gravity and the irony of the situation set in.[78]

Colonel Paul Hill, the 130th Station Hospital's chief of surgical services, took charge when the ambulance arrived at 12:45 p.m. George was in considerable shock—his skin was gray, his lips were blue, and his feet were cold—but his vitals immediately improved upon receiving three units of blood. Informed by Colonel Hill that his uniform needed to be cut open, George told him not to worry as it had been done plenty of times before.

After all, counting his current head-wound, he said he had received stitches seventy-two times in his life, and there was a moment of stunned silence when the staff saw the multitude of scars on George's body, "like a German duelist."[79] Tension filled the room as the thirty-nine-year-old Hill and his nurses tiptoed around their infamous patient, but George immediately put them at ease, "Relax, gentlemen, I'm in no condition to be a terror now."[80]

Major General Albert Kenner arrived at the hospital within the hour. After twenty-nine years of service—including chief medical officer for Operations Torch and Overlord—he had to muster all his professionalism while he examined one of his closest friends, noting that George could neither voluntarily move nor feel anything below the top of his shoulders. Just a few days earlier, Kenner had treated George for a cold, and the lingering stuffiness exacerbated his difficulty in breathing.[81] General Patton's condition was critical, so Chaplain White of the Seventh Army came to administer the last rites.

MORE THAN THIRTY journalists had already gathered in the parking lot of the 130th Station Hospital when the sun rose on December 10. Most had immediately abandoned their coverage of the Nuremberg Trials, but by the time they drove the 150 miles to Heidelberg, the hospital was "guarded like a fortress." By order of General Patton, the press was barred from the building, but its hallways were already crowded "like Grand Central Station."[82] Every Army brass in the vicinity suddenly found his way to the former Nazi Kaserne, but the patient's room was off limits except to Generals Gay, Keyes, and Kenner.

Awake by 7 a.m. after a restless night where he felt a choking sensation every time he began to fall asleep, George couldn't help but remark to his nurse what happened was "a hell of a way to get hurt."[83] He was feeling better but was obviously "apprehensive about his condition." After commanding close to half a million men in his dash across Europe mere months ago, George's world was reduced to a small hospital room, staring at the ceiling and dependent on others for even his most basic needs.

Crutchfield tongs were drilled into his skull, and five pounds of traction was applied to realign his vertebrae, but despite everything, he was "a patient patient, ideal in every way." The only things which agitated him were the people he overheard gossiping in the hallway about his condition and the slow dripping of the IV bottle, so he ordered his hallway to be cleared and the bottle placed outside his line of vision.[84]

Brigadier Hugh Cairns—a close friend of Fred and Dr. Franc Ingraham, and a world-renowned neurosurgeon with the British Army—arrived at 11 a.m. to offer a second opinion at the request of Mrs. Patton. As soon as Beatrice hung up the phone with the AP reporter on December 9, she had called the War Department to confirm what happened and immediately got to work making arrangements, noting in her thought book, "Critically hurt and paralyzed from the neck down. I determined to go at once."[85] Beatrice knew her presence could mean the difference between life and death for her husband, and her place was next to his bedside, no matter what it took to get there.

Getting Beatrice to Germany was a team effort: the State Department issued her an emergency visa within hours, Eisenhower issued orders to find "the very fastest transportation for Big Bee," and a national manhunt was underway to locate Colonel Roy Spurling, an authority on spinal cord injuries and the head of neurosurgery in the European theater during the war.[86] The U.S. Army consultant had just boarded the 1:10 from Louisville to Cincinnati when a conductor informed him that an urgent message awaited him at the next stop. It ordered him to abandon "the train and proceed to the airport in Cincinnati, where an army plane will fly you to Washington, hence to Germany."

The C-54 transport took off from Bolling Airfield at 9:45 p.m. on December 9 despite bad weather across the globe; on board were Mrs. Patton, her temporary aide Lieutenant Colonel Kerwin, Colonel Spurling, a seven-man crew, and seven thousand pounds of mail. Beatrice called Eisenhower just before takeoff to thank him for making it possible for her to go to Germany, but many later wondered if there couldn't have been a better solution. A C-54 transport wasn't meant for passengers and was equipped with just a few aluminum bucket seats without any lining. The cabin quickly became "bitterly cold," and the few blankets Spurling found were hardly enough to keep him warm since he was only wearing a light woolen uniform and trench coat.

A small area in the front of the plane was curtained off for Beatrice's comfort, but she soon joined Colonel Spurling in the back, bringing him a pair of ski pajamas and one of her sweaters. She profusely apologized when she found out he was about to be officially released from military service on December 20. However, the neurosurgeon's misgivings about the hastily arranged trip disappeared once Beatrice's intrepid spirit infected him. "Within five minutes of meeting her," he remembered, "we were friends."

Lieutenant Colonel Kerwin remembered her as a "perky little gal," chattering away as she repeated to herself the words she shared so many times with young army wives whose husbands were injured or missing—"worry is a senseless and evil thing" and "while there's life there's hope."[87] She was concerned about George's propensity for blood clots, though, telling Colonel Spurling that if he "just doesn't get an embolism, I think he may pull through."

Colonel Spurling couldn't help but smile when they landed five-and-a-half hours later in Stephenville, Newfoundland, a busy relay station for transatlantic flights. Whereas in the past, he was merely "herded through the crowds with sharp, curt commands," this time he received a "royal welcome."

The three weary travelers were immediately taken to the Officers' Club, where a warm bed and a bottle of whiskey awaited them. However, within the hour and despite three feet of snow covering the runway, the C-54 took off for the Azores, a tiny Portuguese island three thousand miles away. With just an hour-and-a-half to go before arriving at their next destination, the crew was called upon to keep an eye out for a downed airplane. After circling the area for half an hour, they spotted an orange lifeboat with no sign of life on board.

Upon arrival in the Azores at 5 p.m., the plane was grounded owing to inclement weather on the Continent that closed all airports. Still, the urgency of the mission occasioned a dangerous change in plans just an hour later. After finally receiving a copy of General Patton's diagnosis—"complete paralysis below the level of the third cervical due to a fracture, simple, of the third cervical vertebrae with posterior dislocation of the fourth cervical"—Colonel Spurling had "doubts as to the wisdom of risking the lives of about ten perfectly healthy people in order to get to the bedside of a man who probably had no chance to survive."

Beatrice, however, was ready to keep going despite being on the road for over twenty-four hours, "her eyes alive and punctuating every thought." The Colonel had never seen anyone so unperturbed in the face of adversity, and his admiration for Beatrice grew with each passing hour. At that moment in the officer's club in the Azores, Roy Spurling would have followed the "small, wiry person with an immense amount of vitality," who wasn't "pretty by ordinary standards" but possessed a personality that radiated "like a brilliant gem," to the ends of the world.[88]

BEATRICE'S first glimpse of the Eiffel Tower in over seven years was not as she had imagined. The plan had been to visit Europe upon George IV's graduation in the summer of 1946 and drive the entire route of the Third Army with her husband and son. Instead, she found herself on an army transport with nine strangers, wondering whether she would make it to her husband's bedside in time.[89] It was already December 11, and violent storms were turning an eight-hour flight into an eleven-hour nightmare with no end in sight.

At 8 a.m., Major General Everett Hughes (inspector general of the U.S. forces in the ETO), Lieutenant Colonel Merle-Smith (George's aide), and a contingent of reporters watched nervously from Orly Field as the plane approached, but the fog was so thick that the pilot was unable to land even with the assistance from ground control. Finally, after wasting another fifteen minutes on a second attempt, the controller rerouted the plane to Marseilles, but not before Hughes radioed Beatrice to give her an update on her husband's condition. It was the first update she received since she had heard the news almost forty-eight hours earlier, and Hughes reassured her that George was conscious.[90]

Hermann Göring's former train had been standing by to take Beatrice from Paris to Heidelberg, but in Marseille she transferred to Lieutenant General Lee's luxurious C-47. Since there were no oxygen masks on board, the passengers had no choice but to suffer through the effects of oxygen deprivation when dismal weather forced the plane to climb to 11,000 feet. As they descended to land at Frankfurt's Esborn Airport, the pilot realized he would be unable to do so and flew to Mannheim instead. Unfortunately, by the time he managed to break through the clouds, he saw only pine trees flanking a river, which he followed for a heart-pounding fifteen minutes. The pilot eventually managed to make "a tricky landing" in a meadow, but the navigator admitted that this was the closest call he'd ever had.[91]

The story goes that General Patton ordered Pfc. Woodring to pick up Mrs. Patton at the airport and bring her to the hospital.[92] Woody hadn't left his room in two days; he looked upon the general as a father figure whose "heart was bigger than he was," and he was haunted by the last words he had heard him say, "What a hell of a way to die." George, however, held neither Woodring nor Thompson responsible, and he was unwilling to ruin two young lives over what he knew to be an accident. At his urging, neither driver received disciplinary action despite the accident being attributed to "carelessness on the part of both drivers."[93]

Beatrice's first stop was Villa Reiner—Keyes' residence in Heidelberg as commander of the Seventh Army—to sit down with Brigadier Cairns and Generals Gay, Kenner, and Keyes. Never one to beat around the bush, she immediately asked them to "tell me all about it."

The prognosis was "guarded," but X-rays showed an "almost complete reduction of the dislocation," and his "neurological status slightly improved."[94] George was "resting comfortably," despite Cairns' crude and extremely painful alternative to the Crutchfield tongs, which kept slipping because of the unusual shape of his head. Traction was now being maintained by a ten-pound weight attached to two zygomatic hooks; basically, two debarbed fishhooks inserted underneath the cheekbones.

When Beatrice asked whether George would ever walk again, Albert Kenner—who enjoyed her complete confidence—replied that there was nothing to do but wait, an activity she had plenty of experience with. He explained that George would either regain some function in his arms and be paralyzed from the waist down or remain a quadriplegic for life.[95] His excellent physical condition was why he survived the initial shock of the accident, but his recovery largely depended on his will to live. After years of seeing him get hurt, though, Beatrice was confident his "fighting heart" would carry him through again.[96]

The priority was now to ensure that husband and wife could spend as much time together as possible. Beatrice finally made it to the 130th Station Hospital at 3:30 p.m. on Tuesday, December 11. She made only one comment to the press, repeating what she had told Kenner earlier, "I have seen George in these scrapes before and he always comes out alright."[97]

Notified that his wife was on the way, George ordered the nurse, who was stationed by his bedside twenty-four hours a day, to leave the room. When he heard the door open, and he finally found himself staring into his wife's "darling blue eyes," unable to touch her, all he managed to bring out was, "I am afraid, Bea, this may be the last time we see each other."[98] These were the only words the doctors and nurses overheard until Beatrice emerged from his room half an hour later. What was said between them will never be known, but it was obvious that George was cheered by his wife's arrival, and his vitals improved for the first time since the accident.[99]

Nothing could have prepared Beatrice for what she saw in that tiny hospital room, but her natural resiliency kicked in, and, according to Keyes, "she and he were fine—of course they would be."[100] Beatrice always rose to the occasion when the chips were down, and the moment she walked out of George's room, no one doubted who was in charge. General Eisenhower had instructed the theater commander, General McNarney, to "do everything you can to help her," and Beatrice immediately presented a list of requests.[101]

First, she wanted George's favorite books brought from his traveling library so she could read to him. Second, she wanted complete control of who had access to his room, intimately aware of George's private feelings regarding many of the officers now clamoring to see him. Third, she wanted Fred to come to Heidelberg because there were certain things that her husband felt he could discuss only with his brother-in-law. And fourth, she asked the doctors to always be truthful with her regardless of the news. There were two things she always venerated, "One is intestinal fortitude (the general calls it guts), and another is truth . . . I believe in hoping, but I don't like kidding myself."[102]

George appeared "almost jovial in his manner" when Colonel Spurling walked in, and he immediately apologized for getting the neurosurgeon "out on this wild goose chase." However, the only thing he said during the umpteenth examination was that the accident was "an ironical thing to have to happen to me—after the best of the Germans have shot at me, then to get hurt in an automobile going pheasant hunting."[103]

Beatrice had always seen her husband outwit the pain and shortcomings of his body through sheer perseverance, but now all he managed was "some questionable voluntary movement" in his right thumb, index, and ring finger. Colonel Spurling did note a return of the deep tendon reflexes, giving him hope the spinal cord was merely in shock instead of severed, but he doubted his patient "could live very long with so much restriction of breathing."[104]

After years of practicing medicine, Colonel Spurling knew what was coming when General Patton wanted to speak with him "man to man." Since the doctor could not give a forthright answer at this point, and time felt like an eternity, George simply asked, "What chance have I to ride a horse again?"

This time Spurling's response was unequivocal: "None."

George looked him squarely in the eye, as always "subtly testing out the doctors' statements," and said, "In other words, the best that I could hope for would be semi-invalidism."

He kept quiet for a moment, then thanked the colonel "for being honest," promised to be "a good patient" once explained the "medical problems" of his case, and returned to his "old jovial mood." Aware that they were "surrounded by an awful lot of brass," with "more generals than privates," George wanted his doctor to know that he "was the boss—whatever you say goes."

All of George's "old Army comrades" who were milling around the hospital were "outraged by being kept on the sidelines," so Colonel Spurling suggested issuing an order limiting his visitors to just a handful of people. George readily agreed because "it's kind of hard for me to see my old friends when I'm lying here paralyzed all over." He didn't "like to have people around," except for Beatrice, who had always been the only one he tolerated sympathy from.[105]

Colonel Spurling spent as much time treating George as he did treating the bruised egos of his so-called friends. General Walter Bedell "Beetle" Smith proved to be "particularly persistent" in trying to gain access to the patient's room.[106] Beatrice had made it clear from the moment she arrived that General Smith should "under no circumstances" be allowed to see her husband, and George reiterated that he didn't "want to see the old so-and-so, he's never been a particular friend of mine any how." Ever since Eisenhower's former chief of staff failed to answer whether there were any officers "temperamentally or emotionally in disagreement" with the denazification policy, George could no longer "eat at the same table with General Bedell Smith."[107]

Beetle, however, seemed to think otherwise, and after several days he resolutely informed Colonel Spurling that he was flying over from Frankfurt with some friends. Finally, Beatrice took matters into her own hands and kindly informed him that receiving visitors was too stressful for her husband.[108] General Smith had negotiated the terms of surrender with the German High Command in May 1945, but he was no match for Mrs. Beatrice Ayer Patton.

EVERY MORNING when Beatrice arrived at the 130th Station Hospital, wrapped in fur to ward off the snow covering most of Heidelberg, she first popped into the room across from George's to inquire about his condition. She always did so unobtrusively, "as if she had done it by mistake," but she showed neither nervousness nor tiredness and always "kept her equanimity; nothing ever seemed to ruffle her."[109]

The gloom that had settled over the hospital disappeared with Beatrice's arrival, and she won over everybody with her cheerful demeanor. She was "kind and by no means shy or exclusive," telling a downcast MP to "cheer up [and] stop worrying," and everyone she came into contact with received a warm smile and a firm handshake.[110] Her manner was "quiet and unassuming," Spurling recalled, and she always spoke "slowly, softly and correctly," looking people straight in the eye with a "frank [yet] friendly look."[111]

The armed MP standing guard heard chatter from the tiny hospital room in Ward A-1 day and night. All George wanted to do was sleep and "forget it all," but he was able to do so only in short naps of thirty minutes or less. Waking up was the hardest part, and he always appeared slightly confused until reality set in again. It must have been a living hell for the man who once was the German's most feared general to have each day be a repetition of the one before: his teeth brushed, his catheter changed, his nose sprayed to help with the stuffiness, his limbs moved to ward off muscle atrophy and bed sores.

However, he never voiced "one word of complaint regarding a nurse or doctor or orderly," and "each and every one was treated with the kindest consideration." Colonel Spurling knew General Patton by reputation only—as "the strict disciplinarian, the showman, and the fearless warrior"—but he quickly realized that his "personality was so diametrically opposite to his external philosophy that he seemed in retrospect to be almost a Dr. Jekyll and Mr. Hyde."[112]

After Beatrice coaxed George to eat some breakfast—never more than a cup of coffee, half an egg, and half a grapefruit—she retreated down the hall to answer the letters and telegrams that flooded the hospital. Whether it was President Truman, who knew "faith and courage will not fail you [George]" after winning "many a tough fight," or Mrs. Evelyn Benjamin, "from a humble home in England" who prayed "your husband will recover like mine did," each piece of correspondence warranted a personal reply from "Mrs. George S. Patton."[113] Replying to a cable from Winston Churchill, who admired George's "brilliant services in the common cause," Beatrice believed "the sympathy and concern of his [George's] associates is helping just as much towards his recovery than any other factor."[114]

General Eisenhower initially heard of George's accident "on the basis of rumor and simply did not believe it thinking it was again a story"—George had been involved in a minor fender bender in October—but he consequently learned to his "great distress that it was true." He wanted George to know that he would "always have a job and not to worry about this accident closing out any of them for your selection." By coincidence, on December 8, he had "directed that you [George] be contacted to determine whether you wanted a particular job that appeared to be opening up here in the States."[115]

Beatrice was merely being polite and exemplifying the epitome of "ass kissing," when she replied to "My dear Ike." She had read his "very kind letter to Georgie … and the part about your having a job waiting for him when he can take it, he made me read twice." Until George was able to reply, she wanted Ike "to know that he appreciates it." Beatrice was very much aware of how hurt her husband was by his dismissal from the Third Army, so the conclusion to her short note must have been particularly galling to write, "My trip over was splendid, and—well, all I can say is, I came so fast that I almost kept up the pace with my heart. Thank you for making this possible. Now I'll go and bully him into eating a bit of jelly! Love to Mamie & I am sure glad she's better."[116]

George's world was reduced to a Spartan hospital room, but Beatrice's reading each afternoon allowed his mind to travel where his body couldn't go. The Pattons liked the "mental uplift" reading gave them, and throughout their thirty-five years of marriage, they gathered in the living room after dinner to do just that. George liked it even better when he was read to, fondly remembering lying by the fire at Lake Vineyard as his father and Aunt Nannie planted the seed of his conviction that "a dishonorable death meant a life wasted."[117] Beatrice happily continued the tradition upon their marriage. Her "ability to read aloud was one of her many gifts," and her expressive voice often brought tears to George's eyes.[118]

She kept George's mind occupied by reading the memoirs of Napoleon's confidant, Armand-Augustin-Louis de Caulaincourt, and Clausewitz's *On War*, one of the first books he had bought while on honeymoon. At times he commented on what she read; at other times, he just listened quietly, so quietly that Beatrice hoped he had finally fallen asleep.

Once George finished his dinner, usually nothing more than a few reluctant spoonfuls of broth, Beatrice wished him goodnight and left for Villa Reiner with Colonel Spurling and General Geoffrey "Geoff" Keyes. He was "one of the pleasantest companions and most loyal friends" George had ever known, from the time Geoff served as the 2nd Armored Division's chief of staff in 1940 to his participation in Operations Torch and Husky. Beatrice enjoyed listening to his war stories, many she hoped to hear from George's mouth one day.[119]

While Beatrice's tales of her holidays with George "always brought a misty feeling to both her eyes and mine," what they made most clear to Colonel Spurling was how much General Patton "was a man of action."[120] George never showed Beatrice any apprehension about his condition and tried to cheer everyone "without thought of self," but alone at night, he often became despondent.[121] Captain William Duane Jr., a young neurosurgeon, spent every night at his bedside, listening as his patient reminisced about the first anniversary of the Battle of the Bulge.[122] His nurse thought he appeared mentally confused at night, but Dr. Duane believed he was merely "despairing of recovery . . . His mental attitude is not good. He is greatly concerned about being permanently paralyzed," a terrible prospect in any case, but especially for "an individual who has been so active."[123]

One of George's worst nightmares had come true, and not from "a damned good horse" throwing him, but he was "accepting his condition like a 'true soldier'" and refused to dwell on the why.[124] Beatrice never discussed death with George as she sat by his bedside, but as the doctors took increasingly desperate measures to save his life, she must have wondered whether he wanted to live in this condition. When she once asked him why he was afraid in battle, even though he wasn't afraid of death, George admitted that what he feared was getting maimed and surviving. After visiting countless hospitals throughout the years, he knew that death could be "long, drawn out, and painful."

INSTEAD OF "RIDING TOGETHER AGAIN" at Green Meadows and testing out the new Belgian hunting guns George had bought them, Fred found himself en route to Germany on Pan Am Flight 100, running a 104-degree fever.[125] It had taken him two days to secure a seat because the Air Transport Command (ATC) refused to put him on one of its three daily flights to London, but he persevered because he hoped he "might possibly prove useful."[126]

Freddie, as his sisters called him, was Beatrice's "joy and delight," and one of the few people in the world George trusted implicitly. "Inspite of my faults you have always treated me as a real brother," George wrote on the eve of his departure for North Africa, "and I have felt that way towards you. I do appreciate all you have been and done to and for me."[127]

Fred was "the most completely honest man ... and one of a handful of the truly courageous." At five foot eight, he was only a little taller than his sister, but his courage and tenacity were in no way inferior to George's. Hit on the chin with a polo mallet during a game, he merely took a slug of whiskey and asked Dr. Johnson to sew up his partially severed tongue so he could continue the game.

According to Frederick Jr., there was "nothing flamboyant" about his father's personality. And while he lacked the "true vividness of imagination" that Beatrice possessed, he had remarkable courage, "both physical and moral." George's admiration for his brother-in-law was "without limit," and he enjoyed "complete reliance" on both Fred and Beatrice.[128]

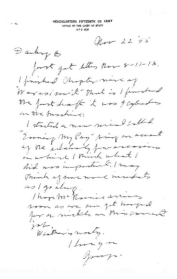

When Fred finally made it to Heidelberg on December 15 amid yet another snowstorm, George suddenly lost the little appetite he had had. Flat on his back with ten-pound weights pulling his cheeks taut and unable to do anything except move his eyes and talk feebly, it was practically impossible for him to swallow without feeling a choking sensation. He coughed almost constantly trying to raise phlegm, but he couldn't produce an effective cough, and his lungs slowly began to fill with fluid. Despite physiotherapy and occasional turning, he developed pressure sores on his shoulders and buttocks. The slight improvement that followed in the days after Beatrice's arrival had dissipated, but despite everything, "his general condition held up remarkably well."

*Figure 87. "I always think of interesting things to tell you while I am driving or flying," George wrote in April 1945, "and then when I get time to write I forget them." (Library of Congress)*

What George could discuss only with Fred is unknown, but no doubt his finances and legacy were two topics of conversation. Worried one day someone would try "to vilify and misrepresent" him, George wrote detailed letters to Beatrice and Fred throughout the war, and he entrusted his papers and diaries to them. Just days before the accident, he finished dictating the last two chapters of a book he intended to call *War as I Knew It*.[129]

Based on his WWII diaries and expounding on his theories of war, by October George had already finished the first draft, which he shared with a select few. Beatrice gave him "hell for making it too short and concise," but he "wrote it so as to interest you and the children and to get my ideas on paper before they faded. Factually it is fine. I don't intend to write a biography but when I am dead someone may find it valuable."[130]

Beatrice was "just as cheerful and lively as ever," and Fred was "a real addition to the party," but George's children were missing from his bedside.[131] Bee and Ruth Ellen agreed they would be of more use at home, especially with Johnnie finally out of the hospital. Young George, however, was terribly disappointed when his mother informed him it would be a far greater comfort to his father if he finished his West Point exams instead of rushing to his bedside.

Plenty of friends and family had broken their necks out riding and pulled through, as Beatrice said, "in fine shape," and the reports coming from Heidelberg were "very encouraging" in the first few days. Colonel Spurling tentatively discussed repatriating George by December 30 to continue his recovery at either Walter Reed or Cushing General Hospital in Boston, and President Truman apparently offered the use of the Sacred Cow, his presidential Douglas C-54 plane, to bring him home.[132]

Letters and daily bulletins kept the family informed. On December 14, Colonel Paul Harkins—George's Deputy Chief of Staff—wrote Bee an account of his recent visit to the 130th Station Hospital:

> Had a grand chat yesterday with Mrs. Patton. I had driven down from Bad Nauheim to Heidelberg to say "hello" and pay my respects to the General. I took Sgt. Meeks with me. I had lunch with General Keyes and then, as he had to go to work, Mrs. Patton and I sat and reorganized the army for about two hours.
>
> She looks tired, but of course, she has a right to be. The General is not in good shape. However, yesterday was the first encouraging day we have had. He asked for a drink and asked to sit up. He got the drink. Of course, it is impossible for him to sit up. They have spikes through his skull and also hooks in his cheek-bones with weights attached, stretching his head and neck to the rear against the 200-pound body pull to the front. His face is quite badly bruised and swollen from being thrown around the back of the car. Mrs. Patton asked that nobody see him until all danger of a crisis is past. I feel confident, with his determination that he will see this thing through and come out O.K. Last night he complained about pain in his back. Although he has felt nothing since last Sunday, and we hate to think that he will have to go into the pain feeling stage, it is good to know that he can feel again. His paralysis, as of yesterday, was still complete from the third vertebra down.
>
> Solid Mrs. Patton, of course, is just the same. She says she's seen "Georgie" in such fixes before and he always comes through. She is as cheerful as she can be under the circumstances and, of course, we will do anything in the world for both of them. It may be she will have to stay longer than she expected. One can't tell how long the recuperation period will be.[133]

When the family first heard the news, they had been "nearly as worried about Mother as we were about Daddy," but Beatrice turned out to be "a great sport."[134] Ruth Ellen wrote Eisenhower that being by George's bedside "has meant more than anything, as you must realize, from your long friendship with them." The Pattons were "devoted companions for nearly 45 years," and their bond had always been special.[135] Captain Duane was "fascinated by the interplay" between the Pattons, and Colonel Spurling thought Beatrice's devotion to her husband was "one of the most beautiful human relationships that I have ever known."

He found General Patton to be "a soft-hearted, kindly man, in fact, almost a sentimentalist," and "a devoted family man" who had evident pride in his children and a profound "love and adoration of his wife." Beatrice "had lived her life for him . . . her boy—a bad boy at times but a very good one most of the time." No one doubted George put up his fight for "Beatrice's sake." She expected him to "fight and win," and even after all these years, "he didn't want to disappoint her."[136]


WHENEVER GENERAL PATTON found himself on the bottom after a peacetime scandal, victory in battle brought him back to the top. There was no war to redeem him from the September conference scandal, but in his battle for life, he was about to emerge the victor in the court of public opinion. His accident was front-page news day after day, and reporters were clamoring for information, but they weren't getting any from Beatrice. She always greeted the press waiting outside with a smile but never spoke to them.

The only public statement she made was released when she first arrived in Heidelberg: "I am very happy to be here with my husband. Now that I have seen and talked with him, I am not in the least worried. He looks very well. His care here at the Seventh Army Hospital has been of the finest, and I thank everybody from the bottom of my heart."[137]

Daily bulletins were released at 11 a.m. and 6 p.m. to control the narrative, but the more brazen reporters "resorted to any type of trickery to get a story." The thought of one of those "damn fools" slipping into his room to take a picture mortified George, and an armed MP stood guard outside his room. While conspiracy theorists later used this as evidence that General Patton needed protection from an assassin, he just needed protection from desperate reporters who even posed as patients and orderlies.[138] Colonel Spurling was exasperated "beyond measure" to read headlines proclaiming his patient yelled for a "Shot of Whiskey" and would soon be walking again.[139]

By December 17, George's neurological condition was still unchanged, and "it became imperative that something be done about the skeletal traction. Not only was the pull on the tongs attached to his skull each day more unbearable but they were losing their effectiveness because of necrosis around them." The fishhooks were replaced by a cast which covered part of his head, neck, and upper torso, leaving George "much happier." His fever broke for the first time since he was admitted, and he was able to sit up at a forty-five-degree angle for an hour, propped up by pillows.

On the day General Patton was supposed to arrive in New York, soldiers across the United States rushed home for the holidays in an ever-greater frenzy. Those lucky enough to return found grateful wives and excited children waiting for them, delicious smells emanating from the kitchen, and presents underneath the Christmas tree. This joyous pandemonium was in stark contrast to Europe. The Continent was devastated by more than five years of war, and those who survived were still picking up the pieces, many going cold and hungry as yet another brutal winter settled in. In a snow-covered Heidelberg, George's first-floor hospital room was the only one that had its curtains closed and the lights dimmed as his condition took a sudden turn for the worse.

Six months earlier, during their tour of Walter Reed Hospital, Beatrice heard George tell the men in ward eight that to win a battle, "you have to make the mind run the body. Never let the body tell the mind what to do. The body will always give up from exhaustion . . . but the body is never tired if the mind is not tired." After countless sleepless nights forced to think about his life and death, George was both physically and mentally exhausted.

There was no doubt he survived as long as he did because of his courage and unconquerable will, continuously strengthened by Beatrice's presence, but "both knew that he was dying." A note on his chart on the afternoon of the nineteenth said he was "very cheerful and talkative, laughing a little," but Beatrice could see right through the bravado. That evening, her fears of an embolism became reality when he suffered "an acute attack of breathlessness and pallor," which lasted about an hour.[140]

"It's too dark. I mean, too late," George whispered to himself, interrupting Beatrice's reading the next day.[141] Those were almost the exact last words spoken by a dying Englishman in *Blood of the Shark*, "It's too late . . . too dark." She waited for him to say something else, but he stayed quiet.

Was it just a coincidence, or was George, who always "learned from everything he read and remembered nearly all of it," thinking back to their times in Hawaii? "When one remembers passages from a book it is a good book," George wrote Beatrice six months earlier as he encouraged her to write more. "I remember passages from both your Hawaiian stories and from the Army experiences. There for they must be good."[142]

He might have been unable to admit it in 1938 because he was sunk deep in depression, but he always felt immense pride in his wife's accomplishments, whether as an author, an equestrian, or a wartime speaker. "In spite of the fact that she devoted her life to him, she still had many accomplishments of her own," Spurling gathered from his many conversations with the Pattons. "She was a student of history, like her husband, except her inclinations followed a different line of thought."

Beatrice continued reading into the afternoon, George listening quietly, "under no emotional strain," until he suddenly said, "I feel like I can't get my breath." Gasping for air as his lips turned blue, "he rallied very fast" when he received oxygen, but the little phlegm he managed to cough up was blood-tinged, an unmistakable sign of "a small infarction of the lung." It was beyond question to Kenner that "a shower emboli . . . hit his right chest and he started to fill up with his own sputum."[143]

General Smith informed a "distressed and shocked" Eisenhower that "death was imminent in the next 48 hours," and Geoff, who never lost hope, wrote his wife that everyone was "in a pretty low state . . . In fact the doctors hold out very little hope."[144]

Kept "reasonably comfortable under oxygen," George suffered through violent coughing spells for the rest of the day as he tried to clear the fluid from his lungs, his legs occasionally spasming uncontrollably.[145] Every time Beatrice touched his lifeless hands—which were "unusually artistic and sensitive for those of a combat General"—she was reminded of all the "sailing, fishing and hunting" he planned to do upon his retirement, all the scrapbooks she had waiting at Green Meadows for him to read.[146]

She always admired how he used to be able to do anything with his hands, from a delicate touch with his horses to the brute force necessary to build a boat, but now he couldn't even turn the page of a book, and all he felt was "a queer sensation in his hands as though the skin was falling away from the bone."[147]

Watching the only man she ever loved slowly suffocate was one of the hardest things Beatrice had ever done. Yet, she was as "plucky and courageous as five ordinary people" and remained undaunted.[148] She spent the night at the hospital and tried to catch a few hours of sleep, but it was hard not to think of George, lying awake down the hall, out of breath just from taking a sip of water. In a last-ditch effort to save him, he was given pure protein and digitalis, but that night he asked Nurse Hohle, "Why don't they just let me die?"[149]

GEORGE ALWAYS BELIEVED "you are not beaten until you admit it (Hence Don't)," but on Friday, December 21, 1945, he refused breakfast and resolutely told his nurse, "I am going to die. Today."[150]

If Beatrice had heard him say this, she would have been reminded of the one Native Hawaiian mystery which always fascinated her the most: the ability "to die at will." Under the right circumstances, the Hawaiians were able to die wherever and whenever they wanted, a phenomenon best illustrated by a story told by Dr. Woods, a plantation doctor on Oahu. When one of his patients saw her deceased grandfather beckoning her, she "promised to go to him at five on Monday." After a big lū'au in her honor, she lay down on her bed at 4:50 p.m. and promptly died ten minutes later. "Death often comes this way to the Hawaiians," Beatrice concluded in her notebook. "I asked my friend Emma Ahuena Taylor if she could explain it. She said: 'It's a gift. We just let go.'"[151]

George lingered through the morning, cooperative and alert, but his breathing was labored, and he became slightly cyanotic. Beatrice sat holding an oxygen mask to his face when he wistfully whispered, "I guess I wasn't good enough." It broke Beatrice's heart to hear him say this after all he had accomplished, but she understood the deeper meaning. His whole life, George told his family that "he hoped he was good enough to warrant" a glorious death on the battlefield, or at least on the back of a magnificent steed like Konohiki; instead, he lingered for thirteen days in a hospital bed. Just as his father said in 1927, "death was the only adventure left for him and [he] yearned for it without fear and with great curiosity, and anticipated being only deterred from so expressing such feelings by his love for his family and his fear of wounding them."[152]

Beatrice continued reading John Steinbeck's *The Red Pony* after coaxing George to drink some eggnog for lunch, but by 4 p.m., he was very drowsy. He assured his wife that "he felt better and very comfortable," but he wanted to sleep a little, so he suggested she get an early dinner and finish the book when she returned. Beatrice waited fifteen minutes until he was asleep before leaving him in the capable hands of Captain Duane and Lt. Margery Randell.[153]

Even though she told Geoff that everything was okay and there was no need for Fred to return after supper, her unease was apparent when she joined Colonels Spurling and Hill in the officers' mess. By now, it was clear to Spurling that Beatrice "was almost clairvoyant" in all matters relating to her husband. So when Captain Duane ran in just before 6 p.m., she jumped up from her chair, "I knew something was wrong—I could just feel it."[154]

Beatrice and the doctors ran across the courtyard to Ward A-1, but it was too late. General George S. Patton Jr. "went out like a light and certainly suffered no pain."[155] He was barely a month over sixty, but as he had maintained from a young age, "Men live in deeds not years."[156]

If George was bothered by being killed in an accident after everything he had been through, his close friend Colonel Codman had the perfect retort, "Do not be concerned, General. Bullet, shell, bomb, shipwreck, plane crash, car crash—all were your daily occupational hazards. In the hearts and minds of every man who served with you the record is crystal clear, and the final words of that record unequivocal: 'George S. Patton, Jr., 02605 Killed in Action.'"[157]

When Fred and Geoff returned from Villa Reiner, they found Beatrice acting "just wonderful." She said goodbye to the man she had dedicated the last forty-three years of her life to, walking out of his room as calm and collected as she had been when she arrived eleven days earlier. She denied Spurling's request for an autopsy, "thoroughly satisfied" that everything was done to save her husband's life and accepting that his death was caused by a "pulmonary embolism followed by cardiac failure." The thought of her Georgie being cut open was unbearable to Beatrice, but it was the wrong decision in hindsight, as an autopsy could have put to rest rumors which persist to this day.[158]

Following the issue of the autopsy, Beatrice was confronted with the prospect of meeting the two people she hated most: undertakers and journalists. Of journalists, there were too many, so George's body was taken to the basement to avoid prying eyes. Of undertakers, there were none, so the best Geoff could come up with was an enlisted officer of the Seventh Army who used to work at a funeral parlor.

A heartbroken Sergeant Meeks came from Bad Nauheim as soon as he received word, bringing General Patton's uniform and "four-star storm flag," which he draped over the General's body.[159] He had been waiting with Willie for the hunting party to return at 4 p.m. on December 9 and had everything ready for their departure at 7:15 a.m. the next day when he heard the news of "that awful accident."[160]

Flags fluttered at half-staff in the foggy night when Beatrice accompanied George's body to Villa Reiner to lie in state. An old German woman placed flowers at the hospital gate just as the ambulance took off, and American soldiers lined the twisting cobblestone streets. Overwhelmed with grief, Beatrice immediately stated her desire to bury George at West Point. However, when General Eisenhower received a confidential message from General Smith explaining the situation, he realized this might cause problems with family members of soldiers buried overseas.

There was always the possibility that "the public might demand that Patton be returned to the United States for burial," but the U.S. Army had not repatriated a single officer or soldier during the war. Geoff was asked if he could "voluntarily" make Beatrice concur with their views, but as a close family friend, he felt uncomfortable doing so and asked Colonel Spurling to do so instead.[161]

Beatrice didn't know that George had asked his daughters back in June "not to let them bring me back." Still, she knew that he considered burying a soldier anywhere but the place he fell as simply catering "to a bunch of snivelling sob sisters retained by those carrion-eating ghouls, the coffin makers and undertakers."[162]

Her reaction was immediate when Colonel Spurling broached the subject, "Of course he must be buried here! Why didn't I think of it? Furthermore, I know George would want to lie beside the men of his Army who have fallen." Given the choice of three cemeteries, she chose the (yet unfinished and unnamed) Luxembourg American Cemetery in Hamm. Central to the Battle of the Bulge, it was where General Patton fought his toughest battle and where the Third Army suffered its highest casualties.

BEATRICE FELT George's isolation and disillusionment in every letter he wrote her the last few months, agonizing with him as he thought it "hell to be old and passé." Until the day she died, she shared his belief that his relief from the Third Army was an effort to "get him," by either the press or SHAEF. Her wrath was instantaneous when she reviewed the list of pallbearers and saw General Smith's name. She replaced the four-star general with George's African American orderly, Master Sergeant Meeks, and scrapped Beetle from the guest list. "He [George] knows I never failed him," Beatrice wrote in her thought book that day, and she wasn't about to start now.[163]

While General Keyes and the Seventh Army took care of the enormous funeral arrangements, General Gay, the soon-to-be commander of the Fifteenth Army, accompanied Beatrice and Fred to Bad Nauheim for an overnight stay on December 22. She requested a quick stop at the scene of the accident, but she was eager to see where George had spent the last two months of his life. His footlockers should have arrived at Green Meadows by now; instead, they still stood in the entryway of his villa at Bad Nauheim.

His "swell little dog" lay listless next to his master's briefcase with a sad look in his eyes, wondering why the man he adored never returned.[164] Willie Patton was just as George described him: a pure white bull terrier, "except for a little lemin on his tail which to a cursary glance would seem to indicate that he had not used toilet paper."[165] It was evident from his letters that the little egghead had been a comforting and loyal presence in George's life, and Beatrice took him home to Green Meadows, where he went as crazy over the school bus's arrival as he used to do when a Messerschmitt flew overhead.[166]

It was comforting to hear Meeks tell stories of how George would be writing her at night and stopping to give Willie a belly rub, but it also brought home how much she had missed. The soldiers of the Fifteenth Army who spent barely two months under General Patton's command had seen more of him during that time than she had in the last four years.

One of those men was staff officer John Eisenhower, who'd known the Pattons since he was a little boy. He was apprehensive when he first heard the news of General Patton's transfer to the Fifteenth Army, very much aware of how "deeply hurt by my father's action" he had been. Still, his new commander "classily hid his feelings," and they got along well.[167]

John was even more impressed with Beatrice, whose actions on the afternoon of December 22 perfectly exemplified "the family nature of the Regular Army at its best." She took a seat behind George's desk and spoke to every soldier of the Fifteenth Army one on one, offering to take home messages for loved ones. Rarely had John "been witness to such a gesture of fortitude and kindness," Beatrice talking little about herself and instead focusing on the soldiers who walked through the door.[168] Anyone who came into contact with

Beatrice during these trying times, no matter the rank or occupation, was confronted with the same fortitude and kindness.

"Viewed from any angle," Colonel Spurling remembered, "Mrs. Patton [was] a grand lady."[169] She asked Geoff to give a case of wine to the hospital mess as thanks for the excellent care her husband had received, and she contacted Brigadier Cairns to ask about payment for services rendered. Cairns just "felt privileged to be able to help a little," but since Beatrice insisted, he suggested a donation to buy medical equipment for the hospital where he worked. A few months later, however, when Beatrice heard of the plane troubles Cairns and his wife experienced when they traveled to the United States, she offered to pay for their return to England in the most luxurious suite on the Queen Mary. Reluctant to accept her offer, Cairns finally did so after Colonel Spurling urged him to.[170]

After all, Roy Spurling knew better than anyone that Beatrice was a headstrong woman who did not take no for an answer. When he told her he planned to stay for General Patton's funeral, she convinced him to try to make it home to Kentucky for Christmas instead. He didn't arrive in time because of bad weather, but "the privileges of knowing General Patton, his family and friends are among the choice memories of these war years."

Three years later, noted gossip columnist Walter Winchell speculated on air that the recently divorced neurosurgeon would now marry General Patton's widow. A furious Beatrice was besieged by phone calls, and Spurling demanded "an unqualified denial . . . In fairness to a splendid woman I am sure that you will want to help correct the embarrassment you have caused her and me by a suitable retraction."[171]

Less than a month shy of turning sixty, Beatrice never considered remarrying. Her "only sweetheart" was the one immortalized in the portrait that was supposed to have been her Christmas gift.[172] Boleslaw Jan Czedekowski was a Polish artist who tried to make ends meet by offering his services to prominent officers living in Europe, and he began painting General Patton in May 1945. Beatrice was moved by the vividness and expressiveness of his work; often so elusive to others, Czedekowski managed to capture the essence of George Patton.[173]

When she looked at the whole, she saw General George S. Patton Jr., the persona of the consummate officer who was temperamental, impatient, and disciplined. When she focused on his face, she saw Georgie as only she ever knew him: sensitive, kind, and loyal. Not a trace of his wartime scowl was visible, and his eyes conveyed both strength and sadness. She would take the painting to Green Meadows, where it remained until June 1999, when George IV donated it to the National Portrait Gallery in Washington.

*Figure 88. George Smith Patton Jr. by Boleslaw Jan Czedekowski. (National Portrait Gallery)*

GENERAL PATTON LAY in state in the living room of Villa Reiner for a day-and-a-half, high atop Castle Hill overlooking the Neckar River and the university town of Heidelberg. Two MPs stood guard day and night around the flag-draped coffin, surrounded by the General's command flags and an abundance of flowers flown in from the Riviera. Keyes did his best to get as many as possible because Beatrice believed a funeral without flowers "is terrible."[174] Officers, soldiers, and civilians paid their respects by the thousands, but no family members were expected to arrive from the States. It was a decision that still brought tears to Ruth Ellen's eyes almost fifty years later and filled George IV with regret.

With just one full day between George's passing and his interment, Johnnie Waters told reporters, "At this late hour, we know of no possible way" to get to Germany in time.[175] However, Bee, Ruth Ellen, and George IV knew it would have been entirely possible to get there—their father completed the trip in less than twenty-four hours just six months earlier—but their mother didn't want them there. Beatrice didn't tell them explicitly not to come, but as grandson Robert Patton wrote, "The funeral was Beatrice's last moment with Georgie."[176] George S. Patton Jr. always came first to Beatrice, and Bee, Ruth Ellen, and George IV were always understanding.

It was 2 p.m. on December 23 when five MPs and Master Sergeant Meeks placed the flag-draped steel casket of General George S. Patton Jr. onto a half-track. The streets leading to Christ Episcopal Church were lined with thousands of mourners; not only a cordon of guards from the Seventh Army who presented their rifles in salute but also many German civilians who took off their hats as the cortege passed.

It was as George imagined it forty-one-years earlier as he struggled through West Point, doubting he would ever have the persistence to make something of himself, but thinking it "worth going in the army just to get a military funeral," hoping "to get killed in a great victory and then have my body born between the ranks of my defeated enemy escorted by my own regiment and have my spirit come down and revil in hearing what people thought of me."[177]

A hush fell over the mourners when the casket was brought into Christ Church, but everyone's eyes were glued on Beatrice, who followed behind. A reporter for the *Boston Globe* described her entering "in black with a grayish sheared beaver fur coat one minute before 3 o'clock. Her frail figure was erect but seemed still slimmer than usual; her face was pale and motionless, empty, worn out." As per Beatrice's wishes, there were no eulogies, neither at Christ Church nor at the gravesite, and the choir sang only two psalms selected by her, "The Strife is Over" and "The Son of God Goes Forth to War." Beatrice did not cry during the twenty-minute service, "but her silence was more heart-breaking than any outburst of grief could have been."[178]

*Figure 89. General Geoffrey Keyes and Mrs. Patton head the procession following the casket as it leaves the Luxembourg train station on December 24, 1945. Fred Ayer and Hap Gay walk behind them. (National Archives)*

Leaving the church on her brother's arm, Beatrice took her place in a black car for the drive to the Heidelberg train station a mile away. Up front were the eighty-eight men of the 84th Infantry Division band who played three movements of Chopin's "Funeral March," followed by seventeen armored cars of the 15th Cavalry Division and the banners of George's three armies (the Third, Seventh, and Fifteenth). Eleven generals walked behind the half-track bearing George's body, including General McNarney, whose train was waiting at the station for the 240-mile journey to Luxembourg. Beatrice's eyes filled with tears watching the casket being loaded onto the first train car under the barrage of a 17-gun salute from a 105 mm cannon and the playing of "Taps." When the train pulled out of the station at precisely 4:20 p.m., Beatrice and her brother were seated in the last train car for the thirteen-hour ride.[179]

Fred was in total admiration of his sister as she stepped out on the train's platform at every stop no matter the hour and "made a short speech in French, thanking the troops for their tribute to George."[180] White-turbaned Algerian troops, playing the traditional French "Sonnerie aux Morts," were waiting in Mainz when the train pulled into the station at 6:52 p.m., a showing of respect repeated at Saarbrücken, Metz, and Thionville.[181] People came to pay their respects to Mrs. Patton while the train was in motion. General Truscott, a longtime friend, needn't have worried Beatrice would hold his replacing General Patton as commander of the Third Army against him. When she immediately offered him both her hands as he entered her train car, Truscott was so overcome with emotion that he threw his arms around her and burst into tears.[182]

The rain finally stopped when the train arrived in Luxembourg at 5:30 a.m. on December 24. The procession to Hamm Cemetery, passing a mere two blocks from George's command post during the Battle of the Bulge, consisted of a motorcycle escort, twenty-one French armored cars, seventeen American jeeps, five American armored cars, a half-track bearing George's body, and several black limousines with dignitaries from eleven nations. The citizens of Luxembourg walked the four miles behind the funeral procession in respect to their "liberator," many of them returning to town to attend the simultaneous memorial service organized by Crown Prince Felix at the Cathédrale Notre-Dame.

A cold wind blew across the cemetery when the funeral procession arrived. Waiting to help Beatrice from the car was General Houdemon, whom she remembered fondly from those evenings in Saumur in 1913. Despite needing two canes to walk, the sixty-year-old general came to say goodbye to his "oldest and dearest friend in good times and in bad."[183]

Six hundred soldiers of the Third Army lined the path from the cemetery's entrance to grave No. 7934, dug the day before by a group of Germans and located next to Private John Przywara from Detroit, killed on the first day of the Battle of the Bulge.[184] At the head of this final procession was the riderless horse with George's boots, as shiny as ever, balancing backward in the inverted stirrups.

This traditional representation of a fallen commander looking back one last time was too much for Beatrice. She had to turn her head away as she walked toward the gravesite, the ground as muddy and wet as it had been during the Battle of the Bulge. Still, the flower arrangements were so copious they covered an area thirty feet long and four feet high. Ironically, the biggest wreath came from the Russian delegation.[185]

An eyewitness described Beatrice standing by the open grave, gripping "General Keyes' left arm with her right hand. Her eyes were glued to the casket, every muscle in her ash-pale face worked, she grit her teeth fighting the tears."[186] The ceremony was short, and only once did Beatrice briefly lose control, when she repeated the words of the Lord's Prayer. No one, however, could fail to notice how her shoulders heaved with each shot of the 17-gun salute. Finally, a lone bugler sounded "Taps" and the flag covering the casket was taken off and folded into the traditional three-cornered shape.[187] Master Sergeant Meeks handed it to Beatrice and saluted her, their misty eyes meeting for a brief moment, "exchanging a final message of condolence."[188]

**Figure 90.** *"What then of death?" George wrote in his West Point notebook at barely twenty. "Is not the Taps of death but first call to the reveille of eternal life." (National Archives)*

CADET PATTON'S "props were knocked right out from under him" when his father died.[189] He was just another face in the crowd on the ferry from Weehawken to Manhattan, but he always remembered, with a "melancholic clarity," the moment he saw the *New York Times* headline, "General Patton Dies in Sleep."[190] Bee and Ruth Ellen were waiting in the capital to pick him up at Union Station, and now four days later, they all stood waiting on the snow-covered tarmac at Washington Airport when the Air Transport Command from Paris landed at 1:30 p.m. on December 25th.

Beatrice had been intent on leaving Europe as fast as possible so she could be home for Christmas. As soon as she determinedly walked away from the gravesite with George's flag tightly clutched under her arm, she and Fred made their way from Hamm to Orly Field near Paris. They were met at the airport by General Walton "Bulldog" Walker, George's protégé and a close friend whom Eisenhower asked to represent him at the funeral. While Walker managed to land in Paris at 4 a.m. on December 24, fog prevented him from landing in Luxembourg, despite flying "all over Europe for six hours." He missed the funeral—the story goes his plane flew over the gravesite during the ceremony and dipped its wing—but at least he got to offer Beatrice his condolences before she and Fred left on the 3:50 p.m. flight to Washington.[191]

Fortunately, they could join a regular ATC, and the return trip took just over twenty-four hours. After a brief stop in Boston to drop off Fred, Beatrice continued to Washington with her two official escorts: Colonel Paul Harkins and Captain William Duane Jr. The plane was forced to land at La Guardia for an unscheduled two-hour layover, but Beatrice greeted all the ATC officers with a "Merry Christmas, boys" as she made her way to the officers' terminal. Her cheery friendliness contrasted sharply with her black mourning clothes, but Beatrice was not someone who easily showed her emotions.[192]

Except for a photographer who snapped a picture of George IV helping a grief-stricken Beatrice down from the plane, the Pattons ignored the press. They immediately left for Bee's home, where the four grandchildren and Christmas dinner were waiting.[193] Christmas was nothing like what she had imagined it would be seventeen days ago, but Beatrice was adamant about celebrating that evening. She did it for the grandchildren and for the same reason Ruth Ellen insisted on celebrating George IV's twenty-second birthday the day before.

Beatrice had learned to carry on valiantly from her mother. Overwhelmed with grief and desperately ill when Frederick died in 1918, Ellie had dressed up with flowers in her hair and given each granddaughter a small gift. Beatrice now acted her part for her grandchildren's sake and helped them open the gifts she brought with her from Germany, including the typical Bavarian costumes George had custom-made for his son and daughters.

After her grandchildren went to bed, a composed Beatrice told her family about George's last days and subsequent funeral. She might have appeared diminutive next to her rugged husband, but she was always the rock in the family. According to Ruth Ellen, her mother was "a very, very tough woman, totally strong but sentimental." Bee wrote her that she wasn't "good at saying stuff—but Ma, you have given all of us something to shoot at. You are as magnificent in adversity as you are in success," and George IV considered his mother "the swellest person in the whole wide world . . . Really you are wonderful which all goes to prove that 'when the chips are down Patton is at its best'—Thumbs up!"[194]

Going through George's diary one day, Beatrice came across his entry from August 10, 1945. That day he felt as if his usefulness to the world had ended, and there was only one thing left for him to do, "sit around and await the arrival of the undertaker and posthumous immortality."[195] Posthumous immortality would indeed come, especially with Beatrice's dedication, which remained as strong in death as it had been in life. She helped shape George, the man and the officer; now, she would create General Patton, the legend.

# 13

## WHEN AND IF

### MARBLEHEAD, MASSACHUSETTS

#### 1946–1953

*WE WOULD BE SPARED THE PAIN OF MISUNDERSTANDING IF WE REALIZED THAT THERE IS NO [MORE] LIMIT TO TRUE UNDERSTANDING THAN THERE IS TO LIGHT, FOR BOTH HAVE NO POINT OF STARTING, NO END TO DEVELOPMENT, AND BOTH ILLUMINATE ALL; LIGHT ILLUMINATES THE DARK PLACES OF THE WORLD, AND UNDERSTANDING ILLUMINATES THE DARK PLACES OF THE SPIRIT.*

On November 5, 1950, the Spanish Riding School and its Lipizzaners were the special guests of the 62nd National Horse Show at Madison Square Garden, a New York tradition in which the Pattons had been enthusiastic participants for many years. Born dark but turning their distinctive gray color—which might be considered white by a layman—between the ages of four and ten, the Lipizzaners were first brought from Spain to a stud farm in Lipizza (in modern-day Slovenia) by Archduke Karl Hapsburg at the end of the sixteenth century. Three hundred and seventy years later, the stallions were visiting America to raise money to ensure the survival of the art of classical riding, first established in 400 BC by the Greek military genius Xenophon.

After the Lipizzaners wowed the audience with their caprioles, levades, and courbettes—balancing on their hind legs and leaping into the air—the lights dimmed across Madison Square Garden, and the fourteen stallions pulled abreast. Colonel Podhajsky, the school's director, rode forward on Pluto, a magnificent gray stallion who years earlier had "cowered under a hail of bombs in Vienna under siege ... and stood without panicking during the horror of an unsheltered air raid outside a train station."[1]

A red carpet was unrolled, and General Tuckerman, the director of the National Horse Show, walked out with Mrs. Patton, who wore a floor-length evening gown and carried a bouquet of red roses. A single spotlight followed Col. Podhajsky as he dismounted Pluto and approached Mrs. Patton, "I am very happy to be able to show you the horses that General Patton, a great American soldier, saved for Austria." Beatrice took a single rose from her bouquet and handed it to Col. Podhajsky as flashbulbs lit up the darkened Garden, "I would give anything if only my husband could be standing here instead of me, for he loved the Lipizzaner so much."[2]

Beatrice, however, knew George found it "rather peculiar" that "twenty middle-aged men in perfect physical condition, and about an equal number of grooms, had spent their time teaching horses tricks" while the world was "tearing itself apart in war." George's role in saving the Lipizzaners from extinction at the hands of the Russians consisted of approving a plan for the Third Army to help rescue hundreds of mares from a Nazi stud farm in Czechoslovakia.[3] To thank General Patton and his men for their help, Col. Podhajsky gave a riding exhibition on May 7, 1945, at Sankt Martin, Austria. "As much as I like horses," George wrote in his diary that evening, "it seems to me there is a place for everything."[4]

Five years after General Patton's death, and to the relief of many, Beatrice was still one of the few privy to his private musings. For months, Fred and Keith came to Green Meadows to help organize George's papers, night after night transcribing his letters and diaries, annotating them to aid future researchers once Beatrice found a suitable institution to donate them to. In the meantime, they looked for a suitable biographer, eventually settling on Douglas Southall Freeman, whom George "held in honor as the greatest military biographer of our time."[5]

George's legacy filled Beatrice with a sense of purpose. She took on many of the roles he would have taken on himself had he lived, ensuring the world would never forget the sacrifices he and his armies had made. She continued to give him "a full and unqualified respect glinting with steel truth." And whenever she spoke of him, her voice held "a sure, unshredded thread of confidence and devotion, the kind you could hang onto if life and death were at stake."[6]

GEORGE S. PATTON IV—WHO would soon legally change his name to George S. Patton—towered more than a head over his mother as he escorted her into Washington Cathedral on January 20, 1946. Beatrice, however, was a formidable woman, and her size belied her strength. She had herself well in hand when she took a seat in the front pew next to her children, grandchildren, and sons-in-law, preferring to keep her grief private, the tears running "down behind my eyes."[7]

Over fifteen hundred mourners attended General Patton's memorial service that snowy Sunday afternoon, including generals, politicians, and hundreds of privates who had fought in the Third Army.[8] Longtime friend and colleague, Colonel (later Brigadier General) Harry Semmes, gave the brief eulogy at Beatrice's request.

Harry painted a picture of General Patton, "our friend, the man ... the soldier ... [and] the symbol of America." His was "a full life dangerously lived," marked by so much unbounded energy that it was a relief to many that he didn't have to spend the rest of his life in a wheelchair.[9] As Albert Kenner wrote to a mutual friend, George "was too grand an old soldier for that sort of life."[10]

Knowing that he "never liked to watch any athletic competition" but "always wanted to be right in it, even when he isn't champ," Beatrice felt that "it was a good thing he didn't have to live as he was."[11] She made her feelings abundantly clear in a letter to General Harbord on January 5, 1946,

> It is so hard to write what one would like to say. Georgie tried hard to live, but he just couldn't make it. His paralysis never really improved, but he never spoke to me of dying—only of coming home. No one would have wanted to have him live a cripple, especially we who loved him best; but why he should have had such a strange accident, with no one else hurt, is impossible to understand. He had planned to continue to work for his country, whether he retired or not, and it seems to me that he still had so much to give when Fate struck him down. I guess the only things really worth praying for are kindness and fortitude and understanding. And if we could have understanding, the others would follow.[12]

The notion "that such a warrior should die in such a routine fashion," was one that many people grappled with and partly contributed to the enduring belief that General Patton had been assassinated.[13] There were many baseless reasons why the idea took root—from a missing accident report to a rumor that Technician Fifth Grade Thompson was intoxicated after a night out—but the Patton family never subscribed to any of the conspiracy theories. Beatrice was satisfied with the Army's conclusion that no foul play was involved. Still, as time progressed, she "got so irritated by people claiming that he had been murdered" that she conducted her own investigation. The report confirmed what she already knew: General Patton died of natural causes, and his death was nothing more than "an incredible irony."[14]

Bee, Ruth Ellen, and George IV were spoon-fed by their father the belief that he was going to die and be buried on foreign soil, and "his conditioning of us since childhood in the inevitability, and the acceptability, of death kept us from a feeling of total loss, which is the lot of some." Ruth Ellen believed death was a blessing for her father, "Both on a personal level and certainly on a historical level, God did him a favor by taking him away in 1945."[15]

"It was terribly sad that it happened," George IV wrote in reply to General Harbord's condolences, "and I didn't think I'd ever get over it. However, I have for the most part. He had a great, full life and the only bad thing about his death, as far as he was concerned, was that he deserved a rest which he probably would have been opposed to. I and my family were the losers on the deal and he was not. Of that I am very glad."[16]

THE TOWN of South Hamilton was plunged into gloom by the death of General Patton. As soon as the news reached Green Meadows, a weeping employee ran outside through the snow and lowered the flag to half-staff while Carmichael, the family's shepherd, dashed into the stable to sit by the trusty Konohiki.[17] A memorial service was held in an overcrowded St. John's Episcopal Church on December 30, 1945. With Beatrice still in Washington, Fred represented his sister and accepted the condolences of the North Shore community and the extended Ayer clan.

In addition to a wife who supported him unconditionally, George had been blessed with in-laws who always had his back no matter the scandal. "All I can say is that Uncle Sam is the meanest man I know to work for," a "disgusted and discouraged" Fred had written upon George's dismissal from the Third Army, "and you know what the public is."[18] The eighty-year-old Chilly—who had lost his wife Theodora in January 1945—best described the family's feelings in a letter of condolences to Ruth Ellen, "I admired, loved, & revered him [George] & his death leaves me very sad & depressed. He was a grand person & is a great loss to the whole country. I shall always miss him terribly."[19]

Beatrice returned to Green Meadows at the end of January 1946, faced with the almost impossible task of organizing George's papers and possessions. It was a task the Pattons would have tackled as a team, especially since Beatrice had wanted her husband "to sit down and continue writing about tactics and strategy." Called "one of the very rare men of action that was capable of expressing himself on paper," George was a prolific writer who kept a diary with an eye on history. If he reached his destiny, he knew people would study him just as he studied those before him.

Beatrice had always saved even the tiniest scrap of paper that had anything to do with her husband, but one day Ruth Ellen saw her mother emerge from the library with tears running down her cheeks. Aware that people would always be interested in General Patton, she had burned some of his most intimate letters because "there are some things that were just between your father and myself . . . I made up my mind that I didn't need to keep the letters because what was written in them is written in my heart."[20]

One letter she did keep for posterity was the one George gave Fred for safekeeping in October 1942. "Darling Beatrice,"

> When Fred gives you this I will be definitely dead. Yet even from that position I find it impossible to tell you how much you have meant to me. Since we were 16 we have been as one most of the time. When we were not it was my fault. In the past few weeks before I sailed for Africa only you understood the strain I was under. Your confidence in me was the only sure thing in a world of dreadful uncertainty. With your help I have convinced thousands of success when in my own mind I cannot see how it will be accomplished. If we landed safely, yours was the victory. I love you with all my heart and hope. George for ever[21]

George was right when he said one "shouldn't feel bad for the person who dies, but for those who stay behind." The letters he wrote in the days before his accident arrived at Green Meadows like messages from the grave, and Beatrice discovered an undeveloped film in his Leica camera. Ever since their first separation at Fort Sheridan, George had shared his life with Beatrice through pictures. He sent her hundreds of rolls throughout the war, asking her to have them developed at the local trustworthy mom-and-pop shop, and then sent back copies for him to annotate. The last picture Beatrice pasted in one of her giant scrapbooks was of a stunt driver performing tricks on a motorcycle, taken in Sweden at the end of November.

Beatrice kept up "an appearance of good cheer and Yankee perseverance," but the words in her thought book spoke volumes, "The star is gone . . . the accompanist is left behind." Their years of separation did not prepare her for the loss she felt. She could always count on a letter, phone call, or radio message, but now there was nothing except the reminiscences of family, friends, and strangers. When she stripped the ribbons of his uniforms to have the clothes refitted for George IV, she wondered why "a beloved one's clothes mean so much? The creases of his body in a coat—and where his legs bend at the groin—it always seems that I must write you what is passing."[22]

Emma Ahuena Taylor once told Beatrice that her husband Albert remained a presence in her life even after he had passed away. She would wake up in the middle of the night to find him staring at her, but she refused to speak to him, worried she would die if she did.[23] Beatrice had no such fears and wanted nothing more than to talk to George, but she could only address the entries in her thought book to him. This was in stark contrast to her daughters, who played Ouija, "and it always says 'Take care of B—Big B.' I [Beatrice] could never work it. They may be psychic, being of your blood—I am only your lover—I don't even dream of you at night, and how I wish I could. Perhaps someday."[24]

Unlike her daughters and husband, Beatrice did not possess the gift of "second sight." Ruth Ellen always maintained that she and her sister were visited by their father on the day he died. She awoke in the night to find him standing by her bedside, dressed in full uniform. When he nodded and smiled at her, she "felt as if some burden had been lifted." Bee had a similar experience, except she received a long-distance phone call, easily identifiable by the buzzing sound on the line. When she checked with the operator, he told her she hadn't received any calls all night.

Beatrice resigned herself years ago to George dying in battle, but his tragic accident was much harder to accept. "He had the finest care . . . ," she wrote a friend in March 1946, "but why he must be taken is past understanding."[25] Her sister Ellen Wood was one of the people who tried to answer that question, and "every word of loving kindness" was a great help. The eighty-six-year-old knew a thing or two about loss; before her husband committed suicide in 1926, Ellen had already lost her daughter Irene and son William Jr. She tried communicating with her children through mediums, but her "Ayer common sense" was stronger than her grief. Despite her efforts to debunk mediums and spiritualists, she always remained friends with Leonora Piper, a blind trance medium who lived in Boston with her daughter Minerva.

Beatrice knew all the tricks of the trade as she often read palms to raise money for the Army at county fairs, and she only reluctantly handed over one of George's gloves and a few of his letters. After years of steeping herself in the culture of Native Hawaii and George teaching her that "there is no death, only change," Beatrice didn't doubt the afterlife, but the power of mediums scared her. When her parents died in 1918, Ellen Wood had suggested a visit to a medium might bring her sister some solace. Beatrice ran when the medium hummed an obscure Irish melody her mother used to sing and wrote the words "Fredk Ayer" on a piece of paper in a shaky scribble that eerily resembled her father's handwriting. Too scared to find out what would happen next, she merely mailed the medium a check for services rendered.

On the other hand, Leonora practiced trance mediumship, whereby intense focus on her part allowed a spirit to talk through her. Beatrice received three letters, a jumbled mess of thoughts and recollections, which she couldn't finish reading. Instead of being comforted, she "felt uncomfortable by the unknown." Taken aback by her mother's reluctance, Ruth Ellen felt more open to the experience and read all three eerily accurate letters. Maybe Ellen unwittingly talked about the Pattons during one of her weekly lunches with Leonora, because few people knew that Beatrice was known as Big Bee. Nor did strangers know that George, having grown up in California, often said adios instead of goodbye and always gave his wife a quick pat on the cheek or the top of her head when he walked by her.[26]

RUTH ELLEN REMEMBERED her mother being "somehow diminished, as if she had lost a part of herself" when she returned from Germany, but Beatrice was determined "to carry on with the old army spirit."[27] So on April 4—the same day it was announced that the Cavalry and Armored Forces would henceforth be one—three thousand people attended the unveiling of Fort Riley's Patton Hall, including Secretary of War Patterson, Little Bee, Ruth Ellen, and Master Sergeant Meeks. He was flown from Rome for the occasion, having been the orderly of Lieutenant General John Lee—commander of the American Forces in the Mediterranean—since George's passing. Devastated by the loss of the greatest man he had ever known, Meeks almost couldn't bear to watch the unveiling "because every time they mentioned the General's name it reminded me that I won't be seeing him again."[28]

**Figure 91.** *Family members at the unveiling of Patton Hall on April 4, 1946: Kay, unidentified, unidentified, Nita, Ruth Ellen, Bee, and Johnnie. (Library of Congress)*

"This is a place of happy memories," Beatrice began her nationally broadcast speech.

In our 35 years of active service in the Army, Fort Riley has been the post nearest our hearts. There is not a corner of the reservation that we Pattons do not know and love. That the first Patton Memorial should be dedicated here is not a coincidence, for whether it is mounted on horses or on vehicles, the Cavalry points the way.

I once asked my husband what he considered the qualities most vital to a successful officer and he answered—imagination, unselfishness, and courage, in that order. Imagination—to picture the situation in all its possibilities. Unselfishness—to bind his men to him by giving each one the credit for his work. Courage—to assume responsibility, not only for himself but for the men under him. His whole life was spent in developing these qualities, pursuing every line of action that contributed to intrepidity and quickness of thought.

When we rode out on the Kansas prairie, he was disposing of imaginary troops in the folds of the hills. In Hawaii, we made landings on beaches where the surveys told us landings were impossible. In France, in 1913, we reconnoitered every hill and hedgerow in Brittany and Normandy. And in Virginia, in 1935, we staged a very famous fox hunt. For the last day of the season, three generals sent word that they were coming down to hunt with us. We called on a local farmer and told him that we would hunt the best piece of our country that day.

"But, Colonel, there aren't any foxes there," the farmer told my husband.

"Well," said my husband, "that's where you come in. You have a mind more like a fox than anyone I know. Take a bag of fox litter and drag it exactly where you would go if you were the fox." That day we had the greatest fox hunt that was ever had at Cobbler.

Imagination is as contagious as prairie fire. One man, who had been following hounds for years, actually saw the fox. If we were still hunting, I should never tell you this story. We might want to use the trick again.

I have been told that my husband's strategy—I use the word strategy advisedly—could not be taught because it depended on personal leadership. This is not true, as the men of his ever victorious armies will testify. His strategy, as fresh as bread, was as old as war. Four little words define it: Imagination—what would I do if I were the enemy? Reconnaissance—where is he weak, for it is there I shall strike him. Audacity—keep him off balance and keep him rocking. Pursuit—keep him off balance, keep him rocking, run him down.

All these are Cavalry functions and will be taught here in Patton Hall, the home of the modern incarnation of the spirit of the Cavalry—going ever forward.[29]

**Figures 92 and 93.** *Beatrice addressing the crowd at the unveiling of Fort Riley's Patton Hall. (Library of Congress)*

LESS THAN THREE weeks after George's passing, the Ayer family was hit with another tragedy. On January 8, 1946, the NYPD received a phone call from a concerned resident at 157 East 52nd Street who smelled gas on the tenth floor. Apartment 10C belonged to a Miss Taylor, but she was visiting relatives in Connecticut, and a friend was staying at her place for a few nights. When police entered the apartment at 1:45 a.m., they found four open gas burners and Jean Gordon unconscious on the kitchen floor in her nightgown. The EMTs worked on her for an hour but were unable to revive her; Jean Gordon had taken her own life just days short of her thirty-first birthday. Beatrice became "a tower of strength" to her sister Louise Gordon Hatheway, who attributed her daughter's suicide to a "sudden impulse." When she left the ETO on October 29, 1945, Jean was possibly "suffering from war nerves," and grew increasingly depressed.[30]

Jean Gordon's suicide remains shrouded in mystery, clouded by a handful of unsubstantiated rumors. Some claimed she had fallen in love with a married captain in the Fourth Armored Division who summarily returned to his family once the war ended, while others believed she was obsessed with her uncle and devastated by his death. Decades later, Beatrice was accused of putting a curse on Jean in a Boston hotel room sometime during the two weeks between her return from Heidelberg and her niece's suicide. There has never been any evidence that Beatrice left Washington between Christmas and the end of January, making it pretty much impossible for her to curse her niece with the following words: "May the Great Worm gnaw your vitals and may your bones rot joint by little joint."[31]

The Native Hawaiians were firm believers in the power of prayers, addressing them "to a great number and diversity of gods and [covering] a wide range of subjects." The kahuna was a witch doctor who specialized in prayers that caused someone's death or sought protection from said practice. He delivered his prayer on his hands and knees, in one uninterrupted breath and surrounded by complete silence.[32] Emma Ahuena Taylor introduced her friend to a kahuna's Book of Prayers, and Beatrice filled her notebooks with many Ka Anaana that cause death by sorcery. The one she supposedly put on Jean was published posthumously in *Love Without End* by a Hawaiian friend, and accessible to anyone looking for a good story. "Needless to say," Beatrice wrote, "both these prayers are incomplete and are therefore useless to anyone [who] would try to use them to invoke harm."[33]

Beatrice forgave George's 1936 Hawaiian indiscretion and attributed it to the follies of a middle-aged man, but she never forgot what happened. When she learned in the summer of 1944 that Jean was going to France to be a Red Cross doughnut girl in the Third Army, she summarily informed George. He quickly replied to his irate wife not to worry, "We are in the middle of a battle so don't meet people."[34] However, three weeks after the Third Army began its spectacular dash across France, he had returned to camp to find "a flock of Red Cross doughnut girls descended on us."[35] After long days of delivering coffee and doughnuts to Third Army combat units, it was a pleasant change of pace for the doughnut girls to be invited to HQ for an entertaining evening with Jean's "Uncle Georgie."

When biographer David Irving (who turned out to be a Holocaust denier) claimed in his 1981 book, *The War of the Generals,* that General Patton "was a ceaseless womanizer who lived in dread of his wife's finding out about him and Jean Gordon," the Patton family was enraged. "Jean Gordon was my best friend," Ruth Ellen told the *Boston Globe.* "Her father died when she was seven. She was bridesmaid at my wedding and at my sister's wedding. She was one of the family. Daddy looked upon her as one of his own daughters. To accuse him of having an affair with Jean is a disgusting lie."

Irving based his claim on the unintelligible diaries of General Everett Hughes, "a thoughtful friend" of the Pattons whose frequent letters during the war allowed Beatrice to create "a perfect picture in my mind's eye" of George.[36] However, one has to question the sincerity of a man who wrote that Beatrice "will never know how many people were involved and how many involved details had to be worked out to get the old soldier under ground into his cement encased tomb where the Luxemburgers won't have as much trouble looking after him as Ike and I have had."[37]

Beatrice later noted in the margins of one of George's letters: "Everett Hughes was a good friend, but with divided loyalties, since he was Eisenhower's Deputy, and, I think, reported things to E. which had been better left unsaid."[38] Hughes was known to be "a notorious and unreliable gossip," noting on July 9, 1944, that George had told him, "She's [Jean] been mine for twelve years."[39] The relationship between George Patton and Jean Gordon was close, but it is by no means certain that it was anything more than companionship during WWII. Prone to exaggeration when telling stories, George might have been boasting like a schoolboy since everyone in the ETO seemed to be having an affair, from Hughes up to Eisenhower. According to Ruth Ellen, her father "kept a watchful eye on Jean, as he would on any member of his family. But to say or imply that Daddy had been sleeping with Jean Gordon for twelve years and that she joined him to continue the affair—that's hogwash."[40]

Betty South was the captain of the Red Cross doughnut crew attached to the Third Army and a close friend of Jean. She could tell that it was "a happiness for General Patton to have a member of the family with him. She [Jean] understood and loved him." They often spoke French together and shared an interest in horses, sailing, and history. "In the rather austere and lonely life he led during the war," Betty recalled, "she was a bright, warm touch, a feminine touch I am sure he needed and appreciated."[41] It was exactly that which Beatrice had wanted to provide herself.

What galled her most about Jean's presence with the Third Army was not the traditional jealousy of a wife whose husband spends time in the company of a younger woman, but a fit of anger that her niece was able to be by George's side at the moment he reached his destiny while she could only read about it in the papers. Desperate to "pick up the sword" but unable to join George in France during WWI, Beatrice found herself stateside once again during WWII, the culmination of all husband and wife had worked toward for over three decades. Beatrice did a magnificent job representing the War Department and keeping her family together, but the dream of standing next to General Patton and sharing his glory eluded her once again.

DESPITE "CHRONIC POSTWAR PERIODS OF CENSURE," Secretary of War Robert Patterson told the 875 graduates of the Class of 1946 to be proud of their new leadership roles as second lieutenants in the Regular Army.[42] On June 4, 1946, he handed out diplomas to the largest graduating class in the U.S. Military Academy's history—including sons of two admirals and twenty-one generals —but he stepped aside when Cadet Patton's name was called. Invited to sit on stage and partake of an honor that should have been her husband's, a beaming Beatrice handed her son his commission in the Infantry.[43] West Point had been a struggle for George IV, but she knew it built up his confidence. He was already "a real man" when he entered, albeit a little "young for his age," and now he would make "a splendid officer" like his father.[44]

Beatrice made it her goal to honor George's wish upon their son's graduation. He had planned to get "you [George IV] and your mother over and, after securing an open car, drive from Avranches to Bad Tolz—provided I can get past the fifteen cities en route of which I am citoyen d'honneur."[45] So, with the help of Generals Gay and Keyes, she prepared "a short pilgrimage" with veterans of the Third Army as their escort.[46]

Mother and son arrived in Paris two years to the day since D-Day, and they were joined by General Gay and Lieutenant Colonel James Hayes, a battalion commander of the 80th Division who came highly recommended by General Keyes. Beatrice also took a copy of the unpublished War as I Knew It, which made for "gripping reading on the very terrain."[47] The foursome began their battlefield tour in Néhou, the Third Army's HQ in July 1944. They followed the route of the Third Army through France and into Germany, ending up at Nuremberg, where they attended part of the Nuremberg Trials.

Hayes loved listening to Beatrice's stories of her trips through France with George in 1912 and 1913, driving along the same ancient Roman roads they were now traveling. It dawned on him how crucial military history was to General Patton, and suddenly many of his former commander's decisions made a lot more sense.[48] Just seven months after his death, only George's closest staff knew history was the driving force behind almost everything he did. Beatrice was often asked "how he 'guessed' so luckily," but what often looked like folly, she knew to be a decision based on profound reasoning and a dash of audacity.[49]

George IV could only marvel at his mother's composure during the trip. After retracing the Battle of the Bulge, they ended their tour in Luxembourg with a visit to General Patton's gravesite at the Luxembourg American Cemetery. Since Beatrice was already at Orly Field by the time the casket had been lowered, it was for her too the first time visiting George's grave. His final resting place lay amid a sea of white markers, bare except for the deceased's name and serial number, and surrounded by flowers.

George couldn't have been more wrong in 1945 when he told Beatrice that "soldiers are forgotten pretty quickly."[50] In every city the Pattons passed through, people welcomed them as if the General were with them. Grand Duchess Charlotte and her husband welcomed Beatrice and George IV to the Luxembourg palace and promised to take care of the General's grave in perpetuity. If ever there were any problems, the Grand Duchess even offered to have him reburied in the national cathedral.

*Figure 94. Beatrice, third from the left, visiting Casablanca in 1949 with her sister Kay, second from the left. (Library of Congress)*

Second Lieutenant Patton's first posting upon his return in July was to Fort Benning, where Beatrice watched him "take his final paratroop jump . . . and receive his insignia."[51] Once he transferred to Germany in the summer of 1947, she often visited, having herself become "a national figure" in Europe.[52] Almost every town General Patton had passed through named streets after him or erected monuments. The most remarkable was the Liberty Road, dedicated in September 1947. At each kilometer along the route the Third Army followed from Utah Beach to Bastogne, a marker (1146 in total) stands to symbolize liberty and the boundless gratitude of the French.

With acquaintances across the globe, Beatrice was never without an invitation. She traveled extensively but always returned to Green Meadows for "a shakedown so as not to become permanently loose-footed."[53]

One of her most memorable visits was to Moscow, which she described in a letter to a friend,

I visited Gen. & Mrs. Grow (he is our military attaché) and though I was there only 48 hours, I saw nearly everything it was possible to see, because it is so restricted. One of the sights was Lenin's [?]. He looks like something from Madame Tussaud's and quite insignificant, considering the trouble he has made for the world. It is said that they give him periodic shots of paraffin to keep him filled out. The churches, now stripped and ticketed 'museum,' are fantastic.[54]

BEFORE GENERAL PATTON even drew his last breath, rumors had begun circulating in Washington regarding what Drew Pearson called "one of the hottest of Patton's hot potatoes."[55] Purported to be filled with "frank comments about the Allies and even about his superior officers," General Patton's diary was also said to contain "the real reason" for curtailing his dash across France and "the manner in which he crossed the Rhine."

The War Department frowned upon its publication and asked Beatrice to keep his papers private. In contrast, others reminded her that "history is entitled to access when the record is kept by one of such rank and eminence as the General."[56] As General Harbord explained to an interested party in January 1946, "She is very wealthy and publication of the manuscript will mean nothing to her in the sense that it would to someone who needs the money, and I have an idea she will take her own good time about making a decision."[57]

The great tragedy of George's untimely death was that he never got to tell his side of the story like many of his wartime contemporaries—which to some might have been a good thing. However, Beatrice was determined to be his voice; she had been fiercely protective of her husband, and she would be even more protective of his legacy. She decided early on that his papers contained too much sensitive material to be released in full so soon, but she was adamant about publishing *War as I Knew It*.

George had just finished dictating the last and most important chapter in the days before his accident—"Earning My Pay" described the "occasions in which my personal intervention had some value"—and discussed his draft with Beatrice while hospitalized.[58] She had all his papers to complete the story, and the help of Colonel Harkins. George's deputy chief of staff advised her on all the details of the Third Army's campaign and supplied the manuscript with invaluable footnotes.

"I am no Lady Burton," Beatrice wrote to General Harbord, "if I do put out anything of Georgie's, I want to do it just as he himself would do it if he were here."[59] She made very few changes to his text so as not to "destroy the style which is inimitably George S. Patton, Jr." The only passages she cut were the ones she knew George would have cut as well because they "do not hurt the story" but "might hurt men he liked." This included the "special treatment for our son-in-law, Waters, when wounded," his account of how General Eddy got drunk, and "Spaatz's remarks on the subject."[60] She also deleted George's reference to *Stars & Stripes* being a "scurrilous rag" but added his candid notes on Morocco and Tunisia to make the book a little longer.[61]

Beatrice kept her plans quiet, hoping to save herself "much persecution."[62] George had been very much aware that the publication of his book would be contentious. When he mailed his son a draft of the first chapter in August 1945, he made it clear that the papers were not to be "left around or shown indiscriminately to your friends. There are many people who would give thousands of dollars to have that paper to publish. If published in the form in which you get it, it would simply make many people unhappy to no purpose."[63] Possessed with "a strong sense of fairness," George wanted his work treated as confidential because he didn't yet "know the other man's side of the story."

Beatrice shared the completed manuscript with Secretary of War Patterson in the spring of 1947 and received his reply sealed in three envelopes. He believed the inclusion of certain critical reflections "would not only be contrary to his [George's] desire, but would lead to bitter controversies and recriminations, a state of affairs that would be altogether unfortunate."

He suggested Beatrice purge those passages concerning George's private feelings toward Field Marshal Montgomery; his belief that Eisenhower caused "the momentous error of the war"; and race prejudice. Since there wouldn't be much left to publish at that point, Patterson proposed releasing *Reflections and Suggestions*—the one uncontroversial chapter—as an essay to be used in training schools.[64]

Military historian Douglas Southall Freeman also had his reservations, but for the exact opposite reason. "You doubtless are wise in saying the diary should not be published until some of the contentious issues have cooled," Freeman wrote Beatrice after meeting with her. "But you have to take into account the virtual certainty that the narrative you sent me will be regarded as 'watered down' and will be received with definite disappointment." However, if Beatrice's "love" and "instinct" told her that "something should be printed now," Freeman suggested she look for a publisher who would emphasize that *War as I Knew It* was "<u>not</u> the full diary."[65]

General Harbord—whom George trusted enough that he shared the first draft of every chapter he wrote—urged Beatrice to publish as soon as possible, thinking *War as I Knew It* "the best war book I have seen, just as I thought George was the best General I have seen."[66] She finally did so in November 1947, acknowledging, "The work of an editor is not easy, especially when that editor is also a wife." Douglas Freeman wrote the book's introduction, and Beatrice chose a passage from John Bunyan's *The Pilgrim's Progress* as its dedication.

The *New York Times* called the book "hastily written." Still, it showed that General Patton "must have been a superb field commander," who was "perfectly willing to sacrifice not only his life but his career and reputation to his duty to his nation's flag."[67] *War As I Knew It* occupied a spot on the *New York Times* bestseller list for sixteen consecutive weeks, but the book was just a decoction of what it could have been had George been able to complete it.

The American public would not get to know General Patton's true character until 1972, with the publication of his complete diaries and correspondence. After many "a knockdown family fight" about whether the contents of the fifty filing cabinets in the basement of Green Meadows should be made public, George's children decided their father's "story had to be preserved as a whole someplace because the jackals have and will continue to drag out the bones."[68]

So they selected military historian Martin Blumenson to catalog the papers and turn them into a two-volume series titled *The Patton Papers*, spanning over a thousand pages. Once Blumenson finished, the Patton family donated all the material to the Library of Congress to be made available for research, hoping it would at least provide a certain context for future historians.

ON THE SURFACE, Beatrice never lost her "enormous zest for living, her interest in everything and everybody under the sun, [and] her innate joyousness." She blossomed when she visited the Tottens at Fort Leavenworth in the winter of 1946, her first extended stay at an army base in over five years. The woman who once contemplated leaving her betrothed because army life was more complicated than she had expected was ecstatic to be on a base again. When old acquaintances weren't showing up on Ruth Ellen's doorstep, Beatrice was out having dinner with friends. Men she had known as children knocked on the door to ask for her advice, and she was more than happy to give them a pep talk, remembering how hard the Command and Staff College was, not only on the soldiers but also on their spouses.

Ruth Ellen turned out to be as stubborn as her mother when it came to having a third baby. James Patton Totten was born by C-section on May 15, 1947, and named Jamie after Beatrice's "dear brother" because the Tottens didn't want another Jim in the family. Once Ruth Ellen recovered from an emergency operation to remove a blood clot, she and her three children moved into Green Meadows for four months while Colonel Jim Totten, the new U.S. Army's Caribbean provost marshal, prepared his family's home in Panama.

Beatrice was a strict disciplinarian, but "she more than made up for it by the fun she helped them [her grandchildren] have." Green Meadows was a magical place for children, and with Beatrice's tremendous imagination, they fought rebels across the lawn and searched for dryads in the woods, her bag stuffed with surprises.[69] She prodigiously read to them—the children's classics that she loved, like *Alice in Wonderland, Kidnapped*, and the *Just So Stories* —sitting on the bed George used for his recovery in 1938.

According to a journalist who interviewed her during WWII, what set Beatrice apart from others was that "so many people are only half alive; so many people go through life wearing blinkers, never getting a glimpse of the broad horizon. They miss so much. This woman [Beatrice] never misses anything. Never refuses anything; packs her days full to the brim . . . with every opportunity for usefulness."[70]

On December 9, 1947, Beatrice left New York on the *S.S. Ancon* for the first of three visits to Panama. She spent the next five months with the Tottens in Quarry Heights, "a most beautiful place—very tropical, hot, and damp, with breathtaking scenery outside and 3 kids and a pet monkey inside."[71] Speaking a mixture of Spanish and French, it took Beatrice only a week to charm everyone at the nearby open-air market. The owner of a local store began carrying her groceries to the car, and she caught the eye of a little monkey, which tugged at her heartstrings until she brought it home.

*Figure 95. Dinner with the 80th Division Veterans Association. (Library of Congress)*

Beatrice also enjoyed perusing the little stalls decked out with local products that women brought from all over the countryside. She fell in love with the molas—a colorful blouse worn by Guna women, the indigenous people of Panama and Colombia—and immediately bought a whole stack to take home to friends and family.

One night when Ruth Ellen organized a party, Beatrice did not turn out to be who the high-profile guests expected. A humble person like her father, who believed possessions "were not the be-all and end-all of life," she just came from the Chinese market, carrying a live chicken under her arm, wearing a scarf around her head, and a molas tucked into her skirt.

On weekends, Beatrice was happy to resume an activity she had enjoyed with George for many years: deep-sea fishing. The Gulf of Panama was easily accessible by boat from the mainland, and filled with thrilling adventures of whales and jumping manta rays. For day trips, the family sailed to Taboga Island, a volcanic island just twenty miles from Panama City and known as the "Island of Flowers."[72]

Overnight trips took them to the Pearl Islands, an archipelago of over two hundred—mostly uninhabited—islands fifty-five miles from the coast. Beatrice brought George's fishing tackle from Green Meadows and managed to catch a record sailfish at some point, but most of all, she enjoyed meeting the guests who joined the Tottens for the weekend.

Ruth Ellen said her mother's "heart was international," and just as in Hawaii, Beatrice became a much-loved figure in the community. When she spent ten days in the hospital with a bout of pneumonia, everyone from the chief surgeon to the cleaners visited her, and she received more flowers and fruit baskets than she could ever enjoy.

People stopped by to tell her stories and they invited her to remote locations of anthropological and archaeological significance. Traveling by canoe up the Charges River in Central Panama and on foot along miles of slippery rock to visit a cave filled with white bats, she was reminded of the ones she had seen as a child near the Temple of Abu Simbel in Egypt.[73]

As Jim spent part of his childhood in Panama—his father, Colonel James Totten, had also been stationed at Quarry Heights—he was able to take his mother-in-law off the beaten path. When he told her of Nombre de Dios—a sixteenth-century port used by the Spanish to transport Peruvian silver—she recognized the name from a Henry Newbolt poem George used to recite to his children.

The governor of the Canal Zone knew how to get to Nombre de Dios, so Beatrice organized an excursion on a tugboat with about forty families from Quarry Heights. Halfway there, she gathered the children around her and began singing Newbolt's "Drake's Drum."

Beatrice looked happy, but she missed her Georgie terribly at moments like this. She never bemoaned her fate or wallowed in self-pity, but continuing without him felt "like learning to live without a leg or arm or eye." No matter how valiantly she behaved after George's passing, Ruth Ellen knew her mother never got over his death.

EVEN THOUGH GEORGE was buried 3,500 miles away, Beatrice felt his presence wherever she went. In line with her recommendation that families of fallen soldiers who "found comfort in a permanent, tangible record near at hand" put up "a simple monument in the family cemetery plot," she and Nita installed a stained glass window in George's honor at the Church of our Savior in San Gabriel and placed a marker near the grave of his parents.[74]

"If I should conk," George wrote Fred at the start of Operation Husky in July 1943, "I do not wish to be disinterred after the war. It would be far more pleasant to my ghostly future to lie among my soldiers than to rest in the sanctimonious precincts of a civilian cemetery." So when Congress passed Public Law 383 on May 16, 1946, allocating $200 million for the Army to repatriate any of the 279,867 fallen soldiers buried overseas, Beatrice vehemently opposed this course of action in a *Boston Globe*'s op-ed piece titled "Let the War Dead Rest."[75]

After WWI, many in the throes of "great emotion" asked for their loved ones to be returned, yet "on the day of burial it was rare to see a family present. Many of them did not come, I [Beatrice] think, because the wound of sorrow had begun to heal, the meaning of the burial ceremony had changed for them and they begun to realize that the broken bodies brought back in sealed caskets bore no relation to the men they had known and loved."

Those buried overseas, in cemeteries marking the "triumphal march of our armies," weren't abandoned, but treated with respect by the locals who cared for the graves of their liberators. "Every good soldier I have ever known wanted to be buried where he fell," Beatrice concluded. "Mine did. Our dead have earned the right to rest in peace."[76]

George, however, seemed not to have earned that right just yet. A few months after he was buried among his men, Beatrice reluctantly agreed to have him moved to a position at the head of his soldiers to prevent nearby graves from being desecrated. Two years later, after hundreds of soldiers had been repatriated, the American Battle Monuments Commission (ABMC) finalized their design for the Luxembourg American Cemetery and notified Beatrice that General Patton's grave was to be moved once again to maintain the cemetery's symmetry.

A yearlong battle ensued between the ABMC and the Patton family, spearheaded by Beatrice, General Gay, and Keith Merrill.[77] At 12:30 a.m. on

December 8, 1945, Keith had delivered $80 million worth of artwork to the National Gallery of Art—discovered by the Third Army in the Merkers salt mine in April 1945. When he returned the art to Germany on May 27, 1948, he visited his brother-in-law's grave. He commended those in charge for their excellent care, but the assurances he received that the General's remains would not be moved again turned out to be false, leaving Keith no option but to take the matter up with the highest authorities.

Commander Merrill appealed to the Army itself with the help of General Gay. On September 9, 1948, he met with General Bradley, a man whose dislike of his former superior and subordinate had only intensified with the release of *War as I Knew It.* The Chief of Staff couldn't interfere with the civilian-run ABMC, nor would he, since he believed high rank was no reason for special treatment.

Keith had no qualms about calling out General Bradley, "The members of the Patton family acquiesce and concur with the reasons underlying the general rule that burials shall be made without regard to rank, race, creed, or color; however, in the case of General Patton, his grave was changed from a position in one of the regular plots to its present location not because of his high rank but to get it completely away from the proximity of the other graves in order to avoid their desecration by the crowds of visitors. The Patton family understood that this was a permanent move and that the remains would not be moved another time."

Since it was plain "illogical" to move the grave from its current "uniform" location to, once again, "the vicinity of other graves," the family would not hesitate to ask for General Patton's remains so they "might bury them suitably and permanently."[78]

**Figure 96.** *No other four-star general is buried at an ABMC cemetery.*

Beatrice was furious as the affair dragged on. Ten months later, she wrote a letter to General Huebner, the Army's liaison with the ABMC, when she heard "that they are still crowing about it. Words cannot express how ashamed I am, that my country should behave in this way toward the grave of a man whose monuments are springing up, unsolicited, in all the liberated countries. I have not spoken of it to my friends in France, Belgium or Luxemburg for this reason: I feel that to do so—except as a last resort—is to let my country down in the face of foreigners." At her wit's end, "if the Commission insists on putting it back in a row, I am tempted to ask Luxembourg for a piece of ground —but I should hate to do this. Georgie should be buried at the head of his men."

Beatrice fought tooth and nail to prevent George's move and eventually persevered, but not without feeling that the Army once again failed her husband. She received spontaneous support from people all across the world, including Princess Charlotte and Prince Felix of Luxembourg, yet she couldn't "bear to ask a favor of Gen. Marshall, he should have done Georgie his honor" without her having to ask.[79]

AFTER TWO YEARS OF PLANNING, the Patton Museum of Cavalry and Armor— now renamed the General George Patton Museum of Leadership—opened at Fort Knox on May 30, 1949. A strong supporter of the museum from its inception (as the family still is today), Beatrice spoke at the official ribbon-cutting ceremony, emphasizing "the necessity of keeping our Armored Forces strong and up-to-date."[80] She was as fierce an advocate of universal military training as George had been, heralding the positive effects on discipline and health of serving in the military for one year.[81]

The Massachusetts branch of the National Security Committee held a conference regarding the issue in June 1947 at Boston's Faneuil Hall, attended by seven hundred people inside and thousands of protestors outside. Dr. Compton, chair of the committee, believed prudence required "on the part of the United States a strong military establishment as insurance" against aggression from any other nation, particularly Russia.

Beatrice took the stage next, speaking "for myself as well as my husband who worked for universal military training all his life." She reasoned Americans insure themselves against everything, "We even insure our insurance. But we have let our national insurance lapse." Universal military training was "an absolute necessity. Why, during the Battle of the Bulge, young men with only three weeks of training were sent across with a terrible loss of life. There is no time during a war to train."[82]

*Figure 97. Big Bee and Little Bee at the opening of the Patton Museum on May 30, 1949. (Patton Museum)*

In a letter to a Boston newspaper in the weeks after the outbreak of the Korean War in June 1950, Beatrice admitted she had asked her husband on his deathbed "when he thought the Russians would start their war." He replied, "Not at all, while they can nibble away at countries like Yugoslavia, create puppet governments and raise puppet armies. Then, when they have got all they can get that way, with many allies, and we are down to two divisions, they'll start marching."[83]

"It would have given Georgie so much satisfaction to know how right he was about the Russians," Beatrice wrote in her thought book, "but it would have made him awfully angry too."[84] George's reputation was Beatrice's "most cherished memory."[85] The more time passed, the more she came to believe that despite thirty-six years of faithful service, her husband was underappreciated and even betrayed by his superiors. She read the books and reports that came out after the war, George often receiving less credit than she thought he deserved. Beatrice was bitter, but she wasn't the only one who believed General Patton was often "a victim of jealousy and manipulation" and had been "treated very badly."[86]

George called his transfer to the Fifteenth Army "a raw deal," but he never believed people to be jealous of him and "[refused] to think about it. I can still close my mind to unpleasant things and it is a good habit as I get quite a few kicks and jabs by little foolish underlings."[87] It angered Beatrice that very few of those in the Army's upper echelons were willing to openly defend or praise George, despite all he had done. He might have kept quiet to his superiors about how he felt, but Beatrice certainly would not.[88]

In an unsent reply to General Marshall's letter of condolence, Beatrice agreed that

> Georgie would far rather have died in battle at the head of his 3rd Army; but we never spoke of death ~~at the last~~, and I know you will be glad to know that ~~after his relief, neither his spirit nor his heart were broken~~. the cruelty of his relief ~~has broken~~ neither his spirit nor his heart. When he died, he still had a great deal to give to his country. I am glad that you wrote me of your aff. [affection?] for him. I wish he could have known that, for he always felt that you did not quite trust him.[89]

The animosity from George's superiors was in stark contrast to the loyalty of his men and the admiration of the towns he liberated. Beatrice received thousands of letters and telegrams in the weeks following George's accident, many of them from members of the Third Army. It took her a while to get up the courage, but she made sure to answer each one personally. The letters kept coming, year after year, eventually going to her children and grandchildren after she passed away. Beatrice felt vindicated when she read the stories of his men, always on the hunt for something she hadn't heard before, something George would have told her himself one day.

Less amusing were the constant appeals for souvenirs, from simple requests like autographs to more personal items like clothing and weapons. "Dear Mr. Holt," Beatrice wrote on November 28, 1947, from Green Meadows to Louisville, Kentucky. "Indeed you are not rude or overbearing by asking for a souvenir of my husband, and I wish that I could send you something for your collection, but I know you will understand when I say that all our keepsakes have gone to either our children or to friends who were near and dear to General Patton. I love to think that you would be proud to have something of his in your collection, and I am sorry that I don't have anything to send."[90]

*Figure 98. Beatrice representing her husband at the Third Army Association Convention in Chicago on August 18, 1951. (Library of Congress)*

Beatrice's greatest pride was meeting the men of the Third Army, who proudly proclaimed—like a badge of honor even to those who bitterly complained of their commander's discipline during the war—"I was with Patton." While visiting Ruth Ellen in Panama, an MP stopped Beatrice to question her pass card, so she showed him her identification bracelet. It was hard to tell who was more excited: Beatrice, who wanted to know if the young man ever had any personal contact with General Patton, or the MP, who was over the moon to have met Mrs. Patton.[91] It reminded her of the times during the war when she met with people who'd seen George, and she felt "like the man who 'shook the hand that shook the hand of Sullivan.'"[92]

The same went for the 2nd Armored Division, whose commanders "felt an urge to report to Mrs. Patton" the latest news, "as they would to him if he had been alive."[93] Whenever she could, Beatrice attended 2nd Armored Division and Third Army reunions. She listened with loving interest to any story people wanted to share, from GIs who described George helping to push a jeep out of the mud in the cold to cooks who saw him lift the lids on their pots to make sure his men were getting sufficient food. This was the Georgie she knew and the Georgie she wanted the world to remember.

On August 19, 1950, Beatrice addressed the veterans of the Third Army at the unveiling of General Patton's statue at West Point, "From now on no one will ever need to ask—how did he look, how did he stand and walk, for your gift, coupled with the genius of Mr. Fraser, has made it possible for even me, his wife, to point to the statue and say, 'There he stands in his glory, at his best.'" She hoped his likeness would forever be an inspiration to West Point's long gray line since "life is a book in which each chapter is different but every chapter is built on those that have gone before. Glory with honor never grows old. May this statue ever stand for Duty - Honor - America."[94]

General Littlejohn, another longtime family friend who served as the chief quartermaster in the ETO during WWII, promised Beatrice at her husband's funeral that he would make it his "business to get a statue of Georgie for West Point." Beatrice immediately was on board, and as soon as she returned from Germany, she began to work tirelessly to get approval from the West Point Academic Board and to raise the necessary funds with the help of General Keyes, and Colonels Codman and Harkins.

The seventy-year-old James Earle Fraser—known for his statues flanking the entrances to the U.S. Supreme Court and the National Archives—accepted the commission to recreate the likeness of a man he called "the perfect soldier." He completed his first sketch in April 1946, a thrilling moment for Beatrice, who was involved with every aspect of the statue's creation, from the look of the pedestal to the choice of inscription—she particularly liked: "There are no practice games in life," and "Do not take counsel of your fears." She collaborated closely with James for four years and then switched her focus to a similar figure he planned to make for placement along the Charles River Esplanade in Boston.[95]

In May 1948, Beatrice approved the statue's design, a perfect likeness of her heroic husband, which James achieved with the help of countless picture albums she shared with him.[96] She loaned him George's revolvers and leather battle jacket, which she still fancied seeing him wear as she looked at the creases in the arms.[97] When George IV joined his mother at the Frasers' West-port, Connecticut, home before heading to Germany, he posed in his father's battle jacket and pants. Melted into the hands of the bronze statue were four silver stars worn by General Patton, which Beatrice threw in the crucible when the statue was cast on July 10, 1950.[98]

Beatrice formed a close friendship with James and his wife Laura, a well-known sculptor in her own right. "How lucky you are to be together and to be the partners that you are," Beatrice wrote upon their wedding anniversary.[99] "You have been able to be together to share the high points in each others' lives —a joy denied to every soldier's wife by virtue of his calling."[100]

**Figure 99.** *Bee, George IV, Ruth Ellen, and Beatrice at the unveiling of General Patton's statue at West Point on August 19, 1950. (Library of Congress)*

"I always feel that one should not mourn for those who have passed on, particularly when they have died a glorious death fighting for the victory of their country," George once wrote a bereaved father, "but that our sympathies, I think, should be extended to those who must live on without their loved ones."[101] Visiting Nombre de Dios with her grandchildren or sailing the *When and If* with Fred were adventures meant to be had with George, the man she shared everything with even when apart. Beatrice missed her Georgie more every year, constantly reminded of all the things they never got to enjoy together. She wished "life weren't so full of goodbyes—but I try to look on them as a starting out, and on myself as a sort of train dispatcher!"[102]

Endowed with an abundance of energy that rivaled George's, Beatrice traveled wherever she was needed most, as devoted to her children as she once was to her husband. "All my babies and children have gone back to school and I am all alone with the dogs, Willie and Powder, for the first time since May 11," Beatrice wrote to the Frasers in September 1949, "catching up on odd jobs and doing a little sailing and hunting for diversion, and listening to the C.B.S World Roundup so as to keep from going to seed. (Talking with Ruth Ellen's parrot includes going to seed.) I go to Panama next month for a month of fishing."[103]

ON THE FIFTH anniversary of his father's death, George IV yearned "for a day with you in which I can tell you my troubles. Just an hour — just 5 minutes — How am I doing? How should I do?"[104] He missed his father, but he had always worshipped his mother and leaned on her just as his father had.

When the twenty-eight-year-old infantry officer was transferred from Germany to Fort Knox in the spring of 1951, he asked Ruth Ellen to keep an eye out for a girl who "was a college graduate, a good dancer, well-dressed, a good cook, potentially a good mother, and, if possible, an Army Brat."[105]

Ruth Ellen stumbled upon the perfect opportunity when she and Jim were invited to a party celebrating the wedding anniversary of Brigadier General Willard Holbrook Jr. and Helen Hoyle Herr (who introduced the Tottens at the Fort Myer Horse Show in 1938).

The Holbrooks' twenty-year-old daughter Joanne, studying at Sweet Briar College, ticked off every box on George IV's list. She came from a military family dating back to the Revolutionary War, culminating with her father, who served in the Third Army. Her great-great-grandfather was the illustrious René DeRussy, and her great-grandmother was Mrs. Hoyle, the grand dame of the Old Army and "one of the most delightful ladies" Beatrice had ever known.[106]

*Figure 100. Beatrice and Joanne at the christening of the Patton 48 Medium Tank on July 1, 1952, in Newark, Delaware. (Patton Museum)*

*Figure 101. Beatrice, George, and Mr. Keller of the Chrysler Plant. Upon their return from honeymoon in Bermuda, Joanne and George spent a few days at Green Meadows, "enjoying a 3-day cruise & a flying trip to the Delaware arsenal." (Patton Museum)*

Within months, George IV felt ready to take Joanne to Green Meadows for the "acid test." The weekend was spent with friends and family on the *When and If*, anchored off Gloucester Bay the first night. Beatrice waited for choppy waters before asking for a volunteer to help prepare lunch, but Joanne had "an iron stomach" and passed the test with flying colors. After an early night, young George took his mother aside the next morning and told her Joanne was the woman he wanted to marry. Beatrice already knew, "The next time you want to whisper sweet nothings in the cockpit, remember that my bunk is right below. I heard everything and I am all for it."[107]

A mere five months after meeting, on what would have been George's sixty-sixth birthday, Brigadier General and Mrs. Holbrook announced their daughter's engagement to Captain George Smith Patton. The two distinguished military families united in marriage on June 14, 1952, at the Washington Cathedral—the only church big enough to house the number of guests Beatrice wanted to invite. Her son's wedding was "one of the greatest joys" since her husband's passing. Ruth Ellen remembered her mother, who was wearing a lavender chiffon dress, "never looked more beautiful than when she danced with George at the reception; she looked like a girl in her twenties."[108]

Peter DeRose, who helped Beatrice compose the "2nd Armored Division March," conducted the orchestra for the newlyweds' opening dance, but he wasn't the only blast from the past. As was his habit whenever one of the Pattons organized an event in DC, Sergeant Meeks showed up ready to help at a luncheon organized by the Tottens. What happened to Virgie is a mystery—during the war she lived with her parents in Junction City and worked as a swing girl in Washington—as was pretty much the entirety of Meeks's life once General Patton passed away.[109]

George made sure his faithful orderly was taken care of, but the death of "the finest man [he] ever knew" left Meeks heartbroken.[110] Just like Beatrice, he had always made sure George could focus on what was important because "every hour he spent caring for the General's equipment and similar time-filling matters was another worry that Patton could be spared." Being together for seven years, continuously during the war as they lived through experiences only they could understand, established an unbreakable bond. Even though Sergeant Meeks officially died on March 8, 1965, Ruth Ellen believed he really died on December 21, 1945.[111]

IF THERE WAS one thing Beatrice learned from her husband, it was that "there was only one direction in which to move—forward." The *When and If* could have become the beacon of an unfulfilled promise, but Beatrice was out on the water whenever she could, going on long-distance sails with friends and family, and teaching her grandchildren to sail along the rocky Manchester Bay, "counting them every minute, not to lose any overboard."[112]

Beatrice enjoyed sharing the responsibility for the *When and If* with her brother, who was as comfortable on the back of a horse as he was behind the tiller of a schooner—unlike Hilda, who was happy to let Beatrice become Fred's "cruising wife."[113] On Wednesday morning, October 22, 1952, the schooner sailed out of Marblehead Harbor on a trip to Norfolk. As brother and sister breezed past the New York coastline, they were blissfully unaware of the drama taking place at Highland Falls.

Major General Waters's appointment in 1951 as Commandant of Cadets at West Point—a job his father-in-law always coveted—was a relief to his wife. Bee never liked change and was happy to settle in the town of Highland Falls for the foreseeable future, until Johnnie was suddenly promoted to Brigadier General in June 1952 and summarily sent to Korea. Beatrice traveled to West Point to say goodbye to Johnnie and ask her daughter to move in with her at Green Meadows, but Bee preferred to stay in the house Johnnie recently bought her.

Beatrice compared Bee to a slender tree, "swayed by passing breezes but strong in the time of storm," yet she always worried her eldest daughter wasn't cut out to be an army wife, requiring "loving support for whatever she did."[114] Despite the strength Bee showed during WWII, the experience of her husband being a POW for two years scarred her for life. As the waiting and uncertainty started all over again, Bee quickly faltered. Obviously, something was terribly wrong, but she kept quiet about the chest pains she experienced and refused to be helped by either her mother or sister.

Just hours before she was supposed to leave for Highland Falls, a phone call awoke Ruth Ellen at two in the morning. "Mrs. Waters just died," the doctor informed her. "I am here with her and the boys."[115] News of Bee's passing was withheld by the Department of Defense (formerly the War Department) until her husband and mother could be notified. It ended up being easier to inform Johnnie in Korea, who immediately received emergency leave to return home, than it was to locate Beatrice on the Atlantic Ocean.

Jim took it upon himself to locate his mother-in-law, but he was unable to make radio contact with the *When and If* and reached out to the Coast Guard for help. Conducting a wireless and shore-to-ship radiotelephone search, the Coast Guard was also unsuccessful. As a last resort, all boats between Connecticut and Virginia were alerted to keep watch for the *When and If*.

The sixty-three-foot schooner was hard to miss, but it still took an emergency call transmitted by a local radio station for Beatrice and Fred to be located.[116] It is impossible to imagine Beatrice's pain when the Coast Guard pulled up beside the *When and If* and informed her that her daughter had passed away almost two days earlier.

Ruth Ellen remembered her mother looking "completely defenseless" when she arrived in Highland Falls with Fred, "smaller and more transparent than I had ever seen her even when she came back after Georgie's funeral." Awaiting Johnnie's return from Korea, Beatrice and Ruth Ellen began tidying up the house, "stunned" to find bottles of liquor hiding in Bee's bedroom. In the end, there was nothing anyone could have done. Bee had been suffering from an unspecified heart ailment and died of heart failure. "My sister was only forty-one years old," Ruth Ellen wrote in *The Button Box*. "It isn't only soldiers who are casualties of war."[117]

"The death of your child is the worst grief of all," Beatrice told Chilly in 1947 when his daughter was thrown from her horse at Green Meadows and died en route to Beverly Hospital. "This is the one thing we don't expect, Chill. We know our parents will die, and we are somewhat prepared for that, but we always expect our children to outlive us."[118]

In reply to a letter of condolences from Laura and Jimmie Fraser, Beatrice wrote that it wasn't "trite to say that the love and sympathy of friends is a real help. I am praying for understanding. Beatrice never knew. She had had a sort of grippe, and must have overdone without realizing it. Johnnie will go back to Korea and the boys [fourteen-year-old Johnnie and eleven-year-old Pat] are here with me until he returns next summer. They are very good and helpful and it is wonderful for me to have them. I am just trying to look ahead & do the best I can for them, but I can well understand David's lament for Absalom."[119]

THE PATTONS WENT into WWII with the same respect they had always felt for the Eisenhowers. Beatrice got together with Mamie at West Point or Washington, and she regularly corresponded with Ike. George, however, quickly became disillusioned by Eisenhower's handling of the war and embittered by his refusal to show him the appreciation he felt he deserved. Always generous with medals and ready to give credit where credit was due, he was especially galled not to be accorded the same consideration from his superiors.

He never received any medals for the Battle of the Bulge, a snub that still angered Beatrice seven years later. When James Fraser received the nation's highest award in the arts, Beatrice wrote the artist that he, James, had "earned the Medal many, many times, but we do not always get in this life that which people wish they had given us while we could still enjoy it."[120]

However, George's dismissal from the Third Army was the straw that broke the camel's back. He was too proud "to reveal his disappointment and dismay" and contained his feelings within the pages of his letters and diaries, which meant "Eisenhower never grasped the terrible hurt he had done Patton in relieving him of his beloved Third Army."[121] The older Eisenhower got, the more he thought of George Patton as an old friend instead of a wartime ally. He relished telling stories of the times they spent together, according to his son John Eisenhower, "a bit of nostalgia for simpler times, a simpler Army . . . Patton did not live to indulge in nostalgia. He died, I presume, still thinking of Ike only as his military superior and tormentor."[122]

General Marshall confided to his biographer that "Mrs. Patton was very bitter at General Eisenhower."[123] She never forgave him for using "Georgie as one would use a pit bulldog," letting him loose whenever there was a problem, only to rein him back in when the battle was won.[124] However, the Eisenhowers also possessed the gift of years. Beatrice felt a little envious when she saw Mamie stand by her husband's side as he was fêted, making plans for the future after years of separation and living the life she had envisioned for herself and George.

Being the excellent hater that she was, time didn't mellow Beatrice. When Mamie called from the presidential campaign trail to offer her condolences upon Bee's death, Joanne picked up the phone. Beatrice, however, refused to speak to Mamie, no matter the urgings of her family. She also refused all invitations to the White House, although she did write President Eisenhower in May 1953 to voice her concern about the proposed budget, which sounded like a "death blow" for the armed services "with the European and Asiatic situation what informed people know it to be."[125]

General Eisenhower's running for president was no surprise to Beatrice. George's diaries and letters were riddled with references to a potential Eisenhower presidency. In October 1945, he had written Fred that

> there was not one iota of truth in any criticism of my governance of Bavaria nor was I relieved for that reason. I was relieved because General Eisenhower is the unfortunate victim of the presidential bee bite, and it is my sincere hope and belief that this malady will prove fatal—not to me but to him because I intend to dedicate some of my declining years to a little highly distilled malice.[126]

On Saturday, June 21, 1952, the phone rang at Green Meadows during little Beatrice's ninth birthday party. Westbrook Pegler, a journalist as controversial as Drew Pearson, was on the line. He wanted to get to the bottom of a rumor that had been going around since the presidential election of 1948, mainly that Mrs. Patton "was gunning for General Eisenhower and would strike him down with dramatic disclosures if Ike ever should be nominated for President."

The idea that Beatrice possessed derogatory papers damaging to Eisenhower originated with journalist Kent Hunter, General Patton's public affairs officer in the Third Army. Seven years after the war, with classified information becoming available, more and more people believed that General Patton "was treated badly," and many hoped his widow would not hesitate to get her revenge on the man many deemed responsible.

General Eisenhower was Supreme Commander of NATO and all its European forces when a new "Draft Ike" movement took hold in January 1952. He finally declared himself a Republican but only agreed to run if he was nominated at the Republican National Convention. With the convention a mere three weeks away, Westbrook Pegler figured Mrs. Patton was best qualified to confirm or deny the rumor that she would boycott Eisenhower's presidential run.

"Mr. Pegler, I am a Republican," she said before hanging up the phone. "Does that answer your question?"[127]

"A MERRY HEART goes all the way, your sad tires in a mile-a," Beatrice often quoted Shakespeare.[128] The first few months after Bee's death were difficult as she once again searched for understanding, occasionally lashing out at her grandsons during the six months they lived with her.[129] However, as she wrote to the Frasers, "Time Marches On," and by the summer of 1953, she almost seemed herself again, proud of her son for receiving the Silver Star for "conspicuous gallantry and intrepidity," and heartened by the birth of her sixth grandchild, Margaret DeRussy Patton.

It had been more important than ever for George IV to gain combat experience. He was finally sent to Korea in February 1953 as commander of the 140th Tank Battalion, leaving his pregnant wife in the capable hands of his mother and in-laws. The old and new Mrs. Patton got along well, and it didn't take long for Joanne to experience firsthand her mother-in-law's forceful but "generous spirit."

When Joanne fell ill not long after her return from Bermuda, Beatrice insisted she stay at Green Meadows to recuperate instead of at George's cramped quarters at Fort Knox. Always eager to keep everyone at their best, she took her daughter-in-law for long walks around the property as soon as she felt up to it. About a year later, on July 6, 1953, while waiting at a hospital in the capital area for Joanne to give birth, Beatrice showed her forceful side. Used to getting things done, she told the doctor to move things along because she needed to get back to Green Meadows. "Mrs. Patton," the doctor replied, "there are some things that can't be hurried, and Mother Nature is one of them."[130]

One month after the birth of her sixth grandchild, Beatrice left for a seventeen-day cruise along the coast of Maine on the *When and If* with Fred, Ruth Ellen, and twelve-year-old Michael. While Beatrice looked happy on the surface and reveled in teaching her grandson about life on a schooner, Ruth Ellen worried about the private conversations she had with her mother. Using her own close relationship with Fred as an example, Beatrice reminded her that "family loyalty was the most important thing in life" and "brother and sister are the closest kin there is." When Ruth Ellen asked whether she was trying to tell her something, Beatrice admitted she was "sending out signals." Now that all three of her children were happily married, she wasn't "needed any more. The doctor hasn't told me anything new. It's just that I have lost my zest. Things are too much of an effort. Things are just not very interesting any more."

She did not go into detail, but the sixty-seven-year-old Beatrice had been worried about her health for a while. Her eyesight had never been good, but neither had her heart. Ever since her youth—and exacerbated during the First World War—she was occasionally troubled by tachycardia, an abnormally rapid heartbeat.[131] Both her mother and daughter had died of heart disease, and she recently learned that she had an aneurysm in her aorta that could rupture at any moment.

Beatrice asked the country's premier cardiologist, Dr. Paul Dudley White, for a second opinion. He explained that she could live a week, a month, or even years, but it wouldn't make any difference whether she stayed in bed all day or continued to live the active lifestyle she had always enjoyed. Beatrice chose the latter and made only one change in light of her diagnosis: she stopped driving George's sports car, worried she might kill someone if the end came unexpectedly.

Beatrice was as private as Bee and kept the news to herself. The only person she ever truly shared with had been gone for almost eight years, and she missed him more each day. She knew George would have been difficult in old age, but it was a cruel twist of fate that he missed out on so much living. After all the years they spent apart, this should have been their time. She never talked about the loss she felt, making a conscious decision to live life and be happy, but deep inside, the nagging pain only grew stronger. When she suffered an attack of tachycardia, she literally felt his loss: "The pounding and tripping of my heart was because you were pulling at the bond between us trying to pull me along and help me bump over the road to where you are."[132]

Death did not scare Beatrice; she learned that from George. Before the start of their grand adventure, he wondered about her strange views on death, even though they were the ones most people held. Her perception slowly changed as George inundated her with glories of the afterlife, asking her at one point, "Did you ever stop to think how much more exciting death can be than life?"

Beatrice continued to hunt twice a week, "[exhausting] people doing things" in the last few months of her life.[133] Living up to the example set by George—whom she still wanted to make proud even in death—Beatrice's driving power increased rather than lessened as she grew older. She began hunting and riding cross-country seriously because of him, "galvanized into action by the dynamism of one man" as his armies had always been, but she didn't give up the practice following his death. "I am afraid no longer," she wrote in her thought book, feeling liberated. "What I live from now on is extra, and if I get hurt it will not hurt anyone else."[134]

Beatrice Ayer Patton spent the last few months of her life as Georgie taught her: passionately doing the things she loved, as unafraid of death as he had always been, hoping to die with her boots on without becoming a burden to her family.

As the riders crossed Walnut Road onto the field of Ledyard Farm, Anna Prince took her position to clear the second jump when a riderless horse suddenly overtook her. She recognized Formaloup, Beatrice's spirited but well-trained thoroughbred chestnut gelding. One of the most renown horsewomen of Virginia, Theodora Ayer Randolph, had found her aunt the Trakehner a year earlier when Beatrice's faithful Quicksilver was put to sleep.[135] "If he did not have already such a distinguished name," Beatrice wrote Ruth Ellen a few weeks earlier, "I would christen him Happy Days."[136]

Beatrice was "in her usual good spirits" when she joined Fred, Hilda, Anna, and twenty-one other riders at the Myopia Hunt Club for a drag hunt on September 30, 1953.[137] "Isn't it a beautiful day," she exclaimed while she mounted her horse, fortified by the raw egg she always had before a hunt. Just the day before, she rode across Green Meadows with her Myopia stable man to make sure there were no woodchuck holes on her property like the one that had brought down Miss Katharine Wellman's horse. "She was very upset over the accident" which sent her hunting companion to the hospital, but "very glad when we couldn't find a single woodchuck hole on her land."[138]

Formaloup was all play at the sound of the hounds as they took off after the scent laid by the field master just half an hour earlier. Riding behind Beatrice as the field entered Ledyard Farm, Fred and Hilda watched in horror as Beatrice was thrown from her horse while clearing a hurdle. To Mrs. Edward Frederick, wife of the South Hamilton police chief, it looked as if Beatrice went "up on his neck and then [slid] off the ground."[139] Some said Formaloup reared and threw his charge, trampling her, while others said the horse bolted, and still others said it stumbled.

By the time Anna made it back down the hill, she could detect neither pulse nor heartbeat. Beatrice Banning Ayer Patton died at 6:45 a.m., at age sixty-seven, near the foot of the hill at Ledyard Farm, her head resting in her beloved brother's lap. She died setting out on the hunt like George, but in the manner he always wanted, thrown "from a damned good horse," enjoying the life of vigorous exercise and dangerous sport.[140]

**Figure 102.** *Beatrice attaching a streamer for discipline to the guidon bearer of Battery C, Harvard ROTC. Harvard University, May 15, 1952. (Patton Museum)*

# LUXEMBOURG AMERICAN CEMETERY, HAMM

## 1957

*WE [MEN AND WOMEN] ARE A DIFFERENT SPECIES; THERE IS NO QUESTION OF EQUALITY, SIMPLY OF QUALITY.*

Ngws of what happened at Ledyard Farm quickly spread to Chilly's Juniper Ridge, where breakfast and spectators were already waiting to welcome the intrepid hunters. Kay called Ruth Ellen from Beverly Hospital, surprised when her niece immediately asked if something "happened to Ma." Told her mother died almost instantly after falling off her horse while hunting, Ruth Ellen's first reaction was, "Thank God." Her father felt he had not been good enough, but "Ma was good enough. In her own way, she died in battle."[1]

Fred knew his sister's death was "just an accident that could happen to anyone while going through a drag hunt or out riding." However, he couldn't stop thinking about how he had instinctively cradled her in his arms after the accident. Only when he became aware of Hilda's yelling not to move Beatrice did he realize he might have made a bad situation worse.

There was nothing Dr. Peer Johnson could do when he arrived at the scene of the accident except pronounce Beatrice dead, at first look, because of a broken neck.[2] The idea caused Fred so much anguish that Ruth Ellen agreed to an autopsy, which revealed Beatrice died of a ruptured aorta, which caused her fall, killing her before she hit the ground.[3]

The aortic rupture Beatrice knew was coming took her while doing what she loved best. Old age never slowed her down, which made her sudden passing even more shocking. The week Beatrice died, "she had been sorting over his [George's] thousands of photographs, and setting his letters and papers into order for possible publication."[4] She had recently collaborated with Harry Semmes on his autobiography, continued pleading for a well-trained Army, looked forward to the release of a commemorative stamp of General Patton—on what would have been his sixty-eight birthday—and planned an extensive trip on the *When and If* to the Caribbean with her five eldest grandchildren, Fred, and Joe Ekeland.

George IV, who spoke to his mother the day before she died, was notified in Tokyo, where he was enjoying some much-needed R&R after the end of the Korean War. He wasn't supposed to return to the United States until early 1954, but he received a priority pass to fly home to Green Meadows, where Joanne and three-month-old Margaret were waiting for him. The Pattons' reunion was bittersweet; George IV met his baby daughter the same day he said goodbye to his beloved mother.

St. John's Episcopal Church was packed for the brief funeral service, which took place at 3 p.m. on October 5, 1953. The bell Beatrice had donated a few years earlier in George's memory pealed across Hale Street in her honor when the ushers—Commander Keith Merrill; Dr. Keith Merrill Jr.; Caleb Loring Jr.; Dr. Robert Seamans; Captain Neil Ayer; Colonel Charles Codman; Frederick Ayer Jr.; Ethan Ayer; John S. King; and Dr. Franc D. Ingraham—entered the small Tudor-style church.[5] Her funeral service was as simple and modest as she had always been, without fanfare and with just a few Army and govern-ment representatives present, in addition to close family and friends.

Possessed by a lifelong hatred of undertakers, Beatrice made it abundantly clear throughout her life that she wished to be cremated. After the funeral service, her ashes were taken to Green Meadows to be buried underneath an elm tree. Or was she? Beatrice had been asking permission for years to be buried with George, but her repeated requests were continually denied. Since George IV and Ruth Ellen knew there was only one place their mother wanted to be, they renewed her efforts upon her death.

In August 1955, President Eisenhower was forwarded a message from Lieu-tenant General Gay, asking permission to have Beatrice's ashes put in or on her husband's grave. "I should think that the subject of Mrs. Patton's ashes would be one better left to the wishes of the Patton children," the president replied. "I don't believe I would want to intervene in the matter; I really don't feel that I would have any right to do so."[6]

The matter dragged on for another year through official channels until the summer of 1957, when George IV, Ruth Ellen, and her son Michael traveled to the Luxembourg American Cemetery. After a few moments of contemplation,

Ruth Ellen took an envelope from her purse and released some of Beatrice's ashes over George's grave.[7] No one ever confirmed nor denied the story, but it is safe to assume that Beatrice Ayer Patton and George S. Patton Jr. were finally together for eternity. What remains at Green Meadows underneath the elm tree is a big rock with a bronze plaque:

*In loving memory of Beatrice Ayer Patton*
*Born, Lowell, Mass. Jan. 12, 1886*
*Died, South Hamilton, Mass. Sept. 30, 1953*
*Devoted wife, mother, grandmother, friend and patriot*
*"I have kept the faith"*

ON THE DAY Beatrice was laid to rest, a Hollywood executive called Green Meadows and asked her children for permission to make a movie about their illustrious father. Beatrice had been fielding these calls since 1950, but she categorically refused every time—as did George when he was first asked in October 1944 by Eisenhower, who had immediately agreed.

No movie studio dared oppose the widow of General Patton, but one man wasn't willing to give up on the project. Brigadier General Frank McCarthy was a movie producer who had graduated from VMI and enlisted in the Army Reserve at the start of WWII. Several times, he had reached out to Beatrice, "a very sweet, attractive, charming lady," but he could tell she "didn't like the movies and had a grudge against the press. It was her feeling that the publicity given to Patton during his career had contributed to his downfall."[8]

Ruth Ellen and George IV were as dead set against a movie as their mother, so McCarthy asked several officers to mediate with the Patton family. General Mark Clark was immediately rebuffed by Ruth Ellen, who thought him interested only in money, and even Major General Harkins made no headway. Besides the publicity of a Hollywood production, the family also worried that a movie "would not properly portray the General but would tend to stress some of the more misleading and dramatic incidents in his life."

Despite the Vietnam War, McCarthy and Twentieth Century Fox finally decided to go ahead with the production of *Patton* after respectfully waiting twenty years. Francis Ford Coppola wrote the winning script, focusing on the General's WWII years. It was based on Ladislas Farago's *Patton: Ordeal and Triumph* and the input of General Omar Bradley, who profited handsomely from working on the movie as a consultant despite speaking less than loftily about General Patton in his autobiography.

John Wayne was an early contender to play General Patton, but the role eventually went to George C. Scott. Ruth Ellen and George IV declined to attend the premiere of *Patton* in 1970, but they did see the movie. Ruth Ellen was brought to tears not only by Scott's portrayal but also by the audience's spontaneous applause. She wrote McCarthy a lofty letter and even published an essay in *Signal Magazine* wherein she admitted the family had been wrong. Not only was *Patton* "more sensitive, more just, and more realistic in their portrayal than any of the contemporary people who portrayed him and judged him," but so many of Scott's "gestures, particularly, his 'mirthless smile' were so true to life that it gave me quite a start."

It was a feeling George IV shared when he went to watch *Patton* with his son Robert. His first reaction upon seeing the iconic opening scene was that George C. Scott sounded nothing like George S. Patton, but watching him walk toward Bastogne surrounded by his men brought tears to his eyes.[9]

Ruth Ellen believed her father would have been happy that "the movie could not strip him to the soul," but many took issue with its lack of dimension and breadth.[10] George C. Scott didn't like the final result either and refused to accept his Oscar for Best Actor.

Sixteen years later, he produced *The Last Days of Patton* with his own money, focusing on the last six months of General Patton's life. While McCarthy had advocated in vain to have Beatrice's influence "more constantly and strongly felt" in *Patton,* she played a major role in its made-for-TV sequel. Eva Marie Saint took on the part of Beatrice Ayer Patton, helped "enormously" in her portrayal by the letters and pictures provided by Ruth Ellen.[11]

In a way, George Patton was as much an actor as George C. Scott, playing his role so well that he eventually became one with his character. Beatrice might have found some solace in the fact that *Patton* helped perpetuate the memory of General Patton, but it would have been disappointing that George C. Scott did such a good job portraying him that he pretty much replaced her husband in the public's mind.

SAILING BACK from Hawaii in 1937, the *Arcturus* had passed a shoal of porpoises—similar to dolphins. Beatrice noted that evening, "I am more than ever determined to be a porpoise some day."[12]

Everyone knew she believed "reincarnation was her ultimate destiny," so when George IV noticed two dolphins swimming next to the *When and If* just a few days after his mother's funeral, he knew she was sending a message. It was the start of a family tradition whereby the Pattons called out, "Hi, Bea!" every time they saw a dolphin.

Bequeathed to Fred upon Beatrice's death, the *When and If* provided pleasure to the Pattons and the Ayers for the next nineteen years. When Neil Ayer inherited the schooner from his father in 1972, everyone agreed with the decision to donate her to the Landmark School in Pride's Crossing to be used in a program for dyslexic children. Eighteen years later, she broke free from her mooring during a gale and crashed into the rocks prevalent along the North Shore. The insurance company deemed the *When and If* a total loss, but a private investor purchased and lovingly restored her. Her current owners are working hard to make the Pattons' dream of sailing her around the world come true, raising money through sunset sails and private charters in Key West during wintertime and Salem during summertime.

Beatrice was the third of the Ayer siblings to pass away. James Cook Ayer preceded her, a few months shy of his seventy-seventh birthday in 1939, as did Ellen Wheaton Ayer Wood, at the age of ninety-one in 1951. She was cursed by a weak constitution since childhood, so no one expected Ellen to survive the tragedies she endured, but her husband's suicide brought her back from the brink of invalidism, and she enjoyed twenty-five more years with her two surviving children (Countess Guardabassi and Reverend Cornelius Ayer Wood), grandchildren, and great-grandchildren.[13]

Louise Gordon Hatheway passed away in April 1955 at Drumlin Farm in Lincoln, Massachusetts, at seventy-nine years of age. She spent most of her life on her farm, breeding Welsh terriers, growing organic and sustainable food, and teaching school children about the "cycles of life and death and the interdependence of people and nature."[14] She bequeathed over $1,000,000 to charities, former employees, and surviving family members. She left Drumlin Farm to the Massachusetts Audubon Society, which continues to run it as part animal refuge, part organic farm, and part livestock operation.[15]

One year after the death of his wife in 1945, an eighty-one-year-old Chilly married the forty-year-old Annabelle Philips—"a grand girl" and "a great contribution to the family," according to Beatrice.[16] Chilly "ruled an industrial empire" for decades, continuing to go into the office five times a week even when his memory began to fail.[17] As director of the American Woolen Company, he built on his father's legacy and ensured the family's trust would provide for generations of Ayers to come. He passed away in January 1956 at his winter residence in Florida at the age of ninety.

Fred died at Ledyard Farm in April 1969, just short of his eighty-first birthday. With a long, illustrious list of directorships across a broad industry and manager of the Ayers' trust, he was also president of the Beverly Hospital from 1927 to 1958, vice president of the Children's Hospital, and a trustee of the Peter Bent Brigham Hospital. Fred left behind his wife, Hilda, three sons, two daughters, thirteen grandchildren, and two great-grandchildren.[18]

Fun-loving and fashionable Kay was the materfamilias of the family, organizing get-togethers for every birthday, wedding, and holiday. Involved in multiple charities, she was a founder of the Planned Parenthood Association of

Washington, a founder of the Frontier Nursing Service of Lexington, Kentucky, and a trustee of The Masters School. She was widowed in 1959 when seventy-two-year-old Commander Merrill fell down Avalon's marble staircase in the middle of the night and fractured his skull. With homes in Washington, Virginia, and St. Croix, Kay spent the rest of her life at Avalon, where she died in 1981 at the age of ninety-one. She was survived by her three children, fifteen grandchildren, and fifteen great-grandchildren.[19]

THE AYERS CARED for neither snobbery nor pretense and emphasized honesty and merit. Despite all the wealth he amassed, Frederick Ayer never gained the notoriety of the Rockefellers or the Vanderbilts, partly because scandal never rocked his family. He was modest, unassuming, and carried "a large heart with him," and just like his daughter Beatrice, he preferred to help others without calling attention to himself.[20] Beginning in Lowell and spreading across the state and the country as the Ayers moved, the family "brought success and civic responsibility," always giving back to the community through volunteer work, philanthropy, and public service.[21]

A curious and forward-thinking man who was not afraid to invest in new technologies, Frederick was also a prudent planner who groomed his sons to care for his legacy and instilled in his children and grandchildren the same work ethic he was known for. He did not want his fortune squandered but wanted it managed so that it "would secure the financial future of generations of Ayers."[22] The biggest chunk of Frederick's inheritance was put in an investment trust managed by Fred and Chilly, a typical Bostonian development where trusteeship formed a part of life. They ran the Ayers' trust until their deaths, slowly growing it through conservative investment, mainly in government bonds.

Fast-forward to 2006, the Ayers' trust had grown to $600 million and close to two hundred beneficiaries. It was managed by Essex Street Associates and Jack Doorly, who went to work for "the family office" in 1973 when he was a twenty-four-year-old college dropout. He slowly worked his way up, taking on more and more responsibility as many of Frederick's descendants branched out into different industries. He eventually gained the family's trust to such an extent that he was allowed to write checks and make investments without explicit consent. It took years to get to that point, but it was "a sweeping degree of latitude that put at risk everything Frederick Ayer had sought to protect."[23]

While several of Frederick's descendants sat on the board of Essex Street Associates, Doorly staffed the office with non-relatives he could trust to turn a blind eye. It allowed him to use the Ayers' money to buy a jet, a penthouse in Miami for his mistress, and a farm in Topsfield, Massachusetts. By 2000, he was spending about $250,000 a month, yet all the money in the world could not buy him admission to the Myopia Hunt Club, which denied his application.

Doorly was always so secretive about what he did for a living that most people thought he was a self-made millionaire. Ultimately, it was his new assistant who blew the whistle in 2006 by revealing that he had asked her to hide certain transactions from the family. The scheme had been going on for so long that Doorly was "the only person who had any true sense of what had become of Frederick Ayer's riches."

Before the trial began in March 2010, the Ayers recovered about $8 million of the $58 million Doorly had stolen. He pleaded guilty to money laundering and fraud and was sentenced to seventeen years in prison, the courtroom packed with thirty of Frederick Ayer's descendants as the judge spoke sentencing.

BEATRICE NEEDN'T HAVE WORRIED that day on the *When and If*; Ruth Ellen and George IV remained thick as thieves for the rest of their lives and even lived on adjoining properties in South Hamilton.

After residing in forty-seven different homes—including in Turkey and Brazil—Ruth Ellen permanently settled at Brick End's Farm when Major General Totten passed away in 1967 after a long battle with cancer.[24] She missed army life every day, so it was a great joy when her sons joined the military and she could visit them across the world.[25]

Like her mother, Ruth Ellen loved gardening and stood ready to defend the Patton name when necessary. Known as the family historian, she wrote a book called *The Button Box,* each button a memory of the remarkable adventures she enjoyed as an army brat and wife. As curious as her mother and as interested in history as her father, she lectured on the Salem Witch Trials, Major General Custer, and the customs of the Army.[26] In addition, she helped found the Army Distaff Foundation—which provides housing, health, and wellness services to widows of veterans—and was a trustee of the Landmark School and the Lab School in Washington, always interested in children with learning disabilities.

Meeting Ruth Ellen was an experience no one ever forgot. She was an exceedingly interesting woman who talked about death as the next big adventure and an army wife to the core like her mother. But, for George IV, she was also a partial link to their father and a "very close friend and supporter." Her death at the age of seventy-eight on Thanksgiving, 1993, "left a great void" in his life, accustomed as he was to having her just a phone call or a short walk away. He missed her continuous support and her ability to put being the son of a famous father into perspective.[27]

After his mother's funeral, George IV returned to Korea to finish his tour of duty, devastated to find several letters and a Christmas stocking from his mother waiting. In the years following the Korean War, he joined the Department of Tactics at West Point, participated in an exchange assignment with the U.S. Naval Academy at Annapolis, and attended the Army's Command and General Staff College at Fort Leavenworth, Kansas.

He also did several more tours of duty in Germany, befriending Manfred Rommel, the son of Erwin Rommel and a well-respected politician who was the mayor of Stuttgart. Following him across the world were Joanne and their five children—Margaret, George, Robert, Helen, and Benjamin. Like her mother-in-law, Joanne was "a wonderful influence" on her husband and the "perfect military wife."[28] Endowed with a philanthropic spirit, she dedicated her time to supporting military families, special-needs charities, the arts, and the environment.

After serving three voluntary tours in Vietnam and receiving the Purple Heart and two DSCs, George IV received his retirement papers when he fractured his hip and underwent multiple operations. However, he fought the decision and was promoted to Major General in 1975. When he arrived at Fort Hood, Texas, to command the 2nd Armored Division—the first time in history that a father and son commanded the same division—the band played the theme song from the movie *Patton*. He felt "it was wrong to interject my dad into the ceremony" and asked the retiring commander why they hadn't played his mother's "2nd Armored Division March." While the commander said he thought it would bore the Major General to hear the march again, the bandmaster admitted he didn't know the music. By the time George IV left two years later, the band was proficient in the "2nd Armored Division March."

Major General George S. Patton retired in 1980 and permanently moved to Green Meadows, where he began to farm organic produce, naming the fields of his farm after his men who had lost their lives in Vietnam. He remained involved with several Army organizations, stayed in touch with his soldiers, and established a scholarship at West Point in memory of his sister Bee. He was eighty-one when he died in June 2004 at Green Meadows after a long battle with a degenerative form of dementia. Major General George S. Patton was buried at Arlington National Cemetery, leaving behind his wife of fifty-two years, five children, six grandchildren, and one great-grandchild.[29]

Joanne, a pillar of the North Shore community, continued the philanthropic work she was known for. She also continued to run Green Meadows Farm as a community agriculture collective and lived at Green Meadows until 2014, when she donated the home to the town of South Hamilton to "support and preserve the historic Patton Homestead as a community asset and provide educational, recreational and cultural opportunities." The Patton Homestead is now open for tours and houses the Patton Family Archives, which the Wenham Museum is cataloging.

Walking around the property today, one can understand why Beatrice chose 650 Asbury Street as the place to grow old with George. One is greeted by unspoiled nature when stepping out on the veranda, exactly as it was almost a century ago. It is possible to walk down to the Ipswich River, passing history along the way. George IV continued his parents' tradition of planting a tree to commemorate significant events in their lives, and in springtime and summer, the meadow explodes with the colors of flowering apple and cherry trees.

*Figure 103. Beatrice at the dedication of the Patton Museum on May 30, 1949. (Patton Museum)*

BEATRICE AYER PATTON WAS AN ORIGINAL. Possessed of a certain eccentricity, it was no surprise she fell head-over-heels for the boy who considered himself "not normal" and "rather strange."[30] Still, George Patton always remained in awe of her willingness to follow him, requiring so many adjustments in "manners, customs, lifestyles, and moral judgements" on her part.[31]

The quality that set Frederick Ayer apart from others was his willingness to try new ventures, a trait both his daughter and son-in-law possessed. Once she made up her mind, Beatrice Banning Ayer unflinchingly stepped into the unknowns of army life, aided by the adventurousness and curiosity she had been allowed to explore since childhood. Army life was "a mixture of thrills and prayers," which reminded her of the togetherness of her own family.[32]

It says a lot about a woman's character when she marries a man who warns her that he doesn't "care for a home and friends and peace and a regular order of life." George Patton was an officer first, then a husband and father. While any other woman might have resented this third partner in the marriage, it fueled Beatrice. She knew from the get-go that George wanted "to fight up to the top and then go off the edge," yet she never tried to rein him in. As a matter of fact, she continuously fanned the flames of his ambition as his destiny became their shared goal.[33]

Her steadfast belief in her husband's greatness was both her strength and her weakness. While she was the anchor George needed to succeed in life, she could be irrational in all manners concerning him. She was fiercely protective and rigid in her defense of him, yet she didn't suffer fools gladly and didn't shy away from standing up to her husband in private when she deemed it necessary. She was a perfect match in spirit to George—more alike than anyone could have ever imagined—yet she managed to maintain her independence. She was a writer of Hawaiian myths, a beacon of hope for army wives worldwide, and the curator of George's life and legacy.

George Patton focused his entire life on preparing for a moment that might never come, yet he was so sure he was destined to be a great battlefield commander that Beatrice never doubted him. Those first days on Catalina Island set the tone for the rest of their lives, and Beatrice followed her husband wherever the Army sent him. The reputation which preceded her from post to post commanded respect because she was kind, interested, and sensible. She always walked with a purpose, charming George's colleagues and defending him with a steely hardness that never bent.

The confidence Beatrice possessed from a young age strengthened the courage of her convictions. Pretense and underhandedness were not in her vocabulary, honesty and straightforwardness being traits possessed by all the Ayers. She accepted every challenge with an open mind and with an energy that was infectious. "Life and love have been so worth living and loving," a reporter wrote of Beatrice, "you know it every minute you are with her and it makes you warm inside."[34]

George spent his entire life hidden behind a mask defined by many as Old Blood and Guts, yet in private he was a sensitive man, "inclined to show emotion." With Beatrice, he could lay down his mask and be himself: hunting in the countryside and sailing the Pacific, engrossed by the vastness surrounding him; writing perceptive letters filled with the romance and beauty of everything he saw around him; sitting with her and reading well into the night; and writing and reciting poetry, often for the woman he considered "my one love, my body and my life."[35] Beatrice showed him there was more to life than the Army, so much so that he realized in 1932 "that I have been so lucky in all the events of this life that I have developed a lust to live."[36]

George Patton awakened in Beatrice a side of her character that might have remained dormant if she had married someone more conventional. Timid by nature, "she first steeled herself to the risks of the hunting field and then learned to be thrilled by them because she thought that in so far as could be done, she should go with her husband, not only in his work but in his play."[37] Fear took hold of Beatrice whenever she mounted her horse; it was the same fear she knew George always felt before jumping into the fray, but he taught her that "courage is fear holding on a minute longer." The Pattons brought out the best in each other, always striving for perfection and hell-bent on never failing one another.

Beatrice was a featherweight who stood only five foot two, but she was a formidable presence who was never dwarfed by the larger-than-life personality of George Patton. She was able to read him "with a tolerance and good humor born of years of experience," a saving grace in their relationship, which allowed her to put up with certain outrageous behavior she would have never tolerated from anyone else. George Patton wouldn't change for anyone, so Beatrice adapted. "In my part of the country," she once said, "domineering women are called Captains. To be a successful Army wife, the only Captain must be the man."[38]

George Patton might have thought himself the captain of the house, but a good officer needs an intimate, and he withered without Beatrice's adoration and approval. His impulsive side was curbed with her by his side, and she gave him the confidence to make the right decisions. Beatrice lived her life for George Patton, turning "right-square-out-of-this-world with enthusiasm" every time she heard of another one of his WWII exploits, but being Mrs. Patton didn't define her. Once she reached Hawaii, her spiritual home, she discovered a part of herself that could excel without her husband. While George seemed to fade away, Beatrice began to blossom.

As the Pattons grew apart during the thirties because of George's self-indulgent depression, the prospect of war forged them back together. Beatrice could have easily walked away, but WWII reconfirmed her belief in their shared destiny. She was not about to abandon someone and something she had worked thirty years for, favoring the Pattons "with a concluding chapter," albeit a short one.

After George's passing, Beatrice marched on like a good soldier without showing her true feelings. Her grief remained profound for the rest of her life, amplified by a lingering sense of unfairness, but it was private. She never made people feel uncomfortable by talking incessantly about her dead husband, nor did she let her grief overwhelm her to the point where she stopped living. Beatrice was devoted to her husband, and she was devoted to the Army, never shying away from her duties. She could have retired to Green Meadows and lived a quiet life; instead she picked up George's sword and made sure he was remembered the way he would have wanted.

If an officer's career depended on his ability, conduct, and wife, then fate had favored him with the perfect attributes. George Patton was a lucky man, but his greatest luck was meeting Beatrice Banning Ayer, and the most fortuitous decision of his life was marrying her. As with the heroes he admired, she was his Josephine (to Napoleon) and Olympias (to Alexander the Great). And like the brave and faithful Penelope who waited ten years for her husband Odysseus to return from Ithaca, Beatrice was loyal to one man only and fiercely so. She was a true soldier in all but combat experience, but she didn't care that "the bugles do not sound for us. There will be no taps at the Army wife's funeral."

Beatrice might never have been a suffragist or a stalwart of social change, but in her own selfless way, her contribution to the world was allowing George Patton to be the man he was destined to be, helping him shoulder the responsibilities of his destiny. She kept his life in order so he could focus on reaching his goal, always sympathetic to his ambitions no matter how crazy they might have sounded to anyone else.

Beatrice Ayer Patton didn't mind being the tail of the kite. As she reminded an audience of newly minted army wives, "How high can a kite fly without its tail?"[39]

# FAMILY TREES

**Figure 104.** *The Ayers, Bannings, and Pattons on Catalina Island in 1902. Front row: Joseph Brent Banning Jr., Hancock Banning Jr., Frederick "Fred" Ayer Jr., Hancock Banning. Second row: William Phineas Banning, Anne Ophelia Smith Banning, Katharine Stewart Banning, Anne "Nita" Patton, George Hugh Banning, Ellen Banning Ayer. Third row: Colonel George Hugh Smith, George, Eleanor Anne Banning, Beatrice, May Banning (Ellie's sister), Martha Craig, Susan Glassell Patton Wills, Katharine Mary Banning, Anne "Aunt Nannie" Wilson. Last row: Katharine "Kay" Ayer, William Banning, Frederick Ayer. (Huntington Library)*

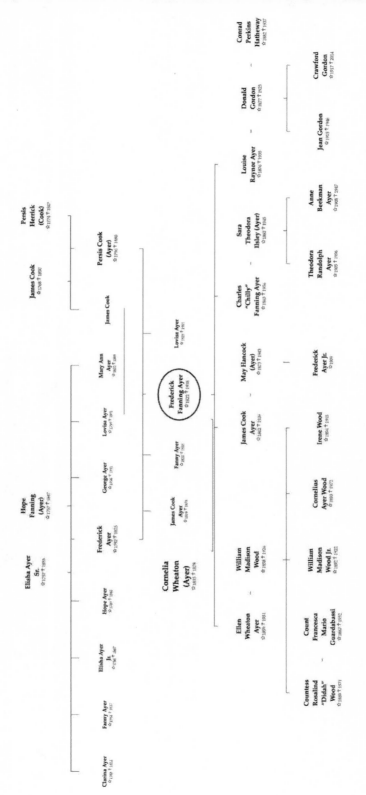

*The Ayers*

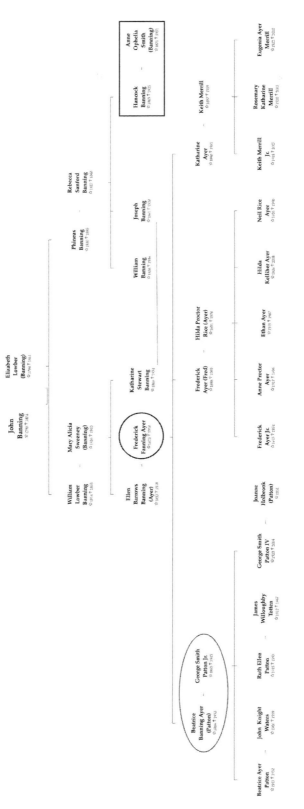

*The Bannings*

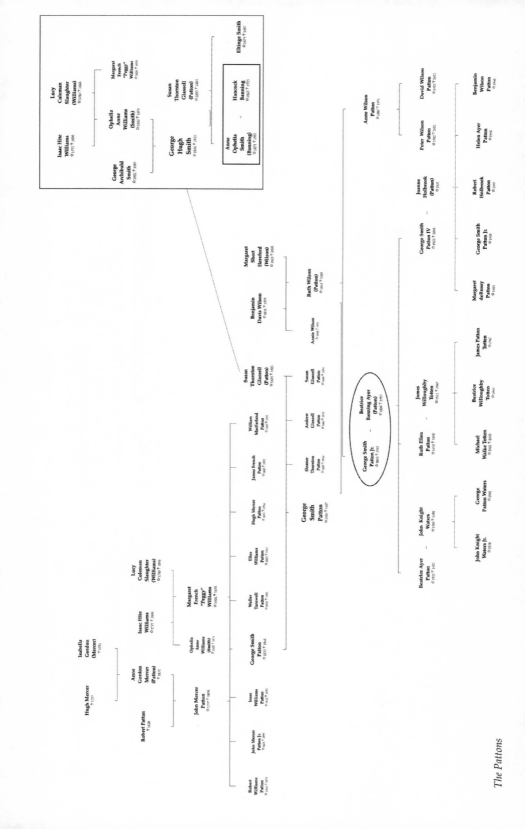

*The Pattons*

# ACKNOWLEDGMENTS

Ruth Ellen Patton Totten spent so many evenings listening to her father expound on the lives and campaigns of military leaders that she felt she could have walked up to Napoleon or Frederick the Great to converse with them.

That sums up the experience of writing a biography; it requires a certain degree of obsessiveness which takes hold the moment you realize you have met your subject. Mrs. Patton was a pleasant companion over the last three years of research and writing—especially during the Covid-19 lockdown.

Writing history, mainly as time marches on, means relying on those who have gone before. So, absorbing information from the hundreds of books and newspapers available, I am indebted to Robert H. Patton's *The Pattons: A Personal History of an American Family* and Ruth Ellen Patton Totten's *The Button Box: A Daughter's Loving Memoir of Mrs. George S. Patton*.

Some initial luck led me to Brian M. Sobel (*The Fighting Pattons*) and Denny G. Hair (*Patton Hidden in Plain Sight*), which set off a chain reaction of similarly exciting interviews. My gratitude goes toward the Ayer and Patton families, who unfailingly agreed to speak to yet another biographer, and provided additional material.

The lockdown made the process of researching and writing both more solitary and global. A sincere thank you to the countless thoughtful staff at the libraries and archives I visited, both virtual and in person. Of those, the George S. Patton Papers at the Library of Congress are the pinnacle, made easily researchable by the transcriptions Beatrice made decades ago and the knowledgeable staff, notably Bruce Kirby.

Bringing a book into the world takes a village, from editors and cover designers—Duncan Murrell and Robin Locke Monda—to supportive friends and family. I got my love of reading and writing from my grandfather, and while it skipped a generation, my father read the manuscript three times—in various stages of completion—and is still excited to read it a 4th time. I left the final read-through for a more impartial participant, Collette Richardson, whom I have gratefully dubbed my proofreader extraordinaire.

I hope you enjoyed reading *Lady of the Army* as much as I enjoyed writing it.

*Figure 105.* The calm before the storm in 1942. (Huntington Library)

*Figure 106.* Trudging through the mud at Fort Knox, a Sherman Tank in the background. (Patton Museum)

# BIBLIOGRAPHY

## BOOKS

Adams, John M. *The Millionaire and the Mummies: Theodore Davis's Gilded Age in the Valley of the Kings*. New York: St. Martin's Press, 2013.

Allen, Robert S. *Lucky Forward: The History of General George Patton's Third U.S. Army*. New York: MacFadden-Bartell Book, 1971.

Allen, Robert Sharon, and John Nelson Rickard. *Forward with Patton: The World War II Diary of Colonel Robert S. Allen*. Lexington, KY: University Press of Kentucky, 2017.

Ambrose, Kevin. *The Knickerbocker Snowstorm*. Charleston, SC: Arcadia Publishing, 2013.

Ambrose, Stephen E. *Citizen Soldiers: The US Army from the Normandy Beaches to the Surrender of Germany*. London: Pocket Books, 1998.

Anderson, Robert A. *Paddy: The Colorful Story of Colonel Harry A. "Paddy" Flint—the Fighting, Fearless Combat Commander of the 39th Infantry Regiment Who Originated the Legendary World War II Call to Battle, "Anything, Anywhere, Anytime, Bar Nothing!."* Westminster, MD: Eagle Editions, 2006.

Atkinson, Rick. *The Liberation Trilogy*. New York: Holt, 2007.

Axelrod, Alan, and Wesley C. Clark. *Patton a Biography*. Gordonsville: Palgrave Macmillan, 2014.

Ayer, Frederick. *Before the Colors Fade: Portrait of a Soldier, George S. Patton Jr*. New York: Houghton Mifflin, 1971.

Ayer, Frederick. *Memories of an Unplanned Life*. Seattle: F. Ayer, 1988.

Ayer, Frederick. *The Reminiscences of Frederick Ayer* . Boston: Privately Printed, 1923.

Ayer, Helen Harrison. *A Diplomat's Daughter*. Hamilton, MA: Privately Printed, n.d.

Ayer, Josephine Mellen. *Josephine Mellen Ayer; A Memoir*. New York: Knickerbocker Press, 1900.

Ayer, Neil Rice. *Wind over Willowdale*. Beverly, MA: Memoirs Unlimited, Inc., 1991.

Barron, Leo. *Patton at the Battle of the Bulge: How the General's Tanks Turned the Tide at Bastogne*. New York: New American Library, 2016.

Bergin, Billy. *Loyal to the Land: The Legendary Parker Ranch, 750–1950*. University of Hawaii Press, 2004.

Beverly Historical Society. *Images of America: Beverly Revisited*. Charleston, SC: Arcadia Pub., 2010.

Blumenson, Martin. *Patton, the Man behind the Legend, 1885–1945*. New York: Berkley Books, 1987.

Blumenson, Martin. *The Patton Papers: 1885–1940*. Boston: Hough Mifflin, 1972.

Blumenson, Martin. *The Patton Papers: 1940–1945*. Boston: Houghton, 1974.

Brandon, Dorothy Barrett. *Mamie Doud Eisenhower: A Portrait of a First Lady*. Whitefish, MT: Kessinger Publishing, 2010.

Brennan, Joseph. *The Parker Ranch of Hawaii: The Saga of a Ranch and a Dynasty*. Mutual Pub Co, 2004.

Cheney, Timothy C. *Reminiscences of Syracuse*. Syracuse: Summers, 1857.

Clarke, Thurston. *Pearl Harbor Ghosts: The Legacy of December 7, 1941*. Novato, CA: Presidio, 2003.

Codman, Charles R. *Drive*. Boston: Little, Brown and Company, 1957.

Coffman, Edward M. *The Old Army: A Portrait of the American Army in Peacetime, 1784–1898*. New York: Oxford University Press, 2014.

Coffman, Edward M. *The Regulars: The American Army, 1898–1941*. Cambridge, MA: Belknap, 2007.

Conner, Virginia. *What Father Forbad*. Philadelphia: Dorrance, 1951.

Cowley, Charles. *Reminiscences of James C. Ayer and the Town of Ayer*. Lowell: Penhallow Printing Company, 1879.

Crosswell D. K. R. *Beetle: The Life of General Walter Bedell Smith*. Lexington, KY: University Press of Kentucky, 2012.

D'Este, Carlo. *Patton: A Genius for War*. Norwalk, CT: Easton Press, 1999.

Dickson, Paul, and Thomas B. Allen. *The Bonus Army: An American Epic*. Mineola, NY: Dover Publications, Inc., 2020.

Dretske, Diana. *Images of America: Fort Sheridan*. Charleston, SC: Arcadia Pub., 2004.

DuRant, Maureen Oehler, and Peter J. Carroll. *West Point*. Charleston, SC: Arcadia Pub., 2007.

Dvorak, John. *Last Volcano: A Man, a Romance, and the Quest to Understand Nature's Most Magnificent Fury*. Pegasus Books, 2017.

Eisenhower, Dwight D. *At Ease: Stories I Tell My Friends*. Doubleday, 1967.

Eisenhower, Dwight D., and Louis Galambos. *The Papers of Dwight David Eisenhower*. Baltimore: Johns Hopkins University Press, 1984.

Eisenhower John S. D. *General Ike: A Personal Reminiscence*. New York: Free Press, 2004.

Eisenhower, Susan. *Mrs. Ike*. New York: HarperCollins, 1996.

Fanning, Edmund. *Voyages Round the World; with Selected Sketches of Voyages to the South Seas, North and South Pacific Oceans, China, Etc. Performed under the Command and Agency of the Author. Also, Information Relating to Important Late Discoveries; between the Years 1792 and 1832*. New York: Collins & Hamay, 1833.

Farago, Ladislas. *Patton: Ordeal and Triumph*. New York: Astor-Honor, 1964.

Farago, Ladislas. *The Last Days of Patton*. Yardley, Penn.: Westholme Pub., 2011.

Fraenkel, G. J., and Hugh Cairns. *Hugh Cairns: First Nuffield Professor of Surgery, Oxford University*. Oxford: Oxford University Press, 1991.

Garland, Joseph E. *Boston's Gold Coast: The North Shore, 1890–1929*. Boston: Little, Brown, 1981.

Glenn, Justin. *The Washingtons: A Family History*. 7. Vol. 7. 1. El Dorado Hills, CA: Savas Beatie, 2016.

Groom, Winston. *The Generals: Patton, Macarthur, Marshall, and the Winning of World War II*. Washington, D.C.: National Geographic, 2017.

Hair, Denny G. *Patton Hidden in Plain Sight Series*. 6 vols. Denny G. Hair, 2018.

Hamilton, Nigel. *War and Peace: FDR's Final Odyssey: D-Day to Yalta, 1943–1945*. Houghton Mifflin Harcourt, 2019.

Hatch, Alden. *George Patton: General in Spurs*. New York: Messner, 1965.

Heefner, Wilson A. *Dogface Soldier: The Life of General Lucian K. Truscott, Jr*. Columbia: University of Missouri Press, 2010.

Heefner, Wilson Allen. *Patton's Bulldog: The Life and Service of General Walton H. Walker*. Shippensburg, PA: White Mane, 2001.

Henley, David C. *The Land That God Forgot . . . : The Saga of Gen. George Patton's Desert Training Camps*. United States: Western Military History Association, 2000.

Hindley, Meredith. *Destination Casablanca: Exile, Espionage, and the Battle for North Africa in World War II*. New York, NY: PublicAffairs, 2019.

Hirshson, Stanley P. *General Patton: A Soldier's Life*. New York: Harper Perennial, 2006.

Hogg, Ian V. *The Biography of General George S. Patton*. Wigston, Leicester: Magna Book, 1982.

Holt, Marilyn Irvin. *Mamie Doud Eisenhower: The General's First Lady*. Lawrence, KS: University Press of Kansas, 2007.

Hoppes, Jonna Doolittle. *Calculated Risk: The Extraordinary Life of Jimmy Doolittle, Aviation Pioneer and World War II Hero; a Memoir*. Santa Monica, CA: Santa Monica Press, 2005.

Hoyt, Cliff, and Linda Hoyt. *A Century of Cures: Dr. J.C. Ayer & Co., Lowell, Mass., U.S.A.: A Reference Guide*. Lowell, MA: Lowell Historical Society, 2018.

Hymel, Kevin M. *Patton's Photographs*. Dulles, VA: Potomac, 2006.

Hymel, Kevin M. *Patton's War: An American General's Combat Leadership*. Columbia: University of Missouri Press, 2021.

Keane, Michael. *Patton: Blood, Guts, and Prayer*. Washington, DC: Regnery History, 2012.

Kipen, David. *Dear Los Angeles. the City in Diaries and Letters, 1542 to 2018*. Modern Lib. Inc, 2019.

Krythe, Maymie Richardson. *Port Admiral: Phineas Banning, 1830–1885*. San Francisco: California Historical Society, 1957.

Laflin, Patricia B. *Indio*. Charleston, SC: Arcadia Pub., 2008.

Lande, David A. *I Was with Patton: First-Person Accounts of WWII in George S. Patton's Command*. Osceola: MBI, 2002.

Letts, Elizabeth. *The Perfect Horse: The Daring Mission to Rescue the Priceless Stallions from the Nazis*. New York: Ballantine Books, 2017.

Lowry, Terry. *22nd Virginia Infantry*. Lynchburg, VA: H.E. Howard, 1991.

Marshall, George C., Forrest C. Pogue, and Larry I. Bland. *George C. Marshall: Interviews and Reminiscences for Forrest C. Pogue*. Lexington, Va: George C. Marshall Foundation, 1996.

Marshall, Katherine Tupper. *Together*. Chicago: Peoples Book Club, 1957.

Merrill, Katharine Ayer. *Keith Merrill, a Memoir*. Privately Printed, 1968.

Michael, John. *Images of America: Fort Myer*. Charleston, SC: Arcadia Pub., 2011.

Miller, Merle. *Ike the Soldier: As They Knew Him*. RosettaBooks, 2018.

Patton, Beatrice Ayer. *Blood of the Shark: A Romance of Early Hawaii*. Honolulu: Paradise of the Pacific, 1937.

Patton, Beatrice Ayer. *Love without End*. Honolulu, HI: Ku Pa'a Inc., 1989.

Patton, Benjamin, and Jennifer Scruby. *Growing up Patton / Reflections on Heroes, History and Family Wisdom*. New York: Berkley Caliber, 2012.

Patton, Béatrice Ayer. *Légendes Hawaïiennes*. Paris: Les Belles Lettres, 1932.

Patton, George S. *War as I Knew It*. Boston: Houghton Mifflin Company, 1947.

Patton, George S., and Carmine A. Prioli. *The Poems of General George S. Patton, Jr.: Lines of Fire*. Lewiston, NY: Edwin Mellen Press, 1991.

Patton, Robert H. *The Pattons: A Personal History of an American Family*. Lincoln, Neb.: Potomac Books, an imprint of the University of Nebraska Press, 2004.

Podhajsky, Alois. *My Dancing White Horses*. Harrap, 1964.

Polk, James H. *World War II Letters and Notes of Colonel James H. Polk, 1944–1945*. Oakland, OR: Red Anvil Press, 2005.

Province, Charles M. *General Walton H. Walker: The Man who Saved Korea*. Charles M. Province, 2011.

Province, Charles M. *The Unknown Patton*. Charles M. Province, 2009.

Pulsifer, Janice Preston. *Changing Town, Hamilton, Massachusetts, 1850–1910*. Hamilton, MA: Hamilton Historical Society (MA), 1985.

Rabalais, Steven. *General Fox Conner: Pershing's Chief of Operations and Eisenhower's Mentor*. Havertown: Casemate, 2021.

Read, Nat B. Don Benito *Wilson: From Mountain Man to Mayor, Los Angeles, 1841 to 1878*. Pasadena, CA: Desert Tide Publishing Company, 2015.

Rickard, John Nelson. *Advance and Destroy: Patton as Commander in the Bulge*. Lexington, KY: The University Press of Kentucky, 2018.

Ritchie, Donald A. *The Columnist: Leaks, Lies, and Libel in Drew Pearson's Washington*. New York, NY: Oxford University Press, 2021.

Roddy, Edward G. *Mills, Mansions, and Mergers: The Life of William M. Wood*. North Andover, MA: Merrimack Valley Textile Museum, 1982.

Rodgers, Russ. *Historic Photos of George Patton*. Nashville, TN: Turner Pub. Co., 2007.

Sarantakes, Nicholas Evan. *Making Patton: A Classic War Film's Epic Journey to the Silver Screen*. Lawrence: University Press of Kansas, 2012.

Schubert, Frank N. *Outpost of the Sioux Wars: A History of Fort Robinson*. Lincoln: Univ. of Nebraska Press, 1995.

Schultz, Duane. *Patton's Last Gamble: The Disastrous Raid on POW Camp Hammelburg in World War II*. Pennsylvania.: Stackpole Books, 2022.

Seamans, Eugenia Ayer Merrill. *Light and Life*. Beverly Farms, MA: Privately Printed, 2003.

Seamans, Robert C. *Aiming at Targets: The Autobiography of Robert C. Seamans, JR*. Washington, DC: For sale by the U.S. G.P.O., Supt. of Docs, 1996.

Semmes, Harry Hodges. *Portrait of Patton*. New York: Paperback Library Edition, 1972.

Showalter, Dennis E. *Patton and Rommel: Men of War in the 20th Century*. New York: Berkley Caliber, 2006.

Sitton, Tom. *Grand Ventures: The Banning Family and the Shaping of Southern California*. San Marino, CA: Huntington Library, 2010.

Snow, Adam, and Shelley Onderdonk. *Polo Life: Horses, Sport, 10 and Zen*. Aiken, SC: NHF Press, 2016.

Sobel, Brian. *The Fighting Pattons*. Bloomington: Indiana University Press, 2013.

Stelpflug, Peggy A., and Richard Hyatt. *Home of the Infantry: The History of Fort Benning*. Macon, GA: Mercer Univ. Press, 2007.

Steward, Scott C. *The Sarsaparilla Kings: A Biography of Dr. James Cook Ayer and Frederick Ayer with a Record of Their Family*. Cambridge, MA: S.C. Steward, 1993.

Summersby, Kay. *Eisenhower Was My Boss*. Werner Laurie, 1949.

Totten, Ruth Ellen Patton. *The Button Box: A Daughter's Loving Memoir of Mrs. George S. Patton.* ed. James Patton Totten. Columbia, Missouri: University of Missouri Press, 2005.

Totten, Ruth Ellen Patton. *The Rolling Kitchen.* Riverside, 1960.

Twain, Mark. *Roughing It.* Orinda: SeaWolf Press, 2018.

Unger, Debi, Irwin Unger, and Stanley P. Hirshson. *George Marshall: A Biography.* New York: Harper Perennial, 2016.

Watson, Frederick, and Paul Brown. *Hunting Pie: The Whole Art & Craft of Fox Hunting.* New York: The Derrydale Press, 1931.

Wellard, James. *General George S. Patton, Jr., Man under Mars.* New York: Dodd, Mead & Company, 1946.

Welsome, Eileen. *The General and the Jaguar: Pershing's Hunt for Pancho Villa; a True Story of Revolution and Revenge.* Lincoln: University of Nebraska Press, 2007.

Westervelt, W. D. *Legends of Maui.* Hawaiian Library, 2021.

Wheaton, Ellen Douglas Birdeye, and Donald Gordon. *The Diary of Ellen Birdseye Wheaton.* Boston, 1923.

Wheeler, James Scott, and Rick Atkinson. *Jacob L. Devers: A General's Life.* Lexington, KY: University Press of Kentucky, 2018.

Wilcox, Robert K. *Target: Patton: An Investigation into the Clandestine Plot against America's Greatest Fighting General.* New York: HarperCollins Publishers, 2010.

Yeide, Harry. *Fighting Patton George S. Patton Jr. through the Eyes of His Enemies.* Minneapolis, MN: Zenith Press, 2014.

## SELECTED ARTICLES AND PAPERS

Ball, Stuart M. "The Piko Club: Hiking O'ahu in the 1930s." *The Hawaiian Journal of History* 37 (2003): 179–97. https://evols.library.manoa.hawaii.edu/handle/10524/145

Benjamin-Constant, J.J. "My Portraits." *Harper's Monthly Magazine* CII, no. DCXII, 1901.

Brown, Nell Porter. "The Scandalous Mansion." *Harvard Magazine,* 2017. https://www.harvard-magazine.com/2017/01/scandalous-mansion

Compiled and Edited by the Historical Association, Wenham Village Improvement Society, Inc. *Wenham in World War II,* 1947. https://archive.org/details/wenhaminworld-war00wenh/page/24/mode/2up

Complete Report of the Board of Health and Board of Consulting Physicians: As Presented to the City Council, December 12th, 1871: To Which Is Annexed Instructions for Controlling Small-Pox Contagion. Stone & Huse, 1871.

Cox, Edward. "Grey Eminence: Fox Conner and the Art of Mentorship." *The Land Warfare Papers,* no. 78W (September 2010). https://www.ausa.org/sites/default/files/LWP-78-Grey-Eminence-Fox-Conner-and-the-Art-of-Mentorship.pdf

Cramer, Stuart W. "Georgie." *Redbook* 81, no. 5, 1943. http://ezproxy.nypl.org/login?url=https://www.proquest.com/magazines/georgie/docview/1847800306/se-2?accountid=35635

D'Este, Carlo. "A Very Special Lady." *Armchair General,* June 28, 2012. http://armchairgeneral.com/a-very-special-lady.htm

Donovan, William H. "Donald Munro Lecture. Spinal cord injury—past, present, and future." *The Journal of Spinal Cord Medicine,* vol. 30,2 (2007): 85-100. doi: 10.1080/10790268.2007.11753918

Drake, Stuart A. "Settings for Plutocrats." *Historic New England,* 2014. https://issuu.com/historic-newengland/docs/historic_new_england_spring_2014/22

Early, Eleanor. "True Confessions Salutes A Hero's Wife." *True Confessions,* 1943.

Emerson, J.S. "Selections from a Kahuna's Book of Prayers." *Twenty-Sixth Annual Report of the Hawaiian Historical Society,* 1918, 17–39. https://evols.library.manoa.hawaii.edu/handle/10524/73

Field, John. "Patton of the Armored Force." *Life Magazine* , November 30, 1942.

Gabel, Christopher R. *The U.S. Army GHQ Maneuvers of 1941.* Washington DC: Center of Military History United States Army, 1992. https://history.army.mil/html/books/070/70–41–1/CMH_Pub_70-41-1.pdf

Gaut, Helen Lukens. "Architecture and Furnishing: Avalon—A Notable Summer Residence." *Vogue,* May 15, 1910. http://ezproxy.nypl.org/login?url=https://www.proquest.com/magazines/architecture-furnishing-avalon-notable-summer/docview/911843635/se-2?accountid=35635

Hamilton Historical Society. "Annual Report for the Town of Hamilton, Massachusetts, 1945." 1945. https://archive.org/details/townofhamiltonan1945unse/page/42/mode/2up

Kushner, Prof. Jack. "The Most Devastating of Life's Disasters." *JOJ Nurse Health Care.* 2018; 6(3): 555687. DOI: 10.19080/JOJNHC.2018.06.555687

Lovelace, Alexander G. "The Image of a General: The Wartime Relationship between General George S. Patton Jr. and the American Media." *Journalism History* 40, no. 2 (2014): 108–20. http://ezproxy.nypl.org/login?url=https://www.proquest.com/scholarly-journals/image-general-wartime-relationship-between-george/docview/1554317389/se-2?accountid=35635

Morris, Nancy J. "Beatrice Pattern's Hawai'i." *The Hawaiian Journal of History* 39 (2005): 75–90. https://evols.library.manoa.hawaii.edu/bitstream/10524/236/JL39081.pdf

Nagle, Mary Dunning. "A Sweeney Sampler." *Minnesota History Magazine,* 1968. http://collections.mnhs.org/MNHistoryMagazine/articles/41/v41i01p029–033.pdf

Park, William B. "Homemade Diving Helmet to Find Lost Motors." *Popular Mechanics,* September 1932.

Patton, Beatrice Ayer. "A Soldier's Reading." *Armor,* 1952.

Patton, Beatrice Ayer. "The Army Wife." *The Atlantic Monthly,* January 1943.

Prioli, Carmine A. "King Arthur in Khaki: The Medievalism of General George S. Patton, Jr." *Studies in Popular Culture,* 1, 10 (1987): 42–50. https://www.jstor.org/stable/23412924

Rovit, Richard, Arlene Stolper Simon, and William T. Couldwell. "Patton: Death of a Soldier." *Journal of Neurosurgery,* JNS 108, 2 (2008): 402-408. https://doi.org/10.3171/JNS/2008/108/2/0402

St. John, Adela Rogers. "Lieut. Gen. and Mrs. George S. Patton, Jr." *Cosmopolitan Magazine* 115, no. 5, November 1943.

St. John, Jeffrey. "Reflections of a Fighting Father." *Patton Society Research Library,* 1985. http://patton-hq.com/textfiles/reflect.html

Stone, James L et al. "Sir Hugh Cairns and World War II British advances in head injury management, diffuse brain injury, and concussion: an Oxford tale." *Journal of Neurosurgery,* vol. 125,5 (2016): 1301-1314. doi: 10.3171/2015.8.JNS142613

Storrs, Francis. "A Stranger in the House of Ayer." *Boston Magazine,* February 3, 2015. https://www.bostonmagazine.com/2007/11/20/a-stranger-in-the-house-of-ayer

Wilson, Harold E. "A Legend In His Own Mind: The Olympic Experience of General George S. Patton, Jr." *OLYMPIKA: The International Journal of Olympic Studies* VI, no. 1997 (n.d.): 99–114. https://www.academia.edu/27607651/A_Legend_In_His_Own_Mind_The_Olympic_Experience_of_General_George_S._Patton_Jr

## INTERVIEWS

Neil Rice Ayer Jr.: April 27, 2022

Beatrice Totten Britton: September 17, 2019

Denny Hair: October 6, 2021

Kevin Hymel: April 25, 2022

Caleb Loring III: April 18, 2022

Helen Ayer Patton: February 2, 2022

Joanne Holbrook Patton: May 2, 2022

Robert Patton: May 4, 2022

Brian Sobel: April 26, 2021

Scott C. Steward: August 2, 2021

James Patton Totten: June 9, 2022

George Patton Waters: October 22, 2021

## COLLECTIONS AND ARCHIVES

Albert W. Kenner Papers, U.S. Army Heritage and Education Center, Carlisle, PA.

American Battle Monuments Commission, Arlington, VA.

Banning Family Collection & George S. Patton Sr. Collection, Manuscript Collection, Huntington Library, California. **HLC-GSP**

Beverly Historical Society, Beverly, Ma.

Dwight D. Eisenhower Presidential Library, Abilene, Kansas.

Everett Strait Hughes Papers, Manuscript Division, Library of Congress, Washington, D.C.

Franklin D. Roosevelt Library, Hyde Park, New York.

General George Patton Museum Of Leadership, Fort Knox, Kentucky.

George S. Patton Letters 1909 - 1945, Patton, George S. (George Smith), 1885–1945, USMA.

George S. Patton Papers, USMA 1909, United States Military Academy Library, West Point.

George S. Patton Papers, Manuscript Division, Library of Congress, Washington, D.C. **LOC-PP**

Hobart R. Gay Collection, U.S. Army Heritage and Education Center, Carlisle, PA.

James Earle & Laura Gardin Fraser Papers, Special Collections Research Center, Syracuse University Libraries. **SUL-GFP**

James G. Harbord Papers, MS 1493, The New-York Historical Society, New York, New York. **NYHS-HP**

James H. Polk Papers, U.S. Army Heritage and Education Center, Carlisle, PA.

Keith Merrill Papers (MS 1480). Manuscripts and Archives, Yale University Library.

Lawrence History Center, Lawrence, MA.

National Archives, Washington, D.C.

New York Public Library: Ancestry Immigration Records, Newspapers.com.

Patton Family Archives at the Patton Homestead, Wenham Museum, Wenham, Massachusetts.

Patton Family Papers, Manuscript Collection, Huntington Library, California.

Paul D. Harkins Papers, U.S. Army Heritage and Education Center, Carlisle, PA.

Truman Papers, Truman Library, Independence, Missouri.

**ADDITIONAL ABBREVIATIONS IN THE NOTES:**

- **AP**: Anne "Nita" Wilson Patton
- **AW**: Annie "Aunt Nannie" Wilson
- **BAP**: Beatrice Ayer Patton
- **BPW**: Beatrice Patton Waters
- **DDE**: Dwight D. Eisenhower
- **EBA**: Ellie Banning Ayer
- **ESH**: Everett Strait Hughes
- **FA**: Frederick "Fred" Ayer
- **FFA**: Frederick Fanning Ayer
- **GP**: George S. Patton Sr.
- **GSP**: George S. Patton Jr.
- **GSPIV**: George S. Patton IV
- **JGH**: James Guthrie Harbord
- **JJP**: John J. Pershing
- **KAM**: Katharine Ayer Merrill
- **RPT**: Ruth Ellen Patton Totten
- **RWP**: Ruth Wilson Patton

# NOTES

## INTRODUCTION

1. Martin Blumenson, *The Patton Papers: 1885-1945* (Boston: Houghton Mifflin Company, 1972), 13.
2. Adela Rogers St. Johns, "Lieut. Gen. and Mrs. George S. Patton, Jr.," *Cosmopolitan Magazine*, November 1943.
3. All maxims are from Ruth Ellen Patton Totten, *The Button Box: A Daughter's Loving Memoir of Mrs. George S. Patton*, ed. James Patton Totten (Columbia, Missouri: University of Missouri Press, 2005).
4. Fred Ayer, Jr., *Before the Colors Fade: Portrait of a Soldier, George S. Patton Jr.* (Boston: Houghton Mifflin Company, 1964), 4.

## BEDFORD ARMY AIRFIELD, MASSACHUSETTS

1. "Patton Arrives Today, Weather Worries Wife," *Chicago Daily Tribune*, June 7, 1945.
2. GSP to BAP, 5 December 1942, box 10, folder 12, LOC-PP. The cannon's provenance is inconclusive. Another possibility is that it dates from seventeenth-century Seville under the reign of King Philip IV of Spain.
3. Eleanor Early, "True Confessions Salutes A Hero's Wife," *True Confessions*, December 1943.
4. Glen Spurling, "The Patton Episode," 1950, box 14, folder 11, LOC-PP.
5. "Mrs. Patton's Comment is: 'I'm on My Knees,'" *New York Herald Tribune*, May 8, 1945.
6. "Mrs. Patton Counts Minutes to Time of Meeting Husband," *The Boston Globe*, June 6, 1945.
7. Joseph Dinneen, "Patton Shakes Hands with 3000 Neighbors," *Boston Daily Globe*, June 25, 1945.
8. George S. Patton Jr, diary entry 4 July 1945, LOC-PP. https://loc.gov/item/mss35634039/
9. Larrry Newman, "Gen. Patton 'Nervous,'" *The Austin Statesman*, June 4, 1945.
10. Brian M. Sobel, *The Fighting Pattons* (Westport: Praeger, 1997), XVI.
11. GSP to BAP, 26 April 1908, box 5, folder 3, LOC-PP.
12. GSP WWII diary, 3 November 1942, LOC-PP. https://loc.gov/item/mss35634025/
13. George S. Patton Jr., *War as I Knew It* (Boston: Houghton Mifflin Company, 1947), 105.
14. "Patton Flying to States," *The Austin Statesman*, June 7, 1945.
15. GSP to BAP, September 1907, box 5, folder 2, LOC-PP.
16. Ruth Ellen Patton Totten, interview by William Heitz, *Hamilton-Wenham's Times Past*, 1987. https://archive.org/details/HWTPSDVD37
17. George S. Patton Jr., "My Father as I Knew Him and of Him from Memory and Legend," 1927, box 23, folder 18, LOC-PP.
18. GSP to BAP, 29 September 1945, box 13, folder 16, LOC-PP.
19. "About the Author," *Los Angeles Times*, November 28, 1943.
20. Harry Semmes, "General Patton's Toast to the Ladies," *Boston Daily Globe*, September 21, 1955.
21. GSP to JGH, 22 October 1945, box 36, folder 15, NYHS-HP.
22. Dorothy Wayman, "Wife Gets Patton's First Kiss, then Cadet Son, Daughters," *Boston Daily Globe*, June 8, 1945.
23. "Gen. Patton Arrives," *Boston Evening Globe*, June 7, 1945.
24. Newman, "Gen. Patton 'Nervous.'"
25. "Swathed in Medals, Pistols, Patton Hailed in New England," *The Washington Post*, June 8, 1945.
26. William M. Blair, "1,000,000 Welcome Gen. Patton Home," *The New York Times*, June 8, 1945.
27. "Big Welcome Given Patton in Boston," *Hartford Courant*, June 8, 1945.
28. Rick Atkinson, *An Army at Dawn: The War in North Africa, 1942-1943* (New York: Henry Holt and Company, 2002), chapter 10, Kindle; George S. Patton Jr., "To Beatrice," October 1916, box 74, folder 1, LOC-PP.
29. "Statesman and GI Pay Patton Honor," *The New York Times*, December 22, 1945.

30. Fred Ayer Jr., *Before the Colors Fade*, 237.
31. Leonard Lerner, "Patton Weeps for His Men at Banquet," *Boston Daily Globe*, June 8, 1945.
32. "Patton: Smiles-Cheers-Tears," *The Christian Science Monitor*, June 8, 1945.
33. Charles R. Codman, *Drive* (Boston: Little, Brown and Company, 1957), 319.

## PART I

1. Beatrice Ayer Patton, "An Invocation To Avalon-Our Isle of the Blest!" box 74, folder 4, LOC-PP.

## 1. THE FARM

1. "Horrible Catastrophe!," *Los Angeles Star*, May 2, 1863; "Obituary," *Los Angeles Star*, July 18, 1863; D.J. Waldi, "Horrible Catastrophe! Disaster in Civil-War-Era Los Angeles," *Kcet.org*, June 6, 2017. https://www.kcet.org/shows/lost-la/horrible-catastrophe-disaster-in-civil-war-era-los-angeles
2. Totten, *The Button Box*, 13.
3. Totten, *The Button Box*, 34.
4. Frederick Ayer, *The Reminiscences of Frederick Ayer* (Boston: Privately Printed, 1923), 10.
5. Elisha Ayer was born in August 1757 in Groton, Connecticut. He was the fifth in descent from John Ayr (an old Scottish word for eagle's nest), who arrived in Salisbury, Massachusetts, in 1635 from Wiltshire, England. The Ayers moved to Connecticut from Massachusetts in 1695.
6. Eugenia Ayer Merrill Seamans, *Light and Life* (Beverly Farms: Privately Printed, 2003), 2. Elisha and his two cohorts had jumped overboard on a moonless night when the ship laid anchor outside of Quebec and swam the three miles to shore with incredible difficulty. They hid in a swamp for a day until the British gave up their search. Then, with the help of a local, the fugitives managed to get passage on a Scottish ship sailing to Halifax, Nova Scotia, where they stole a small sailboat. Once they made it to Boston, they sold the boat and continued their journey to Connecticut on foot.
7. Frederick Ayer, *The Reminiscences of Frederick Ayer*, 3.
8. Totten, *The Button Box*, 7.
9. Charles Cowley, *Reminiscences of James C. Ayer and the Town of Ayer* (Lowell: Penhallow Printing Company, 1879), 14.
10. Seamans, *Light and Life*, 3.
11. "Tribal History," *The Mashantucket (Western) Pequot Tribal Nation*, accessed August 7, 2022. https://www.mptn-nsn.gov/tribalhistory.aspx
12. Frederick Ayer, *The Reminiscences of Frederick Ayer*, 15.
13. Frederick Ayer, *The Reminiscences of Frederick Ayer*, 34.
14. Timothy Collingwood Cheney, *Reminiscences of Syracuse* (Syracuse: Summers, 1857), 7; Frederick Ayer, *The Reminiscences of Frederick Ayer*, 20.
15. Cowley, *Reminiscences of James C. Ayer and the Town of Ayer*, 25.
16. Totten, *The Button Box*, 8.
17. Frederick Ayer, *The Reminiscences of Frederick Ayer*, 40.
18. Cliff and Linda Hoyt, *A Century of Cures: Dr. J.C. Ayer & Co.* (Lowell: Lowell Historical Society, 2018).
19. Cliff and Linda Hoyt, *A Century of Cures: Dr. J.C. Ayer & Co.* (Lowell: Lowell Historical Society, 2018). Ague Cure would ultimately be scientifically proven to be effective against malaria, because it contained quinine.
20. Ellen Birdseye Wheaton, *The Diary of Ellen Birdseye Wheaton* (Boston: Privately Printed, 1923), 309.
21. Frederick Ayer, *The Reminiscences of Frederick Ayer*, 46.
22. Frederick Ayer, *The Reminiscences of Frederick Ayer*, 43.
23. Frederick Ayer, *The Reminiscences of Frederick Ayer*, 50-51.
24. Frederick Ayer, *The Reminiscences of Frederick Ayer*, 60.
25. "Frederick Ayer, Winter Resident, Died Yesterday," *Daily Times Enterprise*, March 15, 1918.
26. *The Complete Report of the Board of Health and Board of Consulting Physicians, As Presented to the City Council, December 12th, 1871* (United States: Stone & Huse, 1871).

27. "Small-Pox: How The Disease Was Exterminated In Lowell, Mass," *The New York Times*, December 25, 1872.

28. *The Complete Report of the Board of Health and Board of Consulting Physicians, As Presented to the City Council*, 6. Lowell's smallpox epidemic lasted eight months, sickened 570, and killed 172. If "duty to the public and the cause of humanity" had been as important to the old Board as economic and political issues, far fewer lives would have been "sacrificed."

29. Richard Howe, "Franco American School: Some History," *Lowell Politics & History*, December 19, 2016. https://richardhowe.com/2016/12/19/franco-american-school-history/

30. Shepley, Bullfinch, Richardson, and Abbott, "Pawtucket Street, 357 - Frederick Ayer Mansion," *Lowell Historical Architectural Inventory*, accessed August 7, 2022. https://lowellhistarch.omeka.net/items/show/751

31. "Mrs. Ayer was famous," *Chicago Tribune*, January 6, 1898.

32. Sometimes also spelled Banning-Coq.

33. "Notes on Ellen Banning and William Lowber Banning," box 4, folder 7, Banning Company Records, Addenda II, The Huntington Library, San Marino, California.

34. Mary Dunning Nagle, "A Sweeney Sampler," *Minnesota History Magazine*, 1968, 29–33.

35. Totten, *The Button Box*, 9-10.

36. Totten, *The Button Box*, 10.

37. Frederick Ayer, *The Reminiscences of Frederick Ayer*, 76-66.

38. Totten, *The Button Box*, 13.

39. Frederick Ayer, *The Reminiscences of Frederick Ayer*, 77.

40. Frederick Ayer, *The Reminiscences of Frederick Ayer*, 70.

41. Edward G. Roddy, *Mills, Mansions, and Mergers: The Life of William M. Wood* (North Andover: Merrimack Valley Textile Museum, 1982), 34.

42. Roddy, *Mills, Mansions, and Mergers*, 15.

43. Totten, *The Button Box*, 19.

44. Virginia Conner, *What Father Forbad* (Philadelphia: Dorrance, 1951), 50.

45. Totten, *The Button Box*, 29.

46. Jean-Joseph Benjamin-Constant, "My Portraits," *Harper's Monthly Magazine*, no. DCXII, May 1901.

47. "Amazing Story of One Woman's Rise to Power," *The World (New York, New York)*, January 6, 1898.

48. "Travelers in the Middle East Archive," *Rice Digital Scholarship Archive*, accessed August 9, 2022. https://scholarship.rice.edu/handle/123456789/1

49. BAP, "Voyage of Arcturus," box 10, folder 7, LOC-PP.

50. Totten, *The Button Box*, 31.

51. Totten, *The Button Box*, 30.

52. BAP to GSP, 4 January 1943, box 10, folder 13, LOC-PP.

53. Frederick Ayer, *The Reminiscences of Frederick Ayer*, 79.

54. The Frederick Ayer Mansion in Lowell stood mostly vacant until 1908 when Frederick sold it to three Catholic priests from the St. Jean Baptiste Parish for a symbolic $1. Since then, it has been an orphanage run by the Sisters of Charity of Quebec, the Franco-American School, and forty affordable housing units. Today, a Massachusetts Bicentennial Marker identifies it as the house where "Beatrice Ayer, the wife of General Patton," was born, built by Frederick Ayer "to reflect his new position and wealth." Two inscriptions were unveiled in 1971: "George: I fought a good fight. I've finished my course. I've kept the faith;" and "Beatrice: Her children are up, and called her blessed: her husband also, and he praised her."

55. "395 Commonwealth," *Back Bay Houses, Genealogies of Back Bay Houses*, accessed August 9, 2022. https://backbayhouses.org/395-commonwealth/

56. Katherine Ayer Merrill, *Keith Merrill, a Memoir* (Privately Printed, 1968), 32.

57. Beth Treffeisen, "Below Stairs at the Ayer Mansion," *Beacon Hill Times*, February 9, 2018. http://beaconhilltimes.com/2018/02/09/below-stairs-at-the-ayer-mansion/

58. Frederick Ayer, *The Reminiscences of Frederick Ayer*, 79. While the Ayer Mansion was considered scandalous and brash upon its completion in 1902, today it is a National Historic Landmark, standing as the last remaining residential commission entirely designed by Tiffany. It is currently for sale for $17 million and has been renamed the Tiffany Ayer Mansion.

59. "Tiffany Chapel," *The Charles Hosmer Morse Museum of American Art*, accessed August 9, 2022. https://morsemuseum.org/louis-comfort-tiffany/tiffany-chapel/

60. Nell Porter Brown, "The Scandalous Mansion," *Harvard Magazine*, January-February 2017.

https://www.harvardmagazine.com/2017/01/scandalous-mansion
61. Treffeisen, "Below Stairs at the Ayer Mansion."
62. Robert H. Patton, *The Pattons: A Personal History of an American Family* (New York: Crown Publishers, 1994), chapter 11, Kindle.
63. Brown, "The "Scandalous Mansion."
64. Seamans, *Light and Life*, 11.
65. Frederick Ayer, *The Reminiscences of Frederick Ayer*, 76.
66. D'Este, *Patton: A Genius for War*, 56.
67. Totten, *The Button Box*, 338; Beatrice Ayer Patton, "The Army Wife," *The Atlantic Monthly*, January 1943, box 11, folder 13, LOC-PP.
68. Interview Robert Patton.

## 2. LAKE VINEYARD

1. Conner, *What Father Forbad*, 51.
2. GSP to RWP, March 1905, box 4, folder 14, LOC-PP.
3. Robert Patton, *The Pattons*, chapter 11, Kindle.
4. GSP, "My Father as I Knew Him and of Him from Memory and Legend." Patton was not his real last name, but it was the one favored by Scottish immigrants seeking anonymity.
5. *The Death of General Mercer at the Battle of Princeton, January 3, 1777.*
6. Robert Patton, *The Pattons*, chapter 3, Kindle.
7. D'Este, *Patton: A Genius for War*, 13.
8. Robert Patton, *The Pattons*, chapter 4, Kindle.
9. George S. Patton Sr., "A Child's Memory of the Civil War," 1927, box 23, folder 18, LOC-PP.
10. D'Este, *Patton: A Genius for War*, 37.
11. Peggy Williams Patton had a sister, Ophelia Anne Williams, who married George A. Smith. Their son was George Hugh Smith, born in Philadelphia in 1834.
12. GSP, "My Father as I Knew Him and of Him from Memory and Legend."
13. Robert Patton, *The Pattons*, chapter 6, Kindle.
14. Robert Patton, *The Pattons*, chapter 6, Kindle.
15. "Death of Benjamin Davis Wilson," *Los Angeles Evening Express*, March 11, 1878.
16. Nat B. Read, *Don Benito Wilson: From Mountain Man to Mayor, Los Angeles, 1841 to 1878* (Pasadena: Desert Tide Publishing Company, 2015), chapter 1, Kindle.
17. Life as a ranchero was no walk in the park either. One time Don Benito was mauled by a bear and was left for dead, but he went back to kill the animal after recuperating. Another time he was shot by a poisoned arrow when he led a campaign into the mountains against the Mojave Indians who were killing settlers and stealing cattle.
18. Read, *Don Benito Wilson*, chapter 5, Kindle.
19. Read, *Don Benito Wilson*, chapter 16, Kindle.
20. Read, *Don Benito Wilson*, chapter 26, Kindle.
21. When Wilson sold Rancho San Jose de Buenos Ayers, it eventually landed in the hands of Burton Green from the Amalgamated Oil Company. He divided the land into smaller parcels and called the property Beverly Hills, after his hometown, Beverly Farms, in Massachusetts.
22. GSP, "My Father as I Knew Him and of Him from Memory and Legend."
23. Read, *Don Benito Wilson*, chapter 24, Kindle.
24. GSP, "My Father as I Knew Him and of Him from Memory and Legend."
25. D'Este, *Patton: A Genius for War*, 35.
26. D'Este, *Patton: A Genius for War*, 37.
27. Tom Cameron, "General's Life Full Of Thrills During Boyhood," *Los Angeles Times*, June 07, 1945.
28. D'Este, *Patton: A Genius for War*, 47-48.
29. GSP to BAP, 8 July 1908, box 5, folder 4, LOC-PP.
30. "Santa Catalina Island: Nearly A Big Fish Record. Tame Tournament. Island Brevities," *The Los Angeles Times*, September 9, 1902.
31. "Crowds Smashing Catalina's Record," *The Los Angeles Times*, August 19, 1902.
32. BAP to AW, 1 October 1902, box 4, folder 5, LOC-PP.
33. BAP to RWP, as quoted in Totten, *The Button Box*, 68.

34. GSP to BAP, 10 January 1903, box 4, folder 6, LOC-PP.
35. GSP, "Facts, dates, and incidents of my life," July 11, 1913, box 5, folder 17, LOC-PP. A blessing in disguise—or "fate," as Mr. Patton called it—because almost the whole force was killed in the Battle of Shaykan.
36. Members of Congress only received new appointments once their previously selected cadets dropped out or graduated, and each member had their own process for choosing a candidate. Moreover, being nominated was still no guarantee of admission because there was also the West Point exam to contend with.
37. GP to Senator Bard, 22 February 1903, box 4, folder 6, LOC-PP.
38. Senator Bard to GP, 3 March 1903, box 4, folder 7, Library of Congress, LOC-PP.

## 3. THE AYER MANSION

1. Seamans, *Light and Life*, 86.
2. Totten, *The Button Box*, 81.
3. GSP to EBA, August 1909, box 5, folder 7, LOC-PP; Totten, *The Button Box*, 81.
4. GSP to BAP, 26 April 1908, box 5, folder 3, LOC-PP.
5. GSP to BAP, 5 November 1909, box 5, folder 8, LOC-PP.
6. GSP to BAP, 21 March 1909, box 5, folder 6, LOC-PP; GSP to BAP, 4 April 1909, box 5, folder 6, LOC-PP; GSP to BAP, 20 February 1910, box 5, folder 6, LOC-PP.
7. GSP, "My Father as I Knew Him and of Him from Memory and Legend."
8. John Mercer Patton to GP, 8 February 1903, box 4, folder 6, LOC-PP.
9. D'Este, *Patton: A Genius for War*, 36.
10. GSP to GP, 14 December 1906, box 4, folder 16, LOC-PP.
11. GP to GSP, March 1904, box 4, folder 11, LOC-PP.
12. GSP to BAP, 10 July 1904, box 4, folder 12, LOC-PP.
13. "Lovely Debutante Party: Presentation Of Miss Beatrice Ayer By Her Mother At Their Home On Commonwealth Avenue," *Boston Daily Globe*, December 16, 1904.
14. "Table Gossip," *Boston Daily Globe*, March 13, 1910.
15. "Table Gossip," *Boston Daily Globe*, December 18, 1904; GSP to BAP, 18 December 1904, box 4, folder 13, LOC-PP.
16. GSP to BAP, 11 December 1904, box 4, folder 13, LOC-PP.
17. GSP to AW, 31 December 1905, box 4, folder 15, LOC-PP.
18. GSP to BAP, November 1904, box 4, folder 13, LOC-PP.
19. GSP to BAP, Fall 1904, box 4, folder 13, LOC-PP.
20. GSP to GP, 15 August 1904, box 4, folder 12, LOC-PP; GSP to BAP, January 1906, box 4, folder 16, LOC-PP.
21. GSP to BAP, 7 March 1905, box 4, folder 14, LOC-PP.
22. GSP to GP, 18 March 1905, box 4, folder 14, LOC-PP.
23. GSP to GP, 27 February 27 1905, box 4, folder 14, LOC-PP. Under the rose comes from the New Latin sub rosa and is defined as secretive and private. Merriam-Webster.com Dictionary, s.v. "sub-rosa," accessed August 28, 2022. https://www.merriam-webster.com/dictionary/sub-rosa
24. GSP to BAP, March 7 1905, box 4, folder 14, LOC-PP.
25. "The Inauguration Will be a Brilliant Spectacle," *Pottsville Daily Republican*, March 3, 1905.
26. GSP to GP, 18 March 1905, box 4, folder 14, LOC-PP.
27. GSP to GP, 18 March 1905, box 4, folder 14, LOC-PP.
28. GSP to GP, 21 May 1905, box 4, folder 14, LOC-PP.
29. GSP to GP, 4 September 1904, box 4, folder 13, LOC-PP; GSP to GP, 1 December 1904, box 4, folder 13, LOC-PP.
30. GSP to GP, 3 July 1904, box 4, folder 12, LOC-PP.
31. GSP to GP, 3 June 1905, box 4, folder 14, LOC-PP.
32. GP to GSP, 10 June 1905, box 4, folder 14, LOC-PP.
33. GSP to GP, 30 May 1905, box 4, folder 14, LOC-PP.
34. GSP to BAP, 10 July 1905, box 4, folder 14, LOC-PP.
35. GSP to GP, 28 August 1905, box 4, folder 14, LOC-PP; GSP to BAP, 9 August 1905, box 4, folder 14, LOC-PP.

36. GSP to GP, 28 August 1905, box 4, folder 14, LOC-PP; GSP to BAP, 1 September 1905, box 4, folder 15, LOC-PP.
37. GSP to RWP, 11 November 1905, box 4, folder 15, LOC-PP.
38. Julie Lasky, "Highland Falls, N.Y.: A Cozy Community Next Door to West Point," *The New York Times,* July 25, 2018.
39. GSP to BAP, May 1905, box 4, folder 14, LOC-PP. Highland Falls only had one hotel, The Villa, which was often booked by the time George could go off campus and get a room for Beatrice. "Truly I am very sorry to have failed," was his frequent apology.
40. Conner, *What Father Forbad,* 51.
41. GSP to BAP, 6 July 1906, box 4, folder 16, LOC-PP.
42. GSP to BAP, 9 July 1906, box 4, folder 16, LOC-PP.
43. GSP to GP, 4 December 1905, box 4, folder 15, LOC-PP.
44. GSP to BAP, 7 October 1904, box 4, folder 13, LOC-PP; GSP to BAP, 12 November 1907, box 5, folder 2, LOC-PP.
45. Totten, *The Button Box,* 73.
46. GSP to GP, 6 January 1906, box 4, folder 16, LOC-PP.
47. GSP to BAP, 21 January 1906, box 4, folder 16, LOC-PP.
48. GSP to BAP, January 1906, box 4, folder 16, LOC-PP.
49. GSP to BAP, 29 September 1908, box 5, folder 4, LOC-PP.
50. BAP as quoted in D'Este, *Patton: A Genius for War,* 88.
51. GSP to BAP, January 1906, box 4, folder 16, LOC-PP.
52. BAP to GSP, July 1907, box 5, folder 2, LOC-PP.
53. GSP to GP, 20 August 1907, box 5, folder 2, LOC-PP; GSP to BAP, 15 October 1908, box 5, folder 4, LOC-PP.
54. "Architecture and Furnishing: Avalon—A Notable Summer Residence," *Vogue,* May 15, 1910, 32; Totten, *The Button Box,* 69.
55. Stuart A. Drake, "Settings for Plutocrats," *Historic New England,* Spring 2014, 16-21. https://issuu.com/historicnewengland/docs/historic_new_england_spring_2014/
56. Totten, *The Button Box,* 69.
57. However, no Ayer would ever dare cross that now invisible barrier. Yet, ironically, Kay's daughter, Rosemary Merrill, would marry Caleb Loring Jr. in 1943.
58. GSP to BAP, 22 February 1908, box 5, folder 3, LOC-PP.
59. GSP to BAP, February 1908, box 5, folder 3, LOC-PP.
60. Totten, Ruth Ellen Patton, *The Button Box: A Daughter's Loving Memoir of Mrs. George S. Patton,* ed. James Patton Totten, (Columbia, Missouri: University of Missouri Press, 2005), 159. Reprinted by permission of the publisher.
61. GSP to AW, July 1908, box 5, folder 4, LOC-PP.
62. Totten, *The Button Box,* 72.
63. GSP, "My Father as I Knew Him and of Him from Memory and Legend."
64. GSP to GP, 3 July 1904, box 4, folder 12, LOC-PP.
65. GSP to BAP, 28 August 1906, box 4, folder 16, LOC-PP; Robert Patton, *The Pattons,* chapter 10, Kindle.
66. Conner, *What Father Forbad,* 52.
67. GSP to FFA, 18 January 1909, box 5, folder 5, LOC-PP.
68. GSP to GP, 10 January 1909, box 5, folder 5, LOC-PP.
69. BAP to RWP, 9 January 1909, box 5, folder 5, LOC-PP.
70. Robert Patton, *The Pattons,* chapter 10, Kindle.
71. GSP to GP, 31 January 1909, box 5, folder 5, LOC-PP.
72. Beatrice Ayer Patton, "Talk for the Third War Loan in Boston," September 20, 1943, box 11, folder 7, LOC-PP.
73. GSP to BAP, 5 November 1909, box 5, folder 8, LOC-PP.
74. GSP to FFA, 3 January 1909, box 5, folder 5, LOC-PP.
75. FA to GSP, 10 January 1909, as quoted in Totten, *The Button Box,* 76.
76. GSP to GP&RWP, 17 January 1909, box 5, folder 5, LOC-PP.
77. GSP to BAP, 23 March 1908, box 5, folder 3, LOC-PP.
78. GSP to GP&RWP, 17 January 1909, box 5, folder 5, LOC-PP.
79. GSP to BAP, 6 January 1909, box 5, folder 5, LOC-PP; GSP to BAP, 27 January 1909, box 5, folder 5, LOC-PP.
80. GSP to BAP, March 1908, box 5, folder 3, LOC-PP.

81. GSP to FFA, 18 January 1909, box 5, folder 5, LOC-PP.
82. GSP to BAP, 17 January 1909, box 5, folder 5, LOC-PP.
83. GSP to BAP, 16 February 1909, box 5, folder 6, LOC-PP.
84. GSP to FFA, 3 February 1909, box 5, folder 6, LOC-PP.
85. GSP to BAP, 17 January 1909, box 5, folder 5, LOC-PP.
86. GSP to GP, 16 May 1909, box 5, folder 6, LOC-PP.
87. GSP to BAP, 3 June 1909, box 5, folder 7, LOC-PP.
88. GSP to BAP, 2 March 1910, box 5, folder 9, LOC-PP.
89. Fred Ayer Jr., *Before the Colors Fade*, 54.
90. BAP to AW, 11 September 1909, box 5, folder 7, LOC-PP.
91. GSP to BAP, 11 August 1909, box 5, folder 7, LOC-PP.
92. GSP to BAP, 16 February 1909, box 5, folder 6, LOC-PP.
93. GSP to BAP, 16 February 1909, box 5, folder 6, LOC-PP.
94. GSP to BAP, 29 November 1909, box 5, folder 8, LOC-PP.
95. GSP to BAP, 3 February 1907, box 5, folder 1, LOC-PP.
96. GSP to GP, 31 January 1909, box 5, folder 5, LOC-PP.
97. GSP to RWP, 20 February 1910, as quoted in Totten, *The Button Box*, 79.
98. GSP to GP, 5 December 1909, box 5, folder 8, LOC-PP.
99. GSP to GP, 9 May 1909, box 5, folder 6, LOC-PP.
100. GSP to GP, 17 January 1910, box 5, folder 9, LOC-PP.
101. GSP to RWP, 20 February 1910, as quoted in Totten, *The Button Box*, 79.
102. GSP to RWP, 6 March 1910, box 5, folder 9, LOC-PP.
103. Totten, *The Button Box*, 81.
104. FA to GSP, 10 March 1910, as quoted in Totten, *The Button Box*, 80.
105. "Ayer-Patton," *The New York Times*, Mar 13, 1910.
106. Totten, *The Button Box*, 192.
107. GSP to BAP, 13 September 1909, box 5, folder 7, LOC-PP; GSP to BAP, 3 November 1915, box 6, folder 6, LOC-PP.
108. GSP to BAP, 9 April 1909, box 5, folder 6, LOC-PP.
109. Totten, *The Button Box*, 78.
110. GSP to BAP, 28 August 1906, box 4, folder 16, LOC-PP.
111. GSP to BAP, 14 October 1909, box 5, folder 7, LOC-PP.
112. Diana Dretske, *Images of America: Fort Sheridan* (Charleston: Arcadia Pub., 2004), 104.
113. Beatrice Ayer Patton, "Army Etiquette," War Department Bureau of Public Relations, box 11, folder 13, LOC-PP; Early, "True Confessions Salutes A Hero's Wife."
114. GSP to GP, 5 April 1909, box 5, folder 6, LOC-PP.
115. GSP to GP, 16 April 1910, box 5, folder 10, LOC-PP.
116. GSP to GP, 1 April 1910, box 5, folder 10, LOC-PP.
117. GSP to BAP, 25 April 1910, box 5, folder 10, LOC-PP.
118. GSP to BAP, 22 May 1910, box 5, folder 10, LOC-PP
119. GP to BAP, April 25 1910, box 5, folder 10, LOC-PP.
120. "Drawn Sabers Form Arch for Bridal Couple," *Boston Daily Globe*, May 27, 1910.
121. GSP to BAP, 26 March 1909, box 5, folder 6, LOC-PP.
122. Totten, *The Button Box*, 17.
123. GSP to BAP, 11 November 1908, box 5, folder 4, LOC-PP.
124. GSP to BAP, 4 April 1910, box 5, folder 10, LOC-PP.
125. BAP to AW as quoted in Robert Patton, *The Pattons*, chapter 11, Kindle.
126. GSP to AW, 27 June 1910, box 5, folder 12, LOC-PP.
127. Totten, *The Button Box*, 105.
128. GSP to BAP, 20 February 1910, box 5, folder 9, LOC-PP.

## 4. CUSTER HILL

1. Edward M. Coffman, *The Old Army: A Portrait of the American Army in Peacetime, 1784-1898* (New York: Oxford University Press, 2014), 131.
2. Frank N. Shubert, *Outpost of the Sioux Wars: A History of Fort Robinson* (United States: University of Nebraska Press, 1995), 49.

3. BAP, "The Army Wife."
4. Alden Hatch, *George Patton: General in Spurs* (New York: Messner, 1950), 46-47.
5. GSP to BAP, 5 May 1910, box 5, folder 11, LOC-PP.
6. Totten, *The Button Box*, 87.
7. BAP, "The Army Wife."
8. GSP to AW, 27 June 1910, box 5, folder 12, LOC-PP.
9. GSP to BAP, 7 April 1910, box 5, folder 10, LOC-PP.
10. BAP to AW, 1 August 1910, box 5, folder 10, LOC-PP; GSP to BAP, 6 September 1910, box 5, folder 12, LOC-PP.
11. GSP to BAP, 6 September 1910, box 5, folder 12, LOC-PP.
12. Totten, *The Button Box*, 86.
13. BAP to AW, 2 October 1910, box 5, folder 12, LOC-PP.
14. Robert Patton, *The Pattons*, chapter 10, Kindle.
15. BAP, "The Army Wife."
16. "National Register of Historic Places - Fort Sheridan," *National Parks Service, U.S. Department of the Interior*, accessed May 31, 2022. https://npgallery.nps.gov/nrhp/
17. GSP to BAP, 6 April 1909, box 5, folder 6, LOC-PP.
18. BAP to AW, 2 October 1910, box 5, folder 12, LOC-PP; BAP to AW, 28 October 1910, box 5, folder 12, LOC-PP.
19. "Patton Widow Recalls Life At Fort Sheridan," *Chicago Daily Tribune*, August 19, 1951.
20. Blumenson, *The Patton Papers: 1885-1945*, 212.
21. Robert Patton, *The Pattons*, chapter 12, Kindle.
22. BAP to AW, 2 October 1910, box 5, folder 12, LOC-PP; BAP to AW, 28 October 1910, box 5, folder 12, LOC-PP.
23. BAP to AW, 1 August 1910, box 5, folder 10, LOC-PP.
24. GSP to BAP, 29 October 1910, box 5, folder 12, LOC-PP.
25. GSP to AW, 22 October 1910, box 5, folder 12, LOC-PP.
26. While the spelling of Little Bee is pretty consistent, Beatrice's name was either abbreviated to Bea or Bee, depending on the person writing the letter. George himself usually referred to her as Bea, although there are some letters where he calls her Bee.
27. GSP to BAP, 6 April 1909, box 5, folder 6, LOC-PP; Totten, *The Button Box*, 89.
28. GSP to AW, March 1911, box 5, folder 13, LOC-PP.
29. GSP to BAP, 29 March 1918, box 7, folder 13, LOC-PP.
30. BAP to AW, 7 September 1912, box 5, folder 14, LOC-PP; BAP to AW, 29 April 1913, box 5, folder 16, LOC-PP.
31. "The 1911 Heat Wave Was So Deadly It Drove People Insane," *New England Historical Society*, accessed July 28, 2022. https://www.newenglandhistoricalsociety.com/the-1911-heat-wave-was-so-deadly-it-drove-people-insane/
32. BAP to AW, 11 July 1911, box 5, folder 13, LOC-PP.
33. GSP to AW, 22 July 1911, box 5, folder 13, LOC-PP.
34. GSP to EBA, 20 April 1910, box 5, folder 10, LOC-PP.
35. Totten, *The Button Box*, 89.
36. George Washington to John Augustine Washington, 31 May 1754, *Founders Online, National Archives*, accessed July 28, 2022. https://founders.archives.gov/documents/Washington/02-01-02-0058
37. George S. Patton Jr., "Report of the 5th Olympiad," September 19, 1912, box 5, folder 15, LOC-PP; *The Fifth Olympiad: The Official Report of the Olympic Games of Stockholm, 1912* (Sweden: Swedish Olympic Committee, 1913), accessed August 12, 2022. https://digital.la84.org/digital/collection/p17103coll8/id/11660/rec/7
38. Totten, *The Button Box*, 94.
39. GSP, "Report of the 5th Olympiad."
40. Harold E. Wilson Jr., "A Legend In His Own Mind: The Olympic Experience of General George S. Patton, Jr," *Olympika: The International Journal of Olympic Studies*, Volume VI (1997): 99-114.
41. Gustaf Wersäll to BAP, 19 December 1945, box 14, folder 5, LOC-PP.
42. GSP, "Report of the 5th Olympiad."
43. GSP, "Report of the 5th Olympiad." All information regarding points is based upon the official report of the Olympic Committee. In his report to his superiors, George exaggerated certain results of the individual competitions: George's ranking: 21 - 6 - 3 - 3 - 3/ Official ranking: 21 - 7 - 4 - 6 – 3.

44. *The Fifth Olympiad: The Official Report of the Olympic Games of Stockholm, 1912*.
45. BAP to AW, 20 March 1913, box 5, folder 16, LOC-PP. George was not the only one; two other participants fainted and one even died.
46. Hatch, *George Patton: General in Spurs*, 46.
47. D'Este, *Patton: A Genius for War*, 136.
48. GSP, "Report of the 5th Olympiad."
49. GSP to GP, 12 April 1911, box 5, folder 12, LOC-PP.
50. GSP to BAP, 2 July 1911, box 5, folder 13, LOC-PP.
51. GSP to BAP, December 1911, box 5, folder 13, LOC-PP; GSP to BAP, 29 August 1912, box 5, folder 14, LOC-PP.
52. GSP to GP, 23 January 1912, box 5, folder 14, LOC-PP.
53. GSP to GP, 5 April 1909, box 5, folder 6, LOC-PP.
54. GSP to FFA, 14 September 1912, box 5, folder 15, LOC-PP.
55. General Houdemon, as quoted in Harry Hodges Semmes, *Portrait of Patton* (New York: Paperback Library Edition, 1972), 201.
56. "Fulk III Nerra," *Encyclopedia Britannica*, June 17, 2021. https://www.britannica.com/biography/Fulk-III-Nerra
57. BAP to AW, 15 August 1913, box 5, folder 17, LOC-PP.
58. GSP to GP, 24 July 1904, box 4, folder 12, LOC-PP; D'Este, *Patton: A Genius for War*, 171.
59. BAP to AW, 15 August 1913, box 5, folder 17, LOC-PP.
60. GSP to GP, 22 July, 1913, box 5, folder 17, LOC-PP.
61. Beatrice Ayer Patton, "A Soldier's Reading," *Armor*, November-December 1952.
62. Blumenson, *The Patton Papers: 1885-1940*, 262.
63. GSP to BAP, 29 March 1909, box 5, folder 6, LOC-PP.
64. GSP to BAP, March 1908, box 5, folder 3, LOC-PP.
65. BAP, "The Army Wife."
66. GSP to BAP, Fall 1913, box 5, folder 17, LOC-PP.
67. GSP to BAP, 2 October 1913, box 5, folder 17, LOC-PP.
68. GSP to BAP, 6 April 1909, box 5, folder 6, LOC-PP.
69. BAP to AW, 15 August 1913, box 5, folder 17, LOC-PP.
70. GSP to GP, October 16, 1913, box 5, folder 17, LOC-PP.
71. "Second Lieutenant Patton Efficiency Report by Captain Richmond," 17 December 1914, box 6, folder 2, LOC-PP.
72. GSP to BAP, 29 September 1913, box 5, folder 17, LOC-PP.
73. Totten, *The Button Box*, 99.
74. "The Permian Period," *National Parks Service, U.S. Department of the Interior*, accessed August 12, 2022. https://www.nps.gov/tapr/learn/nature/the-permian-period.htm
75. Totten, *The Button Box*, 100.
76. GSP to BAP, 11 February 1915, box 6, folder 3, LOC-PP.
77. BAP to AW, 7 September 1912, box 5, folder 15, LOC-PP; GSP to BAP, 18 December 1912, box 5, folder 15, LOC-PP.
78. GSP to GP, 11 February 1915 , box 6, folder 3, LOC-PP. Years later, someone wrote in the margin: "No -- don't cut. We all feel this way! DO NOT CUT!"
79. GSP to BAP, 16 February 1915, box 6, folder 3, LOC-PP.
80. Totten, *The Button Box*, 71.
81. GP to FA, 14 April 1919, box 2, folder 6, HLC-GSP.
82. GSP to BAP, 1 March 1915, box 6, folder 3, LOC-PP.
83. GSP to EBA, 4 March 1915, box 14, folder 16, LOC-PP.
84. GSP to BAP, 2 March 2 1915, LOC-PP.
85. GSP to BAP, 1 July 1915, box 6, folder 4, LOC-PP.
86. BAP to AW, 1 July 1915, box 6, folder 4, LOC-PP.
87. GSP to BAP, 21 June 1915, box 6, folder 4, LOC-PP.
88. GSP to GP, 13 July 1915, box 6, folder 4, LOC-PP.
89. "Found Pinned Under His Car: Lieut. Patton a Victim of Auto Accident. Was On Point Of Asphyxiation When Discovered," *Boston Daily Globe*, August 11, 1914.
90. "Frederick Ayer, Jr., Weds Hilda P. Rice," *Boston Post*, August 5, 1914; "Harvard Man Back from African Jungle with Trophies of Prowess," *Boston Sunday Post*, June 9, 1912.
91. "F.F. Ayer Dies at the Age of 98," *The Ogden Standard*, March 15, 1918.
92. "Woodrow Wilson's Declaration of Neutrality," *World War I Reference Library*, accessed July 12,

20022. https://www.encyclopedia.com/history/educational-magazines/woodrow-wilsons-declaration-neutrality

93. Codman, *Drive*, 159.

94. GSP to General Wood, 3 August 1914, box 6, folder 2, LOC-PP; General Wood to GSP, 6 August 1914, box 6, folder 2, LOC-PP.

95. "Found Pinned Under His Car."

96. Fred Ayer Jr., *Before the Colors Fade*, 65. When Mrs. Rice died at age sixty-three in 1933 from a heart attack (her horse Yellow Turk returned alone from their morning ride, and she was found dead sitting under a tree), George traveled from Fort Myer to be an usher at her funeral. He told Hilda he would have traveled halfway across the world to be there.

97. GSP to GP, 13 July 1915, box 6, folder 4, LOC-PP.

98. GSP, "My Father as I Knew Him and of Him from Memory and Legend."

99. GSP to FFA, 11 November 1915, box 6, folder 6, LOC-PP.

100. GSP to BAP, 23 November 1915, box 6, folder 6, LOC-PP.

101. Ruth Ellen Patton Totten, *The Rolling Kitchen* (Riverside, 1960); Martin Donell Kohout, "Sierra Blanca, TX," *TSHA*, accessed August 12, 2022. https://www.tshaonline.org/handbook/entries/sierra-blanca-tx

102. Stuart W. Cramer, "Georgie," *Redbook*, 09, 1943, 54-55 & 110-112.

103. GSP to BAP, 26 October 1915, box 6, folder 5, LOC-PP.

104. GSP to AW, 10 January 1916, box 6, folder 7, LOC-PP.

105. "General Orozco Shot Dead by Texan Cowboys in Running Battle of Hours," *The News Journal (Lancaster, PA)*, September 1, 1915.

106. Ruth Ellen's account states that no one knew the bullet came from George.

107. Cramer, "Georgie," 54-55 & 110-112.

108. GSP to GP, 21 March 1927, box 10, folder 4, LOC-PP.

109. Robert Patton, *The Pattons*, chapter 12, Kindle.

110. GSP, West Point Notebook, January 1909, box 5, LOC-PP.

111. Robert Patton, *The Pattons*, chapter 10, Kindle.

112. AP to RWP, as quoted in Robert Patton, *The Pattons*, chapter 10, Kindle.

113. Dorothy Wayman, "Gen. Patton's Daring in Sicily no Surprise to Wife Recalling Pershing's Blessing at Sailing," *Boston Daily Globe*, July 15, 1943.

114. "Wife of Gen. Patton for Year's Training," *The Barre Daily Time*, April 5, 1944.

## 5. AVALON

1. Bud Rutherford, "Matinee Games are Exhibitions," *El Paso Herald*, June 5, 1916.

2. BAP to EBA, 5 June 1916, box 6, folder 10, LOC-PP.

3. GSP to BAP, 20 December 1916, box 6, folder 12, LOC-PP; Totten, *The Rolling Kitchen*.

4. GSP to BAP, 6 October 1916, box 6, folder 10, LOC-PP; BAP to EBA, 5 June 1916, box 6, folder 10, LOC-PP; GSP to FFA, 27 June 1916, box 6, folder 10, LOC-PP.

5. "Table Gossip," *Boston Daily Globe*, April 07, 1918.

6. BAP to GP, 25 September 1914, box 6, folder 2, LOC-PP.

7. GSP to FFA, 14 September 1912, box 5, folder 15, LOC-PP; GSP to BAP, 23 September 1912, box 5, folder 15, LOC-PP.

8. GSP to BAP, 5 July 1918, box 8, folder 9, LOC-PP.

9. GSP to EBA, 28 November 1915, box 6, folder 6, LOC-PP.

10. BAP to GP, 16 May 1916, box 12, folder 3, HLC-GSP.

11. GSP to GP, 15 May 1916, box 6, folder 8, LOC-PP.

12. Frank B. Elser, "Cárdenas's Family Saw Him Die At Bay," *The New York Times*, May 23, 1916.

13. GSP to BAP, 14 May 1916, box 6, folder 9, LOC-PP.

14. Frank B. Elser, "Cárdenas's Family Saw Him Die At Bay."

15. GSP to BAP, 17 May 1916, box 6, folder 9, LOC-PP.

16. BAP, as quoted in Robert Patton, *The Pattons*, chapter 12, Kindle.

17. FFA to BAP&GSP, 31 May 1916, box 6, folder 9, LOC-PP; AP to RWP as quoted in Robert Patton, *The Pattons*, chapter 12, Kindle.

18. GSP to BAP, 17 May 1916, box 6, folder 9, LOC-PP.

19. Robert A. Mclean, "Daughter's View Of Gen. Patton," *The Boston Globe*, August 21, 1980.

20. BAP to GP, 16 May 1916, box 12, folder 3, HLC-GSP.
21. AP to RWP, as quoted in Robert Patton, *The Pattons*, chapter 12, Kindle.
22. AP to RWP, as quoted in Robert Patton, *The Pattons*, Kindle edition, chapter 12.
23. GSP to BAP, 18 September 1916, box 6, folder 10, LOC-PP.
24. GP to BAP, 22 September 1914, box 6, folder 2, LOC-PP.
25. BAP to GP, 25 September 1914, box 6, folder 2, LOC-PP.
26. GP to GSP, 20 February 1919, box 9, folder 11, LOC-PP.
27. GSP to GP, 12 March 1916, box 6, folder 7, LOC-PP. Mr. Patton was a lifelong Progressive Democrat and a staunch supporter of Woodrow Wilson (to his Boy's chagrin). He was elected the first mayor of San Marino when the town was incorporated in 1913, the same year he lost out on an appointment in President Wilson's first administration, even with the help of Frederick Ayer.
28. "Beautiful Fight is Brewing in State Democratic Party," *Oakland Tribune*, March 10, 1912; "'Women Are Incapable of Balloting Wisely,' said George S. Patton," *Santa Cruz Evening News*, October 23, 1916.
29. Early, "True Confessions Salutes A Hero's Wife."
30. GSP to BAP, 7 October 1916, box 6, folder 10, LOC-PP.
31. GSP to GP, 14 May 1905, box 4, folder 14, LOC-PP; GSP to RWP, 6 March 1910, box 5, folder 9, LOC-PP; GSP to AP, 26 October 1918, box 9, folder 2, LOC-PP.
32. David Kipen, *Dear Los Angeles: The City in Diaries and Letters, 1542 to 2018* (New York: The Modern Library, 2019), 17.
33. GSP to JGH, 14 January 1944, box 36, folder 16, NYHS-HP.
34. GSP to BAP, 7 October 1916, box 6, folder 10, LOC-PP.
35. Totten, *The Button Box*, 108.
36. GSP, "My Father as I Knew Him and of Him from Memory and Legend."
37. GSP to BAP, 16 January 1917, box 6, folder 13, LOC-PP.
38. GSP to BAP, 19 December 1916, box 6, folder 12, LOC-PP.
39. GSP to BAP, 20 December 1916, box 6, folder 12, LOC-PP.
40. GSP to BAP, 10 January 1917, box 6, folder 13, LOC-PP.
41. GSP to BAP, 9 January 1917, box 6, folder 13, LOC-PP.
42. GSP to BAP, 19 December 1916, box 6, folder 12, LOC-PP; GSP to BAP, 9 January 1917, box 6, folder 13, LOC-PP.
43. GSP to BAP, 21 February 1909, box 5, folder 6, LOC-PP.
44. FFA to BAP, 24 February 1917, box 6, folder 14, LOC-PP.
45. GSP to BAP, 29 January 1917, box 6, folder 13, LOC-PP.
46. "A Lesson," *The Butte Miner*, February 12, 1918.
47. "Frederick Ayer Obituary," *The Boston Transcript*, March 15, 1918.
48. GSP to JJP, April 23 1917, box 6, folder 14, LOC-PP.
49. Merrill, *Keith Merrill, A Memoir*, 21.
50. Merrill, *Keith Merrill, A Memoir*, 24.
51. Merrill, *Keith Merrill, A Memoir*, 31-33.
52. "Table Gossip," *Boston Daily Globe*, May 13, 1917.
53. GSP to BAP, 16 July 1917, box 6, folder 16, LOC-PP.
54. GSP to JJP, 11 April 1917, box 6, folder 14, LOC-PP.
55. George S. Patton Jr., "Diary of U.S. Expedition to France," May 18, 1917, box 6, folder 14, LOC-PP.
56. "President Calls The Nation To Arms; Draft Bill Signed; Registration On June 5; Regulars Under Pershing To Go To France," *The New York Times*, May 19, 1917.
57. GSP to BAP, 8 August 1917, box 6, folder 17, LOC-PP.
58. GSP to BAP, 19 June 1917, box 6, folder 15, LOC-PP; GSP to BAP, 3 July 1917, box 6, folder 16, LOC-PP.
59. Merrill, *Keith Merrill, A Memoir*, 47-48.
60. GSP to BAP, 16 July 1917, box 6, folder 16, LOC-PP.
61. GSP to BAP, 29 July 1917, box 6, folder 16, LOC-PP.
62. BAP to AW, 19 July 1917, box 6, folder 16, LOC-PP.
63. BAP to AW, 16 August 1917, box 6, folder 17, LOC-PP.
64. GSP to BAP, 14 December 1917, box 7, folder 6, LOC-PP.
65. GSP to BAP, 2 September 1917, box 7, folder 1, LOC-PP.
66. GSP to BAP, 29 August 1917, box 6, folder 17, LOC-PP.
67. BAP to AW, 22 August 1917, box 6, folder 17, LOC-PP.

68. BAP to GP, 1 September 1917, box 7, folder 1, LOC-PP; BAP to GP, 11 October 1917, box 7, folder 2, LOC-PP.
69. GP to BAP, 17 May 1917, box 6, folder 14, LOC-PP; BAP to AW, 22 August 1917, box 6, folder 17, LOC-PP.
70. GSP to BAP, 11 October 1917, box 7, folder 2, LOC-PP.
71. BAP to GP, 13 September 1917 , box 7, folder 1, LOC-PP.
72. GP to BAP, 8 September 8 1917, box 7, folder 1, LOC-PP.
73. BAP to GP, 9 September 1917, box 7, folder 1, LOC-PP.
74. GSP to BAP, 24 September 1917, box 7, folder 1, LOC-PP.
75. GSP to BAP, 25 September 1917, box 7, folder 1, LOC-PP.
76. BAP as quoted in D'Este, *Patton: A Genius for War*, 195.
77. Rick Holinger, "River Town Chronicles: Take a Ride through History on Pullman One," *Shaw Local*, November 30, 2020. https://www.shawlocal.com/2017/09/18/river-town-chronicles-take-a-ride-through-history-on-pullman-one/aicov2h/
78. "Mr. Ayer and Family from Mass. Locate Here for Winter," *Daily Times Enterprise*, October 27, 1927.
79. GSP to BAP, 9 November 1917, box 7, folder 3, LOC-PP.
80. Francis Storrs, "A Stranger in the House of Ayer," *Boston Magazine*, February 3, 2015. https://www.bostonmagazine.com/2007/11/20/a-stranger-in-the-house-of-ayer.
81. "Mrs. Frederick Ayer Died Suddenly Today of Heart trouble," *Daily Times Enterprise*, April 3, 1918.
82. "Frederick Ayer, Winter Resident, Died Yesterday," *Daily Times Enterprise*, March 15, 1918.
83. GSP to BAP, 15 December 1917, box 7, folder 6, LOC-PP.
84. GSP to BAP, 23 January 1918, box 7, folder 8, LOC-PP.
85. GSP to BAP, 23 December 1917, box 7, folder 6, LOC-PP.
86. BAP to AW, 15 August 1913, box 5, folder 17, LOC-PP.
87. GSP to BAP, 27 August 1917, box 6, folder 17, LOC-PP.
88. GSP to BAP, 2 December 1917, box 7, folder 4, LOC-PP.
89. GSP to BAP, 20 September 1916, box 6, folder 10, LOC-PP.
90. Conner, *What Father Forbad*, 49.
91. GSP to BAP, 20 December 1917, box 7, folder 6, LOC-PP.
92. George S. Patton Jr., "Rubber Shoes," November 26, 1917, box 74, folder 3, LOC-PP.
93. GSP to BAP, 8 October 1917 , box 7, folder 2, LOC-PP.
94. GSP to BAP, 29 July 1917, box 6, folder 16, LOC-PP; GSP to BAP, 28 October 1917, box 7, folder 2, LOC-PP.
95. GSP to BAP, 14 December 1917, box 7, folder 6, LOC-PP; GSP to BAP, 13 March 1918, box 7, folder 12, LOC-PP.
96. BAP to GP, 11 October 1917, box 7, folder 2, LOC-PP; GSP to BAP, 14 December 1917, box 7, folder 6, LOC-PP.
97. GSP to BAP, 19 September 1917, box 7, folder 1, LOC-PP.
98. GSP to BAP, 23 December 1917, box 7, folder 6, LOC-PP.
99. Wayman, "Gen. Patton's Daring in Sicily no Surprise to Wife Recalling Pershing's Blessing at Sailing," *Boston Daily Globe*, July 15, 1943.
100. GSP to BAP, 23 January 1918, box 7, folder 8, LOC-PP; George S. Patton Jr., "Original Tank Report," 1917, box 7, folder 5, LOC-PP.
101. GSP to BAP, 20 December 1917, box 7, folder 6, LOC-PP.
102. GSP to BAP, 15 December 1917, box 7, folder 6, LOC-PP.
103. GSP to BAP, 8 October 1917, box 7, folder 2, LOC-PP.
104. "Frederick Ayer, Winter Resident, Died Yesterday," *Daily Times Enterprise*, March 15, 1918; GP to FA, 14 April 1919, box 2, folder 6, HLC-GSP.
105. Frederick Ayer, *The Reminiscences of Frederick Ayer*, 80.
106. "Frederick Ayer Dead in Georgia," *Boston Daily Globe*, March 15, 1918.
107. "Frederick Ayer, Winter Resident, Died Yesterday," *Daily Times Enterprise*, March 15, 1918.
108. "Frederick Ayer Obituary," *The Boston Transcript*, March 15, 1918.
109. BAP to GSP, 7 December 1942 , box 10, folder 12, LOC-PP.
110. Beatrice Ayer Patton, "Mrs. Patton's Speech at Dedication of Patton Memorial West Point," August 19 1950, box 23 folder 1, LOC-PP.
111. "Frederick Ayer Obituary," *The Boston Transcript*, March 15, 1918.
112. Frederick Ayer, *The Reminiscences of Frederick Ayer*, 80.

113. GSP to FFA, 20 January 1918 , box 7, folder 7, LOC-PP.
114. GSP to BAP, 20 March 1918 , box 7, folder 12, LOC-PP.
115. GSP to BAP, 22 March 1918 , box 7, folder 12, LOC-PP.
116. "Mrs. Frederick Ayer Died Suddenly Today of Heart trouble," *Daily Times Enterprise*, April 3, 1918.
117. GSP to GP, 19 April 1918, box 8, folder 3, LOC-PP; "Funerals - Frederick Ayer," *Norwich Bulletin*, March 22, 1918; "Body of Mr. Frederick Ayer Will Be Taken to Lowell, Mass," *Daily Times Enterprise*, March 16, 1918.
118. GSP to BAP, 23 March 1918 , box 7, folder 12, LOC-PP.
119. GSP to BAP, April 19 1918, box 8, folder 3, LOC-PP; Early, "True Confessions Salutes A Hero's Wife."
120. Early, "True Confessions Salutes A Hero's Wife."
121. "Mrs. Frederick Ayer Died Suddenly Today of Heart trouble."
122. Telegram from FA to family members, 3 April 1918, box 1, folder 8, mssBanning Company Records, Addenda II, The Huntington Library, San Marino, California.
123. "Mrs. Frederick Ayer Died Suddenly Today of Heart trouble."
124. GSP to KAM, 10 April 1918, box 8, folder 1, LOC-PP.
125. GSP to BAP, 10 April 1918, box 8, folder 1, LOC-PP.
126. GSP to BAP, 4 May 1918, box 8, folder 4, LOC-PP.
127. GSP to BAP, 31 July 1918, box 8, folder 9, LOC-PP.
128. GP to FA, 17 June 1918, box 2, folder 6, HLC-GSP.
129. GSP to BAP, 5 May 1918, box 8, folder 4, LOC-PP.
130. BAP to GSP, 1 February 1943, box 10, folder 14, LOC-PP.
131. GSP to BAP, 3 June 1918, box 8, folder 8, LOC-PP; GSP to BAP, 30 May 1918, box 8, folder 6, LOC-PP.
132. GSP to GP, 19 April 1918, box 8, folder 3, LOC-PP.
133. GSP to BAP, 23 March 1918 , box 7, folder 12, LOC-PP.
134. GSP to BAP, 30 May 1918, box 8, folder 6, LOC-PP.
135. "Warrior Wives Given 10 Rules to Keep Happy," *Chicago Daily Tribune*, November 11, 1942.
136. Early, "True Confessions Salutes A Hero's Wife."
137. GSP to Mrs. Rice, 24 July 1917, box 6, folder 16, LOC-PP; GSP to AW, 22 December 1917 , box 7, folder 6, LOC-PP.; GSP to BAP, 4 May 1918, box 8, folder 4, LOC-PP.
138. GSP to BAP, 19 July 1918, box 8, folder 9, LOC-PP.
139. GSP to BAP, 4 June 1918, box 8, folder 7, LOC-PP.
140. GSP to BAP, 3 June 1918, box 8, folder 7, LOC-PP.
141. GSP to BAP, 9 June 1918, box 8, folder 8, LOC-PP.
142. GSP to BAP, 21 April 1918, box 8, folder 3, LOC-PP.
143. GSP to BAP, 3 April 3 1918, box 8, folder 1, LOC-PP.
144. GSP to BAP, 2 July 1918, box 8, folder 9, LOC-PP.
145. GSP to BAP, 20 May 1918, box 8, folder 8, LOC-PP.
146. GSP to BAP, 28 September 1918, box 8, folder 16, LOC-PP.
147. GSP to BAP, 25 September 1918, box 8, folder 16, LOC-PP.
148. GSP to BAP, September 28 1918, box 8, folder 16, LOC-PP.
149. Beatrice Ayer Patton, "Transcript of speech to V.M.I. on October 28, 1950," box 23, folder 1, LOC-PP.
150. GSP to GP, 28 October 1918, box 9, folder 2, LOC-PP.
151. GSP to BAP, 4 October 1918, box 9, folder 1, LOC-PP.
152. GSP to BAP, 18 August 1918, box 8, folder 10, LOC-PP.
153. GSP to BAP, 26 February 1918, box 7, folder 11, LOC-PP.
154. Early, "True Confessions Salutes A Hero's Wife."
155. Early, "True Confessions Salutes A Hero's Wife."
156. Early, "True Confessions Salutes A Hero's Wife."
157. GSP to BAP, 24 October 1918, box 9, folder 2, LOC-PP.
158. GSP to BAP, 16 December 1918, box 9, folder 6, LOC-PP.
159. GSP to BAP, 7 July 1918, box 8, folder 9, LOC-PP.
160. GSP to BAP, 18 November 1918, box 9, folder 3, LOC-PP. It is the second-highest honor in the US Army and is awarded to those who showcased "extreme gallantry and risk of life" in combat.
161. GSP to BAP, 15 October 1918, box 9, folder 1, LOC-PP.; GSP to BAP, 17 October 1918, box 9,

folder 1, LOC-PP.

162. Christopher Klein, "The False WWI Armistice Report that Fooled America," *History.com. A&E Television Networks*, November 7, 2018. https://www.history.com/news/false-armistice-report-world-war-i-early-celebration
163. Totten, *The Button Box*, 120.
164. GSP to BAP, 26 November 1918, box 9, folder 4, LOC-PP.
165. GSP, "Diary of U.S. Expedition to France," December 31, 1918, box 9, folder 7, LOC-PP.
166. GSP to BAP, 27 June 1918, box 8, folder 8, LOC-PP.
167. GSP to BAP, 26 May 1918, box 8, folder 6, LOC-PP.
168. GSP to BAP, 20 October 1918, box 9, folder 2, LOC-PP.
169. GSP to BAP, 22 November 1918, box 9, folder 4, LOC-PP.
170. GSP to BAP, 7 February 1919, box 9, folder 10, LOC-PP.
171. GSP to JJP, 10 February 1919, box 9, folder 10, LOC-PP.
172. AW to GP, 17 March 1919, box 9, folder 12, LOC-PP.
173. "Tank Corps Heroes Had Heavy Losses: Col Patton Returns with 304th Brigade," *Boston Daily Globe*, March 18, 1919.
174. GSP to BAP, October 4 1918, box 9, folder 1, LOC-PP.
175. Early, "True Confessions Salutes A Hero's Wife."
176. GSP to BAP, 13 April 1918, box 8, folder 2, LOC-PP.
177. Early, "True Confessions Salutes A Hero's Wife."

## PART II

1. George S. Patton Jr, "To Beatrice," October 1916, box 74, folder 1, LOC-PP. Written in Mexico (Colonia Dublan) and sent to Beatrice with a little note: "Darling Beat: There is no news so I wrote the above it is not good for I love you more than the confines of some verse admit of saying."

## 6. SUNSET ROCK

1. "Club History," *Sulgrave Club*, accessed August 15, 2022. https://www.sulgraveclub.org/the-club/club-history
2. GSP to GP, 12 March 1916, box 6, folder 7, LOC-PP; GSPIV to Brigadier General Hobson, "General George Smith Patton, Jr. U.S.A. — A Tribute," box 14, folder 9, LOC-PP.
3. GSP to FFA, 27 June 1916, box 6, folder 10, LOC-PP.
4. Fred Ayer Jr., *Before the Colors Fade*, 43.
5. Totten, *The Button Box*, 132.
6. George C. Marshall, Forrest C. Pogue, and Larry I. Bland; *George C. Marshall: Interviews and Reminiscences for Forrest C. Pogue* (Lexington: George C. Marshall Foundation, 1996), 607.
7. Robert Patton Interview.
8. GSP to BAP, 22 November 1918, box 9, folder 4, LOC-PP.
9. GSP to GP, 1 April 1919, box 9, folder 13, LOC-PP.
10. GSP to BAP, 16 February 1909, box 5, folder 6, LOC-PP.
11. Seamans, *Light and Life*, 193.
12. Semmes, *Portrait of Patton*, 26.
13. Totten, *The Button Box*, 122.
14. GSP to FFA, 18 January 1909, box 5, folder 5, LOC-PP.
15. George S. Patton Jr., "George S. Patton Papers: Diaries, 1910-1945," November 24, 1942, LOC-PP. https://loc.gov/item/mss35634005/
16. "Avalon, Catalina Island, Fire Swept in Early Morning," *The Long Beach Daily Telegram*, November 29, 1915.
17. "Chicago Man Buys Famous Catalina Island," *Woodward Democrat*, March 21 1919.
18. Merrill, *Keith Merrill: A Memoir*, 85.
19. GSP to GP, 17 January 1909, box 5, folder 5, LOC-PP.
20. GSP to BAP, 11 December 1918, box 9, folder 6, LOC-PP; GSP to GP, 1 April 1919, box 9, folder 13, LOC-PP.

21. GSP to BAP, 20 October 1918, box 9, folder 2, LOC-PP.
22. Totten, *The Button Box*, 16.
23. Marilyn Irvin Holt, *Mamie Doud Eisenhower: The General's First Lady* (Lawrence: University Press of Kansas, 2007), 16.
24. Marilyn Irvin Holt, *Mamie Doud Eisenhower: The General's First Lady*, 16.
25. Holt, *Mamie Doud Eisenhower: The General's First Lady*, 115.
26. Totten, *The Button Box*, 123.
27. "Mamie Eisenhower," *University of Virginia, Miller Center*, accessed September 1, 2022. https://millercenter.org/president/eisenhower/essays/eisenhower-1953-firstlady
28. Dwight D. Eisenhower, *At Ease: Stories I Tell My Friends* (New York: Doubleday, 1967), 171-172. The first time a steel cable stretched taut between two tanks snapped, and the flying projectile missed their heads by mere inches; the second time, they were testing the trajectory of machine gun bullets when the gun blocked and began firing at random.
29. GSP to AP, 18 October 1919, box 9, folder 14, LOC-PP.
30. Dorothy Barrett Brandon, *Mamie Doud Eisenhower: A Portrait of a First Lady* (Whitefish: Kessinger Publishing, 2010), 116-117.
31. GSP, "My Father as I Knew Him and of Him from Memory and Legend." Since George was part of the Tank Corps at its inception, if he had remained with it during the interwar years, he, instead of Major General Chaffee, might have earned the epitaph, "Father of the Armored Force." As it was, George's name and contribution would be forgotten in the annals of history until his spectacular drive across Europe in WWII.
32. John S. Eisenhower, *General Ike: A Personal Reminiscence* (New York: Free Press, 2004), 6.
33. Conner, *What Father Forbad*, 109.
34. George S. Patton Jr., "Farewell Speech to the 304th Brigade," September 1920, box 9 folder 18, LOC-PP.
35. BAP to AW, 29 September 1920, box 9, folder 18, LOC-PP.
36. AP to BAP, 29 September 1920, box 12, folder 3, HLC-GSP.
37. GSP to BAP, 28 October 1918, box 9, folder 2, LOC-PP.
38. BAP, "A Soldier's Reading."
39. Kevin Ambrose, "How the Knickerbocker snowstorm became D.C.'s deadliest disaster 100 years ago," *The Washington Post*, January 27, 2022. https://www.washingtonpost.com/weather/2022/01/27/knickerbocker-theater-dc-snowstorm-record/
40. Kevin Ambrose, *The Knickerbocker Snowstorm* (Charleston: Arcadia Publishing, 2013), 39.
41. Kevin Ambrose, *The Knickerbocker Snowstorm*, 60.
42. Brigadier General Bandholtz to GSP, 31 January 1922. Official Military Personnel File for George S. Patton, National Archives.
43. Totten, *The Button Box*, 130.
44. George S. Patton Jr., "The Mercenary's Song," April 1918, box 74, folder 1, LOC-PP.
45. GSP to BAP, 16 April 1922, box 10, folder 1, LOC-PP.
46. Totten, *The Button Box*, 28.
47. Merrill, *Keith Merrill: A Memoir*, 78.
48. BAP to GP, 4 March 1919, box 9, folder 12, LOC-PP.
49. Terry Lowry, *22nd Virginia Infantry* (Lynchburg: H.E. Howard, 1991), 2.
50. GSP to BAP, 7 February 1919, box 9, folder 10, LOC-PP.
51. Totten, *The Button Box*, 119.
52. AP to AW, 25 June 1922, as quoted in Totten, *The Button Box*, 135.
53. GSP to BAP, 26 July 1922, box 10, folder 1, LOC-PP.
54. Robert Patton, *The Pattons*, chapter 15, Kindle.
55. BAP to GP, May 1923, box 12, folder 3, HLC-GSP.
56. Totten, *The Button Box*, 136.
57. GSP to BAP, 20 October 1918, box 9, folder 2, LOC-PP.
58. GSP to BAP, 24 October 1918, box 9, folder 2, LOC-PP.
59. Merrill, *Keith Merrill: A Memoir*, 84.
60. BAP to AW, June 1923, as quoted in Totten, *The Button Box*, 136.
61. Robert Patton, *The Pattons*, chapters 12 & 15, Kindle.
62. George Patton Life-Saving Medal File, Arc Id 568559, Rg 26, Uscg General Correspondence, 1910-35, File Code 181, Box 286, Patton, George S., National Archives, accessed August 15, 2022. https://aotus.blogs.archives.gov/2012/12/14/young-george-patton-the-sailor/
63. Robert Patton, *The Pattons*, chapter 15, Kindle.

64. GSP to BAP, January 1924, box 10, folder 2, LOC-PP.
65. Merrill, *Keith Merrill: A Memoir*.
66. RWP to GP, 17 December 1923, box 12, folder 9, HLC-GSP.
67. AP to GP, 22 December 1923, box 12, folder 2, HLC-GSP; RWP to GP, 21 December 1923, box 12, folder 9, HLC-GSP.
68. RWP to GP, 17 December 1923, box 12, folder 9, HLC-GSP.
69. RWP to GP, 17 December 1923, box 12, folder 9, HLC-GSP.
70. AP to GP, 30 December 1923, box 12, folder 2, HLC-GSP.
71. RWP to GP, 24 December 1923, box 12, folder 9, HLC-GSP.
72. RWP to GP, 24 December 1923, box 12, folder 9, HLC-GSP.
73. RWP to GP, 27 December 1923, box 12, folder 9, HLC-GSP.
74. BAP to GP, 29 December 1923, box 12, folder 3, HLC-GSP.
75. BPW to GP, 27 December 1923, box 12, folder 3, HLC-GSP.
76. AP to GP, 30 December 1923, box 12, folder 2, HLC-GSP.
77. BPW to GP, December 27 1923, box 12, folder 3, HLC-GSP.
78. BAP to GP, December 1923, box 12, folder 3, HLC-GSP.
79. BAP to GP, May 1923, box 12, folder 3, HLC-GSP.
80. BAP to GP, box 12, folder 3, HLC-GSP.
81. RWP to GP, 17 December 1923, box 12, folder 9, HLC-GSP.
82. GSP to BAP, 5 February 1918, box 7, folder 9, LOC-PP.
83. Robert Patton, *The Pattons*, chapters 10 & 16, Kindle.
84. Robert Patton, *The Pattons*, chapter 15, Kindle.
85. Robert Patton, *The Pattons*, chapter 15, Kindle.
86. BAP to EBA, 5 June 1916, box 6, folder 10 , LOC-PP.
87. GSP to BAP, 2 April 1925, box 10, folder 2, LOC-PP.
88. GSP to JGH, 3 February 1925, box 37, folder 8, NYHS-HP.
89. BAP to AW, January 1913/1914, box 6, folder 1, LOC-PP.

## 7. THE PARKER RANCH

1. "Lava Overflow Expected at Pit," *Honolulu Star-Bulletin*, July 8, 1927.
2. B. D. Chilson, "Volcano Active Without Pele's Usual Warning," *Honolulu Star-Bulletin*, July 8, 1927.
3. GSP to BAP, 12 August 1927, box 10, folder 4, LOC-PP.
4. "The May 1924 Explosive Eruption of Kīlauea," *U.S. Geological Survey*, accessed August 15, 2022. https://www.usgs.gov/volcanoes/kilauea/may-1924-explosive-eruption-kilauea
5. "Natives Make Offering to Pele as Kilauea's Lava Flow Increases," *Oakland Tribune*, July 8, 1927.
6. Beatrice Ayer Patton, *Love without End* (Honolulu: Ku Pa'a Inc., 1989), 55.
7. "Dollar steamship line - the president liners 1925," *Gjenvick-Gjønvik Archives*, accessed August 15, 2022. https://www.ggarchives.com/OceanTravel/Brochures/DollarSL-1925-PresidentLiners.html
8. "Notables Sail from Brooklyn for Long Voyages," *Brooklyn Times Union*, May 1, 1925. There is no account of how the concert went, but Al Jolson would make extensive trips to entertain the troops overseas during WWII, at one point even meeting General Patton in Sicily.
9. GSP to BAP, 11 March 1925, box 10, folder 2, LOC-PP.
10. GSP to BAP, 10 April 1925, box 10, folder 2, LOC-PP.
11. GSP to BAP, 27 March 1925, box 10, folder 2, LOC-PP.
12. GSP to BAP, 10 April 1925, box 10, folder 2, LOC-PP.
13. GSP to BAP, 2 April 1925, box 10, folder 2, LOC-PP.
14. GSP to BAP, 6 April 1925, box 10, folder 2, LOC-PP.
15. A. F. Dannemiller, "A Tour of Duty in Hawaii," *Infantry Journal*, XXIV (1924): 381.
16. Totten, *The Button Box*, 145.
17. GSP to BAP, 2 April 1925, box 10, folder 2, LOC-PP.
18. GSP to BAP, 6 April 1925, box 10, folder 2, LOC-PP.
19. BAP to GP, 3 August 1926, box 12, folder 3, HLC-GSP.
20. "A Challenge for the Dillingham Trophy," *Hawaii Polo Club (blog)*, accessed August 15, 2022. https://hawaii-polo.org/2014/08/02/a-challenge-for-the-dillingham-trophy/

21. These nomads formalized the game once they settled in Persia over two thousand years ago, but it wasn't until 1859 that the first game of polo as we know it today was played. British soldiers in India learned the game from the locals and took it back to England, where it quickly became all the rage.
22. George S. Patton Jr., "Polo in the Army," autumn 1922, LOC-PP.
23. According to the newspapers in Hawaii, they played 8.
24. "Best Polo Pony in Hawaiian Department is Maj. Patton's of the 13th Field Artillery," *The Honolulu Advertiser*, March 6, 1926.
25. GSP to BAP, 6 April 1925, box 10, folder 2, LOC-PP; "Here's Schofield's Crack Polo Quartet," *The Honolulu Advertiser*, August 28, 1925.
26. "Polo Players, Cavalry," 1929, box 50, folder 18, LOC-PP. George was a skilled but aggressive polo player with an average handicap of four, negative two being the worst and ten being the very best. The average in the Cavalry was 2.6, while very few scored higher than Walter Dillingham, who averaged a five.
27. GSP to BAP, 28 July 1922, box 10, folder 1, LOC-PP.
28. BAP to AW, 20 March 1913, box 15, folder 9, LOC-PP.
29. Robert Patton, *The Pattons*, chapter 12, Kindle.
30. Dannemiller, "A Tour of Duty in Hawaii," 381.
31. GSP to BAP, Fall 1906, box 4, folder 16, LOC-PP.
32. BAP, *Love without End*, 29.
33. Cheryl Chee Tsutsumi, "The Origin of the Shaka," *Hawaiian Airlines (blog)*, accessed August 15, 2022. https://www.hawaiianairlines.com/hawaii-stories/culture/origin-of-the-shaka
34. Totten, *The Button Box*, 147.
35. BAP to GP, 3 August 1926, box 12, folder 3, HLC-GSP.
36. GSP to BAP, 22 November 1926, box 10, folder 3, LOC-PP.
37. GSP to BAP, 3 December 1926, box 10, folder 3, LOC-PP.
38. Breadfruit was known as a canoe plant, brought to Hawaii by the Polynesians who survived on the fruit during their trip. One breadfruit tree can grow an average of 75 breadfruits per year. It starts off having the texture of a potato but ripens into a kind of custard, gradually sweetening as its starches are converted to sugars.
39. Lee Carson, "Patton's Wife Offers no Alibi for Tough Perfectionist," *The Washington Post*, November 25, 1943.
40. Robert Patton, *The Pattons*, chapter 16, Kindle.
41. GP to GSP, 29 March 1923, box 12, folder 3, HLC-GSP.
42. Roddy, *Mills, Mansions, and Mergers*; GSP to BAP, 1 September 1912, box 5, folder 15, LOC-PP.
43. GSP to BAP, 7 April 1909, box 5, folder 6, LOC-PP.
44. "Table Gossip," *Boston Daily Globe*, September 26, 1926.
45. GSP to BAP, 3 September 1928, box 10, folder 4, LOC-PP.
46. Totten, Ruth Ellen Patton, *The Button Box: A Daughter's Loving Memoir of Mrs. George S. Patton*, ed. James Patton Totten, (Columbia, Missouri: University of Missouri Press, 2005), 159. Reprinted by permission of the publisher
47. GSP, "My Father as I Knew Him and of Him from Memory and Legend."
48. GSP to GP, 17 March 1927, box 10, folder 4, LOC-PP; GSP, "My Father as I Knew Him and of Him from Memory and Legend."
49. GSP to GP, April 22 1927, box 10, folder 4, LOC-PP.
50. "Huntington's Body At Rest," *Los Angeles Times*, June 01, 1927.
51. BAP to GP, 25 September 1914, box 6, folder 2, LOC-PP.
52. "Col. George Patton Dies: Was Noted Figure in History of Southland and Chairman Of Huntington Library Board," *Los Angeles Times*, June 11, 1927.
53. "Another Link Broken," *Los Angeles Times*, June 14, 1927.
54. GSP, "My Father as I Knew Him and of Him from Memory and Legend."
55. Billy Bergin, *Loyal to the Land: The Legendary Parker Ranch, 750-1950* (Honolulu: University of Hawai'i Press, 2004), 224.
56. Totten, *The Button Box*, 166.
57. GSP to GP, 22 April 1927, box 10, folder 4, LOC-PP.
58. BAP, *Love Without End*, 92.
59. BAP, *Love Without End*, 92.
60. Conner, *What Father Forbad*, 103-107.
61. Hawaii was just a territory until 1959, meaning assignment there was considered Foreign

Service.

62. D'Este, *Patton: A Genius for War*, 337.

63. GSP to BAP, 27 April 1927, box 10, folder 4, LOC-PP.

64. Edward Cox, "Grey Eminence: Fox Conner and the Art of Mentorship," *The Land Warfare Papers*, No. 78W (September 2010). https://ausa.org/sites/default/files/LWP-78-Grey-Eminence-Fox-Conner-and-the-Art-of-Mentorship.pdf

65. GSP to AW, 5 March 1928, box 10, folder 4, LOC-PP.

66. "Emma Taylor Passes; Rites Late Tuesday," *Honolulu Star-Bulletin*, November 8, 1937.

67. She wrote many articles on Hawaiian culture, as did her husband, Albert Pierce Taylor, the well-known librarian of the Archives of Hawaii.

68. Nancy J. Morris, "Beatrice Patton's Hawai'I," *Hawaiian Journal of History*, vol. 39 (2005). http://hdl.handle.net/10524/236

69. W.D. Westervelt, *Legends of Maui* (Hawaiian Library, 2021), 10.

70. Mark Twain, *Roughing It* (Orinda: SeaWolf Press, 2018), 460.

71. BAP, *Love Without End*, 58.

72. Beatrice Ayer Patton, *Blood of the Shark: A Romance of Early Hawaii* (Honolulu: Paradise of the Pacific, 1937), Foreword.

## 8. WHITE OAKS

1. Donna Evers, "The Three B's," *Washington Life Magazine*, March 1, 2009; Donna Evers, "Historical Landscapes: The Hostess Wars," *Washington Life Magazine*, December 8, 2009.

2. Totten, *The Button Box*, 194.

3. Totten, *The Button Box*, 197.

4. "Society Will Welcome Two Buds Today: Katrina McCormick and Beatrice Patton to be Presented," *The Washington Post*, December 13, 1930.

5. "Interesting Army Family to Sail here," *Honolulu Star-Bulletin*, May 11, 1935.

6. Totten, *The Button Box*, 241.

7. GSP to BAP, 6 September 1917, box 7, folder 1, LOC-PP.

8. Janice P. Pulsifer, *Changing Town: Hamilton, Massachusetts 1850-1910* (Hamilton Historical Society, 1985), 31.

9. "Hogue And Burroughs Die In East Boston Air Crash," *Boston Daily Globe*, July 24, 1925.

10. "Table Gossip," *Boston Daily Globe*, January 9, 1927.

11. GSP to BAP, 2 November 1926, box 10, folder 3, LOC-PP.

12. GSP to BAP, 2 November 1926, box 10, folder 3, LOC-PP.

13. *Wenham in World War II* (Wenham Village Improvement Society, 1947) 239.

14. "3 Boys Wound Gordon Prince," *Boston Daily Globe*, April 24, 1936; Fred Ayer Jr., *Before the Colors Fade*, 46.

15. "Obituaries: Dr. Anna A. Prince, 77, North Shore Civic Leader," *The Boston Globe*, October 9, 1973.

16. "Three Myopia Cups To Ledyard Horses: Mrs Sears And Daughter Win Parent-Child Test," *Boston Daily Globe*, September 7, 1937.

17. "Myopia Hunt Club Entertains 1500 at 25th Annual Horse Show," *Boston Daily Globe*, September 6, 1921.

18. "Patton's Widow Gives $50,000 Memorial to Medical Center," *The Boston Globe*, June 10, 1949; Neil Rice Ayer, *Wind over Willowdale* (Beverly: Memoirs Unlimited, 1991). Fred also "believed that a certain percentage of your disposable income ought to go toward charity . . . and he encouraged various members of the family to do the same." His vision was to build Beverly Hospital into a premier medical center, and in 1929 a fundraising drive was held to raise $500,000 for the endowment fund. Ten percent was collected in memory of James Proctor Mandell, a nephew of Hilda who died from a severe head injury sustained in a polo tournament. All the advancements in medicine Beatrice witnessed throughout her life came about because "doctors dedicate their lives to saving the lives of others. There are very few rich doctors, except those who inherited wealth. The rest of us must give our money so that they can do their work—have the tools and the room in which to work."

19. BAP, "The Army Wife."

20. Glenn Jeansonne, Frank Haney, and David Luhrssen; "George S. Patton: A Life Shaped by Dyslexia," *Warfare History Network*, September 30, 2020. https://warfarehistorynetwork.com/a-life-shaped-by-dyslexia/

21. GSP to BAP, November/December 1929, box 10, folder 5, LOC-PP.

22. GSP to BAP, 30 June 1930, box 10, folder 6, LOC-PP.

23. GSP to BAP, 21 July 21 1930, box 10, folder 6, LOC-PP; GSP to BAP, 3 September 1928, box 10, folder 6, LOC-PP.

24. John S. D. Eisenhower, *Strictly Personal* (United States: Doubleday, 1974), 9.

25. Fred Ayer Jr., *Before the Colors Fade*, 35.

26. Totten, *The Button Box*, 345.

27. Semmes, *Portrait of Patton*, 185.

28. D'Este, *Patton: A Genius for War*, 77; Kay Summersby, *Eisenhower Was My Boss* (Werner Laurie, 1949), 21.

29. D'Este, *Patton: A Genius for War*, 817.

30. GSP to BAP, 2 March 1910, box 5, folder 9, LOC-PP; Codman, *Drive*, 275.

31. BAP to GP, 3 August 1926, box 12, folder 3, HLC-GSP.

32. Early, "True Confessions Salutes A Hero's Wife."

33. Erin Blakemore, "How American 'Dollar Princesses' Invaded British High Society," *History.com*, A&E Television Networks, May 18. 2018. http://history.com/news/american-heiress-marry-british-aristocrat

34. D'Este, *Patton: A Genius for War*, 345.

35. Early, "True Confessions Salutes A Hero's Wife."

36. Frances Burns, "Pattons most Vivid American Army Pair," *Boston Daily Globe*, October 4, 1953. Reginald "Reggie" Maidment started as the chauffeur, and, once he married, his wife joined the household as a cook; when they had two sons, Buddie and Robert became part of the household as well.

37. Totten, *The Button Box*, 190-191.

38. RWP to GP, 24 December 1923, box 12, folder 9, HLC-GSP.

39. Robert Patton, *The Pattons*, chapter 15, Kindle.

40. John Michael, *Images of America: Fort Myer* (Charleston: Arcadia Publishing, 2011), 84.

41. "Horse shows Loom on Horizon with Spring's Coming," *The Washington Post*, February 23, 1930.

42. "Variety Marks Social Calendar," *The Washington Times*, March 26, 1922.

43. "Ft. Myer Society Circus Is Success; Two Shows Today," *The Washington Post*, April 1, 1933.

44. Cramer, "Georgie."

45. Blumenson, *The Patton Papers: 1885-1940*, 723.

46. Paul Dickson and Thomas B. Allen, *The Bonus Army: An American Epic* (Mineola: Dover Publications, 2020), 37; Robert Patton, *The Pattons*, chapter 15, Kindle.

47. "Joe Angelo Pleads for Veterans," clipping attached to letter from GSP to BAP, 13 June 1930, box 10, folder 6, LOC-PP. Angelo eventually tried to meet up with Patton on July 29, but George was compelled by duty and fear of publicity to have his rescuer turned away.

48. Totten, *The Button Box*, 192. MacArthur hated the mostly peaceful Bonus Marchers even though he fought next to them in WWI. Most people advised against military action, including MacArthur's unofficial military secretary, Dwight Eisenhower.

49. Robert Patton, *The Pattons*, chapter 15, Kindle.

50. Early, "True Confessions Salutes A Hero's Wife."

51. Early, "True Confessions Salutes A Hero's Wife."

52. Frederick Watson and Paul Brown, *Hunting Pie: The Whole Art & Craft of Fox Hunting* (New York: The Derrydale Press, 1931).

53. Semmes, *Portrait of Patton*, 79.

54. George S. Patton Jr., "Cobbler Hunt Diary, 1933-1934," page 13, December 6, 1933, LOC-PP. Referring to the fox's head and tail, the mask and brush of "the old customer" was given to two hunters as trophies, just one of the many social rituals associated with fox hunting.

55. Robert Patton, *The Pattons*, chapter 15, Kindle.

56. GSP, "Cobbler Hunt Diary, 1933-1934," page 16, December 23, 1933, LOC.

57. "On The Line," *The Washington Post*, May 01, 1943.

58. The club disbanded in December 1945 as a silent tribute to their fallen leader, just weeks after they received word from George that he was looking forward to hunting with the Cobblers very soon. There were plenty of other hunting clubs in the area anyway, one of the most famous the Piedmont Fox Hounds, of which Theodora Ayer Randolph served as Master for over forty

years. Chilly's eldest daughter fell in love with the Virginia countryside during her time at Foxcroft, and her name still resonates in the area as "the first lady of fox hunting."

59. Sobel, *The Fighting Pattons*, 8.
60. Fred Ayer Jr., *Before the Colors Fade*, 94.
61. BAP, "A Soldier's Reading."
62. BAP, "A Soldier's Reading."
63. Totten, *The Button Box*, 310.
64. GSPIV to Brigadier General Hobson, "General George Smith Patton, Jr. U.S.A. — A Tribute."
65. Frederick Ayer, *The Reminiscences of Frederick Ayer*, 80.
66. Totten, *The Button Box*, 198.
67. "Lt. Col. Patton's Entries," *Boston Daily Globe*, October 28, 1934.
68. GSP to BAP, 21 July 1930 , box 10, folder 6, LOC-PP.
69. Totten, *The Button Box*, 198.
70. GSPIV to Brigadier General Hobson, "General George Smith Patton, Jr. U.S.A. — A Tribute."
71. Totten, *The Button Box*, 240.
72. Robert Patton, *The Pattons*, chapter 15, Kindle.
73. Totten, *The Button Box*, 109.
74. GSP to BAP, 20 January 1918, box 7, folder 7, LOC-PP.; GSP to BAP, 11 August 1918 , box 8, folder 10, LOC-PP.
75. GSP to BAP, 7 July 1934 , box 10, folder 6, LOC-PP.
76. GSP to BAP, 7 July 1934 , box 10, folder 6, LOC-PP.
77. Evelyn Peyton Gordon, "Miss Patton, Lt. Waters are Married," *The Washington Post*, June 28, 1934; BAP, "The Army Wife."
78. GSP to BAP, 29 March 1925, box 10, folder 2, LOC-PP.
79. GSPIV to Brigadier General Hobson. "General George Smith Patton, Jr. U.S.A. — A Tribute."
80. Totten, *The Button Box*, 246.
81. BAP, "A Soldier's Reading."
82. D'Este, *Patton: A Genius for War*, 358.

## 9. ARCTURUS

1. "Chapter 5 of Hawai'i Revised Statutes: The law of the aloha spirit," *University of Hawai'i*, accessed August 16, 2022. https://hawaii.edu/uhwo/clear/home/lawaloha.html
2. Totten, *The Button Box*, 274.
3. Totten, *The Button Box*, 266-267.
4. BAP, "The Army Wife."
5. Semmes, *Portrait of Patton*, 80.
6. Fred Ayer Jr., *Before the Colors Fade*, 47.
7. "Army Officer Sails here on his Own Yacht," *Honolulu Star-Bulletin*, June 4, 1935.
8. BAP, *Love Without End*, 47.
9. "The Island Murder," *PBS*, accessed August 17, 2022. https://www.pbs.org/wgbh/americanexperience/films/island-murder/#transcript. Intensely disliked and known to have a violent temper, no one was surprised when Thalia slapped one of her husband's colleagues at a Waikiki nightclub on the night of September 12, 1931. She was walking home along the dark alleys of Waikiki Beach when she was dragged into a car and taken to a remote location by five men who beat, robbed, and raped her. When she reluctantly agreed to file charges, someone ensured that her description matched the five young men who were already cited for drunken and disorderly conduct that night.
10. Stuart M. Ball, "The Piko Club: Hiking O'ahu in the 1930s," *The Hawaiian Journal of History*, vol. 37 (2003): 179–97.
11. Piko has two meanings in Hawaiian: navel and summit.
12. Noel Nicholas, "The Officer and the Gentleman," *HanaHou! The Magazine of Hawaiian Airlines*, no. 18.3, 2015.
13. Ball, "The Piko Club: Hiking O'ahu in the 1930s," 179–97.
14. "Col. Patton, Polo Fan, on Return Trip," *Honolulu Star-Bulletin*, May 11, 1935.
15. "Society in the Honolulu Sector," *Honolulu Star-Bulletin*, July 20, 1935.
16. Fred Ayer Jr., *Before the Colors Fade*, 43.

17. "Many Parties in Sector Circles During Week," *The Honolulu Advertiser*, July 21, 1935.

18. "Mrs. Patton wins trophy at Peninsula," *The Honolulu Advertiser*, January 27, 1936; "To Start New Yacht Series," *Honolulu Star-Bulletin*, January 27, 1936.

19. Early, "True Confessions Salutes A Hero's Wife."

20. William B. Park, "Homemade Diving Helmet to find Lost Motors," *Popular Mechanics*, September 1932.

21. Totten, *The Button Box*, 263.

22. BAP, *Love without End*, 92.

23. Morris, "Beatrice Patton's Hawai'i."

24. "Sir Peter Buck," Encyclopedia Britannica, December 11, 2021. https://www.britannica.com/biography/Peter-Buck-Maori-anthropologist-physicist-and-politician. It was possible to track migration patterns from Polynesia to Hawaii based on the shape and size of shellfish hooks.

25. "Best Poloist Showing Here," *Honolulu Star-Bulletin*, August 2, 1935.

26. "Lt. Col. Patton to Play Informal Polo During Duty Here," *The Honolulu Advertiser*, June 9, 1935.

27. Robert Sullivan, "Old B. & G. was Waiting for this War," *Sunday News*, June 10, 1945.

28. "Shafter Polo Team Goes Down in Close Match at Schofield," *The Honolulu Advertiser*, August 27, 1935.

29. "Islanders Beat Shafter in Schofield Polo Tilt," *Honolulu Star-Bulletin*, August 27, 1935.

30. "Polo Season One of Great Social Gayety," *Honolulu Star-Bulletin*, August 17, 1935.

31. GSP to BAP, November 1904, box 4, folder 13, LOC-PP.

32. Fred Ayer Jr., *Before the Colors Fade*, 70.

33. "Maui County Fair," *Maui Information Guide*, accessed August 17, 2022. https://www.mauiinformationguide.com/maui-county-fair.php

34. BAP, *Love Without End*, 96-97.

35. BAP, *Love Without End*, 93.

36. Léo Azambuja, "The Hawaiian Poi Dog," *For Kauai Online*, August 31, 2017, accessed August 17, 2022. https://www.forkauaionline.com/hawaiian-poi-dog/

37. Totten, *The Button Box*, 271.

38. Totten, *The Button Box*, 250.

39. Totten, *The Button Box*, 267.

40. D'Este, *Patton: A Genius for War*, 123.

41. Fred Ayer Jr., *Before the Colors Fade*, 36.

42. Ruth Ellen Patton Totten, interview by William Heitz, *Hamilton-Wenham's Times Past*, 1987. https://archive.org/details/HWTPSDVD37

43. Patton, *Love Without End*, 49.

44. Allyson Chiu, "Hawaii's Volcanoes: How George S. Patton Took on the Lava with Bombs," *The Washington Post*, May 17, 2018; Thomas Van Hare, "Volcano Bombing," *HistoricWings.com: A Magazine for Aviators, Pilots and Adventurers*, May 11, 2021. http://fly.historicwings.com/2012/12/volcano-bombing/

45. "Oahu Blues Flash Too Much Class for Army Poloists," *Honolulu Star-Bulletin*, August 31, 1936.

46. Morris, "Beatrice Patton's Hawai'i."

47. Donald Willard, "Says Mason's Skull Fractured By Blow," *Boston Daily Globe*, Feb 21, 1933.

48. Semmes, *Portrait of Patton*, 25.

49. "Baltic Society to Observe Anniversary of Secret Trip," *The Washington Post*, May 27, 1932.

50. Totten, *The Button Box*, 248.

51. GSP to Arvin Brown as quoted in Patton, *The Pattons*, chapter 15, Kindle.

52. "Patton Yacht Arcturus off Thursday to Visit Palmyra," *Honolulu Star-Bulletin*, September 9, 1936.

53. Fred Ayer Jr., *Before the Colors Fade*, 107.

54. Beatrice Ayer Patton, "Voyage of "Arcturus," entry 17 June 1937, box 10, folder 7, LOC-PP.

55. Sobel, *The Fighting Pattons*, 16.

56. Edmund Fanning, *Voyages Round the World; with Selected Sketches of Voyages to the South Seas, North and South Pacific Oceans, China, Etc.* (New York: Collins & Hannay, 1863).

57. Aaron Elkins, "On The Verge; Fanning Island. Where?" *The New York Times Magazine*, September 14, 2003. The first real tourists did not arrive until 2010 when a cruise ship began making stops. Fanning Island is now known locally as Tabuaeran and is part of the Republic of Kiribati.

58. "Pattons Back from Voyage," *Honolulu Star-Bulletin*, October 13, 1936.

59. "Remains of Pvt. Goins in Shark's Body," *Honolulu Star-Bulletin*, June 5, 1926.

60. Ardis E. Parshall, "Catch of the Day," *The Keepapitchinin*, February 10, 2011. http://www.keepa-

pitchinin.org/2011/02/10/catch-of-the-day/comment-page-1/

61. Daniel Ikaika Ito, "The Cultural Significance of Sharks in Hawaii," *Hawai'i Magazine*, July 10, 2015. https://www.hawaiimagazine.com/the-cultural-significance-of-sharks-in-hawaii/

62. Wailana Kalama, "Why Sharks Are Highly Respected in Hawaiian Culture," *The Culture Trip*, October 29, 2017. https://theculturetrip.com/north-america/usa/hawaii/articles/why-sharks-are-highly-respected-in-hawaiian-culture/

63. "Beatrice Ayer Patton's Novel of Old Hawaii Deals with Totemism, Other Dramatic Human Themes," *Honolulu Star-Bulletin*, December 5, 1936.

64. "Legends Of The Pacific: The Blood Of The Shark," *The Washington Post*, February 24, 1937.

65. Morris, "Beatrice Patton's Hawai'i."

66. Lorna Arlen, "Feminine World," *The Honolulu Advertiser*, June 3, 1937.

67. BAP, *Love without End*, 40; Morris, "Beatrice Patton's Hawai'i."

68. "In Literary Spotlight: Novel of Old Hawaii," *The Honolulu Advertiser*, December 6, 1936; St. Johns, "Lieut. Gen. and Mrs. George S. Patton, Jr"; Adela Rogers St. Johns to GSP, 22 April 1943, box 10, folder 17, LOC-PP. Beatrice did not particularly care for the article in Cosmopolitan Magazine by Adela Rogers St. Johns. In the margins, she wrote, "Georgie! - Such a funny woman! Writes trash, but is most intelligent."

69. Robert Patton, *The Pattons*, chapter 15, Kindle.

70. Sobel, *The Fighting Pattons*, 52. Mr. Patton taught his boy at ten years of age that "drinking [was] common place" by pouring him his first glass of whiskey and explaining that the liquor cabinet wasn't "locked and you can get a drink whenever you want one." (GSP, "My Father as I Knew Him and of Him from Memory and Legend.")

71. Patton, *The Pattons*, chapter 16, Kindle.

72. Patton, *The Pattons*, chapter 16, Kindle.

73. Fred Ayer Jr., *Before the Colors Fade*, 71.

74. Totten, *The Button Box*, 147.

75. GSP to BAP, 7 February 1919, box 9, folder 10, LOC-PP.

76. Notes by BAP on letter from GSP to BAP, 13 September 1943, box 11, folder 7, LOC-PP. George's relationship with women was usually one of old-fashioned chivalry. Driving to his hotel after participating in a Long Island horse show in 1922, George saw three men pull a young woman in a truck. He quickly pulled over, grabbed his revolver, and demanded the men release their hostage. It took quite a bit of convincing before George believed that one of them was the woman's fiancé and they were helping her in the car.

77. Totten, *The Button Box*, 274.

78. Louise remarried in 1925, to Conrad Hatheway, who died in 1937.

79. GSP to BAP, 20 February 1910, box 5, folder 9, LOC-PP.

80. "Leaving Thursday," *Honolulu Star-Bulletin*, December 26, 1936.

81. Totten, *The Button Box*, 261.

82. Totten, *The Button Box*, 261.

83. Patton, *The Pattons*, chapter 16, Kindle.

84. Tim Teeman, "The Price of Being a Patton: Wrestling with the Legacy of America's Most Famous General," *The Daily Beast*, July 12, 2017. https://www.thedailybeast.com/the-price-of-being-a-patton-wrestling-with-the-legacy-of-americas-most-famous-general

85. "Col. Patton to Sail Saturday," *Honolulu Star-Bulletin*, June 9, 1937.

86. BAP, "Voyage of Arcturus," entry 15 June 1937, box 10, folder 7, LOC-PP.

87. BAP, "Voyage of Arcturus," entry 9 July 1937, box 10, folder 7, LOC-PP.

88. BAP, "Voyage of Arcturus," entry 10 July 1937, box 10, folder 7, LOC-PP.

89. BAP, "Voyage of Arcturus," entry 11 July 1937, box 10, folder 7, LOC-PP.

## PART III

1. Beatrice Ayer Patton, "On Growing Older," Patton Family Archives, Wenham Museum, Wenham, MA.

## 10. SAND HILL

1. Haynes W. Dugan, "Down Memory Lane: The 3rd Armored Division, Stateside 1941-1943," *The Writings Of Haynes W. Dugan, Lt. Col., Usar (Ret), 1982,* accessed August 18, 2022. https://3ad.com/history/wwll/dugan.index.htm
2. GSP to BAP, 9 August 1905, box 4, folder 14, LOC-PP.
3. Frances Burns, "Pattons most Vivid American Army Pair," *Boston Daily* Globe, Oct 04, 1953.
4. Fred Ayer Jr., *Before the Colors Fade*, 46.
5. GSP to BAP, 24 November 1909, box 5, folder 8, LOC-PP.
6. GSP to BAP, 10 March 1909, box 5, folder 6, LOC-PP; Burns, "Pattons most Vivid American Army Pair."
7. Spurling, "The Patton Episode."
8. Dorothy G. Wayman, "Gen. Patton Greeted by Wife's Song on His 58th Birthday," *The Boston Globe*, November 17, 1943; Major Verne D. Campbell, "Armor and Cavalry Music Part II," *Armor*, Vol. LXXX, May-June 1971; Beatrice Ayer Patton, "2nd Armored Division March" 1941.
9. Conner, *What Father Forbad*, 106.
10. Totten, *The Button Box*, 286.
11. Fred Ayer Jr., *Before the Colors Fade*, 103-104.
12. "GSP Medical Records, 1904-1948," box 49, reel 2, LOC-PP. His diagnosis: Fracture, compound, comminuted, complete, middle third right tibia./ Fracture, simple, transverse, complete, middle, third right fibula./ Fracture, simple, oblique, complete, lower third, right fibula./ Acute thrombophlebitis of the pelvic veins with resultant edematous swelling of the right leg.
13. Fred Ayer Jr., *Before the Colors Fade*, 104.
14. GSP to JGH, 8 September 1937, box 37, folder 2, NYHS-HP.
15. BAP to JGH, Sunday September 1937, box 37, folder 2, NYHS-HP. The board eventually concluded the accident was incurred in the line of duty and was not the result of any misconduct. Still, George was vexed his superiors had doubted him in the first place.
16. Fred Ayer Jr., *Before the Colors Fade*, 104.
17. GSP to JGH, 8 September 1937, box 37, folder 2, NYHS-HP.
18. Totten, *The Button Box*, 287.
19. BAP to AW, 15 August 1913, box 5, folder 17, LOC-PP; GSP to BAP, 28 September 1912, box 5, folder 15, LOC-PP.
20. Patton, "Voyage of Arcturus," box 10, folder 7,LOC-PP.
21. Gwenn Friss, "Delayed Destiny: Effort Underway to Sail Patton's When and If around the World," *Cape Cod Times*, August 2, 2015. This was a key characteristic of many of Alden's schooners, who had learned firsthand the importance of one person being able to sail during an emergency. When he was still an inexperienced youngster, Alden and three equally inexperienced friends sailed home a schooner whose twenty-three-man crew had fallen ill with smallpox. They almost perished when caught in a terrible storm with not enough people to man the deck.
22. "An Historic Vessel," *Sail When and If*, accessed August 18, 2022. http://sailwhenandif.com/an-historic-vessel/
23. GSP, "My Father as I Knew Him and of Him from Memory and Legend."
24. Leonard Fowle, "Dream Yacht of Pattons Never Fulfilled Mission," *Boston Daily Globe*, October 4, 1953.
25. Peggy O'Connell Parker, "The When and If—Patton's Own," *Army*, February 1978.
26. Seth Salzmann, "I'm Chasing General Patton's Ghost," *True.ink*, February 16, 2021. https://www.true.ink/posts/im-chasing-general-pattons-ghost
27. Frances Burns, "Pattons most Vivid American Army Pair," *Boston Daily Globe*, October 4, 1953.
28. Totten, *The Button Box*, 290.
29. Beatrice Ayer Patton, "Fort Riley Patton Memorial Ceremony Dedication Speech," 4 April 1946, box 75, folder 9, LOC-PP.
30. Frederick Ayer II, *Memories of an Unplanned Life* (Seattle: Privately Published, 1988), 12.
31. "Dr. J. C. Ayer Dies; Retired Surgeon: Practitioner In New York Had Served On Bellevue Staff--Harvard Graduate, '86 Medical Officer In War Distinguished As A Painter," *The New York Times*, March 21, 1939.
32. JJP to BAP, 25 May 1938, box 10, folder 8, LOC-PP.

33. Totten, *The Button Box*, 23. Just a few months after James died, his wife, May, appeared in front of a judge in ill health herself. She was fined $14,000 for avoiding import duties over the last few years when returning from Nassau. She blamed the loss of her husband, who always took care of those things for her. She died in June 1943.

34. Fred Ayer Jr., *Before the Colors Fade*, 106.

35. Sobel, *The Fighting Pattons*, 73.

36. Sobel, *The Fighting Pattons*, 14-15.

37. Transcript of Interview with Major General Patton on May 12, 1987; Folder: Patton, Gen. George; Toland Papers, Series VI: IN Mortal Combat, A Interviews: Lo-Pendas; Franklin D. Roosevelt Library, Hyde Park, New York.

38. Transcript of Interview with Major General Patton on May 12, 1987; Folder: Patton, Gen. George; Toland Papers, Series VI: IN Mortal Combat, A Interviews: Lo-Pendas; Franklin D. Roosevelt Library, Hyde Park, New York; Totten, *The Button Box*, 300. Quote by Richard Steele for The Tatler, possibly in reference to the lady-in-waiting of Queen Victoria's mother.

39. BAP to JGH, 12 November 1943, box 36, folder 16, NYHS-HP.

40. GSP to GP, 12 July 1919, box 9, folder 13, LOC-PP.

41. "Captain Tells How He Halted Italian Flight," *Mount Carmel Item*, December 5, 1918; "How a Modern Horatius 'Kept the Bridge' Alone and Averted Italian Rout," *The New York Evening World*, August 16, 1918.

42. "U.S. Annoys Duce," *San Pedro News-Pilot*, December 30, 1936; BAP to JGH, 12 November 1943, box 36, folder 16, NYHS-HP.

43. Once the Guardabassis permanently left Italy in 1940, they rented the house to the Bulgari family. During the war, it became the headquarters of the German Army (1943-1944) and subsequently for the Allied Troops (1944-1945). It was looted and abandoned for forty years until it was sold and restored to its former glory.

44. GSP to BAP, 24 July 1938, box 10, folder 8, LOC-PP.

45. GSP to Van Voorhis, 29 August 1938, box 10, folder 8, LOC-PP. The Pattons enjoyed Virgie's cooking so much that she was asked to come along. George "bought" Meeks out of the Army (he paid to have his record terminated) and had him reenlist at Fort Myer.

46. GSP to BAP, 24 July 1938, box 10, folder 8, LOC-PP.

47. GSP to BAP, 27 August 1938, box 10, folder 8, LOC-PP.

48. GSP to BAP, 2 September 1938, box 10, folder 8, LOC-PP.

49. GSP to BAP, 4 August 1938, box 10, folder 8, LOC-PP.

50. GSP to JGH, 10 November 1938, box 37, folder 2, NYHS-HP.

51. GSP to FA, 5 May 1943, Neil Rice Ayer Jr. Private Papers.

52. Robert Patton, *The Pattons*, chapter 17, Kindle. Whether General Herr told him implicitly that money was the reason for his transfer is unknown, but according to Robert Patton, his grandfather chose to blame his wife.

53. John Field, "Patton of the Armored Force," *Life Magazine*, November 30, 1942.

54. GSP to AW, 17 January 1915, box 6, folder 3, LOC-PP.

55. FA to GSP, 26 February 1923, box 12, folder 3, HLC-GSP.

56. GSP to GP, 17 January 1909, box 5, folder 5, LOC-PP.

57. GSP to BAP, 19 March 1918, box 7, folder 12, LOC-PP.

58. BAP to GSP, 7 December 1942, box 10, folder 12, LOC-PP; GSP to BAP, 27 July 1939, box 10, folder 8, LOC-PP; GSP to BAP, 3 September 1940, Patton, George S. (George Smith), and Beatrice Banning Ayer Patton. George S. Patton Papers, 1905. USMA Library.

59. Haynes W. Dugan, "George Patton and I," *The Writings Of Haynes W. Dugan, Lt. Col., Usar (Ret)*, 1982, accessed August 18, 2022. https://3ad.com/history/wwll/dugan.index.htm

60. Merrill, *Keith Merrill: A Memoir*.

61. GSP to BAP, 23 January 1910, box 5, folder 9, LOC-PP.

62. Totten, *The Button Box*, 306.

63. Josephine Leavell Polk, "Some of my Memories of Ft. Myer, Virginia," James H. Polk Papers; Box 50, Folder 5. U.S. Army Heritage And Education Center, Carlisle, PA.

64. Seamans, *Light and Life*, 194.

65. Burns, "Pattons most Vivid American Army Pair"; GSP to JGH, 10 November 1938, box 37, folder 2, NYHS-HP.

66. Totten, *The Button Box*, 308.

67. Totten, *The Button Box*, 134.

68. D'Este, *Patton: A Genius for War*, 345.

69. Carson, "Patton's Wife Offers no Alibi for 'Tough Perfectionist.'"
70. GSP to BAP, 27 July 1939, box 10, folder 8, LOC-PP.
71. Patton, *The Pattons*, chapter 17, Kindle.
72. James H. Polk, "The Patton Legend - A Subordinate's View," James H. Polk Papers, Box 54A, Folder 1. U.S. Army Heritage And Education Center, Carlisle, PA.
73. Beatrice Ayer Patton, U.S. Army Heritage And Education Center, Carlisle, PA.
74. Adela Rogers St. Johns, "Lieut. Gen. and Mrs. George S. Patton, Jr.," *Cosmopolitan Magazine*, Vol. 115, no. 5, November 1943.
75. Totten, *The Button Box*, 309.
76. Conner, *What Father Forbad*, 53; "Errol Flynn does some Panting about His Pants!" *The Washington Post*, January 26, 1939.
77. "Errol Flynn Rides Roosevelt Steed and Receives Cup from First Lady," *The Washington Post*, January 26, 1939.
78. Beatrice Patton Ayer Patton, Undated Talk on Military Service, box 11, folder 13, LOC-PP.
79. Totten, *The Button Box*, 312.
80. GSP to FA, 26 September 1943, Neil Rice Ayer Jr. Private Papers.
81. Totten, *The Button Box*, 320.
82. Christopher R. Gabel, *The U.S. Army GHQ Maneuvers of 1941* (Washington DC: Center of Military History United States Army, 1992).
83. "Ft. Myer Gives Big Send-Off to Col. Patton," *The Washington Post*, July 25, 1940.
84. "Mrs. Patton here to Close Ft. Myer Home: Husband Transferred to Fort Benning, Ga., in Charge of Tank Corps," *The Washington Post*, August 1, 1940.
85. Letter, BAP to Priscilla, 24 November 1943.
86. GSP to BAP, 4 April 1909, box 5, folder 6, LOC-PP; GSP to BAP, 1 August 1932, box 10, folder 6, LOC-PP.
87. GSP to BAP, 27 August 1940; Patton, George S. (George Smith), and Beatrice Banning Ayer Patton. George S. Patton Papers, 1905. USMA Library.
88. GSP to BAP, 31 August 1940; Patton, George S. (George Smith), and Beatrice Banning Ayer Patton. George S. Patton Papers, 1905. USMA Library.
89. GSP to BAP, 3 September 1940; Patton, George S. (George Smith), and Beatrice Banning Ayer Patton. George S. Patton Papers, 1905. USMA Library.
90. GSP to BAP, 12 September 1940; Patton, George S. (George Smith), and Beatrice Banning Ayer Patton. George S. Patton Papers, 1905. USMA Library.
91. While he designed them to allow soldiers to escape from a tank without snagging his clothes, the Army never adopted the uniform. Still, they brought many visitors to Fort Benning who wanted to see the "Green Hornet" with their own eyes.
92. St. Johns, "Lieut. Gen. and Mrs. George S. Patton, Jr."
93. St. Johns, "Lieut. Gen. and Mrs. George S. Patton, Jr."
94. Peggy A. Stelpflug and Richard Hyatt; *Home of the Infantry: The History of Fort Benning* (United States: Mercer University Press, 2007), 128.
95. "2nd Armored Division Declared to be Equal of Europe's Best," *The Washington Post*, August 29, 1941; D'Este, *Patton: A Genius for War*, 395.
96. Henry McLemore, "At War (Somewhere in Tennessee)," *The Knoxville Journal*, June 29, 1941.
97. By the time the Carolina Maneuvers concluded in December 1941, the 2nd Armored Division had been on the road for almost six months.
98. Totten, *The Button Box*, 321.
99. "World War II Hepatitis Outbreak Was Biggest in History," *AP News*, April 16, 1987. https://apnews.com/article/ce911d4f173f1c8ade810969005b9e57; Justin Glenn, *The Washingtons: Volume 7 Part 1* (United States: Savas Beatie, 2016), 692. It would take over forty years for the link to be officially made, but this particular vaccine exposed 330,000 soldiers, making it the biggest outbreak in history.
100. Thurston Clarke, *Pearl Harbor Ghosts: The Legacy of December 7, 1941*. (Novato: Presidio, 2003), 134-135; "Interview with Walter Dillingham Alice Sinesky, November 20, 1986," *The Watumull Foundation Oral History Project*, 1987, accessed August 19, 2022. https://core.ac.uk/reader/77119260.
101. "Pearl Harbor," *History.com, A&E Television Networks*, October 29, 2009. http://history.com/topics/world-war-ii/pearl-harbor; "Churchill's Finest Hour- World War II 1939-1945," *America's National Churchill Museum*, accessed September 8, 2022. https://www.nationalchurchillmuseum.org/world-war-ii-churchills-finest-hour.html

102. Early, "True Confessions Salutes A Hero's Wife."
103. James Scott Wheeler, *Jacob L. Devers: A General's Life* (United States: University Press of Kentucky, 2015).
104. GSP to Walter Dillingham, 2 February 1942, as quoted in Blumenson, *The Patton Papers: 1940-1945*, 54.
105. Semmes, *Portrait of Patton*, 83.
106. Burns, "Pattons most Vivid American Army Pair."
107. Patricia Laflin, Images of America: *Indio* (Charleston: Arcadia Publishing, 2001), 7; "Patton's California Home may be Saved," *Chicago Tribune*, May 12, 2002. https://www.chicagotribune.com/news/ct-xpm-2002-05-12-0205120351-story.html
108. BAP to Arvin "Jerry" Harrington Brown, 3 October 1942, box 52, folder 5, HLC-GSP.
109. Seamans, *Light and Life*, 86-87; Vivian Ho, "Eugenia Seamans, 88, Philanthropist, D.C. Socialite," *The Boston Globe*, August 31, 2010.
110. Robert C. Seamans, *Aiming at Targets: The Autobiography of Robert C. Seamans, Jr.* (Washington, DC: NASA, Scientific and Techn. Information, 1996), 36.
111. "Military Myths," *Southwest Living*, March 8, 2017. http://southwestlivingyuma.yumawebteam.com/unique-to-yuma/military-myths/
112. Sarah Seekatz, "Desert Deployment: Southern California's World War II Desert Training Center," *Incendiary Traces*, March 16, 2018.
113. Brigadier General David C. Henley, *The Land that God Forgot* (United States: Western American History Series, 1989).
114. GSP to BAP, 30 July 1942, box 10, folder 10, LOC-PP.
115. BAP, "Letters to me by G.S.P. Jr.," 7 December 1949, box 19, folder 9, LOC-PP.
116. BAP to Arvin "Jerry" Harrington Brown, 23 August 1942, box 52, folder 5, HLC-GSP.
117. BAP to Arvin "Jerry" Harrington Brown, End of August 1942, box 52, folder 5, HLC-GSP.
118. Arvin "Jerry" Harrington Brown to BAP, 31 August 1942, box 52, folder 5, HLC-GSP.
119. George S. Patton, Diary entry 9 August 1942, LOC-PP. https://loc.gov/item/mss35634025; Beatrice Ayer Patton, "Letters to me by G.S.P. Jr.," 7 December 1949, box 19, folder 9, LOC-PP.
120. BAP, "Letters to me by G.S.P. Jr.," 7 December 1949, box 19, folder 9, LOC-PP.
121. BAP to Arvin "Jerry" Harrington Brown, October 1942, box 52, folder 5, HLC-GSP.
122. BAP, "Letters to me by G.S.P. Jr.," 7 December 1949, box 19, folder 9, LOC-PP.
123. BAP, "Letters to me by G.S.P. Jr.," 7 December 1949, box 19, folder 9, LOC-PP.
124. BAP, "Letters to me by G.S.P. Jr.," 7 December 1949, box 19, folder 9, LOC-PP.
125. BAP to JGH, October 18 1942, box 36, folder 17, NYHS-HP.
126. BAP, "Letters to me by G.S.P. Jr.," 7 December 1949, box 19, folder 9, LOC-PP.
127. GSP to FA, 20 October 1942, Neil Rice Ayer Jr. Private Papers.
128. GSP, Diary entry 21 October 1942, LOC-PP. https://www.loc.gov/resource/mss35634.00213/ Black Jack would indeed outlive George, passing away just two years after marrying the woman he had had a secret affair with for over three decades. He had met Micheline Resco, a French-Romanian portraitist thirty-five years his junior, in 1917 at the Crillon Hotel in Paris; at that time, he was still 'dating' Nita.
129. George S. Patton Patton Jr., "Headquarters Western Task Force: Summary of Events," The President's Secretary's File (PSF), 1933-1945. Departmental Correspondence, War Department, Box 83: Patton, George S. Franklin D. Roosevelt Library, Hyde Park, New York, accessed August 18, 2022. http://www.fdrlibrary.marist.edu/_resources/images/psf/psf000334.pdf
130. St. Johns, "Lieut. Gen. and Mrs. George S. Patton, Jr."
131. Semmes, *Portrait of Patton*, 92.
132. Lieutenant General Geoffrey B. Keyes, "Dedication Address Patton Statue Boston," Correspondence with Arvin Harrington Brown, 1953, box 52, folder 5, HLC-GSP.
133. BAP, "Letters to me by G.S.P. Jr.," 7 December 1949, box 19, folder 9, HLC-GSP.
134. GSP to BAP, 23 October 1942, box 10, folder 10, LOC-PP.
135. St. Johns, "Lieut. Gen. and Mrs. George S. Patton, Jr."
136. GSP to BAP, 23 October 1942, box 10, folder 10, LOC-PP.
137. Robert Patton, *The Pattons*, chapter 17, Kindle.
138. George S. Patton Jr., Notebook entry 27 November 1907 as quoted in Blumenson, *The Patton Papers: 1885-1940*, 138.
139. Field, "Patton of the Armored Force"; BAP, "The Army Wife."
140. "Mrs. Patton gives and follows her own advice," *Plumas Independent (Quincy, Ca.)*, December 2, 1943.

141. GSP as quoted in D'Este, *Patton: A Genius for War*, 402.
142. GSP to BAP, 23 October 1942, box 10, folder 10, LOC-PP.
143. GSP, Diary entry 23 October 1942, LOC-PP. https://www.loc.gov/resource/mss35634.00213/
144. Mclean, "Daughter's View Of Gen. Patton."
145. GSP to John Macfarland (the husband of Ellen Banning, daughter of Anne Ophelia Smith), 8 October 1940, HM 78061-78062, The Huntington Library, San Marino, CA.

## 11. GREEN MEADOWS

1. Early, "True Confessions Salutes A Hero's Wife."
2. Peggy Preston, "While General Heads East She's Visiting Family here," *The Washington Post*, November 26, 1944.
3. "Mrs. Patton Sees General in Newsreel," *Boston Daily Globe*, July 17, 1943.
4. BAP to GSP, 18 November 1942, box 10, folder 11, LOC-PP.
5. Robert Patton, *The Pattons*, chapter 17, Kindle.
6. Noel Monks, "Gen. Patton Led Troops in Rout of Nazi Tanks," *The Washington Post*, July 15, 1943.
7. BAP to GSP, 4 January 1943, box 10, folder 13, LOC-PP.
8. BAP to GSP, 2 December 1942, box 10, folder 12, LOC-PP.
9. BAP to GSP, 18 November 1942, LOC-PP.
10. BAP to GSP, 17 January 1943, box 10, folder 13, LOC-PP.
11. BAP to GSP, 8 November 1942, box 10, folder 11, LOC-PP.
12. BAP, "Letters to me by G.S.P. Jr.," 7 December 1949, box 19, folder 9, LOC-PP.
13. Dorothy Wayman, "Gen. Patton's Daring in Sicily no Surprise to Wife Recalling Pershing's Blessing at Sailing," *Boston Daily Globe*, July 15, 1943.
14. BAP to GSP, 8 November 1942, box 10, folder 11, LOC-PP.
15. BAP to GSP, 8 November 1942, box 10, folder 11, LOC-PP.
16. "Advice to Soldiers' Wives: Get a Reliable Newspaper and a Good Map," *The Washington Post*, November 10, 1942.
17. Usher's Diary, 7 December 1942, Franklin D. Roosevelt Library, Hyde Park, New York.
18. Keyes, "Dedication Address Patton Statue Boston."
19. BAP to GSP, 8 November 1942, box 10, folder 11, LOC-PP.
20. BAP to GSP, 5 December 1942, box 10, folder 12, LOC-PP.
21. Early, "True Confessions Salutes A Hero's Wife."
22. Wayman, "Gen. Patton's Daring in Sicily no Surprise to Wife Recalling Pershing's Blessing at Sailing"; "Mrs. Patton Urges Women to get War work," *Boston Daily Globe*, December 10, 1942.
23. BAP to GSP, 25 November 1942, box 10, folder 11, LOC-PP.
24. JGH to GSP, 18 May 1943, box 36, folder 16, NYHS-HP.
25. BAP to GSP, 25 November 1942, box 10, folder 11, LOC-PP.
26. BAP to GSP, 11 January 1943, box 10, folder 13, LOC-PP.
27. BAP, "The Army Wife."
28. "Much Interest in Mrs. Patton's Talk," *Boston Daily Globe*, June 30 1943; St. Johns, "Lieut. Gen. and Mrs. George S. Patton, Jr."
29. "Many Eastern Yacht Clubs to End Season," *Chicago Daily Tribune*, September 19, 1943.
30. "Gen. Patton's Wife in Broadcast Aims Message to French Teacher," *The New York Times*, November 9, 1943; Beatrice Ayer Patton, "Transcript of Mrs. Patton's Weekly Talk #1 to the women of France," October 16, 1943, box 11, folder 9, LOC-PP. Every letter Beatrice sent since then got returned "service interrompu," so she feared Mademoiselle Gogo was dead. However, George eventually heard from her at the war's end and sent her money. (GSP to BAP, 28 July 1945, box 13, folder 11, LOC-PP)
31. GSP to BAP, 23 October 1943, box 11, folder 9, LOC-PP.
32. BAP to GSP, 10 January 1943, box 10, folder 13, LOC-PP; BAP to GSP, 5 December 1942, box 10, folder 12, LOC-PP.
33. "Mrs. George Patton Tells Woman's Club that 'Victory Lies with Us," *Montpelier Evening Argus*, April 6, 1944; BAP to DDE, 2 April 1943. George Patton Folders, Pre-Presidential Papers of Dwight D. Eisenhower, 1916-1952, Eisenhower Presidential Library.
34. BAP to GSP, 1 January 1943, box 10, folder 13, LOC-PP.

35. "Warrior Wives Given 10 Rules to Keep Happy," *Chicago Daily Tribune*, November 11, 1942; Early, "True Confessions Salutes A Hero's Wife."

36. GSP to FA, 2 March 1943, Neil Rice Ayer Jr. Private Papers.

37. "Hail West Point For Role In War: Commanders In Pacific And Africa Join In Radio Tribute On 141St Anniversary," *The New York Times*, March 14, 1943; GSP to FA, 2 March 1943, Neil Rice Ayer Jr. Private Papers.

38. BAP to DDE, 2 April 1943, George Patton Folders, Pre-Presidential Papers of Dwight D. Eisenhower, 1916-1952, Eisenhower Presidential Library.

39. GSP to FA, March 2 1943, Neil Rice Ayer Jr. Private Papers.

40. "Spouse Safe, Patton Daughter Joyfully Relaxes Map Study," *The Washington Post*, April 09, 1945.

41. "Patton Ace North Shore Yachtsman," *Boston Daily Globe*, March 19, 1943.

42. St. Johns, "Lieut. Gen. and Mrs. George S. Patton, Jr."

43. Robert Patton, *The Pattons*, chapter 17, Kindle.

44. "Patton braves Fire of Germans," *St. Louis Globe-Democrat*, March 26, 1943.

45. GSP to BAP, 27 July 1943, box 11, folder 4, LOC-PP; GSP to A. Fletcher Marsh, 16 July 1945, box 13, folder 11, LOC-PP.

46. Harold V. Boyle, "Patton Weeps at Death of Pasadena Aide," *Los Angeles Times*, April 3, 1943.

47. With Meeks and Mims (George's orderly and driver, respectively) as pallbearers, Jenson was buried at Gafsa's military cemetery. He was buried in the sand—there was no wood in the desert to make coffins—together with seven hundred other Americans who did not survive the Battle of El Guettar.

48. BAP to Arvin "Jerry" Harrington Brown, 3 April 1943, box 52, folder 5, HLC-GSP.

49. BAP to JGH, 25 May 1943, box 37, folder 12, NYHS-HP.

50. JGH to BAP, 26 July 1943, box 37, folder 12, NYHS-HP. General Harbord was put in charge of finding a suitable candidate, but after two years, that still hadn't happened. In April 1945, Beatrice donated an additional $5,000 "in the form of 125 shares of Deere & Company Common stock."

51. "Annual Report for the Town of Hamilton, Massachusetts, 1945," *Hamilton Historical Society*, accessed August 20, 2022. https://archive.org/details/townofhamiltonan1945unse/page/42/mode/2up

52. "Wenham in World War II: War Service of Wenham Men and Women and Civilian Services of Wenham People," *Historical Association Wenham Village Improvement Society*, 1947, accessed August 20, 2022. https://archive.org/details/wenhaminworldwar00wenh

53. GSP to FA, 2 September 1942, box 10, folder 10, LOC-PP.

54. "Annual Report for the Town of Hamilton, Massachusetts, 1945."

55. Burns, "Pattons most Vivid American Army Pair."

56. Wayman, "Gen. Patton's Daring in Sicily no Surprise to Wife Recalling Pershing's Blessing at Sailing."

57. Mclean, "Daughter's View Of Gen. Patton"; Burns, "Pattons most Vivid American Army Pair."

58. Totten, *The Button Box*, 238.

59. BAP to GSP, 6 December 1942, box 10, folder 6, LOC-PP.

60. GSP to BAP, October 1929, box 10, folder 5, LOC-PP.

61. Totten, *The Button Box*, 347.

62. Troy Middleton to BAP, 4 May 1943, box 11, folder 1, LOC-PP.

63. BAP to GSP, 4 January 1943, box 10, folder 13, LOC-PP.

64. GSP to BAP, 7 January 1943, box 10, folder 13, LOC-PP.

65. GSP to BAP, 16 August 1945, box 13, folder 12, LOC-PP. By the summer of 1945, he engaged an architect and discussed the plans with Beatrice. He would miss the planning and building, but "when I do get home, we can have the fun of putting the things in." Of paramount importance was fire safety, a thing George IV learned the hard way decades later when a smoldering cigarette caused a trash can to catch fire in the basement of Green Meadows.

66. GSP to BAP, 30 December 1942, box 10, folder 12, LOC-PP.

67. "Gen Patton Writes Bride of Dead Hero to Visit His Wife," *Boston Daily Globe*, April 16, 1944; GSP to Mrs. Sparkes, 9 April 1944, box 12, folder 1, LOC-PP.

68. Hope Ridings Miller, "Just about Washington," *Williamsport Sun-Gazette*, February 8, 1946.

69. Charles D. Herron, "Mrs. George Patton," *The Washington Post*, October 6, 1953.

70. "Work, Buck Hysteria, General Patton's Wife Urges Southern Women," *The Binghamton Press*, December 10, 1942.

71. Wayman, "Gen. Patton's Daring in Sicily no Surprise to Wife Recalling Pershing's Blessing at Sailing."

72. "General's Wife Gives Tips to Army Brides," *Boston Daily Globe*, May 9, 1943; Patton, "Army Etiquette."

73. It means 'How do you do?'

74. "General's Wife Gives Tips to Army Brides"; BAP, "Army Etiquette."

75. "Mrs. George Patton Tells Woman's Club that 'Victory Lies with Us," *Montpelier Evening Argus*, April 6, 1944.

76. "Women Hear Gen. Patton's Wife Speak," *Oakland Tribune*, February 28, 1943.

77. "Rationing Helps Patton: General Writes Wife it Insures Ample Food for Troops," *New York Herald Tribune*, August 3, 1943; GSP to BAP, 2 July 1943, box 11, folder 3, LOC-PP.

78. GSP to BAP, 4 December 1943, box 11, folder 12, LOC-PP.

79. Totten, *The Button Box*, 331.

80. Early, "True Confessions Salutes A Hero's Wife."

81. "Here's Advice for Wives of Service Men From One Who Knows," *Des Moines Tribune*, November 19, 1942. 0

82. Jane Eads, "Wife Tells Real Gen. Patton Story: American Commander In Western Tunisia Not All 'Blood And Guts' Of Popular Tales," *Los Angeles Times*, April 04, 1943; BAP to JGH, 4 December 1943, box 36, folder 16, NYHS-HP.

83. GSP to BAP, 22 August 1943, box 11, folder 6, LOC-PP.

84. GSP to BAP, 21 December 1943, box 11, folder 13, LOC-PP.

85. Noel Monks, "Gen. Patton Waded Ashore To Battle: Leader Leaped Into Surf From Landing-Craft As Tanks Periled U.S. Force," *The New York Times*, July 15, 1943.

86. Early, "True Confessions Salutes A Hero's Wife."

87. GSP to BAP, 5 July 1943, box 11, folder 3, LOC-PP.

88. Christopher Woody, "A Year before the D-Day Invasion, the Allies Took the Fight to the Axis in 'the Soft Underbelly of Europe'," *Business Insider*, July 10, 2020. https://www.businessinsider.com/photos-of-operation-husky-july-1943-allied-invasion-of-sicily-italy-2018-7 Prime Minister Churchill insisted on a second front "in the soft underbelly of Europe." The campaign began on July 19, 1943, when George landed on the beaches of Gela, and ended on August 16 when he beat British Field Marshall Montgomery (the other half of Operation Husky) to Messina.

89. GSP to BAP, 13 April 1943, box 10, folder 17, LOC-PP.

90. GSP to JGH, 14 January 1944, box 36, folder 16, NYHS-HP.

91. GSP, diary entry, 10 August 1943, Diaries, LOC-PP. https://loc.gov/item/mss35634029/. Accessed August 20, 2022.

92. Perrin H. Long, "Mistreatment of Patients in Receiving Tents of the 15th and 93rd Evacuation Hospitals," August 16, 1943. George S. Patton Papers, LOC-PP. loc.gov/item/mss35634029/. Accessed August 20, 2022. It turned out that Private Kuhl was suffering from malaria, and Private Bennett had actually been fighting bravely, but his nerves got the best of him when he watched his friend get hurt.

93. GSP, August 21 1943. George S. Patton Papers: Diaries; Annotated transcripts, LOC-PP. loc.gov/item/mss35634029/. Accessed August 20, 2022.

94. BAP to JGH, 18 December 1943, box 36, folder 16, NYHS-HP; BAP to Arvin "Jerry" Harrington Brown, December 1943, box 52, folder 5, HLC-GSP.

95. BAP to JGH, 4 December 1943, box 36, folder 16, NYHS-HP. In the original, Beatrice jumped from 7 to 10, she never wrote down 8 and 9.

96. Henry Stimson to GSP, 18 December 1943, box 11, folder 12, LOC-PP.

97. Lee Carson, "Patton's Wife Offers no Alibi for 'Tough Perfectionist," *The Washington Post*, November 25, 1943..

98. Early, "True Confessions Salutes A Hero's Wife."

99. GSP to BAP, 10 March 1943, box 10, folder 16, LOC-PP.

100. GSP to FA, 5 May 1943, Neil Rice Ayer Jr. Private Papers.

101. JGH to Colonel John Cocke, 28 December 1943, box 5, folder 15, NYHS-HP; GSP to JGH, 14 January 1944, box 36, folder 16, NYHS-HP. George could "eat crow when he has to—better than anyone I [Little Bee] know. I've never known him to pass the buck or bow out or blame anyone else—when he is at fault," and he "will take any punishment without wincing. However, neither private later resented General Patton for what he did, and always wondered whether he might have been "suffering a little battle fatigue himself."

102. BAP to JGH, 4 December 1943, box 36, folder 16, NYHS-HP.

103. Donald A. Ritchie, *The Columnist: Leaks, Lies, and Libel in Drew Pearson's Washington* (New York, NY: Oxford University Press, 2021), 9.

104. GSP to BAP, 23 August 1943, box 11, folder 6, LOC-PP; GSP to FA, 22 December 1943, box 10, folder 10, LOC-PP.

105. GSP to JGH, 14 January 1944, box 36, folder 16, NYHS-HP.

106. BAP to JGH, 4 December 1943, box 36, folder 16, NYHS-HP.

107. Totten, *The Button Box*, 333; BAP to Arvin "Jerry" Harrington Brown, December 1943, box 52, folder 5, HLC-GSP.

108. Carson, "Patton's Wife Offers no Alibi for Tough Perfectionist."

109. GSP to BAP, 23 January 1944, box 11, folder 14, LOC-PP; GSP to FA, 22 December 1943, Neil Rice Ayer Jr. Private Papers.

110. GSP to BAP, 9 February 1944, box 11, folder 15, LOC-PP.

111. BAP to JGH, 4 December 1943, box 36, folder 16, NYHS-HP.

112. JGH to BAP, 8 December 1943, box 36, folder 16, NYHS-HP.

113. BAP to JGH, 18 December 1943, box 36, folder 16, NYHS-HP.

114. Correspondence pertaining to the Slapping Incident, box 22, folder 13, LOC-PP.

115. Eads, "Wife Tells Real Gen. Patton Story: American Commander In Western Tunisia Not All 'Blood And Guts' Of Popular Tales."

116. GSP to AP, 10 December 1943, box 14, folder 20, LOC-PP.

117. GSP, diary entry, 24 November 1943, LOC-PP. https://loc.gov/item/mss35634030/

118. "Patton's Wife Admits General's Error But Pleads For His Forgiveness," *The Knoxville Journal*, November 26, 1943.

119. GSP, diary entry 17 November 1943, LOC-PP. https://loc.gov/item/mss35634030/ Not a man budged when George told his staff that he "might be on the way out and that if any of them could find a better job [he] would try to get it for them."

120. GSP to BAP, 27 July 1943, box 11, folder 4, LOC-PP.

121. GSP to BAP, 10 December 1943, box 11, folder 12, LOC-PP.

122. Totten, *The Button Box*, 333.

123. Wayman, "Gen. Patton's Daring in Sicily no Surprise to Wife Recalling Pershing's Blessing at Saling"; BAP to GSP, 10 January 1943, box 10, folder 13, LOC-PP.

124. Nigel Hamilton, *War and Peace FDR's Final Odyssey, D-Day to Yalta, 1943-1945* (Boston: Houghton Mifflin Harcourt, 2019); GSP to JGH, 14 January 1944, box 36, folder 16, NYHS-HP.

125. BAP to JGH, 4 February 1944, box 36, folder 16, NYHS-HP.

126. GSP, diary entry 17 November 1943, LOC-PP. https://loc.gov/item/mss35634030/

127. "Gen. Patton's Wife in Broadcast Aims Message to French Teacher," *The New York Times*, November 9, 1943.

128. St. Johns, "Lieut. Gen. and Mrs. George S. Patton, Jr"; Transcript of May 21, 1945 Broadcast, "After the War, What about the Volunteer?" box 13, folder 8, LOC-PP.

129. St. Johns, "Lieut. Gen. and Mrs. George S. Patton, Jr.".

130. GSP to A. Fletcher Marsh, 16 July 1945, box 13, folder 11, LOC-PP.

131. St. Johns, "Lieut. Gen. and Mrs. George S. Patton, Jr."

132. "Patton Envelope Traded for Bond," *St. Albans Daily Messenger*, September 21, 1943.

133. "All Banks in State Open Tonight to Aid Bond Drive," *Boston Daily Globe*, September 27, 1943.

134. GSP to A. Fletcher Marsh, 16 July 1945, box 13, folder 11, LOC-PP; Beatrice Ayer Patton, "Speech Third War Loan Drive Boston," September 1943, box 11, folder 7, LOC-PP.

135. GP to GSP, 20 February 1919, box 9, folder 11, LOC-PP.

136. GSP to FA, 3 July 1944, Neil Rice Ayer Jr. Private Papers.

137. GSP, diary entry 26 January 1944, LOC-PP. https://loc.gov/item/mss35634031/

138. BAP to JGH, 27 October 1943, box 36, folder 16, NYHS-HP.

139. GSP to BAP, 17 June 1944, box 12, folder 2, LOC-PP.

140. John Nelson Rickard and Robert S. Allen, *Forward with Patton: The World War II Diary of Colonel Robert S. Allen* (Lexington: The University Press of Kentucky, 2017), accessed August 20, 2022. https://muse.jhu.edu/book/52609; Morris, "Gen. George Patton through the Eyes of His Aide."

141. GSP to BAP, 29 May 1944, box 12, folder 1, LOC-PP.

142. GSP to BAP, 3 May 1944, box 12, folder 1, LOC-PP.

143. Omar N. Bradley, *A Soldier's Story* (Modern Library, 1999), 230.

144. Robert Patton, *The Pattons*, chapter 17, Kindle.

145. GSP to FA, 4 June 1944, Neil Rice Ayer Jr. Private Papers.

146. GSP to BAP, May Day 1944, box 12, folder 1, LOC-PP; GSP to BAP, 2 May 1944, box 12, folder 1, LOC-PP.
147. BAP as quoted in Robert Patton, *The Pattons*, chapter 18, Kindle.
148. GSP to BAP, 2 and 3 May 2 1944, box 12, folder 1, LOC-PP.
149. GSP to BAP, 5 May 1944, box 12, folder 1, LOC-PP.
150. GSP to BAP, 4 June 1944, box 12, folder 2, LOC-PP; "Mrs. Patton Keeps Watch at her Radio," *Dunkirk Evening Observer*, June 6, 1944.
151. "In Washington, They Took in Very Quietly," *Siskiyou Daily News*, June 6, 1944.
152. GSP to BAP, 6 June 1944, box 12, folder 2, LOC-PP.
153. BAP to JGH, August 1943, box 37, folder 12, NYHS-HP.
154. GSP to BAP, 20 June 1943, box 11, folder 2, LOC-PP.
155. Sobel, *The Fighting Pattons*.
156. BAP to JGH, 19 July 1943, box 37, folder 12, NYHS-HP.
157. GSP to GSPIV, 6 June 1944, box 12, folder 2, LOC-PP.
158. GSP to GSPIV, 19 May 1944, box 12, folder 1, LOC-PP.
159. GSP to GP, 1 December 1904, box 4, folder 13, LOC-PP.
160. GSP to GP, 24 March 1906, box 4, folder 16, LOC-PP.
161. GSP to BAP, 25 August 1944, box 12, folder 7, LOC-PP.
162. GSP to BAP, 14 July 1944, box 12, folder 3, LOC-PP.
163. While it wasn't the role he desired for himself, George was cast as the commander of the fictitious First US Army Group to make the Germans believe that the invasion would happen in the Pas de Calais. Countless lives were saved on the beaches of Normandy when Rommel pulled some of his forces out of Normandy in anticipation of fighting General Patton at the Pas de Calais.
164. GSP to BAP, 8 July 1944, box 12, folder 3, LOC-PP.
165. Peggy Preston, "While Generals make Headlines Wives can't Stay in Background," *The Washington Post*, August 20, 1944.
166. "Patton," *Ironwood Daily Globe*, August 15, 1944.
167. "Mrs. Patton Flies to Capital After Many 'Priorities'," *The Christian Science Monitor*, August 15, 1944.
168. GSP to BAP, 16 August 1944, box 12, folder 6, LOC-PP.
169. BAP to GSP, 10 January 1943, box 10, folder 13, LOC-PP.
170. BAP to GSP, 1 January 1943, box 10, folder 13, LOC-PP.
171. BAP to GSP, 1 February 1943, box 10, folder 14, LOC-PP.
172. D'Este, *Patton: A Genius for War*, 694.
173. Totten, *The Button Box*, 331.
174. GSP to BAP, 24 June 1944, box 12, folder 2, LOC-PP.
175. Beatrice Ayer Patton, "Lucky Shot," *Los Angeles Times*, November 28, 1943.
176. GSP to BAP, 15 September 1916, box 6, folder 10, LOC-PP; GSP to BAP, 26 November 1916, box 6, folder 11, LOC-PP.
177. George S. Patton Jr., box 74, folder 1, LOC-PP.
178. "Gen. Patton Writes Battle Hymn of War," *The Boston Globe*, April 22, 1944.
179. GSP to BAP, 27 September 1944, box 12, folder 9, LOC-PP.
180. Henry Stimson to BAP, 30 December 1944 , box 12, folder 17, LOC-PP.
181. GSP to BAP, 21 December 1944, box 12, folder 16, LOC-PP.
182. Placing great trust in his G-2, Brigadier General Oscar Koch, and his own conviction that the Ardennes was not a "quiet sector," George and his staff prepared three contingency plans.
183. GSP to BAP, 21 December 1944, box 12, folder 16, LOC-PP; "Greatest American Military General of All Time? Public Says Patton, Eisenhower and MacArthur," *Gallup.com*, March 18, 2022. https://news.gallup.com/poll/2236/greatest-american-military-general-all-time-public-says-patton.aspx.
184. Codman, *Drive*, 159.
185. "When Patton Enlisted the Entire Third Army to Pray for Fair Weather," *History on the net, Salem Media*, August 1, 2019. https://www.historyonthenet.com/when-patton-enlisted-the-entire-third-army-to-pray-for-fair-weather; GSP to FA, 12 May 1943, Neil Rice Ayer Jr. Private Papers.
186. Beatrice Ayer Patton, "Broadcast on We the People," July 18, 1943, Box 11, folder 4, LOC-PP.
187. Burns, "Pattons most Vivid American Army Pair."
188. Cramer, "Georgie"; "Patton Has Fear Of 'Another War'" *The New York Times*, June 11, 1945; GSP, diary entry 20 June 1943, LOC-PP. https://loc.gov/item/mss35634027/

189. "Patton Swam Sure Twice to Inspire Men," *The Washington Post*, March 8, 1945.
190. Semmes, *Portrait of Patton*, 238.
191. "He Swam all His Life, Says Mrs. Patton," *Boston Daily Globe*, March 8, 1945.
192. BAP to JGH, 10 February 1945, box 36, folder 15, NYHS-HP.
193. D'Este, *Patton: A Genius for War*, 712.
194. "Mrs. Patton Feels Proud Of General: Cold Forgotten, She Hears Full Story Of Crossing," *The Sun*, March 24, 1945.
195. GSP to BAP, 27 March 1945, box 13, folder 4, LOC-PP.
196. Beatrice Ayer Patton Waters to Frances Elvira Owens, September 23, 1943. Retrieved from the Digital Public Library of America, https://southernappalachiandigitalcollections.org/object/62840
197. GSP to BAP, 2 March 1943, box 10, folder 15, LOC-PP; GSP to FA, 29 March 1945, box 14, folder 9, LOC-PP.
198. GSP to BAP, 27 March 1945, box 13 folder 4, LOC-PP; GSP to BAP, 5 April 1945, box 13 folder 5, LOC-PP.
199. GSP to BAP, 4 May 1945, box 13, folder 7, LOC-PP.
200. Duane Schultz, *Patton's Last Gamble: The Disastrous Raid on POW Camp Hammelburg in World War II* (Pennsylvania: Stackpole Books, 2022), 108.
201. Robert Kelley, "Waters' Rescue Ends Long Anxiety of Gen. Patton Kin," *Boston Daily Globe*, April 8, 1945.
202. FA to GSP, 10 April 1945, box 14, folder 9, LOC-PP; GSP to BPW, 7 April 1945, box 13, folder 5, LOC-PP.
203. BAP to DDE, 8 April 8 1945, George Patton Folders, Pre-Presidential Papers of Dwight D. Eisenhower, 1916-1952, Eisenhower Presidential Library.
204. GSP to BAP, 25 March 1945, box 13, folder 4, LOC-PP. The most damning evidence besides the letters he wrote his family—including the one informing Beatrice that he was hoping "to send an expedition tomorrow to get John"—was the presence of Major Al Stiller on the raid, purportedly to gain combat experience but more likely because he knew what Johnnie looked like.
205. GSP to BAP, 13 April 1945, box 13, folder 5, LOC-PP.
206. GSP to BAP, 9 April 1945, box 13, folder 5, LOC-PP.
207. GSP to BAP, 11 November 1943, box 11, folder 10, LOC-PP.
208. Field, "Patton of the Armored Force."
209. GSP to Colonel Robert Howe Fletcher, 25 April 1945, box 13 folder 6, LOC-PP.
210. Henry Stimson to GSP, 23 February 1945, box 13, folder 2, LOC-PP.
211. GSP to BAP, 31 January 1945, box 12, folder 19, LOC-PP.
212. GSP to BAP, 8 March 1945, box 13, folder 3, LOC-PP.
213. GSP to BAP, 9 May 1945, as quoted in Blumenson, *The Patton Papers: 1940-1945*, 701.
214. BAP to Everett Hughes, VE Day, box II-4, folder 13, Library of Congress, Manuscript Division, Everett Strait Hughes Papers.
215. Field, "Patton of the Armored Force."
216. GSP to BAP, 21 May 1945, box 13, folder 8, LOC-PP.
217. J. Wes Gallagher, "Eisenhower Reveals Patton had Close Call," *The Washington Post*, November 17, 1942.
218. GSP to BAP, 12 January 1943, box 11, folder 14, LOC-PP.
219. GSP, diary entry 3 May 1945, LOC-PP. https://loc.gov/item/mss35634038/
220. GSP to BAP, 8 May 1945, box 13, folder 7, LOC-PP.
221. "Mrs. George Patton Tell Woman's Club that 'Victory Lies with Us."
222. GSP to BAP, Thanksgiving 1944, box 12, folder 14, LOC-PP.
223. GSP to JGH, 22 October 1945, box 36, folder 15, NYHS-HP.

## 12. 130TH STATION HOSPITAL

1. BAP to JGH, NYHS-HP.
2. Totten, *The Button Box*, 350; "Back Injured by Collision on Highway in Germany," *The Washington Post*, December 10, 1945.
3. Hobart Gay, "Account of Sunday December 9th, 1945," box 14, folder 3, LOC-PP; "Transcript Conversation with Gen. Smith re leave," December 5 1945, box 14, folder 3, LOC-PP. It wasn't

such a well-kept secret because newspapers in November had already reported on his interest in retiring from the Army.

4. GSP to JGH, 22 October 1945, box 36, folder 15, NYHS-HP.
5. GSP to BAP, 5 December 1945, box 19, folder 8, LOC-PP.
6. GSP to BAP, 22 May 1910, box 5, folder 11, LOC-PP.
7. In the days following Operation Torch, she even woke up from a dream speaking Arabic. She hadn't spoken it since learning the basics while traveling through Egypt as an eleven-year-old.
8. BAP to JGH, Christmas 1945, box 37, folder 11, NYHS-HP.
9. "Mrs. Patton Learns news from AP," *Bristol Herald Courier*, December 10, 1945. When General Eisenhower heard the news, he instructed his Secretary General Staff, Colonel Bowen, to contact Ruth Ellen in order to notify Beatrice.
10. Marshall Andrews, "George always Comes Out of these Scrapes," *The Washington Post*, December 16, 1945.
11. Robert Patton, *The Pattons*, chapter 18, Kindle.
12. "Patton Heads for Coast," *The Austin Statesman*, June 8, 1945.
13. "Mrs. Patton counts minutes to time of meeting husband," *The Boston Globe*, June 6, 1945.
14. Box 12, folder 17, LOC-PP.
15. GSP to BAP, 30 April 1945, box 13, folder 6, LOC-PP.
16. Blumenson, *The Patton Papers: 1940-1945*, 723.
17. Tom Cameron, "General's Life Full of Thrills during Boyhood," *Los Angeles Times*, June 7, 1945.
18. Robert Patton, *The Pattons*, chapter 18, Kindle.
19. "General's Early Days in San Marino Recalled," *Los Angeles Times*, December 22, 1945.
20. William M. Blair, "1,000,000 Welcome Gen. Patton Home: A Fighting General Back With His Family Once More," *The New York Times*, June 8, 1945.
21. GSP to BAP, 12 April 1944, box 11, folder 17, LOC-PP.
22. Nita to GSP, 19 August 1944, as quoted in Blumenson, *The Patton Papers: 1940-1945*, 519.
23. "Patton Smile? 'Damn It, I'm No Politician,'" *Citizen News (Hollywood, CA)*, June 13, 1945.
24. "Patton Is Just 'Daddy' To His Grandchild, 2," *Chicago Daily Tribune*, June 14, 1945.
25. "Patton Drops Pistols for Truman Visit," *The Washington Post*, June 14, 1945.
26. Jeffrey St. John, "Reflections of a Fighting Father," accessed August 21, 2022. https://pattonhq.com/textfiles/reflect.html
27. Morris, "Gen. George Patton through the Eyes of His Aide."
28. He had been a patient since May 9, when he had been repatriated from Europe.
29. Anne Hagner, "Greets Son-in-Law, Prisoner of Nazis for Three Years," *The Washington Post*, June 15, 1945.
30. GSP to BAP, 17 April 1945, box 13, folder 5, LOC-PP.
31. GSP, diary entry 17 August 1943, LOC-PP. https://loc.gov/item/mss35634029/
32. Totten, *The Button Box*, 349.
33. Fred Ayer Jr., *Before the Colors Fade*, 239.
34. "Patton Gives Little Boy Recount on Autograph Ban," *Boston Daily Globe*, June 15, 1945; "Patton catches 'em napping as he arrives in Hamilton," *Boston Daily Globe*, June 16, 1945.
35. "Horse 'Soft,' Patton Says After 1st Ride," *Boston Daily Globe*, June 17, 1945.
36. BAP to JGH, 16 March 1945, box 36, folder 15, NYHS-HP.
37. Joseph Dinneen, "Patton Shakes Hands with 3000 Neighbors," *Boston Daily Globe*, June 25, 1945.
38. The home Frederick Ayer purchased for his daughter Ellen and her (now deceased) husband William Wood upon their marriage.
39. Seamans, *Aiming at Targets: The Autobiography of Robert C. Seamans, Jr.*, 4.
40. "Here's Advice for Wives of Service Men From One Who Knows," *Des Moines Tribune*, November 19, 1942; GSP to BAP, 31 March 1945, box 13, folder 4, LOC-PP.
41. "Gen Patton's wife tells of unnecessary war casualties," *Boston Daily Globe*, July 7, 1943.
42. GSP, diary entry 4 July 1945, LOC-PP. https://www.loc.gov/resource/mss35634.00312 This was the explanation he gave with regards to Meeks's remark.
43. "California Pastor Assails Profanity in Patton's Speech," *Chicago Daily Tribune*, June 19, 1945; "'Just an Old Bum,' Patton says after Coast Celebration," *The Brooklyn Daily Eagle*, June 11, 1945.
44. "'Be Prepared,' Patton's Reply to Private 'X'," *The Washington Post*, June 23, 1945.
45. GSP to BAP, 21 May 1945, box 13, folder 8, LOC-PP.
46. GSP to BAP, 6 July 1945, box 13, folder 10, LOC-PP.
47. Eisenhower, *General Ike: A Personal Reminiscence*, 72.
48. D'Este, *Patton: A Genius for War*, 721.

49. GSP to FA, Neil Rice Ayer Jr. Private Papers.
50. "Transcript of the Press Conference given by Lt. Gen. Walter B. Smith, at Frankfurt-am-Main, 1100 hours, 26 September 1945," box 13, folder 18, LOC-PP.
51. D'Este, *Patton: A Genius for War*, 762.
52. GSP, diary entry, 16 September 1945, LOC-PP. https://loc.gov/item/mss35634039/
53. JGH to Colonel John Cocke, August 1943, box 5, folder 13, NYHS-HP.
54. Frank E. Mason to Ron Howard, 26 September 1945, box 13, folder 18, LOC-PP; GSP to BAP, 22 September 1945, box 13, folder 15, LOC-PP.
55. Eisenhower, *General Ike: A Personal Reminiscence*, 71.
56. GSP, diary entry, 7 October 1945, LOC_PP. https://loc.gov/item/mss35634040/
57. GSP to BAP, 19 October 1945, box 13, folder 17, LOC-PP; GSP to FA, 11 October 1945, Neil Rice Ayer Jr. Private Papers. It certainly was a 180-degree turn from three months earlier when the Third Army liberated several concentration camps, including Buchenwald and Ohrdruf, and he summarily threw up when he witnessed the atrocities firsthand. "Words are inadequate to express the horror of those institutions," he wrote after taking the press and his superiors on a visit so they could "build up another page of the necessary evidence as to the brutality of the Germans."
58. GSP to JGH, 26 November 1945, box 36, folder 15, NYHS-HP.
59. GSP to BAP, 17 October 1945, box 13, folder 17, LOC-PP.
60. GSP to BAP, October 5 1945, box 13, folder 17, LOC-PP; GSP to BAP, 26 September 1945, box 13 folder 16, LOC-PP.
61. GSP to BAP, 11 October 1945, box 13, folder 17, LOC-PP.
62. GSP to BAP, 22 October 1945, box 13, folder 17, LOC-PP; GSP to BAP, 290 September 1945, box 13 folder 16, LOC-PP.
63. GSP to JGH, 22 October 1945, box 36, folder 15, NYHS-HP.
64. D'Este, *Patton: A Genius for War*, 775. Despite the rumors at the end of 1945, General Patton would have never run for political office. He was very much aware of his own strengths and weaknesses, and governing was not one of them.
65. Robert Patton, *The Pattons*, chapter 19, Kindle.
66. Semmes, *Portrait of Patton*, 142.
67. "Gen. Patton's Wife Tells of Unnecessary War Casualties," *The Boston Globe*, July 7, 1943.
68. Frank E. Mason to General George Marshall (?), 4 November 1945, box 13, folder 19, LOC-PP; GSP to BAP, 5 November 1945, box 13, folder 19, LOC-PP. Commander Keith Merrill worked for the Bureau of Economic Affairs. He spent a few days with George in October when he traveled to Frankfurt-am-Main with the Foreign Economic Administration. He was "working nights on the Bavarian data which Hap [General Gay, his Chief of Staff] collected" and compiled it into a comprehensive report that Beatrice eventually must have read.
69. Fred Ayer Jr., *Before the Colors Fade*, 249.
70. GSP to BAP, 11 November 1945, box 13, folder 19, LOC-PP.
71. GSP to FA, 17 November 1945, Neil Rice Ayer Jr. Private Papers.
72. Codman, *Drive*, 187.
73. GSP to BPW, 24 September 1945, box 21, folder 13, LOC-PP.
74. Hap joined the Army at the outbreak of WWI and, like many Cavalry officers during the interwar years, kept busy playing polo until a ball hit him in the right eye and blinded him. He was Quartermaster of the 3rd Cavalry when George became commandant of Fort Myer. The two had been inseparable except for a brief interlude after Operation Husky. George, however, seemed to be the only one who believed in Hap's capabilities.
75. Gay, "Account of Sunday December 9th, 1945."
76. "General's Condition Critical," *The Austin Statesman*, December 10, 1945. The Army truck suffered no damage, and neither were its driver and two passengers hurt, but the Cadillac had a "smashed radiator and right front fender and the motor was pushed back into the body."
77. Armando DeCrescenzo, "Eyewitness Says Patton was Spunky," *The Austin Statesman*, December 12, 1945; "General Patton Badly Hurt When Car Crashes into Truck," *Stars & Stripes*, December 10, 1945.
78. "Patton In Crash, Spine Hurt," *Boston Daily Globe*, December 10, 1945.
79. GSP to BAP, 8 April 1915, box 6, folder 4, LOC-PP.
80. Blumenson, *The Patton Papers: 1940-1945*, 819.
81. Contrary to popular belief, there is no indication in his medical files the impact with the window broke his nose, and his difficulty in breathing was due to a lingering cold and the fact

that one of his lungs was as good as paralyzed. His medical file does describe "an ancient fracture of nose and cervical vertebral injury in football and riding. Old scar of shell fragment 1918 war right buttock."

82. "Room is crowded like Grand Central Station," *Abilene Reporter-News*, December 12, 1945; "Back Injured by Collision on Highway in Germany," *The Washington Post*, December 10, 1945.

83. Lowell Bennett, "Patton Paralyzed by Injuries: 'Helluva Way to Get Hurt,' Says Patton," *The Austin Statesman*, December 10, 1945.

84. "GSP Medical Records, 1904-1948," box 49, reel 2, LOC-PP; "Patton's Condition is Reported Grave," *Brooklyn Eagle*, December 12, 1945.

85. Robert Patton, *The Pattons*, chapter 18, Kindle edition.

86. Spurling, "The Patton Episode." "Some of the details may be somewhat inaccurate," Colonel Spurling admitted as he compiled his notes a year after the facts; this especially goes for the dates. On August 10, 1950, Colonel Spurling sent a transcript to Mrs. Patton titled "The Patton Episode." It contained the remarks he made to the Conversation Club of Louisville in 1946, describing his trip to Germany the year before to help General Patton.

87. Early, "True Confessions Salutes A Hero's Wife"; Sobel, *The Fighting Pattons*, 54.

88. "General's Condition Critical," *The Austin Statesman*, December 10, 1945.

89. GSP to GSPIV, 12 August 1945, box 13, folder 12, LOC-PP.

90. ESH to illegible [either his wife or mistress], 12 December 1945, box II-4, folder 10, LOC-PP.

91. Spurling, "The Patton Episode."

92. Sobel, *The Fighting Pattons*; Douglas Martin, "H. L. Woodring Dies at 77; was Driver in Patton Crash," *The New York Times*, November 9, 2003.

93. Sobel, *The Fighting Pattons*. It was a big relief to the mother of T/5 Thompson—who was being treated for nervousness after hearing of the accident—that her son was back on the job a few days later. As to Woody, Ruth Ellen reassured him years later that "the family had no ill feelings concerning [his] involvement as the driver of the car," but next to the death of his parents, December 9, 1945, always remained "the saddest day of his life."

94. "Patton Better, Wife Confident of Recovery," *The Washington Post*, December 12, 1945; "General's Condition Critical."

95. "Letter From Major General Albert W. Kenner To Colonel J.B. Coates, Jr., Thanking Him For The Christmas Card, But Regretting The Death Of General George S. Patton," Albert W. Kenner Papers; Box 1, Folder 6, Official And Personal Correspondence, 8 May 1945--10 February 1946, U.S. Army Heritage And Education Center, Carlisle, PA.

96. "Mrs. Patton Radiates Hope in Statement on General," *The Christian Science Monitor*, December 13, 1945.

97. Marshall Andrews, "'George always Comes Out of these Scrapes,'" *The Washington Post*, December 16, 1945.

98. GSP to BAP, 3 December 1916, box 6, folder 12, LOC-PP; Semmes, *Portrait of Patton*, 280.

99. "Patton's Condition is Reported Grave."

100. Geoffrey Keyes to his wife, as quoted in Blumenson, *The Patton Papers*, 823.

101. Dwight D. Eisenhower, *The Papers of Dwight David Eisenhower* (Baltimore: John Hopkins University Press, 1970), Vol. 7, page 609, #532 (WAR 87734, December 10, 1945, OPD TS Message).

102. Early, "True Confessions Salutes A Hero's Wife."

103. Spurling, "The Patton Episode."

104. Essentially breathing with one lung and unable to use his abdominal muscles, he depended on the accessory muscles in his neck to breathe. According to Carlo D'Este, an iron lung had been brought from a hospital in Belgium but was never used.

105. "Patton Fights for His Life: War Hero General Paralyzed from Neck Down and Condition Critical," *Los Angeles Times*, December 11, 1945; GSP to BAP, 1 May 1944, box 12, folder 1, LOC-PP.

106. Colonel Spurling doesn't call General Smith by name, but everyone knew who he was talking about.

107. GSP box 13, folder 17, LOC-PP; GSP, diary entry, 13 October 1945, LOC-PP. https://loc.gov/item/mss35634040 Instead of taking a firm stance when asked whether General Patton was "temperamentally and emotionally" in disagreement with Denazification, Beetle was noncommittal, "General Patton is a soldier and will carry out his orders."

108. D. K. R. Crosswell, *Beetle: The Life of General Walter Bedell Smith* (Lexington: University Press of Kentucky, 2012), chapter 1, Kindle.

109. Spurling, "The Patton Episode."

110. "Mrs. Patton Cheers Hospital; General Still in Grave State," *Washington Post*, December 13, 1945.

111. Otto Zausmer, "Patton's Improvement Triumph For Brave Wife," *Boston Daily Globe*, December 16, 1945; Spurling, "The Patton Episode."

112. Spurling, "The Patton Episode."

113. "Patton's Condition Called 'Excellent'; Temperature 99," *Brooklyn Eagle*, December 14, 1945; Box 38, folder 2, LOC-PP.

114. "Great Contemporaries - Churchill and Patton," International Churchill Society, May 11, 2021, accessed August 21, 2022. https://winstonchurchill.org/publications/finest-hour/finest-hour-129/great-contemporaries-churchill-and-patton/ Even Belgium's Queen Mother Elizabeth called the hospital daily to offer assistance and check up on his condition. She and George had corresponded regularly since meeting in Brussels a few weeks earlier when her son, Prince Regent Charles, awarded him the Grand Order of Leopold.

115. DDE to GSP, 10 December 1945, Vol. 7, Page 608, #532, Dwight D. Eisenhower, *The Papers of Dwight David Eisenhower*. The job Eisenhower referred to was "a proper study of the concept of leadership," for which he thought George was the best qualified "as one of the great troop leaders of this war." (DDE to Joseph Taggart McNarney, December 6, 1945, Vol. 7, page 592, #522, Dwight D. Eisenhower, *The Papers of Dwight David Eisenhower*)

116. BAP to DDE, 14 December 1945. George Patton Folders, Pre-Presidential Papers of Dwight D. Eisenhower, 1916-1952, Eisenhower Presidential Library.

117. D'Este, *Patton: A Genius for War*, 41.

118. Totten, *The Button Box*, 140.

119. GSP, diary entry, 16 October 1945, LOC-PP. https://loc.gov/item/mss35634040/

120. Spurling, "The Patton Episode."

121. GSP, "My Father as I Knew Him and of Him from Memory and Legend."

122. "Gen. Patton At The Peak Of His Career And At His Home-Coming Triumph," *Los Angeles Times*, December 22, 1945.

123. "GSP Medical Records, 1904-1948."

124. Larry Newman, "B&G's Worst Dread was Car Accident," *The Austin Statesman*, December 11, 1945; "Gen Patton Better, Talks with Wife at Bedside," *Boston Daily Globe*, December 12, 1945..

125. GSP to FA, 3 December 1945, Neil Rice Ayer Jr. Private Papers.

126. "Picture News," *The Daily Record*, December 15, 1945; John O'Donnell, "Flying Troubles," *Los Angeles Times*, Dec 14, 1945. While the Air Transport Command had been in charge of taking Beatrice to Heidelberg, a similar request was ignored for days when it came to Fred. Friends and family put pressure on the A.T.C., but they refused to comply in order to make a point. They had often been criticized for making exceptions, most notably when soldiers had to make room for Elliot Roosevelt's [President Roosevelt's son] mastiff.

127. GSP to FA, 20 October 1942, box 10, folder 10, LOC-PP.

128. Fred Ayer Jr., *Before the Colors Fade*, 118.

129. BAP, "A Soldier's Reading."

130. GSP to BAP, 2 October 1945, box 13, folder 17, LOC-PP.

131. General Keyes to his wife, 16 December 1945, as quoted in Blumenson, *The Patton Papers: 1940-1945*, 830.

132. Otto Zausmer, "Patton's Improvement Triumph for Brave Wife," *Boston Daily Globe*, December 16, 1945. Air Force One would not become a standard designation until 1962.

133. Paul Harkins to BPW, 14 December 1945, box 1, folder 11. Paul D. Harkins Papers, U.S. Army Heritage And Education Center, Carlisle, PA.

134. RPT to an unnamed friend, December 1945, box 38, folder 2, LOC-PP.

135. DDE to RPT, 24 December 1945, Vol. 7, page 677, #588, Dwight D. Eisenhower, *The Papers of Dwight David Eisenhower*.

136. Spurling, The Patton Episode."

137. "Mrs. Patton Radiates Hope in Statement on General."

138. Bennett, "Patton Paralyzed by Injuries: 'Helluva Way to Get Hurt,' Says Patton."

139. "Patton Given 'Good Chance' to Walk again," *New York Herald Tribune*, December 14, 1945. The hospital staff was barred from talking to the press, but one reporter managed to speak to Lt. Bertha Hohle, one of the three doting Army nurses who cared for George. "He tells me not to worry about him and go away," she said, "but I have to be there because he never wants to eat or drink. He says he will not unless he gets a shot of whiskey."

140. "Patton to Rest in France," *Boston Daily Globe*, December 22, 1945; Early, "True Confessions Salutes A Hero's Wife."

141. Robert Patton, *The Pattons*, chapter 19, Kindle.

142. GSP to BAP, 9 July 1945, box 13, folder 10, LOC-PP.
143. "Letter From Major General Albert W. Kenner To Colonel R.B. Hill, Surgeon, Chanor Base Section, Regarding The Shortage Of Personnel After The War In The Medical Profession," 20/27 December 1945, Albert W. Kenner Papers; Box 1, Folder 6, Official And Personal Correspondence, 8 May 1945--10 February 1946. U.S. Army Heritage And Education Center, Carlisle, Pa.
144. Cable W 89688. Secret, DDE to Walter Bedell Smith, 21 December 1945, Vol. 7, Page 673, #583, Dwight D. Eisenhower, *The Papers of Dwight David Eisenhower*; General Keyes to his wife, 21 December 1945, as quoted in Blumenson, *The Patton Papers: 1940-1945*, 830.
145. Transmission from Major General Kenner to General Eisenhower, December 21, 1945. "His condition has become steadily worse because of progressive pulmonary edema and congestive heart failure. All laboratory and X-ray findings confirm these diagnoses . . . His situation is extremely critical."
146. "Patton Seriously Hurt in Crash of Car and Truck at Mannheim," *New York Herald Tribune*, December 10, 1945; Codman, *Drive*, XIV.
147. "GSP Medical Records, 1904-1948."
148. General Keyes to his wife, 21 December 1945 as quoted in *Blumenson, The Patton Papers: 1940-1945*, 830.
149. "GSP Medical Records, 1904-1948."
150. "GSP Medical Records, 1904-1948."
151. BAP, *Love without End*, 98-99.
152. GSP, "My Father as I Knew Him and of Him from Memory and Legend."
153. "Patton to Rest in France," *Boston Daily Globe*, December 22, 1945; "Death Comes Peacefully to Patton in his Sleep," *Richmond Times- Dispatch*, December 22, 1945; Spurling, "The Patton Episode."
154. Spurling, "The Patton Episode."
155. "Letter From Major General Albert W. Kenner To Colonel R.B. Hill, Surgeon, Chanor Base Section, Regarding The Shortage Of Personnel After The War In The Medical Profession."
156. GSP to GP, 11 November 1906, box 4, folder 16, LOC-PP.
157. Codman, *Drive*, 319.
158. "Patton to Rest in France." George Patton received the best care available at that time. The consensus is that he probably would have survived if it hadn't been for the embolism. An autopsy could have laid to rest rumors regarding an assassination attempt, and could have exposed the possible effects of the multiple head injuries he suffered over the years.
159. D'Este, *Patton: A Genius for War*, 797.
160. Larry Newman, "Article draft for Cosmopolitan," box 76, folder 3, LOC-PP.
161. Cable W 89688. Secret, DDE to Walter Bedell Smith, 21 December 1945, Vol. 7, Page 673, #583, Dwight D. Eisenhower, *The Papers of Dwight David Eisenhower*. If Beatrice persisted, Eisenhower believed "it would be best for me merely to take it upon myself to make a proper announcement giving the reason as one of public desire and interest and without mentioning her [Beatrice's] desires in any possible way."
162. Sobel, *The Fighting Pattons*, 55.
163. Robert Patton, *The Pattons*, chapter 20, Kindle.
164. GSP to BAP, 23 May 1945, box 13, folder 8, LOC-PP.
165. GSP to BAP, 6 March 1944, box 11, folder 16, LOC-PP.
166. He died in 1954—or 1957 according to Keith Merrill—and was buried in the yard with all the other dogs George loved so much.
167. "Ike's Son Remembers George S. Patton Jr," *American Heritage*, Summer 2012, Vol. 62, Issue 2.
168. Eisenhower, *Strictly Personal*, 115.
169. Spurling, "The Patton Episode."
170. Hugh Cairns and G. J. Fraenkel, *Hugh Cairns: First Nuffield Professor of Surgery* (Oxford University Press, 1991), 173-174.
171. Alfred Mynders, "Next to the News," *Chattanooga Times*, December 12, 1948. "Concerning your broadcast of this date in which a statement was made to the effect that having recently divorced I intend to marry Mrs. George Patton, I wish to issue an unqualified denial. I lasts aw Mrs. Patton in Germany, immediately after the death of her husband. I last heard from Mrs. Patton in January, 1946, when she wrote a thank-you note for my services to her late husband."
172. Jim Dresbach, "The Patton Portrait: The Smithsonian Has the Real Deal," DC Military, March 9, 2017. https://www.dcmilitary.com/pentagram/history/the-patton-portrait-the-smithsonian-has-the-real-deal/article_8abcd113-2329-555d-9880-4020f28c56c4.html

173. BAP to JEF, 15 February 1946, SUL-GFP.

174. Burns, "Pattons most Vivid American Army Pair."

175. "Patton's Services Today; Burial Christmas Eve," *The Sunday Pantagraph (Bloomington, IL)*, December 23, 1945.

176. Robert Patton, *The Pattons*, chapter 19, Kindle.

177. GSP to GP, 15 August 1904, box 4, folder 12, LOC-PP.

178. "Friend, Foe Honor Patton on Last Armored Ride," *Boston Daily Globe*, December 24, 1945.

179. Walter Cronkite, "George S. Patton, Jr., Laid to Rest with Simple Rites in Luxembourg," *The Austin Statesman*, December 24, 1945.

180. Fred Ayer Jr., *Before the Colors Fade*, 51.

181. "Friend, Foe Honor Patton on Last Armored Ride."

182. Wilson Allen Heefner, *Dogface Soldier: The Life of General Lucian K. Truscott, Jr.* (Columbia: University of Missouri Press, 2010), 5.

183. Fred Ayer Jr., *Before the Colors Fade*, 51.

184. "Patton To Be Buried On Path Of Conquest," *Brooklyn Eagle*, December 22, 1945.

185. Cronkite, "George S. Patton, Jr., Laid to Rest with Simple Rites in Luxembourg."

186. "Patton at Rest Among Men he Led to Victory," *Boston Daily Globe*, December 25, 1945.

187. BAP, "The Army Wife."

188. Cronkite, "George S. Patton, Jr., Laid to Rest with Simple Rites in Luxembourg."

189. GSPIV to JGH, 12 January 1946 , box 36, folder 14, NYHS-HP.

190. Sobel, *The Fighting Pattons*.

191. Wilson Allen Heefner, *Patton's Bulldog: The Life and Service of General Walton H. Walker* (Pennsylvania: White Mane Publishing, 2002), 139. Walker took over the Desert Training Camp when George left for Operation Torch. They worked together often during WWII, including with the Third Army, and Walker even took a copy of *War as I Knew It* with him to Korea.

192. "Surgeon Here Praises Patton," *The Philadelphia Inquirer*, December 27, 1945.

193. "Mrs. Patton is Flown here from Europe," *The Washington Post*, December 26, 1945.

194. GSP to BAP, 22 September 1945, box 13, folder 15, LOC-PP.

195. GSP, diary entry, 10 August 1945, LOC-PP. https://loc.gov/item/mss35634039/

## 13. WHEN AND IF

1. Alois Podhajsky, *My Dancing White Horses* (Harrap, 1964), 221.

2. Elizabeth Letts, *The Perfect Horse: The Daring U.S. Mission to Rescue the Priceless Stallions Kidnapped by the Nazis* (New York: Ballantine Books, 2017), chapter 33, Kindle.

3. When the Third Army was stopped at the border of Czechoslovakia as per the Yalta Agreement, they were a mere twenty miles away from the town of Hostau, where a Nazi stud farm used Lipizzaner mares as part of a breeding program to create an Aryan race of horses. The mares were taken from Vienna in 1938 after Germany annexed Austria, but most of the stallions remained in the capital and were slaughtered by the Russians when they captured the city in April 1945. Worried about the safety of the mares with the Russians a mere forty miles away from Hostau, the German commander of the stud farm notified the Third Army that he and his men were willing to surrender on condition that the Lipizzaners were brought to safety. General Patton approved the plan, and on April 28, 1945, an unlikely group of Americans, Germans, and Cossacks managed to bring hundreds of horses to safety.

4. GSP, diary entry, 7 May 1945, LOC-PP. https:///.gov/item/mss35634039/

5. Unfortunately Freeman died before he finished the project.

6. St. Johns, "Lieut. Gen. and Mrs. George S. Patton, Jr."

7. Robert Patton, *The Pattons*, chapter 18, Kindle. To distinguish between his father, the name George IV will be used for the remainder of this book.

8. Robert Allan, "Speakers Eulogize Brilliant Leader; Notables are Present," *The Washington Post*, January 21, 1946.

9. Semmes, *Portrait of Patton*, 284; "Brigadier General Harry D. Semmes: A Matter of Balance," *Museum of Hounds & Hunting North America*, October 21, 2021. https://mhhna.org/brigadier-general-harry-d-semmes-a-matter-of-balance/ Between the wars, Harry pursued a career in patent law. George Patton and Harry Semmes were both members of the first Tank Corps and were both wounded on September 26, 1918. Shot in the head the same day George was shot in

the buttocks, Harry overcame severe balance issues by taking up horseback riding. He was honorably discharged from the Army, but George helped him get detailed to the 2nd Armored Division, and he joined his friend for Operation Torch and Husky.

10. "Letter From Major General Albert W. Kenner To Colonel J.B. Coates, Jr., Thanking Him For The Christmas Card, But Regretting The Death Of General George S. Patton," Albert W. Kenner Papers; Box 1, Folder 6, Official And Personal Correspondence, 8 May 1945--10 February 1946, U.S. Army Heritage And Education Center, Carlisle, PA.

11. Eads, "Wife Tells Real Gen. Patton Story," *Los Angeles Times*, April 4, 1943; BAP to Beverly, 11 March 1946, accessed August 22, 2022. https://www.worthpoint.com/worthopedia/1946-beatrice-patton-george-pattons-487480363

12. BAP to JGH, 5 January 1946, box 36, folder 14, NYHS-HP.

13. Charles M. Province, *General Walton H. Walker: The Man Who Saved Korea.* Ironically, General Walker died on December 23, 1950, on the outskirts of Seoul, Korea, when his staff car collided with a truck.

14. RPT to Dr. Drake, June 26, private collection. Books and movies are still being released on the subject, and the Pattons' grandchildren get asked the same question to this day. Just in 2019, Pat Waters made it clear once again that "there was no conspiracy or foreign power. Why try to change history, perhaps to sell a movie or cause a stir. Please let his death be revered and not questioned."

15. Totten, *The Button Box*, 352; Robert Patton Interview.

16. GSPIV to JGH, 12 January 1946, box 36, folder 14, NYHS-HP.

17. "Hamilton Plunged into Gloom by News of Patton's Death," *Boston Daily Globe*, December 22, 1945.

18. FA to GSP, 10 October 1945, box 14, folder 19, LOC-PP.

19. Chilly Ayer to RPT, 21 December 1945, box 24, folder 17, LOC-PP.

20. Totten, *The Button Box*, 362.

21. Robert Patton, *The Pattons*, chapter 17, Kindle.

22. Robert Patton, *The Pattons*, chapter 18, Kindle.

23. Totten, *The Button Box*, 179.

24. Robert Patton, *The Pattons*, chapter 18, Kindle.

25. BAP to Beverly, March 11, 1946.

26. Totten, *The Button Box*, 360.

27. Totten, *The Button Box*, 353.

28. "Sergeant is Flown from Italy for 'Patton Hall' Dedication," *New York Age*, April 20, 1946.

29. Beatrice Ayer Patton, "Fort Riley Patton Memorial Ceremony Dedication Speech," 4 April 1946, box 75, folder 9, LOC-PP.

30. "Found Dead," *Chicago Daily Tribune*, January 9, 1946.

31. D'Este, *Patton: A Genius for War*, 806. Many believe the unlikely story, but no one knows where it originated. Time-wise, it seems almost impossible to have happened the way it is recounted. There is no evidence Beatrice left Washington between her return from Germany and Jean Gordon's death. The only logical moment would have been the memorial service at St. John's on December 30, which Beatrice did not attend either.

32. J. S. Emerson, "Selections From a Kahuna's Book of Prayers," *Twenty-sixth Annual Report of the Hawaiian Historical Society for the year 1917* (Honolulu: Paradise of the Pacific Press, 1918). https://core.ac.uk/download/pdf/5014342.pdf

33. BAP, *Love without End*, 96.

34. GSP to BAP, 3 August 1945, box 12, folder 5, LOC-PP.

35. GSP, diary entry, 26 August 1944, LOC-PP. https://loc.gov/item/mss35634034/

36. BAP to ESH, V-E Day, box II-4, folder 13, Library of Congress, Manuscript Division, Everett Strait Hughes Papers.

37. ESH to Kittens (either his wife or his girlfriend), 25 December 1945, box II-4, folder 10, Library of Congress, Manuscript Division, Everett Strait Hughes Papers.

38. BAP to GSP, 7 September 1943, box 11, folder 7, LOC-PP.

39. ZBathon, "The Myth of Ike and Kay Summersby Part II," *Armchair General Magazine*, November 1, 2013. http://armchairgeneral.com/the-myth-of-ike-and-kay-summersby-part-ii-2.htm

40. Lloyd Shearer, "Intelligence Report: General Patton and His Niece," *The Boston Globe*, April 19, 1981.

41. D'Este, *The Patton Papers: 1940-1945*, 854.

42. Will Lissner, "Patterson Assails Criticism Of Army: The Military Academy Graduates The

Largest Class In Its History," *The New York Times*, June 5, 1946.

43. "Young Patton Receives Commission from Mother," *Verdun News*, June 21, 1946.
44. BAP to JGH, 1 September 1943, box 36, folder 16, NYHS-HP.
45. GSP to GSPIV, 22 October 1945, box 13, folder 17, LOC-PP.
46. Sobel, *The Fighting Pattons*, 59; BAP to JEF, 8 May 1946, SUL-GFP.
47. BAP to JGH, 10 September 1946, box 36, folder 14, NYHS-HP.
48. Dean Dominique and James Hayes, *One Hell of a War: Patton's 317th Infantry Regiment in WWII* (Virginia: Dean J. Dominque, 2014), 63.
49. BAP, "A Soldier's Reading."
50. GSP to BAP, 12 April 1944, box 11, folder 17, LOC-PP.
51. BAP to JGH, 7 June 1947, box 36, folder 14, NYHS-HP.
52. Sobel, *The Fighting Pattons*, 60.
53. BAP to LEF, 3 April 1951, SUL-GFP.
54. BAP to LEF, Undated (but sometime between 1950 and 1952), SUL-GFP.
55. Drew Pearson, "The Washington Merry-Go-Round," *The Enterprise and Vermonter*, May 16, 1946.
56. Frank C. Waldrop to BAP, 2 January 1946, box 22, folder 3, LOC-PP.
57. JGH to Colonel Palmer, 24 January 1946, box 36, folder 14, NYHS-HP.
58. JGH to BAP, 13 September 1946 , box 36, folder 14, NYHS-HP.
59. BAP to JGH, 16 November 1946, box 36, folder 14, NYHS-HP.
60. BAP to JGH, 3 May 1947, box 36, folder 14, NYHS-HP; BAP to JGH, 2 December 1946, box 36, folder 14, NYHS-HP.
61. BAP to JGH, 16 November 1946, box 36, folder 14, NYHS-HP; BAP to JGH, 7 June 1947, box 36, folder 14, NYHS-HP.
62. BAP to JGH, 7 June 1947, box 36, folder 14, NYHS-HP.
63. GSP to GSPIV, 12 August 1945, box 13, folder 12, LOC-PP.
64. Robert Patterson to BAP, 19 May 1947, box 14, folder 8, LOC-PP. George already shared some chapters with Patterson in the summer of 1945. He received the same reaction, that it "would cause a lot of futile controversy," and he hoped he would alter the text for more general publication instead of family history. (Robert Patterson to GSP, 10 September 1945, box 13, folder 14, LOC-PP.)
65. Douglas Freeman to BAP, 7 May 1947, box 14, folder 8, LOC-PP.
66. JGH to BAP, 2 December 1946, box 36, folder 14, NYHS-HP.
67. Ira Wolfert, "George Patton's Plain-Spoken Diary: War As I Knew It," *The New York Times*, November 9, 1947.
68. Sobel, *The Fighting Pattons*, XIV.
69. Burns, "Pattons most Vivid American Army Pair."
70. St. Johns, "Lieut. Gen. and Mrs. George S. Patton, Jr."
71. BAP to JEF, 17 December 1947, box 19, folder: Patton, Gen. George F. Jr. 1948-1954 - standing figure, SUL-GFP.
72. "Things to Do in Isla Taboga," *Frommer's*, accessed August 22, 2022. https://www.frommers.com/destinations/isla-taboga
73. Totten, *The Button Box*, 367-368.
74. Just two-and-half-miles from Green Meadows, the Myopia Hunt donated a piece of land along Route 1A in the middle of South Hamilton to create Patton Park, and in 1947, Beatrice got the Army to donate a 67,000-pound Sherman tank. The tank stands in Patton Park, with an artillery gun and two Liberty Road Markers in honor of the 83rd Division of the Third Army and the 4th Armored Division. The two pillars, which are exactly like the ones along the Liberty Road in France, showed up unexpectedly one day at the South Hamilton train station in the late forties and turned out to be a gift from the cities of Avranches and Le Havre "in recognition for General Patton and his valiant Third Army."
75. James I. Murrie and Naomi Jeffery Petersen, "Last Train Home," *HistoryNet*, February 12, 2019. https://www.historynet.com/last-train-home/?f
76. Beatrice Ayer Patton, "Let the War Dead Rest," *Boston Daily Globe*, May 29, 1947.
77. GSP to BAP, 25 November 1918, box 9, folder 4, LOC-PP. Her brother-in-law already helped tremendously in transcribing and annotating George's papers, reading such comments about himself as, "Had he not produced an infant I should not have believed him a man at all as it is I think his manhood does not reach above his belt."
78. Keith Merrill Report, LOC-PP.
79. "General George S. Patton, Jr., Buried in Luxembourg American Cemetery," *American Battle*

*Monuments Commission*, December 21, 2020. https://abmc.gov/news-events/news/general-george-s-patton-jr-buried-luxembourg-american-cemetery To this day, at least one of General Patton's descendants is present every year at his graveside for a special memorial service. The city of Luxembourg, and many of the towns the Third Army passed through, still honor him yearly.

80. "Gen. Patton Museum Dedicated by Widow," *Boston Daily Globe*, May 31, 1949. More than just a tribute to General Patton, the museum also has a historical and educational value concerning the Armored Forces, and aims to help "discover and cultivate the leader" within each of its visitors.

81. GSP to Captain Martin, 25 January 1913, box 5, folder 16, LOC-PP.

82. "Military Strength Needed by U. S., Dr. Compton Says," *Boston Daily Globe*, June 27, 1947.

83. "Postwar Strategy of Russians Accurately Predicted by General Patton Before Death," *Avalanche-Journal*, July 30, 1950.

84. Totten, *The Button Box*, 388.

85. Interview with Joanne Patton.

86. Sobel, *The Fighting Pattons*, 82.

87. GSP to FA, Neil Rice Ayer Jr. Private Papers.

88. GSPIV to Brigadier General Hobson, "General George Smith Patton, Jr. U.S.A. — A Tribute," box 14, folder 9, LOC-PP.

89. BAP to General Marshall, undated, box 14, folder 5, LOC-PP.

90. One of those friends was Colonel James Polk, who received a pair of 14K single Brigadier General stars with an accompanying note, "I gave these to Georgie who wore them. You will want to wear them too, and I know you will be worthy of them. B.A.P." (James H. Polk, "The Patton Legend - A Subordinate's View," James H. Polk Papers, Box 54A, Folder 1. U.S. Army Heritage And Education Center, Carlisle, PA.)

91. Beatrice Ayer Patton, "Speech at dedication of Patton Memorial Statue, West Point. August 19, 1950," Box 23, LOC-PP.

92. BAP to JGH, 18 September 1944, NYHS-HP; BAP to Arvin "Jerry" Brown, 3 April, 1943, box 52, folder 5, Patton, George S., Jr. (General) and Family correspondence with Arvin Harrington Brown (1942-1954), HLC-GSP.

93. Semmes, *Portrait of Patton*, 82.

94. BAP, "Speech at dedication of Patton Memorial Statue, West Point. August 19, 1950." Three years later, a copy of this statue would also be placed along the Charles River Esplanade in Boston, where George gave his speech at the Hatch Shell in June 1945 upon his triumphant return from WWII.

95. BAP to JEF, 4 October 1948, SUL-GFP.

96. BAP to Paul Harkins, 22 May 1948, SUL-GFP.

97. BAP to JEF, 15 February 1946, SUL-GFP.

98. BAP to JEF, 5 July 1950, SUL-GFP.

99. BAP to JEF, 24 November 1947, SUL-GFP.

100. BAP to JEF&LEF, 26 May 1951, SUL-GFP.

101. GSP to William J. Mack, 10 February 1945, box 13, folder 1, LOC-PP; William J. Mack to GSP, 22 January 1945, box 13, folder 1, LOC-PP.

102. BAP to JEF, undated, written at Fort Benning, SUL-GFP.

103. BAP to JEF, 8 September 1949, SUL-GFP.

104. Benjamin Patton, *Growing Up Patton: Reflections on Heroes, History and Family Wisdom* (New York: Berkley Caliber, 2012), 81.

105. Totten, *The Button Box*, 381.

106. Totten, *The Button Box*, 100.

107. Joanne Patton Interview.

108. Totten, *The Button Box*, 381.

109. BAP to GSP, 17 January 1943, box 10, folder 13, LOC-PP.

110. On September 10, 1945, George asked Fred to open an account for M/Sgt. William G. Meeks and deposit "$2,220.00 — this being what I owe Sgt. Meeks for pay, etc... and also $500.00 which he handed me in cash..." George wanted to make the deposit "to keep Sgt. Meeks' ill earned gains, mostly from poker, from falling into the hands of Vergie." (GSP to FA, 10 September 1945, box 14, folder 19, LOC-PP).

111. "Sergeant is Flown from Italy for 'Patton Hall' Dedication," New York Age, April 20, 1946.

112. BAP to JEF, undated, SUL-GFP.

113. Totten, *The Button Box*, 382.
114. Robert Patton, *The Pattons*, chapter 18, Kindle; Totten, *The Button Box*, 383.
115. Totten, *The Button Box*, 384.
116. "Radio Search Finds Mrs. Patton's Yacht to Inform Her of Her Daughter's Death," *The New York Times*, October 25, 1952.
117. Totten, *The Button Box*, 384.
118. BAP to Chilly Ayer, as quoted in Totten, *The Button Box*, 384.
119. BAP to JEF&LGF, 5 November 1952, written at Fort Benning, SUL-GFP.
120. BAP to JEF, 18 May 1951, SUL-GFP.
121. Eisenhower, *Strictly Personal*, 114.
122. Eisenhower, *General Ike: A Personal Reminiscence*, 73.
123. George C. Marshall, Forrest C. Pogue, and Larry I. Bland; *George C. Marshall: Interviews and Reminiscences for Forrest C. Pogue*, 547.
124. Jimmy Doolittle, as quoted in D'Este, *Patton: A Genius for War*, 758.
125. DDE to BAP, 25 May 1953, Vol. 14, page 249, #208, Dwight D. Eisenhower, *The Papers of Dwight David Eisenhower*.
126. GSP to FA, 20 October 1945, Neil Rice Ayer Jr. Private Papers.
127. Westbrook Pegler, "Fair Enough," *Santa Cruz Sentinel*, June 27, 1952. It was the end of the conversation, but not the end of the story. Several politicians on both sides of the aisle tried to obtain the incriminating material she most certainly possessed. Still, their efforts were in vain, although some say only because her nephew, Frederick Ayer Jr., was a candidate for Attorney General of Massachusetts. He lost the Republican nomination but served as vice president of the Massachusetts Citizens for Eisenhower committee.
128. William Shakespeare, *The Oxford Shakespeare: The Winter's Tale* (Oxford University Press, 1998), act IV, scene 3.
129. BAP to JEF, undated, written at Fort Benning, SUL-GFP. John "Johnnie" Knight Waters retired in 1966 after thirty-five years in the service, having reached the rank of four-star general and Commanding General of the U.S. Army Pacific. He died of heart failure at Walter Reed Hospital in 1989, with his second wife of twenty-eight years by his side, and survived by his two children with Bee.

    John Knight Waters Jr. graduated from Utah State University with a B.S. in military science and a Masters in Public Administration. He also graduated from West Point and joined the service in 1963, first to Germany and then several tours in Vietnam, where he received, among others, the Silver Star, the Bronze Star, and the Purple Heart. Upon his retirement in 1975, he was the town manager of South Hamilton for several years before moving to a 400-acre farm in Maryland.

    His brother George "Pat" Patton Waters served in the Navy as a lieutenant on the USS Braine from 1965 to 1970 and then started his own real estate development company in Baton Rouge, Louisiana. He often gives lectures on General Patton and represents the family at commemorative ceremonies in Europe.
130. Joanne Patton Interview.
131. Totten, *The Button Box*, 386-388.
132. Robert Patton, *The Pattons*, chapter 20, Kindle.
133. "Gen. Patton's Widow Dies during Hunt: Plunge from Spirited Horse at Myopia Club Causes Instant Death," *The Hartford Courant*, October 1, 1953; Burns, "Pattons most Vivid American Army Pair."
134. Robert Patton, *The Pattons*, chapter 20, Kindle.
135. Burns, "Pattons most Vivid American Army Pair."
136. Totten, *The Button Box*, 383.
137. "Hamilton Rites Await Flight of Mrs. Patton's Son," *Boston Daily Globe*, October 1, 1953.
138. Burns, "Pattons most Vivid American Army Pair."
139. "Mrs. Patton Killed In Fall From Horse: Widow Of General Who Died After Auto Crash Overseas Is Drag Hunt Victim," *The New York Times*, October 1, 1953.
140. Larry Newman, "B&G's Worst Dread was Car Accident," *The Austin Statesman*, December 11, 1945.

## LUXEMBOURG AMERICAN CEMETERY, HAMM

1. Totten, *The Button Box*, 387. The Korean armistice agreement was signed on July 27, 1953, ending a three-year war that killed over one million people.
2. "Gen. Patton's Widow Killed; Thrown by Spirited Horse," *Long Beach Independent*, October 1, 1953.
3. "Gen. Patton's Widow Dies during Hunt."
4. Burns, "Pattons most Vivid American Army Pair."
5. "Mrs. Patton's Rites are Held," *Boston Daily Globe*, October 6, 1953.
6. DDE to John Elmer McClure, 19 August 1955, Vol. 16, page 1829, #1560, Dwight D. Eisenhower, *The Papers of Dwight David Eisenhower*.
7. Patton, *The Pattons*, chapter 20, Kindle.
8. Nicholas Evan Sarantakes, *Making Patton: A Classic War Film's Epic Journey to the Silver Screen* (Lawrence: University Press of Kansas, 2012), 34. McCarthy was General Marshall's aide and eventually the secretary of the General Staff.
9. When Dr. Peer Johnson visited Green Meadows in June 1945, George obliged his old friend and put on his uniform with every medal and ribbon he owned to have his picture taken in the backyard. Twenty-five years hence, the photograph would inspire the opening scene of the movie Patton, but it wasn't characteristic of George to show off his medals like that.
10. D'Este, *Patton: A Genius for War*, 816.
11. "Eva Marie Saint Plays Wife of Patton," *Gettysburg Times*, September 4, 1986.
12. BAP, "Voyage of Arcturus," June 15 1937, box 10, folder 7, LOC-PP.
13. "American Woolen Co. Founder's Widow Left $1,263,495 Estate," *Boston Daily Globe*, December 7, 1951.
14. "For Drumlin Farm, 50 Years of Education," *Boston Daily Globe*, May 1, 2005.
15. "A New Vision for Environmental Education: Drumlin Farm," Mass Audubon, July 2017. https://www.massaudubon.org/content/download/20335/289257/file/Drumlin-Farm-ELC_-Case-Statement_Jul17.pdf
16. BAP to JGH, 16 November 1946, box 36, folder 14, NYHS-HP.
17. "Widow Inherits $5 1/2 Million From Charles Ayer Estate," *Boston Daily Globe*, September 18, 1956.
18. Ledyard Farm continues to be run by Fred's descendants; his son, Neil Ayer, built a world-class cross-country course on the property and put the farm on the map in the seventies when he began organizing international three-day jumping competitions, with Princess Anne and her husband, Captain Mark Phillips, competing in 1975.
19. For the first half of the twentieth century, the rocky shoreline of Massachusetts' Gold Coast was dominated by oceanside estates, of which Avalon was one of the grandest and most private. The mansions lining Paine Avenue in Pride's Crossing—the most exclusive area of Beverly known as the "Valley of the Kings"—began disappearing one by one after WWII, with the rising cost of labor and the difficulty in finding employees willing to maintain homes which sometimes ran over one hundred rooms. Unlike Newport, Rhode Island, Beverly did not try to preserve these Gilded Age jewels. Woodstock was sold after Ellen's death and summarily torn down to build a smaller and more practical home, while Avalon was sold after Kay's death and torn down in the early nineties. It may or may not have been rebuilt someplace else.
20. Frederick Ayer, *The Reminiscences of Frederick Ayer*, 43. The J. C. Ayer Company officially dissolved in January 1943, and the American Woolen Company ceased existence in 1955 when it merged with Textron.
21. Hillary Chabot, "Heirs: He Bilked Us Out Of $58M," *Lowell Sun*, February 23, 2007. https://www.lowellsun.com/2007/02/23/heirs-he-bilked-us-out-of-58m-3/
22. Francis Storrs, "A Stranger in The House of Ayer," *Boston Magazine*, November 20, 2007. https://www.bostonmagazine.com/2007/11/20/a-stranger-in-the-house-of-ayer
23. Francis Storrs, "A Stranger in The House of Ayer."
24. Mclean, "Daughter's View Of Gen. Patton."
25. Colonel Michael Willoughby Totten served in Vietnam and Desert Storm and was the recipient of the Bronze Star. He lived in Syria, Saudi Arabia, and Yemen as military attaché and retired to Maryland after serving his country for over thirty years. He was involved in countless organizations and was a bit of an entrepreneur like his great-grandfather. He died of cancer at age sixty-one in 2003.

His brother James "Jamie" Patton Totten was also a decorated Vietnam veteran and an Army Reserve Colonel. Once he left the Army, Jamie moved to Hendersonville, Tennessee, and became a textile plant manager. A member of the board of the Patton Museum, he is also very much involved with the Ayers' trust, renamed the "1911 Trust" after the Doorly incident.

Beatrice Totten graduated from The Masters School in Dobbs Ferry and Sweet Briar College in Virginia and worked at the Beverly Hospital as a medical technician. She moved to Brick End's Farm after her mother's death, turning the sprawling property into a composting facility with her husband, Peter Price Britton.

26. "Ruth E. Totten, 78; essayist and speaker, daughter of Gen. Patton," *Boston Daily Globe*, December 3, 1993.

27. Sobel, *The Fighting Pattons*, 11.

28. Sobel, *The Fighting Pattons*, 157.

29. General Patton is still revered in Europe, even more so than in the United States. Ettelbruck, a small village in Luxembourg known as "Patton Town," was liberated in 1944 by the Third Army's 80th Infantry Division and is now home to the General Patton Memorial Museum. Ettelbruck has been commemorating the Battle of the Bulge on Patton Day since 1950, and Helen Ayer Patton, the fourth of George IV and Joanne's five children, was present on the 75th anniversary of the Bulge in 2019. Trained as an actress and spending most of her life in Europe involved with veteran affairs, she founded the Patton Foundation to preserve "the legacy of the Patton family and its historical role in world events."

Her younger brother Benjamin Wilson Patton (b. 1966), a filmmaker who graduated from Georgetown University, founded the Patton Veterans Project in 2011, a non-profit which helps veterans cope with PTSD through "intensive filmmaking workshops enabling participants to collaborate with peers to process their service experiences." He is also the author of *Growing Up Patton: Reflections on Heroes, History and Family Wisdom.*

George IV and Joanna's firstborn, Margaret DeRussy Patton, is a Catholic nun in the order of St. Benedict. Mother Margaret Georgina Patton is Subprioress at the Abbey of Regina Laudis in Bethlehem, Connecticut, founded in 1948 by Mother Benedict Duss in gratitude for the Third Army liberating the Abbey of Notre Dame de Jouarre in France. With degrees in both English and Horticulture, Mother Margaret co-founded The Beatrice Ayer Patton School of Montessori in Bridgewater, Connecticut (since closed).

George Smith Patton Jr. was born in 1955—technically the fifth George Smith Patton, but the count started fresh when his father dropped the 'IV' in 1946—and is mentally challenged. He spent part of his childhood at the Devereux Foundation in Pennsylvania and became an accomplished western rider, winning a gold medal at the Special Olympics and running a horse farm in Colorado.

Robert Holbrook Patton (b. 1957) is the author of *The Pattons: A Personal History of an American Family, Patriot Pirates,* and *Hell Before Breakfast,* a history of America's first war correspondents. In March 2021, he opened Green Meadows Farm, a medical and recreational marijuana dispensary in the town of Southbridge, Massachusetts. A commitment to veterans is "a family mission," and Green Meadows Farm, staffed mostly with veterans, will support military organizations and sell medical marijuana to help veterans with PTSD and chronic pain.

30. GSP to BAP, 1 May 1908, box 5, folder 3, LOC-PP.

31. Totten, *The Button Box*, 279.

32. Beatrice Ayer Patton Broadcast on We the People, July 18, 1943. Box 11, folder 4, LOC-PP; Early, "True Confessions Salutes A Hero's Wife."

33. GSP to BAP, 21 February 1909, box 5, folder 6, LOC-PP.

34. St. Johns, "Lieut. Gen. and Mrs. George S. Patton, Jr."

35. George S. Patton Jr., "To Your Picture," 25 June 1918, box 74, folder 1, LOC-PP.

36. GSP to JGH, 21 March 1932, box 37, folder 4, NYHS-HP.

37. Charles D. Herron, "Mrs. George Patton," *The Washington Post*, October 6, 1953.

38. BAP, "The Army Wife."

39. BAP, "The Army Wife."

# ILLUSTRATION CREDITS

All pictures from the Library of Congress are either U.S. Signal Corps or family pictures. They are located in Box 60-64; Box 76-78; and Box OV 1-OV 50. For more pictures and detailed family trees, go to ladyofthearmy.com.

- **Cover.** Banning Family Collection of Photographs Part II - 451.1126. Huntington Library, San Marino, California.
- **Title Page.** U.S. Army Signal Corps. Library of Congress - George S. Patton Papers.
- **Figure 1.** Library of Congress - George S. Patton Papers.
- **Figure 2**. George S. Patton Jr. Collection, Davis Memorial Library, Item #A11-4, The General George Patton Museum of Leadership, Center of Military History.
- **Figure 3**. Library of Congress - George S. Patton Papers.
- **Figure 4.** Private collection of author.
- **Figure 5.** Private collection of author.
- **Figure 6.** Digital image by Stefanie Van Steelandt. Banning Family Collection of Photographs Part II - 451.931. Huntington Library, San Marino, California.
- **Figure 7.** Private collection of author.
- **Figure 8.** Digital image by Stefanie Van Steelandt. Banning Family Collection of Photographs Part I - 180.138. Huntington Library, San Marino, California.
- **Figure 9.** Private collection of author.
- **Figure 10.** Private collection of author.
- **Figure 11.** Banning Family Collection of Photographs Part I - 180.645. Huntington Library, San Marino, California.
- **Figure 12.** Patton Family Collection of Negatives and Photographs - 321476. Huntington Library, San Marino, California. https://hdl.huntington.org/digital/collection/p15150-coll2/id/6069/rec/16
- **Figure 13.** Patton Family Collection of Negatives and Photographs - 321478. Huntington Library, San Marino, California. https://hdl.huntington.org/digital/collection/p15150-coll2/id/6071/rec/17
- **Figure 14.** Banning Family Collection of Photographs Part II - 451.702. Huntington Library, San Marino, California.
- **Figure 15**. Digital image by Stefanie Van Steelandt. Banning Family Collection of Photographs Part II - 451.929. Huntington Library, San Marino, California.
- **Figure 16.** Banning Family Collection of Photographs Part II - 451.926. Huntington Library, San Marino, California.
- **Figure 17.** Banning Family Collection of Photographs Part II - 451.266. Huntington Library, San Marino, California.

- **Figure 18.** Digital image by Stefanie Van Steelandt. Banning Family Collection of Photographs Part I - 180.662. Huntington Library, San Marino, California.
- **Figure 19.** Digital image by Stefanie Van Steelandt. Banning Family Collection of Photographs Part I - 180.140. Huntington Library, San Marino, California.
- **Figure 20.** Library of Congress - George S. Patton Papers.
- **Figure 21.** Joseph Judd Pennell Photograph Collection, Kansas Collection, RH PH Pennell, Kenneth Spencer Research Library, University of Kansas.
- **Figure 22.** Joseph Judd Pennell Photograph Collection, Kansas Collection, RH PH Pennell, Kenneth Spencer Research Library, University of Kansas.
- **Figure 23.** Joseph Judd Pennell Photograph Collection, Kansas Collection, RH PH Pennell, Kenneth Spencer Research Library, University of Kansas.
- **Figure 24.** Private collection of author.
- **Figure 25.** Library of Congress - George S. Patton Papers.
- **Figure 26.** Private collection of author.
- **Figure 27.** Library of Congress - George S. Patton Papers.
- **Figure 28.** Digital image by Stefanie Van Steelandt. Banning Family Collection of Photographs Part II - 451.920. Huntington Library, San Marino, California.
- **Figure 29.** 1978.010.1296. Hopkins Collection, Thomasville History Center.
- **Figure 30.** Library of Congress - George S. Patton Papers.
- **Figure 31.** Private collection of author.
- **Figure 32.** Private collection of author.
- **Figure 33.** George S. Patton Jr. Collection, Davis Memorial Library, Item #A1-97, The General George Patton Museum of Leadership, Center of Military History.
- **Figure 34.** Banning Family Collection of Photographs Part II - 451.1125. Huntington Library, San Marino, California.
- **Figure 35.** Patton Family Collection of Negatives and Photographs - 364. Huntington Library, San Marino, California. https://hdl.huntington.org/digital/collection/p15150coll2/id/6052/rec/15
- **Figure 36.** 2016832341 - National Photo Company Collection, Library of Congress. https://www.loc.gov/item/2016832341/
- **Figure 37.** Banning Family Collection of Photographs Part II - 451.1148. Huntington Library, San Marino, California.
- **Figure 38.** Banning Family Collection of Photographs Part II - 451.1123. Huntington Library, San Marino, California.
- **Figure 39.** Digital image by Stefanie Van Steelandt. Banning Family Collection of Photographs Part II - 451.1152. Huntington Library, San Marino, California.
- **Figure 40.** Library of Congress - George S. Patton Papers.
- **Figure 41.** "Ayer Mill." Photograph. 1902–1907. Digital Commonwealth, https://ark.digitalcommonwealth.org/ark:/50959/6h445j592 (accessed August 27, 2022).
- **Figure 42.** Courtesy of Scott C. Steward.
- **Figure 43.** Library of Congress - George S. Patton Papers.
- **Figure 44.** Private collection of author.

- **Figure 45.** George S. Patton Jr. Collection, Davis Memorial Library, Item #A2-3, The General George Patton Museum of Leadership, Center of Military History.
- **Figure 46.** George S. Patton Jr. Collection, Davis Memorial Library, Item #A2-4, The General George Patton Museum of Leadership, Center of Military History.
- **Figure 47.** Image courtesy of the Patton Family Archives Collection, Wenham Museum, Wenham, MA.
- **Figure 48.** Library of Congress - George S. Patton Papers.
- **Figure 49.** Library of Congress - George S. Patton Papers.
- **Figure 50.** Library of Congress - George S. Patton Papers.
- **Figure 51.** Courtesy of Scott C. Steward.
- **Figure 52.** George S. Patton Jr. Collection, Davis Memorial Library, Item #A2-10, The General George Patton Museum of Leadership, Center of Military History.
- **Figure 53.** George S. Patton Jr. Collection, Davis Memorial Library, The General George Patton Museum of Leadership, Center of Military History.
- **Figure 54.** U.S. Army Garrison Hawaii.
- **Figure 55.** Library of Congress - George S. Patton Papers.
- **Figure 56.** Box 10, folder 7. Library of Congress - George S. Patton Papers.
- **Figures 57 & 58.** (Book signing at Thomas Nickerson Book Shop), Mid Pacnu Photographs, PP-6-11-005 & PP-6-11-008, Hawaii State Archives.
- **Figure 59.** Library of Congress - George S. Patton Papers.
- **Figure 60.** Library of Congress - George S. Patton Papers.
- **Figure 61.** Courtesy of Scott C. Steward.
- **Figure 62.** Library of Congress - George S. Patton Papers.
- **Figure 63.** Library of Congress - George S. Patton Papers.
- **Figure 64.** Library of Congress - George S. Patton Papers.
- **Figures 65, 66, & 67.** Library of Congress - George S. Patton Papers.
- **Figure 68.** Library of Congress - George S. Patton Papers.
- **Figure 69.** 2006686806. Library of Congress - George S. Patton Papers. https://www.loc.gov/item/2006686806/
- **Figure 70.** Library of Congress - George S. Patton Papers.
- **Figure 71.** Library of Congress - George S. Patton Papers.
- **Figure 72.** Library of Congress - George S. Patton Papers.
- **Figure 73.** Library of Congress - George S. Patton Papers.
- **Figure 74.** Library of Congress - George S. Patton Papers.
- **Figure 75.** Library of Congress - George S. Patton Papers.
- **Figure 76 & 77.** Library of Congress - George S. Patton Papers.
- **Figure 78.** Library of Congress - George S. Patton Papers.
- **Figure 79.** Library of Congress - George S. Patton Papers.
- **Figure 80.** Library of Congress - George S. Patton Papers.
- **Figure 81.** Library of Congress - George S. Patton Papers.
- **Figure 82.** George S. Patton Jr. Collection, White Binders, Vol. 11-55, The General George Patton Museum of Leadership, Center of Military History.

- **Figure 83.** Library of Congress - George S. Patton Papers.
- **Figure 84.** Courtesy of the Boston Public Library, Leslie Jones Collection.
- **Figure 85.** Library of Congress - George S. Patton Papers.
- **Figure 86.** Library of Congress - George S. Patton Papers.
- **Figure 87.** Library of Congress - George S. Patton Papers.
- **Figure 88.** General George S. Patton, Jr., Boleslaw Jan Czedekowski, 1945, Oil on canvas, National Portrait Gallery, Smithsonian Institution; gift of Major General George S. Patton, U.S.A., Retired and the Patton Family.
- **Figure 89.** Courtesy National Archives, photo no. 111-SC-223849.
- **Figure 90.** Courtesy National Archives, photo no. 111-SC-223850.
- **Figure 91.** Library of Congress - George S. Patton Papers.
- **Figures 92 & 93.** Library of Congress - George S. Patton Papers.
- **Figure 94.** Library of Congress - George S. Patton Papers.
- **Figure 95.** Library of Congress - George S. Patton Papers.
- **Figure 96.** Private collection of author.
- **Figure 97.** U.S. Army Photo. George S. Patton Jr. Collection, Davis Memorial Library, Item #A16-14, The General George Patton Museum of Leadership, Center of Military History.
- **Figure 98.** Library of Congress - George S. Patton Papers.
- **Figure 99.** Library of Congress - George S. Patton Papers.
- **Figures 100 & 101.** U.S. Army Photos. George S. Patton Jr. Collection, Davis Memorial Library, Item #A3-17 & A3-16, The General George Patton Museum of Leadership, Center of Military History.
- **Figure 102.** U.S. Army Photograph. George S. Patton Jr. Collection, Davis Memorial Library, Item #A3-13, The General George Patton Museum of Leadership, Center of Military History.
- **Figure 103.** U.S. Army Photos. George S. Patton Jr. Collection, Davis Memorial Library, Item #A3-13, The General George Patton Museum of Leadership, Center of Military History.
- **Figure 104.** Banning Family Collection of Photographs Part I - 180.647. Huntington Library, San Marino, California.
- **Figure 105.** Banning Family Collection of Photographs Part II - 451.1126. Huntington Library, San Marino, California.
- **Figure 106.** George S. Patton Jr. Collection, Davis Memorial Library, Item #A16-24, The General George Patton Museum of Leadership, Center of Military History.

# INDEX

Made in the USA
Middletown, DE
22 October 2023

40977731R00298